YOU EAT WHAT YOU ARE

A Study of Ethnic Food Traditions

Thelma Barer~Stein

McCLELLAND AND STEWART

TO THE MEMORY OF MY FATHER
MICHAEL LION BARER

Who instilled in me a lifelong
love of learning.

The Canadian Publishers
McClelland and Stewart Ltd.
25 Hollinger Road, Toronto M4B 3G2

Printed and bound in Canada

CANADIAN CATALOGUING IN PUBLICATION DATA

Barer-Stein, Thelma.

  You Eat What You Are

Includes index.
ISBN 0-7710-8297-5 pa.

1. Food habits - Canada.
I. Title.

GT2853.C2B37   394.1'2'0971   C79-094121-X

THIS IS A WINTARIO PROJECT

Contents

Introduction

Food is only one aspect of ethnocultural traditions, yet it is probably one of the most persistent. The term "soul food," although coined by some Black peoples, by no means applies solely to them. There is no cultural group and no individual for whom at least one specific food – the memory, taste, or smell of which – does not evoke a pang of loving nostalgia.

There are many reasons for the indelible imprint of food customs and traditions on our cultural heritage. Food plays an inextricable role in our daily lives. Without food we cannot survive. But food is much more than a tool of survival. Food is a source of pleasure, comfort, security. Food is also a symbol of hospitality, social status, and has ritual significance. What we select to eat, how we prepare it, serve it, and even how we eat it, are all factors deeply touched by our individual cultural inheritance.

Why do certain peoples eat the foods they eat? Even a cursory look at diets around the world reveals the strange fact that people do not eat only what is available, they eat only *what they consider to be edible*. What is a delicacy in one area may be considered an abomination in another. Sheep's brains and eyeballs, frog's legs, and animal blood are not considered to be universal foods – nor are insects, but they are relished in certain areas of the world. Further, eating food with one's fingers may be considered ill-mannered by some, while eating with a knife and fork may be regarded by others to be absolutely barbaric. It is an indisputable fact that people everywhere carefully select, prepare, and eat their foods in accordance with established tradition.

Tradition seems to be a dynamic package of factors that are imbedded in every group's cultural heritage. Many definitions exist attempting to explain the phenomenon of culture. Perhaps the simplest view embodies all the factors, behaviours, and institutions that are part of a group's daily life which, because of the many variables involved, contain so many differentiating threads. Cultural heritage helps to determine and identify people's values, behaviour, and subsequently their life-style. In a very real sense, then, *culture helps man to select what he eats.*

Most countries of the world are inhabited by peoples of varying cultural backgrounds. Man's habit of migrating is as old as the history of man himself. People move from place to place for reasons of religious or political freedom, for personal and family security, for a sense of adventure. What is often overlooked is the very basic fact that many peoples of the world have moved to another place to find food. Historically, this has frequently resulted in the necessity of relinquishing customary tastes in foods, methods of preparation, etc., according to what is available to them in the new location. Finding new foods and new sources of foods and seasonings also motivated many adventurers and explorers. Man's culture has helped him to select what he eats, and seeking food has made him travel.

Canada is home to more than eighty ethnocultural groups. It has been said so many times that Canada is a land of immigrants. And evidence exists that the earliest inhabitants probably crossed the Bering Strait and came to this land originally in search of food. Much more recent history reveals how peoples came in search of fabled wealth, a piece of land to call their own, and for an opportunity for a better life.

History, too, reveals successive and sometimes overlapping means of coping with these "New Canadians," such as assimilation, integration, hyphenated Canadianism, Biculturalism and Bilingualism, and most recently the policy described as Multiculturalism. But while Canadian government policies swayed regarding the immigrant population over the years, the people themselves went right on with the matters of daily living. Some of the newcomers had brought with them a host of material possessions, others brought education, still others brought only themselves. But all brought with them, consciously or subconsciously, overtly or tacitly, a cultural heritage.

Let us take a closer look at what happens to the generations of Canadians when they arrive in Canada, settle in, and become citizens. Immigrants and homeless refugees concern themselves initially with the basics of human survival: a job, a place to live, food. For the first generation then, the urgency is for survival. The second generation, having survived, concerns itself with the more sophisticated matters of "getting ahead" and "belonging." The first generation didn't have the time and the second generation didn't want to be "different" from what they viewed as "being Canadian." And so cultural heritage for the most part remained in the suitcase in which it had arrived: never unpacked. Some ethnocultural groups such as the Ukrainians, Chinese, and the Jews, clung tenaciously to their language and other traditions but others, like the Icelanders, almost completely lost them. For Canada's third and fourth generations, a combination of complex factors evoked, among other things, the sense that something was missing from their lives. Increased prosperity and leisure time offered a chance for reflection, while the influx of later immigrants, mostly professionals and intellectuals, brought a reminder and often a nostalgia for the richness of past traditions, so long ignored. Reflection brought the need for a sense of individual as well as group identity.

Cultural heritage offers not only a sense of collective identity, but a sense of pride and dignity, purpose and stability, to everyday life. Cultural traditions like classic works of literature and art, and philosophical thought, survive because they offer an answer to man's thirsting soul. We can get along without these, but not for long. In the urgent need for survival, and with pressures to belong and to conform, sometimes these ideals are pushed aside. But eventually, in the pauses of daily life, we each, *in our differing ways*, come to the realization that life is not complete without the enrichment of cultural identity.

In a very special sense, food is not only a nostalgic and persistent part of our cultural baggage, but also a symbol of what we are today. When we stop in at a fast-food outlet for a snack, down a bottle of bubbly cola, chew a wad of gum nervously, or crunch a prepared cereal for breakfast, we are consciously or subconsciously accepting North American food customs. But when we ask grandmother for treasured old recipes or set holiday tables with heirlooms of china and linen, when we idly fantasize over some rare delicacy that makes our mouths water, then we are returning to our inherited cultural food traditions.

Why a book about food and culture? Well, how is it that we have persisted so long in the arrogant assumption that every one eats or likes to eat what we ourselves do? And how is it that food professionals have persisted for so long in the equally arrogant assumption that only certain foods are the "right" foods? The existence of so many ethnocultural groups in Canada has given rise to an emerging awareness of differing cultural heritages; and with this the realization that so-called Canadian food customs may not be so easily defined.

Increasingly, it is becoming obvious that an informed awareness and understanding of many aspects of cultural groups, including their food customs, may be essential not only for professionals in the fields of education, medicine, social work, public health and nutrition, commercial food services, but actually invaluable in any profession or service that involves dealing with people. It has to be self-evident that communication is increased and intensified in direct proportion to knowledge and under-standing. The purpose of this book is to contribute to that understanding.

It is impossible for me to consider that the research for this book began in 1973, when the actual writing began. It has, in fact, been a life-long study. The focussing of my interests on the *diversity* of peoples and their foods began with a realization of the narrow scientific content of both my undergraduate studies in foods and nutrition and my subsequent dietetic internship. Over the years I satisfied my own curiosity about "foreign foods" with informal study, travel and recipe experimentation, the results of which I later incorporated into my professional work as a home service director, on television and radio, and as a consultant and lecturer. The more than four hundred students to whom I taught various courses in "International Gourmet Cookery" further intensified my belief that foods of the world were not only closely related to cultural traditions, but were also a fascinating study. My students were always questioning *why* people ate and served foods in the ways that they did. Interest in the principles of teaching and of learning led me into graduate studies in education, and presently I am a Ph.D candidate focussing on studies relating adult education and culture.

While this book is mainly intended as a useful resource for both the professional and the student, many gourmets may also consider this reference as a step further in their own culinary adventures. Hopefully, each reader will approach with curiosity the chapter of his own ethnic background and then browse through other chapters. To these ends, and mindful of the many stuffy texts that I have had to research, I can only hope that my own interest and enthusiasm have produced a highly readable but also informative book.

So many variations occur in descriptions of food names from one area to another, and even from one author to another, that definitions, like exact recipes, must remain open-ended. Similarly, a wide tolerance in spelling of both terms and food names must be exercised.

Finally, a word about the use of B.C.E. (Before the Common Era) and C.E. (Common Era). This terminology is used in preference to the more common B.C. and A.D. (having specific Christian reference) out of respectful consideration to the many religious and cultural viewpoints represented in this book.

The subject of this book is unique and the scope vast. There will in-evitably be omissions and perhaps areas of contention. I hope the reader will share these with me. It is possible that in focussing on the "strange ways" of others we may fail to reflect on our own entrenched and indeli-ble food customs. But such reflection is invaluable to understanding. It is also possible that we really are what we eat – physiologically – but because each of us is a part of an ethnocultural heritage, it is even more probable that *we eat what we are*.

Thelma Barer-Stein
January 1979, London, Ont.

How to Use This Book

You Eat What You Are is a documented study of ethnocultural food traditions. The book's fifty-two chapters represent main ethnocultural divisions, but in fact these chapters consider the food traditions of more than one hundred ethnic groups.

Each chapter begins with a general historical and socio-cultural background, giving particular emphasis to those factors or events that dictated the food habits of the groups studied. The next section, **Home Life and Facilities**, considers elements in the sociological makeup of family life, the home itself, as well as specific facilities within the home that have direct influence on food traditions.

A specially accentuated section of each chapter, **Foods Commonly Used**, is intended for quick and easy reference and provides an overview of basic dietary preferences. For a more detailed view, these food preferences are then divided into eight categories: **Milk and Milk Products, Fruits and Vegetables, Meats and Alternates, Breads and Cereals, Fats, Sweets and Snacks, Seasonings, Beverages**. It must be emphasized that these represent *traditional* foods and only occasionally mention more recent food customs, where these have become firmly entrenched.

The section **Meal Patterns and Eating Customs** (included in most chapters) deals with the traditional times of meals and snacks, and gives examples of typical foods, where and how they are eaten, and, where applicable, noteworthy elements of hospitality peculiar to the cultural group are included.

The next section, **Special Occasions**, discusses the practices and symbolism of family and religious occasions, with special emphasis on those relating to foods. It is in this section that religious observances of the ethnocultural group or subgroup are given attention.

In only selected chapters are the categories **Cooking Methods** and **Regional Specialties** considered because these factors are not relevant or clearly differentiated in all ethnocultural groups.

Following the last chapter are **Source References**, with the numerical designation of entries corresponding to footnote numbers within the text of each chapter. This listing will serve as a useful and comprehensive bibliography for those wishing to pursue further study. In addition, some of these sources contain information relating to recipes for food preparation.

FOR THOSE INTERESTED, SUPPLEMENTARY FOOD AND COOKING TERM GLOSSARIES ARE AVAILABLE AT COST. PLEASE DIRECT INQUIRIES TO THE AUTHOR C/O McCLELLAND AND STEWART LIMITED, 25 HOLLINGER ROAD, TORONTO M4B 3G2.

ACKNOWLEDGEMENTS

Every project has a beginning, but some need a push to get them going. The Toronto Nutrition Committee recognized the need for a factual reference on ethnic foods and, in 1959, published their first manual, *Food Habits of New Canadians*, followed in 1967 by *Food Customs of New Canadians*. It was with their warm encouragement and firm support that this book was instigated. My thanks especially to three members of the Toronto Nutrition Committee: Nina Burgess, Linda (Beardall) Pickard, and Jennifer Welsh.

Endorsement came from the following, to whom I am most grateful:

Dr. Thomas M.B. Symons, Chairman, Commission on Canadian Studies
Anna Porter, then Editor-in-Chief, McClelland and Stewart Ltd.
Frank Corcoran, Acting Chief, Communications Division, National Museum of Man
Marjorie Hollands, R.P.Dt., Chief Dietitian, Tri-Hospital Diabetes Education Centre, Women's College Hospital, Toronto
Eleanor Sortome, R.P.Dt., Executive Director, Canadian Dietetic Association
William J. Pillsworth, Director Community Services, Fanshawe College, London, Ontario
Pegi M. Walden, President, Ontario Folk Arts Council
Nancy E. Schwartz, Ph.D., Assistant Professor, Division of Human Nutrition, School of Home Economics, University of British Columbia
Patricia Giovannetti, Ph.D., Chairman, Department of Home Economics, Brescia College, University of Western Ontario
Ben G. Kayfetz, Executive Director, Canadian Jewish Congress
E. Margaret Pope, President (1975) Canadian Home Economics Association.

Some very heartwarming assistance and efforts on my behalf were extended by these special people, just when I almost gave up: Robert Siskind, L.L.B.; C. David Carmichael, Timothy Eger, and Andrew Schapiro.

That first push, hopeful endorsements, and special efforts kept me researching, compiling, and writing and then the following people came up with some elusive pieces of information to fill in the gaps: Ann McColl Lindsay, Olga Davidson, Marilyn Chapman, Rhian Haldane, Ayhan Atkay, Melrose Micallef Paquet, Kalja and Asta Loone and their daughter Hilja, Dr. George Wong, Pearl Wong and Helen Beck. Still more information was generously offered by: Estelle Reed, Citizenship Department, Ministry of Culture and Recreation, Toronto; Jessie Rae, Chief Nutritionist, Department of Public Health, Halifax, Nova Scotia; Joy Johns, Nutritionist, Moncton, New Brunswick; Olga Anderson, Chief Nutritionist, Department of Public Health, Newfoundland; Ellen Powers, Executive Director, Writer's Union of Canada; Constance Acheson, Saint John Regional Library, New Brunswick; James A. Draper, Ph.D., Associate Professor, University of Toronto, Ontario Institute for Studies in Education. Credit and thanks to Dr. Harold Troper, professor in the history and philosophy department at O.I.S.E., who coined the term "gastroethnology."

At a time when encouragement was most needed during the five years of research and writing, financial assistance came from a Canada Council Explorations Grant, a Wintario Grant, and an Ontario Arts Council Grant, for all of which I would like to express my deepest gratitude.

And finally, but probably most importantly, my very deepest loving appreciation to my four children, who cried with me over the rejections, screamed with me joyfully over the acceptances and encouragements, and now share profoundly my pleasure of accomplishment. It would have been much tougher (and not so much fun) without them: Debbie, an upcoming dietitian, Lori, an Honours Anthropology graduate, Jody, a Business student, and The Gord, a medical school hopeful. They not only suffered the range of emotions, they also taste-tested so many varieties of foods (depending on which chapter I was working on) that finally the plaintive plea came from The Gord, "Can't we just eat hotdogs like everyone else?" Yes, perhaps now we can.

ONE

African

To place Africa, which is the second largest continent in the world, with more than 270 million people in more than thirty countries speaking 800 languages,[1] all into one small chapter has to be a gross injustice. At best, the information presented here should be considered only a guide to an appreciation and understanding of this vast and fascinating continent, her people and her food.

Over the centuries, other countries have conquered, explored, and exploited both the natural resources and the human beings of this continent who were regarded as pagans to be converted or as merchandise to be shipped as slaves to other parts of the world. And though this mostly tropical and subtropical continent clings for the most part to deeply imbedded cultural traditions of its own, France, the United Kingdom, the Netherlands, Spain and Portugal have left traces of their influence. After centuries of disease and neglect, attempts are being made – by a new and burgeoning middle class – to blend old traditions and modern developments for the benefit of the entire land. But change does not come easily to any country or people. The newborn states of Africa are struggling with problems of political and economic chaos, tribal rivalries, famine, poverty, and lack of education.[2,3]

From the 1500s to the 1700s, African Blacks, mainly from the area of West Africa (today comprising: Senegal, Guinea, Sierra Leone, Gambia, Liberia, Ivory Coast, Ghana, Dahomey, Togo, Nigeria, Cameroon, and Gabon[4]), were shipped as slaves to America, Brazil, and the West Indies. For them, local and tribal differences, and even varying cultural backgrounds, soon melded into one common concern for the suffering they all endured. Music, songs, and dances as well as remembered traditional foods, helped not only to uplift them, but also quite unintentionally added immeasurably to the entire culture around them. In the approximately 300 years that the Blacks have made their homes in America, the West Indies, and Brazil, their highly-honed art of the cuisine so treasured and carefully transmitted to their daughters, has today become part of the great culinary classics of these lands. But all too seldom are the African Blacks given that recognition.

Of African origin are such specialities as GUMBO and PRALINES, WEST INDIAN CALALOO and DUCKANDOO (a dish of greens and a dessert based on sweet potatoes), the Brazilian condiments, DENDE OIL and spicy hot sauces.[5] Jamaica's BAMMY BREAD and the PAN BREAD so beloved in the southern United States are both said to have their origin in the flat round CASSAVA BREADS so typical of Africa.[4] Seeds and the plants of sesame, okra, some melons, and certain varieties of greens as well as yams, together with many techniques of bread making, and the use and combination of spices are also all credited to the ingenuity of the African cook.[4,5,6]

It could be argued that every nation and every ethnic group has its own soul food. But the contemporary connotation of the term "soul food" refers to the gradual blending and developing of a peculiar style of cookery with its own dictionary of food terms: it is a blend of West African cookery begun in the southern United States and now very much a part of the cultural tradition of every African American binding him proudly to his African heritage. "Soul food" incorporates an economical and satisfying cuisine based on cereals, vegetables (greens and yams), pork and pork offal as well as chicken.[4]

In modern times, African immigrants have come to Canada or the United States often as political refugees and many as temporary students who later decide to remain as citizens. Most recent African immigrants to Canada come mainly from Tanzania, Kenya, Nigeria, and Ghana.[7]

When speaking of Africa, it is very important to differentiate between urban and rural populations. Not only are the urban people in many areas still more or less influenced by European customs and manners, but they may also be a part of the growing middle class which is creating a new, independent African image, culture, and cuisine. Although this middle class is growing, still the dominant concern lies with the three-quarters of the African population who are rural and tradition-bound.

Because of the lack of large mountain ranges, the climate of Africa is surprisingly consistent except for the southern more temperate areas. Most of its people belong to a pastoral society where life revolves around the seasons, the crops, the villages, and the tribes. In most areas a subsistence economy predominates: the concern is for survival not profit. This outlook has pragmatic roots. Food is more important than money;

cattle are often more important as a status symbol than as food; food spoilage from rodents, humidity, or insects is prevalent and common; transportation to distant markets for trade or profit is difficult and often impossible because of lack of roads or vehicles or both. In fact, Jacques May reports that: "given better seed, he [the African farmer] will rejoice not because it will give him a better yield, but because he will get the same result from a smaller plot . . ."[8]

The problems encountered by those attempting to introduce scientific agrarian methods are further complicated by general poor soil, lack of storage facilities, lack of trained technicians or available parts for mechanical equipment, and finally, the problems of a population that absorbs more and more land.

While the Canadian or American of African descent is proudly re-learning his heritage and establishing himself as a valued member of the community, the peoples of his African homeland are struggling to ease themselves into the twentieth century socially, economically, and politically; but hopefully with the increasing understanding of a concerned and committed world.

Home Life and Facilities (Rural)

Cookery methods rather than basic foods are what distinguish regional and ethnic dishes in Africa. Foods may be cooked over open fires or in pits heated with stones; either of these methods may be used indoors or outside. Commonly used cookery utensils include: perforated clay steamers, jugs and jars for storage, strainers, mortar and pestle, knives, enamel and clay cooking pots, wooden bowls and spoons (FUFU is always stirred with a wooden spoon), graters, frying baskets. Grinding stones are used to mill grains; dried gourds and calabash shells used as spoons and ladles – and many of these are beautifully decorated and carved.[6,10]

Food storage is a great problem because of the climate and a prevalence of insects and rodents, but elevated platforms, vessels, and cages, strung and held up, and covered clay containers and woven covers of many types are used.

Eating and cooking, if not done outdoors are usually done in a special hut, which usually has floors that have been finished with a paste of dried cow dung.[10] A special ledge along one side may be used to store most of the cookery utensils, especially the treasured clay pots and jugs. In some areas, in addition to pits and the use of open fires, ovens built of dried mud may be used for baking.

Foods are generally used on a day to day basis, and the amount required is judged – seldom asked for by weight. Africa has an oral rather than a written tradition: events and traditions are passed by word of mouth and by careful demonstration, dance, or song. The written word and such things as weights and measures were never important in traditional rural communities. Introduction of weights and measures is a slow process whereas amounts are taught to and somehow learned by young children.[6]

Cutlery is seldom used for eating except in cities and then often only in European company. Even in urban areas, the family evening meal will likely be a traditional FUFU with condiment sauces all enjoyed in the traditional way from community platters and eaten with the fingers.

FOODS COMMONLY USED

Although there are many ethnic groups in Africa, it is possible to make some generalizations in regard to the foods and food customs. In some areas, different names may be used but it is generally conceded that the principal African staple food is a starchy mixture called FUFU which is eaten with spicy sauces and condiments. The starchy mixture may be prepared from any cereal or starchy vegetable or root, by pounding into a paste and then cooking with water like a cereal. It is eaten with three fingers of the right hand by forming it into a ball then dipping into flavourful and spicy sauces. Rice, yams, cassava, plantain, corn, millet, or cocoyams may be used. More sophisticated versions may be formed into small cakes or fritters and fried, or formed into small balls and poached, then served much the same way as dumplings are in other countries.

The condiment sauces are skilfully prepared from locally available spices and herbs and often include onions, tomatoes, meats and bones, fish and seafood, and various root and green vegetables; even fruits, depending on availability. The use of fiery peppers and chilies of many types and distinguishable flavour and hotness is universal. Many a husband judges his wife's love and respect by the hotness of her sauces.[9]

Considerable ingenuity is also displayed in the preparation and variety of breads, fried cakes, and fritters prepared from flours made from cassava, millet, manioc, wheat, and corn.

Soups are the staple food of the nomadic tribespeople, moving from place to place in search of cattle food. They use milk and prepare butter but choose to collect wild vegetables and occasional wild animals rather than their herds for food.

Traditionally, fruit wines, beers made from various cereals, and a slightly fermented beverage made from porridge water (MAHEU) are the beverages usually taken between meals rather than with food. More recently, sugar and honey-sweetened tea and coffee and commercial soft drinks are replacing the traditional and more nourishing beverages.

Milk and Milk Products

Cow's milk, goat's milk and sheep's milk, taken plain or soured or in the form of curds and whey, are used as available. Most often they are used for infants and young children as part of soups, gruels, and puddings. Certain herdsmen are known to drink a beverage of milk and blood. Soured milk is preferred by adults in some areas. Farmers use milk products less often than the nomadic tribes, who prefer to take milk products in the form of soups and buttery sauces.

Fruits and Vegetables

Fresh fruits are eaten in season everywhere as they are available, whether wild or cultivated. Especially plentiful are varieties of mangoes and bananas, used green or ripe, to be eaten as they are or used in sauces. Other fruits include the whole range of tropical and subtropical fruits such as melons, HACHA, BAOBAB, MUSHANGE, HWAKWA (African orange), ONDE, wild plums and berries, wild figs, dates, wild or KAFIR ORANGES, coconut, papaya, avocado, pineapple.[11,9,10]

Most popular vegetables include: plantains, green bananas, pumpkin, okra, yams, cocoyams, spinach, cress, mustard greens, fresh corn. Cultivated vegetables include many varieties of beans, cucumbers, tomatoes, onions, garlic, cabbage, carrots, and potatoes. To these must be added the many local varieties of wild and indigenous roots, tubers, bush greens, and mushrooms.[4,10,11,9]

Meats and Alternates

In most of rural Africa meats from any source are an infrequent part of the usual diet. It will likely be the highlight of a special occasion or given to special guests. Most meats and fowl are tough and stringy and require long, slow cooking with moisture, so are most often used in soups or stewed or braised dishes. It should also be noted that most African women are experts at preserving whatever meat may be available by methods of salting, drying, pickling and/or smoking. In rural areas where cattle are still considered a sign of wealth and status, beef is seldom used for food, but may be in the urban dietary. Some forest animals, pigs (not used by Muslims), goats and sheep, antelope, elephant, and oxen may be used for food.[6] Many varieties of mice are eaten in season and there is also seasonal use of black and red ants and caterpillars as well as some types of grasshopper. Many taboos surround the eating of offal, chicken, and eggs and care is taken to avoid a guest's particular taboo or superstition.

Fish and seafood are commonly only eaten close to their sources, such as in coastal areas, or near lakes, streams, or rivers. Yet many experts have expressed strong feelings about the urgency and the importance of improving fishing methods and storage and transportation facilities since this is an abundant resource that could greatly increase the general protein food supply.[8,12]

There is a very wide variety of pulses used everywhere that form an important part of the diet. Peas, beans, and lentils of many varieties are readily stored and easily cooked into soups, sauces, side dishes, in combination with vegetables, or mashed and fried as cakes.

Varieties of nuts and seeds are used depending on local preference and availability but most popular are GROUNDNUTS, the African name for peanuts. They are used in soups, stews and sauces and as garnishes. GROUNDNUT BUTTER is used as a seasoning.

Breads and Cereals
The staple African food, FUFU, which is prepared from almost any available starchy plant source, forms 80 per cent of the daily calories consumed while the average European diet contains only 30 per cent calories from breads or cereals.[10] It must be stressed, then, that the general African diet is one that is high in fibre and carbohydrates, with proteins and fats forming only a small part.[10] Principal sources for flours and FUFU preparation are: maize, manioc, sorghum, millet, wheat and rice. Plantain, green bananas, and yams are the favourites for FUFU. Many varieties of bread are made from the flours and these are further varied by including recipes for breads that are both leavened and unleavened. Some flours are allowed to ferment first to improve flavour.[8,9,12]

SWAHILI YEAST is the leavening agent prepared by mashing ripe plantain with a little water, sugar, and wheat flour, and allowing it to ferment in a warm place. It not only leavens the dough but adds a sourdough-type flavour to buns, breads, and fried cookies.

Fats
The most-used fats are oils prepared from vegetables, seeds, or coconut. In some areas olive oil or palm oil is used, as available. GROUNDNUTS are sometimes used for their oil but the nuts themselves are more important; the pulp mash left after the oil extraction is also used as food.

Sweets and Snacks
Desserts are mainly fresh fruits in season and as they are affordable or available. They are also nibbled as snacks.[9] More recently there is a large increase in the use of sweetened tea and coffee as well as sweetened commercial soft drinks. An occasional snack or dessert may be of spiced and sugared fried pancakes or cookies; frying more popular than baking because not everyone has an oven. Some honey and preserves are used as sweetening agents.

Seasonings
Blends of many types and flavours in spicy, sweet, and various degrees of

hotness in curries are widely used all over Africa. Many varieties of chilies and hot peppers are savoured.[12,8] Ground sesame seeds (plain or toasted), melon seeds, cotton seeds, as well as fresh and dried types of mushrooms, are also used. Special seasoning pastes are prepared from seeds that have been dried in the sun, then steamed and fermented. Small amounts of the resulting paste are used as a flavouring. One such is called OGILIE.[6]

It should be noted that all foods are not only hotly seasoned but well salted. Salt is obtained by burning certain grasses or tree barks and the resulting ash passed through calabash sieves, then boiled in clay pots until a residue of whitish salt is formed. A third salt source was from certain soils where animals were observed licking; the watery residue from repeated washings of such soil would be boiled and found to leave a salty residue.[10]

Beverages

Although the exact names may differ from one region to another, soured milk (from cow, sheep, goat or camel), beer and wine made locally are all familiar beverages, as is the ever-present hospitable tea and coffee. Coconut milk and juices from fruits are also widely used both as drinks and as cookery ingredients. Commercial soft drinks are now increasingly used.[12]

Meal Patterns and Eating Customs

The majority of rural Africans customarily eat one main meal a day and this is usually the evening meal. Upon arising, coffee, tea or milk or curds may form a small light meal while some may be content to nibble on seeds. Throughout the day snacks of fruits, seeds, or nuts may be accompanied with beverages. In some areas a midday meal of FUFU and relishes may be traditionally larger than the evening meal, which in this case would then be a cereal dish alone of gruel or FUFU.[10]

Infants are usually breast fed on demand up to the age of two years. Attempts to introduce bottle feedings have often met with sad results: sterilization of bottles and formula were poorly understood, formulas were diluted to last longer, and with the abandonment of breast feeding, intercourse was resumed earlier than usual with a resultant increase in children who could be ill-afforded. BOTA is a thin gruel for babies, fed by pouring into the mother's hand and gently easing into the infant's mouth. Some foods and medicinal herbs if deemed necessary are pre-chewed by the mother then given to the infant.

The very young child is taught early that meat is a delicacy, but like other pleasures, he is also taught that he cannot always have everything he may want: meat may be tasted and enjoyed, but it is generally not given until the child is at least three or four years of age.[10]

In most parts of Africa, meals follow strictly specified rituals. At a very young age, children learn that hand washing and clapping of the hands must always precede a meal. Children must be silent while adults eat; further, they must never beg for food. Violations of these rules of manners are punishable by beatings. Men precede women at meals but no one eats alone. Dining is always a group pleasure and a time of calm and serene enjoyment. In some areas it is considered that women are somehow self-sufficient, and no one seems concerned if they are left only the crumbs.

Often if new foods are introduced by aid groups from other countries, the food must be appealing to the men, for if refused by them no one else will touch it.

Hospitality is considered of great importance and also follows a predictable ritual of hand washing, clapping, and the offering of food. Even if one is not hungry, to refuse would be an insult.[9,10]

Totemism is greatly respected and it is considered proper to inquire of a guest what their totem is so that it may be separated from the rest of the food. For example, if the totem of a certain guest is liver, then liver will be removed from the rest of the meats to be served and given to the others so that the guest will not be offended. Other strongly-held traditions concern local clan, family, and tribal taboos: e.g., the eating of certain fish, eggs, or parts of animals or fowl may be taboo, and for the Muslims pork is forbidden.[8,10,12]

While food growing and harvesting is done by the men, women are responsible for collecting firewood and water and for food preparation. So seriously are these daily tasks taken, that young children perform play ceremonies enacting their parts as men and women of the household. This parent-supervised ceremony is called mahumbwe. Very young girls make serious play of helping their mothers and grandmothers at their tasks.

Finally, it is important to remember that the customs and traditions recorded here are a part of traditional and rural African life, but by no means practised consistently. A large and continually-growing population of Africa is the new middle class: freshly-educated, ambitious, sophisticated, and eagerly creating their own culinary and social arts liberally laced with ideas from their rich past, yet at the same time new. Three meals a day, school lunch programs, scientific fishing methods, modern farming techniques have already made many of the traditions seem archaic.

Regional Specialties

West Africa

Long in touch with Europeans, and the most heavily populated area in Africa, West Africa comprises Senegal, Gambia, Guinea, Sierra Leone, Liberia, Ivory Coast, Ghana, Togo, Dahomey, Nigeria, and Cameroon. Like most of Africa, three-quarters of the area's population is rural.[8]

Staples of the farmer's diet include milk and curds and whey, varieties of wild and cultivated green vegetables, dried peas, yams, corn, pumpkin, and types of squash. YAMS, CORN, CASSAVA and GROUNDNUTS are indispensables. CASSAVA is used mainly for its flour – which when slightly fermented is called GARI – and its green leaves are used as a vegetable. GROUNDNUTS are used in soups and stews and flavourful sauces. Eggplants, okra, garlic, onions, and tomatoes are important in many dishes too.

To the more sophisticated West African, FUFU (made from yams or plantains) is still a staple but is prepared in more imaginative forms: fried cakes, dumpling-like balls, thin-fried chips, croquettes and fritters. To add variety, some of these are served sweetened and lightly spiced. The rest of the diet is liberally laced with a wide variety of fish and seafood and there are many chicken dishes flavoured with GROUNDNUTS. Beef and mutton are scarce; chickens require careful cooking to tenderize. Eggs are used liberally and are an important part of many dishes. Both urban and rural dwellers use fruits in season as their means permit: bananas, plantain, papayas, mangoes, pineapples, coconuts, limes and lemons, melons, oranges, and the great variety of local tropical specialties.

Three specialties throughout the area are: YASSA, a general Senegalese term for lemon-marinated chicken, meat or fish dishes; JOLLOF RICE, a favourite special-occasion dish of steamed then browned meats layered with rice, tomatoes, hard-cooked eggs and vegetables, and named for the predominant vegetable; GARI FOTO, a stew-like dish of hard eggs, tomatoes, and onions. Fruit fritters are a popular dessert.[9,11]

This is an area where the new middle class is developing unusual and sophisticated dishes, combining indigenous fruits and vegetables in new ways.

East Africa
The three countries making up East Africa include: Uganda, Kenya, and Tanzania. Strong British influence is felt, although few British or East Indians remain. The British imported European and East Indian cereals, fruits, vegetables, tea and coffee and even domestic animals. Streams were stocked with trout.

Despite the availability of plentiful game, most of the people are vegetarians, living mostly on dairy products, grains, legumes and vegetables and fruits.[11,12] Sorghum, millet, corn, and wheat are widely used but rice remains a favourite in many meals and dishes. POMBE, the national beer, is everyone's beverage, including children.[12] Manioc, sweet potatoes, bananas, and plantain, together with local fruits, round out the diet. In coastal areas, fish and crustaceans are important. Snacks of fruit or sugar-cane are enjoyed; curry forms the favoured seasoning mixture. Other than POMBE, palm wine, tea, and coconut milk are the usual beverages.

South Africa

While the West African nations could be said to combine the most sophisticated of European, New World, and their own indigenous food influences, and the area of East Africa to be principally influenced by British and East Indian food traditions, South Africa is dominated by the influence of the Dutch. As early as 1651, Dutch settlers at the Cape created a colony with the sole purpose of supplying fresh food and other necessities to Dutch ships.

> . . . the richest, most complex and civilized
> contribution to the art of cooking in Africa
> evolved here.[11]

The Dutch Free Burghers and their Muslim slaves from the East Indies, French refugees, Germans, other Europeans and British all added their influence in customs, foods, and culture. The Cape Coloured include those of mixed Black and European background, strongly identifying with the Dutch, the French, and with Christianity. In some of the following typical foods and dishes can be seen the "marriage" of food customs that have created what is now typically South African fare.

The Cape Malay's (East Indies) favourite dishes include:

ATJAR: exotic pickles and preserves prepared from tropical fruits and vegetables which may be packed with brine, syrups or oils and seasoned with varying subtle or hot combinations of East Indian spices.

BREDIE: a specialty and often festive meat or fish stew redolent with onions and colourful with chunks of vegetables such as pumpkin, cauliflower, beans, etc., and taking its specific name from the predominating vegetable, e.g. PUMPKIN BREDIE.

SOSATIES (from the Malaysian SATE): marinated meats, skewered and grilled; snack or main dish.

South African Cape Malay meals may include one of the traditional dishes above as well as salads, pickles, chutneys, and condiments (such as BLATJANG: nuts, garlic, sweet preserved fruits and spices), served with rice and rounded off with sweet bakery and candies. Dates are widely used and a combination of sugar-sweetened dates and sliced onions is a frequent side dish. The ubiquitous TAMELETJE, basically a candy of caramelized sugar, is made in many versions too.

South African wines and brandies are known world wide, as are their fish and shellfish (periwinkles, mussels, crayfish or rock lobster), fowl and pork dishes. Grape-stuffed chickens or roast suckling pigs take precedence and are eaten on Sundays or special occasions by South Afrikaners of European origin. The moderate climate produces vegetables so plentiful and varied and popular that often half a dozen vegetable dishes or salads may accompany the main meal.[11] A plethora of both tropical and temperate fruits may be eaten fresh, preserved into jams and marmalades, dried, or used in desserts and bakery. Cookies of infinite variety (SOETKOEKIE), and many types of buns (MOSBOLLETJE), as well as pies and tarts (TERTS), and doughnuts and crullers (VETKOEKIES) head the list of favourites that are nibbled for snacks or eaten at breakfast time with hot cocoa, tea or coffee. And as with Dutch families the world over, bread on the table is an important element of every meal.

The native Bantu's staple diet includes milk from cattle, millet porridge, and millet beer and MEALIE. So popular is MEALIE, a porridge made from cornmeal but served in many forms, such as puddings, fried patties, etc., that many a South Afrikaner's meal is not considered complete without at least a side dish of MEALIE; with cream and honey it may be breakfast.

BRAAIVLEIS is the traditional South African outdoor meal of grilled skewered meats (usually lamb, huge rolled links of homemade beef and pork sausage) to be grilled, and many vegetable and salad side dishes with the traditional dish of MEALIE.

Special Occasions

For the most part, Africans are a part of a pastoral society and though many adhere to Christianity or Islam they still, to a greater or lesser degree, retain elements of totemism and animism and many of their special occasions revolve around the seasons, planting and harvesting as well as family-life rituals. The land itself has a quasi-religious value to most Africans. This fact alone helps to explain (in spite of forced religious conversions) many cultural and religious ceremonies and the deep emotions relating to the dignity of work and the respect for ancestors. Land is not only the root of their culture and traditions, it also encompasses the whole realm of social relationships from duty to fellow tribesman to witchcraft. "Work is done as much in honor of ancestors and of the system as it is to provide food . . ."[12] Knowledge of these deeply imbedded traditions may help the Westerner to also understand the African's seemingly-stubborn resistance to mechanization, systems, and even to tools that are upsetting age-old traditions, which results in the hateful pitting of one generation against another.

Aside from the cycle of seasons and crops, birth, weddings, puberty, and death – visitors alone are reason enough for a "special occasion," and foods may seem festive merely because of the occasion. Or, depending on the area, the traditions, and the wealth and status, an animal or chickens may be specially slaughtered, special soups may be prepared with special ritual such as the "Blessing Soup" or MILIOKU NGOZI (a rich, hot chicken soup)[6] of West Africa, or simply a more generous quantity of the usual fare may be offered.

TWO

Albanian

Part of the Balkan world lying between Greece and Yugoslavia, the People's Republic of Albania, established in 1945, is said to be "the largest corner of wilderness left on the continent of Europe."[1]

Her people, mostly engaged in pastoral and agricultural pursuits, but barely eking an existence from a harsh, rocky land, have suffered through a 400-year domination of the Turkish Empire – where the food producers were serfs to the Sultan – to the present day where the farmer is now a serf to the State.[2] Problems of famine, malaria in the marshlands, illiteracy, and more currently alcoholism, have all combined to make the Albanian's life a difficult and insecure one.

Accustomed to authority and foreign domination, the insecurity of the Albanians is probably most evident in many of their mountain villages, where the dwellings are so cleverly disguised as to be indistinguishable from the native trees and rocks. Cultural influences include Italian, Greek, Turkish, and more currently, Russian. Progress is being made in medical areas (control of diseases), agricultural irrigation and diversity and there has been an increase in literacy. Cottage industries and increase in crop yields, such as rice, are slowly lifting the general living standard.[2]

While corn is the Albanian's mainstay, rice is also much enjoyed when available and a large variety of cheeses made from goat and ewe's milk supplement the daily diet. In the eastern areas and the plains, Albanian cooking rivals some of the finest in the Turkish and Greek cuisine, but as one moves northward into the mountain areas where poverty and illiteracy increases, the diet is based almost solely on corn, cheeses and KOS (yoghurt).

Home Life and Facilities

Generalization is not possible. Wealth and status vary from almost primitive conditions to a sophistication equal to any European city. Similarly the range of styles of family relationships, types, and styles of foods and food utensils are just as varied, although they may be similar to those found in the neighbouring countries of Italy, Greece, and Yugoslavia.

FOODS COMMONLY USED

The staples of the Albanian diet include: corn, seasonal fruits, such as olives, lemons, figs, and oranges; ewe's and goat's milk from which cheeses and KOS are made.[2,3] The Albanians live simply. Only special occasions or social status differentiate the quantity or variety of daily food. In some areas water for drinking is so scarce that dishes are said to be washed in goat's milk in order to conserve the precious water.[2]

Because draft animals are valued for power and by-products, they have for many thousands of years been considered too valuable to be used merely for food. As a result, the Albanian diet is mainly a vegetarian one except for the occasions or status that permit the use of lamb, pigs in Catholic areas, and sometimes chickens. Unfortunately, a lack of scientific chicken breeding has resulted in only small and sporadic egg production, so that eggs have never formed an important part of the diet. The main source of protein in the mountain areas is cheese, while fish predominates along the coastal areas and in the cities. Everywhere, KOS and cheese are much preferred over the use of fluid milk.

Milk and Milk Products

As already mentioned, milk from goats and ewes is made into KOS and many varieties of cheeses. Both fluid fresh milk and butter are seldom used. KOS is used alone or eaten with other foods.

Fruits and Vegetables

Oranges, lemons, and figs are the main available fruits; some grapes and wild berries are made into fermented beverages. Mixed garden vegetables are used seasonally and as available and these include: cucumbers, onions, peppers, eggplants, zucchini, marrows, okra, squash (KUNGULL), potatoes, and tomatoes. With the establishment of canneries, there has been a gradual increase in the consumption of canned fruits and vegetables.

Meats and Alternates

The favoured meats in the Balkan area (where meat is used) are lamb and mutton and sometimes chicken. Liver is considered a delicacy. Meats are usually prepared in types of stews or as PILAFS with rice, or may be skewered and roasted over open fires. There is also a variety of nuts grown locally: walnuts, almonds, pine nuts, and hazelnuts. These may be used as nibbles, crushed (sometimes with garlic) and used as sauces over meats and/or vegetables. (Please refer also to Greek cuisine.)

Breads and Cereals

The most successful crops of the Albanian farmers have for centuries been their grains. Predominantly corn but also wheat, rye, oats, and barley are harvested.[2] These grains have been used to produce a variety of flours for breads that are used mainly in the coastal areas and cities. But the main type of bread – indeed the main food – is a flat pancake-shaped cornbread broken into pieces and enjoyed with KOS or cheese.

Fats

Olive oil is the main type of fat used everywhere.

Sweets and Snacks

Albanians favour very sweet and rich desserts made with nuts and syrupy sauces. The combination of thin, crisp pastries (identical to the Greek PHYLLO) with nuts, sugar or honey, cinnamon and cloves, and finished with a heavy syrup, or very sweet puddings, are as beloved by the Albanians as they are by the Turks and Greeks.

Seasonings

A people who favour very sweet desserts will almost certainly also enjoy highly-seasoned foods, and the Albanians are no exception. Generous portions of garlic and onions, tart touches of lemon juice or lemon gratings, and the more subtle enhancement of dill and parsley as well as cinnamon and cloves waft through Albanian foods. The combination of crushed or chopped nuts with garlic and oil, to be served with greens or chicken, as well as the combination of nuts and raisins either for nibbling or as part of exotic sauces, are all typically Albanian.

Beverages

Sweet desserts and highly-seasoned foods as well as a difficult life all seem to create a need for strong drink. Cool soups made from pureed or chopped fruit or vegetables plus KOS are often taken as cooling liquid refreshment. Small cups of mint and sugared tea, as well as tiny cups of Turkish coffee, often provide afternoon or hospitality refreshment. Hardier local specialties include:

DUKAGJIN: a drink made from grape juice, sugar and mustard.

HARDIC: a drink made from wild berries.

ORME: an appetizer drink made from fermented cabbage, similar to the juice from sauerkraut.

RAKI: a potent brandy, flavoured from mulberries and served as an aperitif before meals or on special occasions.

Meal Patterns and Eating Customs

Again a distinction must be drawn between the humble farmers and mountain-dwelling herders and the urban upper classes. For the mountaineer, flat cornbread is his staple, and since famine and starvation are not new, a deep appreciation of the importance of bread is expressed by the host, who always breaks the bread first and then shares it with all at his table; then, and only then, are any other available foods placed on the table.

In other areas, it is customary to bring all foods to the table, where they are shared by all the diners usually after appetizers (MEZE) with RAKI or RAKI MANASH have been served. Three meals a day, similar to most western and European styles, are common except, again, to the humbler farmer or mountaineer to whom each meal will likely be the same – and gratefully received: KOS and cornbread.

If a late afternoon tea or coffee break is taken it is called SILLE and may include sweet pastries, nuts, and fresh local fruits.

Special Occasions

Culturally, the Albanians are said to be a "leftover of the Turkish Empire"[2] with approximately 70 per cent practising the faith of Islam, eschewing pork and pork products, but relaxing the usual prohibitions against alcohol: in fact, alcoholic beverages are consumed freely.

Albanians are also strongly influenced in their traits and their practices by their heritage of two main ancestral tribes: the reserved but war-like Ghegs from the north, and the gay, extroverted Tosks from the south.

Among both upper and lower classes throughout Albania, preparation of special occasion fare almost always results in an expansion in the quantity of favoured foods. For the rural poor it may mean their first taste of meat in a very long time (they are vegetarians by necessity, not necessarily by desire), while for others the special occasion may simply be a feast of overabundance, as they eat their way through a formidable list of appetizers and repeated drinks of RAKI, and have to make an effort to continue through the sumptuous and often exotic main dishes to follow.

Since Albania is a land not only of male dominance by custom, but male dominance by population, men are served first and treated with great deference and respect; this is not a custom reserved just for special occasions.

THREE

American

It is for good reason that Israel Zangwill's coinage of the term "Melting Pot," for the name of a play in 1908[1] still serves as an apt description of the United States today. For like Canada, the United States is a nation of immigrants, each ethnic group retaining folk customs, festivals, and food traditions with great pride and yet with a stamp that is different from "home," one that is unmistakably American. Huge areas of fertile land, abundant natural resources, and some of the world's most advanced technology, marketing and transportation systems combine to give America one of the highest living standards in the world.

Though the casual visitor may conclude that America's staple foods are hotdogs, hamburgers, and french fries, washed down with cola drinks, and topped off with ice cream, a more careful examination will reveal regional as well as ethnic specialties that have been adapted to the foods of the New World.

The early immigrants had little concern for Old World traditions. Making a living, creating a home, and raising a family were the basic realities of everyday life. Food was whatever was available and affordable to fill an empty stomach. And yet the newcomers soon found solace in grouping together to help each other in neighbourhoods where the familiar languages, customs, and countrymen somehow gave strength for whatever the future might hold. It was good to share a glass of homemade wine, a pint of beer or a schnapps. It was comforting to smell the familiar scents of cooking and baking and even better to drown a day's hard work and long hours in a homey soup or a familiar stew. For of all the old customs and traditions that somehow no longer "fit" into this new life, the traditions of country foods were and still are a source both of comfort and pride and are recently enjoying a revival everywhere from private homes to restaurants to country fairs.

But long before all the others, bands of Indians whose ancestors had probably crossed the Bering Strait thousands of years before the white man had even heard of America, made their way southward in the great continent, founding villages and developing languages and social systems and adapting to the land in ways uniquely and often ingeniously their own. It was the agricultural Indians of America who introduced to the world such staples as corn, tomatoes, squash, peanuts, tobacco, turkeys, and wild rice.[2] Other American Indians depended on wild animals and fish, seasonal fruits and plants, roots, seeds, and nuts.

It was from the Indians that the earliest pioneers learned how to prepare many foods from corn (which kept them from starvation) and later from pumpkins and squash and even to tap wild maple trees for sweet maple syrup. And in order to avoid cooking on the Sabbath, the Puritans adopted the Indian clambake technique and used it to make slow-simmered beans cooked in the Indian way (today called NEW ENGLAND BAKED BEANS): a sealed bean pot is buried overnight in a pit of embers. In modified version – slow-baked overnight in the oven – it is enjoyed to this day.

As the early pioneers settled into the land, the ethnic foods from the yellowed and often handwritten recipe books they had brought with them, soon became adapted to the variety of new and different produce plentifully available. Ethnic melded into regional specialties and although few writers dare to define the exact borders of these regions, nonetheless distinct food preparations do exist.

Home Life and Facilities

Some of the earliest cooking by European immigrants was done in brick ovens and in iron pots suspended over open hearths. The earliest dishes used were trenchers: carved wooden plates, and deep bowls. Eating and cooking spoons were usually also carved from wood, but toasting forks, waffle irons, and fry pans – all made with long handles so they could be thrust into the fire – were made of iron. Up to 1650, pewterware was imported from Holland, but by 1750 it was made in America.[3] In the South, in the late 1600s/early 1700s cast ironware was favoured for cooking, and foods were prepared and cooked in a slave kitchen, the term used for a small house built apart from the main house.

The Dutch influence began about 1614, with the settlement of New Amsterdam on what was later to be called Manhattan Island. Small flower gardens bloomed with bulbs from Holland and every house boasted a variety of home-grown vegetables from a plot of land near the house. With concern for the lean winter months, the Dutch always built their houses over cellars where an array of home preserves, sausages, head cheeses, root vegetables and pickled meats and fish were safely stored.

Ironware, hearth-cooking and brick ovens have not entirely disappeared from the American scene, but Treen (the variety of wooden cooking and eating ware) and many pewter pieces are now only collectors' items. Probably the most modern kitchens in the world, containing the most in cookery gadgets and small specialty appliances, are to be found in even average-income American homes today. For only imagination and the family budget limit the scope and variety of electrical appliances, plastic ware, cookware, dishes and serving utensils available not only locally as manufactured goods, but as a wide selection of imports as well.

Average American homes boast ranges and refrigerators, ample storage cupboards, cellars and home freezers (or rented freezer lockers) and a host of small appliances from juicers and blenders to yoghurt makers. Supermarkets and specialty stores supply local specialties and fresh produce as well as an incredible array of imported delicacies that permit the gourmet cook to literally "cook the world over." Because of ease of supply and ample storage, American homemakers may shop as infrequently as once a week for their food needs and many of the items they buy will be partially or completely prepared foods.

FOODS COMMONLY USED

With rapid transportation means within the country and superior storage both in private homes and in industry, Americans in almost any area can enjoy not only local seasonal foods and produce but an endless array of imported, frozen, dried, and canned foods available the year round. Almost every small town will have its supermarkets, specialty bake shops and quick-serve fast-food outlets. All types of foods are readily available, so that what is chosen for the day's foods will reflect personal preference, ethnic background, local custom, state of health (special diet), rather than any market or seasonal limitation.

The American may be said to consume a traditional three meals a day, but the prevalence of "coffee breaks" and quick-snack foods make it seem closer to one continual daily meal.

Milk and Milk Products

These products in every form: fluid, fresh, whole, skimmed or partially skimmed milk, buttermilk, butter, imported and local cheeses of many varieties and all types and flavours of sherbets and ice creams are all widely available and used. More recently there has been an increase in the use of yoghurt, both plain and sweetened or flavoured. As interest in travel and international cookery increases, so does the use of pot cheese, cottage cheese and sour cream, and some of the more unusual cheese varieties.

Fruits and Vegetables
Fresh and frozen, canned and dried fruits and vegetables, as well as local and imported produce, are available in most areas regardless of season, although out-of-season produce may be higher in cost. Citrus fruits, melons, and other semi-tropical fruits and vegetables, are shipped to northern climates so that a steady supply of fruit varieties and salad greens is always available. Specialty fruits and vegetables imported from other countries are usually available in larger centres. All root vegetables, such as carrots, potatoes, yams, and beets, are used and available in all parts of the country, potatoes being a great favourite.

Meats and Alternates
Beef is a great American favourite. Consumed in lesser quantities are pork and pork products, chickens, ducks (domestic and wild), geese, game birds, veal, and lamb. Eggs are consumed almost daily, prepared in many specialty dishes such as omelets and souffles and custards, and are used frequently as ingredients in many other dishes. Fish is favoured by certain ethnic groups and especially in coastal regions where freshly caught. Fish may be purchased as fresh, frozen (in many states of full or partial preparation for eating), dried, and canned. Legumes are not widely consumed except as a budget dish, a regional or ethnic favourite. Nuts are used mostly as garnishes or tasty ingredients in desserts or baked goods. But peanuts and peanut butter are used so widely that they could be considered a staple food in some households.

Breads and Cereals
White breads and rolls and dry prepared breakfast cereals are great American favourites. Wheat is most universally used in cereals and baked goods. Corn may be used as a vegetable (corn on the cob), for corn oil, or specially prepared as GRITS, or as cornflour for regional specialty dishes. All grains are readily available but are used more on the basis of personal, ethnic, or regional tastes.

Fats
In the South, lard is the favoured fat for all cookery but butter is used at the table and for special bakery. Elsewhere all varieties of oils, salted and sweet butter, many types of margarine, shortenings as well as lard and drippings, are used according to individual preference.

Seasonings

A common sight in most highway restaurants, quick-serve food outlets and on the "average" American table, are the salt and pepper shakers and the bottle of ketchup or catsup, a spiced thick tomato condiment used to season virtually anything. The average household spice shelf is stocked in amount and diversity by the household cook, and probably reflects an ethnic background.

Beverages

With the exception of very poor rural and urban areas children consume large quantities of fresh milk, sweetened flavoured soft drinks and fruit juices, as well as many kinds of synthetic sweetened drinks. Adults favour coffee and beer, others tea and wine. With increased cost of imported wines, more attention is being given to the fine wines produced in California and in New York State.

Meal Patterns and Eating Customs

In the 1600s meals were served by placing foods in trenchers in the middle of the table and each person ate by spooning up the foods from the communal dishes. Woodenware eventually gave way to silverware and china dishes. Before 1700 it was considered correct to serve dessert or pudding first and each meal was always accompanied with fresh hot breads, milk and butter.[3]

In early times too daily physical exertion was the rule and the hearty meals provided warmth and energy, and often breakfast was indistinguishable in substance from any other meal of the day. But as technology made life simpler and easier, working hours shortened and more and more of the populace became urban dwellers, the heavy meals and rich array of foods were not only no longer necessary, they were impractical and expensive.

Today's trend is breakfast-on-the-run, which usually means simply orange juice and coffee. Typical lunches include sandwich, milk or coffee, and fruit or ice cream. Dinner in the evening is usually the only meal when most families are together, and the usual pattern is soup or appetizer, meat or fish plus vegetables, a dessert, and tea, coffee, or milk completes the meal.

But Americans, like most of the western world, love to snack. Coffee breaks and coffee parties, the easy access of the corner variety store for candy, pop, and chewing gum, or the fast-food outlet with ethnic specialties such as TACOS or PIZZA as well as hamburgers, hotdogs, ice cream, and french fries all seem necessary to keep the American fueled. More and more the pattern of three meals a day is blurring into a day-long fest of nibbling from breakfast to the late-evening show on television. A day of work or play is always accompanied by munching and sipping.

Regional Specialties

The diverse food patterns within the United States differentiate themselves geographically in terms of food, indigenous to particular areas, even though some food traditions discussed may have ethnic roots.

Southern States

"Take two and butter 'em while they're hot!" refers to the southern predilection for a variety of delicious home-baked hot breads and beaten biscuits, which are eaten at almost every meal. As famed as "Southern Hospitality" are Virginia ham, southern fried chicken, HOG 'N HOMINY (pork and pork products served with corn grits), cornbread, hoecake and cornpone, and a delectable array of desserts, e.g. trifle, Sally Lunn, Tipsy Pie, pecan pie, and George Washington cake.

Many specialty dishes of the southern Blacks, enjoyed as "soul food," originated from the humble foods culled from and served with imagination by the early Black slaves. Well-cooked greens of all types, wild and cultivated, such as kale, collard and mustard greens, chicory, etc., are flavoured with bits of salt pork or bacon fat. Other dishes include those made with pork and pork offal (intestines, snouts, tails) and chicken. The main meal of the day is usually a simmered casserole of vegetables and meats served with corn grits or cornbread. Melons are the favoured fruits, eaten sweet, juicy, and fresh.[1,4,5,3]

SOUTHWESTERN STATES

Strongly influenced by traditional Mexican and Spanish cookery TAMALES, TACOS, ENCHILADAS, FRIJOLES all vie with local tropical and semi-tropical fruits and vegetables to create an unusual and distinctive cuisine.

The famed TEXAS CHILI contains no beans but is a slow-simmered stew of diced beef flavoured with a mix of seasoning now known simply as "chili powder" (actually a combination of oregano, hot and sweet peppers, cumin, sugar, and paprika). Thickened traditionally with the same cornflour (MASA HARINA) used to make TORTILLAS, CHILI is popularly served with a side dish of TEXAS BEANS: a flavourful casserole of kidney or pinto beans simmered in water with onions and garlic.[3,6]

Influence of the Hopis, Pueblos, and Papagos Indians have helped also to make beans, squash, chili peppers, and corn true staples of the southwestern diet.

SOUTHEASTERN STATES

Near the region of New Orleans, a combination of French and Spanish settlers, native Choctaw Indians and the ingenuity of the Black slaves have produced a cuisine that is considered to be one of the most unique in America.

The French (both from France and the "Cajuns" or Acadians from Canada) contributed their way with sauces and roux; the Spanish their natural delight in fresh produce and light flavours evoked in meat, fish and seafood. The Choctaw Indians explained the use of the powder made from dried sassafras leaves later called FILÉ and used to thicken soups and stews as well as adding a delicate flavour. The Blacks contributed the use of OKRA and other greens, innovative uses of pork and pork products and cooking with lard. And they favoured heavy cast iron cookware: skillets and pots produce to this day GUMBOS, JAMBALAYAS, deep-fried CALAS (rice fritters) and a host of dishes based on the combination of these food heritages plus the richness of local waters and fields that have made New Orleans one of the gourmet centres of the world.

Eastern Seaboard States

New York, Delaware, New Jersey and Pennsylvania, were variously influenced by the early Dutch, Swedish, Quaker, and German settlers. The latter, by the way, called themselves "Deutsch" (the German word for German), which somehow wended its way into the translation Pennsylvania Dutch.

From around New York, the Dutch-influenced backyard vegetable gardens, storage cellars and many all-American favourite flour mixtures such as pancakes, waffles, donuts, and even cookies are basically of Dutch origin. Even the dollop of coleslaw so prevalent in almost every American quick-serve restaurant is of Dutch origin.

The Pennsylvania Dutch happily produced from their spotless kitchens hearty dumpling dishes, all kinds of sausages, cold, sliced, molded aspic dishes, sauerkraut and pork combinations, pickled eggs and pickled vegetable salads that are now enjoyed all over the United States with little thought to origin.

New England States

Severe climate and non-arable lands probably molded the character as well as the diet of New Englanders. Hearty soups, steamed brown breads, and the famed baked beans all have become synonymous with New England although they really know no regional boundaries. Blueberries and maple syrup, walnuts and persimmons, and the famed simple but hearty New England Boiled Dinner add to the fare.

Pacific Northwest

As if spectacular scenery were not enough, this region is famed for salmon and trout, lingcod and other fine seafood, as well as game, wild berries, and fine apples.

Midwestern States

America's dairylands and famed corn belt. Fine cheeses, butter, fresh milk and cream in abundance come from a country-quilt of well-kept farms. Eastern European delicacies vie with simple hearty "meat-and-taters" (meat and potatoes) meals.

Hawaii and Alaska

The two youngest states of the United States bring an offering of contrasts to the huge American table of foods.

The foods of Hawaii, like the people, offer touches from all the areas of the South Pacific and from America itself. In Hawaiian supermarkets may be found all the familiar products and processed foods known to the U.S. shopper, as well as the delicacies that mark the traditional high points of South Pacific and Southeast Asian cuisine. These are, for example, the sharp-salty fish sauce common to all Southeast Asian tables, the tantalizing scents of exotic spices ready for blending into curries, the whole array of tropical fruits and vegetables – some that are Hawaiian staples such as TARO, from which the sticky POI is prepared, coconut, passionfruit, guava and tangy-sour tamarind – the Oriental additions of noodles and rice and pork and seafood and raw fish, and finally the contributions of the early New England missionaries to Hawaii's eclectic cuisine: hearty stews, cornbreads and fish chowders and pickled meats.

Together with the wild and cultivated bounties of nature: salmon-berries, huckleberries, rhubarb; waters laden with fish and the woods of wild game – beaver, bear, venison, caribou, ducks, and ptarmigan – the early Alaskan pioneers brought with them two staples that still fill hearty appetites in the North. These are pork and beans and the famed SOUR-DOUGH, from which breads and rolls, pancakes and biscuits are made. The sourdough starter – a ferment of flour, yeast, and water – when once begun, lived in a crock in the kitchen, continually added to and a constant source of new doughs with tantalizing aroma and flavour. Northern homesteads were built to stand the weather and provide only the necessities of living, but out of such humble kitchens come simple, hearty, and satisfying foods without frills. This is not to say, however, that Alaskans are still in the pioneer state, for supermarkets and familiar American products for the table are available, if expensive. But to those with a sense of taste, they take second place to Alaska's natural products – and who can compare the ubiquitous tomato catsup to Alaska's wild cranberry ketchup?

Special Occasions

America, though predominantly Christian, probably has representative groups of almost every religious sect in the world and has evolved a few comparatively new ones, such as the vegetarian sects emanating from California.

It is impossible to generalize how any single occasion or holiday is celebrated, for special rituals and special foods depend on personal preferences, region and ethnic and religious heritage. Because of a Christian predominance, the most universally celebrated holiday is Christmas. But each home brings to Christmas special remembrances of this holiday in other lands and other times. For example, Christmas Eve may be celebrated with Polish baked carp, southern Italian octopus dishes, or the Ukraine's twelve dishes, each prepared without meats. The festive day itself may highlight roasted turkey, stuffed goose or duck or whole roasted suckling pig.

FOUR

Armenian

An oval of mountainous land, dominated by the lofty Caucasus Mountains, of which Mount Ararat in the Armenian Republic is the highest, stretches between the Caspian Sea and the Black Sea. This area, commonly referred to as "The Caucasus," is actually made up of three Russian republics: Armenian Soviet Socialist Republic, Georgian Soviet Socialist Republic, and Azerbaijan. Neither the people nor their languages are Slavic in origin, and even their foods bear more resemblance to Eastern Mediterranean cuisine than to Russian. But they do have several factors in common with each other: an incredible zest for life, unsurpassed hospitality, and an ability to use obscure excuses for feasting and merrymaking.

Although it is still a matter of considerable debate whether the Armenian Mount Ararat is actually the one where Noah docked his Ark, what is known is that the Armenians are one of the oldest peoples of history[1] and one of the first to accept Christianity.[2] For about 600 years the people were under Turkish rule. Beginning in May 1918, the people tasted a brief two years of independence and then became enveloped in Soviet domination. The latter has not influenced their age-old traditions, but has brought increased industrialization, modernization and collectivization to agriculture, as well as founding a national university and theatre.[3]

The arable land, though small in area, is highly productive and lovingly attended. The climate varies between subtropical and subtemperate[3] and allows for production of crops not possible in other areas of the Soviet: almonds and walnuts; rice, wheat, and corn, stone fruits (peaches, apricots, plums), citrus fruits, grapes, tobacco, and olives.[3,4] But perhaps more important is their valued production of wool, milk, and cheese from the goats, cattle, and sheep that nibble the tender greens of the high rocky slopes.

The general use of fresh foods (frozen and packaged foods of any type are scorned) in season and the practice of drying, smoking, and pickling to preserve foods for winter is common throughout the Caucasus. But where corn, walnuts, and many types of dried beans are the Georgian staples,[4,5] the Armenians prefer rice, wheat, and pine nuts.[2,4] Many writers feel that the Armenian cuisine combines the finest of Persian (Iranian), Greek and Turkish foods, while others consider that Armenians "cook mostly in the Turkish style."[5]

Researchers have long puzzled over the possible reasons for the almost legendary longevity of the peoples of this area. With an estimated "thirteen times as many centenarians as there are in every 100,000 people in North America,"[6] the question becomes an intriguing one. Our senior citizens are warned of the dangers of alcohol and tobacco, yet strong brandy and wines are daily fare in the Caucasus and many smoke heavily. And although the consequences of over-indulgence in foods are well-documented it is also well-documented that Georgians and Armenians love nothing better than a party.[4,6] One where the dishes on the table are so numerous that they must be piled one on the other. One where each guest vies in toastmaking – everything from the favourable and unfavourable attributes of the host to a salute for world peace – is an acceptable excuse for draining the glass and promptly refilling it. Perhaps these wondrously genial and generous people are so happy and hospitable because they have all also known lean times when bread and beans could constitute a blessed feast. Perhaps most of all their warmth and longevity have to do with their inextinguishable philosophy of living life to the fullest.

Home Life and Facilities
It is the rural and mountain villages that the classically traditional life-style of the Armenians can still be seen. The village is a family, with such an intertwining of caring and sharing that it is difficult to distinguish relatives from friends. Children are loved and respected as much as the oldest grandmother, and each person takes a share in the work and the activities. While modern electrical appliances and utensils are costly though available in the urban centres, home life in the rural areas still revolves around the traditionally simple but practical kitchen where woodenware and earthenware predominate. Heavy earthenware jugs and jars are used to store foods in cold pantries and cellars over the winter months; garlic and onions, dried fruits and vegetables, hang from walls and rafters; women share communal ovens.[7]

FOODS COMMONLY USED

The highly sophisticated and varied cuisine of Armenia encompasses a wide and well-balanced combination of foods. Lamb and chicken are the favoured meats, fresh chopped vegetables are often eaten as salads and vegetables are an important part of many one-dish meals. Soured or cultured milk and many types of fresh and aged cheeses are plentiful and eaten almost any time with breads, fruits, nuts, or just by themselves. Rice forms the basis of many PILAFS and the filling of stuffed vegetables, while wheat is favoured for breads of all kinds and the cracked wheat (BULGHUR) is also used in many dishes. Refreshing yoghurt and soured milk are taken as beverages or snacks, wine often accompanies meals, especially parties, and brandy is taken for any pretence.

Milk and Milk Products
These products are plentiful and form an important part of the Armenian diet. Milk from sheep, goats, and cows is not used fresh but is cultured or soured as buttermilk or yoghurt and used, sometimes diluted with water, as a drink or as a snack and often as part of other dishes. Fresh, hard, soft, and aged cheeses, some flavoured with mountain herbs, are prepared all the time and used generously as appetizers, toppings, and as ingredients for many dishes.

Fruits and Vegetables
Citrus fruits, stone fruits, grapes and melons, quince and apples are all abundantly enjoyed in season and mostly eaten fresh. Some of these fruits may be dried to preserve them for winter use.

Fresh and often wild herbs may be plucked from fields or paths and munched out of hand, minced and used generously in salads, or hung to dry for later use. Garlic and onions are used liberally in dishes and are often enjoyed as they are. Leeks, green beans, squashes, okra, eggplant, salad greens, cucumbers, peppers and tomatoes, zucchini, pumpkin, and cabbages also may be plucked to eat out of hand, chopped into salads or soups, or eaten cooked in casseroles.

Meats and Alternates
Lamb and chicken are the most favoured meats, but beef and goat are also used. There are a variety of game birds that find their way to the table too: pigeon, duck, quail, goose, plover, and partridge, teal, woodcock, and pheasant. Fish may be served boiled, steamed, baked, fried, or split and grilled on skewers. Some seafood is used where available fresh, such as oysters and mussels.[2]

Eggs are widely used in cooking and baking, as a custard-like topping for vegetable casseroles and for the egg-lemon sauce so popular in soups, meat, fish, and vegetable dishes. Many varieties of beans are used but the CHICK PEAS are the favourite.

The plentiful and nutritious nuts are used in sauces where they are crushed or chopped sometimes with garlic and sometimes with spice and sugar. Nut filling for baked goods and nuts nibbled as a snack seem to be always at hand: of pistachios, almonds, walnuts, chestnuts, pine nuts, and filberts. In fact, it is said that whenever two Armenians are talking, there is probably a dish of pistachios between them.[7]

Breads and Cereals
The staple bread is the flat unleavened PIDEH or LAVASH made from wheat flour. BULGHUR, coarse, dried whole wheat is used in soups, as a side dish for meats, or mixed with chopped vegetables in a salad; it is also a frequent ingredient mixed with ground meats (see Lebanese foods) and as fillings for vegetable dishes. Rice is also favoured in many dishes.

Fats
Every home has a supply of olive oil which is used in all cooking, as a basting for meats and fish and as a base to dress salads. Clarified butter is used less frequently, sometimes for vegetables but mostly for special occasions that warrant pastries.

Sweets and Snacks
As well as ignoring the negative effects of alcohol, tobacco and food indulgence, the Armenians seem also to destroy the commonly-held notion that sweets may be detrimental to one's health – at least it doesn't seem that their consumption affects longevity as the Armenians consume more sweets and dessert pastries than other peoples of the Caucasus. The usual dessert is fruit and cheese, but sugared and candied nuts seem always available as snacks and desserts. The traditional syrupy-sweet desserts of thin, crisp pastries layered with nuts, spices, and sugar, so beloved around the Mediterranean, are just as welcomed by Armenians of any age. Other sweet cakes and rolls filled with nuts and sweetened soft cheese fillings and brushed with egg and sugar toppings might even form the excuse for a party.

Seasonings
Garlic and onions head the list of seasonings, closely followed by a wide selection of cultivated and fresh and dried herbs. Nuts and seeds (sesame) add crunch and taste, vinegar and pepper add sharp hotness, while cloves, saffron, and cinnamon evoke the exotic. Greece's famed AVGOLEMONO (egg and lemon juice) sauce adds its tangy touch to many meals. The dribble of clarified butter and the splash of homemade wine or fresh cream may also be a part of the cook's flourish.

Beverages

RAKI (brandy) is commonly taken as an aperitif, just in case any Armenian may be troubled with a lagging appetite, and if so, perhaps two RAKIs would be better than just one. Homemade red and white wines usually accompany meals and are enjoyed by all ages. Yoghurt and soured milk (LEBAN) is usually more a part of lunch or a between-meal refreshment. SOORJ (unsweetened coffee) is the common breakfast beverage.

Meal Patterns and Eating Customs

Hospitality is a way of life and nothing is more enjoyed than inviting guests or wayfarers to partake of whatever food the family may have on hand. Whether the variety is wide or limited, somehow there is always enough to share. The women take great pride in preparing and serving the meals and usually hover in the background while the men feast and drink and merrily toast each other, the weather, the crops, the country, the world. Table service and manners are of secondary importance, shared enjoyment is everything. Even when times are bad, and people have to survive only on bread and beans, these will be prepared in variety and served with the same joy as the most sumptuous meal.

The general pattern of three meals a day prevails. Breakfast is a simple spread of cheese and olives and bread with coffee. The noon meal is usually a hot vegetable or vegetable and meat casserole, while the largest meal, dinner, is usually in the evening between seven and eight o'clock. This meal customarily begins with the potent RAKI and more recently with vodka, to be followed by nibbles of cheeses, various types of olives (black, green, spiced, salted etc.), or sometimes a chopped green salad or a gently-simmered soup. Roasted meat, fish, or fowl, together with more vegetables (often served cooked and cold), rice or BULGHUR PILAF, a choice of wines or LEBAN or yoghurt, to be finished with a dessert of fresh or dried fruits, nuts, and cheeses. Occasionally coffee may conclude a special dinner. Snacks throughout the day will be nuts or toasted seeds to crunch and munch almost continually, sometimes a break of pastries and coffee or wine, if there are guests, or just a humble refreshment of LEBAN and fruit.

Special Occasions

Recognized as one of the earliest branches of the Christian faith, dating from the work of St. Gregory the Illuminator (third century), the Armenians today are divided between the Uniate Church, which is similar to the Roman Catholic but uses an Armenian rite, and the Gregorian Church.[3] A few Armenians are of the Protestant faith and some are Jewish. In America, the Armenian Apostolic Church is most closely identified with the Greek Orthodox Church.[1]

It is the combination of the Armenians' warm family feelings and deep bonds to their faith as well as their inherent delight with parties that make family and religious events occasions for feasting, drinking, and merriment. Usually such a special occasion calls forth a vast array of all the traditional dishes, sweets and pastries, and all the brandy and wine the family can afford (and probably more than anyone can consume). Often a variety of spit-roasted game birds highlight many special occasions, but a specialty of weddings is a huge SAFFRON PILAF made with rice, saffron, and flavoured with rosewater.

FIVE

Australian

On the largest island and the smallest continent in the world[1] almost 13 million people make their home, among unusual flora and fauna and some of the most unique animals in the world: the kangaroo, the dingo (a howling dog-like night hunter), the koala bear and the platypus.[2] One of the driest and most sparsely-populated continents, Australia is mostly tropical in the North and temperate in the South. More than half of the population live in cities and these are located in the irrigated and fertile coastal regions of the East, Southeast, and Southwest. For the most part, the vast interior of plateaus and eroded mountains is all but uninhabited, with many areas remaining untouched and primitive.[1,3]

Many of the great seafaring nations were probably aware of this great land mass in the South Seas, but it remained for Captain Arthur Philip, of the Royal British Navy, to unfurl the British flag at Sydney Cove on January 26, 1788. To this day, this is celebrated as "Australia Day." By the 1800s, almost 5,000 white-men prisoners and their guards formed a colony at Sydney, joining the first 700 convicts who had been unloaded from Captain Philip's ship on that fateful day. They may have been the first "citizens" of the "land down under," but it is estimated that more than 200,000 Aborigines had already been living there in their own neo-Stone Age society.[4] In the ensuing years, with allegiance to Britain, their own parliament attempted to unite the population but it took the First World War to weld the fiercely individual and independent population into a nation.

Unification finally occurred because of the strong link to Great Britain but also because pressures of war caused shortages of essential goods. Self-sufficiency became an urgent necessity. Improvements in agriculture, mining production, and the development of new industries not only helped on the home front but set Australia as an exporter to world markets. Iron ore, coal, and wool, as well as meats, wheat, and sugar became vital economic commodities.

Up to the Second World War, Australia's population was more than 99 per cent of British origin. Following the war, many of the displaced and war-weary of Europe migrated to Australia so that by 1962, more than 1,839,000 immigrants had made their home there. These included Italians, Dutch, Poles, Germans, Yugoslavians, Greeks, Ukrainians, and Latvians.[1] It is not surprising, then, to find that one of the largest Australian cookbooks, *Australian and New Zealand Complete Book of Cookery*[5] should turn out to be a study of international cookery. Many writers claim that Australia lacks a distinctive cuisine, regional cooking styles, or even any great national dishes.[3,6] Nonetheless, the combination of a wealth of seafood, good inexpensive lamb, delicious fruits, and the inspiration and ingenuity of immigrants long immersed in their own traditional cuisines, will soon be recognized as a distinctive Australian cuisine.

Home Life and Facilities
Australian kitchens are similar to those in America, though smaller and probably boasting fewer appliances and gadgets. Electricity is favoured over gas as a cooking fuel, but outdoor picnics and barbecues are frequent and preferred because of the pleasant climate. Home freezers are not yet common, so there are few frozen products available to the consumer. Ranges, refrigerators, and dishwashers are common as are most of the small practical kitchen appliances familiar in America. Most popular is the "hot water jug": available in different sizes, this small appliance heats water quickly to the boiling point – practical in a land where frequent cups of tea are the daily rule.

FOODS COMMONLY USED

The staples of the Australian diet can be described as "steak and eggs," and the preference for simple solid food shows up on the spice shelf too: salt and pepper and a few spices for baking. But some inroads are being made in introducing "health foods," such as whole grains and yoghurt, and the preparation of more vegetables and the use of skim milk powder is becoming more widespread. Price rises in fresh beef will also encourage the use of other meats and meat alternates. Women favour tea, men enjoy beer, and children drink milk at most meals.

Milk and Milk Products

Fresh whole milk is used in quantity by most Australian families: children drink milk at most meals and adults enjoy milk in puddings, soups, custards, and in tea. Skim milk, 2 per cent (partially skimmed) milk, and cottage cheese do not have wide acceptance, nor does the use of skim milk powder. Cheeses are not a usual part of the dietary pattern and usually are only used in specialty dishes calling for cheese as an ingredient. There is a small but noticeable increase in the general popularity of yoghurt.

Fruits and Vegetables

Although there is a great variety of produce in Australia, the variety is mainly seasonal and local. There is even little importing of produce from one state to the other. Part of the reason may be storage and transportation facilities; frequently January floods affect supplies and cause price increases.[8]

Fruits available include passionfruit, pineapples, pawpaws, many forms of coconut, fresh figs, guavas, melons, chokos, tamarillos, mangoes, mulberries, loganberries, lychees, cumquats (Australian spelling), kiwi fruit, feijoas, and a range of citrus fruits.[5,8] Exotic tropical fruits are: persimmon, avocado, custard apples, monsterio delicio. Australia is also rightly famed for its fine quality dried fruits and Australian raisins and currants are widely exported. Other popularly consumed dried fruits include peaches, apricots, pears, figs, prunes, and apples. Australians have a preference for eating fruits with minimum preparation and more dried fruits are commonly eaten as snacks and desserts than in America.[8,9] A favourite accompaniment to a barbecued dinner of steak or chops is a large mixed salad combining fruits and vegetables.[6]

As with fruits, Australians prefer their vegetables with a minimum of "fixing"; not for them mysterious mixtures of creamed or sauced vegetables. Some Australian vegetables are called by names different than those used in North America: beets are commonly called BEETROOTS, CAPSICUMS refer to green or red peppers. Australian "pumpkin" is unlike that found in America, as it is a dark green vegetable with the shape and appearance of the familiar American pumpkin but with a flavour and texture resembling that of carrots.[8]

Meats and Alternates

Beef in the form of steaks and roasts heads the popularity list. Next come other cuts of beef, lamb, veal, and offal. Pork and poultry are not used with any regularity. Roasting, quick-frying, or barbecuing are the usual methods of meat cookery. Other meats used only occasionally include ducks, geese, turkey, wild ducks, marinated Kangaroo meat, partridges, pheasant, venison, and wild pork. A famed dish is CARPETBAGGER'S

STEAK: a thick steak that is split, stuffed with raw oysters, and broiled or barbecued.[6]

There is no shortage of fish and seafood and there is wide variety: oysters, scallops, mussels, tohero (a shellfish with distinctively green colour), trout, salmon, red snapper, mulloway, hapuka, whitebait, tarahiki, gurnard, flounder, and bream. Following the Australian's preference for simplicity fish is served fresh and simply prepared by poaching, baking, frying, or grilling.

Legumes are used only in specialty dishes, but a growing vegetarian community is using legumes and soya bean products extensively.

Finally, it must be noted that STEAK AND EGGS really are a classic favourite and considered the perfect breakfast, lunch or supper and even – for heartier Aussies – a snack.

Breads and Cereals
In home baking there is a definite preference for the use of self-raising flour, that is, flour containing a proportionate amount of salt and leavening agent. Fresh breads are usually purchased daily for meals and for tea time. Wheat flour is the staple but cornstarch is used in thickening desserts and sauces. More recently the Swiss breakfast favourite MUESLI, a blend of toasted oats, dried fruits and nuts eaten with milk, has gained some popularity. Australians do not favour pancakes or waffles and seldom use sweetened breakfast cereals.

Fats
Margarine is the most widely used fat and although generally priced the same as butter, many seem to prefer its flavour to that of butter. COFA is a solidified coconut oil used in making desserts.

Sweets and Snacks
Dried fruits are popular snacks and Health Food Bars, made from nuts, sesame seeds, dried fruits, and honey are enjoyed by all ages. Fresh fruit is taken as a snack in season.

Seasonings
Not for the Australian any complex form of seasoning. Cookery, service, and seasonings can all be described as simple and basic. Salt and pepper and onions would be the staples, for Australians have a strong preference for foods that "taste natural."

Beverages
Australian wine is inexpensive, of excellent quality, and is used widely. Local quality beer is the preferred beverage for most men; women enjoy frequent cups of tea daily; children prefer fresh whole milk but often

have tea or coffee. Fruit cordials are popular, especially in hot weather. Strong spirits, cola drinks, and coffee are not popular.

Meal Patterns and Eating Customs

There are no particular rituals associated with meals in Australia. The three-meals-a-day pattern is prevalent, with morning and afternoon breaks usually consisting of tea or beer with a small snack. The Australian woman taking her lunch at home will eat sparsely; the working person will have an inexpensive hot plate of MINCE, potato, and peas, or a meat pie with beer. Most children eat their lunches at school, buying it at tuck shop or cafeteria and have a choice of cold but satisfying foods such as meat pies, sausage rolls, buns, salads, sweets, drinks and potato chips. The evening meal at home will usually be meat and vegetables, potatoes or bread. Potatoes are expensive and not as widely available as in America. Pastries or fruit or simple puddings will be the dessert.

The Australians, being avid outdoor people, love any excuse for a picnic (the races, any races) or barbecue. Simple barbecued meats or fresh fish, vegetables, fruits, and perhaps biscuits and cakes, together with a good supply of beer spell "good times" and a festive occasion.

Many people still working in the "outback" regions prefer to cook in bush ovens. A hole is dug in the ground and lined with hot coals. A special heavy, covered cooking pot is placed on the coals, covered with more coals, and finally heaped with earth. Although simple in principle, this method requires great skill and for those who know how to do it, anything from meats and stews to cakes and breads can be cooked in this way.

Aside from going to small casual restaurants and local bars for enjoying beer with one's friends, the Australian is not keen about "eating out." Tourists to Australia are often disappointed by what they may consider to be "mediocre hotel and restaurant standards."[3] It is not that the Australians in any way lack hospitality, it is rather that they lack the ability to be servile. To the Australian, even his boss is his "mate," tipping is disliked because of its servile connotation, and great personal pride is taken by each Australian in the fact that his is a "classless society." It is most unfortunate that this pride of independence and love of equality is too often misconstrued as arrogant confidence.

Special Occasions

Freedom of worship prevails in Australia and there are many Protestant groups and Roman Catholics, but about one-third of the population belongs to the Church of England.[1] Since Christmas occurs in the Australian summer, a typical dinner of salads and cold meats, with an ice cream cake or pudding for dessert, would be common. Special occasions such as Race Days, or local sports events, are celebrated with picnics, barbecues, and plentiful beer.

Anzac Day celebrates Australia's birth as a true nation and is marked by a parade of "old diggers" (soldiers) and beer parties. Australia Day, on January 26, is marked by parties featuring barbecues of beef or lamb, salads and the favourite dessert, PAVLOVA: a whipped cream and tropical fruit confection.

SIX

Austrian

Small wonder that the Austrian is said to be daily preoccupied with the subject of food. For over six hundred years the vast Austro-Hungarian Empire enveloped the languages, traditions, and food customs of more than a dozen nations.[1] Even today, Vienna conjures up visions of opulent architecture, lilting waltzes, and mounds of whipped cream. And though 1918 saw the end of the Empire and the opulence, the love of music and the intense appreciation of an Austrian cuisine remains.

With his seemingly-endless appetite, the Austrian *feinschmecker* (gourmet) enjoys pastas, veal dishes, and tomato sauces from Italy, potato dishes and sauerkraut from Germany, dumplings in great array from Czechoslovakia, vegetables and rice dishes from the Balkans, sourcream cookery and soups from Poland and Russia, coffee from Turkey. But from Hungary, the Austrian will only willingly admit to the acquisition of paprika. His beloved STRUDEL and TORTEN, crescents and rolls, and fine breads are, however, of Austrian origin.[2,3,4] When in Austria no one would dare argue otherwise.

If this claim of daily absorption with food seems unjustified, one should consider that although Austria is a predominantly scenic and mountainous country, its manicured farms, pastures, vineyards, and orchards produce all the necessities of the diet and relatively inexpensively.[5] From Austria's granary, in Lower Austria, come wheat, barley, rye, and corn, as well as grapes from the vineyards. From Styria, over 170 branches of the "Fresh Egg Service"[5] supply eggs, while other areas produce fruits and berries, cattle and dairy products. And though Vienna is highly industrialized, the city is surrounded by mixed farming and animal husbandry areas. The smallest Alpine province, Vorarlberg, caters to the complete set of sweet teeth that every Austrian has, and produces famed chocolates and candies.[5,6]

Despite an immersion in food, wine and music, the Austrian history is not a happy one. As in most empires, those who were forcibly made a part of it resented their oppression. Torn between German and Hungarian affiliations, most immigrants solved the dilemma by referring to themselves not as Austrians but as Czechs, Slovaks, Slovenes, Croatians, Serbs, Magyars, Romanians, Ukrainians, Poles, Jews, Italians, or Macedonians.[7] But in 1918, after Austria was established as a Republic, almost 90 per cent of her population was Roman Catholic and almost 99 per cent were German-speaking.[6,7]

Though most Austrian immigrants to America speak German and are German in ethos, they have – with the exception of the groups mentioned above – melded into the general North American society, caring little for Austrian papers or organizations, yet their ties and justifiable pride in Austrian cuisine remain.

Home Life and Facilities

The neat little Austrian kitchen has everything necessary to prepare fine foods lovingly, and everything is in its special place. The kitchen may be the workshop, but the dining-room is the stage; fine linens, fresh flowers, and sparkling dishes have retained their importance.

Even with the presence of supermarkets and availability of prepared foods and mixes, canned and frozen delicacies, traditionally the Austrian homemaker prefers to shop daily in her favourite small specialty shops where she feels certain the proprietor will give her the best. Fresh fruits and tender fresh vegetables are still favoured and their seasonal succulence is treasured. Because of the routine of daily shopping, large refrigerators are really not a necessity, but cold pantries are still filled with a proud array of home pickles and preserves.

Currently there is some deviance from this traditional pattern, as more and more women are taking jobs and finding their cooking and shopping time becoming limited. Supermarkets and the prepared-foods industry are expanding[1,5] and even the traditional pattern of six meals a day is shrinking both in number and quantity of food consumed.[5]

FOODS COMMONLY USED

A post Second World War increase in the consumption of fresh milk and citrus fruits[5] has added nutrients to a traditional diet based on veal, pork, and chicken; large consumption of breads and rich sweets; wine and beer; all somewhat balanced by an intake of seasonal fruits and vegetables.

Milk and Milk Products

Fresh fluid milk is often served boiled rather than cold as a beverage. Sweetened condensed milk is widely used but skim milk and dried milk powder are not favoured. Cheeses of all types, sour milk and thick sour cream are used a great deal, but sweetened, whipped cream is so popular as to almost be classed as a daily staple.

Fruits and Vegetables

A wide range of fresh seasonal fruits are used fresh or prepared as cold fruit soups, compotes, and other desserts, or are used as filling in baked goods. Some imported and canned fruits are consumed. Recently citrus fruits and citrus juices are used regularly.[5]

Seasonal vegetables are purchased fresh and prepared with care as salads, pickles, well-cooked, or well-garnished, never plain. Winter staples include red and green cabbage, potatoes (prepared in an endless variety of ways), beets, sauerkraut, pickles.

Meats and Alternates

Pork, veal, and chicken are the favoured meats; very little fish is consumed. Beef and lamb are usually served well-cooked and accompanied with rich gravies and sauces. Meats are used as main dishes but also form an important part of many snacks, which are often smoked, pickled, or cured meats or many types of sausages.

Eggs are most often eaten boiled, or hard cooked as appetizers, as a garnish or as an ingredient in other dishes. Legumes are of little importance and used only occasionally in soups and sometimes as a side dish. Nuts are used only as garnish or part of rich desserts or candies.

Breads and Cereals

Dried breakfast cereals served cold with milk or hot cooked porridges have no place at the Austrian table. Many types of plain or sweet rolls with hot milk, tea, or coffee would be a common breakfast, but to the Austrian, grains are to be found as flour in the great array of breads of all kinds, dark and light, rolls, buns made with every combination of wheat and rye flours, sweet and soured doughs. Bread is present in some form at every meal and often is part of snacks as well.

Fats

Since sour cream, whipped cream, and eggs are considered to be of such importance in so many dishes, they must also be considered as an important contribution of fats to the Austrian diet. Lard, oil, butter, and margarine are all used in cooking and baking.

Sweets and Snacks

The Austrian sweet tooth is not an easily-satisfied one. It begins with preserves and crisp rolls for breakfast, and requires refuelling at almost any opportune time of the day in the form of chocolates and candies, sweetened coffee and occasionally tea (there is even a preference for sweet rather than dry wines), and of course, the almost legendary consumption of incredibly rich and tempting pastries and desserts, to which the true Austrian will often unabashedly add a generous dollop of SCHLAGOBERS (sweetened whipped cream).

Seasonings
Most typical are paprika, caraway seeds, onions, and garlic, but there is also a learned and judicious use of herbs and other spices. Chocolate is the favourite dessert flavour, also vanilla and freshly-zested rind of oranges and lemons. Wine and sour cream, cream, and fresh butter must also be considered as typical seasonings.

Beverages
There is some consumption of fresh milk, by children, and some sipping of sweetened tea, but coffee in many varieties (flavoured with chocolate, vanilla, or served with cream or whipped cream), is still most popular. When Austrians serve wine with a meal it will almost inevitably be a rich, fruity Rhine wine, this white wine is preferred no matter what the main course may be. Beer is considered a more casual beverage and more favoured by men.

Meal Patterns and Eating Customs
Gracious table manners are part of very early lessons for Austrian children. And these are readily learned, especially when the reward is a slice of SACHERTORTE or APFEL STRUDEL MIT SCHLAG. Meal times are mannered and orderly with the father the first to be served, the leader in conversation, and the one whose opinion on everything from the VORSPEISEN to the MEHLSPEISEN is eagerly anticipated.

Dinner guests are always on time and invariably bring a bouquet of flowers for their hostess. Entertaining and sociability are indigenous to the Austrian personality. If not taking a meal with a friend or entertaining guests at home, the gregarious Austrian will likely feel the need to communicate a few words to a pretty girl or even to a complete stranger at the next table in the *kaffeehaus*. Conversation, conviviality and communication are as much a part of the Austrian soul as food and music.

The day usually begins with an "eye-opener" of small crisp rolls, preserves, and butter, with good coffee. Around 10:00 A.M. a small bowl of hot GOULYASH, or a sausage with bread and pickles, washed down with a beer, followed by a "real" lunch around 1:00 P.M. of soup (a "real" meal without soup is unthinkable), roast meat or chicken, bread, dumplings or noodles, a small salad of greens, followed by cheese, fresh fruit or compote. To sustain one through the afternoon hours, one can always muse on which TORTE will accompany the afternoon JAUSE of coffee and a pastry or two. By 7:00 P.M. businesses are closed and families are together for dinner, a meal suspiciously similar to lunch. After dinner many Austrians will be off to the theatre, opera, or out visiting friends and it would be most unusual if at about 11:00 P.M. one did not find them all chatting over a simple snack of sandwiches, cold salad plates, pastries, and coffee.

In Austria, movable *würstel* stands in strategic locations and cosy *kaffeehäuser*, with their array of sweets, tease and tempt the passerby. Why try to avoid the inevitable? After all who can deny that a little food helps to console and fortify one against the memories of the past and the uncertainties of the future. In almost any Austrian household, that retains even a crumb of Austrian tradition, if there is not a serious discussion of the foods that are being eaten or were eaten, then visions are being conjured up of taste sensations yet to come. And what the father of the household desires will likely be the menu of the evening meal . . . or the next snack.

All of this is a presentation of the traditional Austrian viewpoint when it comes to matters of gastronomy. Traditional should be underlined. The desire by men and women alike for trim healthy bodies, and the fact that more women are working, have made inroads even to the Austrian table: meals and snacks are shrinking, waistlines are becoming increasingly visible. But, despite this, nothing can diminish the opulence of Austrian cuisine.

Special Occasions

The Austria of today is predominantly Roman Catholic, but many Austrians living in other parts of the world may be Jewish or Protestant and will celebrate their religious holidays accordingly. Elegant menus of game are often a part of special-occasion menus together with a great selection of hot and cold garnished platters of other meats, salads, and molds, served with various breads and rolls, beer or Rhine wine, and completed with a tempting array of the famed pastries.

SEVEN

Baltic Peoples: Estonian, Latvian, Lithuanian

The Baltic peoples have many factors in common: a temperate climate and a rich harvest from the Baltic Sea, a land that is primarily agricultural and pastoral, and has had a bitter history of invasions, conquests, and humiliating oppressions. With an approximate population of six million the three countries have known foreign overlords controlling their lands, attempts at Germanization and Russification, and even extermination and deportation of their peoples.[1]

For a period of almost 500 years, and despite other conquerors who were tempted to rule over the loosely-knit tribes of Estonia, it was the Swedes who held predominant influence from as early as the 1500s. To this day, Swedish architecture, names, signposts, and even many Swedish foods carry a strong influence throughout Estonian life.[2] Russification followed in 1721, when Sweden ceded Estonia to Czarist Russia. A burst in Estonian culture resulted in the brief respite after the First World War when foreign influences in the land receded, but returned again in 1939, with the forced establishment of Russian military bases in key Estonian areas.

A glimpse into Latvia's history shows many similar and unhappy parallels. It was the Germans in 1201, who swept over the rich fertile lowlands and sweeping forests of Latvia to conquer the tribes known as Letts, and established the capital city, Riga.[1,3] By the mid-1500s, the German influence disintegrated, but in the ensuing years, the small land became the centre of a struggle of three other powers: Poland, Russia, and Sweden. In 1795, Latvia became officially a part of the Russian Empire although much of her lands remained in the hands of German overlords.[1] Like Estonia, Latvia was to taste brief independence following the First World War until 1939, when it too was forced to accept Russian military bases.

Lithuania's history shows her to be culturally and historically the strongest and largest of the three Baltic countries. Lithuania not only successfully rebuffed early foreign invaders but for a period of almost 200 years (1200-1400), actually expanded to exert control over much of the territory of Byelorussia, the Ukraine, and parts of western Russia. The power might even have extended further with the marriage of Jagelo, Grand Duke of Lithuania and Jadwiga, Queen of Poland, but for a clash in religious convictions. The Polish-Lithuanian Roman Catholicism could not be reconciled with the principles of Orthodoxy of the Russian, Byelorussian, and Ukrainian areas. By 1700, the tide of Russian power and influence was so strong that not only did these latter lands wash back to Russia, but the tide of influence "back-washed" into Lithuania as well. In the First World War Lithuania was occupied by Germans, who seemingly supported the many Lithuanian nationalistic movements. But after Germany's defeat, a pro-Polish government was set up in Vilna (1920), and a part of Lithuania even united with Poland. This period was followed by an alliance with Estonia and Latvia but they too succumbed, as the others had, to Russian domination leading to the establishment of the Lithuanian Soviet Socialist Republic.[1,3,5]

In spite of such a history of dominations and foreign influences, the Baltic peoples still have a rich culture of their own and they are famed for their literature, folk legends, athletic physiques, and joyous choral singing groups. Latvian and Lithuanian peoples share ethnic and language roots in the Slavic-Baltic division of Indo-European languages, but the Estonian ethnic and language roots are to be found in the Finno-Ugric family, relating them more to the Finns and Hungarians.[6,7]

Home Life and Facilities

Since the majority of the peoples of these lands live in rural life-style, it is this tradition that is considered here. While Latvia makes use of her peat bogs to supply fuel, Estonia and Lithuania depend more on the wood resources of their forests. Electricity is costly and electrical appliances are not common except in affluent homes of city dwellers. Wood or peat-burning stoves with built-in ovens are used to cook the family meals and in many cases also form the primary heat source for smaller homes. Heavy cast-iron cookware is favoured for top-of-the-stove cooking; earthenware containers are used for oven baking and also for mixing bowls. The availability of wood makes it the ideal material for many kitchen utensils such as bowls, rolling pins, spoons, chopping boards, work tables, and wooden churns for butter-making. Fresh seasonal foods are preferred and in many areas marketing is done daily, any foods requiring storage are simply placed in a cool area or in an ice box. Extra food provisions for the long winters are frequently prepared in the home by drying, salting, pickling, smoking. Preserves and jams are also prepared.

FOODS COMMONLY USED

The Baltics are noted for their grain crops of rye, wheat, oats, and barley, their high potato production and their daily farms. It is not surprising, therefore, that grains, potatoes, and dairy products form the staple foods, and are supplemented with smaller proportions of fish, pork products, and poultry. German, Scandinavian (q.v.) and Slavic (Polish and Russian) cuisines, because of the historical periods of influence, have all made contributions to the Baltic cuisines. German ethos prevails in the Lithuanian personality, but it is the Slavic influence that prevails in the Lithuanian kitchen, although many so-called typical Lithuanian dishes will be found to be a part of German food traditions. Scandinavian influence, not surprisingly in view of history, predominates in Estonian cuisine, while Latvian cookery clearly shows threads of all three influences. The food of the Baltic peoples differs more in nomenclature than in substance; regional differences and specialties do exist, but many similarities are to be found as well.

Milk and Milk Products
Soured milk, buttermilk and sour cream are staples, while cottage cheese and pot cheese (Lithuanian: SURIS) are widely used for many dishes. Much cheese is also consumed: fresh, aged, and with or without the beloved caraway seeds. Cheeses are prepared from the milk of cows or goats. Most families consider it of great importance that their children consume both milk and products from milk. Milk is also used in many varieties of milk soups and vegetables are often cooked in milk as well.

Fruits and Vegetables
Fruits are plentiful and enjoyed in season, as they are, or stewed with sugar as fruit compotes, or served as fruit soups. Many jams, jellies, and preserves are prepared for winter use. KORVITS is an Estonian sweet preserved relish made from chunks of pumpkin and served traditionally with meat. Estonian "fruit salad," traditionally served in winter, is a speciality of mixed preserved fruits. Berries are especially plentiful, both wild and cultivated, and Estonia's berries are especially noted for their quality and sweetness. The combination of fresh, dried, or preserved fruits, served or cooked with meats and fowl, is also much enjoyed.

Potatoes and cabbage are the staple vegetables and store well for winter use. A favoured form of cabbage, especially in winter, is SAUERKRAUT.

The common root vegetables: carrots, turnips, and beets, as well as the fresh seasonal favourites of cucumbers, radishes, tomatoes, and onions are enjoyed fresh in salads and served with sour cream or a vinaigrette dressing. Wild mushrooms of many varieties are eagerly collected in their season and many are hung and dried to add flavour to dishes all year.

Meats and Alternates

Pork, pork products and poultry are the staples but are not used in great quantity. Domestic and wild fowl and game are enjoyed as available. Jellied pig's feet are a Lithuanian favourite and suckling pig is often prepared for festive occasions. Herring, sprats, and eels are the favoured harvest from the sea. Egg consumption is limited but steadily increasing due to increased supply and lower prices.[9] Some dried legumes are used for soups and Estonian children like to chew dried peas and beans as a snack. KAMA is an Estonian soup served cold in summer and eaten as a refreshment any time of the day: prepared from a flour made from dried, ground, and roasted grains and legumes blended with sour milk and flavoured lightly with salt or sugar.

Breads and Cereals

Grains form one of the most important satisfying and economical staples of the Baltics. Bread is always on the table at every meal and although usually a dark, sour rye bread, other breads made of wheat or combinations of flours may be served. Soups are often thickened with coarse flours or may even be made from grains; porridges and hot gruels are frequently served and may constitute a warming meal. Baked barley is a favourite side dish for meats and soups and barley flour is used for breads.

Fats

Oils are seldom used except occasionally for salads. Lard or bacon fat predominates in cookery while butter is favoured for baking, as a spread, and as a seasoning for foods. Fats are also consumed in the form of creams (sour cream, cream, and whipped cream), sour milk, and in many cheeses.

Sweets and Snacks

The Baltic countries imported French pastry chefs, who opened their own little shops. The tradition of fine pastries, richly and elaborately prepared – by French chefs – is still maintained. Home baking includes satisfying buns, rolls and KUCHENS, based on sweet yeast dough or firm cakes based on eggs. Sugared dried fruits are a favoured snack to be nibbled any time. Plain chocolate, either milk chocolate or bittersweet, is considered a special treat. A common snack in Latvia is paper cones filled with sauerkraut, eaten as ice cream is elsewhere.[10]

Seasonings
Caraway seeds head the list of favourites, and are also believed to be an aid for digestion. Poppy seeds, dill, parsley, and bay leaves add their touch to many dishes as well. Ginger, aromatic honeys, and allspice are used in baking. In general, Baltic foods are not highly seasoned; salty and sour flavours predominate. Most baked goods are rich simply with the aroma and flavour of fresh eggs, butter, and cream.

Beverages
Tea is taken frequently and sour milk is an anytime beverage. Coffee is also used but is considered a luxury in some areas, where a type of coffee may be prepared from ground, roasted cereals such as rye, and sometimes chicory. Beer, wine, and schnaps are enjoyed and vodka flavoured with caraway is a favourite.

Meal Patterns and Eating Customs
Although there is an increasing mobility from rural to urban settings, more than half the Baltic population shares a common agricultural heritage that is reflected in a deep respect for land and nature and a humble religious devotion. Their thankfulness for the gifts of land and nature is shown in their preference for simple satisfying foods unadorned by sauces or excessive seasoning. Breads and soups form the mainstays of many meals. Lithuanians always begin a meal with a prayer of thankfulness and Estonian children seldom leave the table without the words, "Thank you, my Lord, my stomach has been filled." And though Latvian country homes are often isolated from each other, Slavic hospitality prevails in a flow of food and drink shared by all.[9,11,12-15]

Together with individual pride in the family name, care is taken to hand down homemaking skills to the daughters and agricultural skills to the sons. Great respect is shown the father of the household: not only is his opinion consulted in all matters, he is also the first to be served at meals. Party foods are always presented buffet style, while daily meals are commonly served family-style, with everyone helping themselves. Based on the type of work done, heavier meals are usually served in the country, while lighter, more sophisticated meals are favoured in the cities. A simple breakfast of porridge, bread, and a beverage and a similar simple evening meal is balanced with the heavier meal taken at noon and consisting of a hearty meat and vegetable or grain soup with bread and beverage and concluded with fresh or stewed fruits. Many coffee and pastry shops provide snacks for city workers, while soup is often a refreshing snack for country people. Evening guests or quiet family gatherings enjoy tea with home-baked cakes, KUCHENS, or other sweets.

Special Occasions
Religion has a profound influence on the lives of the Baltic peoples.

Lithuanians are mostly members of the Roman Catholic Church, while both Latvians and Estonians are members of the Lutheran Church. Nazi exterminations during the Second World War decimated the Jewish population.[1]

The Christian festivals of Christmas and Easter highlight the festive calendar, but occasions for festivities also include celebrations of seasonal flowers and foods, Saint's Days, harvesting and sowing, and family events such as births, weddings, and funerals. For example, the Estonian celebrations of Leaf Month (May), Juice Month (April), and Candles (February) and many others, indicate the deep ties of religion and nature. Thus the bounty of crops and orchards, religious and family events all intertwine in a heart-felt thanksgiving expressed in humble devotion and happy gatherings.

Traditional customs for Christmas in Lithuania include a meatless menu for Christmas Eve (called *Kucios*), with twelve special dishes prepared from grains, fruits, vegetables, and fish to symbolize the Twelve Apostles. One of the oldest traditional dishes for *Kucios* is a fermented poppy seed soup, AGUONO PIENAS, served with dumplings. Church services, visiting friends, and a buffet menu of ham baked in a sourdough crust, roast goose stuffed with apples and prunes, varieties of homemade sausages, and special winter salads, completed with a display of special cookies and pastries (especially the poppy seed roll called AGUONINES) are part of the festive observances. In the country areas of all the Baltic lands, the slaughtering of a pig for Christmas is followed by the many traditional activities involved in making sausages and blood puddings, curing and smoking hams and bacons, and rendering fat for lard. Again, roasted geese stuffed with apple and prune share the table with salads of chopped herring and beets, potato dishes of many kinds, tart and salted pickles contrasted with sweet fruit preserves and all washed down with homemade beers and wines and even homemade vodka, faintly redolent of caraway. And while other peoples favour richly-sweet desserts to complete festive occasions, the Baltic pastries and yeast doughs owe their fragrance and flavour to roasted crushed nuts and poppy seeds and pot cheese: filling and delicious.

Concern and a special love for animals is exemplified by the Christmas Eve tradition of feeding small amounts of bread and barley to the farm animals before the family's evening meal. This is similar to traditions in slavic countries.

Easter is celebrated with church services and the menu reflects the joy of the spring season. Decorated eggs as well as fruits and berries are hidden for the children to find, and the game of *Koksimine* (Estonian mischievous cracking of hard, and sometimes soft, eggs) is enjoyed by everyone. Communal buffet tables featuring family specialties are set up and prepared well ahead of time: a buffet of salads, meats, and fish and an array of good breads will be enhanced by the presence of the PASHA: Russian-inspired delicate cheese and whipped cream mold.

Weddings are often the excuse for the wearing of regional costumes and the presentation of distinct regional specialities in food, music, and dance. An Estonian country specialty is the serving of soup (PULMASUPP) and farina and milk in wooden bowls traditionally eaten with wooden spoons. This wedding supper is accompanied by specially-made beer drunk from wooden steins.

Similarly, traditional funeral practices often follow local or regional as well as religious customs. In some country areas of Estonia, the path for the funeral procession may be laid out with spruce boughs, with a spruce wreath marking the house of mourning. Following the burial, a large meal prepared by friends and neighbours may include roasted pig, sausages, blood puddings, head cheese, winter salads, or fruit compotes and breads. Home-made vodka will be drunk in toasts to the departed one.

EIGHT

Belgian

In 1830, Belgium, a small heavily-populated country bordering on France, Germany and Luxembourg, detached itself from the Netherlands and became an independent nation. Its history is a long story of other nations marching over Belgian soil, each leaving an imprint upon the people and their traditions: Romans, Franks, Spaniards, Austrians, Dutch, and especially the French.[1]

Belgium is made up of two main groups of people: the Flemings in the North, a Teutonic people who speak Flemish (a dialect of Dutch related to German), and the Walloons in the South who are primarily a Celtic people speaking a dialect of French.[2] It is said that Antwerp, the northern Flemish business city, represents its people's character: "salty, stubborn and proudly provincial,"[3] while Brussels, located in the heart of Belgium, and about four-fifths French-speaking, seems more representative of the more emotional and flamboyant Walloons.[4]

But wherever one goes in Belgium, North or South, despite the differences, some things are universal. Almost everywhere, except in remote rural areas, English is spoken and understood; Belgian husbands become emotional on the subject of food and argue about whose wife is the better cook; and Belgians like their food in ample quantity and of good quality. But although good food well-prepared is a priority, Belgians are not adventurous cooks. They have little interest in experimenting with "foreign" dishes, remaining happily confident that the best is Belgian home-cooking and the best of restaurant food is none other than the *haute cuisine* of France. And although the Flemish favour foods masked with velvety sauces of cream and eggs and the Walloons make extensive use of pork in their dishes the overall tone of Belgian cookery is definitively French.[4]

The meticulous care with which Belgian cooks select their foods can best be illustrated by a walk through a Belgian supermarket, where even everyday items like butter and cream are carefully labelled with the proud producer's name, where an incredible array of exquisitely garnished cold meats, pâtés, sausages, salads, and prepared appetizers delight the eye, and where varieties of canned, packaged, and bottled goods line up in colourful profusion unparalleled elsewhere. Advertisements proudly proclaim:

"Butter from Namur," "Asparagus from Malines," "Pork and pork products from Pietron," "Walnuts from Bastogne," "Strawberries from Wepion."[4]

The tremendous Belgian sweet tooth is not gratified in simply one bakeshop. A distinction is carefully made between the daily baked goods which may be purchased from a *boulangerie* and party specialties, which are selected from a *pâtisserie*. Candies and confections are so important they are sold in specialty stores called *confiseries*, where even just a wanton glance seems to add pounds.

But gradually, as is happening in other parts of the world, some of the high standards of daily shopping and food preparation must be lowered to accommodate the modern life-style; the realities of traffic snarls, working mothers, and a shared international desire to narrow the waistline.

Home Life and Facilities

Most Belgian kitchens, though tiny by western standards, are well-equipped, but freezers and dishwashers are not commonly owned. There is still a strong preference for the use of fresh, seasonal foods and so large storage areas and equipment are really not a necessity. Family meals are often taken in the home, but entertaining may often be in restaurants, further obviating the need for large preparation or storage areas.

FOODS COMMONLY USED

"Coffee is a passion" and FRITES are so popular at home and as snacks everywhere, that coffee and fried potatoes may be labelled Belgian staples.[4] Belgium's national dish is BIFTEK, FRITES, SALADE – also the usual lunch for almost everyone. BIFTEK is not a steak but is the general term used to describe any well-trimmed boneless piece of meat, whether it is beef, veal, pork or horsemeat. The FRITES are eaten usually with varieties of mayonnaise, such as Tartar sauce, Russian dressing or *Béarnaise* sauce, accompanied with pickles or pickled onions. In fact, mayonnaise seems to appear almost everywhere in one form or another. Fish and seafoods are loved, deep-fried foods and potato-based soups enjoyed. The famed WATERZOOI is somewhere between a soup and a stew, made from fish or chicken in a well-simmered broth that is thickened with eggs and cream and served in a soup plate accompanied with potatoes or buttered bread. As it sounds, it is a meal in itself.

Milk and Milk Products
Fresh milk as a beverage is not too popular; even children prefer to drink CAFÉ AU LAIT. Much fresh cream and whole milk are used in preparation of soups, custards, and many sauces. Cheeses are often eaten with breads for breakfast. CRÈME FRAÎCHE, a thick and slightly tangy cream, is used both in France and Belgium for cooking, with fruits and in desserts.

Fruits and Vegetables
Fresh seasonal fruits are preferred and good variety and excellent quality are to be had in supermarkets, specialty stores, and open markets. A typical Belgian touch is to add dried fruits to many meat dishes, especially in the winter when vegetables are scarce and more costly.

Vegetables are of great importance and seldom served without distinction; usually served as a separate course, appropriately sauced and garnished, but often overcooked. Potatoes are a part of almost every lunch and dinner, especially when meat or fish is served. Cabbage, turnips, and potatoes are winter staples. Especially favoured vegetables include cabbage, escarole, BELGIAN ENDIVE, cauliflower, brussels sprouts, CRESSONETTE (watercress), leeks, HOP SPROUTS, and, of course, the ever-present potato, especially in the form of FRITES, served with some variety of mayonnaise.

Meats and Alternates
Walloon cookery is noted for an extensive use of pork, but to all Belgians, meat is an important part of dinner, followed by fish or seafood, which are also much enjoyed. But whether the main dish is meat or fish, the ever-present side dish of some form of potatoes makes the meal always filling. Favoured meats: pork, beef, veal, horsemeat; no lamb or mutton. Game meats are very popular and Belgians love to hunt: *Marcassin* (wild boar), hare, rabbit, roebuck, wild deer, wild duck, grouse, snipe, quail, partridge, and thrush. Favoured fish: salmon, mullet, trout, turbot, skate, flounder, pike, carp, whitefish, dourade, mackerel, lotte, cod, herring. All seafood and shellfish are savoured, especially mussels, which are called "the poor man's oysters."[5] Others are: eels, scallops, clams, crayfish, small CREVETTES and large shrimp, oysters, lobsters.

Eggs are consumed mostly as part of other dishes: rich egg and cream sauces, mayonnaise, etc. Occasionally eggs may be part of light supper dishes. Nuts and legumes are not an important part of the diet.

Breads and Cereals
Dry breakfast cereals or hot cooked porridges are seldom if ever used. Crusty white bread is preferred either as the "Belgian family loaf" or as crusty small rolls called PISTOLETS, which are a favourite late Sunday breakfast treat.

Fats
Unquestionably the Belgians consume much fat in the form of dressings and sauces, mayonnaise accompaniments, fried foods, and butter, which is used lavishly. Butter preferences are as individual as wine preferences and the particular butter is selected by the name of the producer and the area it comes from, but whoever or wherever, the true Belgian will choose unsalted butter as having the superior flavour. Both butter and lard are used in cooking and baking.

Sweets and Snacks
The object of desire – sweets to satisfy the Belgian sweet tooth – are everywhere in evidence. *Boulangeries, pâtisseries* and *confiseries* are never too far away. For any occasion, gifts of exquisitely packaged candies are appropriate and customary. A typical popular snack is the readily-available Belgian waffles, served with butter and sugar or whipped cream and sometimes fresh fruits. Belgians also manage to consume, with ease, great quantities of crisp dry cookies (achieved by using ammonium carbonate instead of an equal amount of baking powder). The frequent cup of coffee is seldom served alone; usually it too is accompanied by a sweet baked product. Late afternoon ladies' gatherings also enjoy "cakes and gossip."[4]

Seasonings
There is only a subtle use of onions and garlic in Belgian cookery and fresh herbs of all kinds are preferred. The favourite herb is chervil while the favoured spice is nutmeg. The richness of butter, cream, and eggs stands alone as the flavouring in many dishes.

Beverages
Estaminets are the popular beer taverns where businessmen are said to down unbelievable quantities of beer. Coffee is served to all ages at all meals and often in between as well. Belgians are very knowledgeable about wine selection and usually purchase their wine with their groceries. Wine is frequently served with dinner.

Meal Patterns and Eating Customs

Belgians are noted for their politeness, which is evident in business and at home. No dinner guest would ever be late, nor would a guest arrive without a bouquet of flowers or a beautifully-wrapped box of candies. A short aperitif hour is customary, followed by a leisurely dinner with wine, and likely one of Belgium's famed liqueurs with the after-dinner coffee: ELIXIR DE SPA (pine-flavoured), or WALZIN or ELIXIR D'ANVERS, both of which are similar to Benedictine.

The usual Belgian day begins with a light breakfast of bread or rolls with jam, unsalted butter and CAFÉ AU LAIT. A mid-morning break of coffee and waffles or cookies is likely for women and the children, while men will enjoy a beer or two.

Traditionally, the noon meal is the main meal of the day: businessmen take a two-hour break and most children come home from school. This is the meal that begins with soup or *hors d'oeuvres*, then a hearty meat or fish dish with potatoes, followed by a separate course of salad or cooked vegetables. Frequently the meat is carved in the kitchen and the platter garnished with the seasonal vegetables. It is interesting to note that vegetables and salads are almost a social status symbol, the higher the level, the more vegetables and salads are used. For most families, however, potatoes are the only vegetable requirement. A usual dessert for dinner would be fruit and cheese, a tart or pudding. Wine or beer is usually served as well.

Throughout the day, snacks of waffles, coffee, and cookies or FRITES to order, dunked in mayonnaise, are generously indulged in. The evening meal is usually a light supper of leftovers or simple egg, cheese, or fish dishes.

As in other countries in the western world, Belgian city dwellers are finding the pressures of urban life make it more and more difficult to enjoy that leisurely noon meal.

Sunday is a quiet day devoted to family and friends and often features a specially prepared dinner. For some families, Sunday is the day for "dinner out," and in Belgium this is a delightful prospect, for all restaurants strive to achieve a high level of renown: many gastronomic societies keep watchful eyes on their menus and specialties.

Special Occasions

All Belgians, with few exceptions, are Roman Catholic; the Flemish being more religious than the Walloons. A specialty of Catholic Flanders' Friday menu is BOTERMELK MET MAVERMOUT, a meatless soup of buttermilk thickened with oatmeal.

Christmas is celebrated with no special menu, but with the best that each home has to offer. For many this may be a rich game dinner, for others pork or beef, but almost all will climax their Christmas dinner with a BUCHE DE NOËL, a log of chocolate cake, trimmed to look like a fallen log, sometimes complete with mushrooms created of egg meringue.

Family christenings are celebrated with afternoon tea or coffee; small packages of candied almonds are often sent to friends as a memento of the occasion. First communions, engagements, and weddings are often celebrated as formal occasions with elegant buffets and dances.

NINE

Bulgarian

Long famed for its exports of fine fruits and attar of roses (used in perfume blending), Bulgaria is probably most noted for the legendary vigorous health and longevity of its inhabitants. The Bulgarians themselves modestly attribute their health and long life to the properties of yoghurt, which they claim was invented in Bulgaria.[1] But a closer examination of their general dietary pattern shows it to be one of the "healthiest in Europe,"[2] basically consisting of varied whole grains, legumes, cheeses, yoghurt, and fresh fruits and vegetables. Whether this diet is due to tastes, tradition, or to the almost "semi-permanent shortage of meats and meat fats," is difficult to assess.[3]

The Bulgarian People's Republic is located in the heart of the Balkans bounded by Romania, Turkey, Greece, Yugoslavia, and the Black Sea. A continental climate of cold winters and hot summers prevails over the mostly hilly and mountainous terrain[4] but the fertile areas of the Dambian Tablelands and the Thracian Plains produce rich harvests of wheat, rye, corn, rice and legumes as well as orchards and vineyards famed for their quality fruits.[2,3,4]

Bulgar means "man of the plow,"[2] and the predominantly agricultural peoples who call themselves Bulgarian are actually a blend of many ethnic groups: tribes from the Asiatic Steppes, and early Slavs who later melded with smaller groups of Turks, Greeks, Macedonians, Romanians, Serbs, Jews, Gypsies, Armenians, and Russians. In fact, most of the Bulgarians who came to America before the Second World War were peasants and labourers of Macedonian origin from the Balkan Mountains. Later immigrants (after the Second World War) were mostly urban professionals and intellectuals who had found themselves dispersed throughout Europe and unwilling to return to their homeland because of Communist domination.[5]

The long history of Bulgaria included acceptance of Christianity by King Boris I in the mid-800s, which led to the development of the first written Slavic in the form of church liturgy and the birth of the Cyrillic alphabet, also used by the Russians. Subsequent wars fought by the Russians and the Serbs all left their mark, but it was mostly the five-hundred-year domination by the Ottoman Empire that left Bulgaria with a lasting Turkish imprint on the traditions and food customs of the Bulgarian people.[2]

Home Life and Facilities
The traditional Bulgarian kitchen is bright with homespun and hand-embroidered table linens and curtains, hand-painted pottery dishes, and carved wooden mugs. Strings of peppers and mushrooms of many varieties add colour and aroma as they hang drying from the rafters. In country or city, the eating area is the centre of the home; hospitality centres around food and people and the sincere enjoyment of both.

In general, the present standard of living, though rising, is still low. A general housing shortage often means that two families may be living in a one-family residence. Average salaries provide for the necessities of life. Typical of most people living under a planned economic regime, many are sacrificing personal comforts for general future prosperity and industrial development and expansion.[3] All of this means that food shortages and rationing are common and kitchen facilities and dining areas meagre. Food storage is not a problem since most foods are purchased on a day-to-day basis; and with most women working outside the home, there is little time for preserving and pickling though Bulgarians are very fond of pickles and thick-sweet preserves.

FOODS COMMONLY USED

The Bulgarian cuisine is mainly adapted from the Middle East – Turkey and Greece – but many native dishes can be traced readily to each of the neighbouring countries. The staple and plentiful vegetables, dried white beans, peas and lentils plus yoghurt, though seemingly simple foods, are used with such ingenuity that they become a variety of hearty and nutritious dishes: GUIVECH, DOLMAS, PILAFS, TCHORBAS, MUSAKA (made with potatoes or the more traditional eggplant). And though onions and garlic are very much favoured, Bulgarian dishes are not highly seasoned, but seasonings and natural herbs are used with a deft hand to bring out inherent flavours of the food. As well as a love for pickles, olives, and peppers as condiments, the

Bulgarians enjoy tartly sour dishes and in these the acid from lemon juice, natural yoghurt or SAUERKRAUT may add tang. Names of dishes vary slightly from one area to another, but the largest percentage of meals is based simply on whole-grain cereals, vegetables, cheeses and yoghurt.[1,6,7]

Milk and Milk Products

Sheep and goat's milk are made into many types of cheeses or used as sour cream, milk, or yoghurt. Yoghurt itself may be used as a cooling refreshment, or as a drink either plain or diluted with cold water. It is also used in soups, vegetable dishes, and served with cooked whole grains, meats, and fish. Sometimes yoghurt is used in desserts or may be served with fruits. Whatever the form of the dish, Bulgarians enjoy milk products at every meal.

Fruits and Vegetables

Fruits and vegetables are also an important part of daily menus. Many main dishes are thick vegetable stews, sometimes including legumes, and sometimes served with cooked grains or hearty whole-grain breads. A meal is considered incomplete without at least one side dish of fresh greens, sliced onions, pickles, radishes, cucumbers, or tomatoes; in winter, olives, and many types of pickles may be used instead. A usual dessert is fresh fruit or a compote of fruits cooked in a syrup.

There is a wide variety and excellent quality of apples, plums, cherries, peaches, melons, watermelons, apricots, figs, and pears. The grapes are so famous that much of their production is exported. Fruits may be eaten fresh, or as jams or jellies or as very thick SPOON SWEETS to be served with glasses of cold water or Turkish coffee, made into fruit compotes, and occasionally into fruit drinks or fruit soups.

When it is necessary to export much of the fresh vegetable produce, the Bulgarian staples become beans, onions, potatoes, and rice.[3] But fresh salad vegetables are eagerly enjoyed when available, and fresh seasonal vegetables become the centre of the meal: eggplant, okra, squash, pumpkin, onions, potatoes, cabbage (SAUERKRAUT is prepared and used widely). When possible, many vegetables are preserved with garlic and brine to create many interesting pickles for condiments, hot peppers being a great favourite.

Meats and Alternates

Bulgarians are probably mostly vegetarians by necessity rather than by choice, but if available, lamb and mutton are enjoyed. Pork and veal are seldom used though pork may be part of a special occasion meal. Fish is mostly consumed near its source: the Black Sea and the rivers. Varieties include turbot, carp, shad, sturgeon, crayfish, mussels, and snails. Eggs are generally in poor supply but are used often as a custard to bake over the top of a vegetable casserole. Legumes are an important part of the diet in good times and bad: small white beans, yellow, red and brown lentils, other beans, and peas eaten fresh and dried. Very occasionally game may be enjoyed roasted or in casseroles with other vegetables: hare, duck, venison, partridge, pheasant, and quail. Nuts of all kinds are an important source of protein. They are chopped or crushed or ground to a fine powder and may be used in soups, salads, meat and fish dishes, with vegetables or with desserts. Locally grown nuts include: green and ripe walnuts, hazelnuts, and almonds.

Breads and Cereals
Many breads are made with white wheat flour, whole wheat flour, rye flour and corn meal. Rice may be cooked into soups, mounded into PILAFS, sweetened and made into desserts. Crushed whole wheat BULGHUR and KASHA (buckwheat) may be cooked as a base for vegetables or as a side dish. The type of cereal or flour preferred depends on the area; nearer Romania corn meal prepared as a baked pudding or as a coarse bread can be as much a staple food as the Romanian MAMALIGA. Grains are also used to stretch the meaty flavour of rarely-used meats (in the same way that meats and vegetables are often combined) especially in meatballs and many types of vegetables stuffed with ground meat and grain filling, then slowly simmered for deep flavour.

Fats
The most-used cooking oil is sunflower seed oil. Olive oil is also widely used both in cooking and as a dressing with garlic, onions, and lemon juice to add zest to crisp fresh salad vegetables. Cold cooked legumes may also be dressed this way and served as a side dish. Butter may be melted and used to prepare the sugary, nut-filled layers of PHYLLO pastry in many forms for rich desserts, and butter may also be eaten with vegetables, but breads are often just broken and eaten plain or with cheeses.

Sweets and Snacks
Bulgarians love to nibble on seeds of all kinds that have been toasted and/or lightly salted, as well as nuts of all kinds. Sweets are very much enjoyed: from licking a spoonful of fresh honey to enjoying thick sweetly-preserved fruits with a glass of cold water or a tiny cup of strong Turkish coffee. Special occasions demand the presence of these rich sweets as well as the full range of delectable crisp and sweet nut-filled Middle East pastries based on PHYLLO dough.

Seasonings
Onions, garlic, and oil are to be found in almost all dishes except desserts. Fresh herbs are used abundantly and often just munched out of hand as they are plucked from the fields. Mint, dill, savoury, and a native tarragon called CIUBRITSA are all used generously. In fact, a combination of

salt and pepper with freshly-chopped CIUBRITSA is used as a dip for bread instead of butter.

Beverages
Plain yoghurt or yoghurt diluted with cold water is the favoured drink with meals, or a between-meals refresher. Wine may be used with meals on special occasions. MASTIKA, a grape brandy and SLIVOVKA or SLIVOVITSA (plum brandy) are taken as a potent aperitif with a variety of MEZE (appetizers) before dinner or for special occasions. Turkish coffee, brewed in a special pot and served in tiny cups, is taken at the end of a meal or served frequently as a refreshment for guests.

Meal Patterns and Eating Customs
Most Bulgarian meals could be easily described as simple, hearty, and nourishing. Breakfast is usually bread with coffee, occasionally cheese and fruit may be added. Lunch would be a salad of chopped or sliced fresh vegetables mixed with nuts and cheese or lightly dressed with oil and lemon juice, followed, if available, by a meat or fish dish, and then by a dessert made with milk and cereal (e.g. rice pudding) or fruit and yoghurt. A dinner may begin with an aperitif of SLIVOVKA, black olives, and cheeses, a TCHORBA (stew of meat and vegetables), a side dish of cold dressed beans or lentils, all accompanied with wine and followed by fruits and Turkish coffee. The main difference between urban and rural meals would be the variety of foods presented and the presence of meat.

Special Occasions
Although the almost eight million Bulgarians include many ethnic groups almost 90 per cent of them belong to the Bulgarian Orthodox Church, a branch of the Eastern Orthodox Church; about 9 per cent are of the Muslim faith, and these include the Turks and the Pomaks (name given to Bulgarians converted to Islam), and a part of the remaining 1 per cent are of the Jewish faith.[4,9]

When possible, Christmas is celebrated with a roasted suckling pig, while a young roasted lamb forms the highlight of the Easter dinner. Fish is especially important in festive menus for "meatless" days: the traditional baked carp, SHARAN SAWREHI, stuffed with a rice and nut filling, or with raisins, walnuts, and onions.

Weddings often occur in civil ceremonies, but with the bride and groom in full traditional dress. A merry time with singing and dancing the circular *horo* or the famed couples' dance, *ruchenitsa*[4], accompanied by heaped platters and full glasses – especially of SLIVOVKA – complete the festivities. The wedding feast itself usually centres around a GUIVECH of cubed lamb and succulent vegetables (an everyday GUIVECH would be of seasoned vegetables only) to be followed by salads, condiments and pickles, and a display of selected fruits in season, BAKLAVA, semolina puddings with rosewater, and finally Turkish coffee.[9]

TEN

Byelorussian

The Byelorussians or White Russians, are members of the Eastern Slav nations which also include Great Russia and the Ukraine. In the early 800s these people made up a part of several independent feudal princedoms, but in 1240, a Mongol invasion captured their territories and they became known as the Grand Duchy of Lithuania or Litva.[1,2] The people we know today as Lithuanians were at that time called Samogitians. With the Treaty of Lublin, in 1569, the Grand Duchy of Lithuania merged with Poland until 300 years later when Poland herself was partitioned between Russia, Prussia, and Austria. The hapless Litvanians were subjected to forcible Russification: the historic name of Litva was changed to White Russia and their language, traditions, and customs were suppressed. Despite ensuing hardships, which continually saw their lands as the battleground for nations around them, a slowly-emerging Litvanian middle class found expression in the nationalistic movement around 1800,[1] climaxing in the Russian Revolution – only to be dashed once again by the Bolsheviks who claimed the land as a Soviet Republic in January 1919.

As if this were not enough, White Russia was again divided after the brief Polish-Russian War of 1919-1920. About five million Byelorussians fell to Polish rule and four million to Russian rule. Following the Second World War, the entire country of about ten million again ceded to total Russian dominance.

Byelorussians who emigrated to America before the Second World War were largely illiterates from the poorer villages (the Tsar encouraged a deliberate state of illiteracy); those who came later were mostly political exiles, professionals, and intellectuals who stimulated the growth of cultural organizations in America aimed at preserving their heritage.

For so long a part of Lithuania, Byelorussia's cuisine most resembles that of Lithuania but also has strong elements of Polish and Russian traditions.[3,4] Festive occasions are marked by devout religious observance: Greek Orthodox Church in the East, Roman Catholic Church in the West, with approximately 10 per cent of the population estimated to be Jewish.[1]

Few differences in food preparation exist from that of Polish or Russian foods, but names of dishes may vary. Foods commonly used include dairy products such as milk, yoghurt, and sour cream; fruits in season, and hardy vegetables, such as beets, cabbages, potatoes, and mushrooms; meats as available but favouring pork and pork products and beef, occasionally lamb, veal, fowl, and fish. Special favourites include varieties of mushrooms and fresh vegetables, such as cucumbers, onions, and radishes to be enjoyed with sour cream and sometimes crisp fresh vegetables may be dipped in honey.[4] Dumplings made from cheese, potato, cabbage or sweet doughs are served ingeniously as appetizers, main dishes, in soups or as desserts. Rye breads and cooked barley or buckwheat are used daily, and few dinner meals are served without side dishes of sauerkraut with apples or cranberries. The Polish influence of adding sugar to heighten the taste of soups and salad dressings is also evident. Like all Slavic food, Byelorussian dishes excel in heartiness, ample portions, and are served with the Slavic tradition of warm and generous hospitality that no amount of hardship can erase.

Please consult the following chapters for further information: Russian, Polish, Baltic Peoples, Jewish.

ELEVEN

Canadian: Atlantic Provinces, Indian, Inuit, Quebec

NOTE: *Canada, like the United States, comprises many different ethnocultural groups. All the ethnic groups studied in this book are Canadian, but considered specifically in this chapter are those groups or regions which, by virtue of their lengthy histories, have established their own distinctive food traditions.*

Canada, like the United States, is a land of immigrants. To really understand the cultural background of Canadians – as well as Americans – it would therefore be necessary to read each chapter of this book, for each chapter represents one or more of the ethnocultural groups, and their food traditions, who consider themselves to be Canadian or American.

Since Canada was first settled by groups of peoples believed to have crossed the Bering Strait from Asia, it is the Indians and the Inuit who first learned to adapt to their new-found environment of varying climate and geography. So symbiotic was the relationship of these ingenious peoples to their environment, that without their help many of the Europeans who came a few thousand years later, may never have survived. For the Indians taught them to use indigenous plants and crops and even brewed a tea from white cedar needles to cure scurvy.[1,2]

In 1497, John Cabot had written in his log: "the shoals of fish off the Grand Banks [Newfoundland] were so great as to impede the progress of the ship. . . ." Shortly after the circulation of this report, eager fishermen from Brittany, Normandy, the Basque provinces, and England all came to reap the sea's harvest.[3] By the early 1500s, small villages were established which soon became not only fishing centres but fur-trading centres as well. By the late 1500s, cod, "the beef of the sea," had become one of the economic staples of Northwest France and each summer as more and more Indians came to the coast to exchange furs for European goods, a gradual transition took place. More and more ships were sailing between France and Newfoundland but their trade soon had little to do with fish.

And although the Basques from Spain had long established a whaling centre at Tadoussac, it became widely known as a fur-trading centre.[2]

By the 1600s, wooden sailing ships were carrying other important cargo: English, Irish, Scottish, Welsh, French, Spanish, and Dutch immigrants, hopefully coming to make a new life in the new land. But life aboard these ships could only be described as grim at best and those who survived the journey by sea had already passed the first test of pioneering. The ship's wood absorbed moisture and made it difficult to keep the stores dry. Rats and insects multiplied rapidly in the dank holds. Aside from the highly-salted pork packed in barrels and small rations of water and hardtack, the ship's stores often included butter, cheese, and beer. But too often before the ship was out to sea, the butter became rancid, the cheese moldy and tough, and the beer spoiled. "Skillygolee," "lobscouse," and "Scotch Coffee" were a few of the nicer names used to disguise the unpalatable slop created by soaking the hard "weavil-ridden" ship's biscuits with water. It was even considered a bit of luck if vinegar or a bit of salt pork were available for seasoning.[4]

Fishing, fur trading, some farming and cattle raising characterized the occupations of the first colonists amongst the diverse cultures of the Maritime region.[5] During the first half of the 1600s while the Europeans were grappling for footholds in the New World, the many Indian Nations, once so free and independent, were in the throes of a cultural and technological revolution. As they became more and more dependent on European goods, their old skills faded: metals replaced flint and bone, muskets replaced lances and bows and arrows, and European trinkets became status symbols. Worse, their old religious beliefs were undermined, wars were fought for extermination not domination, and the white man's diseases and his alcohol decimated, debilitated, and finally degraded them. At this point in history, the mighty Huron Nation was almost destroyed, but the Iroquois and the Algonkins were to be next in the relentless path of fate.[2]

The early 1600s were important years for Nova Scotia. De Monts had begun the work of colonizing Nova Scotia and it was largely from his efforts that the Acadian colony grew.[6] In 1605, the first wheat in Canada was both grown and milled in Nova Scotia in a mill that was claimed to be the first erected on the North American continent.[7] Also about this time, the first cuttings of apple trees were brought to Nova Scotia from France's Normandy province. It did not take long before most farms boasted a small apple orchard and soon specialty apple dishes and apple cider became a welcome part of the settler's fare.[8]

In 1608, Samuel de Champlain founded the city of Quebec[6] and within the next twenty-five years, organized colonization of New France was encouraged by "The Company of New France," or "The One Hundred Associates." This very early attempt to settle New France was met with general apathy but successful French settlement was occurring in small farms in Acadia (Nova Scotia) where the rich soils produced vegetables and grains and wild berries and fruits helped to fill the larders together with the rich bounty of game and fish.[8] The largest period of early growth for New France occurred in the late 1600s, when shiploads of *"Filles du Rois,"* hardy young women arrived from France with dowries of "an ox, a cow, a pair of swine, a pair of fowl, two barrels of salted meat and eleven crowns . . .," together with the addition of 2,000 new settlers and the protection of the Royal Troops. So important was population growth in New France at this time, that early marriage and large families were actually encouraged by annual grants and bachelorhood was not only considered a sorry state, but was liable to fine.[1,9]

As early as the turn of the eighteenth century, the French in New France, deeply immersed in their new life based on a close family life and a reverence for the soil, as well as a verve for ancestral traditions, began the break with the European French. In fact, the factors of tradition coupled with isolation were important in creating and maintaining a proud and independent self-sufficiency which was evident as early as 1675 and steadily increased.[10] Even in 1759, when Quebec (New France) capitulated to the English, she was firmly established as an agricultural society of French-speaking Catholics albeit in an "English Canada."[11]

From 1753 to 1755, the ominous rumblings of conflict between New France and the thirteen British Colonies dealt their saddest blow to the almost 10,000 quiet farm people in the Annapolis Valley: the French Acadians. Refusing to take an oath of allegiance to the British King, probably because they felt this would threaten their loyalties to France, the Acadians were forcibly deported and scattered throughout the British Colonies. Some found their way south to the French New Orleans where they were called Cajuns and soon adapted to the new life.[1,8,9,12]

The English then sent out an urgent appeal for farmers to work the lands vacated by the Acadians. Many Germans came, a large group settling on the good land of Lunenburg. They were called Dutch (as they were in Pennsylvania) as a mistranslation of the German "Deutsch." Their descendants became shipbuilders and fishermen, and although they lost the German language early, they still to this day retain a recognizable Lunenburg accent.[12]

The 1700s also saw the gradual immigration of other settlers from other ethnic cultures. French and British Jews played important roles as early settlers and traders; the French Jews came despite a French decree dating back to 1685 "which prohibited Jews and Huguenots (French Protestants) from settling in Canada or France's other North American colonies. . . ."[13] Nova Scotia counted almost 2,500 Englishmen among its settlers while almost half of Newfoundland's population was said to be Irish – brought in as passengers on English fishing ships calling at Irish ports on the outward journey.[8,14] New Englanders were also among those who came to take up the vacated Acadian farms, and they brought with them their famed trenchers and tureens and baked beans. Many Scots came in the late 1700s because of the severe economic repression and downfall of the chieftains; they settled in Cape Breton Island, in Pictou, Nova Scotia, and in the areas of Prince Edward Island that later became New Brunswick.[15] Groups of United Empire Loyalists, some with their Black slaves, fleeing from the persecution and derision of the Americans for their loyalties to the British, were granted sanctuary and even given lands and some basic provisions to settle in the Maritime area and Upper Canada. A large percentage of these early Loyalists were said to be Germans.[16]

The flow of settlers continued! Polish soldiers and political refugees, Scottish Highlanders from the Thirteen Colonies; German Mennonites from Pennsylvania; Blacks escaping from the American Revolution; Irish fleeing the Irish Rebellion. Swedes joined the flow of British immigrants encouraged by the great areas in the new land, which afforded space that couldn't be found in their homelands, where populations were burgeoning.

In their early struggles for survival, the immigrant settlers clung to familiar customs and made do with available new foods and cherished some old food traditions too. Thus, the 2,000 Blacks who came to Nova Scotia after the War of 1812, had a difficult time adjusting to freedom with its attendant responsibilities, and lived chiefly on rice, molasses, and Indian Meal (corn), making a staple bread pudding called PADANA.[6] The Scots took care to provide themselves with oats, molasses, and eggs; the Irish contented themselves "with a few herring" when they had to; German settlers produced SAUERKRAUT, KOHL SALAD and SCHMIER-KASE. Meanwhile in 1831, the earliest known cookbook published in Canada was *The Cook Not Mad*: but perhaps someone was "mad" when an identical book was found to be published in the same year in Watertown, New York . . .[17]

By the late 1800s, the flow of immigrants became even more varied, not only in their place of origin, but also in their place of Canadian settlement. By the 1840s, a small group of Maltese became Canadian settlers, preceded in 1836 by the first Maltese, Lewis Schikluna, who had established a shipyard at Welland Canal.[1] Groups of Finns settled as far West as Vancouver Island; the Irish potato famine sent the evicted and forced-migrants from Ireland to Canadian soil; the first Hungarian Freedom Fighters emigrated to the United States and then to Canada after the 1848 revolt; Norwegians established settlements on the Gaspé Peninsula of Quebec; peasant immigrants from Prussian-occupied Poland came to flee the resulting oppressions in their homeland – some establishing the first Polish settlement in Wilno, Renfrew County, Ontario.[1]

These later immigrants were probably oblivious to the changes that had occurred agriculturally and domestically in the lives of the pioneers. Food for cattle was widely grown and the ability to keep the animals in barns over the severe winter provided year-round supplies of milk, butter, cheese, and buttermilk. Established settlers soon made cookstoves with ovens a special priority in their homes. And out of the ovens came baked goods leavened with baking soda that was made from burnt corn cobs; or sourdough yeasts prepared from boiled hops or from BARM, a soft dough of flour, salt, and warm water, allowed to ferment. The plentiful pumpkin was simmered into soups, baked into pies and boiled down into molasses. Ingenious pioneers had perfected the making of gelatin from cow hides, and almost every household boasted its own homemade beer and apple cider.[3]

In fact, the later 1850s were characterized by many as a time of "the food supply revolution." Coastal fisheries were expanding; railroad growth and development of new farm implements encouraged farming of virgin lands; improved passenger sailing ships helped to make the dreaded Atlantic crossing a more pleasant experience. The increasing need for labourers in towns and cities, plus the burgeoning landless middle class – all were ready for a wide range and a steady supply of foods.[3] As well as increased technology and increasing need, the "food revolution" extended also to the home kitchen inspiring practical innovations. Catharine Parr Traill wrote a compendium of practical information and encouragement about everything from descriptions of the countryside to recipes for making candles, cheese, pickled beef, and maple sugar "sweeties." She culled ideas from friends and neighbours and wrote of preparing beer from beets, coffee from toasted dandelion roots, processing homemade starch from potatoes and bran, and even how to extract the rennet from the first stomach of a suckling calf and use it to make cheese.[18]

Probably due to the patient persistence of one Alan McIntosh, Upper Canada enjoyed an abundance of apples. McIntosh's patience was evident in his single-minded interest in learning the art of grafting and budding in an attempt to duplicate the apple trees on his father's farm. This one man was personally responsible for acres and acres of crisp red apples known to this day by his name.[19] Gradually apples began to replace pumpkins as a sweet and as a fruit. Dried apples were prepared in "paring bees" or were preserved like small fruits by boiling in sugar then sundrying for winter storage.[3]

The "food revolution" also encompassed the formation of new associations and new types of factories. Flour mills, tanneries, meat-packing plants, and breweries had accounted for most of the gross national product but were being joined by expansion of heavy farm machinery by the Massey family,[19] cornstarch manufacture by W.T. Benson,[20] the first commercial cheese factories, and even the founding of the Canadian

Fruit Grower's Association in the Niagara Peninsula to organize the marketing and storage of fresh fruits.[19]

Changes and developments in Canadian foods and their production were also influenced by events in other lands. In 1860, forty years after the publication of Frederick Accum's book on food adulteration, the first British Food and Drug Act was passed. By 1876 the Food and Drug Directorate of Canada was established with a staff of four analysts – a hundred years later it would employ more than three hundred.[4,21] In Austria, a monk was pursuing a seemingly innocuous pastime that was later to revolutionize agriculture the world over – and in Canada it led directly to the development of rust-resisting, high-yield wheat for which the prairies became famous. The monk's name was Gregor Mendel and he had discovered what was recognized as the basic law of heredity and developed a genetic theory.[22] In 1861, a French engineer, Carré, experimented with ammonia gas as a refrigerant and provided a new means of preserving food without sterilization. By 1868, the first refrigerated boxcar was invented by coupling railroad transportation and the new process of refrigeration; with facilities for shipping, the entire meat and dairy industries expanded rapidly.[22]

But the biggest thrust of energy and publicity that was to affect Canadians occurred in the 1880s and centred around the building of the transcontinental railroad. It not only absorbed every available man for labour, it was even necessary to import labour from other countries. Italians, Chinese, and Finns all eagerly applied their efforts to forge the link between Eastern, Central and Western Canada. Up to the 1890s, Canada's flour exports had steadily decreased but with the new "opening of the West" the whole milling industry was stimulated.[24] Shipping of food products by steamers increased with the development of the railroads and refrigerated boxcars were quickly linked with refrigerated chambers in steamers, making the export of perishables, such as butter and cheese and later even fruits and pork products, a practical enterprise.[24]

The early 1900s were also witness to successive waves of immigrants from the British Isles, the European continent and even from the United States.[1] Ukrainians, Doukhobors, Mennonites, Estonians from oppressed Tsarist Russia, economically deprived Romanian refugees, Greeks, Japanese, Lebanese, and Icelanders, were each groups adding another dimension to the meaning of "Canadian." Italians and Chinese were noted for their efforts in the building of the railroads; Icelanders helped make north-central Saskatchewan famous for its wheat; the Dutch proved their agricultural talents when they introduced strip farming into Southern Alberta and put Western irrigation districts into profitable production.[1,13,25] Japanese settlers worked in British Columbia as farmers, fishermen, and skilled labourers in mining and construction. The simmering political problems of the Austrian Empire brought immigrants seeking calm and stability in their life: Czechs, Serbs, Croats, Ukrainians, Jews, Magyars, and Romanians. In fact, 1913 was recorded as an almost record year of immigration to Canada: more than 400,000 immigrants came.[1]

The experience of the First World War did little to unite Canadians. French-Canadian nationalism exploded against English management even though the seat of the problem was conceded by many to be the French educational system, which was designed to produce priests, lawyers, and doctors but not the economists, engineers, and industrialists that were needed to promote and manage industry and agriculture in the province of Quebec.[1] While Quebec simmered with deep-seated hostilities, "persons of the Asiatic race" – East Indians, Chinese, and Japanese – were denied the vote in British Columbia. Unaware of Quebec or Asiatic "problems" in Canada, immigrants continued their march to the land of hope. Armenians, Hutterites, Byelorussians, Slovenes, and Hungarians fled political insurrections and came to Canada.

Immigrants to Canada in the 1920s were met with the appearance of the first co-op food stores, electric ranges for domestic use, and home ice-boxes to chill foods. They had a few years to enjoy these before the Depression turned North America into a nightmare.[13,27]

Despite immigration and political and even threatening economic problems, industrial history was being forged. Strict grading standards and all the grading acts together were a great stimulus to both domestic trade and export. Canada's per capita egg consumption (in 1928) was the highest in the world and a great expansion of the food industries took place because of an increased public confidence in merchandise purchased.[24] Ethnic tolerance increased as the newcomers proved their expertise in every area of the Canadian economy. And about this time, Quebec eased gradually from a predominantly agricultural and rural society to an urban industrialized one.[1] New developments in agriculture further stimulated optimism, as did development of dehydrated and concentrated food products, such as apples, and the world-wide interest in production and shipment of frozen foods.[21,23]

Canada's story of growth is a closely-intertwined tale of people and food. Representatives of more than seventy-two ethnocultural groups continue to find a place in this land for themselves, their abilities and their hopes. And while making their place, each group adds, in its own way, to the tastes of Canada as a whole.

Regional Specialties

There is little question that home life and food facilities as well as the range of foods commonly used by Canadians closely parallel those of Americans, as do the meal patterns and eating customs and the celebration of special occasions. As in the United States, area preferences blend with age-old cultural customs, personal preferences, status and health, to determine what appears on the table, how it is served, and even how it is eaten. Yet there are two areas of Canada and two distinctive ethnocultural groups, all with such lengthy histories that their food customs stand as distinctive: the Atlantic Provinces and the Province of Quebec and the Inuit and Indian peoples.

Atlantic Provinces

NEW BRUNSWICK

New Brunswick is considered to be the "home of the descendants of the Acadians and the Loyalists," since from earliest times, Acadia had included the areas of both Nova Scotia and New Brunswick.[27] The exception to the area is Edmunston where Loyalists and New Englanders are a part of the population but the distinctly French character of the city is supported by its 85 per cent French population.[27] From earliest times, timber, fishing, and shipbuilding were the most important, and agriculture was, in comparison, neglected.[28] Nonetheless crops of wheat, rye, Indian corn, buckwheat, barley and oats as well as peas and beans were produced; potatoes and root vegetables were popular but scarce; apples, plums, berries, and cherries were carefully cultivated together with small crops of pumpkins, cucumbers, melons, and varieties of squash.[28] Some of the first Loyalists, arriving in New Brunswick in 1783, noted that the Malacite Indians were eating the young fronds of the ostrich ferns and they plucked them too as a food. Today FIDDLEHEADS are eaten as a gourmet delight rather than merely as a hedge against hunger.

For the earliest settlers in the late 1700s, the basis of the daily diet consisted of the rations provided by the Royal Bounty of Provisions:

> . . . one pound of flour per person, half a pound of meat, either beef or pork, an infinitesimal quantity of butter, about half a pound of oatmeal a week, an equal quantity of pease, and occasionally a little rice. . . .[29]

The above-mentioned daily rations could be supplemented with fish and game, and the settlers even became adept at supplementing scarce wheat flour to make delicious corncakes, buckwheat pancakes, and steamed breads of dark flour. In fact, the ritual Saturday night baked beans and steamed bread were (and continue to be) a favourite meal of the entire East coastal area both in Canada and the United States. Wild berries and wild greens and the sweetness of maple sugar added variety too.[29]

Wild fruits of the province include: strawberries, gooseberries, varieties of whortleberries, blackberries, and raspberries, wild cherries and wild plums, and grapes. Some of these were used to prepare fruit cordials, teas and wines; others were made into jams and jellies or sun-dried for winter use. Teas were sometimes steeped from Labrador tea or chocolate root, or sometimes even spruce or hemlock bark.[30,31]

Early settlers enjoyed the abundant fish of the area: herring, both smoked and salted, mussels, lobsters, caplin, and of course cod, which was the main staff of life. Cod heads were preserved by salting down; the cod itself was sun-dried. To use, cod could be soaked then fried in deep fat or boiled and served with fried pork and mealy potatoes.[32] Other fish like mackerel and caplin were spread on flakes (wooden racks) to dry and then cooked when needed.

For the settlers, molasses and maple sugar were the common sweeteners while varieties of vinegar (often made from apple cider) and salt served as usual seasonings. For those with means, the *Halifax Gazette* advertised the availability of imported spices, white wine vinegar, brown sugar and even rum, port, and sherry.

In later years, flour and potatoes became more plentiful and added to the extensive varieties of fish and seafood that were the continuing staples of the New Brunswick table. The ingenuity of the homemakers, then as now, produced cakes and breads and pies to round out the daily fare and preserves and jams for winter months.

NEWFOUNDLAND

Britain's oldest colony, Newfoundland, became Canada's tenth province in 1949.[34] Since before the mid-1500s, English fishing ships had come to the Banks of Newfoundland. It is not known exactly when the crews began to leave men and women ashore to protect their shore buildings (where fish were stored and cured) against the many rival and pilfering crews, but these became the first settlers. The English and the French who created trade intermarried with the Indians of Nova Scotia, the Micmacs, and so came to blend their lives.[34,35] The Beothuck Indians gave no resistance to the settlers and are now extinct. Only the natural elements gave the toughest battles for survival in this land which the English had called "a land of fog, bogs and dogs . . ."[36] By the mid-1700s, about 50 per cent of the population was made up of Irish immigrants, who crossed the Atlantic agreeing to pay for their passage as soon as they had jobs.[34,36]

Bankruptcy, fires, feuds, and "conquerors" – it all mattered little to the Newfoundland settlers who, from earliest times spent their lives with the rhythm of the sea and eked out food from the same substances, potatoes, cabbage and turnips from their little gardens, and somehow still managed to produce a hospitable table of tea, bread, and butter for guests. Living in weather-lashed, isolated fishing communities highlighted human values and daily heroism. Sometimes cod could be traded for flour, molasses, or even clothing; sometimes deer-trapping or seal-hunting could supplement the daily fish-and-potatoes diet.[36]

The rocky island seems, itself, to spurn life. Because they have to be built on rocks, the houses seem asymetrical; fresh meats and vegetables chronically hard to procure ("stringy cabbage and struggling turnips"[36]); there is no place for cows or horses to graze. The extremes of weather were always a problem. In winter, bread was kept in the beds to prevent its being frozen, while in summer the flies and mosquitoes and the stifling heat plagued people and spoiled foods.[36]

Although in Newfoundland "fish" means cod, many other fish are part of the harvest: haddock, redfish, sole, halibut, salmon, mackerel, turbot, swordfish, and herring. The latter may be prepared by pickling, smoking or serving with cream sauce. Occasionally lobsters and shrimp, squid and eels are enjoyed. Hunting may provide rabbits and hares, ptarmigan, caribou and recently small herds of deer provide meat as well. Otherwise main meat is salt beef or variety meats from pork.

Traditions of foods remain a treasured part of the Newfoundland life. Many families have a few chickens, pigs or sheep and even a pony or two, but fish is still cod, and vegetables are still in large part potatoes, cabbages, and turnips.[37] Considered to be the national dish is the one-pot meal of the "boiled dinner," consisting of turnips, potatoes, and cabbage boiled in a pot with salt beef or pork.[38] Strong tea, soft drinks, or rum are the favoured beverages and only small amounts of either canned milk or skim-milk powder are used. The preference for salty foods in the Newfoundland dietary may have come from the wide use of salt cod and salt beef and the flavour of the vegetables commonly cooked with them.[38] Another of the typical Newfoundland dishes is FISH AND BREWIS, prepared from soaked hard bread (similar to ship's HARDTACK), served with cooked fresh or salt codfish, sometimes with a crispy topping of pork fat called SCRUNCHIONS. Few raw vegetables are ever eaten but dandelion greens and turnip tops are cooked in the springtime. Native berries – squashberries, blueberries, partridge berries, marshberries and bakeapples – are used to make jellies and jams, baked and steamed puddings, and many cooked desserts. Homemade breads fill kitchens everywhere with delicious aromas and a commonly-prepared pastry, SMOTHER, covers fruit pies, leftover cooked vegetable dishes, and one-dish meals of fish or meats.[39] Commonly the source of many "in" jokes, the seabird known as the TURR or MURRE is plentiful in coastal regions near the end of winter, and provides a welcome change of fare.

In cultural terms, Newfoundland was considered to be "an island-arrested society and a rich repository of European customs and folklore on the very threshold of the New World." Believed to have derived from British and Irish origins, "mumming," "mummering," or "janneying" are analogous terms for a living folk tradition and are an intergral part of the high-spirited twelve-days-of-Christmas celebrations.[40] Characterized by unique disguises, the groups of mummers go from house to house presenting uninhibited performances and finally identifying themselves and joining in shared food and drink. Adult janneys are treated with beer, the young ones with candies, and all enjoy traditional Christmas SWEET

BREAD, eaten daily during the festive season. Since the kitchen is the centre of the home, guests and mummers are treated to the best chairs around the table, "soup-suppers" and concerts highlight other festive evenings. The "soup-suppers" consist of communally-prepared thick meat and vegetable stews of moose or caribou meat with vegetables selling inexpensively for all to enjoy.[40] SCOFF is the name given to the big meal held at any time, but usually at night and consisting of leftovers from the "soup-supper" plus homemade SWEET BREAD, PORK BUNS, and good strong tea.

NOVA SCOTIA

The area of Nova Scotia and Cape Breton Island was early settled by French (Acadians), English, Scots, Irish, Germans and Negroes, all of whom shared their lives with the native Micmac Indians.[41] The Scottish and French ancestors of the Cape Breton Islanders prepared simple meals consisting of fresh-caught fish or fried eggs accompanied by baked beans or panned potatoes. Occasionally preserved berries were served as dessert or the meal ended with oatcakes or biscuits and pies with tea.[42] For Cape Breton Islanders, breakfast is unchanging: porridge, strong tea, and fresh eggs with bacon.

Since the British government had offered free passage, land grants and even a year's basic provisions, the English coming to Nova Scotia fared well. Although they often had to make do with hardtack and salt beef, the usual fare was hearty beef soup or mutton broths, and status was identified by the type of sweet: ladies used loaf sugar, apprenticed men enjoyed brown sugar, while servants had molasses.[41] Scots came without government support and subsisted at first on shellfish and wild fruits but later added their beloved oatmeal to the dietary when grist mills could be built. Tea with oatcakes and scones marked the hospitality of the Scots, while SHORTBREAD was served for Hogmanay (New Year's Eve) and FORACH marked Hallowe'en when all guests would dip into a communal bowl of fine oats stirred stiff with sugar and whipped cream. The famed HAGGIS would mark St. Andrew's Day and Robbie Burns Night.

The Irish, by 1760 making up half of Halifax's population, submerged their traditions and adopted those of the English and Scots: oatmeal porridge became the morning and the evening meal while fried meat and potatoes formed the midday meal. A treat for the Irish was the serving of thin oatcakes with butter together with a glass of buttermilk.[41]

The dispersal of the Acadians by the British government brought with it an appeal for farmers and it was Germans who came to tend the farms and orchards. They settled in 1753 mainly around Lunenburg where their farms produced barley, rye, and oats and the rich fields yielded potatoes, cabbages, turnips, and cucumbers. The diet of grains and vegetables were well-supplemented with poultry and dairy products, veal and mutton, and many varieties of fish and seafood. German wedding fare consisted of ample servings of soups, mutton, geese, and hams and an array of home bakery. Typical of funerals was the FUNERAL CAKE, a plain cake flavoured lightly with cinnamon.[41] Significantly, German cookery skills added many treasured foods to the tables of Nova Scotia: BARLEY BREAD, CHICKEN NOODLE SOUP, DUTCH MESS or HOUSE BANKIN, SOUSED EELS, KOHL SLAW, SAUERKRAUT, many varieties of homemade sausages and puddings and SOLOMON GUNDY, a type of pickled herring.[43]

Many New Englanders also came to Nova Scotia in the 1760s to take up the farms vacated by the Acadians and added MAIZE to the crops, established the celebration of the New England Thanksgiving Day, and busied themselves brewing beer, wines and making apple cider, candles, soap, starch, and yeast. Some of the Black people in Nova Scotia came with the New Englanders, while others came as slaves to the pre-Loyalists, and still others escaped during the American Revolution. Rice, molasses and Indian Meal (cornmeal) formed the staple foods for the Blacks, with a favourite being PADANA, a bread pudding made from cornmeal.[41]

PRINCE EDWARD ISLAND

As in the other Atlantic provinces, cod and potatoes were synonymous with survival, whether the settlers were English, Scottish, Irish, or French. From earliest times it was apparent that food stores from ships were not dependable and the settlers made ingenious use of shellfish, nuts, wild berries, and various roots.[44] Lobsters, scallops, bar clams, salted herring, and smoked mackerel all were and continue to be important foods and export commodities, but cod is still considered most important.[45]

Although each of the island's cultural groups still retains many traditionally favoured foods, the ingredient that makes them especially "P.E.I." is potatoes. Famed for their fine quality, it is small wonder that potatoes are used in endless ways not only in meat and fish dishes and with other vegetables, but also as an ingredient in dumplings, cakes, breads, and candies. COLCANNON is both Scottish and Irish and is made by mashing together cooked turnips, potatoes, and cabbage. PÂTÉ À LA RÂPURE is a dish of Acadian origin consisting of layered and seasoned mashed potatoes filled with cubed stewed chicken meat and finally topped with crumbled salt pork before baking in the oven. ONESOOE is a one-dish meal of browned pork chops, onions and potatoes. And who on P.E.I. is not familiar with the satisfying POTATO BANNOCK?

In earliest times, bread, molasses, and tea and later oatmeal porridge were the staples that sated hunger. Cordials and preserves prepared from wild berries, an occasional imported orange, and homemade wine and beer were considered special treats. Berries included raspberries, strawberries, bunchberries, blackberries, mulberries, black currants, rose hips, chokecherries, and wild sarsaparilla. These were also used as medicinal remedies, or for teas, preserves, or desserts.[46]

As with the daily menu, potatoes play an important role in many special occasion dishes on Prince Edward Island. Potato pancakes and potato soup are prepared especially for Lent. POTTED MEAT or HEAD CHEESE was served traditionally during Easter week. Traditional Christmas foods consisted of roast duck or goose with side dishes of potatoes and turnips, a special Christmas cake and PLUM PUDDING. The usual scones and sugar cookies would be replaced by POTATO DOUGHNUTS, and MINCEMEAT PIE as special Christmas treats. Oysters are also a favourite of the festive season. P.E.I.'s Acadians prepared a traditional specialty of their own, PATA, to be eaten after the Christmas Midnight Mass. PATA is prepared with a mixture of meats, usually rabbit, chicken, and pork, and topped with a crust of pastry moistened with meat broth instead of water. Crusty rolls called FRENCH CAKES are also traditionally served by the French at Christmas time.[47]

Native Indians

The history of North American Indians, as hunters, gatherers, or cultivators, is one of a tender balance between man and environment. That is, until the white man came. The term "Red Indians" is usually credited to Columbus, who thought he had found the Indies and therefore called the inhabitants "Indians," and the probability that Columbus saw the Beothuck Peoples, who often decorated themselves with a paste of red ochre may explain the "red."[48] So intimately were the lives of the Indians interwoven with their environment, that the distinctive lifestyles of each of the groups were largely determined by the nature of the land itself and the type and amount of food available.

It is important to understand that just as the geographic areas, languages, life-styles, religions, and dialects of the various nations of Europe differ, so do those of various Native Peoples. There are, including the Eskimo or Inuit, seven main groups of Indians in Canada, speaking eleven main languages and about fifty dialects.[48] These groups are:

EASTERN WOODLANDS
Algonquin
Beothuck (extinct)
Cree
Malecite
Micmac
Montagnais
Naskapi
Ojibway (Chipewa)

PRAIRIE (PLAINS) TRIBES
Assiniboine
Blackfoot
Blood

IROQUOIAN
Hurons
Neutrals (extinct)
Tobacco Nation

Cayuga ⎫ Up to 1720 they formed
Mohawk ⎪ League of 5 Nations;
Oneida ⎬ Tuscaroras entered in
Onondaga ⎪ 1720 to form League of
Seneca ⎭ 6 Nations.

NORTHWEST TERRITORIES
Beavers
Dogribs

Grosventre
Piegan
Plains Cree
Sarcee
Sioux

B.C. INTERIOR
Carrier
Chilcotin
Interior Salish
Kootenay
Tahltan

Chipewyan
Hares
Kutchin
Nahanni
Sekani
Slaves
Yellowknives

B.C. COAST
Bella Coola
Coast Salish
Haida
Kwakiutl
Nootka
Tlinkit
Tsimshian

Among the more obvious debts of the white man to the Indian are the knowledge of plant cultivation, uses and techniques of preparation of certain foods as well as implements and medicinal plants. These debts include the cultivation, uses and preparation, and in some cases preservation as well of tobacco, corn (MAIZE), potatoes, peanuts, some varieties of cotton, maple syrup and maple sugar, varieties of beans and squash, pumpkins, sunflowers, tomatoes, pineapples, some melons. Another debt the White Man owes to the Indians is the domestication and cultivation of grapes, strawberries, gooseberries, raspberries, pecans and other nuts. Forest trails and canoe routes, the use and technique of making sleds, canoes, toboggans, and snowshoes are all part of the ancient skills of the Indians of North America.[48,16]

Considered to be "definitely the basis of Indian cooking in Canada"[49] are the many versions of NABOS or soups prepared from whatever is locally available. Although the name BANNOCK is of Scottish origin, Indians have long made a quick bread based on corn or wheat flour that can be baked over a fire or in a pan, and their name for it is PAKWEJIGAN. In fact, this type of bread accompanies most meals, and can be eaten as a snack with preserves or enjoyed with wild herb tea as a breakfast. Traditional Indian desserts are of wild fruits, berries or nuts. Popular among many nations is SAGAMITE: a thick mixture of meats with beans and corn simmered slowly in a cast iron kettle, usually over an open fire.[49] Traditionally, Indians eat when they are hungry rather than following a rigid time schedule; foods are often shared with other families; menus are prepared according to the area, the season, and the availability.

It must be noted again that generalizations about any aspect of Indian life are as difficult to make as generalizations about Europeans would be.

THE EASTERN WOODLANDS

Most of the tribes which inhabited this area shared similar language and culture and lived in the area approximately from the Mississippi River (U.S.) and the western boundary of Ontario to the Atlantic Coast.[48,50] They were knowledgeable in properties and uses of trees and plants: birch, beech, maple, basswood, elm, and ash; made use of many wild foods, such as nuts and berries, fruits and wild rice; and prepared many medicines from flora. Except in the far North, most practised agriculture and raised corn, beans, tobacco, pumpkin, and squash, and based their survival on intimate knowledge of natural resources. The Algonkins were the first encountered by the White Man and also the first to disappear from internal war, disease, and intermarriage. Yet it was from the Algonkins that the Europeans learned about crop cultivation and the taste and use of new foods and also the use of Indian words.[50] Those who were not agriculturally involved depended mainly on hunting and fishing and travelled as necessary for food supplies. These included the more northern peoples.

Both the Ojibways and the Algonkins depended quite extensively on vegetable foods and on maple sugar and wild rice. Wild potatoes, wild onions, yellow water lily root, and milkweed, together with corn, beans and squash, formed the vegetable basics. The Winnebago steamed their corn in an underground pit filled with hot coals and alternate layers of corn and husks with just enough water added for steaming.[50]

Women carried baskets to gather fruits and berries, wild herbs, and nuts: cranberries, gooseberries, June berries, cherries, chokecherries, black and red raspberries, grapes, butternuts, beechnuts, hazelnuts, white and pin oak acorns, hickory nuts. Wild rice was a staple food for the Woodland Indians and would be traditionally boiled and eaten with corn, beans or squash and sometimes with meat, grease or maple sugar added.[50]

Fishing was a year-round occupation and often carried out by women, especially among the Chippewas. Fresh fish and various turtles would be eaten and the methods of preparation varied: spit-roasted, boiled, dried in the sun or over a slow fire, grilled, then smoked and dried and pounded into a powder that could be later added to cornmeal mush, or the fish could be added to cooking wild rice.

Deer, moose, fox, wolves and some smaller animals would be the object of the hunt. The bear was never killed without a special apologetic ceremony for the bear is much revered by the Woodland Peoples. In fact the whole matter of hunting was treated with a preliminary fasting and sacrifice before entering the forest and special charms would be carried for good luck and care taken to perfect the imitation of moose and deer calls.[50] In fact the reverence for animals was underlined in the need to treat even the remains of the game animals with deep respect by cleaning the bones and putting them in a special place.[48]

Feast days were indicated to honour the first fruits, the first crops, or the first game killed by a young Indian. Summer games and family gatherings were popular with the Micmacs, who also enjoyed lacrosse, a game similar to soccer, as well as dancing and storytelling and pipe smoking (in bowls made from lobster claws). The great spirit called po-wah-gen or Manido, believed to inhabit everything, was offered first fruits or game as an insurance for long life, good health, and safety.[48,50]

For those who relied most on hunting, every part of the animal was carefully utilized. The meats were prepared in pottery or metal pots, usually suspended on tripods over fires. In earliest times food was sometimes cooked by dropping hot coals directly into pots made from skins, stomachs, or animal bladders, which were then filled with water. If the food was not sufficiently cooked, more hot coals could be added. Meats could also be spit-roasted or dried over a fire or in the sun, then pounded and stored in birch bark containers. Grease would be rendered and used as a seasoning for rice and other foods; tallow would be rendered and made into soaps; bones pounded into powder, then mixed with dried meat and grease, could be eaten at a later time uncooked.[50] The final debris of meals would be carefully scattered as food for the dogs.

Wild rice has always been such an important staple, especially to the Menomini, that these Indians became known as the "Wild Rice People," and, according to their tradition, they believe the rice to be a gift of the "Underneath Beings." Men pole canoes while the women and children share the task of knocking the ripened grain into the canoes, each family taking care to remain within their own rice area. As with fruits and game, the first collection of rice is cooked and enjoyed with great ceremony by all as an expression of thanks. Traditionally, after the gathering, rice is cleaned and dried in the sun. Then men wearing special "ricing mocassins" dance on the rice till finally it is separated from the chaff and ready to be stored.[50]

As with most of the Woodland Peoples, the bear has always been important, but especially so to the Chippewas. For them the bear meat could only be eaten after specific rituals and ceremonies, the last of which would include the cooking of the bear's head, which had been sitting on a high scaffold for three days. Porcupine skins would be used to store the bear oil and grease, while strips of the bear meat were also preserved by storing in some of the oil. Maple sugar and maple syrup were also of importance to the Chippewas, as the principal part of their diet for almost a month in the springtime, and an important item for barter.[51]

For the Naskapi, the caribou was of prime importance and much formalized ritual was attached to every aspect of the hunt, the kill, and the communal meals. Most interestingly, one man's kill of caribou, valued so highly, was nonetheless ceremoniously and proudly divided into piles of meat and hide and shared with each of his hunting companions.[52] Even today, the communal meal is an extension of this principle of sharing: all or none will be hungry. The communal meal of the caribou, called *mokoshan*, was designed to please the spirit of the animal and ensure future hunting success. The ensuing ritual traditionally began with long bones placed on an outdoor scaffold, followed with elaborate routines of scraping meat from the skin, preparing a broth, crushing bones and marrow in preparation for a paste to be cooked, then freezing in the snow for later eating. Men customarily ate first, followed by women and children. The traditional ritual of the *mokoshan* sometimes took twelve hours, ending with the throwing of bone splinters into the fire as a final gesture to the caribou spirit.[52]

The Cree follow similar food customs, and most Cree still maintain treasured traditions, more so than many other Indian groups. They have a dislike for fishing, maintaining that it is "not worthy of a hunter or warrior."[48] Some Cree, however, make practical use of fish: broth is prepared for infants, fish eggs are used in many ways and may even be blended with BANNOCK dough, and a type of PEMMICAN may be prepared from fish to be eaten with tea by trappers on the trail.[53] Cree enjoy geese as a festive food and occasionally a bride and groom may eat bear meat.[53]

THE IROQUOIANS
In the early 1600s, the settlements of the Hurons were graphically described as "stockaded villages in a fertile land."[54] The people themselves were described as "content with what they have," living basically on corn and red beans. Soups, meal, and bread doughs could all be prepared from the corn, with the addition of fruits, fish, or meats, with fat considered as a delicacy.[54] In fact, the Iroquoians, "alone among the Indians of Canada, seldom had fear of famine."[48]

There was always an abundance of game and fish in the forests and lakes, and the fertile land that produced corn and many vegetables as well as wild fruits and nuts, also yielded sugar and syrup from both maple and birch trees. Cultivated crops included corn, beans, squash, artichokes, tobacco, and pumpkin. Sunflower seeds were used to make oil as a condiment for certain foods and also as a cosmetic; oils pressed from walnuts and hickory nuts formed a thick buttery cream also used with foods; bear grease was used as the White Man used butter.

Corn, the principal crop and staple food, was roasted or steamed and eaten as corn on the cob. Cobs were also buried and allowed to ferment, then eaten as a treat; hominy, succotash (a cooked mixture of corn and beans) and popcorn were all known and enjoyed; corn ground into fine meal or coarse flour was used for breads and for thickening and flavouring soups and stews. It could also be dried together with meats and these, with stored fats, provided good winter fare.

Some Iroquoians ate two meals a day, others one main meal. But for most it seems that food was at hand and eating when desired was the accepted custom. Skulls of old graves show that the Iroquoians had poor teeth (most other Canadian Indians had excellent teeth) and this may be because of their use of soft-cooked foods and the general use of sugars and syrups.[48,55]

As with other Indian Peoples, religion was traditionally part of daily life and the belief in spirits existing within nature (trees, rivers, rocks) as well as a "Chief of all Good Spirits" and a "Chief of all Bad Spirits," was common. Interpretations of dreams and omens, and the importance of thankfulness, prayers, and fasting were and in some cases still are all part of the life-style.[48] Occasionally, wild turkeys would be part of festive meals, more often black bears would be penned and fattened for special feasts. SAGAMITE, the ubiquitous corn soup, formed a traditional part of every feast, together with dishes prepared from clams, fish, turtles. SAGAMITE, to this day, forms the central dish of any Iroquoian occasion.

Traditional mid-winter ceremonials were preceded by several days of fasting (eating *no* foods); then Sacred Ceremonies followed, at which time animal meats – sometimes including fattened dogs as well as bears – would be ceremoniously prepared and shared, to be followed by SAGA-MITE, other meats, and breads.[56,57,58] Other festivals were associated with crops and first fruits and even the successful collection of wild berries.[56]

Among the most important of the festivals was the Feast of the Dead, which was held at ten- to twelve-year intervals. This solemn time would be celebrated by disinterment of corpses from temporary graves: flesh and skin would be stripped from the bones and burned, then the bones would be buried in a mass burial ground.[58] Accompanied by great lamentations and tears, these tasks would be undertaken in the belief that the soul would take flight after the great ceremony ended. Long processions, bearing the bones to the burial area, would be followed by speeches and distribution of foods.[57]

Keen agriculturalists with unique social and political patterns, the Iroquoians were "much superior in cultural development to all other Indian tribes with the possible exception of the Haida in B.C." They valued and practised charity and hospitality and often welcomed large groups of impoverished peoples, even portioning land to them.[57]

THE PRAIRIE (PLAINS) TRIBES
There were few animals that these tribes would not eat, but they were mainly dependent on the bison or buffalo. Some groups avoided fish; the Blackfoot considered bear too sacred to be used as food; others disdained dogs as food except for special occasions.[48] The nourishing buffalo meat could be used fresh, or dried and powdered, and could even be preserved for years if necessary.

In fact, the uses of the buffalo were staggering in their variety and ingenuity. Not only was every part of the flesh and offal converted to food (fresh or dried) but the hides were used for blankets, bedding, clothing, wigwams, and furniture. Skins were stretched and treated for use as bridles, thongs, saddles, and lassoes. Horns could be shaped into spoons, ladles, and drinking cups. Bones were used for their marrow (which could also be dried and stored), or crushed and boiled to collect fat, which would be skimmed off and stored in bladders. Dried sinews could be used as threads for garments or for bow strings. Feet and hooves could be boiled to extract glue; even tail hairs were useful as a brush to kill flies and mosquitoes.[59]

It takes great skill to prepare PEMMICAN. Large thin sheets of flesh are hung to dry over open fires, with the sun speeding the drying process. The dried and smoked sheets are then pounded into a powder and mixed with marrow fat, then packed into strong skin bags and sewn with sinews. The dried strips of meat are called JERKY. Sometimes dried fruits, such as chokecherries or saskatoomin (blueberries) may be added to the PEMMICAN mixture before storing.[59]

Elk, deer, sheep, bear, wild fowl, and many varieties of fish supplemented the staple bison. Some tribes used wild rice and vegetables when available; most groups enjoyed chokecherries, service berries, red willow berries, prairie turnips, wild rose haws, bitter root, as well as the wild lily bulbs called CAMAS.

Nearly all the Prairie tribes shared similar beliefs concerning great spirits present in all things, especially the spirit Napi, the Old Man. Shamanism, charms, amulets, dreams and magic were all an important part of daily life.[48,60]

Hospitality has always been traditionally extended to anyone coming in peace. Common welcoming phrases include: *ta-ta-wah*, meaning "there is always room for you," and *kes-poo*, meaning "may it satisfy you," or "refresh you."[59] The importance of hospitality is underlined by the formalized three-step ritual traditionally followed. Strangers were commonly called "cousin" or "brother-in-law," and were bidden first to share a smoke together, then speak to others present and, finally, share in food. In fact, the high point of most celebrations is the free distribution of foods that have been communally prepared.[61] Refusal of hospitality or eating only sparingly is considered rude.

NORTHWEST TERRITORIES TRIBES

The peoples of this area still living in dense forests and open tundra have a difficult life and experience many periods of food scarcity. All speak dialects of Athapaskan and are basically hunters and fishermen.[48]

Caribou and salmon are the most important staples, but when available, other animals and fish are also used for foods: moose, buffalo, bear, musk ox, mountain goats, and sheep, smaller animals, and any other fish that can be caught. Very few vegetable foods are used, occasionally berries, bulbs, and some tender spring shoots are enjoyed. Most foods were cooked by the method of adding water and food to skin pouches then dropping in hot coals till cooked to desired doneness. Fish and meats were also dried and stored in caches, high platforms built on poles; PEMMICAN preparation also served as a means of food preservation.[62] In some areas the sea mammals form an important part of the tribe's existence, both for food and for skins: sea lions, sea otters, seals, and the beluga or white whale.

BRITISH COLUMBIA INTERIOR PEOPLES
Although the languages of the B.C. Interior Indians belong to three different language stocks, the customs of the people are similar. The most important food is salmon. Other foods include deer, moose, elk, caribou, bear, mountain sheep and goats, as well as roots and berries in season. Smaller animals such as rabbits, groundhogs, beaver, gopher, and porcupine as well as fish such as pike, types of trout, whitefish, may be all part of the dietary too. In some grassy areas, where grasshoppers are plentiful, the Indians pluck them and eat as a snack.[48] Some berries may be pressed and dried for winter use; inner bark of certain trees may be cut off in juicy slivers and also dried for winter use. Smoking, drying, and then pounding is a common method of food preservation and because of the prevalence of fish, a type of FISH PEMMICAN was commonly prepared for winter use.[48]

Women of all ages traditionally had the difficult task of finding, digging, and preparing all types of roots and berries for winter storage. These included tiger lily roots, bitter root, sunflower roots, yellow lily roots, and chocolate lily roots (SA-QWA-AKS).[63]

Traditionally, two principal cookery methods were preferred: boiling of foods with the use of hot stones, and pit steaming. The latter was done by digging a deep pit then layering it with hot rocks, grass, and the roots to be steamed, then packing over with earth, leaving a long stick buried down one side. This stick would later be pulled up to provide an air hole for all the layers.[48,63] Rush mats or animal skins find uses in sleeping, cooking, or eating and even today many of these tribes people prefer to sit on mats rather than chairs when eating.

BRITISH COLUMBIA COASTAL INDIANS
Because of their isolation caused by the Rocky Mountains on one side and the Pacific Ocean on the other, these peoples evolved their own unique patterns of culture. Although there are at least four distinct groups of six languages, they share many common traditions. These include an elaborate mythology, scanty clothing, high respect for their leaders, and the practice of lavishing them with gifts; the building of complex rectangular houses made from cedar planks (durable and aromatic); and their dependence on food from the sea.[48]

Several species of salmon form the staple food and were traditionally caught by means of spears, dip nets, and dam-like traps. Halibut was next in importance and was taken by barbed hooks or clubbed with hardwood clubs.[64] Other fish included cod, whales, sea lions, oolichan, porpoises, sea otters, sea urchins, cuttlefish, and clams. Land animals formed only a small part of the dietary: deer, caribou and very occasionally bears, mountain sheep and goats (found inland). Plant foods included berries and roots, inner bark of hemlock and other trees, edible seaweed, eel grass and CAMA.[48]

As with the B.C. interior peoples, the coastal Indians used two principal methods of cookery: boiling with hot rocks and pit steaming. Some fish was cooked by spearing on a stick and roasting over a fire.[65] In earlier times, water-tight wooden boxes and woven baskets sealed with spruce gum were made by the Haida Indians and used both as storage utensils and cooking pots (hot-stone method).[64]

Foods such as fish and berries could be readily preserved for winter use either by sealing in oil or by drying. Salmon and clams could be smoked then dried; seaweed and berries could be dried then pressed into cakes; berries sometimes being simply stored in oil.[48] Although some tobacco was grown, it was not smoked but was dried, pounded to a powder, then chewed with lime made from burned clam shells.

Of great importance as a nutrient and as a condiment was the use of grease in the form of animal fats, and especially the use of oil from oolichans. These tiny fish were valued for their very high oil content, which could also be used as cooking fat. Sometimes they were called "candle fish" because a dried one, when lit at one end, would burn like a candle.[48] Because of the prevalent custom of dipping foods, especially dried fish, into oil before eating, White explorers coined the name "grease feast."[64]

Special diets were a traditional part of special ceremonies for both boys and girls upon reaching maturity. Boys were secluded with their uncles for a time and ate no "meat containing sinews or muscles"; it was believed that to violate these taboos might have affected their prowess as hunters.[64] During her initiation period a girl would be secluded under a grandmother's care, would sleep only in a sitting position, and would step out of doors only if her head was covered so as not to offend the sea and land spirits. During this time, too, girls would not be permitted any fresh salmon and could only eat dried strips from the previous year's catch.[64]

The most famed ceremonial of the B.C. Coastal Indian Peoples was the potlatch. This was an elaborate ceremony held for important events such as bestowing gifts, property or inheritance, but perhaps most important, to establish the status of a group or certain individuals within it.[65,66] For this occasion, foods were prepared in a huge quantity – in fact, using the hot stone method, foods could even be cooked in canoes, then spooned out with huge wooden ladles.[48] Typical foods to be served would be smoked salmon, caribou or venison, bear meat, berries prepared in various ways, tasty roots, small cakes made of dried berries and fruits and SQUAW CANDY (braided strips of smoked salmon).[64]

In their arts and industries, customs and beliefs, these peoples differed greatly from all other Indian groups of North America in having one of the most sophisticated cultures of any Indian group.[65] Their variety of mechanical and architectural skills were only matched by their skills in woodcarving (totem poles), song writing, and the staging of elaborate dance productions, often as special events for the potlatch.[64] But this description scarcely does justice to the complex intricacies of games and pastimes and elaborate rituals or orders and status that were an integral part of each potlatch.[67]

The west coast Indians believed in a pantheon of deities of earth and heavens, some beneficent, some evil. The priest-doctor functions were traditionally performed by the local "shaman," or medicine man, whose rituals included beneficent magic, amulets, and medicinal herbs. Unlike other Indian peoples, the west coast groups also believed in a class of weird monsters, dwarfs, ogres, and even in huge rocks of quartz that were believed capable of attacking man with electric-like charges. Considered to be the most powerful of all was the "thunderbird," believed to live on mountain tops and control man with lightning as the "ultimate master of the natural world."[66]

The west coast peoples, with their abundance of food and elaborate culture, recognized an aristocracy more sophisticated than the chief-systems of other groups. Their celebration of the potlatch and their "well-organized system of slavery" also serve to make them distinct. As Leechman[48] states: "Prairie tribes put war deeds first – west coast people made wealth and gift distribution important in life."

INUIT (ESKIMOS)

The very name "Eskimo" conjures up visions of husky dog teams and glistening igloos, furry parkas and mukluks, and vast drifts of blinding white snow whipped by howling winds. Actually "Eskimo" was the name used by Europeans to represent the peoples they knew as "eaters of raw flesh." "Inuit" is the people's name for themselves and it means the "chosen and true people," while the singular form, "Inuk," means simply "man."

The more than 50,000 Inuit are scattered in the northern hemisphere from Greenland to Alaska and Siberia, speaking a single but complex language, and traditionally travelling in search of food and living off the land with unparalleled skill. Although there had been contact with Europeans as early as the 1500s, it was in the 1950s that the white man had the most shattering effect upon the tranquil Inuit life-style. With the sudden and rapid expansion of airlines, telecommunication systems, and settlements complete with homes, schools, stores and even churches and hospitals, snowmobiles began replacing sled and dog teams, woollen clothing and rubber boots replaced traditional dress, permanent modest wooden homes replaced snowhouses and igloos and skin tents. Worse, sugar and tea, lard and flour quickly replaced much of the protein-filled meat/fish diet of the Inuit and by this time the serving of carbohydrate foods has become almost a status symbol.[68,69]

Today's Inuit live mainly in coastal areas, making forays inland primarily "to hunt caribou, or to fish in the lakes, to cut timber . . . or to quarry soapstone for lamps and pots, returning always to the coast as their real home."[48] Inuit diet traditionally relied upon fish and sea mammals and land animals (depending upon the season), with small amounts of seaweed, some sorrel leaves and other greens in the summer as well as some berries and sometimes the partly-digested greens from the stomach of land animals.[48] Very occasionally some ptarmigan or ducks or small game animals supplemented the diet.

Raw meats and raw fish may occasionally have been nibbled as snack food or out of necessity, depending upon conditions, but traditionally, hot meat or fish, and the broth, was the usual fare. A soapstone pot simmering almost continuously over a seal-oil lamp with bubbling broth of meat or fish provided a warm and satisfying meal to anyone who was hungry. Specific hours or times of meals mean little to a people who never had timepieces and where, because of a far north location, wintery nights sometimes last all day or summery evenings know no sunset. One ate or nibbled as hunger and food supply dictated.[48]

Foods in excess of daily needs were always diligently preserved by freezing in caches, drying, smoking or preserving with oil bags made of seal skin called SEAL POKES. Fats were rendered for use in heating and lighting, some used for snacks and others used as a preservative for foods, such as seal meat or berries.[68,70,71]

There seems to be little evidence of special festive or ceremonial foods as such. Special occasions are marked by increase in the quantity of foods consumed and shared communally rather than by different types. Some sources indicate that fermented berry juice was drunk to help mark special events.[72] Many Inuit have accepted Christianity yet still cling to beliefs in fortune telling, the "Shaman" (medicine man), charms and amulets, inner spirits present in many objects. Traditional offerings of useful objects, such as tools or cooking utensils, indicate a belief in life after death.

The changes that have occurred in the traditional Inuit way of life have been so sudden and irreversible that today only the drifts of snow and the howling winds and all-too-brief northern summers can remain aloof from the unrelenting clutch of white man's twentieth-century "civilization." Tea and flour, sugar and lard, together with canned and prepared food mixes have made tragic inroads into the traditional Inuit dietary. Most foods are still boiled, most men still retain autonomy in their families, but together with white man's "civilization," the Inuit are suffering increasingly from white man's obesity, acne vulgaris, dental caries, diabetes, atherosclerosis, breast cancer, scurvy, and heart disease.[69]

QUEBEC

Quebec may be described as the area in Canada "where ancient France lingers," but it has attained a heritage and tradition distinctly its own.[10] Modern growth and development, economics and politics may intrude but cannot erase the deeply-rooted evidence: white-washed stone houses, Roman Catholic churches with belfries and spires, outdoor bake ovens and wayside shrines, and most of all the sense of home and family that is Québécois. The vitality of ancestral traditions coupled with isolation both from France and from the English in Canada served to direct Quebec on an independent course where often the spoken word, preserved in traditions of lore and songs and folk tales as well as homey recipes passed from mother to daughter, made the oral tradition more important than the written word.

The food traditions of Quebec date back more than 350 years and were known for their traditional richness: abundant eggs and meats, fresh rich cream and sugary maple syrup laced through a diet of plenty. The staple harvests of the early pioneers of corn, barley, oats, peas, lentils, beans, and asparagus combined with the plentiful game and fish. Potatoes (called "root") were not too popular in early times but maize, adopted from the Indians, became an important mainstay: coal-roasted and eaten off the cob; as a hearty stew with game or fish; ground into flour for pancakes and some breads; or as SAGAMITE, a soup made from cornflour, dried fish, and dried peas. In fact, the mashed maize could be frozen and kept throughout the winter, often forming the base of the now-famed HABITANT PEA SOUP.[11] Abundant wild fruits were carefully picked and preserved as jams and jellies, relishes and compotes. Probably dating back to the basic stores of the "*Filles du Rois*" (of the 1600s), salt pork is considered to be the "mainstay of Quebec cuisine."[11]

In fact, the traditional foods of Quebec and their method of preparation represent well their history. They blend English foods such as salt pork, beans and peas, molasses and spices, and many puddings and pies together with traditional favourites from France with dishes learned from the Indians and culled from the new lands.[73] From the traditional black cast-iron kettle came POT-AU-FEU: beef cooked in water with root vegetables and served with homemade bread; SOUPE AUX QUATORZE AFFAIRES: traditional pea soup with four main ingredients of corn, bread chips, salt and butter[73]; the BOUILLI: early vegetables simmered with chicken; FÈVES AU LARD: simmered beans with pork.

Sugary fruit desserts and recipes with maple syrup abound in the repertoire of any Québécois kitchen, for the "French love sweets."[74] Cakes of maple sugar were stocked by the earliest colonists to last from one spring to the other. Syrup-drenched cakes and pies, butters and endless confections, as well as specialties such as GRAND-PÈRES AU SIROP: dumplings served with maple syrup; LES TOQUETTES: hot maple syrup sprinkled on the snow to form a hard candy; (even eggs poached in maple syrup);

chickens prepared with maple syrup; and servings of pancakes, bacon, and bread – all doused generously with syrup.[11,73,74] Finally, the irresistible BEURRÉE DE SUCRE D'ÉRABLE: fresh heavy cream poured over inch-thick crusty fresh bread, then sprinkled with crushed maple sugar and topped with seasonal fresh berries.

For a people whose lives centre in home and church, it is not surprising that the calendar is happily dotted with festive occasions. Although traditionally, "family life is lived in a world of rules, the definitions of which are taken from the Church's teachings,"[75] the rules for festivities take into account the joys of family and friends and good foods. Christmas menus vary only slightly according to local traditions and family specialties, but most include a Christmas Eve – RÉVEILLON – buffet of assorted pickled vegetables, breads and biscuits, soup or stew and, especially TOURTIÈRE: a savoury thick pie of minced pork; CIPÂTE (also called SIX-PÂTES, CIPAILLE and SEA-PIE): a pie or casserole made with several pastry layers filled with game birds or other meats. Both of these dishes may be eaten hot or cold and served, sometimes alone, with homemade wines or coffee as the sole dish of the RÉVEILLON. Another favourite traditional dish is CRETONS: a pork pâté made from the crispy residues of rendered lard, sprinkled with spices (cloves, garlic, and cinnamon), and stored by covering with fat.[73] The festive Christmas meal is ended with maple syrup desserts of dumplings or pies and cakes, a BUCHE DE NOËL (chocolate-coated Christmas log), tea, coffee or milk.[76] For many the traditional Christmas Eve sweet is the QUEBEC APPLE DUMPLINGS: whole apples stuffed with mincemeat, covered with pastry and baked with butter, brown sugar, and cream, then served warm with rum-flavoured cream.[73]

Winter Carnival takes place before Lent begins and abounds in hearty dishes, such as roast pork lion with apples, thick pea soup with ham bone, roasted fowl with mashed potato stuffing, bread soup, spicy gingerbread, roasted and buttered squash or fried pumpkin, and of course crusty breads baked in outdoor ovens.[74]

Weddings and baptisms, Lent, Easter, Autumn Harvest, Christmas and Winter Carnival all embrace the best of cookery and the generous hospitality so typical of Quebec. Typical too is the Saturday night supper of home-baked beans with pork, served with brown bread – and the resulting Sunday breakfast of pork and beans.

TWELVE

Chinese

There is a pervading sense of classic timelessness in everything Chinese. About one quarter of the peoples of the world – about 800 million – are Chinese.[1] They have actually emerged from a blend of many races and groups and theirs is considered to be one of the oldest civilizations extant, dating back more than 4,000 years.[2] Their culture is firmly and deeply rooted in the history of the earth.

Dynasties and kingdoms, religions and philosophies, and even droughts and floods came and went; but one element remained steadfast: the humble peasantry. Long before invaders mounted their chariots or nomadic tribes saddled their horses, the peoples of Northern China tended their crops of millet, rice and barley, and shepherded their flocks of sheep. Earliest evidence of rice cultivation dates back to 1800 B.C.E.[2] By communal effort, fields were irrigated, tripod cooking pots of earthenware were constructed, and wine was made from fermented millet.[1] Despite increasing numbers of invasions and political turmoil, the agrarian lifestyle of the Northerners – tending cattle as well as their pigs, dogs, and hens; rearing silk-worms; making plain white pottery, even their intense devotion to family – remained relatively undisturbed.[2]

The earliest recorded period of Chinese history is sketchily referred to as the Shang Kingdom, some time before 2000 B.C.E.: the people were late Stone Age Chinese whose communal efforts were in many ways superior to those of primitive tribes and peoples around them. This Kingdom became overrun by rough tribesmen from the West, and began China's longest dynasty: the Chou Dynasty. It was in this period (1027-256 B.C.E.)

that the plough and chopsticks were introduced, and the people called their group "Central Nation," thus distinguishing themselves from the other peoples whom they referred to as "Barbarians." It must be noted, however, that this distinction was a cultural rather than a political one[1] and it was actually by cultural influences (not domination or wars) that many of the bordering communities became gradually incorporated into the Chou Dynasty. The Chou evolved a feudal pattern of agriculture, traded with Turkestan for jade, and celebrated important agrarian seasonal rituals; their ruler designated spring by ceremoniously turning the soil with a jade hoe and designated winter by making sacrifices to heaven.[1]

The overthrow of the Chou Dynasty signified a shift from central authority to the stronger peripheral areas and began a period of almost continuous warfare aptly called the "Warring States Period" (481-256 B.C.E.). To add to their miseries, nomadic invaders were such a relentless source of turmoil to the warring but agrarian states, that antagonism towards nomadic peoples has been a "feature of Chinese thought ever since."[2]

But as so often occurs in history, out of darkest times come some of the greatest cultural achievements. So it was that while warriors battled amongst themselves and nomadic invaders, peasants tilled fields and tended flocks; great minds began to philosophize on man's existence. This was the era of prophets in Palestine, Zarathustra in Persia, Homer and Plato and Heraclitus in Greece, Buddha and Jina in India, and Confucius and Laotse in the Central Nation. The period was 550-280 B.C.E.

"You know so little of the world, how can you concern yourself with spirits?" It was with such words that the most influential of all Chinese philosophers, Confucius, laid a groundwork of moral and ethical codes exhorting man to concern himself with earthly matters and human relationships, yet at the same time not to deny the existence of spirits.[1,2] It was Laotse, reputedly the founder of Taoism, who taught followers the gentle philosophy of "Tao, the Way": a path of righteous living leading to happiness and peace of mind.

The period from 221-206 B.C.E. was the short but very influential rule of the Ch'in Dynasty, during which the Great Wall of China was built. It replaced feudalistic states with official-ruled commanderies and also began the first of several "literary inquisitions" in China's history by burning both books and scholars. Paradoxically, this was also the period of the establishment of standardized character writing or ideoforms. Thus was laid one of the most important bases upon which the cultural family of China exists and survives: a method of written communication understandable to every citizen, regardless of dialect in spoken language. To this day it is the tie that culturally binds all peoples on whom the Chinese have had influence: Japanese, Korean, Vietnamese, and much of the rest of Southeast Asia. And though the Chinese themselves have never used the name "China" (they have called themselves "Central Nation"), it is from the Ch'in Dynasty that the name China originates.[1]

Yet it was the Han Dynasty that was destined to be proudest of all. Even today among the many peoples who form the People's Republic of China, which includes the Mongols, Uigurs and Tibetans as well as the Huis (Han peoples of the Muslim faith), the main body of the Chinese distinguish themselves as Han.[1,4] To the reforms begun by the brief Ch'in Dynasty were added the books of Confucius called "The Classics" as well as a stable political structure destined to last for 2,000 years. In fact, it was the features and conditions of the Han Empire that made it possible to speak of Chinese people and Chinese culture. Further, it was (as in olden times) a system in many ways superior to those of its neighbours, and hence became China's influence outward. The system was to remain largely unchanged until the arrival of the Europeans in the early 1500s C.E.[2]

Perhaps most important, it was the firmly entrenched characteristics of the Han period that were responsible for China's difficulty in adapting to modern times.[2] China's ruling minority was chosen by competitive examinations based on The Classics of Confucius. While this principle made people regard education solely as a means to advancement, it also stifled creative and particularly scientific thought. Traditionally, any independence in the middle class or signs of liberalism in the commercial class that did not serve the ends of this ruling minority was persecuted and exterminated.[2]

All of this is not to say that technological achievements were not important. During this period, Chinese minds devised gun powder, porcelain, paper money, a simple seismograph as well as complex irrigation schemes, techniques of slope-terracing, the use of animal droppings for fertilizer and had even developed the wheelbarrow with its simple central wheel.[1] In fact, as early as the first century, a harness had been developed that did not interfere with an animal's breathing, thus enabling animals to be used for draft.

Conquests of Vietnam and Korea, around 1000 B.C.E., brought the use of tea into China first as a medicine and later as a sociable and pleasing beverage. In turn, Chinese character writing was adopted by Korea and Vietnam and later introduced into Japan.

Between 1,000 and 700 B.C.E., the age of poetry with Li Po and Tu Fu flourished, tolerance and interest in religions spread, and at the same time a new invention was changing the people's eating habits: the stone roller. Rice had been the staple food of the people of the South and was planted wherever possible in the North but the new stone roller made wheat more popular and more practical as a crop for the North China Plain. The wheat flour was prepared into doughs to form noodles, steamed buns and dumplings with many types of fillings, as well as lacy pancakes enfolding tidbits of meats, fish and/or vegetables.

Tea drinking first appeared in China after the conquests of Vietnam and Korea[1] but it is believed that tea drinking probably originated in ancient Tibet.[2] It was during the 700s C.E. that Lu Yu wrote his classic *Ch'a Ching*, which described every detail of tea from its cultivation to its ritual preparation and his writing probably led to the national acceptance of tea as a beverage.[5] To this day the Mongolians still use the method of pressing dried tea leaves into bricks and breaking off pieces as needed and boiling together in water which was the popular method in Lu Yu's time. It was about three hundred years later (Sung Dynasty, 960-1280 C.E.) that the method of preparing tea by whisking powdered tea with hot water evolved. To this day, the Japanese use this method in the honoured classic tea ceremony and for preparation of rare teas.[5] An abridgement of Lu Yu's classic text by Chen Chien in 1475 led to the ritual steeping of tea, popular in most of the world today.

There was never any defined period of stagnation in Chinese history but there was a period of general languidness (about 900 C.E.) when educated men grew long fingernails (indicating their disdain for manual labour) and contented themselves with watching a flower unfold while women hobbled about on tiny bound feet. But, as always, the stalwart masses tended fields and flocks and minded the voice of their fathers while their lives spun out in "unremitting labour."[1]

While it is said that "the enquiring mind died with the Sung Dynasty,"[1] it was then that the southward-pointing compass needle was invented, the abacus used for counting, and acupuncture developed into a fine art of healing. Cities boasted clean streets, pure water, and even public bath houses for the poor. Many varieties of tea and rice were readily available and delicate fruits were sent from distant provinces, packed in ice for city markets.[1] Families enjoyed outdoor picnics and restaurant dining and the wealthy homes boasted tiled walls and floors, and many servants.[1]

The fall of the Mongol Empire (1200s to mid-1300s) brought a period of population increase but also famine, peasant revolts, and the rising of secret societies. The Ming Dynasty came after the fall of the Mongol Empire. Having successfully overthrown the Mongol invaders, the Chinese, more convinced than ever of the superiority of their own culture, made isolationism a policy of the entire Ming period. They felt their own culture to be the ultimate, neither willing to give nor needing to take anything from the rest of the world. But this was not to last long either, for the clash with the great European naval powers was yet to come.

The Portuguese were the first to reach China by sea, settling in the port of Macao in the late 1400s and setting up an enviable trade that was to last three hundred years, despite competition of other sea powers, particularly the Dutch and the British. Oranges, peaches, limes, and corianders, but mainly huge shipments of tea filled the holds of Portuguese ships and gave Europe a taste of China.[2] Jesuit priests entered Macao with the Portuguese and made their way to Peking, the capital city, and later became allies of the Manchus who were to overthrow the Ming Dynasty in the mid-1600s.[1]

The first evidences of faltering strength of the great Han-inspired tradition began to show with the establishment of strict Manchu rule: contacts with the West were to be only religious or commercial; all Chinese males were forced to braid their long hair into a single pigtail or queue. By the early 1700s the Manchu influence had spread over China, Mongolia, Manchuria, Turkestan, Formosa (Taiwan), and Tibet. Paradoxically, in time, the Manchus themselves were to become "more Chinese than the Chinese," as a result of their eager adoption of Chinese culture.[1]

A combination of factors inevitably and gradually led to a period of downfall. The clash with European ideas and powers coincided with the end of the orderly Confucian system that had characterized the 2,000-year influence of the Han Dynasty. Savage wars, famines and floods, and widespread poverty were bad enough, but huge population increases added the final blow.[2,6] Lack of arable land led to measures attempting to increase intensity of cultivation: new crops were introduced such as groundnuts, maize, sweet potatoes, and the new technique of market-gardening was used wherever feasible. But increase of population density led to a sharp decline in living standards as well as to a growing problem of the middle society of minor officials and impoverished gentry who had no future opportunities.[2] Strengthened in their ideals and resolve by previous minor revolts, the worsening living conditions led to renewed and more vigorous revolts of the once placid peasantry. With ugly measures the Manchus repressed the peasant revolts and blamed their troubles on the most convenient scapegoat: the foreigners.[2]

The antiquated rigidity of the Confucian order proved not only inadequate but stultifying in the face of the machine age and industrial revolution occurring in the West. There was no middle class, no bureaucratic freedom, no liberation of new energy sources. The tragedy of the loss of millions of lives when the Yellow River changed its course was added to the humiliation of Hong Kong ceding to Britain in 1842 and British and French forces daring to enter Peking. The rumblings of the T'ai P'ing Rebellion, then the Sino-Japanese War of 1894-1895, exploded in 1900 into the Boxer Rebellion, out of which the seeds for change began to sprout.[1,2,6]

Into this confused, chaotic and humiliating atmosphere, rife with corruption and simmering revolts, came Sun Yat-Sen, who cut off his queue as an act of defiance against the Manchus. He attempted to cure his country by making China into a republic. Meanwhile, western ideas of free enterprise and pursuit of personal profit gained ground as the Chinese became involved in world trade, which in turn led to the growth of a new middle class: the merchants. It was this group who strongly questioned the old Confucian order and patriarchal hierarchy. In fact, "the claim that 'all men are equal' shook the very foundation on which the Confucian edifice rested."[2]

Chiang Kai-Shek (married to the sister of Sun Yat-Sen's widow) helped foster the new national spirit and increasing westernization, but seemed blind to the desperate plight of the once stable peasantry.[1] Increased Japanese advances and atrocities to China and the seeming inertia of Kai-Shek's government stirred the growing spirit of Chinese Communists in Yenan whose leader, Mao Tse-Tung, perceived that it is really the peasantry which holds the key position in all Asiatic countries. He determined to Sinify Marxism, took the slogan "Chinese do not fight Chinese," and proved the validity of his ideals when he proclaimed the People's Republic of China on October 1, 1949.

Following this declaration it must be realized that there are four distinct divisions of the Chinese populace. Mainland China, or the People's Republic of China, is politically separate from the Chinese of Taiwan, which has been regarded both as a U.S. puppet and as a bastion of the Chinese Nationalists.[3] Both are also politically distinct from the Chinese populace of Hong Kong, still under British rule and most influenced by the West, and yet the area in which most of the old flavour of Chinese traditions is retained.[3] The fourth "division" consists of "Overseas Chinese." These include the many early emigrants who left their native China in the 1800s, to seek their fortune in Canada and the United States and Australia as well as in other areas. Their dream was to return home one day, but for various reasons they stayed on to become citizens of these other lands.

Nonetheless, no matter where the Chinese may be located in the world and no matter what their position or profession, they still view Mainland China as the source and centre of their great culture. There have been changes in the past and there will be changes in the future, but despite this, the timelessness and continuity that are China's heritage will continue.

Home Life and Facilities

Perhaps part of the success of the People's Republic of China lies in the adaptation of Marxist-Lenin values to Chinese values and the viewing of allegiance to the state as simply an extension of the age-old allegiance to the family.[3,7] More than 2,000 years of Confucian values cannot be removed readily, but adaptation is possible and it is this that is seen not only in Mainland China but also in family life wherever the Chinese make their homes. (See Special Occasions.)

Traditionally, it was always Hsiao–filial piety or family duty – that dominated one's life.[6] Certain factors were common to all segments of society. Age demanded and received respect and the submission of youth. Women had no equality with men, and each extended family unit was autonomous in all life decisions such as education, religion and festival observances, social organization, and economic activity.[6] In contrast to that of the western world, Chinese society has always been and is composed of families rather than individuals. One of the most treasured values was family harmony and all family activities were responsibly disciplined to achieve this goal.

Overseas and Hong Kong families blend western ideals and values with their own traditions. The "new way" changes occurring in Mainland China include: love matches replacing arranged marriages; family devotion replacing state authority and devotion to society's welfare; a levelling of opportunities for women; and increased status and opportunity as well as living standards for the common man.[3] To achieve this, it was necessary to overcome "the respect for the intellectual elite who kept the masses on the edge of survival for literally thousands of years."[3]

The traditional Chinese respect (bordering on reverence) for the scholar can be understood more clearly when the Chinese view of a "scholar" is clarified. Because, traditionally, high posts were attained by competition in government exams of The Classics, education became synonymous with an elite upper class. Once the post was attained, election of family members to influential posts followed (familial piety). A family's sacrifice to educate one promising member could pay off and benefit all. Ideally, any son could aspire to such a role no matter what his origins. This principle of family sacrifice to aid one talented member is much a part of Chinese practice even today.

About one-fifth of the Chinese population today live in modest but modern accommodations in cities. But a look into the traditional homes and life-styles, especially the Chinese "courtyard system," is significant to basic understanding. Typical northern farmhouses were built of sun-dried bricks or pounded earth, wood being too expensive and scarce.[1,8] Houses were closely integrated around courtyards with the main living area facing south so the warming rays of sun could be caught. The few windows faced only to the inside of the courtyard and were covered by translucent oiled papers. To discourage thieves, no windows would be visible from the outside of the compounds.[8] This system was widely copied in other lands because of its efficiency and practicality.

Most such homes consisted of a kitchen and separate living-bedroom called the *kang* room, so named because of the fire-heated brick platform in the centre of the floor. Families always sat and slept with feet towards the warming *kang*. Generally, furnishings would be kept to the barest necessities. Outside in the courtyard would be located the privy building and the water well. Pigs, chickens, and draft animals would be housed in a stable nearest the kitchen area. The kitchen area of the courtyard home is of utmost importance. Since fuel is scarce and expensive, classic Chinese cookery methods demand that all food be bite-size for quick cooking and all preparation be done before cooking begins. Simple, utilitarian utensils (still in use today) are stored on open shelves or hung on walls.

Many families in Mainland China still live in such traditional homes. But though others may enjoy more modern accommodations, kitchens are still the centre of practicality since, even in cities, one kitchen may have to do for three families, even though they may have the convenience of gas or electricity to replace small fire-braziers.[1]

Housing and facilities vary according to location. Yenan and Shensi people still make their homes in caves dug in the loess cliffs, yet some of these now have electricity.[1] In Mongolia, people live in *yurts*: strong tents made of layers of felt supported on a lattice frame and anchored with ropes. In the centre of smoothed earthen floors a stone area is set apart for fires made with dried dung and a central chimney carries the smoke upwards. Many people in the South live in primitive huts thatched with palm while still other families live in bamboo homes. And many other families make their homes aboard houseboats, eating and sleeping on the bobbing waters.[1,9] Most important of all, North or South, wealthy or poor, the main difference in facilities was and even is today more a matter of the number of working hands than the type of modern convenience available.

The Chinese kitchen is remarkably the same the world over. To the western eye it is incredible that such few implements can achieve such variety and artistry. Of course the answer lies in the heritage of thousands of years of techniques of preparation rather than actual recipes. Every Chinese kitchen will contain the basic tools for Chinese cookery. These include bamboo or aluminum steamers, a WOK (or large skillet or even electric frypan), a cleaver, a firm, heavy chopping block, and various sizes of strainers, skimmers, ladles, spatulas – many with bamboo handles that do not conduct the heat.

Perhaps most versatile of all is the Chinese cleaver: massive and awkward in appearance but incredibly practical. Depending on how foods are placed and held, the cleaver can be used for slicing, cubing, chopping, mincing, scoring, and the flat of the blade or handle used for crushing and grinding. The dull side of the blade can be used to pound and tenderize meats; the edge of the wood handle can be used to crush and grind spices; the broad, flat blade can be used to scoop up all prepared foods and transport them neatly to the cooking pan. The dome-shaped WOK is also a marvel of ingenuity. It may be used for deep-fat frying, stir-frying, boiling, or simmering foods, or even as an improvised steamer. When special brown sugar is placed in the bottom with a rack of food above, and well-sealed with a cover, it is possible to smoke-flavour any meat or fish. Using regular steamers, or an improvised steamer, it is possible to set layers of dishes one above the other in bamboo perforated racks and steam-cook an entire meal of many courses using only a small single heat source.[5,9]

Food storage is seldom a problem in any Chinese home. Long ago the Chinese developed methods of food preservation that are unsurpassed even today: smoking, pickling, drying, and salting. Further, despite availability of food storage facilities, it is a matter of great pride to use ingredients that are as fresh as possible. This might often mean bringing home a live squawking chicken or a still-wriggling fish. Food storage is only considered in more modern Chinese homes, which may utilize many western-style foods and beverages, and a greater variety of fruits than commonly used in traditional Chinese homes.

FOODS COMMONLY USED

The traditional Chinese diet is confined almost entirely to foods of plant origin. The staples of grains, legumes, and vegetables exist as such for the simple reason of economy.[3] Imagination, necessity, and ingenuity have made satisfying and delectable dishes from a wide range of seeds, roots, tubers, and plants of many kinds. Rice is produced more readily in the South, hence it is the southern staple. Northern climates favour wheat production, so wheat flour made into noodles and pastries are staples of the North. There is no milk in the Chinese diet, but Chinese living in other countries do consume some. Traditionally, 98 per cent of the diet is of plant origin, while only 2 per cent is of animal or fish origin.[8,11] Regional specialties and foods of minority groups represent interesting departures from usual daily menus. Seasonings are often limited but used deftly to enhance and add variety to natural food flavours. Cooking techniques also help to make similar foods taste and look different. Local rice wines and many varieties of teas are the common beverages.

Milk and Milk Products

The Chinese have historically had a distaste for milk and milk products.[10] Although there are many learned speculations as to the reason, none are conclusive. Logic points to the use of animals for work rather than for either milk or meat consumption; it is also possible that diseases and intestinal discomforts may early have been related to both milk and water sources; in early times too cattle were considered sacred in certain areas. All that can be sensibly concluded is that the aversion to dairy products, especially milk, occurred very early in China's history. "It is not known why they did not use milk as a food."[2]

With the encouragement in modern Mainland China of minority folk customs, the pastoral peoples of Mongolia and Sinkiang have been encouraged to market many varieties of cheeses in city areas.[1] Although dairy products have never been a part of the Chinese menu, recently some desserts are served with whipped cream, and ice cream is fast becoming a favourite treat in Mainland China.[9]

Concerned nutritionists should take note of the fact that Chinese delight in munching fish and poultry bones made tender by marinating and slow cooking. Soups and stocks are often prepared from simmered bones. Some regional customs include the serving of pig ribs cooked in a sweet and sour sauce of sugar and vinegar to new mothers. The acid of the vinegar and slow cooking process may help to make the calcium in the bones more readily assimilated.[8] (See Fruits and Vegetables and Meats and Alternates for uses of soybeans.)

Fruits and Vegetables

Good varieties of fruits and vegetables are probably more plentiful than ever before in Chinese Mainland markets.[1] Fresh fruits and vegetables are eaten in season, but fruits preserved and dried have always been considered a delicacy. Unless dried or salted, preference is given to vegetables purchased as late as possible before cooking. Nutrients are well-retained by quick stir-frying, by steaming, or by adding vegetables to soups minutes before serving.

Problems of storage, climate, and transportation led to development of preservation methods for vegetables: salting, pickling, and drying.[5] Famines led to discovery of ingenious use of any edible plant substances: buds, roots, fungi, sprouts, flower petals, seeds, and barks.[12]

Peaches, apricots, apples, pears, and plums, as well as oranges and other citrus fruits, many varieties of melon and cherries are all grown in China and eaten mostly at the end of a meal or as a refreshing snack. Canned loquats, lichees, and pineapple are used in some areas together with meats and poultry. Fresh, cooked or preserved (often spiced as well as dried and sugared) fruits are especially savoured on festive occasions.[12]

The following list indicates some unusual Chinese vegetables:

BAAK CHOY: Chinese chard or Chinese cabbage: thick succulent white stems topped with deep green leaves and sometimes tiny yellow flowers.

CHUNG CHOY: salt-preserved turnips; only small slice used to add flavour, often to soups.

DOON GWOOH: blackish dried mushrooms requiring washing and soaking before use.

GAW PAY: thin sun-dried strips of mandarin orange peel, especially used in duck dishes. Oldest and most flavourful is most expensive.

GUM JUM: also called "Golden Needles," these are dried brown lilies, soaked then snipped into thin strips to add a delicate flavour to fish, poultry, or vegetable dishes.

HAW LAAHN DOW: tender green snow peas. Ends may be snipped and threads pulled in preparation for cooking, but they are cooked (usually stir-fried) and eaten, pods and all.

HOONG JO: these look like wrinkled, red dates; also called "jujubes." Used for colour and sweetness in poultry and pork dishes or in soups. Must be pitted, washed, and soaked before use.

JAR CHOY: preserved and spiced turnip greens used as a flavour accent in steamed or stir-fried dishes.

JEET QUAR: a hairy melon similar to fuzzy zucchini; used for soups.

JOOK SUEN: fresh or canned bamboo shoots.

KAIR: Chinese eggplant with a purple or white colour and a cucumber shape; they are usually finer grained than large eggplants.

LAW BOK: Chinese turnips: large and creamy-coloured, these may be used grated raw as a vegetable, a garnish or a condiment.

LIEN GOW: Lotus root. Actually the underwater stem of the common Water Lily plant. Exterior is pinkish-brown and the interior is fibrous and mottled with holes.

LOM GOK: these are the very pungent cured strips of dried black olives and are used mostly in steamed dishes.

LUT GWOH: dried Chinese chestnuts prepared by soaking then cooking in water until tender.

MAH TUY: crisp white water chestnuts, usually sliced very thin or cut in narrow strips before adding to dishes.

MAH GWOOH: whole button mushrooms.

SAN GEUNG: fresh ginger root.

SEEN SUN YEE: pickled bamboo shoots, usually canned in brine and used for marinated and steamed salad-type recipes.

SUN HA: dried bamboo shoot membranes requiring soaking before use when they turn from dark reddish-brown to ivory.

WUN YEE: also called "Cloud Ears": a type of fungi requiring washing and soaking before use.

YIEN WAW: the nests of small birds or swallows. These are sold as dried cup-like nests which expand on soaking and are famed for the soup they are added to, BIRD'S NEST SOUP. The natural glutinous quality of the nests gives the soup a clarity and thickness. A costly but epicurean delight.

YUEN SAI: coriander leaves, also called "Chinese parsley." Used preferably fresh and sometimes dried.

It should be noted that all vegetables are carefully washed, and trimmed before cooking is begun. Trimmings may be used as part of a stock pot to prepare a soup, broth, or sauce. If vegetables have been dried or salted, they usually require soaking before use. Vegetable pickles as well as their juice can be used as ingredients in dishes or served separately. The final step in vegetable preparation is the most time-consuming (for the cooking time itself is usually short): cutting, slicing, chopping, stripping, or dicing or roll-cutting exactly as may be required for each specific dish.

Meats and Alternates

There is no question that animal foods are enjoyed and even preferred, but for the majority population the cost of meats relegates them to use mainly on special occasions.[10] Pork, poultry, and eggs are most favoured; mutton and fish are consumed regionally when available.[6,10] Except for the Huis, there is a general "disinclination" toward beef-eating, probably related to ancient practices when cattle were much more important for work purposes than for food.[10] Beef is seldom eaten, veal "almost never."[5]

Because of its general wide use and availability (most rural homes have a few pigs), pork can be considered the staple meat. Every part is carefully prepared for utmost flavour. For example, a full-flavoured broth is commonly prepared by browning a few bits of pork in oil and garlic then adding cold water and simmering. Chinese sweet pork sausages are commonly steamed on top of a pot of rice; ham is usually used as a flavouring for other dishes or as a garnish.[5] Lamb and mutton are used primarily in the North where sheep-herding is common.

The customary bite-size or thin strips of meats are used because they cook quickly and spread flavour to other ingredients. Tougher meats are sliced as thin as possible then marinated. Large pieces of meats or whole ducks or chickens are commonly cooked in commercial establishments where the consumer may then purchase any desired amount. (Home ovens are rare: top-of-stove cooking is common.) Whole roasted ducks or crispy-roasted pigs are specialties for festive occasions.[5]

Poultry is enjoyed and is symbolic. Chickens, ducks, squabs (pigeons), geese, and pheasant are enjoyed from the skin to the bones and entrails. Male birds are considered to represent the positive and aggressive *yang* while ducks symbolize fidelity and happiness. Pigeons are considered not only for their intelligence but also for their filial devotion and longevity.[5]

Use of fish is increasing with development of the 3,000-mile coastline and numerous inland lakes and rivers as well as cultivation of artificial lakes for fish breeding. Dried fish and seafood (especially shrimp) are traditional favourites and available everywhere. The Chinese name for fish, *yu*, is pronounced the same as the idiogram for "bounteousness," and because fish are known for their rapid ability to increase as well as for their speed and unconfined life-style, they further symbolize regeneration and freedom. Whenever a whole fish is served, it is customary to place the head of the fish (a succulent savoured part) facing the guest of honour.[9]

Buddhists frequently serve fish at funeral banquets as a symbol of the departed person's new freedom from earthly restraints.[5] Freshness in fish and seafood (unless preserved) is essential, so live purchase is preferred. Fishy taste and smell is abhorrent and is intriguingly disguised by marinating the fish in a splash of wine or sherry plus fresh sliced ginger, garlic and scallions, before cooking.[5,13]

Some unusual delicacies include: dried shark's fin, which may be purchased in a whole piece, or shredded and pressed into a block, from which small amounts may be used; dried jellyfish, thin and translucent and preserved in salt and alum; tiny dried shrimps; dried scallops. All dried foods are soaked before use.[14]

Eggs may be used freshly beaten into small pancakes or omelets incorporating other foods; in steamed baked custards (not sweet); in prepared batters, coating foods to be fried. Egg "noodles" may be made by cooking beaten eggs in thin sheets then shredding or by swirling beaten eggs in hot broth to create "egg drop." Eggs may be smoked; eggs may be hard cooked then cracked and simmered in strong tea to give the whites a veined appearance – attractive as appetizers. THOUSAND YEAR EGGS are those that have been coated in lime clay and stored for six-to-ten weeks. This is enough to give them a shiny-black look and soft smooth consistency. Used as appetizers, their flavour is more like fish than egg.[9]

The soybean is called the "Chinese Cow" for good reason: the uses vary tremendously. Soybeans, like many other legumes, are used as dried beans or as bean sprouts. Fermented, soybeans are used in the preparation of the favourite condiment: soy sauce. They may also be prepared into a firm white curd (called CHINESE CHEESE) which can be braised, coated and fried, pickled, steamed with other ingredients, or eaten with sauces or as a garnish to soups. Soybean milk may be used often in the same way as westerners use cow's milk.[6] Chinese vermicelli, called BEAN THREAD is prepared from the soybean starch, is translucent and truly thread-like, but does not fall apart with long simmering.[14] Nor is this all. BEAN CURD SAUCE is fermented bean curd that is packed in jars and sold as red bean curd sauce or white bean curd sauce, both types having specific uses. Spiced, smooth bean pastes (almost like a date filling in texture and appearance) may be used to fill festive pastries. Here are some other examples of uses:

MIEN CHIANG (MISO in Japanese): thick syrup-like bean paste used for flavouring.[13]

DOW FOO: bean curd or bean cake, usually kept covered in water. Fermented and sold in jars it is called FOO YU.

TIEM JOOK: soybean milk sediment dried into thin sheets, broken, and soaked before cooking.

WOW DOO: dried black beans used in soups and slow-cooked dishes.

DOW SEE: salted, fermented black bean paste often garlic-flavoured and used in small amounts for poultry, pork and seafood dishes and especially with steamed fish.

Finally, nuts are also an important protein source: usually purchased shelled and blanched, browned by stir-frying, and then added to dishes. Nuts may also be used as sweetmeats and treats but commonly are added to dishes in small amounts to give flavour and texture. GINKGO NUTS (BOK GOR) are used in soups and braised dishes while walnuts, almonds, peanuts, and cashews are usually browned and crisped with stir-frying, then used.[5,12]

Breads and Cereals

Rice is the southern staple grain and wheat is the northern staple. But as grain production increases, both rice and wheat flours are used in steamed breads and dumplings to add menu variety. For all Chinese, rice is an important symbol of food. "Have you had your rice today?" is almost the same as the western "How are you?"[9] For the poor, rice may be the main part of the meal; for the wealthy it may be served at the end of the meal as a symbol of plenty. To all, each grain of rice is sacred for all are aware of the labour that went into producing it, and many bear memories of lean times when every grain of rice was treasured. Upsetting a rice bowl is considered bad luck while deliberately spilling a rice bowl is the worst insult. Rice is a symbol of all food, of all good omens and of fertility.[9,12] Long-grain rice is favoured; glutinous rice is used mostly for desserts while rice flour is a frequent thickener of sauces and soups. Most Chinese do not feel "satisfied" unless a meal includes rice.[9]

Wheat flour is eaten in the North mostly in the form of noodles. (Southerners consider noodle dishes as snacks or quick lunches.) Noodles and rice are never eaten at the same meal. Very long noodles are often served as a symbol of longevity. Barley, millet, maize, and buckwheat may all be used in the form of flours to be made into noodles, steamed breads, buns, and filled dumplings of various symbolic shapes, or thin pancakes served rolled, and filled, or to be filled by the diner at table. CONGEE is a thick rice gruel, almost a breakfast mainstay taken with pickles or condiments.[5]

Fats

Peanut oil, corn oil, and oils prepared from soybeans and rapeseed are all commonly used. Lard is sometimes used for frying but is not as popularly used as are oils. Butter is not used. Sesame seed oil is used in small amounts and mainly as a seasoning, especially in vegetable dishes. JOH YOW, strained pork suet, is used in pastry making.[5,6]

Sweets and Snacks

The Chinese have no real penchant for sweets. Tea is taken clear, and even sweet dishes are less sweet than usual western tastes dictate. Desserts, if any, will be fresh or preserved fruits, sometimes in a light syrup touched with anise or cloves. Savoury nibbles such as steamed buns, egg rolls or spring rolls, WON TON, thinly-sliced pickled or barbecued meats, vegetables and eggs or noodles are favoured as snacks. Sweet and sour sauces served with meat or fish dishes are enjoyed for their contrast in a menu. Occasionally, sweet preserved fruits may be served between courses at a banquet to arouse the appetite; but more likely hot broths or slightly-sweetened soups will be served for the same purpose.[12]

Seasonings

The amount and use of seasonings varies with regional tastes, as do the names – but the basic seasonings are the same throughout China. Onions of every type: scallions, leeks, chives, cooking onions as well as fresh garlic are a part of many dishes. Others include: fresh ginger root, rice wine, bean pastes (MIEN CHIANG), and fermented pastes, sesame seeds and sesame seed oil, sugar, many types of vinegars. Spices include black pepper, star aniseed, cloves, FIVE SPICE POWDER (fennel, clove, anise, cinnamon and Szechwan pepper blended together). The flavour-enhancer, monosodium glutamate, is used only sparingly by good cooks and is derived from wheat protein and more recently from corn or beets. It is called MEE JING or WEI CHING. CHO is rice vinegar and both pale and dark types may be interchanged with cider or malt vinegar.[5] Not to be overlooked as flavourings are the many preserved, pickled, and salty-dried foods used in small amounts.

Chinese condiment sauces are as important in cookery as other seasonings and are used sparingly. Some are composed with other ingredients into dipping sauces to be used at the table, others may be used for cookery, some are used in both ways.

JEUNG YOW (soy sauce): not to be confused with SHOYU sauce, which is Japanese soy sauce and too sweet for most Chinese dishes. Used in all Chinese cookery and adapted in other lands. In use for more than 2,000 years.[5] SANG CHO is delicately light, while CHAN YOW is considered the best general type. CHU YOW is dark and heavy and only for special tastes.

HOM HAH: shrimp paste with strong flavour and aroma, used especially in Fukien cooking.

DUK JEUNG (plum sauce): similar in taste and use to chutney sauce and is used mainly as a dipping sauce.

HO YOW (oyster sauce): has velvety, chicken-like flavour and is used widely.

HOY SIEN JEUNG (hoisin sauce): widely used as a flavouring ingredient. Excellent as a barbecue sauce for ribs.

MIEN SEE JEUNG: pungent brown bean paste, salty and redolent of garlic. Used especially in steamed dishes for flavour.

Beverages

Chinese seldom drink either water or milk. Most commonly enjoyed is clear hot tea as a beverage after meals and at any time. Wines are served at special or formal occasions and also used in cookery for the express purpose of neutralizing some flavours (as in fish) or to blend others.[5]

Tea as a beverage was first known in China in the first and second centuries C.E., but considered medicinal at first. Tea drinking as a general custom was promulgated with Lu Yu's classic called *Ch'aching.*[5] *Cha* is the northern Mandarin name for tea, *chai* is the Russian name for tea (they got it from China), while the Amoy dialect on the southeastern coast called it *tay*. From this latter name the Dutch traders, who sold tea to the French, called it *thé*, then the English called it tea.[5] By any name, there are Chinese connoisseurs of tea that could vie with any world authorities of wines in their ability to distinguish quality, flavour, variety, and even the location of growth. Some of the varieties include: CHANG, green tea; HOONG, red tea (we call it black, but red has happier connotations to the Chinese); then a range of smoked, fermented, and partly-fermented teas. The finest of green teas are considered to be CLOUD MIST and WUN MO. KEMUN is one of the finest of the black teas, while LAPSANG SOUCHONG is a well-known strong smoky tea. OOLONG is semi-fermented: the best grades make a clear straw-coloured tea, lower grades yield a brownish-red brew. Scented teas such as JASMINE, LICHEE, CHRYSAN-THEMUM are shunned by purists, but enjoyed nonetheless as an afternoon tea taken with pastries.[12]

Cooking Methods

Chinese cookery dates back several thousand years and China has probably one of the few cultures where "scholars wrote learned treatises on food and poets wrote cookbooks."[12] Having approximately 80,000 distinct and separate dishes, Chinese cuisine stands unparalleled for its variety, ingenuity, originality, and practicality. Nothing edible is ever discarded and in times of famine even dogs and rats were prepared with some delicacy.[10] Cookbooks per se are almost unknown in China. Instead, teaching was always by demonstration from mother to daughter or from chef to apprentice.[12] A classic Chinese recipe is basic and from it variations may be made according to necessity and preference. Minimal facilities and utensils are required for usual day-to-day meals. However, for occasions where many people are to be served, it is common to use the foods and services of commercial establishments. For example, the barbecuing of meats and preparation of holiday pastries are seldom tasks for the home kitchen.

The following methods of food preparation may be used singly or sequentially to prepare almost any Chinese dish. Soups and rice cookery are not included here:

STIR-FRYING: all ingredients are prepared before cooking, by washing, and cutting into bite-size pieces. Usually all the foods for one dish are assembled in piles on a plate ready to cook. A small amount of oil is heated in a WOK, seasonings and flavourings added, then prepared ingredients are added and tossed and stirred, adding those requiring the longest cooking period first. (Sometimes tough meats or vegetables may be lightly par-boiled to tenderize or meats or fish may be marinated for the same reason before stir-frying.) The food is then heaped on a serving platter and served with suitable garnish. A quick rinse and the WOK is ready to prepare the next dish.

DEEP-FRYING: out comes the same WOK, only this time a cup or two of oil is added and allowed to heat till very hot. (When a wooden chopstick is placed in the oil and bubbles disperse rapidly from it, the oil is considered ready.) Again, prepared foods await on a plate; these may be filled doughs (such as spring rolls, egg rolls, or won ton) or they may be batter-dipped food morsels. To facilitate placing in the hot oil and removing when done, a bamboo-handled brass mesh strainer is used; its wide shallow bowl very efficient for scooping up the crisp-browned foods. Usually sauces or dips are served with fried foods.

STEAMING: layers of lattice-bamboo or perforated aluminum trays that nest into each other and are covered with a tight lid are set over a pan or WOK of boiling water. Into each layer of the steamer goes the serving plate or bowl with the food to be steamed cut into bite-size morsels (cut through bone and all) with a sprinkling of the desired seasonings, sauces, and garnishes on top. Those foods requiring longest cooking are put on first. Leftover foods may be easily reheated this way without drying or flavour loss. A whole meal of several different dishes can be steamed over one heat source. This can be used for rice, meats, fish, poultry, dumplings, and pastries as well as individual steamed egg custards.

SLOW-COOKING: this term really refers to methods of braising (sautéeing in oil first then adding liquid), or stewing (cooking with water). "White stewing" refers to cooking with water or clear stock. "Red Stewing" refers to cooking with the "master sauce," a mixture of soy sauce and spices, in which whole chickens and chunks of pork may be slowly cooked; the sauce is then cooled and stored for use again, increasing in strength and flavour and said to be good for one hundred years![12]

ROASTING or BARBECUING: meats are oiled then brushed with marinade and always elevated or hung from hooks on racks so heat flows evenly around. Water pan may be set below to catch drippings. This is a commercial technique, as Chinese homes have seldom had ovens as part of the kitchen facilities. In any case, the convenience of being able to buy even very small portions of such meats is typical of any Chinese community.

SMOKING: more a method of adding interesting flavour than a cookery technique. Burning brown sugar or moistened burning tea leaves are used to flavour and char previously cooked (usually by slow-cooking or steam-cooking) meats or fish. Smoked eggs are an appetizer treat.

Regional Specialties

It was always the Chinese royal courts that had the finest chefs and could afford to produce magnificent, even legendary banquets. With the overthrow of the Ming Dynasty in the 1600s, court officials fled with their chefs. In this way the northern styles of cookery went with them and were adapted to the regional foods. Regional styles developed for the same reasons as in other lands: climate, food production, local religion and custom. Taoists teach that foods should be served as close as possible to their natural state: Buddhists abhor the taking of life, so are vegetarians often in the strictest sense; Muslims use no pork. Yet another reason for differentiation was difficulty of transport or storage between areas of production. Yet travellers have historically been the purveyors of traditions, foods and customs as well as goods for trades, and so too in China, where many previously distinct regional dishes have been adapted to other areas, often making origins difficult to distinguish.

Opinions even differ as to whether the regional specialties should be grouped by general area, by chief cities, or by province. Common Chinese restaurant terminology, such as Shanghai or Mandarin, used in western countries, is also misleading as the terms may be inclusive of many styles and as good as the restaurant itself. The age of Chinese culinary traditions also makes origins difficult to pinpoint.[5,9,12]

PEKING (NORTH and NORTHEAST)

Considered the classic Chinese cuisine, and most delicate, Peking is the most sophisticated and elegant. Onions, garlic, and leeks are used; steaming and poaching are the favoured cooking methods. Wheat flour dishes, such as noodles of all kinds and steamed breads, buns, and pastries are served with most meals while rice is reserved for banquets. Also included in the foods of this area is the Mongolian specialty, the Mongolian HOT-POT: a steaming pot of broth is set in the centre of the table and all diners dunk thinly-sliced meat and vegetables to cook in the broth, and then eat them with condiments. All northern nomadic peoples favour HOT-POT

cooking and eat lamb and mutton. Peking's famed dishes include: PEK-
ING DUCK, CHICKEN VELVET, SPRING ROLLS, and YELLOW RIVER CARP
with SWEET AND SOUR SAUCE.[12,5]

CANTONESE AND FUKIENESE (SOUTH)

Following Taoist principles, most foods are stir-fried or steamed. Because
of nearby coastline and rivers, fish and seafood are a specialty and sugar
is used in many dishes (to flavour not to sweeten), because it is grown in
this region. Canton was the first port open to westerners and the em-
barkation point for many emigrating Chinese, therefore it has adopted
western foods, such as tomatoes, peanuts, and corn as well as French
pastries.[12] Cantonese specialties: DIM SUM (steamed filled dumplings),
SHARK'S FIN SOUP, BIRD'S NEST SOUP. Chicken broth is often used as a
cooking medium and flavouring and prized for its sweetness and delicacy.

SHANGHAI (EASTERN)

Not really a distinctly different cuisine but often singled out; there are
many red-stewed dishes here, an abundance of sugar and fruits (like Cantonese), fine pickled and preserved foods. Pickled and salted greens are
often cooked with meats. Most famous of these dishes is pickled cabbage,
adapted in other lands as KIMCH'I in Korea and SAUERKRAUT in Germany. Both Cantonese and Shanghai residents are fond of noodles,
pastries, and dumplings: these are all sold as snacks by street vendors.

SZECHWAN (CENTRAL AND WESTERN)

As the climate gets colder, the foods get spicier and oilier. This cuisine is
famed for its liberal use of hot pepper and hot pepper sauces as well as for
its rice-paper-wrapped chicken. Many enjoy the flavour of chicken fat to
stir-fry vegetables.[5,12]

Meal Patterns and Eating Customs

In Chinese tradition, nothing is more cherished than an old friend. Love
between a man and a woman is considered to be simply a need of body,
while friendship involves the widest and highest range of human emotions.[15] Thus, sharing the pleasures of food can never be greater than
when in the company of old friends.[12] So much care is taken and consideration of flavour and colour and artistry exercised by the cook, that a
diner at a Chinese table would be considered barbarian if he asked for
added seasonings or a knife. Seasoning and cutting are to be done in the
kitchen. The diner may enjoy foods from any plate, eat them in any
order, dip into any sauce or condiment or spiced salt according to taste.

An almost universal Chinese breakfast is a bowl of CONGEE or JOOK:
hot rice gruel cooked with small tasty tidbits or served with pickles, salty
side dishes and always tea. Northern Chinese breakfasts are more likely to
be steaming noodles or a wheatcake or hot steamed dumplings. In

Mongolia, brick tea, cheese, and acrid butter may start the day while Tibetans may wake with a meal of buttered hot tea and TSAMPA (roasted barley or CHINGKO flour).[1] For most of the Han Chinese, the local cereal grain is the central part of the meal, while anything else reflects either local custom or economic status.[1]

The noon meal in most areas is a smaller version of the evening meal: soup, a rice or wheat dish, vegetables, and fish or meat, if possible. For some, a favoured noon meal may be varieties of DIM SUM, served with many cups of tea. For others, lunch is just right if it includes a bowl of noodles with condiments.

The Chinese are great snackers and enjoy nibbling on toasted seeds and nuts of all kinds, fresh fruits, dumpling dishes, assorted small plain cakes, and innumerable cups of tea. Snacks are important not only when a hunger pang strikes, but also just whenever *not* eating becomes too monotonous.[12] The preference is always for light savoury foods, never for rich sweets.

The main meal is the evening or family meal but with the addition of friends it can easily become a banquet. Tables seating eight to ten are favoured since this makes eating and serving easier. Each diner's place is set with a rice bowl, tea cup, chopsticks, and small dipping dishes as needed. Heaping bowls and platters are brought in several at a time and centred so all may reach. Soup served from tureens may alternate with other dishes if the meal is lengthy. Normally the host will raise his chopsticks as a sign that the meal may begin with serving of soup.

In a typical family meal care will be taken to consider variety in flavour, texture, cookery technique, type of food, and the meal will include at least one soup. Soup is a usual beginning but may be preceded by a cold selection of small appetizers. Small bites of foods are selected with one's own chopsticks and eaten over one's own rice bowl; the blend of flavours from casual drips of many sauces and juices makes the rice a flavourful dish to enjoy between other bites of foods. Holding the rice bowl close under the chin is also practical. Incidentally, vegetables are never eaten raw but may be served cold after cooking and seasoning.[12]

The general etiquette of a meal is important too. Each person's rice bowl is held with the left hand, thumb resting on the top rim and always close to the chin; rice may be scooped into the mouth without wasting any and other morsels may add tasty juices to the rice itself. Eating rice from a plate is difficult and wasting rice is an affront to any Chinese. Chopsticks are always used in pairs for eating but may be used singly to fold or stir in cookery. Each diner selects a morsel and either eats it at once or drops it in the rice bowl. Slippery noodles may be scooped into the mouth with chopsticks, while holding the bowl close to the mouth. It is not polite to select the best tidbits for yourself, but someone else may pick up a special bit for you with the square end of the chopsticks and place it on your plate.

To the casual observer, the use of chopsticks may seem awkward but like everything else Chinese, they are both ingenious and practical. Like the porcelain wide-bowled soup spoons, they never burn the mouth, or taste metallic. The general pace of eating is slow since only tiny morsels can be eaten at a time. Foods can never be drowned in sauces because as the small piece is lifted up, excess sauce immediately drains off. Children use slightly shorter chopsticks than average and sometimes the host or hostess may use longer ones so as to reach and place special pieces on the plate of their guests.[12]

Meals are concluded with the passing of small hot towels, damply fragrant to clean the fingers and refresh the diners. A lengthy banquet may include both the passing of hot towels and the nibbling of dried preserved fruits part way through the meal, or the serving of hot soups.

Special Occasions

In traditional Chinese life, it is sometimes difficult to separate the calendar into specific occasions because there are many days that are deemed special only for certain family members, others are for the entire family and still others are shared by the community.[6,17,18] These revolve around the life cycles, business ventures or family or communal enterprises. Each may involve food offerings, incantations, spells, magic potions, or consultations of special calendars according to the family or local custom.[18] In present-day Mainland China such matters and quaint customs take little importance in everyday affairs.[6]

Calculated on a lunar calendar, it is unquestionably New Year's that evokes the greatest celebrations. Celebrated on the first day of the first month with dragon-led parades, incense and fireworks and banners of red everywhere (signifying good luck), New Year's is traditionally ushered in by family feasting, gifts of money in red envelopes for all unmarried children, and much visiting. Friends and relatives wish each other "*hsin hsi*" or "New Year happiness," or "*kung hei fat chey*" or "May you make money."[19] Actually New Year's is celebrated for the first fifteen days of the new year, especially for agrarian families who take this period as an annual rest as well as one for visiting, feasting, and wearing new clothes.[8] It is also a time when crowds throng to see theatre and film in "cultural palaces and watch chess tournaments, soccer, and other events.[6]

In ancient times palace dignitaries were presented with purses embroidered with eight Buddhist symbols called "Eight Treasures," which they proudly hung on their chests.[18] In more recent times this is recalled by the serving of a fruit-filled rice pudding called EIGHT TREASURES RICE PUDDING.[13] Customary too at this time is the setting around the room of small bowls of lichees and longans, platters of steamed rice cakes and jujubes (red for luck) and salted seeds.[9] During the festive dinner itself, red sweet and sour sauce is sure to be part of at least one dish be it pork or fish.[20] This is also the time to give the "Kitchen God" some sticky sweets so he won't give a bad report on the family.[9]

Because of its strong connotations, the Chinese consider the New Year as a male festival or one of *yang* spirit. But the Moon Festival, second in importance, because of its cool *yin* connotations is left to the girls and women.[17] In some areas it was traditional to include many fertility rites and sacrifices to the Old Man in the Moon as the one who arranges all marriages on earth.[6] In other areas, especially those under Taoist influence, it was believed that the moon was inhabited by a rabbit "forever busy pounding out the elixir of life."[17] For this latter reason many moon effigies and rabbit images are burned with incense and money. Together with special parties for moon-viewing and the giving of boxes filled with MOON CAKES (round, filled pastries), symbolic lanterns made of paper are also used for gifts and for decorations.[9]

For every special occasion, small cups of rice wine are served to family and guests and feasting marks the special time. "Food makes the occasion . . . food means contentment, even happiness, and happiness in turn calls for food to emphasize it."[9] For those unable to add meat or fish to their usual daily foods, the major and minor special occasions of the Chinese calendar will surely bring the possibility of several special dishes rich with the welcome flavour of meat or fish.

Ch'ing Ming is the Chinese spring holiday. It is also called the Feast of the Tombs and is a time when the families make a special effort (as at New Year's) to be together to make offerings to the dead in the hope that they may offer assistance to the living. There is also some evidence that this may originally have been a festival of spring rites which marked the renewal of life with many mating celebrations, although in time this was superseded by the cult of Ancestor Worship.[17] In more recent times it has been taken as the time of remembrance for all who gave their life to worthy causes.[6]

Some contemporary changes in the Chinese calendar have occurred in Mainland China: International Labour Day on May 1 and National Day on October 1. New Year's is still celebrated with a blend of both new and old traditions.

Other traditional days are marked with picnics of rice cakes and steamed dumplings. An old tradition of the fifteenth day of the seventh month, called the Festival of Lost Souls, is marked by setting lighted candles adrift in rivers and lakes, chanting Buddhist scriptures and eating bitter foods.[17] Other occasions mark change of clothing for the season and agricultural events, such as harvesting or planting, and cold spells or hot spells of weather indicate special foods. For example, in *shu fu* (hot period), chunks of fresh fruits and ices are sold on the streets and many enjoy sour soups or drinks cooled with ice water. Most of these older traditions, however, are now relegated to history.

THIRTEEN

Czechoslovakian

Czechoslovakia was born in October 1918. It would simplify our understanding of the people and the country if we could say that the mother was Czech and the father Slovakian. But it was not that elementary.

The name Czech derives from the language they speak,[1] and this most westerly branch of Slavs make up 70 per cent of the urban population of the region of Bohemia, Moravia, and Silesia. Bohemia's name is believed to have come from the early peoples who inhabited the area: the Boii.[2,3] For four hundred years, Bohemia was an Austrian province whose cuisine was strongly influenced by both Germany and Austria. Vienna was the spiritual capital for Bohemia and the people's ethos was predominantly Teutonic in nature: disciplined and orderly.[2,4]

The Slovaks, on the other hand, speak a different though related language and their cuisine and their culture carry strong influences from their neighbour, Hungary.[3,6] Most Slovaks were engaged in rural rather than urban pursuits, such as farming, lumbering, and cattle raising. And they take great pride in their traditional local dress and festivals.[6,7]

Up to the 1300s there was much German immigration into Bohemia and also considerable immigration of Magyars into Slovakia. The hopes for a peaceful way of life seemed futile. Up to the mid-1800s continuous strife between ethnic groups, oppressive taxation, and forcible Germanization all made their daily life one of constant suffering. It cannot be said that the Austro-Hungarian monarchy was sympathetic to any cause but its own, with the result that the period up to the end of the

First World War was a tug-of-war between Hungarian and German dominancy.[2,3]

The joy at Czechoslovakia's birth was to be short-lived. By 1939, Hitler had forced the surrender of Czechoslovakia to Germany and once more the people were torn and dispersed. Ruthenia went to Hungary, Bohemia and Moravia became German protectorates and Slovakia, a puppet state.[2,3,7] Forcible colonization, exploitation and brutal oppression became routine again. In May 1945, with the end of the Second World War, a brief period of freedom was hungrily enjoyed as Soviets entered Prague from the East and Americans from the West. But by 1948, the Communists' "bloodless takeover" occurred.[3]

The food situation in any land under stress, bears little resemblance to the traditional fare. Heavy exportation of food products and a frequent shortage of milk and dairy products have made the current Czechoslovakian diet one that is predominantly carbohydrate, consisting mainly of bread, winter vegetables (cabbage and root vegetables), and potatoes.[6] But strong in Czech memories are gravy-rich pork and veal dishes, famous hot sausages of endless variety, dumplings that appeared from the beginning to the end of a meal, and a large choice of some of the finest beers in Europe.[5,6] The land satisfied these tastes in abundance: Bohemia, traditionally an area of well-balanced industry and agriculture; Moravia, long the centre of animal husbandry, with rich yields of wheat, corn, barley, and sugar beets; Slovakia, always well-supplied from her own natural resources.

Sooner or later, no matter where Czechs may be, conversation is bound to turn to nostalgic arguments regarding the choice of the finest of beers, the lightest of dumplings and, among PARKY (sausage) connoisseurs, which *uzenazstvi* (beer and sausage tavern) was the best of all.

Home Life and Facilities

Present conditions of crowded housing facilities and working parents as well as general scarcity of appliances, make the Czechoslovakian kitchen one which contains barest necessities. Food storage is not a consideration for most families because foods are usually purchased on a daily basis. Traditional home cooking is likely to be limited to weekends or holidays and further limited by what is available. Tiled ranges heated with locally-mined coal have been the centre of most Czech kitchens, complemented by hand-woven table linens and brightly-painted earthenware or fine china dishes. In better homes, the family's treasured collection of fine Czechoslovakian crystal would be used to grace the table for special occasions.[5,6]

FOODS COMMONLY USED

The traditional Czechoslovakian cuisine borrows heavily from

both the Austrian and the Hungarian tastes and leaves no question as to satiety and richness. Plain meats, fresh crisp vegetables, fresh fruits, or small servings have no place here. The rich production of dairy products find themselves as ingredients in many baked goods, creamy gravies, and smooth sauces. Both vegetables and fruits are preferred well-cooked and probably well-garnished with appropriate sauces, syrups etc.: sour-cream-smothered vegetable dishes and fruits cooked in syrup predominate. A great variety of grains and flours are used in many types of breads and rolls, cereal side dishes, and especially in the many dumplings that find themselves in soups, beside sliced gravy-rich meats, or on a dessert plate graced with a sweet fruit sauce or whipped cream. Whether one turns to Austria or to Hungary, there was never a lack of richly elegant desserts. Beer is considered to be the national beverage for Czechs, while the Slovaks prefer wines.

Milk and Milk Products

Sour cream, pot cheese, sour milk, and buttermilk, are used widely in many dishes, but milk is seldom used as a beverage per se. Frequently hot milk is added to the breakfast coffee. Occasionally BRYNDZA, a sheep's milk cheese, finds its way to the table and sometimes the Slovakian peasant specialty of LIPTOVSKY SYR (Liptauer cheese), made with a soft blend of sheep's milk cheese and seasonings, is heaped on rye bread, but for the most part, simple pot cheese heads the list of favourites.

Fruits and Vegetables

Fruits and vegetables are used mostly in their cooked state. Fruits are served as compotes, fruit sauces, or fruit fillings for baked goods and sometimes poached as a garnish for meat dishes. Vegetables are usually well-cooked or served as pickles of many kinds. Berries and stone fruits are popular but citrus fruits are seldom used. In public dining places, ascorbic acid has been added to salt to make up for this lack.[6] Apples are widely enjoyed and used in compotes, fillings, and as sauces. The staple vegetables include potatoes, green and red and savoy cabbage, sauerkraut, wild mushrooms, rutabagas, cauliflower and kohlrabi, onions and garlic. Some fresh seasonal vegetables are also used sparingly, such as radishes and cucumbers.

Meats and Alternates

Pork is the favoured meat and every part of the animal is used. Other meats include beef and veal, hare, all offal, geese, ducks, and chickens, smoked and cured meats, and a great variety of sausages, served hot. Fish and seafood are not popular and are seldom served. Although carp and herring are usually available, they are mostly served just on traditional Christmas Eve.

The preference is that meats be cooked until tender and juicy, and always served with a thick rich gravy – often including sour cream. Any meats that are not suited to this type of cookery are used in sausages, dumplings or as a base for soups.

Eggs are used mostly as an ingredient for other dishes. Occasionally omelets are served, which incorporate bits of meats, vegetables, even potatoes, or pot cheese and sometimes fruits and fruit sauces. Legumes are of no importance in the diet and nuts are used only in bakery and desserts.

Breads and Cereals

Wheat and rye predominate. Most breads are made with whole grain flours, either wheat or rye, or a mixture of both, incorporated into a sourdough. Bread is never wasted. In fact, the Czechoslovakian uses of slices or crumbs of stale bread vary greatly: in soups, in sauces, in cakes, and most often in dumplings. Much wheat flour is consumed in bakery sweets. It must not be overlooked that the many types of dumplings are as much of a staple food as bread itself.

Fats

Preference is shown for butter and rendered pork or goose fats. More recently use is made of margarines.

Sweets and Snacks

Desserts and candies have always been available and they are a very popular snack. Women consume the most sweets both in the form of candies to nibble and rich desserts to take with a coffee break.[6] Men prefer a snack of beer and hot sausages.

Seasonings

Spices and herbs are used with a light touch; foods are rich in natural flavours, they are not heavily seasoned. The classic seasonings include poppy seeds, caraway seeds, garlic, onions, and mushrooms. Often dried or toasted bread and/or cake crumbs may also be used as a seasoning. Nor can it be overlooked that much of the rich flavour and aroma of Czechoslovakian cookery is derived from the rich and abundant traditional use of fresh dairy products.

Beverages

Beer is said to be the national beverage and the particular favourite of the Czechs, who will heatedly discuss the quality and merit of one beer over another. Both red and white wines are made locally but do not travel well so are not usually exported. Many wines are homemade, especially by the Slovaks, who prefer wine over beer.[4]

SLIVOVITZ is a clear and very potent brandy made from plums. It is taken straight with any excuse from appetite stimulation to medicinal use.

Coffee or a coffee-flavoured brew made from malt or chicory is taken for breakfast hot and strong, often liberally laced with hot milk or even rum.[6]

Meal Patterns and Eating Customs

Traditionally, Czechs and Slovaks prefer all meals to be served hot. When food varieties are not abundant, satisfaction is found in a coffee beverage with breads for breakfast; a quick hot lunch based on sausages or a potato or vegetable dish; dinner may be a soup with a second course of meat and gravy and a small dessert of dumplings, or it may be a quick meat sandwich with pickles and potato salad.[6]

These three simple meals will be complemented by hot snacks of sausages and beer or assorted pastries with coffee. *Gastronom* counters and taverns as well as pastry shops and coffee houses and the famed *uzenazstvi* are present everywhere in cities and towns.

Friday was traditionally a meatless day, not as much for religious reasons as for a way to economize on meats. Friday dinner would be a traditional "false" soup with fruit dumplings for dessert. A "false" soup is made with a meatless vegetable stock, often starting with browned onions to add a pseudo meat flavour.

Even in difficult times the Sunday dinner is almost always the biggest hot meal of the week. A hearty rich soup is followed by a special dish of pork or beef (or roast fowl), floating in smooth thick gravy, garnished with poached fruit or a huge sliced dumpling, to be completed with light sweet fruit dumplings served hot.

Special Occasions

Most Czechoslovakians are members of the Roman Catholic faith, celebrating traditional feast and fast days, while only about 10 per cent are Protestants of the Reformed and Lutheran churches. Of the more than 350,000 Jews living in Czechoslovakia before the Second World War, few remain: those that were not killed during the Nazi regime emigrated.[3]

The usual festive fare consists of roasted goose or duck served with steamed dumplings, gravy, and red cabbage. Trout or carp, especially the spectacular KAPR NA CERNO (a whole baked carp served with black sauce made of beer, prunes, raisins, sugar, and vinegar) may grace the festive table for Christmas Eve.

FOURTEEN

Danish

The mainland of Denmark, together with its surrounding islands, juts out into the cold and stormy waters of the Skagerrak and the Kattegat, the North and Baltic Seas, yet there is within the hearts and the homes of the Danes a special warmth. The Danes have their own word for it: *hygge*. It describes, in one word, that pleasant sensation when one is at ease with oneself and the world. *Hygge* is a feeling, an atmosphere, and a way of life. It is evident in the meticulously groomed dairy farms of the low rolling countryside. It even seems to be reflected in the apparent contentment of the animals the Danes raise. The cows are said to produce some of the world's finest milk, which is churned into butter and fermented into cheese, the pigs, which are cured into pork products, are of unparalleled quality, and chickens produce eggs so fresh, they are proudly date-stamped.[1,2]

Today's farmers are related to early conquerors and rulers of England (1013-1035) and later expansions saw them ruling many shoreline areas of the Baltic Sea, Iceland, and even for a brief period Norway and Sweden (the Kalmar Union, which lasted until 1523).[1] Sweden won her independence then but it was not until 1815, that Norway, by the Congress of Vienna, was taken from Danish control only to find itself then ruled by Sweden. About this time, Danish trade expanded to the West Indies. (Perhaps the Danish fondness for rum desserts dates from this time.[3]) But in 1917, Denmark sold the Virgin Islands to the United States and about the same time granted Iceland her independence.

But the adventures of the Danes were not limited to northern Europe or even to the West Indies. As early as 1619, Captain Jens Munk landed at what is today Churchill, Manitoba, and claimed the land for Denmark, calling it Nova Dania. It is uncertain why his claim was not taken seriously, but what is known is that all of his crew succumbed to scurvy. Captain Munk and only two members survived that tragedy. More than two hundred years later, more Danish ships brought settlers to establish what is today a community of about nine hundred people: New Denmark, New Brunswick.[3,4]

Home Life and Facilities

The old Danish proverb: "First flowers, then food on the table"[5] explains the Danish delight in well-designed table appointments and cookware. These, together with a collection of candles and accessories that is in most Danish homes, makes it difficult not to set an appealing table. And if flowers are not already a part of any setting, they will likely be brought by dinner guests.

Although Danes are practical enough to readily accept many convenience foods and labour-saving devices, they still enjoy certain tradition-tested customs. Probably from her mother and grandmother the Danish homemaker has learned to adjust the embers in her iron stove to the perfect heat for AEBLESKIVERS (round puffed cakes) or for a cast iron pot of yellow pea soup.

But if the coal stove is still a part of the country kitchen, the city kitchen, presided over by a working mother, is more appropriate to the times. Small appliances are widely used, colourful and lightweight cookware is preferred, and gas stoves and refrigerators are all very much a part of the modern kitchen. In fact, many new additions to the traditional Danish kitchen and way of cookery have combined to make Danish dishes just as good as mother's but prepared more quickly than grandmother's! Ekkodanmark, a branch of the Department of Agriculture set up to promote Danish foods, advises on canned and frozen goods, imported foods, and new recipe ideas.

The problem of food storage and preservation in Denmark, as in most of the northern countries, has always been carefully considered because extreme climate conditions can so easily spell hunger. Curing, salting, pickling, drying, and smoking were arts learned quickly because these techniques allowed meats and fish to last over long voyages or through periods of famine. Today, modern technology and storage methods lessen the need for these age-old methods, but a distinct preference for salty foods persists, and even today salted meat and fish as well as dried or smoked foods are distinct Danish favourites.[2,6,7]

FOODS COMMONLY USED

Good Danish food can be found both in homes and in

restaurants. Both types of fare are prepared from fresh ingredients with simplicity and care taken to enhance the natural flavours. Danish food is considered by some tastes to be bland; even the occasional curries are never spicy hot. Coffee and pastries are great favourites and all dairy foods have a daily place in the meals. Pork is the favourite meat; potatoes the favourite vegetable, but there may be a problem deciding between AKVAVIT or beer. Solution: take both.

Milk and Milk Products
Milk, whey, or buttermilk are freely used often as refreshing beverages and also in soups and gravies. Cream is used generously in ice cream, whipped cream sauces (savoury not sweet), as well as in desserts as sweetened whipped cream. In fact, plain cream, whipped cream, and sour cream are to be found in almost every dish: soups, salad dressings, meat and fish casseroles and sauces, and certainly in desserts. Coffee however, is preferred black.

Danish cheeses, noted for their buttery richness and mild nutty flavours are exported all over the world. The Danes themselves enjoy cheeses for breakfast, cheeses as part of lunch menus and often as a dessert with fruit or as a late evening snack.

Fruits and Vegetables
Fresh fruits in season are preferred, but fruits are also enjoyed when stewed then thickened with corn or potato starch and served with cream. The staple vegetables are potatoes and red or green cabbage, although the former are definite favourites. String beans and white asparagus are enjoyed when available, as are pickled cucumbers, pickled beets, a variety of summer vegetables, canned or fresh peas and carrots. To the staples of potatoes and cabbage, are added pickles or root vegetables in winter and greens in summer. Salad to the Danes means a mixture laden with meat or fish and bound with mayonnaise: tossed salads with light dressings are largely ignored except by aristocrats.[7] Danes have other favourite vegetables, which are lovingly prepared: cauliflower, Belgian endive, onion of every type, kale, celeriac, and a great variety of local mushrooms.

Meats and Alternates
Danish meat dishes are served moist and juicy; if the meats are naturally dry then they are accompanied by gravy or a sauce. Broiling or dry roasting methods are seldom used in meat or fish cookery. Though fish is plentiful, meats are the staple. Of these, pork is the favourite and all parts are used; offal, sausages, and ground meats are often served for economy. Blood is used in soups and for sausages. Fish include: shrimp,

eels, herring (in countless ways), salmon, trout, mackerel, turbot, plaice, cod (fresh, dried or salted).

Eggs are used occasionally for a light meal such as an omelet but mostly they are used as an ingredient in or garnish for other dishes. The only legumes used widely are dried yellow peas, used at least weekly for a soup, GULE AERTER. Nuts are used in bakery and then almost always almonds.

Breads and Cereals

Gruels or porridges of barley or oats are used only in rural areas or by children or invalids. Rice and pasta are also seldom used. Some oats are found in desserts or as oatcakes accompanying the traditional buttermilk soup. Most grains are eaten in the form of breads, rolls and crispbreads. Heavy dark and moist rye bread is sliced especially thin for SMORREBROD.

It should be noted that gruels and porridges of barley or oats still do form the staple peasant diet together with cabbage and potatoes and the very occasional addition of small amounts of fresh or cured home-raised pork.

Fats

Butter is the favourite and is used for everything and everywhere generously. Unsalted butter is preferred. Danish margarine is also of fine quality and flavour and is being used increasingly.

Sweets and Snacks

Danes enjoy cakes, pastries, and crisp cookies often as snacks with coffee. The characteristic lightness and crispness of Danish bakery is attributed to HARTSHORN SALT (ammonium carbonate) used instead of baking powder. In Canada and the United States it can be purchased in drug stores. Thick and sweet preserves as well as powdered sugar are often used to garnish desserts, especially pancakes.

Seasonings

Danish food is not highly seasoned. Cream, butter and eggs, mustard, horseradish, dill, onions, and leeks are favoured. Poppy seeds and caraway seeds are used mainly in or on breads or rolls. For baked goods, the aroma familiar to Danes is the pungent one of cardamom, saffron, and toasted almonds.

Beverages

Black coffee in copious quantities vies with beer and AKVAVIT as the favoured drinks. AKVAVIT is a strong clear liquor distilled from grain or potatoes and always served icy cold. In fact, it is traditional to serve AKVAVIT from a frozen block of ice, syrupy, thick and potent. Taken straight, it is often followed by a chaser of beer and then nibbles of salted foods. Children consume large quantities of pop; this is recent, not traditional.[7] In cases of overindulgence, the Danes take a "cure" in the form of GAMMEL DANSK BITTER, a medicinally bitter brew (suspected of being alcoholic), said to clear head and stomach.

Meal Patterns and Eating Customs

Although Danes adapt readily to new ideas, they still relish foods in season like tiny shrimps, which they heap on buttered white bread; the first delicate strawberries; new potatoes; fresh white asparagus. They still believe firmly that the best lunch is SMORREBROD and that beer is the best chaser for the best drink: AKVAVIT. Some things are too good to change.

Danes love a good joke and a hearty laugh but they show their sophistication in elegant table settings and in their fondness for formal entertaining. It is almost second nature to set a table with candles and flowers. Dessert spoon and fork will be placed above each setting; no water glasses will be on the table; no host will wrestle with meat by carving at the table; the artfully arranged main dish platter is prepared always in the kitchen. The success of a dinner party will be judged by the abundance of food, the lateness of the guests' departure and whether or not they asked for recipes.[7]

Breakfast for Danes is usually very early since schools and business often begin at 8:00. Lunch is invariably the SMORREBROD: quite literally any artistic and flavourful combination of thinly-sliced foods deftly balanced on thinly-sliced pieces of dark rye bread. With beer or coffee who needs more? Dinner may be a hearty soup and dessert or a multi-course meal introduced with AKVAVIT and beer, nibbles of salted or smoked foods followed by one or two hot dishes and later fruit and pastries with coffee. More usually dinner at home is a simple two-course meal of meat and potatoes or poached fish with sauce and potatoes or soup and dessert.

Danes seldom stay at home and enjoy any excuse that takes them out: to have a beer or have a coffee, to take a walk, to see friends. They love people and conversation and what better way than to enjoy both at the many small snacking restaurants, sidewalk cafes, stalls and booths and pastry shops? But who counts the number of drinks, snacks or nibbles in any given day? In speaking of his own meal patterns, the average Dane doesn't consciously include them either.

Special Occasions

Most Danes are Lutherans and the majority of those who aren't are Roman Catholics. But festivities celebrated are not always of a religious nature. Birthdays, Midsummer Eve, even the start of the crayfish season are all celebrated as avidly as Christmas, Easter, weddings, and christenings.

Drinking itself can be a special occasion and has a proscribed ritual. All Scandinavian countries share the custom of *Skoal*. The host begins by meeting the eye of his guest, together they wordlessly down their drinks without changing their gaze. When complete, the glass is raised with a slight bow of the head and lowering of the eyes. A woman, particularly a hostess, is usually not part of this custom.[2,8]

Although there are some distinctive characteristics in foods and customs from one Scandinavian country to another, festivities bring a delicious blending of wondrous smells and a happy sharing of the very best one has. Typically, repeated *Skoals* echo through any occasion, are washed down with beers and endless helpings of foods, ending finally with coffee and sips of CHERRY HEERING or maybe even a GLOGG or two.

Early in December, kitchens begin bustling with the furore of Christmas cookie baking, preparation of hams, LUTEFISK (traditional Christmas Eve dish made from lye-cured cod served with mustard sauce), liver pâté – the list is endless. Then there is the special Christmas SMOR-REBROD with its array of fish, pickled and smoked dishes, salads, cold meats and hot dishes, breads of every kind, cheeses, cream-filled cakes and crispy cookies.

Christmas foods are unquestionably the most outstanding but every festivity is celebrated with the best one has and always with one more helping. This can be fully understood when it is remembered that even a gathering of friends is a special occasion to the gregarious Dane.

FIFTEEN

Dutch

In almost everyone's mind "Dutch" is synonymous with the clopping of wooden shoes, children skating to school in winter, and a lone boy somewhere with his finger in a dyke. Some think of the Dutch as staid and solid and settled placidly to a life of agriculture with days in the fields and evenings with the *goude frouw* knitting and the *burgher* puffing contentedly on his pipe . . . In fact, wooden shoes are worn only in the muddy countryside; the Netherlands' year-round climate is so damp and misty that there are few days when ice does form on the canals. Finally, in place of a little boy with a very sore finger, Dutch engineers have a network of well-engineered dykes, dams, pumps and sluices that are not only keeping back the North Sea, but are also draining and reclaiming the 25 per cent of the Netherlands that is actually below sea level.[1]

Even the briefest glimpse into history will reveal the Netherlands as a once-important seafaring nation with global possessions: from the Arctic Ocean to Asia, Africa, Latin America, and even Staten Island in the United States.[1] It was the Dutch East India Company that was credited with introducing, in 1625, the Holland-Friesian breed of cattle to America and in the 1800s it was Amsterdam bankers who were credited with being the first to invest in railroad building in Canada.[2] It was outspoken Dutchmen in the 1500s who fought the evils of the Inquisition and even to this day offer their land as a haven to religious and political refugees. Daring explorers, shrewd businessmen, and independent thinkers, the Dutch have also historically contributed their skills to world art and literature.

It may be true that the image of the contented Dutchman persists over the reality because so many of the Dutch contributions to our daily lives relate to the home. It was the early Dutch pioneers in New Amsterdam on Manhattan Island who introduced flower gardens with imported bulbs from Holland, built their homes over food storage cellars, and even served pancakes and waffles and cookies to neighbours who had never sampled such delights.[3] Even the ubiquitous mound of cole slaw on restaurant plates is of Dutch origin. Credited with introducing strip farming in southern Alberta, developing Western irrigation districts, and starting market gardening in the Holland Marsh area of York County in Ontario, sturdy Dutchmen emigrating to the New World from the most densely-populated area of Europe found vast areas of good land awaiting their industrious ingenuity.[1,2]

Because of the imports of the Dutch East India Company, the Dutch were among the first Europeans to make tea drinking a daily ritual. In fact, the Dutch are credited with initiating the 4:00 tea break, the rules of steeping for five minutes, and even the serving of tea from a tea-cosy-protected pot.[3]

There are many who would argue that the most important Dutch contribution is the beloved tradition of Santa Claus. Although the Dutch Sinterklaas[4,5] is the antithesis of the western world's commercially-exploited Santa, he arrives annually in the Netherlands on December 6. (See Special Occasions.) Far from having any religious connotation, Sinterklaas is a Dutch tradition specifically for the enjoyment of the children regardless of religion.

Dutch family life is of prime importance, and closeness of friends and relatives is retained with much visiting. In the Netherlands this poses no problem since more then twelve million people live in no more than 16,000 square miles.[1] In Canada and the United States this visiting is maintained, regardless of distance one has to travel. The sports-loving, health-conscious Dutch are also famed for their appetites. Though many are overweight, they still claim "Western Europe's longest life expectancy and one of the lowest death rates in the world."[6] Perhaps then the image of the *goude frouw* knitting and the *burgher* puffing on his pipe is more a symbol of inner peace and a strength contributing to the Dutch health and longevity.

Home Life and Facilities

The spotless Dutch kitchen, boasting shiny rows of plates in the cupboards and a collection of spoons hung in a spoon rack, that was always so much a part of pioneer Dutch kitchens[3], is often still to be found today. Many Dutch have a fondness for delftware – earthenware dishes glazed in white and blue – as well as a penchant for copper utensils and accessories.

North American home-styles are very much a part of Dutch life too, but the tradition of gathering around the kitchen table for good food and talk persists.

A part of Dutch homes that is shown with pride is the food cellar. Rows of home-canned fruits, vegetables, pickles, pickled meats, head cheeses, and bins of root vegetables are very much a part of homemaking skills. Modern homes make full use of freezers and refrigerators, but the traditional pride in home preserving remains.

FOODS COMMONLY USED

The Dutch eat traditional hearty fare at home, but prefer international dishes when they dine out. Cheese is one of the most important dairy products and usually eaten for breakfast. Fruits and vegetables are well-cooked and usually enjoyed in season although preserves are popular. Potatoes in endless forms and breads of every type stand apart as the most important staples. Meats are used more sparingly and pork and beef are favourites. Of fish, herring is used most widely and in many ways. Seasonings are limited because natural flavours of fresh ingredients are preferred. Tea, coffee, beer, and gin are the usual adult drinks, while children enjoy milk. It is customary that all cooked foods are well-cooked.

Milk and Milk Products
Milk and buttermilk as beverages are taken more by children than by adults although a substantial amount of milk is consumed in tea and coffee. The cheeses of the Netherlands are famed, such as EDAM, GOUDA, and the spiced LEIDEN, which are all named for the towns where they are produced. The Dutch prepare few dishes with cheese, nor is cheese used as a dessert; the Dutch enjoy their mild nutty cheeses thinly sliced and served with bread either for breakfast or as a snack with gin.

Fruits and Vegetables
Frozen and canned vegetables are readily available, but there is a distinct preference for fresh seasonal fruits and vegetables.[5] Potatoes are used in infinite ways: boiled, mashed, pureed, fried, as a souffle, pudding, or else baked or sauteed. Van Gogh's famous painting, "The Potato Eaters," is still representative of some rural areas where the evening meal may consist of a huge bowl of potatoes centred on the table, each person spearing his own and dipping into gravy or bacon fat before eating.[5] White asparagus, red and green cabbages, cauliflower, Belgian endive, brussels sprouts, leeks, onions, kale, and carrots are favourites.

Apples are the most widely used fruit. Other fruits are usually expensive and therefore used sparingly. Dried fruits often accompany cooked meat dishes.

Meats and Alternates

Meats are cut and sold differently in the Netherlands than in Canada. Beef and pork are preferred and offal and variety meats are imaginatively and frequently used for economy and flavour. All types of cured, smoked, and pickled meats and sausages are enjoyed also for flavour and because of economy. There is only occasional use of fowl and hare.

Favourite fish: herring, in many forms. Green or spring herring is lightly smoked and brined and called HOLLANDSE NIEUWE. These are usually purchased from street vendors, sprinkled with raw sliced onions and eaten as a snack. Cod, haddock, plaice (flounder) and SNOEK (pike) have a place, too, as well as shrimp and an abundance of eels. It is a New Year's custom to down as many oysters as possible.

Legumes are sometimes a part of several vegetables that are cooked and mashed and served with butter or gravy. More usual is the serving of dried peas in the soup called ERWTENSOEP. Nuts are only seen in bakery and then almonds are favourites.

Breads and Cereals

A great variety of breads made from wheat and rye flours are served at every meal and customarily eaten in quantity. Hot cooked cereals or cold prepared cereals are not used. The exception is PAP, a hot cereal of oatmeal and milk, but more usually prepared from stale bread with hot milk poured over and served to children for breakfast.[5,7]

Fats

Unsalted butter is the preferred fat. All the well-cooked meat and vegetable dishes are always served together with gravies or sauces or drippings or butter. "Dry" meats or vegetables are not served.

Sweets and Snacks

Chocolate, cocoa, and candies are considered special treats. A great variety of baked goods, especially cookies and unfilled, un-iced cakes are taken with tea or coffee as between-meal breaks. Red currant jellies and jams are favourites on bread or as dessert sauces. Snacks are often hearty meat sandwiches of fish specialties.

Seasonings

Daily Dutch home cooking may be described as well-cooked but never highly seasoned. Onions, salt, and pepper with the added flavour from butter or drippings provide zest to soups, meats and vegetables. Some fresh herbs are used when available. Ginger and cinnamon are used in baked goods with honey and molasses often providing sweetness as well as distinct flavour in such things as honey cakes and honey and gingerbread cookies.

Beverages

Milk is the children's beverage while adults prefer tea or coffee taken with milk and sugar. Afternoons find the ladies enjoying tea and cookies while men take a few beers. Traditional dinner aperitif is Genever gin, sometimes called BORREL by the Dutch; the rest of the meal will be served with water or mineral water and, on special occasions, wine.

Meal Patterns and Eating Customs

The average day in the Netherlands ("Holland" being the unofficial but popular name) begins with an ample breakfast of many breads, unsalted butter and jams, sliced cheeses, and occasionally a fried or boiled egg. Young children may be served PAP. The morning drink is tea with milk and sugar while the youngsters have milk or buttermilk.

Lunch, called *koffietafel*, is also cold meal consisting of breads, cheeses, plus sliced meats and sausages and the addition of one small hot dish (baked casserole, souffle, or omelet), perhaps a dessert of fruit or rice or farina pudding. One thing is certain: lunch will be concluded with "endless cups of coffee," taken with milk and sugar.[7,8] Note that both breakfast and lunch are "sandwich meals" and these are accompanied by either tea or coffee.

Six o'clock in the evening is time for a quick aperitif of Dutch Genever gin (strongly juniper-flavoured) preceding the usual dinner time of 6:30 P.M. The often damp and chilly weather makes hot soup a popular first course, followed by fish or meat plus gravy and one of the many hot potato or vegetable dishes. A simple dessert pudding or FLENSJES (small crêpes) will finish the meal. Accompanying dinner will be water or mineral water and sometimes wine but never tea or coffee. Juices or soft drinks also have no place at the dinner table. Occasionally men may have beer.

But the legendary Dutch appetite could hardly be appeased with a mere three meals a day. So about 10:30 A.M. everyone stops for coffee and hot milk served with KOEKJES (cookies). Again at 4:00 P.M. a universal break for tea and cookies. But in between if the suggestion of a hunger pang should strike, all is in readiness: *pannekoekenhuisje* (pancake houses) dish up huge pancakes a-shimmer with butter and preserves; *broodjeswinkel* (delicatessens) stand by to serve sandwiches, especially the famed UITSMIJTER, a Dutch "snack" of bread and butter topped with sliced meat, fried eggs, and pickles. Then there are always vendors with herring and eel snacks.

Dutch cooks seldom experiment: simple and hearty traditional dishes are well-loved. Most popular dining-out meal is the *rijstafel* or Indonesian "rice table." This is a traditional feast centring around mounded rice flanked by platters of shrimp or pork or beef ready to be accented with an array of hot, sweet, spicy, crunchy, or cool condiments. What a contrast to the daily Dutch fare! Such exotic tastes were brought home to the Netherlands by colonists living for a time in previously Dutch-owned Indonesia. Three hundred years of Dutch occupation was long enough to bring home some Oriental food tastes. Many quick lunch counters also feature a few of these specialties; the names and flavours are familiar to the Dutch. The fact that most western Dutch import shops feature a section of specialty foods for the *rijstafel* is proof that adventurous Dutch will occasionally attempt this cookery at home.

Special Occasions

More than two-thirds of the Dutch population belong to Protestant sects and the majority of these are members of the Dutch Reformed Church. Of the remainder some 27 per cent[2] are Roman Catholics and about 5 per cent are Jews.[1]

Easter is celebrated with daffodils and tulips, HONINGKOEK (honeycake) and KRENTENBOLLEN (currant buns)[4] while Christmas is quietly celebrated by going to church with family. New Year's Eve calls for happy family parties with APPEL BEIGNETS (fried apple fritters), OLIEBOLLEN (deep-fried yeast donuts), and APPELBOLLEN (apples baked in puff pastry).

But the happiest and most important celebration of the year is, surprisingly, neither religious nor patriotic and is celebrated by everyone regardless of age or religion. This is the delightful festival of Sinterklaas or St. Nicholas Eve, on December 5. Marzipan and fondant candies, special cookies called BOTERLEITER, SPECULAAS and TAAI-TAAI, rich with honey and fragrant with nuts and spice, mark everyone's place at the table while gifts, treasure hunts, and even practical jokes make the evening. The climax of the merriment comes with the arrival of Sinterklaas and his helper Svart Piet, carrying a huge sack of toys for good children and reprimands for the bad ones. The children eagerly prepare for their arrival by placing one of their shoes, filled with hay, carrots, or cookies, in front of the fireplace – Sinterklaas and Piet may arrive by horse, barge, car, or even bicycle.

SIXTEEN

East Indian

On August 15, 1947, the Republics of India and Pakistan were born amid cheers and parades. The sub-continent of India has a history of warring kingdoms drawn into temporary peace only to burst again and again into cultural or political explosions.

It was historically the northern provinces of India, centring around the capital of Delhi, with its fabled riches and benign climate, which proved to be the most tempting area for conquests both militarily and ideologically. Greek thought in 300 B.C.E., Buddhism in the 200s B.C.E., were followed by the Hindu ideals in 100 B.C.E., and gradually filtered throughout India and Pakistan.[1] Later battles by Huns and Turks only added to the anarchistic state of affairs that had prevailed for several hundred years.

By 1,000 C.E., yet another power arose: united by the beliefs of Islam, a series of Muslim rulers prevailed as Delhi Sultans for several hundred years. They in turn were followed by the Mogul Dynasty, led by Baber in 1526.[1] This period of religious toleration and cultural splendour peaked in the mid-1600s, when the famed Taj Mahal was constructed, then declined abruptly by early 1700, coinciding with the firm entrenchment of the Sikhist faith.[1] Later, Persian plunderers only added to what was a chaotic and violent era fraught with political, economic, and religious warring factions.[2]

The indigenous crops of fine teas and spices made Northern India into an arena for European conquest – ostensibly for reasons of trade. The Portuguese in the 1400s, were followed by the Dutch East India Company in the 1600s, with the British taking a share of the trade monopolies in the late 1600s.[1]

But the diversity of religious faiths is only one factor in the great complexity that is India. In the huge tropical sub-continent of India and Pakistan reside more than one-sixth of the world's population, representing eight distinctive ethnic groups, many religious and religious sub-groups, endless local and regional cultural traditions, and over 200 different languages and dialects. Add to these figures the staggering population growth rate, food production problems, and the difficulties of education and communication, and it can be seen that the problems created are indeed complex.[3]

Increase of food production is a slow, uncertain process. Despite a continual lack of financial resources and technical skills, continued efforts are aimed at increasing the crop yields of present arable land.

Most of the area's agricultural lands are deficient in organic matter and frequently lacking in water. Other countries of the world use compost from crop residues and other organic wastes. In India crop residues are used together with animal dung for cooking fuel and building materials.[3] Irrigation systems have been introduced, but frequently primitive farming methods prevail often with family hand labour. Since animals and fowl compete with man for the land and the food, animals are lean, milk production is low, chickens are scrawny and their egg production is also low.[3]

Common to other areas where subsistence agriculture is practised, the low crop production as well as dairy and eggs are usually consumed in the local villages. There is seldom any kind of surplus. Transportation is often simply bullock cart and often over primitive roads to far-distant markets. Storage facilities are limited and often non-existent. If it seems that discussions of the food problems of India and Pakistan focus on the poorer classes, it is because they represent 80 per cent of the total population, and their dietary intake is also controlled by local availability, economic status, traditional religion and culture, plus the vagaries of nature, which can bring drought or flood.[3]

Unlike many other lands and cultures, the most decisive factors in India's cuisine are *not* the influence of invaders and conquerors, but rather natural resources available, local tradition and custom and status, as well as the complex stipulations of the religious groups. It is for these reasons that the statement can be made that India's cuisine is set apart mainly by use and varieties of spices and that although the foods of different areas appear to be different, they are in fact only different in methods of preparation rather than composition.[3,4]

Home Life and Facilities
Home life and facilities depend, like most other matters, again upon the region, the cultural traditions, and the economic status.

There are more than a half-million small villages in India and Pakistan with populations just under 2,000, which are run by *panchayats* or local councils. People in the villages subsist on local produce mostly secured by hand labour, dependent on the weather. Sometimes women may be left behind as the men leave the village to seek work. For most life is hard and primitive methods prevail in home and field.

The kitchen and dining areas of most homes are held in some degree of reverence and shoes are never worn there. Kitchen facilities may vary but most have open shelves to store copper and brass utensils as well as spices, seasonings, and staples, such as cereals, legumes, flours and pickles.[4] Cooking will be done over small charcoal or dung-burning "stoves," usually a container to hold the burning fuel fitted with a grate on top. Cooking utensils include some type of griddle for breads and a deep pot to be used for rice cooking, heating water, deep-frying and pickle making.

The rounded griddle is called a TAVA, while the dome-shaped utensil specific for frying is called KARHAI. Some method of grinding and crushing the many blends of spices used for different dishes is a vital part of the facilities. These may be as simple as a long flat stone with a smooth round one to roll over the spices or a stone vessel with a deep pit and a stone pounder to form a type of mortar and pestle. City homes of some stature would use electric blenders. CHIMTA is the name given to long tongs with smooth flat edges. These and several sizes of ladles and mixing spoons constitute basic equipment. Especially popular in the Punjab area is the TANDOOR, a clay oven used for barbecuing meats and also to bake breads, which are slapped onto the sloping sides of the pit-like oven.[4,5]

A collection of small bowls and individual THALIS (trays) will be used for meal service and these will reflect the status of the home. Most households will also have at least one PARAAT, a wide-brimmed brass tray used for kneading bread doughs, but it can also be used for serving foods on special occasions.

Just as the kitchen facilities vary according to status, so do storage facilities. These are non-existent for most of the population. Dry flours, cereals and legumes are stored high on shelves in closed jugs and jars to keep free of vermin and insects – always a problem in tropical climates. Thus, fruits and vegetables in the form of pickles and seasoning sauces and chutneys, oils and other condiments keep well. Oil, brine, or sugar may be used to preserve the fruits and vegetables as pickles; they may vary from salty to very sweet, spicy, and hot or sour. Only in the wealthiest of urban homes do electrical appliances, and especially refrigerators, make an appearance.

FOODS COMMONLY USED

The most important factors differentiating East Indian foods are

the use of seasonings and the methods of preparation, while the variable factors include economic status, local traditions, religion, and availability. All areas depend mainly on cereals followed by legumes and only small amounts of vegetables and fruits. Dairy products are enjoyed as often as possible by all. Meats and fish pose problems: the poor can seldom afford them and religious taboos affect usage. Some taboos may be locally overcome. For example, Hindus (especially in coastal areas) may eat fish by considering them "fruit of the sea" rather then flesh; other may eat beef in restaurants but never allow it to be cooked in their own homes.[5] More frequently vegetarians are such for economic reasons rather than by choice.[3,5]

The basic cereals are rice, wheat, corn, millet, and barley. Pulses are commonly used in at least one daily dish, often in a thick sauce called DAL, which can be served over grains, used as a side dish or as a thickener for other dishes.[6] Vegetable oils are the staples but GHEE (clarified butter) is preferred by the upper classes. Potatoes and onions are the staple vegetables, other vegetables and seasonal fruits are consumed mostly in the form of condiments, sauces, and pickles. Tea is the favoured beverage in the North, while coffee has preference in the South.

Milk and Milk Products

Milk is a staple of some vegetarian meals, when available. Fresh milk, whether from cows, buffalo, or goats, is always boiled before using. Yoghurt relishes, milk desserts, and drinks prepared with buttermilk or yoghurt sometimes diluted with water are used as often as possible.[5] British introduction of tea drinking replaced many traditional frothy hot milk drinks and cool fruit beverages.[5]

Milk also forms the base of most of the very sweet desserts made by combining boiled milk, sugar and spices with grated carrots, flours, or raisins. KULFI is similar to ice cream, made with frozen boiled milk, chopped nuts and cardamom. KHOYA is evaporated milk boiled to an almost solid cream. GULAB JAMAN (fried milk balls) are prepared from boiled milk blended with cream of wheat then formed into balls and deep-fried and finished with a plunge into hot syrup.[4] Many desserts are also made from fresh curds, similar to cottage cheese.

Fruits and Vegetables

Fruits and vegetables are eaten in season only sparingly; more is consumed in the form of pickles, condiments, and chutneys. The latter may be made from any fruits including tomatoes, mangoes, dates, lemons, melons, citrus fruits, coconuts and flavoured with tamarinds, ginger, mint. These are preserved with both sugar and spices. ACHAR, or pickles, are made by all women in a household when seasonal vegetables are in their prime. Cleaned and cut vegetables are prepared in combinations that may be cherished family recipes and, together with distinct seasonings, are preserved in brine or one of several types of oils. Condiments may include fresh or dried fruits or vegetables prepared sometimes just before the meal as taste-tingling and complementary side dishes to the meal.

General vegetable consumption is low,[3] but greens of all kinds are used whenever they may be found: mustard greens, fenugreek greens, spinach, radish greens, gram and chickpea greens. A Punjabi favourite is creamed mustard greens served with cornbread and buttermilk to drink.[5] When fresh greens are not available, pulses may be soaked and sprouted; they are often eaten in their fresh form.[3] In many areas it is also common to preserve vegetables by cleaning and slicing then drying in the sun. Aside from greens, onions and potatoes are frequently used. Other vegetables (but not widely used) may include cauliflower, okra, eggplant, many types of mushrooms, lotus stems, water chestnuts, tomatoes, radishes, cucumbers.

Fruits also include many of those available in America: varieties of apples, pears, cherries, berries, melons, plus the great variety of tropical fruits including CHEEKOOS (like brown persimmons) and KULU PEARS.

Meats and Alternates

To most East Indians, it is the "alternates" that are vital. The Brahmins (upper-caste Hindus) are said never to touch meat, eggs or fish, but examples do exist where the traditions are sometimes stretched. Buddhists and Jains are strongly against killing; a few Jains go so far as to wear masks lest they inhale any minute insects. Muslims do not use pork. Most Indians, however, are so poor that they cannot afford meat of any kind; they are vegetarians by need not choice. In fact, the term vegetarian is misleading since the bulk of their diet is not vegetables but rather cereal grains, pulses, and dairy products.

It is said that "when an Indian sits down to eat meat, it is nearly always goat meat."[5] But whether it is goat, lamb, buffalo meat, or chicken, the likelihood is that the meat will be finely chopped or ground or well-marinated before cooking because most available meats are lean and tough. A great favourite is any kind of meat cooked on the bone so that diners may eat with fingers and enjoy sucking out marrow and nibbling tid-bits.[5] Many ground meat dishes are popular: KOFTAS (of Persian influence), which are many sizes and types of meatballs served with special sauces; KHEEMA is a spiced ground meat sauce served with rice or CHAPATIS, DAL, or sometimes vegetables. Other meats may be prepared as barbecues (TANDOORI), or curried.

Chickens are usually bought in the cities, ready for use, fresh, or frozen. In rural areas they will be purchased still live from markets or poultry men hawking their wares from door to door. Most chickens are skinned before use in cookery, then cut up, leaving the bones for nibbling. Generally chickens are considered a luxury food and reserved for special occasions.

Fish and seafood are used mostly in the coastal areas, where caught, and in cities where refrigeration is available. Fish production and intake are low.[3] Eggs are in short supply and even when available, often fall under so many religious taboos that they are not used. Nuts of all kinds are widely used and served toasted and salted as ever-present nibbles or appetizers and are often crushed or ground to form part of sauces, confections, desserts.

Of great importance are pulses (legumes), called by the general name of DAL in most of India. (DAL also refers to a sauce of cooked pulses.) Varieties and uses are many. There are several varieties of lentils, peas (called GRAM): BENGAL GRAM, BLACK GRAM, GREEN GRAM, RED GRAM. Beans are of many varieties too, including soybeans. DAL is eaten minimally at one meal each day and everyone eats some form of DAL; cooking methods and seasonings vary by locale.[5]

DAL is usually thick except in the South where it is traditionally served soupy-thin. Cooked DAL is served in tiny bowls or poured over rice, then seasonings that have been precooked in oil are poured over. In Punjab, whole unhulled DALS are cooked slowly in the TANDOOR and often a spicy dish of chick peas served with puffy deep-fried bread accompanies a meal and is called CHANA BATURA. In Delhi the DAL may be cooked as hulled and split MOONG DAL, spiced with cumin and browned onions and given a tangy splash of lime juice. In Bombay, a hot, sweet and sour TOOVAR DAL is prepared by adding JAGGERY (raw sugar) and tamarind paste to the cooked DAL. The oil and spice mixture used to finish the DAL may be called: TARKA, BAGHAR, or CHHOWNK.[5]

Beans and chick peas and other pulses may also be marinated in peppery mixtures of tamarind and hot spices and nibbled as snacks.[7] Cooked mashed DAL figures prominently in many fried snacks. Also there are flours made from legumes and these are used in making desserts, breads, noodles and snacks. Legumes may be also served as CURRIES in small side dishes and often sold by street vendors in may forms as quick snacks, such as BEELPURI: a mixture of lentils and puffed rice well-seasoned and served with wheat-flour chips.[4]

Breads and Cereals
In the South and the East rice is the staple grain. In the North and the West, many varieties of breads are made from their staple of wheat. In wealthier homes, both rice and wheat may be used while the poorest may eat only barley or millet.[3] Valuable nutrients are lost when rice is well-washed before using, cooked in large amounts of water and the water is drained off. In some areas, though, the drained rice water is saved and used for breakfast.[3]

BASMATI or BASUMATI rice is considered the best of long-grain rice, is usually well-aged and comparatively expensive. But like pulses, rice too comes in many varieties in India and each to be used in special ways. It may be polished or unpolished, brown or parboiled; it may be long, short or round grain; may be freshly harvested green rice or rice that has been aged for several years in clay-walled store rooms.[4,6] There is also pressed rice, puffed rice, rice flakes, beaten rice, and rice flour. Rice flour blended with varying amounts of ground lentils, then cooked flat like little pancakes, or baked, could form almost endless varieties of hot little breads popular in the South for breakfast, following coffee and fruit.[4]

Rice is commonly cooked into fluffy mounds and served garnished with DAL and seasonings or with curried accompaniments or may be made into rice balls, rice gruel, or sweet rice desserts. The latter are prepared from sticky or glutinous rice. Two popular rice preparations are pillau or pilaf, in which meats, fish and/or vegetables with seasonings are cooked together with the rice. BIRYANIS are similar, but more ornate and garnished with nuts, flowers, raisins, VARKA (silver leaf). Many sweet dishes may be made with rice or rice flour in the form of puddings or sweet confections. Saffron, coconut milk, and milk are most commonly added to rice for flavour.

At Hindu weddings rice is thrown into a fire to symbolize fertility. One explanation has it that rice is not fertile until transplanted to another field. A girl therefore becomes fertile when transplanted to her husband's home.[5]

Breads are mostly made from wheat flour and cooked unleavened. But they can also be made from chick pea flour, maize, millet or barley flour, bean, rice or lentil flour, and from white or various types of whole wheat flour. Most breads are deep-fried or griddle-cooked as ovens are usually improvised by heaping a covered pan with hot coals. CHAPATIS are made with only whole wheat flour and water then rolled into flat rounds – which puff when cooked on a griddle – and then held over a flame with tongs. PURIS or POORIS are the same as CHAPATIS, only they are puffed by deep-frying. PARATHAS are similar to pancakes. Two richer breads are BHATURA (favourite of the punjabis), a deep-fried bread made with white flour, yoghurt, baking powder and egg, and NAAN, a yeast and baking powder-leavened rich white bread baked in huge flat ovals by slapping quickly on the sides of the TANDOOR or under a broiler.[5] ROTI is the general name given to all Indian breads.

Fats

Average intake of fats is very low; butter and GHEE (clarified butter) is mostly confined to the middle and upper class. Mustard oil is popular in the northeast, peanut or groundnut oil is used where cultivated, while coconut oil is restricted mainly to the west coast.[3] Northern India uses GHEE where it can be afforded, but peanut oil and GINGILLI OIL (sesame seed oil) is widely used. Seasonings are always first well-cooked in fat or oil before other ingredients are added. Oils are used for deep-frying, a popular method of cookery where fuel and space is limited. Oils are also used in the preparation of ACHAR, various types of pickles and condiments.

Sweets

East Indian sweets may vary greatly in composition but they all have one thing in common: they are very sweet. Sweet desserts may be made from cooked thickened milk, from a rice base with added raisins and nuts, from very thin Indian vermicelli cooked with milk and flavoured with rose water, almonds and JAGGERY (unrefined palm sugar). Sweets may also be made from doughs prepared with legume or rice or wheat flours – even cooked mashed vegetables, such as eggplants, potatoes, sago palm – all deep-fried in different shapes then plopped into hot spicy syrups to give them a fragrant and sticky glaze. Many of these sweet treats are purchased from street vendors rather than being made in the homes.

There is also a definite taste for spiced, salted, and even sour snacks. These may include green or unripened fruits dipped into spicy sauces or simply salted and then nibbled. Crisp, thin flakes or chips can be made from various fruits and vegetables then salted and eaten as snacks. Of course salted roasted nuts are high on the list of nibbles too.

Coffee and tea are always taken well-sweetened, and bottled sweet beverages are also being used.

Most meals are ended with a light dessert of fruits, usually peeled or cut into pieces by the women of the family, and passed first to the children.[5] Really sweet confections and desserts are saved either for tea time, for between meal snacks, or for special or festive occasions.

Seasonings

It is the unique use and preparation of freshly ground seasonings that set the East Indian cuisine apart. In fact, it is the *vasana*, or aroma, of food that is of prime importance to the Indian.[7] This is not to say, however, that appearance and flavour do not also play an important part. Each household has its special treasured recipes of exactly what type and amount of spices or herbs may be used in preparing each dish. The mixture of freshly ground seasonings is called MASALA. The Indian palate carefully distinguishes between a full range of tangy, sour, piquant, peppery, hot, briny flavours, as well as sweets.

The much-misused all-encompassing term "curry" actually refers to a "highly seasoned stew with plenty of sauce."[4] The word "curry" is said to have originated from the Tamil word *kari* meaning simply meat or food – but that which is prepared in a manner to appeal to all of man's senses.[6] Bottles of seasoning sold in the western world as "curry powder" consist of a blend of spices and herbs and vary greatly both in their flavour and quality. In India the term "curry" refers to a meal based on rice with a spiced and sauced meat or fish dish surrounded by several smaller bowls of accompaniments such as chopped vegetables, nuts, chutneys and pickles, toasted chips or flakes of fruits or vegetables – all to be eaten in the order desired and usually with a spoon and a fork.

Sometimes fresh or green spices may be ground with liquid such as water, coconut milk, etc., in which case they are called "wet MASALAS." Wet MASALAS blend smoothly into sauces, but one rule should be noted: all seasonings are always well-cooked, whether in fat or oil or liquid, before being added to a dish.

The list of spices used is almost endless: cardamom, cloves, cinnamon, mace, nutmeg, saffron, turmeric, many types of peppers and chilis, fennel, dill, cumin seed, mustard, bay leaf, aniseed, coriander seeds, dried garlic, ginger. The MASALA may be hot, spicy, burning, tangy, mellow, rich, light, but never on any account should it "catch the throat!" Many arguments can begin and probably never end on the subject of which spice or herb, how much, and whether fresh or dried should be used for what dish.

Beverages

Tea is the favoured hot drink in the North, coffee in the South; both are served well-sweetened, and usually with boiled milk. Yoghurt and buttermilk are much enjoyed as cooling beverages as well and are often served diluted and sometimes lightly salted or sweetened. LASSI is the name given to salted or sweetened diluted yoghurt. Hot tea and coffee are commonly served as a breakfast beverage but may also be taken at other times of the day between meals. They are rarely served at the end of meals. Some wines are made in India but are not highly regarded or served often. There is also Indian beer, but of lesser importane as a beverage. Frequently after a large feast a glass of water may be served and this is taken with the left hand.[8] Some fruit drinks, called SHURBUT, make a cool refreshment. These are made from fruit juices or crushed fruit pulps and iced.

Regional Specialties

There are many common characteristics shared by East Indians and Pakistanis, both in their food customs and in their basic diets. For example, there is a strong preference (whether for religious, regional or economic reasons) for cereal foods, legumes, and milk products, with little meat, fish, fruits, or vegetables actually being consumed by the majority of people. Yet there are some interesting regional preferences and differences that are worth noting. Included in this section are the general customs and food specialties of East, West, South, and Northern India, and Pakistan as well as Sri Lanka (formerly Ceylon). The cuisines of all these areas, however, may be called East Indian.

East India

This area includes the northern part of the eastern coastal provinces of India, centring around Calcutta and the Bengal province. Here par-boiled rice is the staple food. Fish is important because the area is really a maritime state and many types of fish are used, as well as fish meal.[3] Plantains, potatoes, tubers, beans and water lily roots are eaten more here than anywhere else. Thinner and sweeter curries, usually including fish and vegetables, are served for one meal of the day. In general foods and food preparation are simpler than, say, the central northern region.[8] The favourite bread is called LOOCHI (elsewhere known as PURI), and is prepared from white or whole wheat flour, fried until puffed. Mustard seed oil and GINGILLI (sesame seed oil) are used predominantly. Milk sweets include SANDESH, RASGULLA, GULAB JAMUN: well-boiled milk sweetened and served as thickened puddings. DUM ALOO is a dessert made from potatoes with almonds, raisins, and yoghurt.[8] One typical meal may be LOOCHI, DUM ALOO, and fried eggplant, another may be a fish and vegetable curry with rice and DAL and fruit in season.[8]

West India

This is the area on the northerly part of the west coast of India which includes the provinces of Gujarat and Maharashtra, with Bombay the principal city. The vegetarian peoples here are the Gujaratis and the Maharashtrians, while the Parsee (see Special Occasions) and the Goans (from Goa, under Portuguese influence) are non-vegetarians. Rice is favoured especially in the coastal areas.[3] Both the Gujaratis and the Maharashtrians serve a sweet dish as a first course with a vegetable dish and PURI. However, the Gujaratis like to eat wheat dishes first and rice dishes last, while the Maharashtrians reverse this order.[8] The Parsee specialty is PANEER, like firm cottage cheese, served first and last at every wedding feast, and prepared frequently in every home.[9] The Parsees also like DHAN SAK, which is plain fried rice, and it is served with any combination of meats or fish, vegetable or DAL dishes. BOMBAY DUCK, taken as a salty, fishy-tasting condiment, is enjoyed frequently by the Parsees: it is a small fish that may be served fresh either curried or fried.[8]

The Goans have their food preferences too. Accompanying their rice they enjoy finely chopped fresh vegetables dressed with salt and lime juice.[8] FOOGATHS is the general name given to many mild mixtures of coconut and vegetables, while VINDALOO is a vinegar-marinated meat and spice dish.[8]

Throughout the West India area, NEERI, a drink made from coconut palm, is sold everywhere. Breads called BEL PURI and KHASTA KACHURI are sold by vendors everywhere for snacking. Milk sweets are also a favourite here, and are called JALEBIS; BARFI, a type of fudge; DOODH PAK, a type of milk rice pudding; and SHRIKHAND, a semi-solid sweetened yoghurt.[8]

South India

The people of the South are considered to be great rice eaters, who prefer their foods cooked simply. However, their MASALAS (curries) are much hotter than in other areas. Some say that where the standard of living is the lowest there is an increase in the intake of sharp flavoured spices and condiments[3] as though the increased depth of flavours somehow helps one to overcome the oppressive heat of the tropical weather and the monotony of simple meals. GINIGILLI OIL, or sesame seed oil, is predominantly used, and most foods are thinned with coconut milk. SAMBAR is the general name given to all vegetable and legume or pulse dishes. PACHADI is a cooling "salad" made of chopped fresh vegetables or fruits blended with yoghurt – similar to a RAITA. RASAM is a clear spicy broth much enjoyed here but unusual since soups and broths are not generally a part of the East Indian cuisine.[5] Desserts are commonly made from a base of rice, vermicelli or pulses that have usually been boiled in milk then sweetened well with sugar or molasses and served at the end of most meals. The southerners are great coffee drinkers and hot well-sweetened coffee served with fruit begins most days. They are also fond of snacking and enjoy IDLI, fermented and steamed mounds of pulses and rice, or MASALA DOSA, crisp-fried potato-filled pastries served with sweet or sour chutneys.[8]

The poorest of the area eat millet, called RAJI, or SHOLAM, which is small millet ground into flour then boiled or steamed in little balls. Wheat for breads is available only in wealthier homes.[3] In the area of Cochin, in Kerala province, foods are very plain and rice and coffee prevail. Rice and fish and vegetables and seafoods make up the dietary and the use of much coconut and coconut milk make their foods milder than in most other areas of the South. Tropical fruits are freely available here and form an important part of the diet: bananas, pineapple, papaya, custard apples, mangoes.[8]

Northern India

This is the area of India most influenced by the cuisines of the conquerors, for Delhi seemed historically like a magnet: here came the Greeks, under Alexander the Great, the Kushan Kings, the Muslims, the great Mogul Empire adding Bengal and Kashmir to the domain, then the Persian kings. From the courts and palaces came the cuisines that were to influence the cookery of all of India. The Delhi cuisine is said to be considered the epitome of India's cuisine.[5] The people of the area admired and happily adopted dishes from the Persian cuisine: pilafs, imported fruits such as melons, pomegranates, figs, plums, dates and nuts. They also traditionally used ice from the Himalayas to cool their drinks and prepare chilled dishes. This area was ideal for the creation of a great cuisine because of its fertility and climate which are most conducive to crops and orchards.

For modern-day Delhi residents, conveniences of electric appliances and efficient kitchen facilities as well as a wide variety of prepared food mixes make the preparation of traditional meals a simple matter.

Of Punjabi origin is the TANDOOR: the clay oven partially submerged in the ground and used for barbecuing skewered meats and baking flat oval breads by slapping them against the hot sides.[4,5] The brick and plaster charcoal stove called CHULA is mostly used. In some areas the CHULA is made from smoothed mud.

Here is the great wheat and tea area of India. However, rice dishes, meats and fish are used as are fruits and vegetables, all as lavishly as income permits. Cereals and pulses take their place nonetheless as an important part of all meals. Here the fabulous BIRYANI and rich PULLAO or PILAFS are served, and there are a great many wheat breads, each with similar ingredients yet prepared differently so they add great variety to the menu: CHAPATIS, PULKAS, PARATHAS, and NAN. KORMA is a thick, rich curry, well-browned with added poppy seeds and coconut flavouring, of meat that has first been tenderized by a yoghurt marination.[8]

Pakistan

The areas of Pakistan are more than 80 per cent of Muslim population. Here, the rules of Islam prevail and when available, meat is the main part of the meal. Pakistanis have many beef, lamb, and chicken dishes, but do not eat pork. The KABABS and KOFTAHS, and even the BIRYANIS, seem to have more of a hint of the Arab lands than of India, although the taste for rice and for seasonings is definitely Indian. Rice and wheat are the main crops and of the pulses, chick peas are the most popular. Small quantities of fruits and vegetables are available, mostly in West Pakistan: both fruits and vegetables represent temperate and tropical produce.

There are some differences between East and West. Bangladesh, (formerly East Pakistan) is densely crowded, has abundant water, and is in constant threat of floods while rice and tea are the principal crops. People of Bangladesh speak Bengali.[3] Pakistan includes a much larger area which is sparsely populated and lacks water to the point where droughts are common. Wheat is the main crop in the West, but corn, rape, mustard, sugar cane, barley and chick peas are also produced. Pakistanis speak Urdu.[3] Hydrogenated vegetable oils are used in both areas, principally mustard and rape seed oil. In both areas, although meats are much favoured, production of meat and poultry is sparse: the animals again compete with man for the land, meat is lean and chickens yield few eggs.[3] Sadly, the Pakistani and Bangladesh peoples' diets are considered among the poorest in the world, being low in calories and low in nutrients.[3]

Breads, cooking of rice, and milk and milk products are similar in name and preparation to those in most of India. HALWAH may be sweet wheat or carrot puddings, called HALWAHGAJAR. Pakistanis enjoy their foods highly spiced[3] and often their pilaus or BIRYANIS are flecked with beans or split peas (KISHRIS) or with vegetables and lentils, called BHA-JIAS. Sometimes in West Pakistan wheat flour is used to prepare lamb and potato-filled pastries, resulting in a SAMOSA.[3]

Sri Lanka (Ceylon)

In the hot, humid equatorial island country, two main groups struggle: the Tamils, of southern Indian descent, and the Buddhist Sinhalese. Both in language and religion (the Tamils are Hindus) the groups differ. Curries, onions, red chilis, and fish dominate the dietary, together with rice and wheat flour. Torrid curries with rice or "stringhoppers," fried noodle patties, are favourites.[10] The third main group of the island are the Muslims. Dietary habits differ mainly according to religious custom: the Buddhist Sinhalese do not eat meat, although there are some exceptions; the Muslims have the widest range of foods eschewing pork but permitting beef and have no strong objection to milk; while the Hindu Tamils refrain from eating any flesh, but drink milk whenever possible.[3]

A meal pattern of four meals a day is commonly followed by all. A morning meal, prepared from rice or rice flour or occasionally wheat breads, a noon meal consisting mainly of rice with grated coconut as the curry base, with MELLUM, a well-spiced preparation of shredded vegetable leaves cooked with grated coconut as the usual accompaniment. Number of dishes varies according to the economic standard. Sometimes accompanying the breakfast cereal food is a SAMBAL made of various spices with onions and chilis and usually grated coconut – and if income permits a curry may also be part of breakfast. The end of each meal is sweetened tea. A late afternoon small meal will consist of sweetmeats and sweetened tea, while the evening meal will be similar to either breakfast or the noon meal.

Cereals and spices form the main part of the diet, and there is a general lack of fruits and vegetables.[3]

Meal Patterns and Eating Customs

The majority of East Indians have two main meals a day. The morning meal is usually based on the regional preference of rice or wheat and this is accompanied by the regional preference of either tea or coffee. Region, however, plays no part in what is added to the beverage: all enjoy their tea or coffee well-sweetened and preferably served with boiled milk. Sometimes SAMBALS (sauces) of spices may accompany the rice breakfast and either fruit or ACHAR (pickles) may also be a part of the meal. In most areas the evening meal is based on rice plus DAL plus vegetables, then, according to religion, means, and area, a meat or fish curry and a sweet milk dessert may complete the meal. The time between morning and evening meal is often sated with the many foods hawked by vendors in almost every part of the country: beverages, milk sweets, fresh fruits, or snack foods made from a cereal or pulse base served with spiced sauces.

In most of India, it is the custom to sit on the floor or the ground and the area used as the table is covered with carpets which in turn are spread with cloths. In the South, it may simply be a cool area and smoothed ground may be the table. In hotels and in upper-class homes, meals may be taken on large tables or on short-legged individual tables. Most commonly each diner is served a THALI (tray) of metal, upon which rests many small ornate metal bowls, each containing a different sauce, dish, or condiment. It is up to the diner to mix the foods and eat them in whatever order may prove pleasing. In the South, banana leaves may substitute for the THALI and portions of foods may be placed directly on the diner's leaf or placed in small earthenware bowls that are discarded after the meal.

But North or South, hands are always washed before and after eating, and foods are always prepared and eaten only with the use of the right hand. If any cutlery is ever used it will be a spoon or a fork, knives never make an appearance except in the kitchen to prepare the foods. Northerners pride themselves on their ability to eat deftly with only the fingertips of the right hand, while southerners eat their foods with great relish and use their right hand right up to the wrist if need be.[5]

In the entire domain of East Indian cookery, there is one further custom that is greatly enjoyed by all. This is the nibbling of fragrant, piquant PAAN after a meal. The PAAN is a heart-shaped leaf which is wrapped around special spices and usually served to guests as they are departing, or else purchased on the street from vendors. It is said to freshen the breath and aid digestion. Many homes have an ornate box called a *paandaan*, especially made for storing PAAN, or for keeping a loose mix of after-dinner spices to be nibbled.[5,4]

Religion and Special Occasions
Probably in no other country in the world do many diverse religions play such a prominent part in the daily lives of so many people as they do in the life of the East Indian.

It is important to bear in mind that religious restrictions alone seldom are responsible for malnutrition. According to Dr. Rajammal Devadas, principal of Sri Avinashilingam Home Science College for Women in Coimbatore, India, "People used to think cultural factors affected better nutrition, but the absence of nutritional education and poverty are the deciding factors. If these are remedied, people will eat better."[11]

While there is a small minority group of Christians in India, the majority populations may be represented by Hinduism, Buddhism, Muslim, Parsis, and Sikh religious disciplines. While general principles of each can be outlined, it must be born clearly in mind that there are many adaptations and variations within each group as to beliefs and practices, particularly where food is concerned. Sometimes it is the family tradition that is followed, sometimes the local traditions, and frequently availability and necessity dictate dietary patterns.

Hinduism

Hinduism is the religious denomination of 80 per cent of the Indian population and has roots reaching back to the Indus Valley civilization which flourished some 3,000 years before Christ. There is a mixture and a borrowing of many customs and beliefs and the Hindus themselves represent diverse elements from many ethnic sources. Although in modern times efforts have been made to abolish several tenets of the ancient religion, such as *purdah*, the separation and seclusion of women; *suttee*, the mournful self-cremation of a widow on the funeral pyre of her husband; and the caste system, remnants of each still remain in some areas.[2]

The chief features of the newer Hinduism are the movement towards social purpose and a type of puritanism.[12] Many other ancient traditions are slowly being dissolved either by newer tradition, or in some cases by India's newer legislation: child marriage, animal sacrifices, and the concept of untouchability. The caste system developed from the belief that an individual was born into a certain class station and was destined to remain in it for all his life.[13] There are four main classifications: the Brahmins, representing the upper or priestly class; the Kshatriyas, representing the warrior class; the Vaisyas, representing the traders and agriculturalists, and finally the Sudras, or menial classes, who were considered destined to serve the other three castes who together were called the Aryans.[2]

Hinduism embraces an enormous pantheon of gods and lesser gods in three main groups, called *vaishnava, saiva,* and *sakta*. Many seemingly contrasting principles and beliefs can often be held by one individual. This becomes even more complex when it is understood that the many gods can also be worshipped in any of their incarnations (of which there are eight). In addition, there are also many local divinities and demigods, and some of the incarnations may also have sons. Animals as well as plants may be considered sacred, for example the cow, one of Hinduism's best-known deities which is considered holy as a representative of "Mother Earth herself."[12] Even parents and teachers are considered as gods – as is the husband by his wife.[12] Further, there are two main writings: the *Vedas* and the *Puranas*, as well as six different schools of philosophy emphasizing different means for the individual to achieve the main spiritual goal of rising above the "cycle of transmigration and achieve union or close contact with the ultimate Being." Tradition (*aryan dharma*) punctuates the life of the Hindu with frequent ritual acts and disciplines. Subordinate to *moksha* (the winning of salvation), are the three aims of religious merit, prosperity and pleasure – the Hindu's general ethics. Strict vegetarianism is held by the upper classes, and this includes abstention from beef, in fact all flesh or that which may have the seed of life, such as eggs. However, these rules vary with some considering water-buffalo steaks appropriate to eat, and fish as the "fruit of the sea."[5]

The vast complexities of the ancient Hindu faith can be further appreciated by any attempt to catalogue the number of festivities and special occasions celebrated. Unlike the Muslims or Christians or Jews, there are no singular festivals celebrated universally. Instead, there are regional festivals, local temple feasts and traditional family occasions. However, these are not always celebrated annually, often there is a space of several years between the celebrations and many may be based on differing lunar calendars with differing intercalations. Eight popularly celebrated occasions will be considered here.

DIVALI (OR DIWALI)
Perhaps the almost universal Hindu festival, it is a time of renewal, of bright lights, of new clothes and painting of homes, games of chance, of fireworks and the distribution of sweetmeats to all. A modern addition is the sending of cards wishing: "A Happy Divali and a Prosperous New Year."[2]

DUSSARA
A festival celebrated differently in different areas. This can be more readily understood when it is realized that this is the ten-day festival worshipping Devi, Shiva's wife, who is widely considered to be all things to all men. Generally it is considered a festival celebrated with pomp and pageantry.[2]

HOLI
A springtime festival having elements of primitive fertile orgies, and sometimes pranks are played similar to those on April Fool's Day. The festival is presided over by Kama and Krishna, the deities of pleasure. There are many lively dances and singing and the scattering of colour dyes in powder form so everyone and everything is bright and colourful.

SHIVARATRI
A solemn all-night vigil with hymns and the reading of sacred texts. It is believed to bring material prosperity and life after death for those who keep this festival sacred.

JANMASHTAMI or GOKUL ASHTAMI
The birthday of Krishna, believed to be the eighth incarnation of Vishnu. This is celebrated with pyramids of young men reaching high to break hanging curd pots. This unusual celebration practice is based on the legend that the child Krishna was particularly fond of milk products and used to steal, with the help of friends, butter and curds, hung high in earthen pots in the kitchen to be out of reach of children.

GANESHA CHATURTHI
Celebrated as the birthday of the jovial elephant-headed Ganesha, whose
well-rounded pot belly symbolizes a god of plenty and appetite. Offerings
of milk, fruits, and puddings are presented. The centre of these festivities
is Bombay where three-day processions crowd the roads.

RAKHI PURNIMA
Mainly a festive occasion for upper castes, i.e. the Brahmins, who
ceremoniously discard old sacred clothing and put on new ones. The
coconut plays a special symbolic role for it is believed to represent the
three-eyed Shiva. It is therefore considered auspicious to break a coconut
at a shrine or whenever one is embarking on a new enterprise. An amulet
called *rhaki* is tied on men's wrists by women to signify that from that
point on their relationship will be only brotherly.[2]

RAMA NAVAMI
The seventh incarnation of Vishnu, Rama is one of the most beloved of
deities and this is the celebration of his birth. This is one of the most important festivities and it is celebrated by all castes and sects. Because he
was believed to have been born at noon, a coconut is placed in a cradle
and a priest announces the birth of Rama to the rhythmic incantations of
the name Rama. Afterwards, dancing and stage shows and effigy burning
of evil spirits take place.

Buddhism
Many legends surround the birth and life of Siddhartha Guatama, the
Buddha and founder of Buddhism some 500 years before Christ. He de-
nounced animal sacrifices and the caste system and pronounced his
philosophy in the form of four "Sublime Verities":

1. that sorrow is inherent in life
2. that sorrow has a cause
3. that removal of sorrow leads to cessation of sorrow
4. that removal of sorrow can be affected by RIGHT LIVING.

"RIGHT LIVING was all that the Buddha wanted of his followers."[2] His
teachings were especially appealing at a time when it was considered that
only royalty or the upper castes had an opportunity to attain *nirvana*, and
his teachings were easily adopted but were confined to India during the
Buddha's lifetime and for about 300 years afterward, then gradually
became a world religion largely due to the missionary zeal of Emperor
Asoka who spread it to China and Japan and most of Southeast Asia.
However, in India itself, Jainism and a newer version of Hinduism strug-
gled for supremacy over Buddhism. This was followed by the Muslim invasion.[2] Most Buddhists refrain from eating meat because of their belief
in the sanctity of all living things.

The most radical sect of Buddhism is Zen Buddhism, described as ". . . what I do and my mind and my soul are one . . . anything that absorbs one fully is in effect – ZEN."[14] Severe dietary restrictions believed to help one on the way to achieving *satori* (enlightenment) are roundly criticized by food professionals because the special dietary system claims that there is "no disease that cannot be cured by 'proper' therapy which consists of natural food, no medicine, no surgery, no inactivity."[15] The special dietary regime recommended begins at the lowest level with an intake of 10 per cent cereals and gradually reaches the "highest level" of 100 per cent cereals with the documented result of emaciation, starvation, and death.[15]

Muslim

The Islamic faith has much in common with both Judaism and Christianity and indeed recognizes all the sages of both the Old and New testament. Muslims make up approximately 80 per cent of the population of Pakistan. While Sunday is the holy day for Christians and Saturday for the Jews, the Muslims hold Friday as sacred. It is obligatory that they abstain from work on this day and say the main prayer in the mosque.

All Muslim celebrations are based on a purely lunar calendar with no intercalations, so that the named months do not necessarily fall in the same seasons. For example Ramadan or Ramzan Id may occur in winter or summer. Indian Muslims celebrate similarly to others but add some local festivals such as death anniversaries of saints.[2]

Generally, Muslims abstain from the eating of pork and any flesh that has not been ritually slaughtered. Although alcohol is also a part of the abstentions, many make concessions.

UD-UL-AZHA or BAR ID
Enjoined in the holy writings of the Koran, this is the festival commemorating Abraham's willingness to sacrifice his son as a sign of obedience to God's command. (In the Muslim version of the account it is Ishmael – believed to be the progenitor of all Muslims – not Isaac who is the object of sacrifice.) This day is celebrated with the sacrificing of animals by the wealthy to give meat to the poor. Special benedictions are repeated while killing the animal as the meat of an animal not killed according to sacred ritual is not considered fit for human consumption.[2] Generally, it is a day when new clothes are donned and there is widespread feasting.

RAMZAN ID or RAMADAN
Celebrated by abstention from food, drink, and smoking, from the hours of sun-up to sun down for the whole of this month is one of the important pillars of Muslim faith. Those who are ill may make up the fast days at another time.[12] Light meals are taken before dawn and after sunset, while communal prayers are often accompanied by the gift of a set amount of

alms in the form of grains or fruits. It is believed that those who do not keep these traditions will remain after death suspended between heaven and hell.[2,16]

Parsee

The Parsee are a group of people who came to the Bombay region of India when the Arabs conquered Persia and imposed the faith of Islam on all. In order to preserve their beliefs and customs, these people of ancient Persia, members of the faith of Zoroaster or Zarathustra fled. From the early 600s C.E. they made their home in the province of Gujarat, spoke Gujarati, and absorbed many of the manners and customs of the Hindus around them. However, they retained certain characteristics of their own despite an adoption too of many western ideas from the British. They still believe in a supreme deity called Ahura Mazda and a lesser evil power called Ahriman and they consider that the universe is a battleground of continuous warfare between Ahura and Ahriman (good and evil). They believe also that the path of heaven is over an "accountant's bridge," where each person's good and evil deeds are said to be balanced and the decision made on his entry to heaven or hell. Most Parsee disputes centre around the dates of festivals and these disputes have led to three sect divisions, each with their own calendar.[20] Most festivals are marked by parades and pilgrimages and charity to others.

Sikh

This is the newest and most liberal of Indian religious groups and was founded by Guru Nanak in 1469 after the Muslims had established their power in North India. This was a period of some moderating influences: many Hindus were personally troubled by their polytheism and idolatry and yet many Muslims found their ideas being "tamed" by Hindu influences.[2] These changing ideals found expression in two cults that came into being about this same time: the Hindu Bhakti cult and the Muslim Sufi Cult. Both actually developed many mystical ties in common by referring to a loving God-man relationship and it is felt that the Bhakti Cult influenced Nanak in founding his religion.[2] Further, these new cults found leadership from the common people not the intellectuals, and the principles they propounded were general enough that they found sympathy with both Hindus and Muslims.

Nanak's followers were known as Sikhs, from the sanskrit Sishya (disciple) while Nanak himself was known as the teacher or Guru. The concept of the Guru developed until he was not only the acknowledged teacher but also the head and leader of the community. Gobind Singh, the tenth Guru, is credited with building the Sikhs into a powerful community and instituting the Granth (literally, the book) in place of the series of Gurus.[2]

Because Gobind Singh's father, the ninth Guru, had been slain by Moghuls, Gobind swore vengeance and developed the militant aspect of the religious order. It was he who developed the institution of the five Ks that are still a part of the Sikh community:

kes – unshorn hair
kirpan – sword
kacha – short pants
kankan – steel bangle
kangha – the comb

Together with the rejection of the caste system, the advocacy of monotheism, and the rejection of idols for worship, most Sikhs have also added the suffix of Singh ("lion") to their personal names to further designate their pride and beliefs.[2,17] In general, their faith is a flexible one with none of the Hindu's elaborate taboos. Sikhs observe many Hindu festivals as well as their own.

BAISAKH or VAISAKH

The first day of the month of Baisakh (April-May) is most important for Sikhs and is celebrated as the day that Guru Gobind founded the Khalsa. The Khalsa is an "elect" group of five men. The formation of this group is based on the story that the Guru wanted to create a special council and asked for the lives of five men only. It is said that 80,000 men came to offer their lives. Of these, five were selected and after each selection, the Guru entered into a tent with the man and came out with a sword dripping with blood. At the end the whole ceremony was revealed to be merely a test, for the five brave men were alive and five goats had been sacrificed. The five great men came to be known as the *Panch Pyare*, ("beloved five") and these five are represented for their devotion and bravery in all important Sikh festivals.[2]

This festive occasion is marked with processionals and religious music, usually led by five leaders with drawn swords in memory of the *Panch Pyare* of the Guru Gobind Singh. Following this everyone joins in feasting and dancing.

Gurpurab represents the many festive days marking the births of all the Gurus which are observed by all Sikhs as holy days.

SEVENTEEN

Egyptian

Sphinx, pyramids, Pharaohs, and slaves all evoke vividly the images of ancient Egypt. But so should a sip of cool frothy beer or a bite of warm crusty bread, because both are credited to the ancient inventive genius of Egyptians: an unnamed brewer and an equally obscure baker.[1]

Perhaps it is from the land of Egypt that the expression "the sands of time" originated. It would be entirely appropriate. The study of Egyptology and the science of archaeology have discovered keys to the ancient civilization under layers of dry sand. It is one thing to read about the histories of ancient peoples, it is another to view actual implements, original writings, artifacts, clothing, and even dried foods that were part of everyday life several thousand years ago. Credit must be given the exceptionally dry climate of Upper Egypt (Southern) and the ease with which excavations may be made in sand.[2]

Said to be the direct living descendants of the ancient Egyptians are a group of present-day Egyptian Christians known as Copts. They clung to their faith even though in the 600s A.D. almost all Egyptians embraced Islam under the powerful influence of the Ayyubids, who established Egypt as the political and cultural centre of the Islamic world.[2] Although the overwhelming population of Egypt is Arabic, the other groups including the Bedouins, Turks, Greeks, Syrians, French, Italians, and British remain in Egypt almost as historical footprints of past conquests and dominations.

Those foreign dominations have for the most part been subtly blended into the general Egyptian culture but some threads may be noted in the area of gastronomy. Excavations have yielded foods and writings about the foods that graced ancient Egyptian tables: leeks, onions, and okra; the large flat round yeast breads that are a staple of the Middle East even today; cakes rich with honey and dates; FOOL or FUL – the slow-simmered beans; and TAMIYA, the seasoned mashed bean patties, deep-fried. Even though thousands of years old each is a part of Egyptian cuisine today.

The processed BURGHUL, used in many dishes, is likely of Syrian origin, but Greek and Turkish influence is evident in: MEUSHTI, stuffed vegetables; SHOURBA, egg yolks laced with lemon juice and whisked into clear soup stock; and the many varieties of honey-drenched and nut-studded pastries made with phyllo dough. A popular classic Bedouin dish of lamb and rice, called MANSAT, is also much enjoyed on Egyptian tables. It is served over layers of carefully-baked whole wheat sheets called SHRAK. COUSCOUS is a Moroccan staple used in Egypt more as a dessert than a main course dish.

History credits both the Arab civilization and the spread of Islam with bringing coffee to the tables of the world as a stimulant, refresher, and symbol of hospitality.[4] Thought to have originated from Upper Ethiopia and Egypt, from an area called Kaffa, the Arabs first brewed it for use as an energizer and stimulant. Gradually the Greek and Roman Bacchic culture (so called because wine was their favourite beverage) was uprooted together with their vineyards as the Arab world spread its influence, and coffee came to be known as "the wine of Islam."[40] It was not until the 1500s that coffee lost its exclusivity and its fame and aroma spread over Europe and coffeehouses became second homes. Coffee's importance never waned in Egypt: so important is the role of this beverage that businessmen commonly have the name of their favourite coffeehouse inscribed on their business cards.[5]

But of prime importance in Egypt and the entire Middle East is the oldest liquid of all – water. Egypt itself has been described as "a long fertile valley surrounded by desert."[6] Only to the extent that water can be encouraged for irrigation can food be provided. Newer systems of canals and dams are helping to increase agricultural output and lessen the age-old dependency on the Nile's annual flooding. More than 60 per cent of the population is engaged in agriculture with the principal crop of cotton yielding not only high quality fibre but also cottonseed oil used in cooking.[2]

Berseem, the Egyptian clover, is used as a rotation crop for fodder to feed cattle, sheep, goats, and chickens as well as pigs, though pork is consumed only by the Copt community as the Muslims do not use it. The milk produced by these animals is used for yoghurt and many types of cheeses. The gentle *gamoosa* (water buffalo) provides milk and is a dependable beast of burden and may even live with humble families as the winter heating unit.[6] Donkeys are the preferred beasts of burden.[6]

While upper-class Egyptians converse in Arabic, French, and English and enjoy a cosmopolitan life-style, the *fellaheen* (peasants) continue a way of life that has known little change in centuries. Working in fields with their gentle *gamoosa*, they tend crops and vineyards and orchards and care for their animals and poultry but seldom eat what they produce. Meat, poultry and eggs as well as most vegetables and fruits are sold; the *fellaheen's* staples are bread, onions, and legumes and copious drinks of very sweet tea. Their main protein source other than grains and legumes is MISH, a white skim milk cheese stored in earthenware jars to ripen.[6]

No one has torn down sphinx or pyramids in order to erect modern skyscrapers in Egypt. It remains as it has always been: a land and a people quietly aware of their ancient roots but absorbed in their daily tasks, all carried out with typical Mediterranean disdain for time, bustle, or punctuality. There must always be time for a sip and a chat.

Home Life and Facilities
Both the life-style and the facilities are sharply defined by class distinctions. Modern ideas and technology have made great inroads in the educational, economic, and agricultural spheres, but the roles of male and female have changed little from olden times. Upper-class women enjoy higher education and the help of servants but seldom accompany their husbands to restaurants or coffeehouses.[1] Class is synonymous with wealth: servants, appliances, and the hand labour of many Muslim wives in a household (Muslim law allows a man four wives) indicate a family's status. *Fellaheen* conditions parallel those of many in subsistence economies, where most perishable foods are neither preserved nor stored but are consumed locally and seasonally as they are available. For this reason starvation may result when crops are poor.[6]

FOODS COMMONLY USED

Although there is a marked difference in the foods of the upper classes and the *fellaheen*, the general Egyptian fare is vegetarian: even the wealthy only serve meat once or twice a week, while the poorest may only taste meat on a special occasion.[6] Bread is the staple of all groups, from the leavened wheat breads of the upper class to the *fellaheen's* staple of unleavened corn breads flavoured with FENUGREEK (similar in flavour to Anise). Meat, fish, legumes, and milk products are a part of urban diets, skim milk cheese and legumes are the most important protein foods for the *fellaheen*, who supplement their diet with onions, tomatoes, and some wild greens as well as very small amounts of local fruit. The wealthy consume fruits and vegetables according to taste. Tea is the rural drink, coffee is the urban drink, and all groups consume sweetened carbonated drinks.[6]

Milk and Milk Products

Fresh fluid milk is rarely used except occasionally in cooking. Some goat's milk is used but cow and buffalo milk are preferred. In the cities milk is sold from door to door and is always boiled before using. A variety of products are available in cities: pasteurized milk, condensed milk, butter, and cheeses. Yoghurt but primarily MISH is the rural staple. MISH (flavoured with red peppers and FENUGREEK) is considered peasant food, it is also much enjoyed by upper classes.[6] A dried paste of soured milk blended with flour and seasonings, such as red peppers, is called KISHK and is commonly cooked with water and eaten as the evening meal at rural tables with corn bread, onions, and sweet tea.

Fruits and Vegetables

Fruits are generally produced in small quantities and enjoyed mainly by the upper classes. In rural areas, the seasonal fruits, such as guavas, figs, and dates are used. Though quantity is limited, there is a wide range of tropical and subtropical fruits produced with peaches, pears, citrus fruits and apricots being the most important. In addition, there are crops of apples, loquats, cherries, nectarines, plums, and quinces. Egypt ranks sixth in world production of dates, and there are also large crops of citrus fruits. PORTOQAL are oranges and limes are called LEIMOON. Smaller crops of olives, bananas, pomegranates, grapes, and mangoes are also grown.

Onions and leeks are the most popular vegetables grown, dating from ancient times, and used year-round by all classes of people. Tomatoes are plentiful but eaten cooked rather than fresh. Other vegetables are eaten only in very limited amounts in rural diets and only used seasonally on urban tables. Okra, potatoes, eggplants, cauliflower, cabbages, and spinach are other staple crops.

In cooler months, wild and cultivated leafy vegetables are eaten by all but special favourites in the spring are the tender seeds and leaves of chick peas and broad beans. MILLOKHIA (spelled in various ways), is a green similar to spinach, and is especially popular in a classic soup of the same name which is based on chicken stock flavoured with tomato paste, garlic, coriander, and pepper.[1,5]

Occasionally radishes, carrots, lettuce, purslane, cucumbers, and even tomatoes are eaten raw as a side dish. Where storage is available some vegetables may be pickled in brine or vinegar during season: carrots, turnips, radishes, tomatoes, cucumbers, sweet peppers. Okra and MILLOKHIA are the only two that may be stored and preserved in dried state for later use in soups, sauces, and slow-cooked casserole-type dishes.[6]

Meats and Alternates

Meats are not a frequent part of the dietary. When they are used, meats and fish are most often well-seasoned, and eaten mostly as part of a dish with legumes or cereal grains. Muslims not only do not eat pork but also prefer meats that have been ritually slaughtered. Beef, lamb, kid, commercially-raised rabbits, and even camel may be used by them as well. Since chickens are allowed to forage, their meat is stringy and tough and their egg production is low. Most popular of all fowl are pigeons. The young squabs being a special delicacy, pigeon nesting is encouraged everywhere.

Legumes are universally popular. Two classic Egyptian dishes: FUL, the slow-simmered beans and TAMIYA, the fried bean patties, are a popular dish at home and frequently purchased from vendors or restaurants. Lentils, chick peas, broad beans, horse beans, vechling or the prass peas and MOKI or lima beans are all used in soups and thick or thin stews. Sometimes they are mixed with meats or vegetables – always they are well-seasoned.

Because of its perishability, fish is used where caught. BOURI is a form of mullet fish most used: FESSIKH is salted BOURI.

Small amounts of almonds, pistachios, and pecans are grown. They are used mainly as snacks or in rich desserts and pastries. Pine nuts may be used in some meat/vegetable dishes, or sometimes served with rice.

Breads and Cereals

Corn, wheat, barley, rice, sorghum, and millet are the cereal crops produced in Egypt. BALADI is the wheat indigenous to the land, while LINDI is a variety introduced from India which has better baking qualities.

Bread is the most important staple food for all the population groups and the poorer the family, the greater is the proportion of bread consumed to other foods.[6] Wheat breads are considered the finest and BETTAI or BETTAWA is the classic Arabian bread leavened with yeast and baked in a fourteen-inch flat circle. The *fellaheen* make their breads from corn, millet, or sorghum (depending upon area) and flavour it liberally with FENUGREEK. On special feast days they may add wheat to their usual breads to make them more festive.[6]

Rural delta communities use corn as the staple, with only occasional use of wheat and rice. Rural southern Egyptians make breads from millet or sorghum with some wheat flour added. In common to all breads of rural areas is the sweet and fragrant flavour of FENUGREEK (similar to anise in flavour).

Rice, BURGHUL, and COUSCOUS form the main ingredients of many festive dishes and are often used as stuffings (well-seasoned) for meats, poultry, including pigeons, and vegetables. BURGHUL is a nutritious whole grain prepared from boiled, dried, and cracked wheat. It can be purchased from fine to coarse and has many uses. Cooked it can be used in many ways as rice; uncooked it is used by soaking first, then it may be combined with chopped vegetables and dressed with oil and seasonings.

(See also chapters on Lebanese and Syrian foods.) Another very similar grain dish is FARIK or FIREEK, which is made from green wheat.[5]

COUSCOUS is the favoured dish all over North Africa, especially in Morocco. (See Moroccan chapter.) Rural Egyptian families prepare it because it is economical and satisfying: other Egyptians may make it as a sweet treat or dessert to be eaten with sugar and flecked with peanuts. Classic COUSCOUS is served with stewed meat and vegetables and a side-dish of very hot-seasoned sauce.

As if proof were needed that not a crumb of bread is wasted, witness ESH ES SARAYA, "Egyptian palace bread": made with bread crumbs stirred into a heavy syrup then poured out to cool. When cut into triangles and served with whipped cream, the flavours of honey and butter from the syrup and the richness of the cream fit the name.

Fats
FOOL SUDANI (peanuts) and SIMSIM (sesame seeds) rank as the important crops used especially for oil production. Cottonseed is the source for most of the vegetable oil consumed in Egypt. Butter is usually used in the form of SAMNA or MASLI – clarified butter.

Sweets and Snacks
Large quantities of sugar are consumed in the very sweet desserts and confections, the well-sweetened tea and coffee, and the many carbonated beverages that are enjoyed. The pastry of the Mediterranean phyllo, makes its sweet appearance in pastry shops in the familiar array of honey or syrup-drenched sweets. Exquisite sugared confections are sometimes specially created for desserts, but only in well-to-do homes.[5] Sugar-coated nuts and sweets like HALWAH, which is a confection made from ground nuts and sesame seeds and sugar, are snacked whenever possible.

Seasonings
The aromas wafting from the bazaars of Cairo and Alexandria form a rich, heady blend of henna, sandalwood, myrrh, camphor, opium, and hashish.[5] The rich scents wafting from Egyptian cookery may include coriander, mint, cumin, cinnamon, and the rich warmth of buttery honey syrups. Regardless of class, two favourite seasonings used are FENUGREEK and sesame seeds and sesame seed oil. While all of these lend their flavours to various dishes and breads, the most-used blend is that of garlic and onions with tomato paste or tomato juice. Egyptians love the sharp pungency of garlic and onions. In contrast is the love of very sweet drinks and desserts. Delicate pastries and fruit desserts will be enhanced with nuts, butter, honey and often rose water or orange flower water.

Beverages

Sweetened coffee is the mainstay of the urban Egyptian while sweetened tea is the frequent refresher of the rural family. Both beverages are enjoyed after meals and often as a "pick-up," or served just to express hospitality. Water is traditionally served with meals.

Soft drinks, carbonated beverages, and drinks made with prepared fruit syrups and plain water are used frequently. Meal beverages also include the following: ERKESOUS, non-alcoholic beer flavoured with anisette; TAMBRAHANDI, made from date palm juice; SHAIER, made from barley; SOUBYA, drink made from fermented rice; LUBKI, drink similar to gingerale.[5]

Meal Patterns and Eating Customs

The abundance of gracious words, multiple cups of coffee and proliferation of heaped dishes that are all so typical of the unfailing Arabian hospitality can be explained in one word – *shaban*, meaning total satisfaction.[3] The *shaban* of the guest is the joy of the host and nothing is spared to achieve this. Age, place, or wealth mean nothing. The best of what is available is proffered to the guest – and in great quantity.

Guests are seldom surprised by unusual foods. Age-old traditions of food preparation, serving and even eating are well-enshrined in Arab hospitality. City dwellers often prefer to take their meals in shaded courtyards during very hot weather. But whether indoors or out, the ritual is the same. Diners seat themselves informally on layered carpets while platters of food are placed on low wooden tables within easy reach. There are no individual plates, no cutlery. Foods are traditionally eaten with the fingers of the right hand only or are deftly scooped up with broken pieces of flat Arabic bread (from that big fourteen-inch flat circle). Just in case there are some sticky fingers, bowls or brass jars filled with scented water are passed by servants between courses of the meal.

Because the sheer quantity of foods offered is an important part of hospitality, some special dinners could have as many as forty varied dishes, each one heaped and garnished in lavish display.[7] Water or some form of light drink will be served with the meal. Sweet honey desserts might conclude a special meal, but fruits are the usual dessert. Small cups of Turkish-type black sweetened coffee and the smoking of the *narghile* or *hookah* (waterpipe) may be an after-dinner pleasure for some.

Hospitality is consistent, but foodstuffs may vary considerably. The humble home of the *fellaheen*, often shared by the family's animals, may be able to offer only bread, MISH, and sweetened tea. A few dishes based largely on legumes and occasional soups or vegetables would be the only addition to the daily fare. Contrasting this, Egyptian city homes may rival the sophistication of gourmets anywhere with the exotica of the typical Middle East specialties.

Morning begins very early for the *fellaheen* with a light breakfast of FUL, bread, olives, MISH, and sweet tea. In some areas local fruits may be eaten in season accompanying the bread and tea.[5] Urban breakfasts are identical but coffee substitutes for tea.

The *fellaheen's* lunch will be a repeat of the earlier meal while the evening dinner may include a legume-based soup (e.g. thick lentil soup) or KISHK cooked with water. Olives with fresh onions and bread will complete the meal, while cups of sweet tea will be sipped to satiety.

There is usually not great variety of types of foods in the peasant meals but the staple legumes are prepared in many different ways and the adroit use of pungent and hot seasonings, plus generous bread and tea intake gives variety and satisfaction. Dried boiled legumes can be served as soup or stew, or drained and served as a "salad." Sometimes mashed cooked legumes are heaped in a mound and served with small amounts of meats or vegetables. Or they may be deep-fried in patties: TAMIYA. FUL NABIT is yet another main dish prepared from sprouted beans.[6]

Urban lunches also favour dishes prepared from legumes and these are often taken in restaurants. Dinners in upper-class homes feature all courses on the table at once and diners casually select each course to their own taste: a soup (eaten with a spoon), a legume dish, stuffed vegetables, COUSCOUS, with meats and hot sauce, a plentiful supply of breads and finally fruits, and then coffee.

Snack foods abound on city streets and even along roadsides and again the favourites reflect the Egyptian love of legumes: FUL MEDAMIS, simmered seasoned beans served with olive oil and lemon juice; TAMIYA, fried bean patties served with spicy-hot sauces; KUSHARI, pasta, rice, and lentils topped with spicy tomato sauce and flecks of crisp browned onions.[1] Vendors of sweet confections vie with those selling fresh fruits, toasted nuts, and crispy seeds. Coffeehouses locate themselves conveniently too. And at any time of the day, sweetened cola drinks and other carbonated drinks as well as fruit mixtures are available to slake the thirst.

Special Occasions

Since the majority of Egyptians are of Arabic origin (the Ayyubid, Muslim sect), it is the Muslim feast days and fast days that rule the Egyptian calendar. The small group of Egyptian Christians (about one and a half million) dating their lineage to the ancients, celebrate Christian festivals. Very small other groups include Protestants, Orthodox Christians, and Jews.

Feast days for the *fellaheen* are marked whenever possible with the inclusion of meat. This is usually ritually slaughtered with ceremony fitting the occasion. The meat itself may be chicken, lamb, water buffalo (although rarely because the animal is more valued for work and for milk), and occasionally even a "very old camel – so tough it must be stewed for days before it can be eaten . . . ."[6] Since wheat breads are considered of the finest quality, the inclusion even of some wheat flour into the daily bread is considered a treat for many *fellaheen*.[6]

For many, however, special feast days are marked not only by the inclusion of many friends and relatives for special visits, but also by long days of preparation of the speciality dishes. These include FETA, a classic holiday dish of layered bread, rice, and meats all moistened with rich garlic-flavoured broth; ESH ES SARAYA, the rich sweet made from bread crumbs, honey, and butter, and served with ISHTA (whipped cream); heaping platters of MEHSHI, which are seasonal vegetables (e.g. eggplants, zucchini, peppers) stuffed with savoury rice and meat mixtures; variations of garnished sweetened COUSCOUS. The most dramatic dish of all, worthy of any festive occasion, has to be the FERAKH BEL' BORGHUL. This is prepared by stuffing chickens with FARIK, or rice, then poaching them to tenderness and browning them to crispness and finally cooking them inside a boned turkey or lamb. With great ceremony the chickens are extracted as the awesome *pièce de resistance*, then carved in small pieces for the diners.[1,5]

EIGHTEEN

English

It has been said that no person in the world exhibits and exemplifies dignified self-control as does the upper-class Englishman. It is an image carefully cultivated. Appearance is everything. No matter what storms may rage in their minds or what chaos surrounds them, the English will quietly proceed with their reassuring cup of tea.

"British is best." "The Royal Navy always travels first class." "Britons never never shall be slaves." These are more than mere slogans or sayings or songs. This is the stuff of which tradition is made and nurtured. Although the English aristocracy of dignified mien, elegant dress and cultured manners actually represents a minute proportion of the population, it is their image that is considered typical of all Englishmen. It is a unique mixture of snobbishness and aloofness; a firm conviction of superiority that resides in even the humblest Englishman that leaves him with no doubt that the "stiff upper lip" will conquer all adversity.

How such a tiny island nation could have exerted and maintained so much influence on the rest of the world must be further tribute not only to the qualities they have but also to those qualities that they themselves believe they have. The quintessence of Englishness may be summed up in a description by Winston Churchill: "tenacity, national pride, and a sense of history."[1]

But while a selective "sense of history" seems to buoy up the English image of the English, history in cold hard facts offers an impartial viewpoint. The far-reaching effects of the Magna Carta in 1215; diplomacy and nationalism in Elizabethan times (1500s); and the great surges of industrialization and colonization in the early 1800s are indisputable historical highlights but they are intertwined with class and religious struggles, with poverty and disease.

The early Celts and Germanic tribes that inhabited England – Angles, Saxons, and Jutes – were a brawny, boisterous mix of warring kingdoms and it was only the threat of Danish invasions in the 800s C.E. that united them. After the Battle of Hastings in 1066, when William the Duke of Normandy came from France to reign as King, some semblance of order and manners prevailed. French became the language of the aristocracy and this is when French words for meats came into use: mutton from *mouton*, pork from *porc*, and poultry from *poularde*.

Medieval times were characterized by the building of castles and siege warfare, by the Peasant's Revolt and the Black Death. And while the lords dined on gargantuan banquets of whole roasted animals, huge sausages and many puddings made with blood, and fruits and flowers preserved in honey, the peasants huddled in their mud-daubed wooden houses and munched on coarse bread and a pottage of peas or beans washed down with homemade barley ale.[4] Yet even in those early times it was the upper classes who projected the image that made the continental Europeans refer to the English as "prodigious meat eaters."[3]

The 1300s and 1400s saw a gradual movement of the peasants from their humble status as tenants-on-the-land towards the growing cities, where they became involved in craft guilds, industries, and merchandising. Slowly, prosperity and trade were making England into a solidified nation and the English spoken in London became official "English" by the 1500s. With increased income, more and more people were able to make meat the centre of their diet and increasingly the "cooked dish" became the centre of the meal.

It was both timely and lucky that the penchant for meat-on-the-table coincided with Elizabethan England's emergence as a great maritime power. For while onions and garlic, wild and home-grown herbs flavoured meats through spring and summer, imported spices from the Far East were almost a necessity to make meat palatable through the winter. In fact, it was so difficult to keep meat fresh after the customary September slaughterings (winter fodder was scarce), that the Elizabethans actually became accustomed to eating spoiled and even putrid meats and even to this day many maintain a preference for "high" game.[3,5]

Salting down meats or spicing them heavily all became standards of Elizabethan cookery. In fact it was considered meritorious if diners could not recognize what they were eating. But probably most of all the popularity of the spiced "cooked dish" could be explained in the fact that it was so easily spooned up and could be eaten without chewing. These are factors of prime importance when dental fillings, artificial teeth and dental care were scarcely known – the first metal fillings were used in 1542[3] – and most of the population suffered inflamed gums, dental decay and a resultant general lack of teeth.[3]

The Elizabethan Englishman had little dignity, elegance, or manners. He was in fact rough and tough. In the late 1500s, foods were eaten with huge long-handled spoons (the forerunners of today's cooking spoons), knives were used to cut the tougher pieces, and unconcealed belching was commonly accepted. In fact, table cloths were used mainly to wipe greasy fingers – if there were table cloths at all.[3] Even Elizabeth I herself was known to spit at courtiers, interrupt religious sermons, and she even ended a feudal uprising by executing 1,000 people.[2] Yet she did institute the Poor Law in 1601, which was the first governmental aid for the poor. She also tried to help the lagging fishing industry by instituting a three-day annual fast during which no meat could be eaten.[2]

In the ensuing years manners did not improve. Gargantuan meals were accompanied by excessive drinking. The huge cupboards and sideboards common in the dining-rooms of the time held chamber pots for use as soon as the ladies left the room.[5] (The after-dinner division of men and women had more utilitarian purposes than talk and brandy sipping.)

If manners didn't improve, the variety of food on the English table did. Increasing travel and trade brought new imports to the English table. Cane sugar and fresh turtles came from the West Indies while the East Indian influence brought the taste of curries, spicy pickles, and tangy condiment sauces to add zest to the traditional bland English dishes. "Cheap and murderous gin" remained the most popular drink.[5]

Meanwhile, evidence of yet another English characteristic was becoming obvious, at least to non-Englishmen. This was the peculiar quality of insularism. No matter where in the far-flung British Empire the Englishman chose to make his home, he carefully packed his language, manners and traditions together with other belongings. He never considered it important to learn either the language or the customs of the "foreigners," much less eat their food. Boiled mutton and steamed pudding was the menu in steamy cities of India, jungles of Africa, or the mountains of New Zealand. Early housekeeping books published in England even as late as the 1800s showed little evidence that the English kitchen had contact with anything but English food.[5,6]

In the 1600s, England's East India Company established a monopoly on tea, but English people at the time were enjoying coffee when they weren't imbibing gin.[3] Some 2,000 coffeehouses dotted London's streets by 1725. Some were the favourite haunts of the Whigs or Tories, others were frequented by academics or physicians. It was going to take another one hundred years before tea with its rituals of steeping, straining, and sipping, would overtake coffee and become entrenched as an English tradition. Presently, the average English adult brews and sips eight pounds of tea a year, while the Scots, Irish, Welsh, and English together brew and sip more than half the world's production of those tiny dried leaves.[3,5,7]

From 1837, until her death in 1901, Queen Victoria reigned.[8] Those sixty-four years, covering three generations, uncovered the excesses of the aristocracy and revealed a powerful and burgeoning middle class that was to be responsible in great part for England's world supremacy on the seas, in industry and in banking and even as a model society.[2,6] The nobility continued to live in the grandest of styles and vied with each other for French cooks, Italian pastry chefs and gardeners. They were seemingly oblivious to child labour and the horrors of working conditions in the mines and factories that paid for their fripperies. A dandy called Beau Brummel became the gentry's idol. His elegant dress, exaggerated speech and mannerisms and his proliferation of "delicacy of tastes" and "refinements of the palate" supplanted the previous coarseness and vulgarity. There is a tale describing his abrupt dismissal of a mistress because he "found out that she had eaten cabbage . . ."[5]

Generally, the Victorians were confident and self-satisfied. They had good reason. Education, arts, and literature flourished; workers became organized and vocal and even won a nine-hour day by striking. London's banks made her the financial capital of the world while her merchant marine and her colonizers fortified the image of England as a supreme world power. The Victorian ideal centred around a happy home life and servants, ample families and ample tables. Mother, like Queen Victoria, ruled over all while father provided.

The example of the aristocracy, however, filtered gradually through the whole population and proved that one excess was as bad as another. A gradual change was occurring which often has been attributed to the Victorian era but in fact became noticeable in the late 1800s. Perhaps as a retaliation against the excesses of the past, the English developed a veneer of fastidious control and modesty that extended into every facet of life. A grey-brown pallor settled over conversation, homes, clothing and even the food they ate. Food, like sex, was considered an "unfortunate carnal necessity to be endured . . ."[5] Visible enjoyment of *anything* was synonymous with sin. Formality at meals, dressing for high tea and for dinner, hushed dining-rooms and silent eating became the national style. The subjects of food and cooking were considered bad taste and the pleasures of the culinary arts were considered unladylike. Children were banished to the nursery to eat their overcooked vegetables and bland milk puddings in the company of a grey-uniformed nanny. The ideal of genteel behaviour metamorphosed into polite rigidity and an emotionless composure that left the English with an almost guilt-ridden viewpoint of anything at all pleasurable.

Perhaps the legendary British Empire is shrinking; but the traditionally English view of the English is not. The English have successfully taken the excesses and the eccentricities of the past and blended them with present practicalities. Perhaps it is the traditional qualities of tenacity, national pride, and a profound sense of history, that still enable the English to believe that any discomforts are only temporary.

Home Life and Facilities

English food is honest and simple and so are English kitchens. There is a place for substantial wooden spoons, earthenware mixing bowls, pie pans and pudding bowls; but there is no place for exotic cookware or complex gadgetry. The biggest pot in the kitchen will likely be a soup kettle, but it will be used for cooking jams and jellies and shimmering marmalades. (The English are not given to soup-making.)[5] Most important will be a kettle of boiling water, a teapot – beloved even if it is stained and a bit cracked – and a collection of tea cups.

Thick frypans and electric or gas ovens have all but replaced hearth ovens and iron griddles or bakestones; but teacakes, biscuits and pastries are as expertly made and as much enjoyed as ever.

Although electrical appliances and gadgetry, and a wide range of exotic imported foods are available, especially in the larger cities, English people prefer their home preserves, home-grown fresh fruits and vegetables and local meats, fish, and seafood. The English larder (a cool storage pantry) is still just as important as the refrigerator. Purchasing in small quantities is favoured, so storage areas are not as important in general as they are in those areas where food variety is not available all year round.

FOODS COMMONLY USED

English cookery is not complex; the preference is for simple fresh foods well-cooked and unadorned. Meats, especially pork and pork products, beef and game as well as locally-caught fish and seafood together with well-cooked vegetables form most of the main dishes. Tea is indispensable. Tea with milk and sugar is served at all meals and at work breaks. White breads and rolls and many quickbreads and biscuits and a great variety of cakes, pies, and steamed puddings form a large part of the general diet. Bland meat and fish main dishes are sparked with pickles, condiments, and spicy bottled sauces that are added to the foods at the table. Fruits are consumed more as marmalades, preserves, and cooked desserts than fresh in their natural state. Many fine cheeses are produced in England and often form the "savoury" part of a meal (at the beginning or the end) or are eaten as a snack.

Milk and Milk Products

Milk is mostly consumed in the form of fresh whole milk served with tea. Almost daily children are served cream soups and milk puddings while adults prefer their milk with tea or taken as cheese. Cheddar, Cheshire, Stilton, and Caerphilly are some of the best-known and locally produced cheeses. CORNISH CREAM and DEVONSHIRE CREAM are thick-clotted creams usually eaten with breads and jams at tea time.

Fruits and Vegetables

The English countryside and the many small home gardens yield a variety of fruits, berries, and vegetables. Pears and apples (commonly pippins) peaches, apricots, cherries, quinces, rhubarb, and green walnuts all are occasionally enjoyed as fresh fruits but most often are eaten in some cooked and sweetened form. The most popular vegetables are potatoes, brussels sprouts, turnips, and cabbage. Salad and salad vegetables are not as popularly used. Many berries, fruits, and even some vegetables are made into jams, preserves, pickles, and chutneys. Vegetables are well-cooked (usually in much water), and sparingly seasoned. Sometimes they are cooked together with meats and fish or sausages to make a quick one-dish meal.

Meats and Alternates

There is no shortage of meat in the English diet. Inexpensive cuts of meat form the basis for slow-cooked casserole-type meals. Steaks and chops and many types of sausages are fried or grilled for quick suppers. Pork, beef, lamb, and mutton together with seasonal game give much variety. Meats are usually grilled or pan-fried, stewed in a pot with vegetables or oven-roasted. Game is usually well hung before cooking to tenderize. A "joint" of meat will likely be the centre of the Sunday dinner table. Tastes run conservative when it comes to fish and seafood. Batter-fried FISH AND CHIPS is a great favourite either as a snack or a supper. Jellied eels, cockles, and whelks are often bought from street vendors, but in the homes simple poached or fried fish or even occasionally "soused" (pickled) fish may include a selection from: kippers (smoked herring), flounder, salmon, sole, haddock (FINNAN HADDIE). Excellent dried, pickled, and smoked fish as well as crabs, prawns, crayfish, and oysters are all readily available.

Eggs appear frequently on the English menu: with bacon and/or pork sausages, or "mumbled" (scrambled) eggs for breakfast. Many a pub's "fork platter" (a lunch dish on one plate eaten with a fork) will include a poached or fried egg atop anything from spaghetti to beans or even a steak. Eggs are a part of the many custards and puddings, form the batter coating on fried fish, and are an integral part of the puffy YORKSHIRE PUDDING.

Legumes are not frequently used; beans being considered a food of necessity rather than one of choice.

Breads and Cereals
White breads and rolls made from wheat flour are preferred over whole grain or rye breads. The English homemaker is adept at making many types of quickbreads, leavened, but not with yeast. Bakery with yeast is seldom attempted at home. PORRIDGE is oatmeal and it is almost always a part of breakfast as is cold toast. Preferring toast crisp (the English place it on toast racks after toasting), when it is cold it is spread with butter, thick preserves or marmalade. Plain baked goods, lightly-flavoured and un-iced, accompany tea and form the major part of the four o'clock tea ritual.

Fats
During war time, the English rendered and clarified fat from meats and poultry to be used in baking and cooking. But lard is preferred in cookery and butter finds a place on all tables as well as in much cooking too. Oils are seldom used.

Sweets and Snacks
In the English vernacular, "sweet" may refer to dessert or to taffies or hard candies. Such is the weakness of the English sweet-tooth that almost half a pound of "sweets" (candies) are consumed per person per week.[10] Sweet shops are everywhere and a little package of candies is to be found in almost every pocket or handbag for "quick energy." Much sugar is consumed in baked goods and many prefer their tea so sweetened as to be syrupy.

Seasonings
For several hundred years the spice shelf in the English kitchen was very important. Heavily seasoned foods were not only enjoyed – spices were frequently a necessity to cover rancid and fermented flavours of spoiled meats and fish. Since the Victorian era, however, salt and pepper, onions and a few home-grown herbs such as thyme, rosemary, sage, and garden savoury have comprised the seasonings.

Beverages
The most important English beverage is tea. Tea, well-steeped and hearty of flavour and aroma, is served with fresh or canned milk and sugar many times during the day – at the slightest provocation – and after meals. Tea is considered a comfort and consolation, a break from work or other routines, a sociable time for friends, a cure or at least a comfort during illness, even a meal in itself. Pubs (short for "Public Houses," where simple sandwiches or one-platter lunch dishes are served with draft beer or

ale as well as other alcoholic beverages) are so popular in England that most Englishmen have "their pub" just as most Parisians have their café. Beer is the most popular alcoholic drink, but a wide variety of imported wines, gin and whiskey (Scotch) are also consumed.

Regional Specialties
Regional specialties are highly developed in England, a few still available only in certain areas, but more being enjoyed widely with the increase in transportation, communication and the widespread interest and publication of regional pamphlets describing these dishes. Some are old favourites, beloved in almost every English kitchen: BRAWN, BUBBLE AND SQUEAK, TRIPE AND ONIONS, JUGGED HARE, TOAD-IN-THE-HOLE, VEAL AND HAM PIE, SOUSED MACKEREL or HERRING, KIPPERS, KEDGEREE, FISH AND CHIPS, TREACLE TART, TRIFLE and MINCE PIE. The most famous of the almost endless list of breads, biscuits, and cakes to accompany tea are: CRUMPETS (PIKELETS in the North), MUFFINS, HOT CROSS BUNS, SWISS ROLL and VICTORIA SPONGE.[11]

North England

COUNTY OF CUMBRIA:
Mutton, CUMBERLAND HAM, and the long strip sausage made of herb-flavoured pork called CUMBERLAND SAUSAGE, are this area's famed meats. The Westmorland TATIE POT is a lamb and vegetable stew cooked with BLACK PUDDING (blood sausage), and served traditionally with pickled cabbage. YARB PUDDING, a combination of leeks and spring greens boiled in a muslin bag with barley to form a pudding, can be served with meats or chilled and sliced then fried with bacon. ATKINSON'S BISCUITS, made with butter, honey and almonds, GRASMERE GINGER-BREAD and HAVVER BREAD (oat bread) vie with WESTMORLAND PARKIN (an oatmeal sweet) and WESTMORLAND PEPPER CAKE (a rich spiced fruitcake sharpened with black pepper) as tea-time treats. Local MALLERSTANG CHEESE satisfies the savoury taste, but the local sweet-tooth may enjoy CUMBERLAND TOFFEE, KENDAL MINT CAKE, or a rich thick sauce called RUM BUTTER or BRANDY BUTTER. The latter two are eaten on biscuits or scones or used as a sauce for mince pies or steamed puddings.[11,12,13]

COUNTIES OF CLEVELAND, DURHAM, NORTHUMBERLAND, TYNE AND WEAR:
From the Kielder forest comes venison, popular for steaks, roasts or stewed in casseroles with vegetables. NORTHUMBERLAND PIE is made from several meats: beef, bacon, and BLACK PUDDING flavoured with onion and sealed in a pastry crust. STOVEYS, is a dish prepared from leftovers of meats flavoured with bacon and onions and browned in a skillet with sliced potatoes. Leeks, potatoes, and dried grey peas called CARLINS

are the most traditional vegetables served. Suet pastry, smothered with sliced leeks is boiled in a cloth or "cloot" to make a LEEK PUDDING, while the CARLINS are soaked and boiled until soft, then fried and flavoured with rum. This latter dish is a specialty for Passion Sunday or Carlin Sunday, said to have originated when a siege, laid on Newcastle by the Scots, was broken by a French ship delivering a load of dried grey peas.

Tea favourites include GRANNY LOAF, a quick bread made with citron, raisins and currants, NORTHUMBRIAN ANISEED CAKE, a delicate brown sugar and honey cake flavoured with anise. Probably most famed is the SINGING HINNY: a large round scone-type of cake baked on a griddle where it is said to "sing" as it cooks.

FLITTIN' DUMPLING got its name because this hearty steamed fruit pudding could be sliced and carried as a satisfying snack wherever the farmers worked. NORTHUMBRIAN SWEET PIE is a Christmas tradition made as a deep dish pie of mutton chops, sweetened dried fruits and peel flavoured with spices and rum all baked under a pastry.

LINDISFARNE MEAD, a honey wine, and COTHERSTONE CHEESE as well as LINDISFARNE MEAD SAUCE, made from mead and blackcurrants, are famed.

NORTHWEST COUNTIES OF CHESHIRE, DERBYSHIRE (HIGH PEAK ONLY), GREATER MANCHESTER, LANCASHIRE, MERSEYSIDE
Three meat dishes are unique to this area: HINDLE WAKES, a poached chicken stuffed with prunes and bread crumbs and flavoured with marjoram, is served cold with a lemon sauce; the LANCASHIRE HOT POT, a slow-simmered stew of lamb, lamb's kidneys, onions, and potatoes and sometimes a few oysters; and the LIVERPOOL LOBSCOUSE, a stew of mutton and/or vegetables topped with biscuits or barley and served with pickled red cabbage.

BLACKBURN FIG PIE is a tart filled with stewed figs, treacle, and spices, while MANCHESTER PUDDING consists of layers of apricot preserves and thick egg custard topped with meringue. From the Knotty Ash section of Liverpool comes WET NELLY, a syrup-soaked pudding made from cake and pastry scraps.

The tea cakes of this area are widely known and available in many bake shops. BURY SIMNEL CAKES are spiced fruit cakes, the DERBYSHIRE OATCAKES are more plebian and can be served with butter and preserves or fried with bacon and eggs. ECCLES CAKES are round pastries rich with dried fruits and sprinkled with castor sugar (white granulated sugar).

CHESHIRE and LANCASHIRE CHEESE are enjoyed locally and exported.

YORKSHIRE
BLACK PUDDING, a staple in most of North England, and YORK HAM, cured by oak smoke, are widely enjoyed.

CURD TARTS or YORKSHIRE CHEESE CAKES are small tarts filled with curd (cottage) cheese, flavoured with sugar and currants. An old traditional Christmas Eve dish, especially in Durham and Yorkshire Dales, is FRUMENTY, a type of porridge made from soaked unhusked new wheat, oven-baked for three hours, and served with milk or cream. If served for Christmas Eve it would be followed by apple pie and cheese and gingerbread. Yeast fritters flavoured with spices, currants, and apples are the traditional dish for Shrovetide Tuesday and called PATELY FRITTERS. FAT RASCALS is the endearing name given to raisin scones, and YORKSHIRE PARKIN, a spicy ginger cake made with oatmeal, is traditionally served around the bonfire on Guy Fawkes' night, November 5. But most famous of all is YORKSHIRE PUDDING, a light crisp batter baked in a smoking hot pan. When eaten in Yorkshire it is said to have a top and bottom but nothing in the middle. Traditionally it is served as a first course with gravy or raspberry vinegar, followed by roast beef and roasted brown potatoes, and likely the meal will be topped off with a stew of dates and rhubarb, or apple tart and the local creamy, tangy cheese: WENSLEYDALE.[12] WENSLEYDALE CHEESE and BRONTE LIQUEUR made from herbs, honey, and brandy, are local treats.

The Plain or Heart of England *(central region)*

COUNTIES OF GLOUCESTERSHIRE, HEREFORD, WORCESTER, SALOP, STAFFORDSHIRE, WARWICKSHIRE, WEST MIDLANDS:
Meat pies are a great favourite here, but two other meat dishes are also specialties: SHREWSBURY LAMB CUTLETS, butter grilled lamb covered with aspic and served with green vegetables and mayonnaise, and STAFFORD BEEFSTEAKS, braised steak and onions served with a rich gravy and mushroom or walnut ketchup. FIDGET PIE is a harvest specialty of gammon (ham), onions, potatoes, and apples while HEREFORDSHIRE PIGEON PIE is a pastry-covered pie of pigeon and beef and carrots. SHREWSBURY PIE is made with rabbit meat, dumplings of liver, baked under a pastry with a spiced wine sauce. HEREFORDSHIRE COD, cooked with cider and mushrooms and sprinkled with cheese and lampreys (similar to eels), are the famed fish dishes.

Desserts include WORCESTER BEASTINGS PUDDING, a baked egg custard made from the first milk after calving (called beastings), and TEWKSBURY SAUCER BATTER, individual saucers of stewed sweetened fruit baked in the oven with a batter topping.

WARWICK SCONES are rich with honey, SHROPSHIRE MINT CAKE is pastry filled with currants and mint, while CLIFTON PUFFS are puff pastry triangles filled with chopped fruits and nuts flavoured with nutmeg and brandy. COVENTRY GODCAKES were originally baked especially for presentation to godchildren on New Year's Day, and are pastry triangles filled with mincemeat. SHREWSBURY SIMNEL CAKE also has a festive connotation: this spiced round fruit cake, filled and topped with marzipan, and decorated with twelve marzipan balls representing the twelve apostles (but sometimes only eleven to exclude Judas), is baked especially for Mothering Sunday, the fourth Sunday of Lent and often for Easter.

Cider is not only a popular drink, it is also much used in many desserts and meat dishes, while DOUBLE GLOUCESTER cheese, similar to cheddar, is the local specialty together with the world-famed WORCESTER SAUCE.

East Midlands: Derbyshire, Leicestershire, Lincolnshire, Northamptonshire, Nottinghamshire:
The most famous pork pies of all, MELTON MOWBRAY, are made in this area from an age-old recipe that is widely copied elsewhere.

Many dessert pies and puddings are made from the local Bramley apples or green gooseberries, but probably the most unusual is a pie with a pastry crust that is filled with a sweetened mashed potato filling flavoured with lemon and nutmeg. Dark tea cakes are the favourite here, often containing mixed dried fruits: MELTON HUNT CAKE, LINCOLNSHIRE DRIPPING CAKE (dripping is the fat used), and LINCOLNSHIRE YEAST PLUM BREAD, which is cake-like in texture and flavour though rich with fruit and dried peel.

DERBY, COLWICK, LEICESTER and STILTON are the cheeses produced here. A white wine, called LINCOLN IMPERIAL, is produced from the vineyards in Stragglethorpe.

Thames and Chilterns
Ducks from Aylesbury are famed, and the plentiful rabbits are often made into AYLESBURY HARVEST PIE: not a pie at all, but a rabbit stuffed with prunes and roasted with bacon and onions. A BACON CLANGER is a boiled suet pudding of bacon and onions, and BEDFORDSHIRE, or HERTFORDSHIRE CLANGER, is a filled pastry with a savoury meat mixture at one end and a jam filling at the other end – a practical lunch in one piece! Baked marrow bones eaten with a long thin spoon and STOCKENCHURCH PIE, made with minced meat, macaroni, and hard eggs are served as simple hearty suppers. POOR KNIGHTS are fingers of egg-and-milk-dipped bread, fried, then sprinkled with sugar, while HOLLYGOG PUDDING consists of a flour and lard (or margarine) pastry spread with treacle, rolled up and baked in milk. BANBURY CAKES are similar to ECCLES CAKES; oval pastries filled with dried fruit and spices.

East Anglia
Norfolk turkeys and quail are highly prized, but the area is most famed for the great variety of quality seafood: crabs, mussels, whelks, cockles, red and black herrings, while COLCHESTER OYSTERS can be dated back to Roman times. Local asparagus in season is so plentiful it is sold on roadside stands, and similar in flavour, with a slight touch of chive, is SAMPHIRE, a type of grass.

IPSWICH ALMOND PUDDING, a light custard flavoured with almond, is a frequent dessert sweet.

Mustard is said to have originated here, and the world-famed Colman Mustard has its plant in Norwich.

Southwest England

WILTSHIRE HAM and WILTSHIRE BACON gained great fame even though the processed pork included not only local swine but also that imported from Ireland. CORNISH PASTIES originated in Cornwall, and the same pastry from Devon is called TADDY OGGIES. Both are elongated cases of pastry filled with meat and potatoes and onion. DEVON PORK PIE is also a meal in a pie dish: pork chops are topped with sliced apples and seasonings and covered with a crust. Warmed cream poured over the baked pie just before serving is the finishing touch. Devon is also famed for its fine salmon as well as snails, SEVERN ELVERS (tiny two-inch eels), and STARGAZEY PIE: a two-crusted pie having stuffed herrings in the centre arranged so the heads are at the outer edges and all the tails meet in the centre. The name describes it aptly.

SYLLABUB originated in this area: a soft dessert of cream and brandy flavoured with lemon, sugar, and nutmeg. Large buns filled with candied dried peel and sugar coated (BATH BUNS) and the sweet rolls split and filled with fresh clotted cream and jam and called DEVONSHIRE or CORNISH SPLITS, are all part of the tea accompaniments.

A seaweed, called LAVER, is often eaten as a savoury for breakfast either as LAVER BREAD or oatmeal coated and fried with bacon. SALLY LUNN, well-known throughout England, is a light golden cake split and buttered while hot.

Southeast England

STEAK AND KIDNEY PUDDING, beloved English dish, is said to have originated in Sussex.

CHERRY BRANDY and SLOW GIN are produced in this area as are wines from local grapes.

LONDON

All the regional specialties find their way to London, but the city itself is also famed for food specialties. JELLIED EELS are often bought from street vendors, while BEEF AND CARROTS is boiled beef with carrots and onions served with PEASE PORRIDGE and SUET DUMPLINGS. WHITEBAIT is the local name given to young herring, sprats or pilchards, batter-dipped and fried and served with lemon wedges, brown bread, and butter. Tea-time or snack favourites are CHELSEA BUNS and LONDON BUNS: sweet dough sugar or icing crusted.

The Isle of Man

KIPPERS (smoked herring) and QUEENIES (scallops) are exceptionally good here while a favourite tea treat is DUMB CAKE: simply made from flour and water and baked in the ashes of a hearth fire. Legend suggests that young women eating a piece of DUMB CAKE while walking backwards will dream of their lover.

Meal Patterns and Eating Customs

The well-bred Englishman's reputation for composure under all circumstances is based on strict emotional control. It has even been rumoured that it is only in their relationship with their pets that Englishmen "let themselves go."[3] Seldom do they touch each other in public, even for a handshake, and the cool "how do you do?" though spoken as a question is never expected to be answered. This same control pervades conversations. Englishmen are careful to converse in a way that steers clear of the emotional or the heated argument, or even the intellectual. The delight of every Englishman is a sense of humour and the ability to take things and themselves not too seriously.[12] But most of all, this composure is not only noted at mealtimes, it is a point of etiquette. It is understood that one chews only small bites at a time, never speaks with food in the mouth, and uses knife and fork throughout the meal (setting the knife to rest while eating with the fork just isn't done). But it is also just as much understood that displaying any interest in the food on one's plate, whether of delight, distaste, or simple curiosity would be most ill-mannered.

More than a meal, a snack or a drink, tea is an English tradition. Tea is also a snack at 11:00 A.M., called "elevenses." It is often a meal that brings out regional specialties when served at 4:00 P.M. and it is *the* English beverage. It also starts the Englishman on his day, and there is even an automatic bedside tea machine that can be set to have tea brewed and piping hot for the first morning stretch.[7]

There is a traditional way to prepare tea, and every Englishman considers himself the undisputed expert. Fresh cold water must be poured into the kettle and only when it reaches a rolling boil is a little poured off into the teapot to "hot the pot." With the teapot thus warmed, the water is poured out and measured black tea leaves are placed in the pot. The pot is taken to the bubbling kettle (never the other way around) to be filled. The lid is then placed on the teapot and a cosy (a cloth or knitted cover to keep the teapot hot) covers all but the spout while the five minutes' steeping time is carefully waited out. The food accompanying the tea may be as simple as bread and butter or as elaborate as a buffet with hot savoury dishes (often local specialties), to be followed by a variety of buns, biscuits, and cakes. The fare may be varied but the talk is not. Conversation around the tea table is as traditional and ritualized as the tea itself: the art of small talk is shown here at its artistic peak.

Most Englishmen start their day with a simple breakfast of tea with milk and sugar, and some type of breads or buns. This is identical to the "elevenses" tea break. In the cities, especially London, lunch is taken at a favourite pub. Here, sandwiches with thin fillings (a slice of cheese or beef), together with a pint of ale are a usual lunch. Pubs also offer a variety of hot one-plate lunches, which may include almost anything served on toast, or anything hot (creamed meat or fish, spaghetti, beans), very often with an egg on top. From 4:00 P.M. to 7:00 P.M. is considered "tea" time or if the meal is to be ample, "high-tea." A light evening supper may include roasted meat and well-cooked vegetables with a sweet, of a steamed or baked pudding, and tea.

It is considered good taste to serve foods in small, even portions. Second helpings may be offered but usually are declined more out of what is considered good taste than from lack of appetite. Among the upper classes it is still traditional for ladies to leave the men alone at the table after dinner for their brandy and cigars (chamberpots being long out of date).

Special Occasions

Church of England, a Protestant denomination, is the state church and has a membership of over two million. Other Christian denominations include Roman Catholic and smaller groups, such as Methodist and Baptist. Freedom of worship prevails.

In England, as in much of the world, many festivals of the year, though outwardly religious or secular, often trace their origins to ancient mystical pagan rites. Although the real Guy Fawkes was hung for attempting to blow up the Houses of Parliament in 1605, all of England commemorates the occasion on November 5, with huge bonfires and burning effigies – similar to the ancient Druid rite of building fires to replenish the waning strength of the autumnal sun. And instead of human sacrifices of the Druids, gingerbread cookies shaped like men are gleefully consumed while the bonfires roar. Similarly, October 31, called All Saints' Eve or All Souls' Eve is celebrated mostly in fun, although here and there one can still find a household that quietly sets out glasses of wine and little buns called SOULCAKES to satisfy wandering spirits.

Shrovetide is the name given to the days immediately preceding Ash Wednesday. This period is characterized by the "cleansing" of one's home and one's soul: houses are meticulously scrubbed and often painted; souls are cleansed by being "shriven," or subjected to confession of sins. Shrove Tuesday is the traditional pancake day and in many areas races are held with ladies running while they flip pancakes in a skillet. The fourth Sunday of Lent is called Mothering Sunday, traditional day for flowers and SIMNEL CAKES. Currently the twelve marzipan balls that decorate the top of the cake are said to represent the twelve apostles. But it is interesting to note that there are records of such a cake with similar distinct decorations dating to ancient Greek and Roman times. Even the fragrant HOT CROSS BUNS, so typical of the Easter season, can similarly be shown to have pre-Christian origins – the cross representing the four seasons and the roundness of the bun, the sun.

But whether or not it can be proven that Christmas too has its origins in ancient mid-winter rites, there can be no doubt that it is the most beloved festival. Christmas in England is rich with traditions that are tenderly preserved and deeply cherished. It is a family time with wintery snows and cheering fires, warming punch bowls, caroling, gifts, and Santa Claus, but most of all the Christmas Feast. Traditional hot wine punches are merely the prelude to a festive dinner of roast goose or turkey filled with fragrant sage dressing, accompanied by potatoes and turnips and brussels sprouts. Somehow room is left for port wine and nuts and dried fruits as well as for mince pie. But the highlight in every English home has to be the CHRISTMAS PUDDING: a brandy-drenched sweet of fruits, nuts, and spices, served warm and flaming with cooling hard sauce or rum sauce. Almost as important as the pudding is the traditional ENGLISH CHRISTMAS CAKE, prepared weeks in advance with fruits and nuts in a rich cake batter, all carefully set aside with a sprinkle of brandy and rum now and then to aid in its mellowing. No one remembers exactly why anymore – perhaps for luck? – but everyone stirs the cake or the pudding at least once and only in a clockwise direction.

NINETEEN

Filipino

A partially submerged mountain range in the southeastern Pacific Ocean forms a grouping of 7,100 islands and islets called the Philippines. Tropically hot and humid and frequently struck by torrential rains and earthquake tremors, more than 90 per cent of these islands are an uninhabited tropical wilderness. In fact, more than half of them remain unnamed. Luzon and Mindanao are the two largest islands upon which more than two-thirds of the population of the Philippines lives and works.[1,2]

The natives of the Philippines call themselves Filipinos. Originally this term denoted a person of Spanish descent born in the Philippines, similar to the Creole of the Spanish-American colonies, but the name has been applied to the 80 per cent of the population of Malays Christianized since the 1800s.

Arriving from the many Malay Islands and tracing their origins to approximately 3,000 B.C.E., the aboriginal inhabitants arrived in successive waves and formed their own unique customs, lore and dialects. Today these dialects number more than 80 per cent, although most people are fluent in English and often Spanish as well. Since 1946, when the Philippines became independent, Tagalog, a Malayan dialect, has been declared the official language.[1,2]

Although the Filipinos have long had trade contacts with the Chinese, Japanese, Portuguese and East Indians, the strongest influence has come from the Spanish and the Americans. In the 1300s Arab missionaries brought the faith of Islam to some of the smaller southern islands and those who adopted the faith are called Moros. Perhaps the first Christian influence was Ferdinand Magellan's landing in 1521, but the strongest was the Spanish rule and colonization which began in 1565 and lasted 333 years until the Treaty of Paris in 1898 when Spain gave the Philippines to the United States for twenty million dollars.[2]

So powerful was the influence of the Spanish rulers and the Roman Catholic missionaries, that the small feudal units called *barangays* were not only quickly and easily conquered – they also rapidly embraced Spanish names, customs and foods. Enraptured by the colourful Roman Catholic ceremonials, the Filipinos readily converted to the religion of Spain as well. Many vestiges of this lengthy influence are still much a part of daily life in the Philippines. Women stress modesty in dress and primness in behaviour and girls from fine families make public appearances usually only when discreetly chaperoned.

The Spanish custom of the late afternoon *merienda* is much enjoyed by the Filipinos and may include a variety of small or light savoury snacks or dishes. The *merienda* is never considered as a meal because it does not include rice. The Asian heritage insists that only when rice is present, at least in one of its many forms, is a meal a proper meal. Late evening meals followed by city-strolling is an older custom more recently replaced by earlier dinner hours as the newer American influence presses in on older customs.[3]

The 25 per cent of the land under cultivation yields vital subsistence crops of corn, sweet potatoes or yams, and from ancient hillside terraces comes rice. Many tropical fruits including coconuts, bananas, mangoes, oranges, papayas, and CALAMANSI (similar to lemons and limes) are grown. Each crop takes a place in an interesting cuisine that blends influences from China, Malaysia, Spain and, most recently, the U.S.

China's staples of rice and noodles are also staples for the Philippines but in a form not used in China: served together as PANCIT. Many of Spain's dishes that mix ingredients in one casserole for a hearty main dish have found a place on Filipino tables: PUCHIDAS and PUCHEROS are hearty variations on Spanish stews called COCIDAS which are mixtures of slow-simmered legumes and vegetables with meats included whenever possible; the Spanish CALDERETA is a fish stew which becomes the Filipino KALDERETA, a stew made with goat meat. The Spanish *conquistadores* brought chocolate from their Mexican conquests to Spain and the Spaniards brought it to the Islands. Filipinos often enjoy a frothy hot chocolate for breakfast and a bitter-chocolate richness in the sauces of many chicken or duck dishes (similar to the Mexican MOLE). One of these is called PATO NG MAY TSOKOLATE.

The marriage of Chinese and Spanish cuisines together with the native tropical fruits and vegetables produces other interesting dishes. Chinese spring roll skins, those delicate, tissue-like pastry leaves, are used to produce LUMPIA. These are similar to spring rolls but are filled with a mix of ingredients that leave no doubt as to their Philippine origin: garlic, pork, chicken, bean sprouts, shredded cabbage and finely shredded coconut palm hearts – a tropical touch with a nod to Chinese origins!

From 1898 to 1946, when the Philippines gained their independence, American influences added yet another dimension to culture and customs. Freedom of speech, free elections and free enterprise found a place in everyday Philippine life together with some incursions of American slang, hurry-up living and the appearance of convenience snack foods such as hamburgers and hot dogs and the slabs of meat Americans call "steak."[3] In fact, in deference to American tastes, many native dishes tempered their garlic flavouring and removed the Filipino condiments made from fermented fish – pungently strong in taste and odour for American palates – PATIS and BAGOONG.

But the intricacies of a fine cuisine are not part of every Filipino's table. Though the tropical climate is a benign environment, many poor people subsist on little more than rice, sometimes stretched with the addition of corn. Others manage with rice lightly flavoured with PATIS or BAGOONG SAUCE. Sometimes stomachs ache for days. Every grain of rice is treasured – as it is in all rice countries – and appetites are appeased by many types of dishes from gruels to puddings and treats made of glutinous rice as well as the more familiar fluffy rice.[5]

Home Life and Facilities

In government and in the home, many examples exist of the influence of American and Spanish occupations. The Spanish occupation brought with it increased religious participation especially by the women in the families. But the newer patterns did not replace ancient Asian kinship ties: the importance of family relationships and responsibilities are of prime concern. The new religion remained family-centred, not church-centred as in Spain.[6] Family shrines became the worship centres, and on special occasions the entire family would join a procession carrying their own personal statues rather than those belonging to the community church. Again, it was through the women's interest and devotion to Roman Catholicism that European ideas of dress, customs and music made inroads in Philippine family life.[6]

Though Philippine women enjoyed equal status with their men, and frequently are the "family treasurers," nonetheless like Spanish women they manage in a very feminine way to make their males feel dominant.[60] The father makes all family decisions concerned with the outside world: schools, voting, business and community affairs.

The Filipino's family is of great importance for it represents the only source of love, sustenance and security: there is almost nothing one will not do for the sake of his family. *Lamangan* is a Filipino expression meaning more or less: "by hook or by crook to get on top . . ." It is also an expression that gives some suggestion of the difficulty of accepting loss or defeat and the intense importance of self-esteem, pride and dignity. In fact, the Filipino's supersensitivity is often considered to be a Malay trait called *hiya* and may be the underlying reason for the difficulty in giving or receiving criticisms.[6]

As has already been mentioned, it was mainly through the women that European ideas were introduced, including ideas about food and its methods of preparation. Filipinos have always been alert not only to new food ideas but also to methods of sanitation and food preservation. In the larger cities modern kitchens and appliances abound but contrast sharply with low-income homes where the barest minimums of food and equipment are available.

FOODS COMMONLY USED

Filipinos enjoy salty flavours and cool, sour tastes. They love to combine many different ingredients in one dish, favour onions and garlic as a base to most preparations and consider frying one of their favourite methods of cookery. Tropical fruits and vegetables blend happily with pork, chicken and seafoods in an ingenious variety of dishes that borrow from China and Spain but end up definitely Philippine. Sourness is added with the frequent use of unripe fruits, the juice of the tart CALAMANSI, or vinegars plain or spiced with chilis. Saltiness is most frequently added with the generous addition of either PATIS, the amber liquid prepared from fermented and salted fish, or from BAGOONG, a popular fish paste also fermented and salted. These two condiments are on every meal table, much as the western salt and pepper shakers are. Rice heads the staple list, closely followed by fish and pork as can be afforded.

Milk and Milk Products
The gentle *carabao*, similar to the water buffalo, is the farmer's work horse and also provides milk from which a delicate white cheese is made. This cheese is widely used, especially at the end of meals.[3] Fresh milk and milk products are increasingly available, using milk from cows, but canned evaporated milk and condensed milk are widely used in cookery.

Fruits and Vegetables
Tropical fruits are abundant in most tropical climates. Coconut is used in many ways: coconut oil, shredded fresh and dried coconut (COPRA) – even the gelatinous pulp of green coconuts called BUKO all find a place in the cuisine. Bananas too are used in many ways: wrapped in bacon, broiled, fried in slices and even hawked by vendors as skewered barbecued treats.[7] CALAMANSI and mangoes also find many uses.

Generally fruits find their way into a variety of dishes whether or not they are ripe. The Filipino's penchant for cool sour flavours makes use of many green or unripe fruits, while over-ripe fruits are happily mashed together to make ice cream or cool fruit mixtures for refreshing desserts.

Fruits and vegetables are often used interchangeably. It is typical to find both fruits and vegetables combined in meat or fish dishes.

In fact, fruits are so widely used it is difficult to say which is most important: mango, banana, or coconut. Other native fruits include breadfruit, dayap, atis, anonas, jackfruit, guava, star apples, many varieties of bananas, tamarind. Also to be added to the long list of fruits are: chicos (similar to dates), Mindanao grapefruits, pomelo, avocado pears, magosteens and even pineapples. These latter are believed to have been introduced by the Spanish and are mostly grown for export.[6]

Most of the vegetables presently used were introduced by the Chinese from the Asian mainland, brought by the Spanish either from Mexico or from the Mediterranean, or grown for American tastes - such as leafy greens and some root vegetables.[8] Eggplant, taro root, ampalaya and patola are examples of vegetables probably indigenous to the islands. Tomatoes and squash and some varieties of beans were almost certainly introduced by the Spanish, while mung beans (and sprouts) are of Chinese origin together with some types of cucumbers and melons, and perhaps some varieties of edible bamboo and bulbs.[8] Like the fruits, many vegetables are used when still green, some when just sprouting, others when ripe.

Meats and Alternates

Pork is the most widely used meat: most farms have pigs, a few chickens and several *carabao*. It was the Spanish who added beef to the Philippines' traditional cuisine of rice-fish-pork-chicken, and the later influence of the Americans accentuated the taste for beef, as well as dairy products.[8] Very insignificant amounts of ducks, geese, pheasants, pigeons and turkeys add to the dietary.

Fish consumption usually far exceeds available local supplies and much fish is imported to meet the demand.[6] One of the favoured special dishes is INEHOW: a whole baked fish (BANGUS) stuffed with PATIS and tomato-flavoured rice and onion and garlic sauteed in oil. The whole stuffed fish is then wrapped in banana leaves and oven or pit-baked.[9]

Lumbag nuts, pili nuts and betel nuts as well as the more familiar cashew nuts form very small crops on the islands and not a large part of the cuisine. Of minor importance too are the bean crops: soybean, mung beans, garbanzos, and other varieties used mainly in some mixed dishes such as soups and stews, sometimes mashed with fruits as in HALO-HALO. This is a popular dessert of alternate layers of mashed fruit pulp (sometimes with mashed beans) and shaved ice, topped with cream.[7,9]

Breads and Cereals

Without rice, it is not a meal. So say the Filipinos. But rice is more than a mound of perfectly cooked fluffy granules. Rice may be found in fillings and stuffings, in soups and stew dishes. Glutinous rice will often be the base of many confections and sweet desserts such as SUMAN, a sweetened glutinous rice steamed in rolls or squares of banana leaves and eaten anytime as snack or dessert, or MALAGKIT, a sweet pudding made with glutinous rice and coconut milk. Rice flour can be made into cakes and puddings and delicious noodles as well. The delicate thin LUMPIA skins are made from a mixture of rice flour and water then filled and fried to a golden crispness.

Rice is the chief food crop, followed closely by corn and sweet potatoes. But while corn and sweet potatoes will be found in many of the combination dishes that the Filipinos are noted for, there is no question that rice is the prime staple food.

Fats
Coconut oil and oil made from many local seed crops are widely used in cookery. Use of lard and olive oil became more prevalent under the Spaniards, while butter together with other dairy products increased in favour under American influence.

Sweets and Snacks
The Filipinos' eclectic mix of foods and cookery techniques creates unusual combinations also in the taste for sweets.

The mid-afternoon break called the *merienda* follows a Spanish tradition of sweets in the form of a small afternoon meal. This was practical when the other Spanish tradition of a very late evening supper was also popular. Many Filipinos now follow American patterns of working hours and three meals a day. Yet for many others, the *merienda* is a custom too pleasant to break. Sweet cakes, tarts, fritters are a part of this tradition, but Filipinos also add small savoury foods like UKOY, deep-fried fritters of shrimp and bean sprouts held with a light crisp batter.

Many sweet treats are made from a base of glutinous rice, richly sugared and often flavoured with coconut. Ice creams and fruit mixtures also form snacks or desserts. Confections include those made of rice bases with added nuts and fruits and sometimes flavoured with chocolate. The very sweet Spanish FLAN (baked custard) is almost a daily dessert.

Seasonings
The base of most dishes is a mixture of onions and garlic sautéed either in oil or lard. A Malay dipping sauce of garlic, vinegar and seasoned salts is frequently used. Most kitchens boast an array of Chinese-inspired seasonings such as soy sauce, fresh ginger root, fresh garlic and onions, salt and several types of pepper.

The general love of cool, sour flavours is achieved with the use of tart green fruits, vinegar or the juice of tangy citrus fruits or the favourite CALAMANSI. The ultimate perfection of sour-seasoning is in the SINIGANG, a sour soup made with fish or meat and a combination of green tart fruits such as tamarind, guavas, green mangoes, CALAMANSI or KAMIAS, a sourish fruit resembling a cucumber. Seldom are two recipes for SINIGANG the same.

Beverages

Probably the most traditional beverages of the Philippines are those from the indigenous coconut tree. Both the milk from green to ripe coconuts and the sap that comes from the cut growing-tip of the tree can be consumed as sweet fresh drinks or fermented into an alcoholic drink called TUBA. TUBA can also be made from the sap of the buri or nipa palm trees and likely is one of the oldest national drinks.[8]

Cacao and coffee plants were introduced by the Spanish and have continued to be cultivated as the popularity of coffee as a beverage and the use of chocolate both as a drink and as a flavouring increased.[8]

A great variety of cool fresh fruit drinks are popular any time of the day. Milk is increasingly used by children. Adults favour fruit drinks and also coffee with meals or as a refreshment break, while hot chocolate may often be a breakfast beverage. Tea or coffee may accompany *merienda*.

Meal Patterns and Eating Customs

As in all other areas of Philippine life, it is not difficult to trace the origins of eating customs and find their threads in the history of the islands themselves.

As in most Asian areas, rice is the staple and most respected food, for hunger is always a reality. Although many in the Philippines enjoy a prosperous life and happily mingle foods, meal patterns and eating customs that blend Malay, Chinese, Spanish and American patterns, there are still many who cook and eat their meals squatting on the ground and savouring every grain of rice and the slight taste of fishy condiment. Native fruits and vegetables in season fill many plates.

Traditional Filipinos begin their day with a meal of fish and rice, others enjoy fresh fruits and ENSAIMADA, sugary yellow buns that are the Filipino coffeecake. For still others, frothy cups of hot chocolate accompanied by crusty white sourdough bread (PAN DE SAL) mean breakfast.[7]

Diversity of tastes is less apparent in the other meals of the day, depending, of course, on economic circumstances. Both lunches and dinners tend to consist of several dishes served buffet style, followed by fruits in season and then a variety of sweet desserts of which the flan is always one. The dishes presented at the meals often span several cultures and end up somehow being unquestionably Filipino.

The *merienda*, the small, sweet meal served in the late afternoon with tea or coffee, is suffering competition from the many street vendors, cafés and restaurants as well as quick snack bars in the American style. One can snack in almost any language, or at least with enough diversity to satisfy any taste, whether the hunger pangs arrive in morning, afternoon or late evening.

Despite the penchant for rice, the Philippines are not part of the "chopstick culture"; Western or European eating customs prevail. Hospitality is always gracious and the best dishes proudly presented to guests. Many Filipinos will even temper their own tastes for fermented fish condiments and heavy garlic to please what they believe to be an "American" palate; saving their traditional seasonings for when they are dining with family.

Special Occasions
The population of the Philippine Islands is 80 per cent Roman Catholic.[2] About 4 per cent of the population follow the Muslim faith and are called (much to their resentment) Moros. The latter group live in independent groups faithfully following Islamic ceremonies and customs and are ruled by their own chieftain or sultan called the *datu*.[6]

Mestizos is the name given to those of mixed native and Spanish inheritance but more recently this term is used to denote any mixed racial background. Mestizos are also sometimes called Cacique.[6]

The predominantly Christian population of the Philippines is unusual in that it represents the largest body of Asiatic peoples converted to Christianity.[2] Both the Spanish and American periods of influence have also left the islands with a more Western or European culture than any other Asian country.

Thus it is natural to expect that the Christian festivals of Easter and Christmas will have a special significance. Religion is more family-centred than church-centred and this makes for a special festive spirit on any occasion. Families gather and share special foods and their preparation brings a spirit of happy anticipation.

Sunday is a time of family relaxation, and is often celebrated with a special Sunday dinner of PUCHERO. With a PUCHERO, other courses are hardly necessary! This special dish is a loving combination of several meats and many vegetables cut in large chunks glowing with a rich golden sauce of well-simmered tomatoes and yellow yams all bathed in a rich blend of sautéed onions and garlic. Served with mounds of rice, it is a Sunday meal for leisurely eating and one conducive to rest afterwards.

Pork usually holds the centre of attention for Christmas and Easter. Despite an ample array of many classical dishes arranged in bountiful buffet, the JAMON DE NAVIDAD, a baked Christmas ham glazed with fruits and spiced with brown sugar, or the LECHON DE LECHE, charcoal-roasted suckling pig, will probably steal the scene. INEHOW, the whole stuffed banana-wrapped baked fish, and LUMPIA will likely be other specialties on the menu. A full array of fresh fruits, CARABAO (cheese) and special sweet custards, puddings and cakes as well as the LECHE FLAN will complete any festive meal.

TWENTY

Finnish

Six hundred years of Swedish rule and one hundred years of Russian domination have left their stamp of the language and food customs of Finland but the character of the people remains uniquely Finnish.

The difficulty in understanding the Finn becomes apparent when writers vary in their descriptions from "honest yet stubborn" to "slow and very quiet."[1,2] Of course there are regional and individual differences, but certain characteristics are evident. Finns are noted for their strength and athletic prowess, and Finnish names will be found in the lists of pioneers clearing sites and building towns and highways in the U.S. In Canada the Finns are famed for their work on the Canadian Pacific Railway and the Welland Canal. Their apparent slowness may be attributed more to their meditative and philosophical natures, and their noted long periods of silence readily explained by saying "There is nothing to talk about."[3] Most of all the Finns possess a quality that can best be described by their own word: *sisu*. It has been described as courage, stamina and stubbornness rolled into one package. Others call it more simply, "guts."

It must have been *sisu* that gave the Karelian Finns the endurance to move from their own homes en masse during the Russian invasion of their beloved province of Karelia in World War II. It must have been *sisu* that caused the rest of the Finn population to open their homes to these 420,000 refugees, to feed and clothe them and donate their own money and precious possessions to help the Karelians eventually build new homes.[2] And surely it is *sisu* that provides the Finn with the kind of moral and spiritual sustenance to live in a rugged country visited by summer only two months of the year.

The Finns call their country Soumi, literally "marshland." Laced with more than 60,000 lakes, less than 8 per cent of the total land surface is fertile. This small arable portion consists mainly of the coastal regions, the rest of the land being mainly stony or covered with forests. Crops are therefore limited. Principle ones are those that form the staple foods: potatoes and a fine variety of grains including rye, oats, barley and wheat. Flax is also an important crop and the country women are famed for their hand looms that produce rugs, cloths, mats, curtains and even clothing from the linen threads.[2,4]

The exact ethnic origins of the Finns are obscure but they are believed to be of Mongolian origin. Yet their height and fair skin makes them seem closer to the Teutons. Although 98 per cent of Finns now speak Finnish, it was the publication of Finland's epic *Kalevala* in 1836[1] that led to the establishment of Finnish as the official language. Finns learn Swedish and Finnish in schools and many also learn German, English or Russian. Estonians and the Hungarian Magyars are the only other peoples speaking languages from the Finno-Egric root, but only the Finns are presently a part of the free world.[2] Perhaps this too has something to do with *sisu*.

It is said that there are three things for which the Finn will be most homesick: the sour rye bread, the sauna, and the luminous summer nights when the sun forgets to set. RUISLEIPA - the sour rye bread baked flat and crisply hard with a hole in the centre (western Finland) or thick, round and crusty (eastern Finland)- is the staple of every meal. The sauna is the eagerly anticipated Saturday night relaxation of Finnish families and is much enjoyed by many others who have come to appreciate the pleasure of its warm steamy ritual. Both RUISLEIPA and the sauna may be duplicated wherever Finns live, but the strangely mystical light of summer nights when the sun does not set below the horizon can only be appreciated in Finland and cherished in the memories of those who have witnessed it.

Home Life and Facilities
Because of the many rivers and streams, electrical power is common all over Finland, even in country barns. But wood and coal continue to be the common fuel for heating and cooking. RUISLEIPA is still baked in brick ovens: several times a week in eastern Finland where the softer loaf is preferred but sometimes only twice a year in western Finland where the thin hard bread is preferred. The latter version is punched with a hole then hung on long poles to dry. It can be stored for months.

The most important room in the country house is the *tupa*. It is a combination living room and kitchen with typically scrubbed wooden floors, wooden furniture and handwoven mats, table linen and curtains. The important and often huge brick oven for baking bread is built into one wall of the house and the bread is placed and removed with a large wooden paddle.

Preferring fresh fruits and vegetables, homemakers in the cities market frequently but everyone makes preserves of berries and pickles of vegetables such as beets and cucumbers. All Finns have a strong preference for natural simplicity in their foods, enjoying the natural taste of wild berries and mushrooms while fish and meats may be flavoured only with salt or smoke. Although the sauna is primarily a bathhouse, legs of lamb and sides of bacon and ham are often smoke-cured there; quick post-sauna snacks of sausages are often grilled over a small fire and enjoyed there with KALJA, the light Finnish beer.

FOODS COMMONLY USED

Breads and cooked grains form a part of almost every Finnish meal and are often accompanied with herring, potatoes or dairy products. Milk and cheeses are used generously. Because of the short growing season, fruits and vegetables are prized especially in season and accompany meats and fish in the form of preserves, pickles and stewed dried fruits during winter. Meats and fish are used frugally, with nothing wasted. The staple fish is herring, prepared in many ways and used as appetizer or main dish. The Finns do not consume much concentrated sweets, preferring snacks of sandwiches or very plain cakes and cookies. Coffee is the national beverage but beer, vodka, cognac and strong tea have their place.

Milk and Milk Products
Much milk is consumed as a fresh whole beverage, clabbered milk, called VIILI PIIMA, or fresh buttermilk. Finland is famed for its great variety of quality cheeses: EMMENTHAL, TILSITTER, KREIVI, KESTI, AURA. There are also many local fresh-milk cheeses similar to pot cheese or cottage cheese and called simply "breakfast cheese." Both fresh rich cream and sour cream are used in many dishes.

Fruits and Vegetables
Because of the short growing season, fresh local fruits (mostly berries) and seasonal vegetables are greatly enjoyed. Preserves of berries and dried fruits (lightly sweetened or even quite tart) are often served with meats. Local fruits include blueberries, raspberries, cloudberries, lingonberries, cranberries, strawberries and gooseberries, while citrus fruits are imported. Apples, rhubarb and rosehips as well as dried fruits are also used. Fruits are eaten fresh, atop cereals, or as fillings in pastries and sometimes cakes. They are also served as dessert in the form of tart fruit soups, thickened puddings, whips, custards and snows (with whipped egg whites). Fine liqueurs are made from some of the berries.

The staple vegetables are potatoes and cauliflower. Cucumbers, onions, beets, carrots and radishes are used but not in any quantity and there is some resistance to the encouragement of wider use of vegetables.[2] Salads of fresh vegetables are almost unknown. Many types of wild mushrooms are used both fresh and preserved in salt brine for winter use. Most vegetables are consumed as pickles while potatoes and cauliflower are eaten in long-cooked (sometimes four to five hours) casseroles.

Meats and Alternates
All parts of beef, pork, veal and lamb are used: roasts, stews, jellied meat loaves, sausages, soups ("slaughter soup" is made from offal and blood). Bottled blood is sold as an ingredient for other dishes.[5,6] Chickens are not plentiful. The Laplander's domesticated reindeer is considered a great delicacy, especially reindeer tongue. Occasionally game birds, bear meat and elk are used.

Although herring is the staple fish, other fish used include sprats, sardines, whitefish, bream, flounder, pike and salmon. Freshwater fish are most common from local rivers and lakes. RAPUJA are the tiny freshwater crayfish served in midsummer while MUIKKO are the tiny lakefish eaten whole.

Eggs are consumed mostly as an ingredient in other dishes, bakery and desserts. But MUNAVOI is a smooth spread of mashed hard-cooked eggs with butter. Legumes, other than the dried peas for soup, are not used.

Breads and Cereals
Whole grain bread is a part of every meal: slightly sour-flavoured and filling. Porridges and gruels made from various grains are often the main dish at lunch and sometimes are eaten as desserts in smaller servings with berries added. Plain tasty yeast breads and crisp plain cookies are always served with coffee. Rye, barley, oats and wheat are used singly or in combination for the many grain breads and dishes.

Fats
Much fat is consumed in the form of whole milk, butter, cheeses, cream, and sour cream. Butter is the main cooking fat although salt pork and bacon fat are also used.

Sweets and Snacks
The Finns are not great sweet eaters, preferring VIILI PIIMA, KIISSELI (fruit soups) or fresh berries in season as a dessert. Between-meal snacks will usually be coffee and a sandwich or a variety of plain crisp cookies or yeast breads, pound cakes, or other un-iced baked goods. Really rich and elaborate desserts are seldom served except on special occasions or for

guests. Even the many types of berry preserves enjoyed with meats are only slightly sweetened.

Seasonings

Finns prefer natural flavours but like them on the robust side. From the sour rye bread and soured-milk dishes to the tart pickles and fruit desserts, the Finnish preference is not a sweet one. Favoured seasonings are dill, onion, garlic, juniper berries, and pine needles which may be rubbed on game or fowl. Because smoked meats and smoked fish are so popular, smoke must be considered a flavouring as well as the abundantly used fresh milk and cream.

Beverages

Coffee is the national beverage but milk, buttermilk and clabbered milk are popular. There are a variety of homemade fermented beverages, especially KALJA which is similar to beer but is non-alcoholic and not sweet. Vodka is called RYYPPY and is served icy cold. Finland is reputed to be the largest importer of fine cognac from France.[6] Tea and herbal teas are occasional beverages, but the Finns enjoy their tea brewed strong.

Meal Patterns and Eating Customs

Throughout Finland, Finns wake up to a morning coffee, PULLA (braided yeast bread) or open face sandwiches of cheese and meats. Many Finns prefer coffee only and save their appetites for a lunch of PUUROA (cooked cereal) or, in the country, a heartier meal of meat or fish with potatoes and gravy, bread, butter and cheese. Not long after the noon meal comes a break when coffee, breads and cookies or sometimes open-face sandwiches are served. The evening meal is likely to be a baked casserole of meat and cereal, or potatoes, bread and butter, all served with fruit preserves, beets and cucumbers. Later in the evening coffee will again be accompanied by yeast breads and cookies.

VOILEIPÄPÖYTÄ is the name given to the Finnish "sandwich table." In Sweden this is called smörgäsbord, in Denmark it is called smørbrød and in Norway, koltbord. The basis of them all is bread and butter and upon this is built the rest of the meal – usually lunch, but occasionally a simplified version serves as breakfast. The Finnish sandwich table is similar but differs with the inclusion of more freshwater fish dishes which abound in Finland, and small, hot, stuffed pastries. The ritual of the sandwich table requires that the smoked and salted fish (usually herring dishes) are eaten first, then a fresh plate taken for other fish dishes and cold roasted, smoked or cured meats and jellied meat loaves. Still another fresh plate is taken for the variety of hot dishes. Finally fresh fruit or a compote of fruits with cheeses form the dessert. Coffee is served later, sometimes accompanied by simple yeast cakes and cookies.

The other Finnish standby is the "coffee table," the favourite break of the day, anytime in the afternoon or evening, and the favoured way to entertain guests. Although usually just a simple serving of yeast cake (PULLA) and cookies with excellent coffee, it can be more elaborate for special occasions or special guests. In this latter case, the fare will likely include PULLA, un-iced poundcake, several types of cookies and a layered filled cake. Fine china coffee cups and a bread and butter plate will be placed before each guest and it will be expected that not only many cups of coffee but also a generous helping of *each* of the cakes and breads will also be consumed. Not to have tasted each of the baked goods (together with as many cups of coffee as needed) would be considered an insult. And while the plain cakes and cookies alternate with the cups of coffee, somehow room must be saved to enjoy a generous helping of the rich layered cake as the finale!

The roles of mother and father in Finnish life are well-defined. The country woman will consider not only the house cleaning and weekly baking as part of her work, but also the daily meal preparation and barn chores as part of her share; while the menfolk do the heavy work in fields and forests. City women also accept a heavy work-load of daily meals, weekly (usually Saturday) house cleaning, baking, as well as shopping. Most city people live in apartments. All Finnish women follow routines of housekeeping with almost religious fervour; but the bustle of Saturday's activities is rewarded and soothed with the relaxation of the Saturday night sauna.

The ritual of the sauna occupies such a central place in the lives of the Finns that often, as in pioneer times, it is either the first building to be built or the first item a Finn will seek out when he emigrates. The sauna is a small house built of wood inside and out and often located near a lake or a backyard pool. One enters into a small dressing room and from there into the main room where the bathers rest or sit on sturdy wooden shelves. Heat is supplied by a small stove with hot rocks. From time to time water is splashed on the heated rocks to add steamy moisture to the air, and the bather may also douse himself with cool water as a refresher. A soap and water scrub is followed by a shower or a leap into a lake or pool. Some hardy Finns have been known to run outdoors and roll in the snow. But the sauna is more than merely a bathhouse. Because of its scrupulous cleanliness, the sauna has been known to be the scene of a birth. Because of its relaxed atmosphere, it has also been the scene of many business discussions and even sauna parties. Also sauna-cured and smoked meats are common. A snack always follows the sauna ritual: sausages are grilled over an open fire or snacks of salty fish with rye bread and butter may be washed down with homemade KALJA.

The daily menus differ slightly between country and city dwellers. Commonly, the rural Finns awaken early to coffee and PULLA. This is followed between 10:00 and 11:00 A.M. with a substantial breakfast of potatoes, meat, and gravy (or fish) then rye bread and butter and a dessert of porridge. A rest period after this meal is followed by a "coffee table" and then all return to their work. The country evening meal is served in the late afternoon (usually after the cows are milked) and is similar to breakfast. Later in the evening the country Finn relaxes and completes the day with yet another "coffee table." In actual practice, then, the rural meal pattern consists of two hearty meals interspersed with coffee and plain yeast breads and cookies.

Just as the country meals follow the routine of daily labour, so too the city meals adapt themselves to the working hours of the people. It is not practical for city people to have only two meals and to eat them at the odd hours popular in the country. Although breakfast for most is still little more than coffee and PULLA, men often will have one or two open-face sandwiches of garnished sliced cheeses and meats or fish. The city noon meal depends on whether it is being eaten at home or in a restaurant. A home luncheon will be little more than a bowl of cooked cereal (PUUROA) and milk or buttermilk; while lunch eaten out will almost surely be the VOILEIPÄPÖYTÄ: an array of fish and sliced meats, small hot dishes and then fruits and cheeses, all served with sliced dark breads. Often milk is the noon beverage, but men may take mild beers or KALJA.

The city dinner will be eaten when the men come home from their work so that the family can dine together. If this is to be a late meal, then the family may enjoy a late afternoon "coffee table" to appease hunger. Dinner will likely be a slow-baked casserole with potatoes and served with pickles followed by a porridge or fruit dish for dessert. Coffee and breads will be enjoyed still later in the evening as a snack before retiring.

Special Occasions

Religious freedom prevails in Finland. The Evangelical Lutheran Church claims a membership of 95 per cent of the Finnish population while only 2 per cent belong to the Greek Orthodox Church.[4]

Christmas, Easter and May Day are the main festivals but the Finns are also much affected in their mood and social life by the seasons. The long dark days of winter, relieved only by visitors or special family occasions, seem to cause a cloud of solemn quiet to fall over daily life. Even alcohol consumption increases dramatically in an effort to dispel the national winter depression. The joyousness of the first of May is celebrated with singing and dancing and a great sense of communal relief that the end of winter is in sight. SIMA, the tangy fermented lemon drink, is served everywhere to happy visitors and even on streets together with the crispy-fried TIPPALEIPÄ.[2] Midsummer Day, though less exuberant than May Day, is celebrated with special menus featuring fresh cheeses. Happy parties with crayfish feasts and sleepless nights during late spring and summer celebrate "the time of the long days" or *Pitkiä Päiviä* when the lingering mysterious lights add their special quality to the festivities.

Christmas is celebrated on December 24 with church services and a festive meal of well-cooked vegetable casseroles, LUTEFISK or LIPEÄKALA (the specially-prepared salt cod dish), baked ham, garnished with dried fruits, and a creamy rice pudding. Later in the evening cookies and coffee are enjoyed while Santa Claus gives gifts to the children.

An Easter buffet is centred around a display of home-baked yeast breads. The most famed of these is the PÄÄSIÄISLEIPÄ, baked in a high round tin, which strikingly resembles the Russian KULITCH. This bread is of Karelian origin. From the rich spring butter and creams come the special cheeses that are served on the Easter buffet as well. One of the oldest traditional Easter dishes is served either as a pudding or a beverage depending on the area. EASTER MÄMMI is prepared from a mixture of molasses, water and rye flour flavoured with raisins and orange peel, and the pudding version is traditionally baked in baskets.

TWENTY-ONE

French

Impossible. Impossible to think of France without at once being pleasantly assaulted with a sensuous vision of velvety wines and tempting foods. Is this reputation a carefully nurtured legend or does it indeed have some basis in fact?

A great cuisine can only be developed where there are suitable and abundant natural resources, diligent and imaginative cooks and enough sensitively appreciative palates to taste and enjoy the results. It would seem that France can give a nod to each point.

Watered by numerous rivers, blessed with a temperate climate and a fertile soil, the rolling plains and valleys of France are dotted with orchards and vineyards, yield grains and varieties of delicate vegetables, and nurture cattle, sheep and fowl all in such abundance that, under normal conditions, France is actually self-sufficient in foodstuffs.[1] Farmers, fishermen and sheep herders have learned from centuries of diligent care and lessons handed down from one generation to the next how to coax the finest quality from their produce, be it grapes or chickens. And in a nation that can honour a chef with the Légion d'Honneur[2] it is not surprising that the taste for fine wines begins with the very young at the family table, and the arts of the kitchen begin near *maman*. . . .

Few nations boast culinary histories, gastronomic maps and qualities of foods and wines that set world standards. Such is the case for France. Any library of cookbooks, while acknowledging the cuisines of most of the world, will have the weightiest shelves of books on French cookery. Not surprising when one glances at such tomes as Curnonsky's *Cuisine et Vins de France*, Brillat-Savarin's *La Physiologie du Goût*, the epic 2,984-recipe collection of Auguste Escoffier, or the meticulous cataloguing of foods, techniques and recipes by Antonin Carême. And it is indisputable that France's brandies and wines have set world standards and her cheeses defy imitation.

But it was not always so.

It was Auguste Escoffier who said: "When we examine the story of a nation's eating habits . . . then we find an outline of the nation's history." France's history of food might begin with the meats boiled in huge pots together with fish and vegetables, or with whole wild boars spit-roasted and served with an assorted garnish of game and fowl.[3] It was the comparatively civilized Romans who introduced their own spices, wine and wheat to the Gauls. And in those early days before the Common Era, not only new foods but table manners also proved to be a novelty; the Romans taught the Gauls to drink from cups instead of human skulls and to seat themselves at rough tables instead of squatting on the ground. But there was an exchange too. The Romans enjoyed milk-fed snails, oysters and FOIE GRAS made from the artificially enlarged livers of geese,[1,3] and they introduced these new luxuries "back home." But it was to take many years of history until both Romans and Gauls learned to eat with anything else but their fingers, their teeth and possibly a sword.

Charlemagne is credited with being perhaps the first gourmet in the history of French cuisine, ruling his feudal empire while dining on four-course meals and savouring the smoothness of brie cheese which he had "discovered" in a little abbey near Paris. He is also credited with helping establish France's wine industry, planting many orchards and even developing fish ponds teeming with eels, carp and pike.[3] He left his intellectual mark as well, founding numerous schools and becoming a patron of scholars and artists as well as a devout Christian.[1] In the late 700s C.E. Charlemagne struck a very early blow to male chauvinism when he allowed women to share his dinner table – a previously unheard of circumstance.[3]

The pages of history from France's Dark Ages echo the plight of peoples all over Europe: gluttony and luxury for the upper-class few and almost unparalleled misery, poverty and near-starvation for the masses. Wars, diseases and meagre crops that failed resulted in the people scrounging for food from roots, barks, and even mixing earth with flour to make bread and as a last resort the eating of human flesh.[3]

France's "sense of mission" was perhaps born in the eleventh century with the Crusades.[4] The First Crusade was made up totally of French knights inspired to destroy all of Christendom's enemies, and as they marched under the theme "God wills it," they massacred populations, set towns in ruin, and even plundered Jerusalem.[4] They did, however, also find time to enjoy dishes made with rice, and brought back to France not only rice but many oriental spices: cinnamon, cloves, thyme, aniseed and bay leaves. At the same time, the feudal system was disintegrating and while some peasants retained small plots of land, many others moved towards the towns.[3] While small markets sprang up, storage, transportation and food preservation were hardly adequate. The arrival and the use of spices greatly enhanced the palatability of available and inexpensive foodstuffs such as whale meat.[3]

The Middle Ages were characterized by gargantuan feasts and gross table manners: eating with hands, belching and tossing scraps on the floor were all commonplace. However, many ate simply and it is even said that bread and soup was a common meal. Joan of Arc herself is said to have enjoyed soups so much that she was known to eat five different soups at one meal and nothing else.[3] Perhaps as a further influence from the Middle East, candied fruits, sugared nuts and other sweetmeats became popular and Auvergne gained fame for its fine quality DRAGÉES (sugared almonds). About the same time a growing interest in food and its preparation was indicated by the publication of the first cookery books in French: *Menagier de Paris*, and Taillevent's *Viandier*.[3]

But the real turning point in the gastronomy of France was the arrival of a plump fourteen-year-old girl named Catherine de Medici. She arrived in Paris to become the queen of Henry II in 1533. It was not she who revolutionized the tastes of France; it was her retinue of chefs, pastry makers and gardeners, the finest from Florence. To realize what an impact this must have made, it is necessary to look for a moment at the culinary accomplishments of France's neighbour.

The gastronomic arts had reached their epitome in Florence; the first modern cooking academy, the Compagnia del Paiolo ("Company of the Cauldron"), had been founded there in the early 1500s.[5] Cookbooks had been commonplace in Rome since the first century C.E., with the writings of Apicius. Consumption of vegetables, especially cabbage, common boiled greens and fava beans were all commonplace as was a variety of fruits such as apples, apricots, peaches, cherries, figs and many types of melons.[5] Herbs, spices and many blended sauces were used both in cooking and as flavouring to be added at the table.

The Romans are said to have invented cheesecake: both a savoury and a sweet dessert type using honey. More than a dozen varieties of cheese were known; they were used often after the meal as a dessert with fruits.[5] Breads made with flour and yeast, pasta made from flour and water and shaped in a variety of ways then dried, even the use of tomatoes and corn, newly arrived from the ships of the *conquistadores*, had some of their first experimental tastes in Italian kitchens.[5]

While Catherine de Medici dazzled the French courts with her sumptuous banquets of unusual dishes, the greatest shock must have been her introduction of the fork! Spoons and knives had been used before, but to dine with a fork was revolutionary. The art of making breads, cakes and pastries, the preparation of fresh vegetables and the serving of fruits and cheeses were appreciated but a great favourite was to be ices and ice cream.[3] There seems some contradiction as to whether the first ice creams were introduced by Catherine de Medici or by a Sicilian in Paris, Francisco Procopio, who is said to have opened the first café selling ice creams and ices of many flavours.[6] For sure, it was Catherine who introduced the French courts to the iced delicacies, but perhaps Procopio deserves credit for presenting it to Parisians.

From the kitchens of Marie de Medici, Catherine's niece who married Henry IV, came the present French classics: SAUCE BÉARNAISE and SAUCE MORNAY.[3] By now the culinary arts gained even wider appreciation, and while the next king, Louis IV, gorged on endless courses and enormous quantities of foods, Parisians were beginning to enjoy a new stimulation: the first public cafés (in 1669) serving coffee.[3]

The 1700s saw many fads and fancies such as BOMBE GLACÉE, PETITS POIS (actually introduced by Catherine de Medici), ANIMELLES (ram's testicles), and truffled FOIE GRAS (imported truffles from Italy had started the French on a search for their own underground delicacies).[3,5] But it was through the efforts and writings of a French agronomist and economist, Antoine Parmentier, that the humble potato was finally accepted as a food.[6] About the same time restaurants began appearing much to the consternation of the *traiteurs* or caterers who had more or less a monopoly on the selling of cooked meats. In 1765, an innkeeper named Boulanger is said to have used sheep's feet to flavour his soups which he sold as *restorantes*. This was construed by the *traiteurs* as an illegal way of selling cooked meats, but when the furore died down more and more Parisians were enjoying eating out and by the turn of the century more than 500 "restaurants" had opened their doors, each boasting long and different menus.[3] It was not uncommon, then as today, that cooks trained in the palaces and wealthy homes and retired by opening their own fine little restaurants.

The New World was opening up and its new foods trickled into Paris: roast turkey, squashes, tomatoes and corn; even Indian corn pudding had its vogue on French tables. Both Benjamin Franklin (1706-1790) and Thomas Jefferson (1743-1826) brought enthusiastic impressions of the French cuisine back to America, not only in the form of recipes, cookbooks and a newly-honed sense of taste, but also in the form of cuttings from French vineyards with which it was hoped to begin an American wine industry.[3] However, credit for the first California vineyards goes to Spanish missionaries who, as early as the mid-1600s, had imported vines from France and Germany to assuage their well-developed wine-thirst.[7] But more than the influence of either American leaders or European missionaries, the arrival in Louisiana of the worn and weary Acadians, routed from their homes in Nova Scotia by the English in 1755, gave Americans a true taste of the art and ingenuity of French cuisine. Having wandered for more than ten years and finally settling in the area of New Orleans, the French (called "Cajuns" in the area) had preserved little else but their bodies, their language and their culinary skills.[8] These they blended and adapted with the best that was at hand – and their "hand" proved a strong one in creating what is known today as the distinctive "Creole Cuisine."[8]

The French Revolution did little to restrain the wonders of the French cuisine. In fact, there is some evidence that had Napoleon been more of a discriminating eater, he might not have suffered the *débâcle* of 1813. He was suffering such a *crise de foie* (a digestive disorder so common among the French that it is listed in most gourmet glossaries) he felt he must have been poisoned, and he ordered a retreat.[3,4]

The post-revolutionary years saw a surge of technical progress together with such an interest in the culinary arts that many famous names became associated with food. Napoleon's prime minister Talleyrand and his chef Antonin Carême ("the king of cooks and the cook of kings") may not have been the first in history to combine diplomacy and gastronomy, but Carême quickly became famous for his splendid creations of architectural confections and his detailed books on cookery which included his own illustrations.[6] While foreign courts enjoyed the secrets and the results of Carême's creations from the kitchen, Talleyrand was busy receiving diplomatic secrets from Carême!

Other names, trailing through French history, left immortal imprints on the gastronomic map. Marie Antoinette brought to Paris the recipe for a curved little bun, originating in the Turkish siege of Budapest in 1686. It became transformed into the buttery, flaky CROISSANT.[3,6] The deposed Polish king Stanislaus Leszczynski's favourite dessert of liqueur-soaked cake served with whipped cream became the BABA AU RHUM.[4] François Appert won a prize offered by Napoleon with his invention of preserving foods in jars; pirated by the English and the Americans, the canning industry was born. Another Frenchman, Louis Pasteur (1822-1895), seeking to preserve wine and milk, stumbled on the process that bears his name. Another Frenchman, Charles Tellier (1828-1913), perfected the refrigeration system which has revolutionized the food industry.[3] Still another Frenchman, Mege-Mouriés, affected the world's eating habits with his invention of margarine in 1872. But powerful butter interests kept his product in disrepute for years. In fact, only during World War II did margarine gain respect.[3]

Always inventive, adaptive and willing to try something different, the French gradually standardized their cuisine so that eventually, with the mention of the name of a dish, everyone knew what it was and what it contained. Food discussion, then as now, centred mainly around the menu for the next meal or the exact degree of seasoning in a dish. The "settling" of the French cuisine, however, was preceded by some intriguing new tastes: in 1855 horsemeat was sold in Parisian markets for the first time and the *boucherie chevaline* is a common sight today. During the siege of Paris in 1870, the flesh of dogs, cats and even rats and donkeys was sold as meat.[3] About forty years earlier a more palatable dish in the form of COUSCOUS was introduced after the French took over Algeria, and in various forms it is still a part of Parisian menus.[3]

During and after the great world wars, universal austerity both in economics and in general outlook made some of the extremes and excesses of the past seem more out of place than ever. While the war-weary soldiers yearned for the local wines and the good hearty cooking of *maman*, restaurants changed their fare too. Not only were the gargantuan displays and lengthy menus of the past distasteful because of the seriousness of the times; they were also no longer a necessity because the new modes of transportation and food preservation brought fresh foods to every home. Expensive and time-consuming techniques were no longer practical or necessary.

The weighty gastronomic discourses by Carême and Brillat-Savarin were to move to the back of the bookshelf with the advent in Paris of a new philosophy propounded by a young chef from Angers, Maurice Sailland. He called himself Curnonsky, an appropriate variation on the Latin *cur non*, meaning "why not?" In 1927, 5,000 Parisian gourmets elected him prince (and he was to call himself Prince Curnonsky thereafter), whereupon all his pronouncements on food became legendary. Some, like the reduction of the menu to one main course from the previous three, were sensible. Others, like his statement that one should "never eat the left leg of a partridge, for that is the leg it sits on, which makes the circulation sluggish," detract from some of his more contemporary views.[3,4]

Curnonsky classified the French cuisine into four categories: *haute cuisine, cuisine bourgeoise, cuisine régionale,* and *cuisine impromptu.*[9] He said of *haute cuisine* that "like our *haute couture* it is the most beautiful manifestation of our national activity," and noted that it was not only the privilege of the elite clientele to enjoy, but it was propagated throughout the world by master chefs trained in the great French tradition. He defined the *cuisine bourgeoise* as cooking in the family style, for "in France one always eats well."[9] He defined *cuisine régionale* as being the best specialty dishes of the forty regions of France. His final category may be the most prevalent throughout the world: *cuisine impromptu,* or the hasty improvisations or what some cooks call "pot-luck" – a meal put together quickly from whatever is at hand.[9]

Curnonsky not only ate well and cooked well, but he also took his position as " the Prince" very seriously. His book *Cuisine et Vins de France* states in precise detail recipes representing the four types of cuisine, as well as strictly prescribed rituals for table service, carving, wine art and wine service that in many places are still the guiding principles.

But considered to be the greatest of all culinary authorities was Auguste Escoffier. He was decorated by the French government with both a Chevalier of the Legion of Honour and the Rosette of the Officer of the Legion.[6] Of all the sayings and writings of the gastronomic greats of France, it is the words of Escoffier that were destined to point the way to the newest phases of French cuisine: the *nouvelle cuisine* as articulated by Paul Bocuse, and the *cuisine minceur* with which Michel Guérard experimented.[2] The great master had entreated his students and readers to *fait simple*, and nearly thirty years after Escoffier's death in 1935, at the age of eighty-nine, French chefs and fine cooks the world over realized the timelessness and practicality of his words.

Home Life and Facilities

Just as "much of French history is simply Paris history presented as a *fait accompli* to the provinces,"[4] so the lessons of life are simply the family viewpoint presented as indisputable fact to the child. The principles of a sense of "belonging" and "favouritism" are inculcated early. In many ways, French mothers teach their children suspicion of life-styles outside the family circle; schools teach a wariness of that which may be new; from families to schools to organizations the "French way" is carefully taught so that one will not "go astray."[4] In some ways the French mother is as important a symbol to the family as Paris is to France herself: the occupation of Paris by a foreign power means defeat for the nation, while the liberation of Paris represents a victory for every French person in the entire world![4]

There is little question of *maman's* importance in the French family. She is often characterized as being hardworking and frugal. While all of this may be true, what is indisputable is her skill with food and every aspect of it. If she can afford to hire servants to do the work of marketing, preparing, cooking and serving there is no doubt that she will nonetheless be astutely knowledgeable on every detail and be able to offer criticism as well as factual advice. If she is the one to do all the chores accruing to the table, then she will consider it her duty to rise early and shop almost daily for small quantities of the freshest and best herbs, bread, meats, fish, fruits and vegetables she can procure. Freezers and supermarkets and many brightly packaged quick-mixes are found in Paris, but there will always be a place for the farmer's and fisherman's market and for the small refrigerator; for the French there is no substitute for the freshest, the seasonable, the local and the best.

In a French kitchen nothing is ever wasted. Bits of stale bread, the last of vegetables, the trimmings from the meat or the fish, all will find a place as stuffings, garnishes, sauces, or soups. French kitchens are frequently small and seemingly inefficient, but the miracles of cuisine they produce are never disappointing. The *batterie de cuisine* usually begins with a gas stove, although many have both gas and electricity just as in the "old days" the large country estate kitchens used gas ranges for fast cookery but the old reliable wood stoves were preferred for slow simmering.

Quality pots, pan, skillets, double boilers and casseroles are important. Purchased once, they should last a lifetime (if not longer). A battery of sharp specialty knives, wooden spoons and wire whisks, the TAMIS (drum sieve), food mills and graters and mortar and pestles to pound, grate and purée foods are also found. More recently the electric blender has taken the place of some of the older utensils, and a still newer electric appliance from France combines many kitchen functions in one unit.[10]

FOODS COMMONLY USED

It does not matter which food you name: if it is prepared by a French cook it will look and taste "French." Therefore, we must conclude that the foods themselves are not French, but surely the technique of their preparation, the seasonings that enhance their flavours and the way they are served make all the difference. "*Vive la difference*!" Mainly the French enjoy foods that take time and care and are as lovingly prepared today as they were a few hundred years ago: sauces, soups and stews. It is understandable too, that bread in many forms but especially the ubiquitous BAGUETTE must be a staple food. How else to mop up those sauces, savour the soups, and accompany those stews!

Vegetables are treated with the respect they deserve and are always fresh, freshly cooked and served as a separate course; while salads are stark in their simplicity, quivering with crispness, aglow with the shimmer of a simple VINAIGRETTE.

Fruits may be served in many forms but none so eloquent as the choicest served on a plate with nothing but a drop of dew to assure its freshness and a wedge of cheese to accompany its juiciness. Water is for bathing, cleaning, and occasionally an ingredient of necessity, but to the French it is not something one drinks. The beverage of France is wine, which graces the table, whets the appetite, and enlivens food flavours – what could be more basic than wine? Ah, and the seasonings! Fragrant fresh herbs, a whiff of scallions or shallots, chives or leeks and, with a gentle hand – a little garlic.

Milk and Milk Products

Milk by itself is not a common beverage except for very young children; even so it is more likely that they will join the rest of the family for the breakfast CAFÉ AU LAIT (sweetened coffee with hot milk) and CROISSANTS or BAGUETTES with preserves. In the Basque area, foamy hot chocolate with whipped cream and golden warm BRIOCHE is the likely start of the day.[11]

The French, however, make much use of milk and cream in soups and sauces. Cheeses are a frequent part of the menu, often in casseroles and sauces, and as a light meal or snack with bread and wine. But most often cheese is served as a dessert with fresh or stewed fruits. There is scarcely a region of France that does not produce some cheese specialty, either fresh or aged and made from the milk of cows, sheep and goats or a mixture (see Regional Specialties). Some of the sweetest disguises of milk and cream appear in the guise of SOUFFLÉS, MOUSSES, CRÈME ANGLAISE (bland custard sauce) and the gentle pyramids of sweetened whipped cream atop desserts.[12]

Fruits and Vegetables

Fruits are savoured for their natural beauty and fresh flavour and for this reason are purchased in small quantity and in season. To end a meal with one's last bite of bread spread with a creamy cheese and then to add the juicy coolness of any luscious fresh fruit. . . . But the French also prepare fruit tarts, fruit soufflés and fruit puddings (CLAFOUTI) as well as many types of homemade fruit wines, brandies and clear potent liqueurs from many types of fruits.

The diligence of French cooks is similar to that of French farmers. Nothing is wasted: both manure and composts of trimmings, leaves and kitchen wastes are returned to the earth with rhythmic precision. The reward is a seasonal delight of a great variety of fresh vegetables of every type.

Cooked vegetables are always served as a separate course, especially the first-of-the-season. Others are cleaned and trimmed and appear at the table as the natural garnish of the meat or fish platter. All green or brightly-coloured vegetables are traditionally prepared by a short boiling then after draining they are plunged into icy cold water. The last step is a quick reheating just before serving by sautéeing in butter.[10,12] It should be noted at once that the vegetable water is not poured away, but will be used as the liquid addition to soups, stews or sauces. Vegetables may also be served with sauces, tucked into crêpes, simmered in soups or puréed into soufflés. They may also be chilled with oil, vinegar and herbs (VINAIGRETTE) to be served as a cold appetizer or salad. Artichokes, asparagus, green beans, green peas, cauliflower, brussels sprouts, endive (Belgian), broccoli, and spinach are special favourites. Potatoes, carrots, and tiny onions are most enjoyed lightly glazed with butter and sugar. A special vegetable *mélange* called RATATOUILLE blends the flavours of tomatoes, eggplant, zucchini with garlic and onions.

Mushrooms (CHAMPIGNONS) have a special place of honour at the French table. Finely chopped and blended with minced onions they form a flavourful thick sauce called DUXELLES, used alone or as the base for many other dishes. Mushrooms may be carefully sliced, chopped finely, or spirally fluted before using. They may be stewed, grilled, sautéed or stuffed, but most elegant of all they may be served in simple splendour under a glass bell: CHAMPIGNONS SOUS CLOCHE.

Wonderful things happen to potatoes in the French kitchen, too. Although it took the writings of Parmentier to make the French take potatoes seriously as a food, they then made up for lost time. Mashed, scalloped, baked, and of course french fried, stuffed, made into crispy pancakes, hashed, rissoléd, the list is almost endless. But the French top all the potato dishes with two triumphs of technique: POMMES ANNA and POMMES SOUFFLÉES. If these are not enough, the American potato and leek soup VICHYSSOISE is based on an old French favourite potato soup but served chilled. The French penchant for classification is clear even on the matter of potatoes; for each different shape, seasoning, and technique, there is a separate recipe.[6]

Whether it is prudence, frugality or simply an appreciation of food, the French give fruits and vegetables a place of great distinction on the daily menu. Freshness and care in cookery assure optimum nutritional content.

Meats and Alternates

From the *boucherie* come the cuts of beef, pork, lamb and veal as well as brains, liver, tripe, kidneys, tongue and heart: meats as well as innards, each prepared with common-sense thriftiness. *Charcuteries* (prepared meats) provide a huge variety of prepared, cured, smoked and pickled meats and loaves and sausages of every type. Meats are often larded, that is, poked through with thin strips of fat to increase juiciness and flavour. Larding and the cooking technique of braising rather than dry roasting are most commonly used for large meat cuts to flavour but mostly to increase tenderness.[12]

Although there is a recent tendency to enjoy small cuts of meat that can be quickly prepared such as steaks and chops – served very rare – most French prefer to use age-old recipes for braising, stewing, and soup-making that take time but provide worthwhile flavour while at the same time calling for the least expensive cuts of meats as well as offal.

Chickens, ducks, geese as well as rabbits, horsemeat and any available game or fowl are all enjoyed in season and economical. Special occasions may call for "a good piece of meat" but the type of meat depends more on the favourites of the region.

"Plainly almost anything that lives is edible, in France at least."[12] The list includes snails (ESCARGOTS), mussels (MOULES), frog's legs (CUISSES DE GRENOUILLES), smelts or minnows (GOUJONS), and sea urchins (OURSINS). More familiar to other tastes are crabs, shrimp, lobster, LANGOUSTE and a variety of fish found in French waters. Eels (ANGUILLES) and scallops (COQUILLES) may also be added to the list of edibles eaten, like all fish and seafood, in a great variety of ways: grilled, deep-fried, ragoûts, stuffings, etc. From Marseilles comes the famed BOUILLABAISSE, a richly-flavoured soup-stew of fish and other seafood served with crusty bread and a spicy hot ROUILLE. (But it is from the ancient writings of Atheneus that we learn it was the early seafaring Greeks who introduced their KAKAVIA to the fishermen of Marseilles where it quickly gained favour as BOUILLABAISSE.)

That eggs are a useful addition to the French menu can be seen by the 282 separate recipes for egg dishes found in *Larousse Gastronomique*. Such a staggering list does not include the many variations of soufflés, omelets and custards which are largely based on eggs! Incidentally, it should be noted that the omelet thought of as French was another of the many dishes introduced by Catherine de Medici's Florentine chefs: the origin seems to be an ancient Roman dessert of honeyed eggs called OVA MELLITA.[5] Eggs both as a dish and as an important cookery ingredient find themselves in many dishes but seldom at the French breakfast table.[13]

Legumes and nuts are not an important source of protein in the French dietary but are used in some dishes. The most famous of bean dishes is the CASSOULET, a specialty of Languedoc. Small white beans are well-cooked and layered with several types of meats and sausages to form a richly flavoured and filling dish. Nuts are used in desserts and confections.

Breads and Cereals

For the French, the importance of daily bread cannot be overestimated. Crusty bread, usually still warm from the baker's oven, starts the day with steaming hot chocolate or coffee with milk. The main meal at noon would be incomplete without the bread basket – and it is only removed at the very end of that meal. The hearty soup that is the usual evening meal would be inconceivable without bread and many a French snack relies simply on bread plus a few squares of chocolate.

French homemakers do not bake their own breads or rolls and seldom trouble to make pastries or cakes. Why should they when experts have opened shops in every neighbourhood just for the express purpose of providing the staple of the French diet? Meticulously demanding about the length, the width, the type of crust and of course the freshness of their breads, bakeries cater to every whim. Most popular are breads made of white flour, and only when bakeries close do some families condescendingly nibble on "health bread" (that is, anything but white bread). CROISSANTS and BRIOCHES are the best known of small rolls, while the BAGUETTE in many sizes and shapes is the favourite of breads although many varieties of each exist to tempt the mealtime tastes.

The French bother little with whole wheat or rye or other flours, and never concern themselves with the category of food others call "cereals." Hot or cold cereals are almost unknown and even where known are not popular. Rice is used occasionally, mostly in combination with other ingredients to form sweet or savoury dishes but seldom as a dish of any importance. France's ties with Algeria brought Algerian COUSCOUS to Paris in varying forms, some better than others.

Fats

Olive oil, butter, chicken fat, goose fat and lard all have a place in the French cuisine; mostly the preference is a regional one.

Sweets and Snacks

The range of French desserts from light to rich is as impressive as the number of egg dishes, yet the favourite dessert is fresh fruit and cheese followed by a demitasse of black coffee. Pastry shops and cafés abound so sweet snacks are available almost everywhere. Crusty white bread sandwiching a few squares of chocolate is a favourite of school children.

Seasonings

French food is often judged by *haute cuisine* and seldom by the more common *cuisine bourgeoise* or *régionale*. For this reason, the image of trays laden with heavily sauced and garnished foods and cold platters of stuffed extravaganzas masked with CHAUD-FROID and glittering with GELÉE brings sighs of wonder and groans of, "Oh, I could never cook like *that*!" In fact, most French do not cook like that either.

Most vital to French cooking is the quality and freshness of the ingredients at hand. Invariably this means local produce that is seasonally fresh. Menus are never conceived ahead of time, but are mentally assembled at the market as the freshest foods and the best of buys are combined with prudence and skill. For this reason too the French have little use for large refrigerators or freezers.

Used with the taste and skill of generations of patience, French cooks add to their basic foods only those seasonings necessary to enhance the original flavours. Scallions, shallots (with their delicate garlic-onion flavour), leeks, onions and garlic all have a special place. A tiny plot for a fresh herb garden is common and so too is a kitchen shelf near a bright window with freshly-growing chives, tarragon and chervil in small pots. If the herbs cannot be purchased fresh, they will be dried. Most used are: tarragon, chives, rosemary, sage, thyme, savoury, fennel, marjoram, bay leaf, parsley, chervil, and basil.[14] Most commonly, several aromatic herbs will be tied together in a little bundle and placed in the cooking dish, to be removed just before serving. This is called a BOUQUET GARNI.

Two other commonly-used techniques for seasoning are the BRUNOISE and the MIREPOIX. Finely diced mixtures of vegetables are lightly browned in a small amount of butter or other fat and this mixture is added to other dishes to enhance flavour: soups, stews, casseroles, etc. The names can almost be used interchangeably except that the BRUNOISE is always a vegetable mixture whereas sometimes the MIREPOIX may contain a fine dice of meat such as ham or salt pork.

Another category of seasoning techniques is the ROUX. Basically, the ROUX is the flour and fat mixture used for thickening but depending on whether the ROUX is white, blond or brown, different flavouring results are obtained.[6]

Sauces could also be considered as seasonings and here again the list is almost endless. Some of the better-known are: MAYONNAISE, HOLLANDAISE, BÉARNAISE, VINAIGRETTE – in fact, "every kind of liquid seasoning for food"[6] and Carême is said to have categorized more that 200.

Finally, the simplest and often considered "the most French" is the addition of wine to enhance flavour. A common misconception is that the poorest quality of wines may be used as "cooking wines." This is in fact a fallacy since in the process of cooking the alcohol evaporates and the flavour essence of the wine remains – either to enhance or ruin the original flavours. Commonly, the wine used in preparing a dish is also the wine served with the meal at table.

Beverages

CAFÉ AU LAIT or hot chocolate are the favourite morning beverages for the French. Meals are almost always ended with a demitasse of fine black coffee, and probably the French take as many coffee breaks during the day as their taste dictates. Water is never seen on a French meal table unless it is in the flower vase. Wine is not only the beverage of France, France's wines are of such quality as to set world standards in many categories. Regions have their distinct specialties, and certain wines are traditionally savoured with special foods but the final decision on what to drink with which dish is still a personal one.

Regional Specialties

Although processed and imported foods are available in most areas of France, the majority prefer to cook and eat in the traditional manner. This "preference" is of course strongly conditioned by climate and geography and in border areas by the influence of neighbouring countries. And naturally when local markets offer the freshest and finest of local produce – young vegetables, ripe fruit, fragrant honey and freshly-cured *charcuterie* – who can resist? Each community also boasts its own bakeries, daily serving an array of breads, rolls and the special pastry delights of the locality. (Special bakeries in Paris also tempt with careful reproductions of provincial specialties.) Although no longer recognized as duchies or kingdoms, the provincial divisions of France mostly denote differences in culture, language, and cuisine.[6,12,13]

Normandy and Brittany

Reaching out to the English Channel in the northwest corner of France, these two provinces are famed for their rich production of milk, cream and butter.

From the sea comes a wide variety of fish, shellfish and seafood. Conger eels are made into the favourite of the Breton fishermen: a soup-stew called COTRIADE. Shad, salmon and trout are especially delicate.

Mutton and lamb feed in the salt marsh areas, giving them a distinctive flavour. The residents prefer to serve their lamb and mutton rare and bloody: MOUTON PRÉ SALÉ.

The common beverage is hard cider made from the bounteous apple crops. The potent apple brandy, calvados, as well as the liqueur, Benedictine, are made in Normandy.

Brittany's pancakes and griddle cakes are famed, but especially the high thin lacy ones called simply CRÊPES BRETONNES and served in casual folds enclosing sweet or savoury filling. Buckwheat is used in soups and as a flour in some of the Breton pancakes and griddlecakes.

Almost all the culinary specialties of the area are noted for their use of cream. In Normandy, GRAISSE NORMANDE (seasoned pork fat and suet) adds distinctive flavour as well. Normandy's cheeses have international fame, among them: CAMEMBERT, PONT-L'ÉVÊQUE, and the rich double-cream: GERVAIS PETIT SUISSE.

Artois, Flandre, Picardie

Meats, orchards and produce of these ancient provinces in the north of France are not of exceptional quality and the main food resources come from the sea. Beer and hard cider are the principal beverages. Beer and leek soup, hotch-potch, and jellied eel have a strong flavour and resemble similar dishes of Flemish origin. There are a great variety of herring dishes: baked, fried, pickled, smoked with hazelnut leaves salted and oil-cured. Apple and red plum tarts and preserves are found among the sweet specialties. Pork and rabbit and especially the ANDOUILLETS (pork sausages) are among the best meats of the area.

Alsace, Lorraine

Alsatian pork and geese are famed for their quality and succulence. The pork is made into a variety of sausages and prepared meats, while geese livers are processed into TERRINES and PÂTÉS. The hearty foods of the table include PÂTE DE FOIE GRAS, CHOUCROUTE DE STRASBOURG, and a string of dishes with German overtones: KUGELHOPF, KAFFEEKRANZ, SCHENKELE, noodles, red cabbage with chestnuts and POTATOES À L'ALSACIENNE.

Plums, berries and cherries are distilled into fine liqueurs: KIRSCH (cherry), FRAMBOISE (raspberry), MIRABELLE (yellow plum), QUETSCHE (red plum) – all clear, potent and fragrant. The wines of the area, frequently disturbed in the past by political unrest, are returning to their deserved glory: spicy reisling, sweet velvety traminer, rich gentle gentil, the musky muscat and the light sylvaner.

The rich, satisfying foods of the Lorraine kitchens echo many of the same tastes found in Alsace: fine pork products, rich geese and geese livers, red cabbage and sauerkraut, potato and noodle dishes, filling soups. But most famous of all is QUICHE LORRAINE, a rich custard of eggs and cream baked with strips of bacon in a tart shell. Coffee cakes, macaroons, but especially the MADELEINES from Commercy deserve special note. Light and dark ales are the favoured beverages together with a selection of fine Moselle and Meuse wines, fruit liqueurs and specialty cheeses.

Lyonnais, Franche-Comté, Savoy

The Lyonnais district is a small plains area with fertile fields and much industry. Fine vegetables, orchards with stone fruits, chestnut trees flourish. Especially fine potatoes produce notable dishes such as meats, tripe, potatoes or onions in LYONNAISE SAUCE or "à la lyonnaise." Typically this is a fine cream sauce flavoured with onion, white wine and white vinegar.[6] Lyons sausage, chicken sausage, black sausage, dishes with chestnuts or walnuts (both plentiful) and delicate chicken and veal dishes are all well-known. QUENELLES, poached balls of ground fish (especially pike), are also a specialty. Desserts include pumpkin cake and MATEFAIM, a coarse, heavy pancake, and fritters of acacia blossoms.

The area of Franche-Comté shares many gastronomic specialties with the neighbouring area of Switzerland. In fact Comté cheese is considered a type of French gruyère. Almonds, chestnuts and walnuts find their way into many desserts and sweets. Hearty culinary specialties include a type of cornmeal porridge, a purée of cooked bread and butter served as a soup, and a range of soups made with garden-fresh vegetables and fruit soups, especially cherry soup. Many pork products such as variety meats, hams, sausage and bacon are of excellent quality. Cheese dishes, hearty breads, simmered meat and fish dishes with wine, and preserves of local fruits - quinces, bilberries and whortleberries - as well as some rare and unusual wines are produced here.

Mostly mountainous, the area of Savoy produces cereal grains and potatoes and some cattle for beef, milk and cream. Orchards on the hillsides supply temperate climate fruits such as apples, pears and plums as well as chestnut and almond trees. In the shadows of the woods are found mushrooms and tiny wild strawberries. CIVET is a specialty dish of hare and pork with a sauce combining spices, wine and animal blood with cream. The abundant crops of nuts make nut oil a favourite for cooking, adding a unique flavour to many dishes. Satisfying cheese dishes, noodle dishes and potato specialties also resemble many dishes of Switzerland.

Champagne

This is the area of chalky soils, vineyards and cool caverns yielding the sparkling wines that have made the province's name synonymous with elegant special occasions.

There is a distinct and interesting difference between both the people and the cuisine of southern and northern Champagne. The tall, blue-eyed blonds in the north of the province prefer substantial dishes of cabbage and potatoes, enjoy strong cheeses and relish the strongly-flavoured wild boar and prefer to wash it all down with beer. The shorter, dark-haired populace of the southern area of the province have lighter tastes, showing a preference for fish and chicken dishes and wine as their beverage. Pork products of fine quality, mutton and poultry as well as local cheeses, fine fragrant honey and of course the famed hillside vineyards are the produce of the land.

Île-De-France

This area literally pulses with Paris at its heart. Here, all the culinary specialties as well as the finest produce of land, sea and rivers come together with the historically great chefs to produce the *haute cuisine* for which all of France is world-famed. Further, the very area surrounding Paris is said to be one of the most fertile in all of France, and from here come the freshest delicacies of the earth to Parisian markets. Pork, beef and poultry specialties are too numerous to mention, fish and seafood dishes, such as SOLE MARGUEY and COQUILLES SAINT JACQUES À LA PARI-SIENNE are imitated throughout the world. Sweets such as PARIS BRIOCHE, aniseed breads, barley sugar and candied almonds and the countless VOL-AU-VENTS, FLANS and TARTS. . . . The name Paris is at once the impetus for and the summary of fine cuisine.

Burgundy

There are always those who will dispute it, but it is the considered opinion of the experts that the province of Burgundy is "undoubtedly the region of France where the best food and the best wine are to be had."[6] Certainly with so many dishes known as *à la Bourguignonne*, with such famed wines and even the fine mustard known as DIJON, named for Burgundy's capital, there is substance to the claim.

The sauce which has added fame to the region is prepared from the local dry wine to which is added a garnish of fluted mushrooms and tiny whole glazed onions. Meats prepared with this sauce are usually enriched with lardoons and a whiff of garlic, but the sauce is also used for fish and poultry (COQ AU VIN) and ESCARGOTS. Rich is the word not only for the arrays of wines, but also for the fine poultry from the district of Ain, and the fine cattle, winged game and the famed ESCARGOTS from Bresse. On-ly the fish found in Burgundian waters can be described as delicate. Fruits are of exceptional quality and the black currants are made into a liqueur called cassis. Pigeons, duck, hare, woodcocks, all are prepared with special skill. Fine preserves, jams, biscuits and cakes, and sweets such as meringues, macaroons, fondants and nougats stand high on the gastronomic list. Côte de Beaune region produces white as well as red wines, while the Côte de Nuits area produces the great reds.

Loire Valley

The Loire Valley is an elegant region where ancient castles and estates dot the landscape of sweeping fields and gardens. Fine salmon and trout, truffles from nearby Périgord, an abundance of cream and butter and tiny shallots to flavour almost any savoury dish as well as the lesser-known dry or sweet vouvray wines are the regional specialties.

Bordeaux
Masterful cooks and winemakers, the people of the Bordeaux region have fine produce from both land and water as basic ingredients. Originating from this region are many dishes made with BORDELAISE SAUCE: the sauce itself is made from a base of white or red wine enriched with marrow, but the term can also refer to a dish with the addition of mushrooms called CÈPES, or the sauce may be based on a MIREPOIX, or finally the dish may be garnished with tiny potatoes and artichokes. Many dishes also contain more than a taste of garlic, and as one moves southward towards the Spanish border, many fine Basque dishes have found favour in Bordeaux such as the PIPERADE, an omelet of eggs and vegetables, and the thick cabbage soup flavoured with salt pork: CARBURE. Specialties include ENTRECÔTE, lampreys and lamb as well as chicken served à la Bordelaise. Game and the flavourful CÈPES abound in the forests. And here too is the home of armagnac and cognac, the finest brandies in the world.

The Basque Country
The Basque are different. They speak their own language called Euskera, populate three provinces in France and four in Spain, and consider themselves at once citizens of both countries and individualists above all. They dance the *fandango* in their rope-soled shoes called *espadrilles*, place a rakish beret on their heads and defiantly claim their gourmet clubs (for men only) are the finest in the world. TRIPOCHKA and LOUKINKA are two of their mountain sausages; CHIPIRONES is a type of cuttlefish served in its own ink, and TTORO is a savoury fish stew related to BOUILLABAISSE. It is here too that the Basques sip their foamy hot chocolate and munch tender egg-rich BRIOCHE for breakfast; play *pelota* at the *fronton*; find time also for the church which is very important in their lives, but forsake everything each autumn to hunt the *palombe*, a wild pigeon with a delicious flavour.

It is believed that the taste for hot chocolate as well as chocolate in other forms was brought to Bayonne, the capital city of the Basque region, by the Jews escaping from the Inquisition in Spain and Portugal in the early 1500s. They had brought with them their secret recipes and from here introduced the taste of France.[11]

Rousillon, Languedoc
Pungent flavours and hearty foods with a definite Spanish and Mediterranean taste are to be found in this region. "*À La Languedocienne*" applies to the many dishes that are served with a sauce or garnish of tomatoes, mushrooms and eggplant. Garlic is one of the most-used seasonings.

Soups that are substantial meals in one pot are those which include in the broth a whole stuffed chicken; beef ribs and other meats with white beans and cabbage; stuffed goose neck, etc. Potatoes, cabbage and beans occur again and again in combination with omelets or poached eggs, veal, beef and mutton. Most famous of all is the roquefort cheese and the ancient dish of Roman times, CASSOULET, a layered white bean casserole with many meats. A little further north, Auvergne gives its name to cabbage specialties coming so abundantly from the good soil: POTÉ AUVERGNATE, a hearty cabbage soup, and OEUFS À L'AUVERGNATE, poached eggs served on a bed of sausages and cabbage. Other pleasures include mushrooms and truffles, chestnuts and snails. Good local wines from heavy and rich to sparkling and rosé as well as white accompany the meals.

Provence
Formerly a part of Italy, Provence still retains the flavours of olive oil, garlic, tomatoes and black olives. Garlic is used generously but it is not considered to be either as strong or as bitter as that found elsewhere. AÏOLI is a type of mayonnaise sauce made with mashed garlic, egg yolks, oil and lemon juice, and it is served with many things but especially as a sauce for the fish in a BOUILLABAISSE or the simpler BOURRIDE. Provençal foods include the aforementioned and also MARIAGE, a thick meaty soup with rice, and PISTOU, a thick vegetable soup with green beans, potatoes, pasta, garlic, and tomatoes served with basil and grated cheese. LOUP is a wolf fish prepared in many ways, while BRANDADE DE MORUE is an appetizer of finely puréed codfish with oil and garlic. The PAN BAGNA is similar to a favourite lunch of Malta: crusty bread moistened with olive oil and layered with anchovies, tomatoes and capers. PISSALADIÈRE is an open tart (similar to a pizza) laid out with sliced onions, anchovies and black olives. PANISSO is a cooled mash of cornmeal or chick peas fried in oil then eaten with sugar. Not only the olives, olive oil, garlic and tomatoes but also the chick peas, rice and many forms of pasta add up to satisfying pungent food with the taste of the sea and Italy.

Meal Patterns and Eating Customs
Food is a subject of prime importance to every French person. It is not uncommon for suggestions for the day's menus to be discussed by family members at the breakfast table over a hot drink, breads and preserves. Traditional recipes are treasured and the happy purchase of a young vegetable or a fine piece of meat will send the whole family into rapturous anticipation of the "special dish."

The morning meal is light but each of the simple items must be "just so." The exact proportion of hot milk to well-prepared coffee, the freshest bread of exactly the length, width and crust favoured by the members of the family, and choice preserves to each one's taste. The noon meal is usually dinner, the special meal of the day, although in cities this pattern is changing somewhat as women move more into the working world and out of the homes.

Traditional dinner would begin with *hors d'oeuvres*, literally "aside from the main work," and meant to be small flavourful appetite teasers. These may be taken with a light apéritif, a favourite being KIR; directions for its preparation include opening a lightly chilled bottle of chablis and pouring off one drink (for the server) then replacing that amount of wine in the bottle with CRÈME DE CASSIS which gives the pale wine a rosy glow.

The fish course would be followed by a course of meat, poultry or game, never carved at the table, in homes usually the carving is done in the kitchen and the foods presented attractively arranged by a servant holding spoon and fork in what is commonly called "French Service." Carefully prepared vegetables may be cooked and served as a garnish to the main course or immediately after as a small separate course.[14]

A serving of salad greens, cool, crisp and shiny with a simple VINAIGRETTE, will always follow the main course. Family dinners will end with cheese and fruits either fresh or poached and a demitasse of coffee. One wine may be chosen that will complement all the courses or a separate wine will be served for each course, always proceeding in the order from light dry wines to heavier and sweeter. Wine is never taken with a green salad (the vinegar in the salad would disturb the palate's appreciation of the wine).

The staple food to the French is bread. At every meal, the bread basket is placed on the table and remains as a part of each course, the last crust to be enjoyed with cheese. Only the fruit, the sweet dessert (if there is one for a special occasion) and the demitasse coffee will be taken without bread. Bread is not only considered a symbol of hospitality and satiety, it is also viewed as important to cleanse the palate for the appreciation of the flavours of the various courses.

Water is never on a French table; wine is served throughout the meal to everyone at the table (regardless of age), and black coffee signifies the end of the meal. The French also do not add water to sauces or casseroles – how can one add water when stocks, vegetable juices and wines are always at hand?

French banquet menus follow traditional patterns too. The courses are usually multiplied, depending on the grandeur of the occasion. Commonly, soup either hot or cold followed by hot *hors d'oeuvres* then a course of cold *hors d'oeuvres* would precede the fish course. A course of poultry or fowl may precede a more substantial entrée of roasted meat or game. Carefully chosen vegetables garnishing the entrée will accompany the meat. Or a course consisting of cooked vegetables by themselves or in the form of small casseroles may be served preceding a small course of green salad to clear the palate. Cheese and fruit would then be followed by an array of sweet desserts, usually the choice depending again on the type of occasion. After-dinner liqueurs may accompany the demitasse coffee. In a gathering of true gourmets, it would be considered bad taste to smoke during a meal as this would disturb the taste sensations and thus the appreciation of the diners.

French table service differs only slightly from that in other western countries. It is customary to place cutlery with the fork prongs and soup spoons facing downwards to the cloth. Dessert spoon and fork are placed above the dinner plate setting with the fork at the top and the spoon below.[9]

French family supper menus most frequently consist of a good satisfying soup or casserole, bread and wine. It is a lighter, simpler meal than that served at noon.

Special Occasions

The majority of the population of France is Roman Catholic with a minority being Protestant and some of the Jewish faith. The two most important religious festivities of the year for Christians are Christmas and Lent. Christmas is ushered in with the celebration of midnight mass in the church followed by RÉVEILLON, a festive meal at home for all the family. This meal is usually a carefully prepared series of dishes that reveal not only traditional family favourites, but regional specialties as well. White or black puddings (made with light meats and fats or blood) will almost always be a part of the dinner. A fat goose or a stuffed turkey will be the centre of the menu while family specialties may shine after the nuts and cheese course. Special desserts such as BÛCHE DE NOËL may represent generations-old recipes or the best from the *pâtisserie*.

In contrast to the feasting of Christmas, Easter is preceded by forty days of fasting from Ash Wednesday to Easter itself. In early times the fasting prohibitions of this time forbade the inclusion of any foods of a "live nature." Thus breads, fruits and vegetables as well as legumes made up the limited menus. Meats, fish and seafood as well as butter were all excluded.[6] In more recent years fish and seafood have been permitted together with the use of eggs and butter, yet there is a sense of restraint in the forty days of fasting menus. In many French homes, the foods of Lent are considered an individual matter.

TWENTY-TWO

German

He who doesn't love wine women and song
remains a fool his whole life long.

– old German proverb

As early as 100 C.E., Tacitus wrote of the Germans as a "warrior nation, hard-drinking, honest and hospitable." He spoke of German food as being "simple," but the diet was a hardy one that included breads and gruels made from oats, millet and barley, wild fruits and berries and wild game and fowl roasted whole on huge spits.[1] Milk and cheese added variety, especially on the occasions when game was lacking. By 800 C.E. it was Charlemagne who had joined the many tribes together in a huge empire that included not only present-day Germany but also France and parts of Italy.[2] It was Charlemagne too who encouraged monasteries in their cultivation of vineyards, orchards and garden, especially herb gardens.[3]

Charlemagne's Holy Roman Empire continued to exist for a time, but parts of it were fated to break away and become distinctive united nations. This was also to be the fate of Germany.[2] In fact, at the time of Tacitus' writing, the term "Germans" referred rather loosely to all the "barbarian" tribes north of the Alps and the Rhine River including what are today known as English, Dutch and Scandinavians.[1] The Latin word *Germania* used in so many early Roman and Hellenistic writings is believed to be of Celtic origin[4] while the later term *Deutsch* has a more complex origin linking both early Teutons and Saxons and referring to language as well as people.[4] It is thought that by a mistranslation of the word *Deutsch* the Germans emigrating to Pennsylvania came to be known as "Pennsylvania Dutch."[5]

Although Charlemagne had tried, and the people themselves dreamed of it, the hope of a united Germany was not to be. There were early problems which prevented unification: lack of natural boundaries was one problem and the second was the fact that the German language was also spoken in other lands, so it too could not be used as a unifying factor.[2]

However, the influence of the Romans and others brought improvements at least in the foods. By the Middle Ages, Germans were quaffing their hot spiced wine from gold- and silver-plated vessels and downing not only spit-roasted oxen but also spiced sausages and blood puddings, smoked meats and pickled fish, a great variety of fresh and dried fruits and even spiced honeycakes.[6] Because of the strict adherence to church fasting days which prohibited the eating of meats, fish was in greater use and prepared in even more ways than in present times.[3] Spices were especially important not only to help preserve foods but to help improve the flavour of spoiled meat.[3]

Accepted Germanic manners and customs date from Charlemagne's time, and although there were some gradual adaptations, the prevailing pattern of manners was rigidly adhered to by all. It was believed that Charlemagne introduced the custom of dining alone with his faithful leaders while the servants were the last to eat.[3] Later, couples often dined together, sometimes sharing a plate and eating with the fingers (before cutlery became popular), but the women would retire promptly after eating, leaving the men to their drinking and singing.

In the Renaissance period, the establishment of the Hanseatic League helped to organize and increase trade, bringing a greater variety of fish, spices, fruits, oil and even precious sugar to the German tables.[3] Cattle and poultry production was increased both in amount and quality by special breeding. Following the ideas used in the kitchens of noblemen, foods were cooked in cauldrons suspended on hooks over open fires, there were even some primitive kitchen ranges with metal rings over wood fires to hold huge pots in which bubbled mixtures of meats, vegetables and fragrant herbs.[7] Local inns served sausages with white and black radishes with mugs of wine, cider or beer, and favourite dishes included lentils or beans cooked with chunks of cured and smoked pork.[7] In cold weather, dried fruits were served with cured meats, and pears, apples and plums were commonly set into banked ovens to dry after the bread had been baked.[7] Two other dishes were already old favourites: steak Tartar, adapted from the scraped raw meat of the marauding Tartar horsemen from Mongolia, and the winter use of salted shredded cabbage – a tart fermented dish the Tartars had learned from the labourers on the Great Wall of China.[8]

Germany as a political entity came into being on January 18, 1871, when peace was finally signed with France and Bismark welded the nation together. But the area itself was still far from unified.[9] There were still pronounced regional differences that included religion, customs, dialects and even temperaments.[1] Wars and dissension had torn the land: the Thirty Years' War (1618-1648) had produced incredible devastation and starvation – people ate dogs, cats, rats, acorns and grass.[3] Generally, it was felt that the unification of 1871 was only a superficial one.[4] Despite every effort, the fiercely individualistic areas could seldom reach agreement and the result was a lack of national identity.[4]

The discovery of America had brought many new exciting foods to European tables. But it took almost 200 years, and the strong insistence of Frederick the Great in 1744 that German peasants plant potatoes against hunger, before the potato found a firm place in German cuisine. It now appears in dozens of delicious forms from soups, thick sauces, pancakes, dumplings and puddings – even to the making of schnaps.[3,7] Cocoa and turkey came to be known, but coffee was to suffer a lack of popularity because of the preference for beer. Brewed everywhere and drunk everywhere, beer was considered as a food in liquid form, evidenced by a corpulence seldom seen before.[10] It began and ended the day, was a part of many dishes – BIERHALS, BIERFREUND, BIERSACK, etc. – and was the beverage for all gatherings from weddings to funerals. It's thought the beer preference has to do with Germany's long history of strife and wars, for the processing of beer is quicker and easier than the culture of wines.[10]

The 1700s not only saw new foods enter the German cuisine, there were also some new customs. French influence was becoming paramount in everything to do with food and drink. Small glasses replaced huge drinking mugs; coffee, tea and chocolate came to be sociable drinks and were served from specially made porcelain sets. Fine light bakery and flaky pastries replaced the heavy honey and spice cakes of old. The carving of huge roasts became refined to an art and matching silver sets of cutlery and carving utensils came into vogue.[3] Even Frederick the Great of Prussia preferred speaking French to German; French cooks and cookbooks, French manners all became an intrinsic part of the cultured upper classes and, as always, this newer protocol was rigidly adhered to.[3,7]

But the German peasants, workers and the many poor made do with their homemade beer and filled their stomachs with KRAUT and bacon, lentils and peas, firm satisfying breads and light dumplings.[3] By the 1800s more than four-fifths of the German population were peasants and their own pigs were the mainstay of their diet. Thanks to Frederick the Great, it could be said that by the end of the 1800s, "potatoes were such a regular item that smoke coming from a cottage chimney at night was almost a certain sign that inside, potatoes, bacon and onions were frying."[7]

Kaiser Wilhelm II ruled from 1888 to 1918. It was he who introduced many English customs since his mother was a daughter of Queen Victoria. Most popular was the introduction of large satisfying English-style breakfasts, and inns called *weinstube* featuring lodging and good food and wine.[7] Kaiser Wilhelm also insisted upon menus being written in German instead of French – and he was not above enjoying robust peasant dishes.[3] It was not long before the tastes and manners of the court were reflected in fine hotels and the burgeoning middle classes.

The industrial revolution that swept Great Britain took another 100 years before it took hold in Germany. For too long, the Germans lacked well-established political and economic systems: Germany's many fragmented provinces and states often had separate currencies and different trade tariffs.[9] But within three years after the 1871 unification, more mines, iron works and blast furnaces were producing than had been even seen in the past seventy years.[9]

The expansion and power of the great Krupp works paralleled the growth of Prussian power. Educational systems were keyed to industrial education and research, and this trend together with the vast riches of natural resources and the growth of fast communication systems spurred German genius. Welding industrial development to scientific research and careful use of resources were vital factors in Germany's success. But so was another point: business and industries were enriched by aggressive personalities who regarded politics as too conservative.[9]

Yet the dream of a unified Germany was still shared by political conservatives, intellectuals, and powerful businessmen.[4] The gradual rise of the Social Democrat Party and a large working class that chafed under the collar of hard work and submissiveness expected of them caused rumblings of concern.[9] In their gigantic industrial leap forward, they had pushed aside the periods of Classicism and Romanticism that other nations had gone through, and this lack "added yet another rift to the many inner conflicts of the German people."[1]

After the First World War, the great progress of the Second Reich was abruptly ended. New interpretations and fabrications of German past history attempted to overcome the sense of national failure. These theories drew largely on old popular legends, on Wagner's revival of Germanic mythology and on Gobineau's race theory, and not least on Nietzsche's "superman" and "blond beast."[4] Every misfortune came to be attributed to the deceit of others: "the crafty Jews, the perfidious British, the treacherous Italians and so forth."[4] Lacking established bounds and traditions and leaning heavily on a lack of reality and with a sense of despair and inferiority, the ground was laid for the horrors that came with World War II.

Today, Germany is split yet again into East and West, but the Germans of both areas have more than demonstrated that their deep traditions of respect for authority and orderly living as well as their great zest for life has brought them industrial and agricultural advances as well as one of the highest standards of living to be found anywhere.[1] Gone are the luxurious and even aristocratic manners and customs and in their place has come a new sense of the pleasures of regional German cuisine, dialects, and festivals. Yet some admirable old ways remain: politeness and formality especially in names and titles, the importance of cleanliness and neatness in dress, and an admirable sense of responsibility even in young children.[1,3]

Home Life and Facilities

The German home is an orderly one and German cleanliness is legendary. Children are taught very early to be polite, courteous and responsible. There are some regional differences that are noted by the Germans themselves. Northerners feel that the Bavarians (in the south) take life too easily, are too fond of good living, and speak with an unintelligible dialect. But the southern Germans counter this with the opinion that the northerner is too dour and serious even if he is grudgingly admitted to be honest and very hard working![2,1]

But whether from the north or the south, in most German households there is little argument that father is the head. More recently the traditional view that the "woman's place is in the home" is fast disappearing as more and more women join the work force.[2]

Kitchens are small but efficient and make use of modern gadgets and electrical appliances. In fact small appliances are of high quality and often perform several functions. Earthenware mixing bowls, strong wooden spoons, pudding and cake molds, rubber, wooden and metal spatulas as well as wire whisks all find a place in the German kitchen. Even if the weekdays are busy ones, the *hausfrau* will find time to prepare a special dinner at least once a week while home baking for the holidays is traditional. Many kitchens boast specialty baking utensils: the KUGELHOPF tube pan with its diagonal spiral fluting, springform cake pans and flan and torte pans and probably a SPRINGERLE roller or wooden SPRINGERLE molds for cookies. Utensils are chosen for use and for quality and all are bought to last.[11]

In rural areas cold cellars are used for winter storage of root vegetables, fruit, the family crocks of pickles and sauerkraut and shelves of home preserves and jams. But food storage is not such a necessity in the city. Germans prefer their foods fresh. Baked goods, and often vegetables, fruits and meats as well, are bought daily.[2,3] Besides, many specialty stores, small open-air markets, and huge supermarkets and *Hypermarkets* with incredible selections of local and imported goods make shopping a delight.[2] Still other specialty shops feature a wide range of fine foods such as imported cheeses, different breads and rolls and sausages and meats of every description. Milk too is not delivered to homes and is often fetched daily from nearby dairies.[2]

FOODS COMMONLY USED

Pork, beer, potatoes, sauerkraut and black bread are not only German staples, they are simple hearty foods that German in-

genuity has raised to gastronomic heights of perfection and diversity. Newer trends to lightness and simplicity in dishes and meals have brought the tendency to forego soups as being fattening, and people are tending to eat less bread and potatoes but more eggs.[2]

It is a pity that soups are losing popularity for German soups were always richly satisfying, based on vegetables, flour-thickened, and flavoured with smoked pork. No part of the pig is wasted and much of the pork produced finds its way into the dozens of varieties of sausages as well as hams, bacon, chops and roasts.

Beer is the national drink and is of exceptional quality everywhere with many areas specializing in several distinctive types. Potatoes are served in every conceivable form and guise but none so wondrous as the fluffy dumplings of Thuringia. Sauerkraut, too, shows up in soups, stews, blended with fruits or dotted with caraway seeds – the perfect bed for roast goose or plump sausage.

German bakery is renowned not only for its flavour – the honest taste of good fresh ingredients – but also for its lack of colouring, additives or chemicals which the Germans dislike. Throughout, honest natural flavours of good fresh foods in hearty servings all washed down with fine beer represent German cuisine at its best.

Milk and Milk Products

Milk is not a favourite beverage except for children, pregnant women and nursing mothers.[12] Milk is used in custards, puddings, and cream fillings. In East Germany where the cuisine tends to retain its traditional flavour, tastes include a much more prominent use of sour cream than in the rest of Germany.[3,13] In Northern and East Germany buttermilk may often be used to marinate and tenderize game.[13] Breakfast and afternoon KAFFEE (coffee) is taken preferably with canned milk.[3] Sour cream called SCHMAND is added to soups and gravies.

Many fine imported cheeses are available and these are enjoyed mostly as a dessert, especially after a cold meal. Sometimes sliced cheeses join platters of assorted cold meats and sausages for a light supper with rye bread to form open-face sandwiches which are eaten with a knife and fork. TOPFEN, the dry pot of farmer's fresh cheese, is widely used in baking and cooking. QUARK is a creamy form of fresh cottage cheese.

Fruits and Vegetables

Apples, pears, cherries and plums are produced in quantity in many areas of Germany. The Rhineland is of course famed for grapes and these are pressed into many varieties of fine wines. Fruits are enjoyed fresh as a snack but most often are cooked into compotes, that is, wedges of fresh fruits poached in sugar syrup sometimes lightly flavoured with fresh lemon zest or lightly spiced.

Dating from olden times, dried fruits still play an important and interesting part in the German cuisine. They can be made into jams and spreads, fillings for tarts and yeast doughs, and they can also add their natural sweetness and colour to many meat and game dishes. Fruits such as crushed pineapple, orange wedges or chopped apple are often also added to sauerkraut dishes.[3] Cold fruit soups and soups made from fresh crushed berries, sweetened and slightly thickened with cornstarch, are popular especially in Northern and East Germany.[13] Dried fruits may also be cooked as a colourful compote and then served as a side dish with game or meat roasts. Raisins and apples are frequent tasty partners to quick suppers of liver or sausages.[7] And of course fresh fruits and nuts are a special treat at holiday time.

In Germany, vegetables are treated with the respect due their special "status." Cabbage, turnips and potatoes can be mashed, sliced, grated, shredded and cooked, boiled, fried and braised into literally dozens of delicious dishes. But the highest praise is reserved for Germany's flavourful wild mushrooms and exquisite white cultivated asparagus. Mushrooms and asparagus are considered company treats.[3] Many varieties of cabbage, cauliflower, hop sprouts and cabbage sprouts, carrots, turnips and peas find their way into the German vegetable pot. If the vegetables are not intended to add their flavour to a soup or a stew then they are cooked in the special German way. First a thorough cleaning then shaping and cutting as desired, a quick tossing in hot bubbling butter, a little addition of moisture and the vegetables steam to a perfect tenderness, forming their own sauce. Old or fibrous vegetables may be cut up and boiled first then given the glorious butter and steam treatment. Sometimes a little flour, toasted breadcrumbs or a dollop of sour cream adds the final flourish. Vegetables cooked this way are served separately as they deserve to be.[11]

Meats and Alternates

All over Germany pork reigns supreme. So many delicious ways have been found to serve every morsel of pork that the dishes are endless. When it comes to describing Germany's sausages another book is needed. Beef and veal find a smaller place on the menu, but Germany's plump chicken, ducks and especially the geese are famed. There is also some competition from wild game and fowl which is plentiful in Germany's mountains and forest areas, and which is marinated to tenderness and slowly cooked in covered dishes that bring out the best flavours. Every part of the animal is used: tongue, brains, ears, kidneys, heart, lungs, tripe, milt, sweetbreads, palates, heads, shanks, tails, hocks, trotters and udders.[3] The quality of smoked bacon and cured hams is legendary.

The seemingly endless varieties of WÜRSTE (sausages) can, however, be placed in general categories. ROHWURST is cured and smoked sausage ready to slice and eat; BRÜHWURST is sausage that is smoked then scalded and usually eaten heated; KOCHWURST is smoked sausage already well-cooked and may be eaten as is or heated; BRATWURST is the large category of sausages that are sold raw (but may be spiced, smoked and cured for flavour) and usually pan-fried before eating.[3] Animal intestines are often well-cleaned and used as casings for sausages; blood too finds a place as fried blood (GERÖSTETES BLUT) or more commonly in black or blood pudding (sausage).[11]

Almost as important on the menu (but not quite) is herring. In Emden it is even possible to be served an entire meal with appetizer, main dish and salad made with herring.[1] Fresh-caught herring is called "green" and is often served fried. Herring salad may be prepared by mixing diced herring with chopped cooked potatoes; herring may also be served jellied, grilled, cooked *au bleu*, grilled or fried in wax paper packets, chopped and spread on toast.[14] Nor does the list end there. There are also ROLLMOPS or BISMARK HERING, fillets of herring rolled around onions and pickles; BRATHERING, fried sour-pickled herring and MATJESHERING, a quality fat herring served simply with boiled potatoes.[1]

Nor is herring the only fish. German waters provide crayfish, lobster, eels, mussels, flounder, plaice, turbot, sole, and the noted salmon and trout especially from the Rhine River. FORELLE BLAU or TROUT AU BLEU is a method of fish cookery said to be devised in Germany: live fish (scales and all) are plunged into acidulated water to cook briefly and then are served immediately. Traditional German accompaniments to all fish dishes are potatoes in some form, usually simply boiled and garnished with minced parsley or chives and fresh butter. Other partners with most fish meals are cucumbers, asparagus and green salad.[11]

Eggs are widely used not only soft-cooked for breakfast but also at other times in many forms, most under the heading of EIERSPEISEN. These include scrambled, fried (SPIEGELEIER), poached, as plain or fluffy omelets, eggs with sauces, and KAISERSCHMARREN – "torn" (pulled into irregular pieces with two forks) egg pancakes served with cinnamon sugar and buttered raisins.[14] Eggs are also used generously in savoury and dessert soufflés, blended into soups and sauces, and add their golden richness to the many fragrant baked goods.

Legumes are important too. Yellow and green dried peas are used in thick soups or as side dishes of puréed peas. Lentils and white beans are also used both in soups and in many one-dish EINTOPF meals.

Breads and Cereals

Bread is on the table at all meals whether in the home or at a public dining room and it is the undisputed "staff of life," only slightly more important than the ubiquitous potato. While chewy dark breads made of rye flour come immediately to mind, German bakeries also turn out an incredible array of soft and hard, crisp and chewy, seeded or plain breads and rolls of every shape and size. Rye and wholewheat flour, barley and oats all have a place in breads and rolls. Many are sprinkled with cracked wheat grains, coarse salt, and crunchy sesame or poppy seeds. With such an array to choose from it is not surprising that dry breakfast cereals are not too popular although children are sometimes served hot cooked oats or rice at breakfast, usually sweetened with sugar and raisins and sometimes flavoured with cinnamon.

Fats

Lard, bacon fat and butter head the list of most-used fats in Germany. Olive oil is used only infrequently for special salads or dishes. Vegetable shortenings and margarine are gaining popularity among health-conscious Germans. Many homes (especially in the country) still enjoy the flavour of fats rendered from geese, ducks and chickens and these are used as spreads on breads and in general cooking. Fats for deep-frying include lard, rendered fat from fowl and even horse fat.[7]

Sweets

Sweet preserves with the breakfast bread, plenty of sugar in the *kaffee*, something sweet to finish the midday meal – and how depressing it would be to contemplate a day without afternoon KAFFEE that included at least a little KUCHEN, STRUDEL or TORTE! And what kind of a holiday would Christmas be without the warm aromas of WEIHNACHTSGEBÄCK and KONFEKT?

It is all right to list beer, sausages, kraut and potatoes as hardy old traditional German staples but let no one forget the rich baked goods are available if not from mother's oven, then from any number of exquisite *Konditoreien*, where one can relax, chat a while and sip delicious KAFFEE while choosing from a bewildering display of sweet nibbles.

One is further reminded – in the nicest way – of the German sweet tooth with the serving of many meat and fish dishes gently afloat with sweet and sour sauces and sometimes including a melange of dried fruits to heighten the tart-sweet flavours. Don't forget, too, that not only are many popular German summer soups made with fresh fruits, but if none of these is available the canny *hausfrau* will use sugar and vinegar.

Seasonings

After Charlemagne encouraged the monasteries (in olden times very advanced in both the growing and preparation of food) to plant herb gardens, it did not take long for the people to adapt the fragrant herbs into many dishes: lovage, woodruff, parsley, chives, garlic and dill. Seeds quickly found a place too: caraway, dill, sesame and poppy seeds.[7]

German cookery could generally be described as hearty but bland. Strong flavours and strong seasonings are not the rule – even garlic is used with a heavy hand only in certain sausages, while onions, chives and leeks are preferred. Adding a distinctive touch to the German cuisine is the prevalent use of sweet-sour flavours usually created by blending vinegar or lemon juice with brown sugar. The best of German cookery relies on the delicate natural flavours of fresh ingredients: fresh eggs and butter, choice meats and fish, young tender vegetables, fragrant ripe fruits. Sweet and sour dishes are often further enhanced with the addition of raisins or currants and spices like cinnamon and nutmeg or the dried crumbs from honey cake or gingerbread. Other frequent tastes include: anchovies, apples, capers, fresh dill weed, horseradish, juniper berries and many varieties of mustards.[3,7,11]

The tang of sour cream and dark rye bread and the smoky taste of bacon permeates many meals especially in Northern and East Germany.[1,13]

Beverages

Beer is the favourite German beverage and if natural thirst and good fellowship are not enough, there are any number of salty, sour, tangy or tart VORSPEISEN to lure on the thirst. German thirst is not only first and foremost quenched by frothy mugs of beer, the containers come in different sizes and materials and the beer itself comes in many tastes and brews from mild to strong. If that is not enough, there may be a SCHNAPS to drink before the beer and even fruit syrups to add to them for variety. Germany is considered to be "the greatest brewing country in the world and Munich the greatest brewing city" but every area and every town and in many cases most homes brew specialties of their own.[1,3] Types of beer include: HELLES, light Munich beer; DUNKLES, dark; HELLER BOCK, strong and light; DUNKLER BOCK, strong and dark – and many more. Further, it is possible to order one's beer in anything from a small glass to a huge *stein*.[1]

Many fine German wines are also produced, both reds and whites, but the whites are more widely known than the reds. Rhine and Moselle wines offer many delicate flavours. The sweetest ones are for sipping while the drier, fruity types are for special-occasion meals. Generally, the Germans have a preference for sweet rather than dry wines.[2,3]

KAFFEE begins the German day as a warming, stimulating breakfast drink. The coffee served in the late afternoon usually has the connotation of a friendly hospitable gathering to which is added the sweet touch of fine pastries. Coffee and a sweet is a German tradition.[13] Tea has a medicinal connotation and is usually taken to "cure" something; of the many types of herbal teas, camomile and mint are among the favourites.

Regional Specialties

While the various regions of Germany were independent and autonomous communities, until relatively recently, it is not surprising that they also developed special regional foods. Yet there is a common factor: almost everywhere these regional foods are based on the country's favourite staples of beer, pork, potatoes and cabbage - yet they are different in the technique of cooking, seasoning or the way they are served. In general, three main divisions of German cuisine can be distinguished: North, Central and Southern.[3] The Northern area, influenced by its proximity to the Scandinavian, Baltic countries and the Netherlands as well as by the damp, cold climate, is characterized by thick soups, pickled and smoked meats and fish, dried fruits, smoked bacon, sour cream and many dishes with geese and eels. Most interesting is the traditional North German meal of LABSKAUS: a one-dish meal of meat *and* fish plus vegetables which became a sailor's specialty and earned the name LOBSCOUSE. SCHLACHTPLATTE or "slaughter plate" is also a Northern specialty of a variety of meats and sausages - the byproducts of a slaughtering day - served with bread and pickles.

Berlin, considered part of the Northern cuisine district, is famed for its ground meat dishes: STRAMMER MAX, a snack of buttered rye bread with a thick slice of ham and two fried eggs resting on top; BERLINER PFANN-KUCHEN, luscious plump jam-filled donuts (the inspiration of those in other countries), and BAUMKUCHEN, rich eggy Christmas layered logs glazed and browned with chocolate.[3] Here too, KÜMMEL (caraway, as a flavouring and as a liqueur) is important and beer is taken with schnaps accompanying most foods and occasionally beer *mit schuss* indicates a shot of raspberry syrup in the beer for a change.[7] Every Berlin bar carries a good supply of KURFÜRSTLICHER MAGENBITTER, a bitter potent cordial said to do wonders for the stomach.[7]

The central region also includes hearty meals and foods, especially the famed Westphalian ham and dark heavy pumpernickel bread.[3] Pork is important here and many dishes favour a heavy touch with freshly ground black pepper. Gravies are thickened with dried breadcrumbs more often than with flour. PANNHAS is a thick, simmered porridge made from buckwheat and may be eaten hot or cold and sometimes sliced and fried. PANNHAS may have been the origin of New England "scrapple," only cornmeal was used in America rather than buckwheat.[3] Frankfurt has a special herb-flavoured green sauce, GRÜNE SOSSE, bearing much similarity to the PESTO ALLA GENOVESE based on basil.

One cannot think of Thuringia without fluffy round images of plump dumplings, for here is the home of the feathery KLÖSSE, made only from potatoes and flour - the best made even without the leavening help of eggs.[3,7] The foods in Saxony are similar but they take even more pleasure in sweets: SCHNITTEN, STOLLEN, and fruit KUCHEN in delicious variety.

Apple cider in different alcoholic potencies is a familiar drink throughout this region.

The southern German cuisine has a characteristically lighter touch enhanced by the grape cuttings planted by the Romans almost 2,000 years ago. They call their dumplings KNÖDEL here, and they make some special potato dishes: puddings, pancakes, diced potatoes and bacon and the famed HIMMEL UND ERDE: equal amounts of pan-fried sliced apples and potatoes with crisply fried slices of blood sausage.[3]

German cuisine can also be divided into that based on wine and that based on beer. At one time only the aristocracy was permitted to hunt and dine on game and wine; today it is only a question of taste and preference. Wines are served mostly in a *Weinkeller* and foods are more apt to be light and delicate from main dish to airy desserts. Beer is served in a *Bierlokal* a *Brauhaus*, or a *Keller* and is the hearty partner to filling savoury dishes usually served in generous portions.[6]

Meal Patterns and Eating Customs

Early risers, the Germans like a light breakfast of bread or rolls with butter and preserves and coffee with canned milk and sugar. Children may be served a porridge of oats or rice flavoured with raisins and cinnamon.[11] But since that first meal of the day is served before the real German appetite has fully awakened, most people take a few sandwiches of meat or cheese to work or school, these to be eaten around ten o'clock as the second breakfast or snack. In some areas a few sausages with beer fill the hunger "pocket."

Traditionally the noon meal is the largest of the day and many try to eat at home with the family, although this is becoming increasingly less likely with more and more women working outside the home. A hearty soup, a meat and vegetable EINTOPF and a dessert (SÜSSPEISEN) make up the midday meal.

Since the evening supper is customarily served about 7:30 P.M., an afternoon snack of "coffee and a sweet" helps tide one over. A light evening meal of soup and a dessert or simply a selection of cold meats, sausages and cheese provide sustenance. Occasionally a late evening hunger pang may be assuaged with sausages and beer or a thick goulash-type soup.[3,11] Restaurants serve every variety of food in generous portions and "eating-out" is almost a form of sport to many Germans.[3]

One can understand the delight in eating out with only a glance of what is offered: good eating places have special names such as *Gasthöfe, Ratskeller, Weinstuben, Bierhallen, Restaurants, Schnellimbiss-Stube* (quick lunch counter), *Milchbars* for cool milk or milkshakes, *Eissalons* for refreshing ices and ice creams of all types, *Konditoreien* for pastries and coffee, summer beer gardens and even special canteens at places of business to provide especially that hot midday meal.[2,3,11] And there is a *Würstlerei* just for beer and sausages.[1]

There is another reason not only for "eating out" but also for taking guests out to dinner. The German hostess retains a vivid memory of the strict formality and rigid code of etiquette of former times; casual entertaining does not come easily to her. Further, it does not add to one's composure that German women are perfectionists in matters of cleanliness and order, and often may feel nervous at the thought of guests. There is a definite preference for entertaining by asking guests for coffee or after-theatre snacks. Yet even these casual entertainments are still beset by rituals.[3] It is most important that guests arrive punctually; some hand-kissing is still customary, and most likely a bouquet of flowers will be proffered to the hostess. Handshaking is a definite point of etiquette and more handshaking goes on in Germany than in many other lands.[2] Hostesses always serve with their finest linen and if possible any fine treasured pieces of china, especially coffee sets. Rhine and Moselle wines may be sipped with little nibbles of salted pastries and nuts or a punch bowl may be prepared for the guests.

Before the evening closes, the hostess usually serves casually prepared sandwiches or plates of sausages with beer. The more sophisticated may sip scotch, bourbon or brandy but generally cocktails are not in the German entertaining tradition.[3] Dinner parties at home usually are prompted by some special family occasion such as confirmation or an engagement.

A particularly delightful custom is that of presenting a child with a huge gaily-decorated cone filled with sweets for his or her first day at school. Perhaps this sweet beginning adds pleasure to learning.

Special Occasions

Present-day West Germany is almost equally divided between Roman Catholics and Protestants and each celebrate not only religious and saint days but also join in beer and wine festivities, regional holidays and, in some areas, harvesting and planting festivities.

Literally hundreds of local and regional festivals and holidays are celebrated throughout Germany and vary according to locale as do customs and foods. The South is predominantly Catholic while the North is mostly Protestant. Plain cakes, bread and cheese are served at funerals, while the happier family occasions such as weddings, engagements, and confirmations call forth wines and opulent meals from the best of the regional and family specialties.

The wedding-eve party is called *Polterabend* and, aside from the special treats and wine that are served, guests traditionally bring baskets or armloads of old crockery and these are cheerfully smashed because "broken dishes bring good luck."[3] Humorous and teasing speeches and songs for the new couple help make a boisterous and fun-filled evening. Another traditionally German evening is the *Herrenabend*, an evening for men only. Not quite the same as the familiar "stag party," the *Herrenabend* is usually for the purpose of discussing business or politics while eating and drinking. Of course no one minds if, towards the smaller hours of the evening, the drinking predominates over the conversation.[3]

Spring and fall sees the proliferation of many local beer and wine festivals but none as overwhelming as the Munich *Oktoberfest* held annually for a sixteen-day spree of beer-drinking, singing to the oom-pah-pah bands, dancing and snacking on roasted chickens, sausages and whole spit-roasted oxen all in gargantuan quantities. The fest, originated in 1810 to celebrate Crown Prince Ludwig's marriage, proved to be such a good idea that it has been carried on ever since. The boisterous good fellowship has spread to other countries where citizens of German origin make their homes, and, like the Irish St. Patrick's Day parade, everyone regardless of ethnic background happily joins in. Together with the fun and frolic, eating and drinking, nearby amusement parks offer all manner of games and rides as well.

The German's annual calendar is rung in with a quiet family evening on New Year's Eve centred around the traditional speciality of Polish carp: a whole carp gently poached in a rich sauce of beer, gingerbread crumbs, lemon peel, almonds and raisins all traditionally served with KARTOFFELKLÖSSE and KRAUT.[11,14] The festive meal is served with a flaming punch bowl and completed with an array of baked treats. Catholics eat no meat on New Year's Eve, Protestant families may enjoy other local food favourites.

Three King's Eve, Epiphany or *Dreikönigsabend* signifies the end of the Christmas season (Twelfth Night) and is greeted with the serving of wine or punch and KÖNIGSKUCHEN, a loaf cake with raisins, almonds and rum.[3]

Arriving in bleak mid-winter is the brightest carnival of them all: *Fasching* (elsewhere called Mardi Gras and Shrove Tuesday), usually a three-day bash of costumes, masks, parades, processions, parties and carefree revelry unmatched at any other time of year. Crullers called FASTNACHTKRAPFEN are the special treat everywhere but feasting and drinking before the Lenten restrictions is the general rule. The new spring beer, called BOCK, is celebrated during this time as well and is enjoyed with BOCKWURST sausages that are the specialty of the season.[11] Holy Thursday (just before Good Friday) is also called *Gründonnerstag* and the spring festival is heralded with the serving of a green vegetable soup made of fresh spring vegetables while other dishes made with eggs and spinach are also traditional. Good Friday or *Karfreitag* is a solemn day when all businesses and shops are closed. For the pious, no meat is eaten and only fish dishes are taken. Churches open their doors revealing huge displays of fresh flowers and flickering candles.[11]

Easter or *Oster* arrives with the special aroma of home-baked fruited breads and cakes, candies in the form of eggs and rabbits and a traditional Easter dinner featuring ham served with puréed peas. For the children, the Easter bunny annually does his job of hiding coloured eggs throughout the house and in gardens.

A pleasant ritual of spring is the Whitsun Festival or *Pfingstausflug*, a traditional spring outing when good luck is considered to be the prize of the first person to hear a cuckoo, and everyone enjoys communing with nature.[2,3]

In the land where the Christmas tree originated, as well as many Christmas legends and nostalgic carols, the holiday begins early with the many fairs, especially the one held annually at Nürnberg. Here is to be found every conceivable decoration and toy for Christmas: a fairyland of colour, design and fun. And for those who get hungry while shopping there is always the famed Nürnberg LEBKUCHEN and PFEFFERKUCHEN.[3] Some of the earliest stagings of Christmas nativity scenes and primitive Christmas plays were said to be presented by Saint Francis of Greccio in 1223.[15]

While the first taste of Christmas may be at the fairs, the real beginning of the festive season is on Saint Nikolaus' Day, December 6. The evening before all children hang up socks or boots and find them filled in the morning with sweets and small gifts. But the real excitement is the house-to-house visit of Saint Nikolaus himself with his helper, Krampus, a horrid furry little monster who carries a switch for bad children. But most children have been good and therefore happily receive the Saint's good cookies and good wishes.[15] Delicious smells drift from every home as mothers prepare almost daily batches of honeyed and spiced cakes, cookies and fragrant breads all called WEIHNACHTSGEBÄCK. And everywhere little *Naschkatzen* (pilferers of sweets) are nibbling tastes of STOLLEN, LEBKUCHEN, SPRITZ COOKIES, SPRINGERLE and SPEKULATIUS.

Christmas Eve brings tree-lighting and carol-singing and most families go to church. Surprise gifts from Kris Kringle appear mysteriously under the tree after everyone returns from church services. Since pious Christians refrain from meat on Christmas Eve, the traditional dinner of Polish carp baked in all its glory with beer, nuts and raisins is usually the highlight of the meal surrounded with potato dumplings and dishes of KRAUT. Punch or wine and fine bakery end the meal while others still nibble on fruit and nuts. Christmas Day is a quiet family day in Germany and the special dinner will likely be the regional speciality of roast hare, roast pork or a fine fat roasted goose. Marzipan fruits and little figures are part of the decorations and the nibbles too.

TWENTY-THREE

Greek

. . . pleasures drive out pain and excessive pain leads men to seek excessive pleasures . . .

– Aristotle[1]

It was spoken by a Greek, and more than twenty centuries later it is still the core truism of Greeks everywhere. No characteristic is more typically Greek than the inherent ability to balance pains and pleasures delicately and live life to the fullest.

Eight and a half million Greeks living on the land and on 1,400 Greek islands suffer the daily realities of existence in a harsh meagre land where political problems simmer unresolved and where poverty and hardship are old neighbours. But while the body may subsist on bread, cheese and olives as rural daily fare, the Greek soul is spiritually nourished by the mystically dazzling landscape of endless blue skies, the clarity of a strong white sun and the warmth of rustic red earth.

These are the same elements that bore witness to the "Glory of Greece," a brilliant span of 200 years from 500-300 B.C.E. that saw Athens become the light-source of the Western world and spawned a plethora of literature, philosophy, mathematics, democracy and a sophistication in the style of living that has seldom been equalled. While the rest of the world gnawed on roasted meat, the Greeks were savouring many varieties of fruits and seafoods, experimenting with cooked mixtures of meats and vegetables, developing sauces and dressings (white sauce, mayonnaise, marinades of oils and seasonings), blending seasonings – and even writing cookbooks.[2,3]

Because reminders of Greece's past greatness are everywhere visible in the civilized world of today, the past and the present are one reality to the Greek. It doesn't matter what subject is under discussion, Greeks will have an opinion – and a word for it. It is the incredible blending of past greatness, of living the present to the fullest, and of unflagging faith in the future that makes simple survival the ultimate Greek pleasure. With bold words and classic gestures, with intense curiosity and endless enthusiasm together with an age-old ability to dramatize, the Greek brushes aside pain and troubles, gently disdains time and plunges fully into the enjoyment of life.

Others may point to the closeness of Greek family life or to the stability of the Greek Orthodox Church as central factors for the Greek's optimism and self-confidence. But it is all of these factors and something more. It is an ancient tradition that Greece is somehow more than a land or a people but rather a special image that was nurtured by the ancient gods of Greece and preserved for all eternity by an omnipotent "god of Greece."[1] That innate Greek faith is rooted firmly in the belief that while other gods may be alive or dead, the "God of Greece" will somehow forever intervene just when things seem hopeless. And a glance at Greek history seems to bear out this philosophy.

When the great Hellenistic age came to a crushing end with the Roman Conquest of 197 C.E., Greek schools declined, Greek democracy disappeared, yet Greek language and culture survived. The novelty of Greek cuisine – varieties of wild animals, fruits and seafoods, the ingenious uses of sauces and seasonings, recipes and utensils – was a revelation to the Romans. They unabashedly adopted Greek foods, together with Greek art and architecture, Greek philosophy and refinements. And they valued their Greek chefs above all.[2,4] While the Greeks helplessly watched as Athens gave way to Rome as the centre of the Western world, they must have also had some satisfaction in seeing that Hellenistic influence proved stronger than armies.

The threads of Greek language and culture that flickered during the Roman domination were fanned to a bright flame during the thousand years after the fall of Rome. The period of the Byzantine Empire with its centre in Constantinople actually took its name from the ancient Greek community on which it stood: Byzantium. Christianity was introduced by the Emperor Constantine as the state religion of the Roman Empire around 325 C.E., and it is probably to the credit of the early Christian theologians' incorporation of many Greek philosophical ideas that Christianity flourished even though Rome was later sacked by hostile pagan tribes.[3]

Again, however, this Greek flowering of influence was to be nipped abruptly in 1204 C.E. as the Crusaders captured Constantinople and parcelled it out to Frankish knights. The new rulers crushed everything Greek. Latinization was the goal, Greek ships and trade were turned over to the Venetians and strong attempts were made to impose Catholicism. It did indeed seem that the Franks dominated every aspect of life – with one exception. Greek women quietly saw to it that the children they bore never forgot that they were Greek.[3]

The continuing benevolence of the "God of Greece" was about to meet the strongest test. On Tuesday, May 29, 1453, the Byzantine Empire was crushed completely with the capture of Constantinople by the Ottoman Empire. So deep is the memory of that terrible day, that even to the present, Greeks consider Tuesday a bad-luck day and the entire month of May fraught with grim symbolism. Yet historians see a brighter aspect and believe that the mass exile of thousands of Greeks throughout Europe (as a direct result of the Turkish conquest) may have been responsible for the revival of learning that led to the Renaissance period.[5]

The suppressions and cruelties of the Ottoman domination were to last 400 years. And while the Greeks learned, among other things, to enjoy sipping Turkish coffee, smoking the *narghile* (water-filtered smoking pipe) and preparing meat on skewers which they called SOUVLAKIA (from the Turkish SIS KEBAB), the Turks who were previously a nomadic people very quickly developed a taste for all of Greek cookery. Not surprising then, in the manner of all conquerors, they also gave Turkish names to classic Greek dishes.[2,5]

It seems the Greek's hopeful confidence, that age-old faith in the "God of Greece," was to be renewed again. In their 400-year dominance, the Turks made two fateful errors: they gave the Greeks concessions in trade, shipping and administration, at once unwittingly creating Greek leadership and a Greek navy; and secondly they decided to place the Orthodox Church leaders in charge of their communities. The Greek leadership and navy were to be the seeds of subsequent Turkish downfall, while the authority and strength of the Church in small communities unified the Greek peoples everywhere and served to preserve their language and their culture. While the rest of the Western world at that time became a blend of Roman and Turkish culture with only echoes of Greek taste apparent, to the Greeks themselves their vital roots remained strong.

It is worth remembering that when people are suppressed, their only daily concern is survival. There is not time or freedom of mind to devote to the arts, to literature, to philosophy or to delicacies of the palate. Choice lands were cultivated by the Turks and the Greeks were forced to retreat to barren rocky lands and mountain areas, often surviving on cheese made from the milk of mountain goats, wild herbs, olives and whatever crops they could nudge from the unwilling land. The Turks called the Greeks *Rumis* and it is from this bitter time that the Greek still refers to the noble and creative part of himself as *Hellene* and any bursts of stubbornness or selfishness as being the *Romios* part of his person.[3]

Of necessity, then, Greek cuisine became an art of the past. It was so successfully adapted, transformed and renamed mostly by the Turks and the Italians that its Greek origins were all but forgotten. Yet one piece of ancient writing remains: *The Banquet of the Learned* (*Deipnosophists*), written in 200 C.E. by Athenaeus, an Egyptian living in Rome. His detailed descriptions of foods eaten, their methods of preparation and even cooking utensils and cutlery as well as menus for dinners and banquets are remarkable in their sophistication. It is from Athenaeus that we learn of KAKAVIA. A seafood stew introduced to Marseilles by seafaring Greeks, KAKAVIA later became world-renowned as BOUILLABAISSE. Sauces are discussed in loving detail: that emulsion of eggs, lemon juice and olive oil called mayonnaise, a thick white sauce called BÉCHAMEL, and even cruets of oil and vinegar to be set on the table and used to dress fresh or cooked vegetables. The use of blends of curry probably was introduced in Alexander's time after his conquest of northern India, but Greek cooks were already long-familiar with fragrant thyme and oregano, mint and marjoram and the Isle of Rhodes was noted for a ginger-flavoured bread.

There is more. The general acceptance of small nibbles of food with drinks as "provocatives to eating" not only added graciousness to dining but may even be the ancient root of the fact that Greeks never drink without the accompaniment of food. Athenaeus further describes many stuffed, baked vegetables and leaves, tiny meatballs called KEFTHEDES, light crusty breads and thin crispy pastries, polenta and dumplings, capers and pine nuts, force-fed geese, herb-grilled fish and seafood and unusual combinations of meats cooked with vegetables. The flavoured beverage was a light drink of wine diluted with fresh water and sometimes flavoured with honey or spices.[2,3,5,6] It is incredible to think of these commonly known culinary cornerstones of today being part of daily fare even before 200 C.E.

The Greek peoples have been supressed and forced to survive on meagre rations for so long, that it was often the Greek emigrants rather than the native Greeks who revived culinary interest and pride. The first large wave of Greek emigrants followed that fateful Tuesday in May, 1453. But other events in Greek history have spurred waves of emigrants, especially to North America. In 1891 a combination of serious crop failures especially in Laconia and Arcadia, as well as fear of conscription in Turkish lands, sent emigrants in waves that continued even after the First World War.[9] The combined shortages and suffering that the Greeks endured during the Second World War and during the subsequent civil strife, once again sent Greeks to seek a better, more peaceful life elsewhere.[9] It is probably this recent memory of pain that motivates Greeks in North America to take every advantage of the results of hard work, enterprise and education.[10]

The Greeks are a people who know and treasure their deep roots in the past. Against a backdrop of painful history, their own pride and determination – together with the help of the God of Greece – have kept alive and vital a culture, language and cuisine that have few equals. Despite an occasional fretful fingering of the worry-beads, the Greek has learned to find pleasures in day-to-day living and to brush aside the painful events with a hopeful sigh to the future. It is a feat of survival and pride that

Aristotle himself would enjoy reading the many Athens newspapers of to-day, Greeks from the Byzantine Empire would be at home in the worship and rituals of the Greek Orthodox Church, and even Athenaeus would be happily familiar with today's Greek table.

Home Life and Facilities

A definite factor in Greek survival has to be the close sense of family ties and responsibilities. There is no doubt that the Greek male is favoured and loved by mother and sisters but in later years he returns this affection with a strong devotion which often includes the postponement of his own marriage in favour of seeing his sisters provided for. And the Greek male's lifelong devotion to his mother is legendary: it is said that with the slightest look or gentlest sigh from his mother, the Greek male capitulates to her wishes.[3]

Every Greek feels himself a strong part of an extended family that even includes concern for someone from the same village or area. A Greek emigrant does not need to be told where to seek advice or help; he will automatically seek out relatives no matter how distant, and former villagers or neighbours. This kind of help and shared responsibility comes naturally to a people whose history is flecked liberally with examples of the need for mutual aid without which survival would have been im-possible.

Except for the upper classes, where women exhibit considerable in-dependence, the male and female roles in the Greek family are clearly defined. The men not only enjoy their favoured position, they carry this loving confidence with them into their work and into their male-oriented leisure hours. Every village, no matter how small, boasts a *plateia* or village square where the men congregate to enjoy a Turkish coffee, a sip of RETSINA or OUZO, or simply sprawl over the chairs and read the papers or listen to the talk. It is a male preserve and the women neither complain nor intrude. In fact most Greek women contentedly follow the saying of Euripides: "A woman should be everything in the house and nothing out-side it. . . ."

The women concern themselves with homemaking and crafts, with child-rearing, with the kitchen garden and the nearby goats, sheep and chickens. Not for them the problems of fields or businesses, of money or education. Nor do they envy the male social life. They find fulfilment in their weekly visit to the church, and their daily trip to the village well or market.

The rural Greek family home commonly comprises two large rooms: one for sleeping (Greek children usually go to bed when their parents do), and one for everything else. Firewood and stores are kept under the house. Large earthenware jars are used to store and cool fresh water taken daily from the local wells. In the main room of the house the walls are lined with open shelves displaying cooking and table utensils, strings of garlic and onions and colourful jars of sweet preserves (spoon sweets). Day-to-day baking is done out of doors in beehive-shaped ovens, while the local *fourno* (bakeshop) shares its facilities for special-occasion baking. This is also one of the few times that young boys share in household tasks: it is their job to bring home the fragrant baked foods from the *fourno*. Villagers also share wine and olive presses, for each home makes its own olive oil and ferments its own wines.

Recent government programs are encouraging the arts of butter-, cheese- and yoghurt-making and dispensing information on nutrition as well as attempting to increase the methods of food preservation such as drying, canning, salting and pickling.[8] Traditionally, Greeks have favoured fresh seasonal foods. This is an understandable preference considering that storage and transportation, together with low annual incomes, frequently meant that the available food was the day's menu.[8] But it should also be noted that preference for fresh seasonal foods is also distinctly shown by those with a discerning palate.

Modern methods of food storage and preservation are available to those in the larger cities as of course are an increased variety of foods both local and imported.

FOODS COMMONLY USED

To the casual observer, it seems that Greeks are either enjoying a feast day, or submitting to yet another fast day. The Greek calendar is studded with both. Foods for fast days coincide with the foods that are the staples for most rural Greeks: bread, olives and olive oil, fruit and nuts and legumes. Food for feast days includes roasted meats such as lamb or chicken, varieties of fruits and vegetables, cheeses and yoghurt and specialties of delicate pastries and cookies. The abundant fresh lemons and wild herbs season most dishes while homemade wine is the favoured beverage.

Milk and Milk Products

Milk is not a favourite beverage for the Greeks, who prefer yoghurt and cheese when it comes to milk products. Yoghurt, usually made at home, is considered a snack, or an ingredient in many dishes. Cheeses vary from mild to strong and may be grated for use in cookery, or cut in cubes for salads or as appetizers. Most popular is FETA, a pungent goat's milk cheese preserved in brine. But there are many other cheeses: mild KASSERI; MIZZITHRA made from ewe's milk and resembling cottage cheese; and KEFALOTIRI, which is a salty and hard grating cheese. MANOURI and GRAVIERA are used much like FETA; all three lend a pronounced flavour to TYROPITAS and SPANAKOPITAS, a marriage of PHYLLO pastry with the cheese as filling.[2] SAGANAKI is an appetizer of deep-fried flour-dusted cheese squares served hot and sprinkled with fresh lemon juice.

Fruits and Vegetables

As in most Mediterranean countries, Greek fruits are noted for their luscious ripe flavours and are enjoyed fresh or lovingly preserved in thick heavy syrups to be served to guests accompanied with a glass of fresh cold water. Served in this way, fruits are called spoon sweets. Sometimes these may also be made from selected tiny vegetables such as tomatoes.[6] Lemons and other citrus fruits are used most widely. In season there is also a choice of grapes, figs, quinces, strawberries, cherries, apricots, plums, peaches and many types of apples. Special autumn favourites are PEPONI, a Greek melon resembling both a honeydew and a cantaloup, and KARPOUZI, a richly-flavoured type of watermelon.

Vegetables have a special place in the Greek menu and their use is frequent. Carrots, potatoes and small beets are year-round staples, while aubergine (eggplant) and courgette (zucchini) head the list of seasonal favourites. These may be made into pickles, or they may be stuffed and baked or sliced and layered into casseroles with sauce and cheese. Even the zucchini flowers are considered a special treat and served batter-dipped and fried. KOLOKITHOKORFADES is a zucchini-flower specialty where the flowers are gently filled with a cheese mixture before being dipped in batter and fried. Artichokes, okra, broad beans and lima beans, cauliflower, fresh peas, tomatoes and cucumbers as well as many wild greens such as mustard, dandelion, spinach and others are collectively known as HORTA.

HORTA is cleaned, chopped and boiled, then served with lemon juice and oil. But other vegetable preparations may be more elaborate, including BÉCHAMEL SAUCE and cheeses; layered between PHYLLO pastry and cheeses; or scooped out and baked with fillings. DOLMADAKIA are meat and rice-stuffed vine (grape) leaves. Vegetables can also be a part of PILAFS (with rice), yeast doughs and sometimes breads (ZUCCHINI BREAD) and vegetables can be a light meal when combined with eggs to make omelets or soufflés.

A meal (other than breakfast) without fresh or cooked vegetables of some kind is rare. A main course of meat or cheese is accompanied by SALATA. This term is loosely used to include cooked, chilled vegetables served with oil and lemon and a sprinkling of herbs or the GREEK SALATA, a carefully constructed mountain of fresh greens (sometimes over a mound of potato salad), garnished with black olives, cubed FETA, tomato and cucumber chunks all shimmering with oil and lemon juice and fragrant with fresh oregano.

Olives are of special importance in Greece. Greeks prefer their olives black, but these may be brined, pickled or even spiced and are a part of almost every meal. Sometimes bread and olives may form a simple meal.

Meats and Alternates

Goats are plentiful in Greece but because they are generous with their milk, they are seldom used as food. Goat's milk, and the FETA cheese made from it, are important staples. Some pigs and chickens are available, but the staple Greek meat is lamb. Meat is generally scarce and expensive, so every part of the animal is utilized and the main cookery methods promote tenderness and "stretch" the flavour. The sweet nutty flavour of lamb blends well with all vegetables, and often a dish is considered different because of the different herbs used: spearmint, rosemary, oregano and even cinnamon. Lemon juice and/or yoghurt flavour as well as tenderize.

Eggs are not plentiful in Greece but are used in pastries, omelets and the famed AVGOLEMONO SAUCE used to finish soups, glaze fish and meat dishes, top casseroles and add a golden lemon touch to vegetables.

People living on the islands and near coastal regions enjoy fish and seafood dishes prepared from recipes that date to Greece's Golden Age: grilling with herbs, oil and lemon juice; baking in parchment, and baking fish on a bed of chopped vegetables. Dishes may include eels (a traditional Christmas dish), squid, octopus, prawns, cod, red mullet and sun-dried PETALIA. Those who do not live near the sea make every effort to obtain fresh fish and seafood for they are great favourites.

Fish roe is considered a special delicacy and may be made into small cakes and fried in oil: TARAMA KEFTHETES; or made into the popular dip used as an appetizer: TARAMOSALATA. This creamy mixture is made by puréeing soft white bread, fish roe, onions and olive oil and lemon juice. It is served either from a bowl garnished with bread chunks and black olives, or as a filling for scooped-out cucumbers and small tomatoes.

Another valuable source of protein in Greece is in the many varieties of nuts: almonds, pine nuts, walnuts, pistachios and chestnuts. These are used in pastries and confections and often mixed with rice as a stuffing for vegetables or as a PILAF. Sometimes choice nuts will be arranged on a serving platter and honey poured over to be served as spoon sweets for guests.

Thick and hearty lentil soup (FAKI SOUPA) and bean soup (FASOLADA) are favourites in the Greek cuisine. They have often satisfied appetites in hard times, and also are the Lenten staples when meat is forbidden.

Breads and Cereals

Bread is on the table for all meals. KOULOURA, a crusty white bread baked in a ring-shape and sprinkled with sesame seeds, is typical. Some whole grain breads are used with appetizers (MEZEDAKIA) and some specialty dishes, but white breads are preferred. Wheat flour is used for breads and pastries.

Rice and pastas are eaten in small quantities, mostly in soups, in occasional casserole dishes or in PILAFS to add variety to the menu. PILAF is the name given to a rice-based dish of Turkish origin where sauced meat and/or vegetables are served either with molded rice or over a mound of rice.

PHYLLO pastry is one of the most versatile. Modern Greek women buy the commercially made paper-thin sheets (literally, "phyllo" means "leaves"). Liberally spread with oil or melted butter, they can be folded, rolled, layered or twisted into endless sweet or savoury delights.

Fats
Olive oil is of prime importance in the Greek kitchen. Some fats and margarines are made with olive oil and flavoured like butter. Butter is used especially for its flavour in baked goods.

Sweets
The traditional ending to a Greek meal, and a favourite snack in itself, is fresh fruit. But this is not to say that Greeks don't have a special sweet tooth. The offering of sweets is an important symbol of hospitality in the home, and a sweet pastry with Turkish coffee makes a pleasant break any time of day. Special breads and baked goods are made for festive occasions and these are crunchy with nuts and spiced with cinnamon, ginger and cloves. BAKLAVA (layered nut-filled PHYLLO), KATAIFIA (sweetened shredded wheat) and even a simple semolina cake called RAVANI are all enhanced with a soaking of hot thick syrup right after baking. Other confections include fritters (LOUKOMATHES), rich buttery cookies (KOURABIEDES), beignets (SVINGI) and sugared nuts and dried fruits.

Sweets are always served with a drink: Turkish coffee, OUZO, or a simple but welcome cold glass of water.

Homemakers take great pride in preparing treasured recipes for spoon sweets. Choice fruits in season are carefully preserved in thick sugar syrups and enjoyed with guests anytime but especially in winter when fruits are not available. They may be made from citrus peels (lemon, limes, oranges), grapes, fresh figs, cherries, and even eggplant or tiny tomatoes.

Seasonings
Garlic, leeks and many types of onions are widely available and used in most fish, vegetable or meat dishes. In fact the classic STEFADO (beef stew) owes its rich flavour to slowly simmered onions. Except for SKORDALIA – a potent garlic mayonnaise, forerunner of the French AÏOLI – garlic is used in moderation. A surprise to some tastes is the use of cinnamon, either stick or powdered, in many meat dishes.

Mostly the fragrance of Greek cooking has a pleasant freshness that comes from the generous use of fresh lemons and wild herbs. Together with lemons, garlic and onions, parsley and celery leaves, mint, oregano and green dill (not the dill seeds) are most used. Camomile and sage are used as herbal teas, while both marjoram and basil are used as potted plants rather than seasonings. In fact, most Greek homes have a little pot of basil for good luck and to give as a sign of affection – and to keep away the flies and mosquitoes.[4]

English	Greek	Uses
oregano	RIGANI	seasoning
mint	THIOSMOS	seasoning
dill	ANITHO	seasoning (not the seeds)
bay leaves	DAPHNI	seasoning and also boiled with linens to impart fresh smell
rosemary	DENDROLIVANO	for seasoning, especially with lamb. Also used to freshen black dresses.
thyme	THYMARI	leaves fed to snails to impart flavour, also added to oil-preserved olives.

Greeks were among the first to use capers pickled in wine vinegar and used in sauces or as a garnish. Baked with bread, sesame seeds are a favourite, and sesame seed oil is used in the confection called HALVA (there is also a cake called HALVAS made from semolina). Puréed seeds are used in the appetizer called TAHINI, a popular dip in many Mediterranean countries.

Three other flavours tease the palate: ORANGE FLOWER WATER, RETSINA and MASTIC. Orange flower water is a flavouring extracted from the oil of orange blossoms and it is used to flavour delicate sweets. Retsina is pine-flavoured resin extracted from pine trees and gives its name to the well-known white Greek wine. Mastic is made from a resinous shrub and gives its clean pungent flavour to sweets, breads and even chewing gum and is popular in many Balkan countries too.[2] The most widely known use of mastic is in the potent drink MASTIKA distilled on the Greek island of Chios.[7]

Beverages

Water, thirst-quencher, refresher and symbol of hospitality, is the most frequently used beverage in Greece. Natural well-springs are respected and cherished and most will be found to mark the location of monasteries and villages. Water and a sweet will be offered to a stranger even before his name is known; water brings men to the *tavernas* and the *zacharoplasteion* (pastry shops) where sometimes the classic water may be replaced with OUZO or Turkish coffee prepared exactly to taste. Water brings women to the wells to fill their jugs but also to socialize.

OUZO, said to be the favourite drink of Alexander the Great and believed to be the inspiration for pastis and pernod, is prepared by infusing distilled grape spirit with a blend of fennel, aniseed, saponaria and mastic. The predominant flavour is licorice-like; it can be taken straight or with water when it turns milky.

Turkish coffee is a pleasant relic from the Turkish occupation and is always prepared to individual preference: *glikos*, very sweet; *metrios*, half sugar and half coffee; *schetos,* black. Actually "to taste" means that there are over thirty precise levels of flavour and preferred sweetness.[3]

The usual beverage with meals is either cold water or homemade wine; more recently children have been encouraged to drink milk. RETSINA, the white resin-flavoured wine considered so typical of Greece, is actually only one of many varieties, both red and white – and not all are treated with resin. Many legends tell of the origins of the resin-flavoured wine but the most persistent tells of Greeks pouring the resin over their wines during the early part of Turkish domination to prevent their conquerors from taking their wines. Later when the Greeks tasted the resinous wine, they enjoyed it. Most visitors react like the Turks and drink something else. FIX and ALPHA are Greek beers; imported ones are preferred.

Meal Patterns and Eating Customs

The Greek doesn't like being alone and doesn't think that anyone or even anything should ever be alone. For example, a drink must always be accompanied with food and food must always be enjoyed with friends. Greek men can always find an excuse to be with other men and consider it an unparalleled honour to have guests – even strangers – to share their home and food. Greek women seriously value their reputation as hostesses and the very finest will be provided to the guest even if it may sometimes mean that the family must do without.

So deeply valued is the concept of hospitality that it is closely interwoven with a sense of self-esteem in the Greek word *philotimo*. Since a part of hospitality is a display of generosity, members of the Greek family happily extend every courtesy and the best of their food to their guests. This can have adverse effects. Greek women may be insulted if only one helping of food is taken; they firmly believe in an old Arabic saying, "The food equals the affection." Greek men may feel shamed if their offers of hospitality are refused. Moreover, it is often true that any failed gesture in the ritual of hospitality on the part of guest or host can be construed as either a personal insult, a family or communal insult or even disdain of the ancient gods themselves.[3]

Perhaps it is not even correct to suggest that the treatment of guests is any kind of "ritual" to the Greeks, for their enjoyment of people and their warmth of affection are sincere. Thus, if one's appetite is limited it may be best to visit during the late afternoon rather than at a mealtime. From five to nine o'clock is considered in Greece as late afternoon when visitors would be treated to spoon sweets, fresh cool water and perhaps OUZO and pastries. The Greeks delight in their children and it is expected that visitors will admire the little ones and probably bring small gifts for them.

But should the guests' admiration extend to a particular object in their home – in the generosity of most Mediterranean peoples – the Greek family would probably make you a gift of the admired item.

Age-old tradition even accompanies the offering of refreshments to visitors. It is the Greek hostess who serves all food and drink while the host remains at all times to converse with the guests. The oldest guest is served first. Traditionally, a spoonful of the homemade sweet is taken together with a glass of water and, before partaking, the honoured guest extends good wishes to the entire family and ends with the expression: "*Yiasus!*" This means, "To your good health!" Everyone then sips the water and tastes the sweet preserves. This will be followed by general conversation. OUZO or whiskey may then be served accompanied by the tasty small pastries that Greek homes never seem to be caught without – especially when guests arrive.

The pattern of the day's meals varies from rural to urban dwellers. The Greek farmer rises early, often with little more than grape juice or fruit brandy to start his day. His noon meal will be brought to the fields for him by his wife or daughter and the basket will contain a hot soup, bread and cheese, perhaps olives and raw onions, tomatoes and cucumbers and occasionally a sweet pastry or fresh fruit. The farmer's evening meal will be after sundown when the chores are completed and the meal itself will be similar to the noon one except that a meat dish may be added if meat is available or if it is not a fast day. The table will be set with colourful woodenware and the womenfolk will place the meal on colourful cloths woven from goats' wool.[11]

Turkish coffee will begin the city-dweller's day, while the noon meal may extend for much of the afternoon and even include a siesta. Many cosmopolitan menus are available to those in cities, and it is only in private homes that often the really authentic Greek dishes are preserved and treasured. The visit to the coffeehouse or *taverna* ends the work day typically from the smallest villages to the cities and is a habit continued even in emigrant countries – but only for men. Dinner is traditionally very late in the evening – ten o'clock considered the usual time. And even after dinner at home it is not considered too late for an evening visit to the *taverna* or *kafeneion*.

Although the mealtimes form a pattern there is always time for snacking, always a place to provide what the mood dictates. The *kafeneion* is the Greek café where Turkish coffee in all its many varieties will be individually ceremoniously prepared in a long-handled pot called a BRIKI. It is also a place where a man may enjoy animated conversation or a quiet snooze while sprawling himself over several chairs. *Zacharoplasteions* are always strategically located shops which offer tempting varieties of honeyed pastries, nutted sweets and fabled candy confections to be enjoyed with Turkish coffee whenever the urge for sweets insinuates itself. Hunger – whether for a meal or just a hearty snack – may be assuaged at the *psistarya*, those eateries whose specialties include charcoal-roasted lamb rotated on spits and served with simple green salad, Greek bread and the husky red house wine.

And then there are the *tavernas*, second home to most Greek men. Why not? For it is here that anything from a small drink to a complete meal can be enjoyed with conversation and often with debate and frequently with the insistent and soulful rhythms of the *bouzouki*. It is in the Greek *tavernas* that the guests are expected to walk directly to the kitchen to make their selections of food (a word or two of advice to the chef is in order too). Platters are placed on a table and diners help themselves or they may choose their foods directly from the cooking pots. The meal is always enjoyed with crusty white bread and wine. It is also in the *tavernas* that the lusty combination of good food and drink, good friends and music together well up in the Greek souls and burst forth in the controlled exuberance of impromptu dancing. The Greeks have a word for that impulsive ecstasy of the spirit – they call it *kefi*.

The Greeks are a people to whom the word *zenos* means both stranger and guest; to whom *philotimo* expresses the sincerely natural rituals of hospitality; and to whom the height of spiritual pleasure blends people, food, drink and music into a spontaneously joyous burst of *kefi*. Why shouldn't the Greeks have the right words for the things they do so well?

Special Occasions

To outsiders, it seems that "Greeks are always either feasting or fasting." There is good reason: 98 per cent of the Greek population is Greek Orthodox and the calendar revolves around the fasts and festivals of the Church and all public and private activities are geared to it. Feasting preceded by fasting actually only occurs during five important holidays of the year: Christmas, Carnival Time (Lent), Saint George's Day, Assumption and Easter. Other festive days are usually marked with special foods, most significantly with the inclusion of lamb or kid.[12] Other occasions include Name Days, Saint Days, weddings, funerals, baptisms, planting or reaping crops, or the opening of a new business.

Fasting, in Greek Orthodox tradition, is a strictly observed discipline which includes vegetables, fruits, grains (bread) and olives but no animal products such as meat or fish and not even wine or oil. Greek homemakers are scrupulous in their observance of fast days even though their ingenuity in preparing meals is heavily taxed.[3,12]

Such devoted observance can be understood when it is realized that for the Greek, the Church is not just a Sunday matter, the Church is an integral part of traditional everyday life. *Papas* (the priest) with his long hair, beard and flowing robes is deeply involved with every family, and presides over every occasion with ceremonies, blessings and often advice. During the 400-year Turkish occupation, the Church was credited with saving Greek culture and language and became the source of hope and security to each Greek family. Having proven itself in the most difficult times, this faith is still a source of comfort. When talk and worry-beads can't solve a problem, many Greeks will prayerfully light a candle to a special saint, consult the *papas*, or (when in Greece) make a special pilgrimage to a holy site.[3,7]

Although the traditional daily life of the Greeks is strongly interwoven with the Church, there is also a deep belief in the immortal "God of Greece." And within this fabric of mysticism are also some threads of ancient superstitions that are so much a part of Greek life that it is difficult to draw a line between custom and belief.

The ten or twenty beads on a string commonly called Greek worry-beads do not have the religious significance of the Catholic Rosary; they are used by all classes of people as an aid to meditation, a substitute for nervousness, or simply to "chase the bitterness away."[1] Furthermore, the casting of spells, the fear of the "evil eye," the shaken concern for "bad-luck Tuesdays," or the grim connotation given events in May – like the worry-beads – are often practised more as a custom than out of any tangible conviction. Nonetheless they exist. Countryside children and animals often wear necklaces of blue beads and May Day wreaths often have whole buds of garlic, the blue beads and fresh garlic considered effective means of warding off the "evil eye." Cutting of cloth for clothes, scheduling of weddings, and even the planting of flowers during the month of May are all considered activities fraught with bad luck. The memories of 400 years of Turkish domination, which began on a fated Tuesday in May, could be at the root of these persistent customs.

One of the most prevalent of superstitions occurs each year in the days between Christmas and Epiphany (January 6). This is considered to be the time when those strange crippled ghosts known as *kallikandzari* rise up from the earth's depths to poison foods and frighten people. For this period of time all edibles may be carefully hidden or disguised; torch-light searches from house to house and strong crosses nailed on doors and over windows are believed to help ward off evil attacks. In the evening sieves are placed on windows and in doorways because it is believed that the ghosts become fascinated by the holes in the sieves and spend the night counting them rather than inflicting harm.[1] The frightening season of the *kallikandzaris* comes to a close when the *papas* blesses the waters on January 6, and all the ghosts are believed to return from whence they came.

For the Greeks and for many other peoples with ancient roots and traditions and profound religious feelings, ancient myths and even pagan traditions have become such an integral part of daily life that distinctions or rationalizations are often difficult to make and the prevailing principle seems to be quite simply, "Why take a chance?"

The most important festival for the Greeks is Easter, with its emphasis not on Crucifixion, but on Resurrection.[3] *Apokria* (carnival time or a "farewell to meat") is gaily ushered in with parades, costumes and many parties filling two weeks of merrymaking before Lent. The forty days of Lent itself are solemnly observed with a diet of bread, olives, vegetables, grains, legumes and fruits. Invertebrate seafoods are used in coastal areas. Most Greeks observe these fasting traditions strictly during the first and last week of Lent, while the devout follow the ascetic diet for the full forty days. But even for them, the usual daily fare of bread and olives and boiled beans and sliced raw onions may be relieved by a traditional sweet called HALVAS, made from farina or semolina, and flavoured with almonds and sugar.[3,4,12]

The week preceding Easter Sunday is called Holy Week and is busy with the preparations of the holiday which even include "spring cleaning" indoors and the exterior whitewashing of all homes. On Maundy Thursday or Holy Thursday the lambs are killed and hung, and eggs are hard cooked then dyed red and rubbed with oil to make them shine. On Good Friday the TSOUREKI (Easter bread), fragrant with caraway seeds and nestled with the red eggs, is baked. The evening meal is traditionally bean or lentil soup flavoured with vinegar to represent the vinegar believed given to Christ when he thirsted. Saturday includes the joyful marketing and preparations of the festive foods for Easter Sunday. But through all these preparations, the fast continues with the austere bread, olives, legumes and fruits.[4,12]

The spiritual climax of the Easter festival is the midnight service on Saturday when all lights in the Church are extinguished while the *papas* chants. Finally the announcement of *Christos anesti* is greeted by the lighting of everyone's candles from the priest's three-branched candelabra. Then, carefully shielding the flame, each candle is carried home to be reverently placed before the family's icon. Now the happily traditional midnight meal of MYERITSA SOUP, olives, TSOUREKI and citrus fruits is enjoyed by all. After the meal, the game of egg-cracking keeps everyone laughing.

Easter Sunday finds most of the men busily preparing a shallow trench filled with glowing charcoal over which the *souvla* (spit) of lamb will be cooked with an occasional basting of olive oil and lemon juice. Soup, stuffed vegetables and many sweet pastries will be a part of the festive meal. Understandably, after the austerity of Lent, it will be the MAYERITSA and the roasted lamb that will be relished most.

Christmas by comparison is a much quieter and less significant festival on the Greek calendar. Fish is traditionally eaten on Christmas Eve and eel dishes are especially popular. Special sweets such as KOURABIEDES (buttery cookies), CHRISTOPSOMO (walnut and sesame-seed breads topped with a cross of dough) and fried treats such as DIPLES and LOUKOMADES, those crispy fritters dusted with cinnamon sugar or served with sugar syrup, are the highlights of the season.

January is called Saint Basil's (Vassilio's) Day and this is the day not only for exchanging gifts (Saint Basil was known to be a philanthropist), but also for enjoying old rituals designed to foretell fortunes in the coming year. Splitting open a pomegranate and counting the seeds is used to suggest the abundance of the coming year. The evening is spent singing *kalandra* (carols) and then at midnight *Vasilopeta*, Saint Basil's Cake, is served. Everyone watches the serving with suspense for somewhere in the cake a good luck coin is imbedded. Tradition states that the first slice is for Christ, the next for Saint Basil and if one of these should have the coveted coin, a donation must be made to the Church. But if one of the family or guests receives the slice with the coin, good luck is said to be theirs for the coming year.[3,4,6]

Like other Greek occasions, funerals too have a share of both religious and superstitious ritual. Surviving family members usually eat a quiet meal of fish, bread and wine followed by Turkish coffee. Special memorial services are held on the fortieth day after the death and also on the first- and third-year anniversaries of the death. A special plate of KOLYVA is prepared for blessing at the Church, then it is eaten by all the family. KOLYVA represents one of the most symbolic dishes: the wheat for everlasting life, the raisins for sweetness and the pomegranate seeds to symbolize plenty.[3] A very old tradition holds that when a Greek leaves a house of mourning, he must sprinkle himself with water to drive away the spirit of death. Modern-day Greeks leaving a funeral will seldom return directly home, but will stop at a pastry shop to eat and drink. This seems to be a form of ritual purification similar to the older one of water-sprinkling.[1]

TWENTY-FOUR

Hungarian

Hungarians do not take anything lightly, least of all food. The romantic, volatile and soulful Hungarian uses food the way most other people use psychology, politics, literature, material acquisitions and even medicine. Food is the prelude to a mood, the buffer for difficult situations and the solace – even the cure – for adversity. Food elevates the spirit, food promotes confidence, food is a comforting symbol of success and status. But most of all, in the Hungarian mind, food, love and music are inextricably interwoven with one's very existence.

The Hungarian coffeehouse symbolizes the uniquely Hungarian viewpoint. Softly-lit and comfortable, well-supplied with sumptuously sinful pastries and good coffee, it is here that the Hungarian finds inspiration and sustenance, even on occasion solace. No Hungarian could survive a day of business without repeated fortifications of smoothly rich pastries and sensuous whipped cream floated gently down on a wave of strong coffee. And how could one sustain oneself in the suspenseful prelude to a love affair, the inner strength required and then the agony at the breakup – without a coffeehouse?

The Hungarian restaurants are so much a part of daily life that not even the vicissitudes of wars, the reversals of economics or the upheavals of politics could empty their tables or close their doors. When all else in life falters, food, love, and music remain steadfast in the life of the Hungarian. It would be unthinkable to make love on an empty stomach, conclude a business deal or even survive a normal day without fine food and wine to the accompaniment of Gypsy violins. Who but the Gypsy violinists could understand one's every mood and knowingly accompany it with melodies that can be at once tender and passionate or haunting and sad?

And when on those rare occasions all seems to be moving well in his life, the Hungarian can still find a reason for sadness that requires consolation. It seems that no Hungarian ever had a happy childhood. Mournful recollections of that "unhappy childhood" are always considered suitable excuses for further gastronomic indulgence. Just why there seem to be so many unhappy Hungarian childhoods is uncertain. Perhaps mother and father were too preoccupied with love and food? Perhaps a rich little pastry became the substitute for parental love? Perhaps too the unhappy childhood is fabricated. No self-respecting Hungarian could indulge in food and love (with musical accompaniment) without reasons.[2,13]

Given such vital significance, can the finesse of the Hungarian cuisine ever be underestimated? Hungary's history is witness to the many influences that resulted in the complex subtleties so much a part of the Hungarian table.

A part of Hungary's earliest history concerns the Khazar Kingdom which occupied a strategic position between Asia and Byzantium and spread to much of the area that is Hungary today. In 740 C.E., these tribes dramatically converted to Judaism. Although many reasons are given, the most logical seems to be that both Islam and Christianity were backed by political or military forces while Judaism allowed the Khazars to retain neutrality. For a long time they maintained the Jewish laws of Kashruth and no pork was eaten.

Although the Khazars were believed to be of Magyar origin, they were defeated in 896 by seven other Magyar tribes. Finally driven to a small area near the Bosporous Sea, the Khazar Kingdom came to an end, defeated by the Russians. Many Hungarian towns still bear names believed to be of Khazar origin (Kozar and Kozardie), the language of the Khazar Jews is still spoken in parts of Poland, Lithuania and Hungary, and the agriculture, handicrafts, commerce and wine making that they introduced are still much a part of Hungary.[2,3,4]

Hungary's appeal to conquerors was not only its strategic location but also the fertility of the vast Hungarian Plain. Here a mellow climate and a rich land yield orchards and vineyards, grain fields and pastureland – a plentiful reservoir of abundance that probably more than anything else has made the Hungarian a lavish and appreciative cook.[5] It would be difficult to find a farm without pigs, an abundant supply of fruits and vegetables and grains and cool pantries without fresh cream, sour cream and butter.

To this natural abundance, the 150-year Turkish occupation introduced to Hungary not only many tropical fruits and nuts but also coffee and many seasonings the most important of which was PAPRIKA.[2,5] Today Hungary's production of quality paprika is highly regarded; only a

Hungarian uses paprika with the deft understanding of a connoisseur. Although paprika, a favoured seasoning, is not used exclusively, it is used widely in Hungarian cookery.

While the Hungarians are willing to admit that many things were the result of the Turkish influence, it would be more difficult to gain an admission that the beloved Hungarian RÉTES (identical to the Austrian strudel) probably had its origin in the paper-thin crisp Turkish pastries made from PHYLLO – the most famous of which is BAKLAVA.[6] And these Turkish pastries, in turn, originated from Greek influence.

Further influences on the Hungarian cuisine now so deeply imbedded that they are difficult to separate are Slovakian, Serbian, Croatian, Romanian, Russian, Polish and German. This vast span of influence was mostly due to the fact that Hungary was for almost 200 years more or less under Hapsburg rule and a part of the Austro-Hungarian Empire until its breakdown after the First World War. Extended uses of sour cream, dumplings, noodles, sauerkraut and the art of soup, pastries and sweet delicacies may well be the most pleasant aspects of this period for it was also one marked with almost continuous inner strife and feudalism.

If nothing else, both the very rich and the very poor in Hungary always shared a love of food. Just as a laden table was essential to the Hungarian aristocracy, so the filled larder was essential to the Hungarian peasant. In fact, it was the Hungarian Baroness Orczy who lived both in Hungary and in England who coined the much-quoted phrase: "I would say the Englishman lives like a king and eats like a pig, and the Hungarian lives like a pig, but God knows he eats like a king."[2] To this day, good eating is synonymous with good living to every Hungarian regardless of background.

Finally to the many influences of colourful and hearty foods that found their way into the Hungarian cuisine came the refining influences of the sophisticated Italian cuisine from Queen Beatrice, and the subtle French culinary arts from Queen Anne. King Matthias wed the Italian Queen Beatrice in 1475 and enriched Hungarian aristocratic cuisine with all the delights of the Italian courts – including ice cream and forks. The gentling effects of French and Italian cuisine still evident in Hungarian cookery include wider use of sweet cream instead of sour cream, a preference for butter, especially in bakery, and a general lightening of seasonings, especially the use of garlic.[2]

Where else but in Budapest could so many cukrászdas (coffee and pastry shops) flourish? And where else but the Hungarian capital could the world's first museum of catering be opened, or a holiday be declared to celebrate a cake – the DOBOS TORTA?[1,7]

But the history of the Magyars, speaking their Hungarian language of Finno-Ugric origin, is not just one of gastronomy. It is also one of defeats and partitions, of conversions and peasant uprisings. Hungary was defeated by the Turks in 1526 and partitioned into three main areas: the part that is half of today's Hungary and partly Czechoslovakian and partly Russian, the area west of the Danube; secondly the Great Hungarian Plain which is today also part of Romania and Yugoslavia; and finally Transylvania in the Eastern Carpathian Mountains which is today mostly Romania.

In the early 1700s, fighting between the Turks and the Hapsburgs (Germans) resulted in a tug-of-war with Hungary, forced conversions to Roman Catholicism and even compulsory Germanization.[8] It had been King Stephen who, in 1001 C.E. had converted his people to Christianity, so the main objection 700 years later was not to religion, but rather to the enforcement of the German language and customs.

The first Hungarian to emigrate to Canada was Stephen Parmenius De Buda who accompanied Sir Humphrey Gilbert to Newfoundland in 1583. But the first real wave of immigration came after the 1849 Hungarian defeat against the combined strength of the Austrian and Russian armies. The date of October 6, 1849, is still remembered as a day of mourning in Hungary.[9] These first "freedom fighters" were to be followed by many subsequent emigrations of fiercely independent peasant rebels seeking a free life. Most came to Canada via the United States, working as miners, farmers and industrial workers.

It is interesting that up to 1930, 90 per cent of the Hungarian emigrants were from the poorer classes of Hungary, especially the rural areas. After 1930 up to World War II the class of Hungarian emigrants changed to include many professionals, intellectuals and members of the aristocracy – mostly Jews or those whom Hitler classified as being Jewish – fleeing from Naziism.[10] Even after 1945, the flow of the upper class continued, culminating in 1956 when the October Revolution was crushed by the Russians, and 175,000 people left the country.[8]

Although Hungarian organizations in America have attempted to unite all Hungarians, they have met with only limited success. The reasons burrow deeply into the Hungarian culture where until very recently feudalism and class distinctions were a way of life. These differences in manners, customs and even appearance survived the pressures of the American or Canadian way of life. Further, the importance of the kinship patterns, similar to those in Poland, Germany and Italy, have had a profound influence on family life. These kinship patterns include primarily one's obligation towards helping and maintaining the status of the "family" – which may include relatives, in-laws, godparents plus all their families – rituals of marriage, birth and death and assistance in education or business. To add to this complexity, the once-privileged classes have reconciled themselves only slowly if at all to the democratic way of life in North America. Many still cherish dreams of returning to the life they once knew.[11]

The final difficulty in attempting to unite Hungarians lies in the frequency of historical changes in the Hungarian borders which at various times included Poles, Serbs, Germans, Romanians, Jews and Austrians. Although each of these peoples was officially classed as Hungarian when they emigrated because of their having shared for so long in the social and political culture of Hungary, once they reached a new land they chose to revert to their former identity and unite with cultural groups other than Hungarian.

But the Hungarian pattern of life in the New World has closely followed that shown by many other ethnic groups. The first generation of immigrants clung together not only with their kinship patterns but also in their manners, appearance and language. The original intention of many was to work hard and save money in order to return to the former homeland. In many cases, as in the case of the Hungarians, the conditions that they had left behind them changed, but not for the better once they had escaped from the system of land estates and rigid class distinction where there was no hope of owning more land, advancing their position in life, or gaining an opportunity for education. Later emigrants sought to escape religious persecution and the Communist regime which seemingly favoured the labour classes, but further suppressed personal, religious and political freedoms.

The changes that occurred in North America were gradual but profound. In Hungary the kinship pattern promoted the success of the whole "family" as a unit rather than individual success. In the new country, schools lauded individual achievement, newspapers and store catalogues advertised materialism, and the opinions of neighbours and peers gradually took on more importance than distant members of their "family." Gradually, too, Hungarian calendars marked with special name days and saint days were lost and with them went many holiday rituals.

As ties with the Old World and the old traditions weakened, the Hungarians regarded themselves more and more as Americans and Canadians. But the Hungarians together with many other ethnic groups have witnessed and are happily participating in a partial reversal of this integration for there is currently a new-found pride in old crafts, songs, customs and traditions and increasingly these are being revived.

There may be evidence of the Hungarian adapting and even integrating into the community that is his home. There may even be intermarriage. But one thing is certain: so long as there is even a trace of Hungarian soul there will be an appreciation of fine food and wine, and somewhere a Gypsy violin will play the haunting melodies that will bring tearful reminiscing about unrequited love and unhappy childhoods – and the consolation of sumptuous pastries.

Cooking Facilities
Distinction must be made between the past and the present. Class distinctions were very much a part of Hungarian daily life until shortly after World War II. In the aristocratic homes, lavish meals of many courses,

each with intricately prepared dishes, were possible because of the availability of cooks, gardeners and servants. Finely crafted tableware and luxurious eating began as early as the late 1400s. It was the influence of King Matthias and his Italian wife Queen Beatrice that soon made the work of artisans and the arts of gastronomy very much a part of the life of the upper classes. Abundance of good produce, servants and the appreciation of good foods well-prepared were the true beginnings of the excellence of the Hungarian cuisine.[2]

But while the nobility wined and dined on what the world came to know as "Hungarian cuisine," the peasant people lived on their monotonous diet (except for festivals) of bacon, bread and soup. The bacon was often cooked on an open fire, the bread baked in outdoor communal ovens, and the soup slowly simmered in a big kettle called a BOGRÁCS. The delightful food specialties of the upper classes – known as "national dishes" – likely were unknown to the rural family because they had neither the time to prepare the more traditional complex foods nor the money for the ingredients. To this day many white outdoor ovens, still used for cooking and baking, may be seen in the countryside.[6,10]

Class distinctions with their inevitable luxury and poverty no longer exist. Huge kitchens with fine facilities and many chefs prepare meals for workers. Individual homes have minimal kitchens as most meals are taken outside the home. Except for special occasions and restaurant fare (especially for tourists) food in Hungary is simplified to pork and poultry dishes, potatoes, cabbage and much bread. Cattle, pigs, poultry, eggs and wine are mainly for export.[12]

The Hungarian cuisine is seen at its finest in restaurants, and only occasionally in Hungarian homes when time permits the loving attention that great cookery requires. Hungarian women tend to prepare traditional foods mostly on weekends and of course for festive celebrations.[10]

FOODS COMMONLY USED

The staple foods of the nomad Magyars in earliest times included meat from their herds of sheep (lamb, sheep, mutton), game, millet and groats, some fish and ZSENDICE a fresh cheese made from sheep's milk.[2] Foods were cooked mainly over open fires on sticks or in huge kettles. Later, pork, lard, paprika and sour cream were added to these staples. As the Magyars settled down, adaptations from other cultures were added to the staple diet: more fruits and vegetables, onions and other seasonings, noodles and dumplings. But the cornerstones of the Hungarian cuisine continue to be pork and lard, onions and paprika and sour cream. Tea and KUMIS (fermented mare's milk) were the earliest

beverages, and are still used; but coffee and the fine locally produced wines are today's staples.[14]

Milk and Milk Products
Fresh milk is not a popular beverage and is seldom used; but milk is used in many dishes, especially puddings, custards and milk soups. Variations of ZSENDICE – a staple so long ago – are still popular in certain areas and fresh curd is the type of cheese most used both as a spread with added seasonings or as an ingredient for fillings in baked goods and dumplings. Fresh sweet cream and sour cream are used liberally whenever possible.

Fruits and Vegetables
Traditionally fruits and vegetables have been produced in fine quality and great quantity. More recently most have been used for export, leaving those available for local sale often too expensive for large or even adequate consumption.[12] Apples, plums, apricots, peaches, and many types of melons are not only available in season but are also used as preserves and in the production of fine fruit brandies.

Cabbage, potatoes, onions, green pepper, tomatoes and cucumbers are not only the staple vegetables, they are the most popular, most used and the basis for many stews, soups and pickled vegetables. Raw salads with fresh greens are seldom if ever used. As income increases a much greater variety of vegetables is used, preferably those that are fresh and seasonal. Vegetables are never served simply boiled; they may be braised, baked or boiled then drained and blended with a sauce of onions, paprika and sour cream, buttered crumbs, or prepared as stuffed vegetables, vegetable puddings, vegetable soufflés or fresh vegetable soups.

LECSÓ is a well-cooked blend of lard, onions, tomatoes and green peppers. This basic sauce is of South Slav origin[14] and is used throughout Hungary not only as a basic sauce but also as an appetizer. With added sausages or meats it becomes a main dish. By itself a little may be added to stews and soups or vegetable dishes to enhance flavours.[2,14]

Meats and Alternates
The time of the Kingdom of the Khazars was the only time in Hungarian history that pork was not the number-one meat. In many areas, especially Transylvania, DISZNOTÓR, or pig-killing day, is set aside as a feasting holiday and every part of the animal is either used fresh or preserved by smoking, brining, drying or sausage-making.

Cattle-, sheep- and pig-raising are basic industries and game is widely available so meat is usually a big part of the diet if income permits. Hungarians are very fussy about the freshness of their fish and would rather eat locally caught fresh fish than any imported varieties. Fish may be prepared as a soup, smoked or baked whole as a main dish; but fish is not consumed in great quantities. Most fish used in Hungarian dishes are those caught in the Danube and Tisza Rivers: carp, perch, pike, sturgeon, trout, FOGAS, SILURE or catfish and small amounts of tiny crabs and crayfish, the latter usually used for soups.[2,5]

All types of offal and variety meats are used efficiently in sausages, stews, soups and casseroles with vegetables. Goose liver is considered a luxurious treat, comparable to caviar in Russia.

Legumes are not an important part of the dietary, being only occasionally used in soups or a bean casserole called SOMOGYI. Nuts and poppy seeds are an important ingredient in the many fine cakes, tortes, RÉTES, yeast pastries and breads. Nuts and poppyseeds tossed with buttered noodles are often a side dish to meats.

Breads and Cereals

Bread is much revered in Hungary and seldom is a table set without a display of a variety of breads and rolls made from wheat or rye flours. In fact BANKOTI (Hungarian wheat) is considered one of the finest in the world and high in gluten content. In the 1840s the introduction of iron rollers for milling white wheat flour caused the wheat germ to pop out without crushing, thus resulting in the whitest milled flour available anywhere. Breads, cakes and pastries baked with this new white flour quickly became a prestigious status symbol.[15]

TARHONYA, one of the staple foods of the nomadic Magyars and still a favourite accompaniment to meat dishes and a soup garnish, is made from eggs and flour blended to a stiff dough then grated to form tiny pellets. After drying, these tiny pellets or grains may be stored for long periods of time and cooked as needed. Noodles and dumplings are widely used as well. Cereals in the form of dried breakfast flakes or cooked porridge are not used.

Fats

Lard is the most widely used fat in Hungary. Butter is used, especially for baked goods and sometimes to add flavour. Hungary's margarines and oils are considered of inferior quality and are seldom used.[12]

Sweets

The Hungarian sweet tooth prefers cakes and rich pastries over candy. The national preference for temptingly sweet baked goods both as a snack with coffee and as dessert (as well as reward, consolation and medicine) makes the intake unquestionably high. Sugar is also a major ingredient in the fruit brandies, wines, preserved fruits and even the many cups of coffee enjoyed daily.

Seasonings

Paprika, onions, tomatoes, green peppers and sour cream are the staple seasonings of the Hungarian kitchen. But the range is much wider than that, including many herbs such as dill and tarragon, and in some areas black pepper takes precedence over even paprika. Poppy seeds, apricot preserves and nuts often form a part of the flavours or fillings of desserts and pastries, and chocolate and whipped cream are great favourites.

Beverages

Coffee, wine and brandy are the main beverages consumed in Hungary and by Hungarians everywhere. They are not tea drinkers and seldom is beer consumed.

Breakfast coffee is often served with hot milk. Afternoon coffee with a dollop of whipped cream seems the only fitting accompaniment to the staggering array of pastries. But by evening perhaps a little guilt has set in for the coffee after dinner is usually served black.[5]

Hungary produces many fine wines and is famed for her tokay variety. Wines and fruit brandies are produced everywhere but Transdanubia and Northern Hungary are famed for their vineyards and it is the area in Northern Hungary called Palóc that produces the red wine called bull's blood or EGRI BIKAVÉR.

Regional Specialties

Budapest

The capital of Hungary, Budapest is actually a union of three cities, Buda, Pest and Obuda, which joined in 1873 to form, among other things, what is probably the pastry and coffeehouse capital of the world. Said to be the city of "romance, wine and Gypsy music," Budapest is also the city where the pastry and confection makers happily cater to at least two million connoisseurs.[1] All of Hungary's great dishes and regional specialties may be tasted here in fine restaurants, coffeehouses (*cukrászdas*) and stand-up strudel shops where strudels may be sampled crisp and warm in a great variety of sweet fillings: fruit, nuts, noodles with cheese, poppyseeds and even with savoury fillings of cabbage, potato with onion and cheese, and many others.

As has been mentioned, it is Budapest that staged a festival to honour a cake – the incomparable DOBOS TORTA, and even opened a museum dedicated to the history of catering and the gastronomic arts.

Transdanubia

The area west of the Danube is famed for its vineyards and matchless wines. But the residents like to drink, in addition to their own wines, bottled mineral waters. This is one of the few places in Hungary where milk is drunk as a beverage, and milk and home-baked breads are a usual lunch.

Many mushrooms grow wild in this area but most famous of all are the truffles carefully sniffed out by trained dogs. The area is also noted for its

many goose farms, especially for the huge goose livers from specially fattened geese.

Local specialties include WHITE HURKA, a sausage made more from
grains than meat. It is first boiled and then fried. Curd cheese and
browned onions fill noodle squares that are pinched together then
poached and eaten with a thin sauce of paprika cooked in lard. Many
simple milk soups (meatless), pastries, strudels and dumplings using fresh
curd cheese are much enjoyed here.

Northern Hungary

From the Danube River to the Soviet border, this area is called Palóc, and
is as famed for its many local crafts and embroideries as for the wine
called bull's blood or EGRI BIKAVÉR. Here in small villages, life has continued with little change almost since medieval times. Baking foods in
ashes, collecting the eggs of wild birds and even grinding flour continue
unchanged. Fish caught locally is still dried, salted or smoked for use during the winter, and cheeses are dried and smoked in sausage shapes and
hung from the cottage rafters. The planting and harvesting of both wheat
and grapes to make wine are intertwined into many local and colourful
festivals which go back to ancient times.

Transylvania

This area, populated by the Székely people, has variously been considered
Hungarian, German and Romanian. Presently it is a part of Romania.
The forests and mountains as well as the people themselves have con-
tributed to the lore that is part poetry, part legend and part mythology.
Stories of ghosts, trolls and spells abound and seem somehow to fit into
the atmosphere.

But a fine cookery tradition is also prevalent and it includes many
dishes or versions of dishes that taste differently than the general cuisine
of Hungary. From Romania, the Transylvanians have adapted cornmeal
and use it for breads and dumplings, and from their own fields they have
plucked tarragon and summer savoury and use them as abundantly in
their cookery as the rest of Hungary uses paprika.

Sauerkraut is a part of the Transylvanian SZÉKELY GULYÁS and forms
the base of many casseroles with pork or noodles. TOKÁNY is a delicious
pork and beef stew simmered with wine and finished with sour cream.
Flax is eaten as a vegetable and many main dishes are created around
grape leaves or cabbage leaves stuffed with imaginative mixtures of finely
chopped and seasoned meats and vegetables. Cross-cut wooden slabs provide the wooden platters for the famed grilled dinner of pork and
sausages, pickled cabbage (especially CIKA, the cabbage core) and
cucumbers with potato salad. This grilled dinner on a wooden platter is
called FATÁNYÉROS and is often served as a specialty in many Budapest
restaurants.

Pork is an important staple and pig-killing day means much work in slaughtering the pigs, smoking, curing the meats and in the preparation of many types of sausages. But it also means special feasting foods, almost all based on pork: PAPRIKÁS, soups, roasted meats, sausages, all accompanied with pickled vegetables and much wine.

The area also makes good use of locally prepared fresh curd cheese, cream and sour cream. Often these too differ in flavour because they may be prepared from sheep's or even buffalo's milk.

The Hungarian Plain

The rich, fertile Hungarian Plain is populated mostly by peasants and shepherds having little formal education and living in isolated villages. Paprika, grains, orchards and rolling pastures with sheep and cattle all add to the produce of the area. It is one of the few areas that does not produce noteworthy wines, but the fruit brandies are so good they are a part of the daily peasant breakfast together with bacon roasted over an open fire and eaten with bread. Often the lunch and dinner of these people will be identical to the breakfast. Cabbage and sauerkraut, pickled cucumbers and many potato dishes add some variety to the usual meals. A fresh sheep's cheese called GOMOLYA is also enjoyed.

It should be noted that Hungary's paprika is not only considered among the finest in the world, it also ranges in flavour from sweet to very hot. Because of its sugar content, it is always allowed to cook with great care together with the melted lard and gently simmered onions to create the base for so many fine Hungarian specialties. No Hungarian cook would ever turn his back for even a moment on the careful simmering of this lard-onion-paprika combination. A touch too much heat or a little too long cooking and the mixture may well be discoloured or taste bitter.

Meal Patterns and Eating Customs

The dishes comprising the Hungarian cuisine form the distilled essence of centuries of adaptations based on their native ingredients and the fine recipes from other peoples that have been a part of Hungarian history. What sets them all apart and makes them so distinctly Hungarian is more than a matter of lard, paprika and onions – it is passionate attention and appreciation.

Sauces and salads are of little importance in the Hungarian menu. Soups, main dishes, cooked and pickled vegetables, fine breads and pastries – these are the cornerstones. Probably most important of all is the art of soup-making. Hungarians can make a flavourful and satisfying soup from literally almost anything: an onion browned in fat, flour browned in fat, milk and noodles, cabbage and sour cream, endless combinations of simple and complex vegetable soups and of course soups made with meats or game. Given so many types of soups, so many satisfying main dishes – TOKANY, GULYAS, PAPRIKÁS and many others – and desserts of incredible delicacy and richness, is it any wonder that appetizers join sauces and salads as being of little importance? In fact, appetizers are only served in aristocratic homes or in restaurants.

Whether Hungarian breakfasts are the peasant meal of brandy, roasted bacon and bread, or the urban meal of coffee with hot milk, rolls and preserves – they are small. Mid-morning snacks are common everywhere: factory workers may have a small bowl of GULYÁS, shepherds may pause for bread and onions, others may take coffee with bread or rolls, similar to a breakfast.

The largest meal of the day is usually at noon. Invariably it begins with soup, and if it is in a poor home, it may be only soup and bread. The main dish following the soup will likely be of meat with cabbage, potatoes or noodles forming a part of the dishes or a side dish. Dessert is almost as necessary as soup and may be stewed fruits, thin dessert pancakes called PALACSINTÁK, dumplings served with sweet sauces, fritters or noodle desserts, soufflés, custards or puddings. Traditionally, the noon meal is eaten at home with all the family together. More and more, however, children are taking this hot meal in school cafeterias, industrial workers in factory restaurants.

The afternoon coffee will be taken with honeycake or coffeecake if it is just for the family. But there will be a choice of fine pastries, cakes, STRUDEL and TORTAS if there are guests or if this snack is taken in a coffeehouse.

The evening meal is usually a light supper of leftovers from the noon meal. Sometimes soup and dessert are enough, other times soup with bread or light dishes made from eggs will be taken. The evening meal is traditionally eaten between seven and nine o'clock.

Special Occasions

It is estimated that two-thirds of the Hungarian population is Roman Catholic, the remainder Protestant. The large Jewish population that was for so long a part of Hungary was either exterminated under the Nazis or escaped to other lands; few remain. Religious practice is not encouraged under the Communist regime and most religious orders and monasteries are now state properties.[9]

The Magyars have always been noted for their colourful costumes, spirited music and lavish feasting. No matter what the rest of the year may be like, a festival is for merrymaking, eating and drinking, friends and music. This includes religious occasions, weddings, christenings, funerals, name days and saint days and many special celebrations associated with the crops and the seasons. Although the agricultural celebrations are usually local events, they represent old traditions and are much cherished.

Probably the most important religious holiday in Hungary is Easter. Húsvét literally means "the taking of meat," and begins on Shrove Tuesday. This date also coincides with the time of much spring planting: vegetables, poppy seeds and the preparation of maize for sowing. Dwellings are cleaned and often painted. In preparation for Lent when no meats or greasy foods may be eaten by the devout, even the dishes and pots used to cook meats and greasy foods are carefully set aside and replaced with others.

Ash Wednesday marks the start of Lent and the abrupt ending of all festivities. Even the customary bright tablecloths are exchanged for sombre dark ones.

The traditional pancakes enjoyed on Shrove Tuesday actually begin the forty days of meatless and greaseless meals. But ingenious Hungarian cooks provide an imaginative supply of breads of all kinds and baked goods, filling noodle and dumpling dishes, meals based on fish or cottage cheese, and many soups and main dishes based on cabbage and/or potatoes. The fare is simple but it is satisfying. Sour eggs and herring salad are the symbolic foods for Ash Wednesday.

The Easter week after Lent is the time to enjoy new spring vegetables, layered Easter cakes and painted eggs all culminating in a Good Friday dinner of wine-flavoured soup, stuffed eggs and baked fish. The chiming of bells on Holy Saturday signals the end to Lenten restrictions and the eagerly anticipated Easter Eve feast. This is considered to be the biggest and most important meal of the year. A rich chicken soup is served with dumplings or noodles followed by roasted meat (ham, pork or lamb) then several pickled vegetables, stuffed cabbage rolls and finally a selection of sweet cakes and black coffee. Easter Sunday is a continuation of the feast with roast lamb and "blessed" ham as the traditional main dish and more cakes and pastries served to all.

April 23 is an annual country festival celebrating the rounding up of the flocks and the hiring of shepherds all accompanied with feasting and drinking.

A week of celebrations everywhere in Hungary centres around August 20, the birthday of the beloved King Stephen. November 1 is All Saint's Day and it is also the final day for sowing winter wheat – and more feasting. Mid-October brings the vintage festivals, for wine is the national drink as the Hungarians remind themselves in an old folksong:

The Slovaks all drink brandy
The Germans all drink beer
The Hungarians drink wine only,
The very best, my dear.[5]

Christmas is celebrated quietly with the day preceding it observed as a fast day – that is, no meat is eaten and the Christmas Eve meal is traditionally a simple one based on fish and potatoes and the serving of cakes and tortes made with nuts and poppy seeds.

It was King Matthias and his Italian wife, Queen Beatrice, who introduced turkeys and they have been popular ever since (when available) for the Christmas Day dinner. The turkey is accompanied with roasted potatoes, stuffed cabbage and desserts of brandied fruits or fruit compotes with wine and more cakes of nuts and poppy seeds. In more modest homes, chicken or goose will be the main course, but everyone enjoys cakes.

Weddings are gala occasions involving not only many days of preparation but often three days of celebration.

Perhaps one of the best examples of local festivities is the DISZNOTÓR or "pig-killing" day celebrated in most rural areas but especially in Transylvania. The day begins with spiced wine or brandy and coffeecakes and then the work begins. By 11:30 A.M. a PAPRIKÁS has been prepared from pigs' brains and pork is roasted with potatoes or layered cabbage. The meal itself will begin with a cabbage or potato soup. Throughout the day pigs are slaughtered and prepared into cuts to be separated as fresh meats and as those to be used for brining, smoking, curing and sausage-making. Most trimmings go into the latter but some such as the snout and ears are saved for a special soup for the evening meal. The pig soup, freshly prepared sausages and roasted pork are eaten with bread and wine as well as pickled peppers, cabbage and cucumbers.

In order that urban dwellers may not miss this type of pork feasting, many restaurants make a feature of DISZNOTÓR presenting a special menu of soup made from pigs' trimmings and a main dish of varied fresh pork sausages and FLEKKEN (loin pork slices flour-dipped and crisply fried) served with rice, noodles and assorted pickled vegetables.

TWENTY-FIVE

Icelandic

Ingolfur Arnarson guided his Viking ship towards a northerly land and threw some logs overboard. Wherever they would drift would be the location of his settlement. Whether it was the will of the gods or simply the drift of the tides, Arnarson found that his logs had drifted ashore at a place he called Reykjavik. That was in the year 874 C.E. Today the city is the capital of Iceland and with a population of about 90,000 it can claim to hold one-third of the country's population in its tree-less, dog-less but sun-filled streets.[1]

The name "Iceland" is a misnomer. But perhaps the Icelanders will keep the name in order to ensure their pleasant way of life and avoid the influx of tourists and new settlers. Moderate winters, coolish summers and only one-eighth of the country covered with glacial ice seem to prove that the name is inappropriate. Since only 1 per cent of the land is arable, the main harvest is from the sea, while meat is obtained from the sheep and cattle that nibble seaweed and mosses from between lava rocks.

Iceland is located just south of the Arctic Circle and there is evidence that, before man arrived with his sheep and his goats, his fire and his axes, there were woods of birch trees. Mostly because of man, but also because of wind erosion and volcanic eruptions that scorched the earth with fiery lava, vegetation is minimal.

The Vikings, however, were not the first to step on this land. There is evidence that adventurous Irishmen were there first.[2,3] These early Irishmen were said to be Celtic monks in search of solitude. As the Viking settlements grew, they brought with them not only logs and provisions, but also animals for food (there were no herbivorous animals on Iceland) and Celtic women and bondsmen. It is said that the Norse and Celtic strains remained without change for a thousand years. Later, very small groups of other immigrants came to the land and intermarried.[2] But all continue to live in a tolerant and classless society.

Early Icelandic history matched the pattern of the country and its climate. Tribal blood-feuds, fiery volcanic eruptions, silent snowy winters followed by glacial floods, the plague of the Black Death, the ravaging raids of English and Algerian pirates and finally cattle disease and famine gradually took their toll of hope and life.[1,3] The Black Death in the early 1400s killed two-thirds of the population but it was not till the "greatest recorded eruption and lava flow in history" in 1783-84 – a horror that decimated horses, sheep and cattle as well as people – that the first groups of emigrants left Iceland for America.[1,3] Many of those first settlers made their homes in Saskatchewan and it is said that today more Icelanders reside in Manitoba than in Iceland's capital.[4]

It is understandable that their past history would give Icelanders an empathy for the suffering of others, as well as a fierce desire to maintain their independence. Offers of aid from other countries are met with the reply, "We'll do it ourselves when we are able." And so they have. They have built roads, highways, and huge greenhouses heated with piping hot spring water. In fact the heating of all homes in Reykjavik is by the same system of harnessing the heat and water of the many underground springs. Where else in the world can one turn a tap for instant hot water and enjoy hot-water heating all supplied from deep underground springs?

Another characteristic of the Icelanders, whether in their native land or abroad, is their insatiable love of books and reading. The humblest home displays with pride a well-stocked bookshelf, and Icelanders are said to have more publishers, more published books, and more daily newspapers than any other country in the world.[1]

Their capacity for alcohol does not quite match that for books, but it is considerable. Icelandic wives dutifully bring the black coffee – it is still a man's world in Iceland.[5] This is clearly visible in the after-dinner separation: men in one corner to talk, while women gather in another to "chat." Many parties finish only in the small hours of the morning, for the men take great pride in "finishing the bottle."[5]

Icelanders adapt well into almost any society and though they are said to be living in almost every Canadian province, their rapid integration both by intermarriage and by lack of ethnic papers or organizations has made them a valued part of the Canadian life-style. The deep importance in their daily lives of books and their deep desire for self-education has always placed them on an intellectual level even though they may make their living at humble tasks. Most Icelandic families enjoy the custom of evening and Sunday reading and take great pride in their shelf of books.

Cooking Facilities

Since wood is scarce and bricks expensive to import, most homes in Iceland are built of concrete blocks. Most tend to keep the living room for company and the kitchen as the centre of family living and eating. Actual food preparation areas are described kindly as "step saving": tiny by any standards.[5] Yet Icelandic women retain a proud tradition of home cooking, baking and preserving.

Electrical appliances tend to be expensive, but the Icelandic homemaker will save her money for a first purchase of an electric iron, tea kettle and electric mixer; later acquisitions may include a toaster and a vacuum. Some homes have refrigerators with freezers, but most homes manage with "cold closets." These are small alcoves built into the kitchen wall, enclosed with doors and ventilated to the outdoors. They are fine in winter, but of little use in summer.[5]

Because of inadequate storage, the homemaker shops almost daily for the needs of the family. Department stores and supermarkets are increasing, but most still shop in the specialty stores: the milk store for fresh milk, the meat store, the bakery for bread and cakes, and the grocery store for vegetables (mostly potatoes) and other needs.

FOODS COMMONLY USED

The Icelandic cuisine revolves around the plentiful sea harvest supplemented by dairy products, whole grain and white breads and potatoes. Vegetables and fruits are often scarce and expensive, but canned products and the produce from local greenhouses, which include bananas, grapes and tomatoes, are helping to increase the variety.

Vitamin supplements are widely used to help make up for the lack of greens and fruits. Lamb, the favoured meat, is prepared in unusual ways. The traditional Scandinavian cold buffet and love of coffee together form the favourite ways of entertaining: buffet and coffee parties are common.

Milk and Milk Products

A glass of fresh cold milk is a common accompaniment to almost every meal, and soups made with milk and dried, puréed fruits are often enjoyed. But the favourite dish of all and an Icelandic staple is SKYR. It is made from pasteurized skim milk fermented with rennin. The resulting curd is eaten with a sprinkling of sugar both as a snack and as a dessert. The slightly soured whey is used to preserve many types of meats and fish.[6] A brownish, smooth-spreading cheese called MYSOSTUR is eaten as a spread on bread much as peanut butter is used in America. Other cheeses are sliced and enjoyed in open-face sandwiches or as part of the cold buffet. Cream is used in cookery and whipped cream is a part of many cakes and desserts.

Fruits and Vegetables
Wild berries and rhubarb grown locally and imported dried fruits such as raisins, prunes and apricots are used. These may be made into preserves with sugar, sugared fruit soups (with added cream or milk) or dessert puddings that are sweetened with sugar and thickened with potato flour.[5,7] Fresh fruits are scarce.

Use of imported and canned vegetables is increasing, but potatoes are the staple vegetable and are served daily, often at more than one meal. Salads are all but unknown.

Meats and Alternates
Icelandic lamb, the staple meat, is sold ground, in fresh cuts, spiced, smoked, salted, and in the form of many varieties of sausages and frankfurters. It also comes in a meat paste made with ground mutton or lamb blended with potato flour. This paste is used to make fried meat patties.

Smoked, salted mutton is a Christmas tradition, while BLODMÖR, a sausage made from salted sheep's blood thickened with barley or rye flour and boiled in the cleaned sheep's intestines, has been made from earliest times. Another sausage called LIFRAPYLSA is made from sheep's liver. Still another old traditional dish that is often the Sunday dinner is SVID – smoked or fresh whole lamb's heads served boiled. SVID is sometimes prepared into head cheese – meat from the lamb's heads jelled in its own aspic.

Cattle are mainly used for milk products, rarely for beef. Pigs are all but non-existent; pork is rare and expensive and said to have a fishy taste because of the pig's diet.[5] However, horsemeat is a frequent part of the menu and is more available and tenderer than beef.

Icelandic fish is of excellent quality, relatively inexpensive and abundant. Herring in many forms – salted, fried, pickled, smoked, raw, baked – form an important part of many meals and especially the cold buffet table. Whole baked stuffed fish and Icelandic fish cakes FISKIBOLLUR, made with minced fish, eggs and seasonings fried to golden brown patties, are special treats. HARDFISKUR is a traditional Icelandic dish of wine-dried fish – usually haddock. This fish is not cooked, but is pounded until it reaches a soft crumbly texture, then it is dipped into butter and eaten with the fingers.[6] Still another uniquely Icelandic fish dish is HAKARL – cured shark meat. Shark meat is not considered edible until it has been cured. The meat is cut in strips and laid in clean gravel beds for several weeks. Finally it is washed and air-dried in special sheds. As is the case with most pungent but delicious foods, the taste is an acquired one; however, it is widely agreed that washing it down with icy Icelandic BRENNIVIN (brandy) adds to the pleasure.[6]

Icelanders have a deeply rooted objection to eating birds of any type, so the poultry that is raised supplies eggs but not meat to the Icelandic table.[7] Eggs are often served with the smoked mutton in the same way that bacon and eggs are used. Eggs are also used widely in the many fine baked products and also blended with sugar and milk or cream to make a type of eggnog soup.[5]

Dried legumes and nuts are used only minimally.

Breads and Cereals
Grains in the form of porridges, flour for thickening and baked goods form a large and important part of the Icelandic dietary. Oatmeal together with bread and butter is an almost daily breakfast, while breads made from whole grain wheat flour, barley flour, rye flour or white wheat flour are present at every meal and often accompany coffee.

Homemakers pride themselves on the many breads, cakes and cookies they bake at home and there always seems to be "a little something baked" to go with coffee, no matter the hour. Potato flour is used for thickening soups, gravies, sauces and puddings. Rice is used seldom and then only in the form of a milky dessert pudding.

Fats
Much fat is consumed in the form of cheeses, coffee and dessert cream, ice cream, and also in many fried foods where any fat – from margarine and butter (all unsalted) to sheep's fat and horse fat – may be used. Icelanders like the rich flavour of fat fish and meats and seldom skim soups or gravies.

Sweets
Icelanders do not hedge about their love of sweets. They add granulated sugar to almost everything from appetizers to soups and even in mashed potatoes.[5] They sweeten their many daily cups of coffee and enjoy them with a great variety of sweet baked and fried cakes, often adding an extra sprinkle of white or brown sugar on top.

Seasonings
The Icelandic spice shelf is a minimal one. Salt, pepper and onions are the few added seasonings – most food is enjoyed for its natural fresh or smoked flavour. Salt is seldom added, and to most other tastes Icelandic food often seems like part of a salt-free diet. But it should be remembered that Icelanders enjoy many salted meats and fish so that the contrast of bland dishes is a welcome one. Fresh cream and fresh unsalted butter are frequent flavour additions, but most often sugar is used to heighten natural flavours – and with a liberal hand.

Beverages

Young and old enjoy a glass of cold milk with almost every meal, but there is little doubt that good strong coffee with cream and sugar is the number-one beverage. While milk accompanies meals, coffee does too but goes on to be the snack beverage as well as the drink to discuss business, chat over old times and entertain friends.

Icelanders, together with most Scandinavians, also share a predilection and capacity for alcohol seldom equalled elsewhere. The idea of a "good time" is never complete without the other idea of "finishing the bottle," and the men are quietly indulged by patient wives waiting with the sobering strong coffee. Imported wines sometimes accompany meals, though beer and ale are more common. The favourite national drink is BREN-NIVIN, similar to brandy and taken straight and icy cold.

Meal Patterns and Eating Customs

The normally reserved, independent and industrious Icelanders become talkative, gregarious and even humorous after a few drinks. But it should be noted that the usual alcoholic beverages are confined to meals and most especially to evening gatherings in homes or night clubs. Morning breaks are not the rule, but an afternoon coffee break with bread and butter and several cakes and cookies is enjoyed. Snacking and street vendors are not as much a part of Icelandic life, but coffee shops are as popular as anywhere else.

Mornings begin with a breakfast of oatmeal porridge, bread and butter, milk and coffee. Lunch is usually a hot meal of meat or fish with potatoes, followed by a sweet fruit soup and a glass of cold milk. From about 2:30 to 4:00 P.M. most Icelanders will be enjoying their coffee with open-face sandwiches or bread and butter, and/or a variety of layer cakes, tortes, quick breads and cookies. At seven the family enjoys either another hot meal based on meat or fish and similar to the noon meal, or maybe sliced meats and cheeses to be enjoyed as open sandwiches with rye and wheat breads. SKYR will be the usual dessert eaten with a sugar topping or sugar and cream. The day would not be complete without an evening coffee and pastries around 9:30 P.M. If there are guests, the evening will not be concluded till all have enjoyed coffee, though probably much later than 9:30.

Icelanders are casual about meal service, preferring to place food on the table and allow everyone to help himself. Bread and butter is part of every meal. It is understandable that the Icelanders have a great love for flowers and these are a part of the table setting whenever possible. Preferring to talk in separate groups, men and women disperse after the meal, it still being considered "odd" or "forward" if women join in men's conversations.[5]

Special Occasions

Most Icelanders are of the Lutheran faith. They are not devoutly religious, but may attend services and keep Sunday as a day of rest and reading. They enjoy a special Sunday dinner, usually boiled smoked lamb's head.

Perhaps it is their Viking heritage but many Icelanders carry strong convictions about psychic phenomena such as communications with the dead and a belief in haunted houses. Ghost stories are a favourite pastime and they are listened to with more than casual interest.[7] Though not strict in their own religious beliefs, Icelanders are most tolerant of other beliefs.

Christmas is the main annual celebration with HANGIKJÖT (smoked mutton) being the specialty of the feast together with a variety of special sausages, many cured and smoked meats and fish and an array of special baked treats. All in all, it is a veritable "groaning table" of hot and cold buffet dishes to please all family tastes and those of callers. ASTAR-BOLLUR are baking powder doughnuts made as a Christmas specialty and richly flavoured with currants.

Aside from Christmas, most Icelanders make Sunday a special day of quiet with the family. Many go to church services but many others prefer to listen to the services at home by the radio. Others spend the day quietly reading. But almost all Icelanders know it is Sunday when SVID (lamb's heads) and potatoes appear as the main dish and the favourite SKYR as dessert.

TWENTY-SIX

Iranian

In 1935, the Shah Mohammed Riza Pahlevi changed the name of his country from Persia to Iran. Changing a name is simple, but shifting an ancient nation into the high gear of modern Western civilization is a monumental and complex task.

Beginning with the shedding of women's veils and the doffing of men's traditional fezzes,[1] the Shah's reforms spread widely and thrust deeply into many aspects of Iranian life.

Yet in this harsh dry land, despite illiteracy and poverty, conquerors and religious disputes, one thing remains constant: the innate artistry of her people. Ancient Persian culture abounds with eloquent tales of wit and exquisite paintings. Her cities reflect the genius of sculptor and architect and her peoples participate in crafts of carpet weaving, delicate metalwork and pottery that have been handed down from generation to generation since prehistoric times.[3] Persian artisans throughout history absorbed the new and subtly blended it with the familiar old ideas, perhaps with some inner vision that their skills would long outlive conqueror and conquered.

While the ancient Persian artisans worked at their crafts, Persia like many other lands knew periods of power and times of suffering. It was the Persian, Cyrus the Great, who united the tribes of Medes and Persians and established the Persian Empire about 540 B.C.E.[1] By the time of Darius in the fifth century B.C.E., the mighty Persian Empire dominated the countries from India to Greece and its power was only subdued with the might of Alexander the Great in the early 300s B.C.E. This was the period of great commercial expansion: increased trade, use of coins, building of roads and irrigation tunnels all of which also included the exchange of ideas. Long ago Oriental tea and rice had revolutionized Persian cuisine[4] and Persian expansion in turn had spread crafts and arts. With Greek conquests, Hellenistic influences touched everything from the foods on the table (sauces, stuffed vegetables and methods of food preparation) to architectural designs.[3]

A change in religion came with the Arab domination in 640 C.E. Zoroastrianism had been the Persian faith since being founded by the Persian prophet Zoroaster (about 600 B.C.E.). The dualistic faith of Zoroastrianism, teaching that the principles of good and evil struggle for mastery in the universe, was suppressed and replaced by the faith of Islam which appealed to the Persians because of its simplicity and emotionalism.[5] Small pockets of Zoroastrian believers are still to be found in areas of Iran and the Near and Middle East as well as among the Parsees in Bombay.

But foreign influences and dominations were not to end with the Arabs. In the next 800 years, Turks and Mongols vied for control of Persia. It was a period that all but wiped out the ancient culture and artistry. In the crumbled small kingdoms of the ancient Persian land, only small pockets of learning kept alive arts, science and literature, while in the homes parents quietly passed their skills on to their children.

The brief Persian resurrections, under Ishmail I in 1499, who established the Persian Islamic sect of Shiism, and later the rule of Shah Abbas I, who restored order and even promoted trade with the British East India Company, were squelched in 1722 by an Afghan army. Later a tug-of-war between Russia and Great Britain further weakened Persian rulers and increased foreign influence to the point where the despair of the people resulted in the growth of a nationalist movement. This climaxed in 1923 with the election of Riza Kahn Pahlevi as prime minister. The shift to independence, renewal of ancient pride and vitality had begun.

Home Life and Facilities

The traditional walled-in houses and picturesque gardens of Iranian homes reveal a deep respect of old ways. While the men pursue their trades, crafts or other work, the women spend long hours lovingly preparing fresh seasonings and the intricate ingredients for favourite dishes. Besides meal preparation, their work includes the care of children, animals and often work in the fields. The week's routine of work is broken by the Muslim day of rest: Friday. On this day, picnics are customary and the men of the family take turns accompanying a chattering group of girls, aunts, mothers and grandmothers for a country outing. As in most other Middle Eastern countries, men prefer to enjoy the company of other male friends in local *ghavakhane* (a name meaning "coffeehouse" although tea is the favoured beverage).[6]

In a land where ancient arts are prized, it is no surprise that the ancient arts of the kitchen are also prized and taught with great pride by mothers to their daughters. In the larger cities, modern conveniences and appliances are becoming increasingly available; but to many Iranians the arts and skills of the kitchen are still best performed in the old way – squatting on rug-covered floors and working on trays, blending seasonings in mortar and pestle, cooking foods with patient care over a small stove.

FOODS COMMONLY USED

The classic Middle East staples of lamb, wheat bread, eggplant and yoghurt are also the staples of Iran. But Iranian cuisine sets itself apart by the cultivation and use of rice for almost every meal. "A loaf of bread, a jug of wine" may have satisfied Omar Khayyam, but the fact that the Iranians themselves pay highest tribute to their poet Firdausi, who wrote the *Shah-nama* – an epic poem to the ruler said to have invented cooking – clearly marks their valued appreciation of gastronomy.[4,6]

Thus the Iranian dietary, along with a base of expertly cooked long grain white rice, includes seasonal fruits and vegetables, meats and fish, all subtly touched with fragrant spices and herbs and accompanied with liberal servings of some form of yoghurt as well as flat wheaten bread. Very little seafood is used and pork is forbidden since it is a Muslim land. It should be emphasized that Iranian foods are *mildly* seasoned often using saffron or turmeric and the aromatic cinnamon, clove and cardamom, while orange-flower water and rose water perfume many confections. Sweet hot tea in tiny cups is the anytime beverage; while succulent sweetness keynotes not only the tea but also snacks and treats and even some of the fruit sauces that are part of meat dishes.

As in most Middle East countries, the disparity is great between the diet of the wealthy classes and the low-income groups both in rural and urban areas. The fine intricacies of the Iranian cuisine and selection of many dishes for a meal are the privilege of the upper classes alone. For others, cereals supplemented with dairy products, and small amounts of fruits and vegetables in season washed down with huge quantities of sweet tea form the basic diet. Meats are used rarely. In the wheat-producing areas rice – the staple of most Iranians – is considered a luxury for the poor; while in the rice-producing areas, the poor enjoy wheat bread like cake.[7]

Milk and Milk Products
Ten per cent of Iran's population consists of nomadic tribes who herd

goats and sheep. Fresh milk is not practical in a hot climate; goats and sheep can forage for food in dry scraggy areas where cattle could not survive. Hence the title of "poor man's cow" bestowed on the goat, the producer of milk that makes excellent cheeses and which is fermented also to produce the rich buttery yoghurt. Most homemakers prepare their own yoghurt, simply by adding a little yoghurt to fresh milk and allowing it to ferment. Spread on a cloth and allowed to dry in the sun, the yoghurt culture can be transported as a dried powder then reconstituted.[6] Yoghurt is used as it is or diluted with water and lightly salted to form a refreshing beverage. It is also used as a marinade to tenderize meats, and as an ingredient in many dishes.

Fruits and Vegetables

While the climate of the Middle East is conducive to the growing of fruits, the orchards and vineyards of Iran produce fruits of legendary flavour and size. These are not only enjoyed fresh and ripe as desserts but are also imaginatively combined with meats and form unusual accompaniments to the main dishes. When fresh fruits are not available, a large variety of excellent dried fruits such as dates and figs, dried apricots and peaches are used instead. The list of fruits includes fresh dates and fresh figs, many citrus fruits, apricots, peaches, sweet and sour cherries, apples, plums, pears, pomegranates and many varieties of grapes and melons.[7,8]

While the eggplant is "the potato of Iran," Iranians are fond of fresh green salads dressed with olive oil, lemon juice, salt and pepper and a little garlic.[9] Vegetables such as pumpkin, spinach, string beans, varieties of squashes and carrots are commonly used in rice and meat dishes.

Tomatoes, cucumbers and green onions often accompany a meal. A small sweet variety of cucumber is popularly served as a fruit. The term DOLMEH is used to describe any vegetable or fruit stuffed with a rice or rice-and-meat mixture: grape leaves, cabbage leaves, spinach, eggplant, peppers, tomatoes, even apples and quince (BEH).[9]

To underline both the skill and imagination of Iranian cookery, a few examples of the main ingredients in Iranian specialties would include duck, pomegranates and walnuts; lamb, prunes and cinnamon; spinach, orange and garlic; and chicken and sliced peaches sautéed in onions and butter, seasoned with cinnamon and lemon juice.

The above are only a few examples of the combinations of meats and vegetables, or meats and fruits plus unusual seasonings that may go into CHELO KORESH, the favourite Iranian dish that is served at least once daily. This dish of crusty baked rice is topped by one of the sauces listed, or one of dozens more limited only by price and availability of ingredients.

Meats and Alternates

Lamb is the favoured meat. Young, sweet and tender, lamb is treasured for its flavour and texture and is usually combined with rice to form CHELO KORESH, TAH CHIN (layered rice, yoghurt and lamb) or the many DOLMEH dishes. Next to lamb in importance is kid (young goat), and very occasionally beef and chicken. Many varieties of local fish are eaten, but almost no seafood.[8]

An important source of protein is to be found in the large quantities of beans, legumes and nuts consumed almost daily. Chick peas, dried fava beans, white and red beans and lentils are used not only in stews with vegetables and bits of meat but also mixed with rice and even toasted and salted to be enjoyed as appetizers. Nuts in rich profusion, especially pistachios, walnuts and almonds, are used widely as ingredients or garnishes as well as appetizers or to nibble lightly toasted and salted like the beans.

Iran's beluga caviar, lightly salted sturgeon roe, deserves special mention for it is world famous. Sturgeon and swordfish are served skewered as a specialty dish of the Caspian Sea region, but the fish are also good smoked.

Breads and Cereals
Unpolished long grain rice or PATNA is an Iranian staple and many say that the preparation of rice in Iran is unequalled elsewhere in the world.[6] The exact method of cookery – whether or not to presoak, and how long to cook – depends on the age of the rice. The scores of unusual food combinations are actually based on two simple rice dishes: CHELO, in which the brown crustiness of the rice is encouraged with the addition of melted butter and egg yolks, then the rice is topped with sauces; or POLO, similar to *pilaf* in which the many ingredients are mixed and cooked together with the rice. KHORESH is the name given to the many sauces that can top a CHELO and these are usually only limited by season, not by imagination.

Aside from main dishes, rice may also be heavily sweetened with sugar, syrup or honey and flecked with almonds and pistachios to prepare a type of SHEKAR POLO, a very sweet POLO used for special occasions. Finally, rice will likely be the principal ingredient in the many stuffed fruit or vegetable dishes called DOLMEH.

Second only to rice is the production and use of wheat. There are said to be more than forty types of wheat breads from very dark to very light, from crisp to limp, and at least one type of flat bread will be a part of every meal. NÂNE LAVASH is an example of the thin crisp bread with good keeping qualities, while NÂNE SANGAK is a fresh yeast bread, baked on hot stones and eaten while still warm.[9,10]

Some barley is produced but it is used mainly as food for animals and only occasionally for human food when wheat crops are poor.[7]

Fats
Olive oils, clarified butter and fat from the "fat-tailed sheep" are used in

cooking and salads. Butter is clarified mainly to remove the milk solids and enhance its keeping qualities.

Sweets and Snacks
Fresh fruits are the usual dessert, but the insatiable Iranian sweet tooth finds some satisfaction in the many fruit KHORESHES used in CHELO, the many cups of hot sweet tea (herbal and regular), candied and dried fruits, and the special occasions when SHEKAR POLO and pastries like BAKLAVA are prepared in profusion.

Seasonings
One of the distinctions of the Iranian cuisine is the subtlety of the seasonings. The traditional Iranian politeness even extends to the limiting of garlic in cookery so as not to offend others.[10] Onions and garlic are used only with discretion, but cinnamon, cloves, cardamom, saffron, paprika, nutmeg, turmeric and dill are used with artistry: never overpowering, always gently enhancing the main ingredients.

To balance the natural sweetness of fresh and dried fruits used so often in cookery, the Iranian cook adds judicious amounts of tartness by using one of the following: VERJUICE, the sour juice of unripened grapes, lemon or lime juice, strips of dried limes, dried tangerine peel or tamarind. Powdered SUMAC, with its chili-powder appearance and sour taste, is a seasoning often used for broiled meats. Pomegranate juice and seeds are often used both for colour and tartness.

Beverages
The national beverage of Iran is sweet clear tea, often sipped through a sugar cube. Sweet tea starts the day, breaks the work hours, may accompany social or business engagements and sometimes meals. Tea called CHÂI is always appropriate. But so are the special herbal teas called TISANES, used for a variety of medical "cures," steeped from flowers such as roses, violets, jasmine, camomile, and spices such as ginger, saffron and anise: all fragrant, flavourful and aromatic.

Next in importance is coffee – more important in some areas than in others. Special rituals surround the preparation and serving of tiny cups of coffee (see "Meal Patterns and Eating Customs") but it is taken with little or no sugar.[11]

Yoghurt, diluted with water or sparkling mineral water and lightly salted, is served as a refreshing drink – often with meals – and is called DUGH or ABDUG.

Although Muslims do not drink wine, they sometimes allow themselves beer (often taken with the addition of salt), cognac, or AARAK, a clear potent liquor redolent of anise. Large quantities of carbonated beverages and soft drinks are also consumed.[6,7]

Meal Patterns and Eating Customs

Consideration of others and refinement of manners are as much a part of the Iranian character as appreciation of and dedication to artistry. Shoes are traditionally removed before entering a room and the main meal of the day is always preceded by ceremonious hand-washing and the serving of tea.[8,9]

Traditional Iranian dinner is set out in serving dishes set on a large white cloth spread over many beautiful carpets. The diners sit around the cloth on soft cushions. It is customary for the diners to eat all foods with the fingers of their right hand. Special short-handled spoons are used for soups and soft desserts, and sometimes visitors are given forks. However, all food is prepared and served in such a way that knives are never needed or used at the table. A simple meal would traditionally observe all of these customs, a more elaborate meal or banquet would differ only in the number and variety of dishes presented.

Where coffee still takes precedence over tea, there is a special ritual to its preparation and serving, and special implements are used. For the purist, the coffee beans are roasted and crushed immediately before brewing. MIHMA is the special spoon for roasting the beans, QÃSHUGA is the name of the long rod to stir the roasting beans, while HAWAN is the special brass mortar used to crush the hot, freshly roasted coffee beans.[11] In fact, in some homes, the early morning pounding of the coffee beans is a pleasant awakening for the family.

The rounded Iranian coffee pots, with their long spouts and narrow necks, seem always ready with a fresh brew, whether the housewife is being hospitable or the merchant is doing business. In fact to refuse the offer of coffee is considered an insult.[6] Traditionally, coffee is offered three times after the guests' arrival and always it must be drunk. This is not a difficult matter as the handle-less cups are very tiny and when one excludes the sediment, there is really not too much to drink. Like eating, the cup of coffee is always received and drunk with the right hand. The use of the left hand is considered impolite, but the noisy sipping of the beverage, or rather the thick brew, is indicative of pleasure.[11]

Three meals a day are usual and they begin with a light and early breakfast of sweetened tea or coffee and breads. Sometimes the breads are served with local cheeses. Lunch and dinner are usually similar meals based on hearty portions of rice either made as CHELO or as a POLO and usually accompanied with fresh seasonal vegetables, bread and cheese. Iran has a small but fine repertoire of soups but these are not as popular as dishes prepared with rice as a base. In fact, ASH, the word for soup, is really part of the Persian word ASH-PAZ or "cook." This literally means "the maker of the soup."[9] For most meals, fresh ripe fruits are the usual dessert.

Throughout the day nibbles of crunchy toasted nuts of all kinds, crisp dried seeds, and roasted beans all lightly salted are enjoyed everywhere.

Juicy snacks of fresh fruits and the frequent social sipping of tea or coffee allow little opportunity for real hunger. AJEEL is a favoured mix of nuts and seeds that have been simmered in lime juice then salted and toasted. The familiar arrangement of selected fresh fruits that graces tables and is sold by vendors is called MIVEH.

Special Occasions

The largest religious group in the ancient land of Iran is the Muslim with much smaller groups of Christians, Jews and Zoroastrians.

Friday is the Muslim day of rest and women relax by enjoying a form of a country picnic where the traditionally favoured dish is KUKU or KUKUNE. This is like a large omelet or soufflé cooked on top of the stove and prepared from vegetables and eggs. It may be eaten hot or cold accompanied by breads, cheeses, and fruits.[6,9]

The Persian New Year is joyously celebrated on March 21, the Spring Solstice. Iranian families prepare many special sweet dishes and always among them are the SHEKAR POLO, a sweet and syrupy rice dish flecked with almonds and pistachios, and the traditional BAKLAVA. Shoots of wheat to symbolize the very roots of life adorn the festive table together with a mirror on which eggs are arranged. The first jiggle of the eggs symbolizes the very moment when the legendary bull tosses the whole earth from one horn to the other. There follows a happy time of family visits and gift-giving and many sweets and treats to nibble and munch for thirteen days of festivities when all schools and businesses have a holiday too. Traditional outdoor picnics end the days of New Year celebrations.[6,9]

TWENTY-SEVEN

Irish

The Irish are one with their land. Warm, sprightly and whimsical on the outside, the Irish character occasionally surfaces to reveal mercurial ups and downs of temperament firmly rooted in steadfast stubbornness. The land is the same. A moderately moist climate gently washes over the idyllically green land, which is dotted with lakes, encircled with mountains and only occasionally breaks to reveal the limestone of the plains or the granite and basalt of the Highlands. Even the softness of the peat bogs belies their vital importance for fuel and power. The Irish people and their island homeland both exhibit tenderness and strength and bear witness also to the contrasts inherent in their history.

After the arrival of St. Patrick in 432 C.E., Christianity spread over the many separate kingdoms of the Emerald Isle and for the next 400 years Catholicism, oatmeal, milk, leeks and the building of monasteries occupied the souls, and filled the stomachs and the working days of the Irish. Aside from those occupied in the religious life most of the population were farmers and shepherds. Then this somewhat peaceful existence was shattered with Viking raids and even the brief establishment of Viking rule. Although seldom openly attributed to the Viking conquest of 832 C.E., could it be possible that the Vikings left an inheritance of mischievous trolls and bottomless imbibing that remains to this day so much a part of the legends and customs of the Irish?[1]

For the next 700 years after the Viking occupation the Irish had to stave off raids, invasions and pressures from, first, the Normans (who had already established themselves in England) and then the English. Both Queen Mary and Queen Elizabeth in the 1500s and early 1600s gradually followed a practice of supplanting the Irish landowners with Scottish and English owners. The Irish (Catholics and Protestants alike) now became tenant farmers on what was their own land. This non-resident ownership of land together with strong grievances in many other areas of Irish life came to a head and erupted in the rebellious outbursts of the 1700s.

But a spectre more ominous than religion or politics was looming. The wheat, oats and barley that the Irish grew for their landlords, and the pigs, mutton and beef pastured on their lands never saw an Irish hearth. Adopted by the Irish peasants as their staple food, potatoes in every possible form became the basis of every meal. The usually gentle climate became endless days and nights of alternately drizzling and torrential rains and in that year of 1821, the uneducated, misgoverned pauper peasants suffered famine, fever and death from the first failure of the potato crops.[2] Increasingly, the majority of the Irish population lived on reboiled tea, potatoes and misery. Some, at this point, assured of priests and potatoes, set out for a new life in North America.

Those Irish who decided not to emigrate managed to survive and the next year enjoyed – if nothing else – a profusion of potatoes so plentiful that it is said they were even used as fertilizer.[2] But the respite in the form of food for all hardly made up for the almost slave-labour conditions in the cities and the general oppression in the countryside. England and Scotland were glutted with unskilled labour; beggars, disease and death were commonplace. And the blighted potato crops of 1845 were only the foreshadowing of the disastrous total crop destruction in 1846. The beleaguered government decided on eviction and forced emigration; it was far less costly than attempting to support the starving disease-ridden thousands in workhouses.

So it was that almost two million Irish – almost 40 per cent of the population – prematurely aged, haggard, sick with cholera, typhus and dysentry, allowed themselves to be herded onto filthy ships to the New World.[3] Many died on board the ships, others soon after landing. Those who managed, by miracle or inner fortitude, to survive were given three-quarters of a pound of bread and the same of meat for six days and then they were on their own.

While the Irish back home fought mainly for survival but also for independence from the English, those in the New World applied their inner stubbornness to building roads, homes and sawmills and clearing land for their own farms.[4] Others became soldiers or leaders in political and religious affairs. But always the lilt of Gaelic (Irish language) and laughter could be heard over the clink of glasses wherever Irishmen gathered. And as memories of the misery of their lives in Ireland softened gradually with time (although it is said the Irish have a long memory) they kept alive too the memories of leprechauns and the Blarney Stone – whoever kisses it will have a "golden tongue" – hearth-baked soda bread and St. Patrick's Day. What other holiday is celebrated with such wistful sadness and uninhibited joy? Who but the Irish could turn their St. Patrick's Day Parade (wherever in the world it is held) into an event felt and celebrated by all ethnic groups? Perhaps it is that March 17, St. Patrick's Day, is more than "the wearin' o' the green," more than parades and drinking and sad lamenting songs; perhaps St. Patrick's Day is celebrated by so many because most of all it portrays a yearning memory of a dear homeland, beloved in spite of suffering. Most peoples of the world can share that.

The struggle for independence from the English culminated in the Foundation of the State in January 21, 1919. Disagreements, treaties, and violence were not to end. It was not until 1948 that the Republic of Ireland finally gained British recognition, albeit with some regrets. The Irish flag, a tricolor of green, white and orange, was adopted in 1848. The green was representative of the Gaelic and Norman-Irish while the orange symbolized the William of Orange supporters, mostly English and Scottish. The field of white on the flag then – as now – was meant to symbolize peace between the Irish factions.

Sadly, religious violence still disrupts the Emerald Isle. The Irish people – like their land – appearing so softly mellow, occasionally erupt in granite stubbornness.

Home Life and Facilities
The emigrant Irishman may dream of potato fields, turf-roofed cottages and a hearth with bubbling stew, and he could return to Ireland today and see the whole picture unchanged. Irish cities are as noisy, crowded and modern as most around the world, but one need not travel far into the countryside to find an example of life as it was and likely will continue to be for a long time. Accustomed to a frugal life and hard work, the rural Irish find deep contentment in simple daily life. The rain barrel for water, the huge hearth for cooking and heating a cottage, and open shelves to store dishes and groceries are the same now as they were several hundred years ago. The term "to take pot luck" is said to have originated with the three-legged iron pot that the Irish housewife hangs over her fire to cook potatoes, make a soup or a stew, and even bake breads and cakes. Skill is necessary to bank the coals of the fire just so, and to raise or lower the "bastable oven" as the three-legged pot is sometimes called. A kettle for boiling water, a churn for butter, and a sturdy wooden board for making dough (mostly quick breads) as well as mixing bowls and stirring spoons comprise the important utensils of the country kitchen.

City kitchens, like most in Europe, are efficient and compact, but contain as many electrical or gas conveniences as needed. (Many country cottages still use no gas or electricity.) However, the Irish cook, like the Scottish, prefers simple substantial meals with no frills so there is little need for the gadgets and "conveniences" found in many Western kitchens.

Conservative Irish cookery has not moved far from the traditional staples known and enjoyed for centuries. The earliest staples were oatmeal, milk products and leeks. Oatmeal is still used; milk and milk products are still favoured, although tea and stout are more popular as beverages; while leeks, although still appearing in traditional dishes, have been widely replaced by onions. The biggest change over the centuries was the replacement of oatmeal with potatoes. Fish was and continues to be the principal source of protein (next to milk) because it is readily available and generally less expensive than meat. To most Irish, "meat" most often means variety meats, sausages or pork products, not by preference, but for economical reasons. So adept are the Irish at putting together a satisfying meal economically, that at least this Irish saying is based more on fact than legend: "When it comes to knocking up a light savoury meal you can't beat the Irish."[5]

Milk and Milk Products

Milk is used in cooking oatmeal and making soups. Buttermilk is a beverage often taken with a light vegetable meal. Cottage cheese, called "curds," is eaten occasionally and used in IRISH CURDCAKE, a type of cheesecake made with curds, eggs and flavoured with butter and lemon, all baked in a pastry shell.

Fruits and Vegetables

Apples are the most popular fruit and are used in applecakes, FRUIT FOOLS, FLUMMERY, and the toffee apples prepared especially for Hallowe'en. Oranges are a special treat, not daily fare. Blends of fruits, such as plums and apples, are made into preserves.

Potatoes are the number-one vegetable; although many others are available, they are not used in quantity. Cabbage, carrots and onions are used year around because of their keeping qualities, but purple broccoli, asparagus, chicory (Belgian endive), endive (curly green leaves), leeks, kohlrabi, marrows, mushrooms, peas and parsnips also are used. SLOKE is a sea "spinach" which must be cooked four to five hours, and DULSE (also called DILLISK or DILLESK[6]) is a type of reddish brown seaweed often added to soups, fish or vegetable dishes or mashed potatoes (DULSE CHAMP).

The variety of delicious and satisfying dishes produced from and with potatoes makes their popularity understandable. People near the sea enjoy potatoes freshly boiled in sea water, and boiled potatoes often form the main part of a meal. Whether boiled in seawater or saltwater, their appeal is national. CHAMP is a mound of hot mashed potatoes served in a soup plate with a pool of melting fresh butter; each spoon of potatoes is dipped in the butter. COLCANNON is a dish of Scottish origin, using mashed potatoes and other vegetables (usually cabbage or turnip) well-cooked and blended with the potato. Leftover cooked potatoes may thicken a soup or stew, or be blended with flour to form a potato dough or bread, or formed into patties to be fried as pancakes: BOXTY BREAD or BOXTY PANCAKES. CUMBERLAND PIE is a hearty dish of two layers of the potato pastry filled with rolled slices of bacon and beaten eggs, all well-baked. HAGGERTY is another main dish made with thinly sliced potatoes and onions fried in bacon fat to form a large crisply browned cake. DUBLIN CODDLE, a traditional Saturday night dish guaranteed to prevent hangovers,[6,8] is a piping hot casserole (like a thick soup) of bacon and sausages topped with sliced potatoes and onions.

Meats and Alternates

Pork is the country mainstay and a favourite throughout Ireland. But budgets seldom permit roasts, chops and other expensive cuts. The ingenuity of the Irish cook, however, produces a proliferation of delicious dishes based on TROTTERS (pig's feet), BATH CHAPS (cured cheeks and tongues eaten breaded and fried), BRAWN (pig's head cooked in spicy broth then chopped and jelled), GRISKINS (odds and ends of pork trimmings pounded flat then breaded and fried), and the wide use of bacon fat to flavour dishes based on cereal or vegetables.

Beef is enjoyed but expensive for frequent use. MINCE is the name given to ground beef, brisket is used for simmered CORNED BEEF AND CABBAGE, while SPICED BEEF is a traditional Christmas favourite. Chickens are used occasionally, mostly in soups or stewed dishes, and geese are a holiday favourite. Game finds its way to the table less often: quail, grouse, hare, pheasant, snipe, partridges, woodcocks, ducks and venison.

Herring is a regular part of the diet and Irish fish soups are a specialty. LOUGH NEGH POLLAN (a freshwater herring) and POTTED or SOUSED HERRING make good companions to potatoes. Fish that is baked slowly in a pickling mixture keeps well and may be eaten hot or cold: this is called POTTED or SOUSED. Many other fish are readily available: mackerel, trout, cod, haddock, whiting flatfish, and smoked or fresh eels. WILLICKS or WILLOCKS are winkles or periwinkles that have been boiled in seawater then eaten out of their shells with a pin, sometimes accompanied with vinegar and salt or lightly dipped in fine oatmeal.[6] BLOCKING and LYTHE are two fish commonly sold dried and filleted. Crab and lobster are available but the large DUBLIN PRAWNS, whose fat tails are sometimes exported as SCAMPI, are special favourites.[7]

Eggs are enjoyed with ham, bacon or sausages, often as a breakfast dish, but more often as a dinner. Eggs also are a frequent ingredient in other dishes. Peas and dried beans are used less frequently. Nuts cannot be considered a protein source as they are infrequently used in baking, and never as a snack or food.

Breads and Cereals
A hot cereal for breakfast in Ireland means oatmeal. Oats and wheat flour (often whole grain wheat) are used widely in preparing the many breads and biscuits that are a part of most meals and always accompany tea. Frequently, fine oatmeal or coarse wheat flour kneaded into leftover mashed potatoes will form the dough for a stomach-filling bread or even a main-dish pie crust.

Fats
Bacon fat is the most widely used fat for cooking and baking and even as a spread. Butter is used when it can be afforded, most often to lend flavour.

Sweets and Snacks
Simple cooked fruit desserts, custards and milk puddings made with CARAGEEN (a fresh moss used as a thickening agent), and bread puddings are the usual desserts. Cakes are for special occasions only (Christmas and weddings) and most baked goods are not heavily sweetened if they are indeed sweet at all. Honey, treacle (molasses) and white sugar are the usual sweeteners. YELLOWMAN is the traditional Irish sweet: a hard candy similar to the brittle in "peanut brittle." Sugar is also consumed in tea. The Irish also enjoy homemade jams and jellies eaten with breads and biscuits.

Seasonings
The Irish spice shelf is a small one. Salt and pepper together with onions and leeks are the daily seasonings. Caraway seeds are used in breads, cakes and pancakes, cinnamon and nutmeg and mace flavour rich festive fruitcakes together with nuts, dried fruits and currants. Butter and bacon fat must also be considered to add flavour to vegetables and fish.

Beverages
Tea is the beverage accompanying every meal and most snacks. But the Irish have a reputation for their love of alcoholic beverages – stout being the usual, but occasionally whisky or mixed drinks too. Irishmen don't linger over their drinks, the reason perhaps being found in one of their many sayings: "Don't sip a cocktail, drink it quickly while it's still smilin' at you!"[5]

Of the milk drinks, buttermilk is favoured over whole or skim milk as a drink for refreshment or with meals.

Meal Patterns and Eating Customs

It is easy to romanticize Irish home life as being "quaintly traditional." It is painful to be realistic and speak of it as bluntly as Thomas J. O'Hanlon: "Anybody who lives in Ireland can testify to the absence of love in the average home." Poverty, drunkenness, violence, families with many children and little food – small wonder that the Irish staples of food are as meagre as their often suffering lives.[9]

From a many centuries' tradition of "having to endure," the Irish have found some consolation in their "pint o' stout," their pot of potatoes and probably even in the whimsical names lovingly given to the humblest of their dishes. Three meals a day is a fine pattern to follow if you can. But many Irish can make little distinction from one meal to the other so long as it is warm and filling. Tea, potatoes and SODA BREAD (made from flour, buttermilk, leavened with soda and marked off into floury FARLS) may well serve as breakfast, lunch and supper with only an occasional fish or two as a supplement.

The Irish like to awaken to a steamy cup of tea taken with milk and sugar. For some, breakfast may also include oatmeal, bacon and eggs, soda bread and preserves. Around eleven, most people pause for a "wee bite of pastry" taken again with tea and sometimes with coffee. The main meal is often about one o'clock and may include a hot and hearty soup of fish and vegetables or a casserole. Either dish is accompanied by soda bread, potato bread or potato pancakes. Irish stout or fresh buttermilk is the likely beverage, and a pudding the likely dessert. Late afternoon tea may include a few small sandwiches and little cakes or even a hot fish dish. The evening supper around eight o'clock is light and often cold, prepared from the leftovers of the noon dinner.

Special Occasions

Most Irish are of Celtic origin and about 90 per cent are of Roman Catholic faith. Freedom of worship is guaranteed by the constitution. The Orangemen represent the Protestant Irish.[4]

Being a Christian country, Ireland celebrates Christmas and Easter, but since there is still more than just a small belief in the "wee people" and in spirits and fairies, Hallowe'en is also still very much a part of the festival calendar.[7]

Christmas is the most lavish family celebration of the entire year with many specialty dishes that are not only favourites in Ireland but are also very much a part of holiday tradition in Canada and the U.S. The traditional dressed boar's head is sometimes replaced with a potato-stuffed roast goose or turkey, and homemade spiced beef is a frequent holiday favourite. Spicy-sweet plum puddings, hot mince pies and traditional iced rich Christmas cake round out the meal. New Year's is a more important celebration in Scotland than in Ireland, but the Irish do celebrate it with the Scots currant bun and Scottish shortbread.

The austerities of the Lenten season are ushered in with Shrove Tuesday, when pancakes highlight every meal and housewives happily attempt to win the many pancake-flipping races held locally. Lenten dishes are based on fish, cereal and vegetables and are really not too different from the rest of the year. For most Irish, meats are too expensive to be a regular part of the diet. Soups like BROTCHAN and BROTCHAN ROY made from an oatmeal-thickened vegetable broth and sometimes garnished with grated cheese as in the meatless COTTAGE SOUP, CHAMP and COLCANNON and dishes like MEALIE GREACHIE (pan-fried, flaked oatmeal served with fried eggs) are all examples of filling and meatless dishes. Easter itself is welcomed with the spicy warm fragrance of HOT CROSS BUNS, SIMNEL CAKE (marzipan-topped fruit cake) and EASTER BISCUITS made with currants, grated lemon rind and egg yolks.

Hallowe'en is celebrated with parties and fireworks. Roast goose is part of the traditional menu, topped off with apple cake, toffee apples and nuts in the shell. Often tiny charms are wrapped in paper and baked in the cake or in dumplings to add to the fun of the evening. A must with the goose dinner is the making of dozens of BOXTY PANCAKES, gobbled as fast as they are fried. The large potatoes grated for the pancakes are usually too big for storage and no one objects to this method of storage. BARMBRACK is the fruited yeast bread for Hallowe'en.

There could not be an Irish wedding or Christening without a many-tiered darkly rich fruitcake, beautifully iced and decorated. It is considered good luck to share this cake with the guests so all are given a small finger of the cake, often specially wrapped. The top tier of the wedding cake is the smallest one and is often stored away to be used for the Christening of the first child, and sometimes the middle tier is saved for the twenty-fifth wedding anniversary.[7]

TWENTY-EIGHT

Israeli and Jewish

> *. . . and to bring them up out of that land unto a good land and large, unto a land flowing with milk and honey . . .*
>
> – Exodus III[1]

It is touched with Biblical mystique and drenched in history, but on any map of the world you can hardly see it. This small strip of land called Israel is strategically located between three continents: Asia, Africa and Europe. It has known the conquests of almost every great civilization in ancient history and is revered as the Holy Land by three great religious groups: Judaism, Christianity and Islam.

In earliest times it was Canaan and was divided into many fragmented kingdoms inhabited by various Semitic groups known as Canaanites, Ammonites, Moabites, Amorites and others as well as the historically more important Phoenicians, Philistines and Israelites.[2] The gradual conquest of Canaan by the Israelites took place over a period of several hundred years (around 1200 B.C.E.) when most of the world would be later dated as being between the Bronze and Iron Ages.[3,4]

It is to the credit of the Israelite monarchy (1000 B.C.E.) that the dissident tribes and kingdoms finally achieved political unity and historic significance.[5] Under King Solomon, the Hebrews made pilgrimages to the Temple in Jerusalem bringing offerings of fine flour, first fruits and the fattest of their calves to celebrate the three main festivals of the year: Passover or *Pesach*, Pentecost or *Shavuoth,* and Tabernacles or *Succoth.* Jewish dietary laws regarding the eating of clean and unclean flesh were strictly observed and the Sabbath (Saturday, the seventh day of the week) was honoured with rest, prayer and simple food cooked ahead of time. An orderly life-style prevailed.[3] Trade and commerce flourished on land and sea with Solomon's merchant fleet of ships and his camel caravans.

But idol worship and the increasingly luxurious life-style of the wealthy caused rumblings among the workers and farmers of the Hebrew nation. They were not content with their "fragrant brown loaves and roasted goat meat, their barley, oats, vegetables and olives."[3] Finally, full-scale anarchy and idolatry broke out; the nation was disrupted and fragmented leaving it vulnerable to the devastating conquest of King Nebuchadnezzar of Babylon. In 586 B.C.E., he swept through the Kingdom of Judah, destroyed the great Temple of Solomon and exiled most of the Israelites to Babylon as captives.[2,5] The few poor farmers remaining had to eke a living from the destruction left; their exiled countrymen, mindful that Jerusalem and the Temple had been the symbol of their faith, intoned: "If I forget thee O Jerusalem, may my right hand forget its cunning. . . ."

While the Jews agonized over their fate, other parts of the world were awakening to the inspirational words of philosophers. Already Confucius was propounding his ideas and ideals in China; Zoroaster was prophesizing in Persia; soon in India, the great Gautama Buddha would reveal his profound wisdom. But the Jews already had known more than 1,200 years of history recording ideas and ideals, prophecies and revelations.[3]

In fact, the Jews did not fare so badly in Babylon. Most importantly, they were to set a pattern of Jewish survival for the next 2,500 years. Without a Temple, Jews grouped together wherever they could to pursue daily study and worship. Study, worship and prayer – the direct communion of man and God – replaced Temple offerings and sacrifices; in many cases, teachers replaced the priestly ruling class. These were the steps that provided the means of survival and created a spiritual and democratic bond within a people unparalleled in history.[2,7]

Many Jews were later allowed to return to Jerusalem and the Temple worship was restored. But the Greek Empire was now rising, and the Syrian Seleucids under their king, Antiochus Epiphanes, attempted to Hellenize all their conquered territories. The Kingdom of Judah was no exception. Greek ideals and aesthetics, customs and modes of food and eating, even dress and gymnastics all held much to allure the culture-conscious Jews. The Hellenic conquest threatened to be a spiritual and cultural one as well as one of land.

This threat became the impetus for a small band of Hebrews – zealots who called themselves Maccabeans – to rally the Israelites to the cause of religious freedom. In what was at that time an almost unprecedented form of guerilla warfare, they succeeded in routing the Syrians and restoring a semblance of order to the Temple and a rededication to the symbols, worship and principles of the God of Israel.[2,5] It must be noted that this revolt was probably the first example in recorded history of a battle fought for religious and spiritual freedom: as much an attempt to rally the Israelities together as to stem the tide of Hellenization. From this episode in 165 B.C.E. Jews the world over celebrate the festival of

Chanukah with lighting of candles and eating of pancakes and sweet fritters.

The Romans were the next to bring desolation, suffering and slavery to the inhabitants of this tiny strip of land. In memory of the second destruction of the Temple in 70 C.E., the ninth day of the Hebrew month of *Av* is a day of fasting (total abstinence from food and drink for twenty-four hours) and mourning for all Jews. At that time, stripped of their homes and their lands, the Jews were shipped as slaves to Rome where they built the great structures for the Emperor Titus.

In the fourth century C.E., Jerusalem was rebuilt again, this time with churches and monasteries to celebrate the official religion of the Roman Empire: Christianity.[3,5] While Hebrew and Aramaic continued to be the languages of the Jews and the lands they inhabited, yet a third language and influence was rising: Arabic, the Arab Empire and the faith of Islam. Muhammed had founded the religion of Islam in the 600s C.E. and, like the Christian church, modelled the Mosque after the Synagogue.[2] For a time, there was great affinity between the Arabs and Jews since many customs including prayer, circumcision, dietary laws and family life all followed Jewish models and precedent.[2,3,5] With the Arabic conquest of Palestine in 638 B.C.E., Islamic holy sites were added to the others and the Arab caliphs ruled for almost 500 years.

In the ensuing years, fraught with the desire to set down roots but continually singled out for their "isolationism", Jews were to be found in Italy, France, Germany, Spain and Portugal. No longer able to own land and pursue a life as farmers or shepherds, Jews turned to whatever trades were open to them.

Jewish communities were also to be found in the British Isles (until the Expulsion Edict of 1290 C.E.) The Jewish entry and subsequent expulsion from the British historical stage represented, in microcosm, the tale of Jewish life in almost every other European land. First came the encouragement to enter and settle because of their known ability as statesmen, councillors, physicians and merchants. Secondly came the rumours, allegations and edicts leading to their victimization, degradation and persecution. The final step was the command to leave, usually with the penalty of loss of possessions as well as home.[8] This repeated saga may have been the reason for the preponderance not only of the educated professionals among the Jews, but also of the continuing emphasis of the individual home as a sanctuary and haven of Judaism.

It was the Inquisition that caused a turn in the movement of Jewish emigration. From steadily westward, now it was back to the only direction left, to the area known as the Levant: Egypt, North Africa, Arabia, Syria and Palestine. In 1178 C.E. the area was taken over by the Muslim leader Saladin, and Muslims subsequently reigned for 300 years; by 1517, it became part of the Ottoman Empire. The tormented Jews of Europe were offered help by the Ottomans and were welcomed for their linguistic abilities, and their business and professional acumen. The Turks were mostly militarily or agriculturally inclined and content to leave matters of trade and business in the hands of the Armenians, Greeks or Jews.[8]

But it was to take yet another 300 years of persecution, pogroms and probably the seeds of human rights sewn by both the Russian and the French Revolutions that instigated the first utopian plans to return to Palestine and create a new Jewish homeland.[2]

The new city of Jerusalem, begun with the suburb of Yemin Moshe in 1860 as a religious settlement, grew slowly. There and in other areas, settlers experimented with vegetables, orchards and chickens on lands that had been dustblown and neglected for centuries. Ancient lands yielded to the persistent but increasingly familiar coaxing of Jewish farmers. In the 1880s, vineyards financed by Baron Edmund de Rothschild and cultivated from French vineyard cuttings were to start a new industry.[10] The long-forgotten "Turkish province" began to bloom with the toil of these new-style farmers: mostly idealists with intellectual and professional training who had to learn the hard way how to work with their hands.[11]

Set aside too were the languages and even the familiar foods of the lands the settlers had come from. Hebrew was revived as the daily language, agricultural schools were established, and the typical meals were garnered from whatever the land and cattle offered: mostly dairy foods, fruits and vegetables.

The Turkish Empire broke down completely during the First World War, and in 1917 Turkish rule in Palestine was turned over to the British Army as a British mandate.[2,5,8] While political Zionists pressed leaders to implement the Balfour Declaration of 1917, which viewed "with favour the establishment of a Jewish homeland," the League of Nations also gave recognition to the Jews' right to settle in Palestine.

Now a new European immigration wave joined the early pioneers (*chalutzim*) and many of these were merchants, artisans, and labourers eager to ply their trades. It was they who gave impetus to factories, industries, schools and research institutes. This new wave joined not only the *chalutzim* but also the Oriental Jews who had long lived in the land and devoted their lives to study and strict religious and ritualistic observance of Judaism.[11] The population of Palestine was now made up of Arabs as well as Jews from Russia, Poland, Lithuania, the U.S. and Canada and the Oriental communities from Yemen, Arabia, Persia, Syria, Morocco, Turkey and the Balkans as well as the Sephardic Jews from Spain, Italy and Portugal.[11]

After the European Holocaust, the small state absorbed as many of the homeless, orphaned and war-weary souls as it could. The new citizens of Israel had come from more than 100 countries of the world, speaking almost as many languages and bringing with them (if nothing else, and often it was nothing else) their culture: language, customs and foods. Thus this tiny "new" nation once again made a historical impact on the same land shown to them by Moses: the little strip of land he called the Promised Land some 3,270 years ago.[9]

In Abba Ebans' words: Israel is not a new "esperanto" nation writing its history on a clean slate. It is the only state in the world which speaks the same tongue, upholds the same faith, and inhabits the same land as it did three thousand years before.[8]

Home Life and Facilities

The earliest Israelites were mostly farmers and herdsmen living in simple homes with simple furnishings. In hilly, rocky areas they were able to build homes of stone; in the plains they built out of sun-dried mud bricks. The poorest homes in country areas were put together with thatch and straw, using smoothed clay for the floors.[2] In towns, the more permanent dwellings were often joined at the rooftops and this became the place for strolling and meeting one another after the working time. Rural homes would be furnished with tables, stools, straw mats for sleeping, and with vessels of earthenware, clay and wood in the kitchen. Town homes would use some metal utensils as well as the earthenware ones both for cooking and for storage. (To this day, huge porous earthenware jugs are used to keep water cool.) Small clay dishes filled with olive oil and lit with a flaxen wick would provide light in the evenings.[2]

Women had much to occupy their time in those early days of Israel's history. It is believed that the secret of yeasts for baking was discovered by the Egyptians, but the ancient world had long known the secret of fermentation to produce wines. Wheat and barley grains were ground in stone millstones then pounded in mortar and pestle to make fine flours. Kneaded bread doughs were then baked by laying them in hot ashes (a technique still used by modern-day nomadic peoples), or by placing them into rudimentary earthenware ovens heated with charcoal embers.[2] Oil was pressed from both olives and sesame seeds; cheeses and butter were prepared from the milk of cows and goats; wine was made from fermented grapes. (Later this art fell into disuse in the Middle East because of the Muslim prohibition against wine; Israel today has the only flourishing wine industry in the area.[10]) Onions, leeks, garlic and cucumber were commonly used and fruits such as dates, figs and grapes added some variety to the diet. Natural honey was the source of sweetening.

Modern-day Israel, like the many peoples that make up the nation, has many kitchens. It is not enough to consider merely foods that are "Israeli" or that are "Jewish." One must ask the further questions:

— "What is your country of origin?"
— "Do you keep the laws of Kashruth?"

A Yemenite Jew following orthodox observance will eat and serve differently than a reform Jew of German origin. Yet, all are Jews – or Israelis. Tastes and origins may vary, but the observance of the Jewish dietary laws (called Kashruth) also varies from strict to negligent. And the observance of these laws further affects not only the foods on the table, but the facilities within the kitchen itself. There is no more complex set of food rules in the world than those which govern the "kosher kitchen," and they are observed voluntarily.

The laws of Kashruth were first described in the book of Leviticus in the Five Books of Moses, and were later codified and amplified by schools of the learned into what is known as the Shulchan Aruch and the Talmud. Observance of Kashruth varies not only between Jewish households (as it did throughout the Diaspora), it also varies in observance between the cooperative settlements. The matter of food and eating is one that affects us many times each day, and it is widely considered that discipline as well as thankfulness in regard to food has played an important role in Jewish awareness and survival.

In following the interpretation of the rule that states, "thou shalt not seethe a kid in its mother's milk," strict separation of meat foods and dairy foods is observed even to the point of separate dishes, cookware, towels and cutlery. Thus in the observant kosher kitchen, each item required in the preparation and serving of foods (as well as the clean-up) will be stored in duplicate – often in different colours – one set for dairy and one for meats. This rule carries on to the meal itself, for no dairy foods may be served at the same meal with meat foods.

There is a classification of both foods and dishes that may be considered to be *pareve*: that is, they are inherently kosher and are considered "neutral," neither meat nor dairy. This covers grains, fruits, vegetables, beverages (except milk or milk products), and seasonings. As far as dishes and utensils, all glassware is considered to be *pareve* or suited to both meat or dairy use (but at separate meals). Packaged or processed products may be marked "PAREVE" on the package; often soaps and detergents may be so marked as well.

Yet another duplicate set of dairy and meat dishes and utensils may be found in the strictly observant kitchen – stored in a separate cupboard – and these are for use only during the eight days of *Pesach* (Passover), when the prohibition of all leavened foods adds still more restrictions.

Kosher or Kashruth, meaning "fit for use," covers all foods used in accordance with the biblical laws. The term *glatt kosher* signifies the observance of the strictest rules.

In effect, the Jewish dietary laws place foods into three categories: those that are inherently kosher or *pareve*; those that require some processing to make them kosher, as in preparation of meats; and those that are not kosher. Foods that are not kosher include pork products, shellfish, any fish without scales or fins and any meat from animals that do not have split hooves or chew their cud.[1] This prohibition is also concerned with the ingredients in prepared products; for example, gelatin in dessert products or candies must be from a kosher source. To distinguish prepared products that may or may not be kosher, several international label markings are used – K, U, or COR – which indicate the designation of rabbinical approval.

Depending on degree of Judaic observance, then, the kosher kitchen may have to be a large one, and in some cases may mean two separate kitchens (as in many institutions) in order to observe the letter of the laws of Kashruth.

FOODS COMMONLY USED

There is an incredibly complex blending of food and culinary habits together with variations in Kashruth observance, and as yet no clear-cut Israeli cuisine has emerged. However, there seems to be a preference for the age-old food favourites of the Middle East: legumes, lamb, fresh and saltwater fish, *leben*, the unsaturated oils of seeds and nuts, olives and grapes as well as the produce of local fields and orchards.[11]

This low-cost, nutritive and well-balanced diet is not enjoyed by all. For example, many Europeans consider vegetables (with few exceptions) as "mere grass." However, the newly emerging general cuisine shows a strong preference for meat soups with rice or noodles, salads of all kinds, eggplant in many forms, HAMOUT-ZIM (pickled vegetables), lamb on a spit or in kebab form, HOUMOUS, TEHINA, FELAFEL, cottage cheese and LEBENIA in many forms and combinations. Those of Oriental background (from North-African and Mid-East countries) prefer rice and oil while the Europeans enjoy potatoes and margarine. Canned, quick mixes and frozen foods sell primarily to Westerners or are for export; Israelis have no doubt about their strong preference for fresh foods.[11,12]

In reference to Israeli foods and food customs definite distinctions exist between the three main divisions of Jewish people. These are divisions which distinguish cultural differences only – and not religious – for they are all Jews. The Jews from central and eastern Europe are Ashkenazic, those from the countries of the northern Mediterranean and those who speak Spanish or Ladino (a mix of Spanish and Hebrew) are called Sephardic Jews, while those from the North-African and Middle Eastern countries are called Oriental Jews. In common, all use Hebrew as the language of prayer if not of study as well, have special local foods for all the Jewish holidays, and use the Torah (the Five Books of Moses or the Pentateuch) as their holy book.

Milk and Milk Products

Milk and milk products are plentiful and of excellent quality in Israel. LEBEN is made from skim milk, LEBENIA is prepared from whole milk. Other refreshing cultured milk drinks include ZEEVDA, yoghurt and KEFIR. All these clabbered milk drinks are nutritiously similar but are made from different cultures yielding slightly different flavours and textures. All have proven historically to be good ways of using milk in hot climates.[11] Cottage cheese is one of Israel's favourite foods, appearing in countless dishes and frequently eaten for breakfast.[13] Filled pastries of many types (and with origins from many countries) use cottage cheese as their basic ingredient: BLINTZES, KNISHES, strudel, tarts and turnovers as well as cheese pies and cheesecakes. Cottage cheese smoothed with sour cream may also be blended with other ingredients to form tasty snack spreads that may be colourful with vegetables, spicy hot, salty with olives or anchovies or sweet with carrots and honey.[13] Other cheese favourites include mild firm cheeses of the gouda, edam and Swiss cheese types.

Fruits and Vegetables

Among Israel's principal crops are citrus fruits, olives, figs, corn and tomatoes.[15] Although citrus fruits and drinks made from fruits head the list of Israeli favourites, varieties of melons, dates, bananas and grapes are also produced as well as smaller amounts of other fruits.[14] Apples, pears, plums, peaches, apricots, pomegranates, avocadoes, pomelos, mangoes, rhubarb, quinces, pawpaw, strawberries and persimmons are quickly becoming not only a part of the dietary but an addition to the lists of exports. Compotes of stewed mixed dried fruits are Sabbath favourites because they can be slowly simmered, keep well – and smell delicious. Dried fruits include prunes, raisins, dates, figs, apricots, apples and pears.

The most widely used fruits are the citrus, especially oranges. Wedges of juicy orange are used in many salad and fresh fruit dessert mixtures. The *tapuach zahav* (golden apple, the name given to the orange) is also made into preserves and marmalade, refreshing drinks and iced sherbets. The peel is shredded for flavouring other dishes, for use in baked goods, and candied as a special treat called POMERANTZEN.

The most symbolic fruit is the SABRA. Although with sharp prickles on the outside, once peeled this juicy fruit from the cactus-type plant is a joy to eat. Native-born Israelis are called Sabras after this plant because they too, though prickly on the outside, are soft within.

To many tourists and visitors it must seem that Israelis are vegetarians. Many interesting and nourishing dishes are made from vegetables, which are even a part of the breakfast menu, while tomatoes served with milk as a beverage are a common morning snack in homes for older citizens.[11]

The popularity of vegetables stems from the bountiful growing season and new agricultural techniques which combine to produce as many as three crops in a year.[11] The *kibbutz* way of serving vegetables (sometimes called a Ben-Gurion salad) is to place whole washed vegetables on the table. Each diner selects and peels his own – peels are placed in a special bowl called a KOLBONICK that is standard on most tables – then dresses his vegetable selection with fresh lemon juice and oil.

Tomatoes and potatoes are the largest and most enjoyed crop of vegetables. But many others come year around or in seasonal plenty, including greens of all types, cabbages, cauliflower, cucumbers, peppers, onions, eggplants and carrots. Potatoes, tomatoes and onions are popular with all the population. These and other vegetables are often cooked in combination dishes that form hearty soups or stews, sometimes in combination with meats, fish or legumes. Vegetable consumption, both raw in salads and cooked, is greatly increasing despite the original distaste of the central Europeans.[14]

Other vegetables include asparagus, artichokes, fresh peas and green beans of many varieties, especially the favourite PUL or broad bean of antiquity, brussels sprouts, beets, cabbage made into sauerkraut and carrots sweetened with honey and made into TZIMMES, leeks, KHUBEISA or HAALAMIT (greens), okra or BAMIA, squash or KUSA or KISHUYIM (plural in Hebrew), marrows, calabash or Israel's pumpkin-like squash, yams and sweet potatoes, turnips and celery.[11,12,13]

One has only to think of the blend of cuisines and cultures that make up Israel's population to understand that it would not be difficult to think Israelis were indeed vegetarians. The range of non-meat dishes includes savoury stuffed vegetables of the Mediterranean countries, the dozens of legume soups and stews of the Orientals, the endless potato and cabbage dishes from European Ashkenazis, and the new flavours and recipes that are being developed and that combine such tastes as carrot and orange.

Meats and Alternates

In Israel, it is mostly the "alternates" that are important on the menu. Land is too scarce and too valuable to be able to support large herds of beef cattle. While lamb, mutton, poultry and fish are more frequent on the menu, beef is much enjoyed when available and within the family budget.

The rules of Kashruth demand that only meats from those animals that chew their cud and have a cloven hoof may be eaten. The animal must be slaughtered in the ritual manner by a *shochet* and *kashered* (made fit, in this case especially in regard to blood removal) by soaking in cold water for one half-hour. Then the flesh must be salted with coarse salt for one hour on a slanted board so that the released blood may drain away. After a final washing, the meat is considered *kashered* and fit for use.

In most lands where Jews make their homes, the hindquarters of animals are part of the prohibition. But in Israel, the hindquarters are used because skilled butchers are able to cut the meat free of the main blood vessels. Thus the meat is called *treibert* and is fit for use.[13] Most modern-day kosher butchers, both in Israel and in other countries, perform the added service of *kashering* meats for their customers.

Those of European background prefer to roast or stew their meats and like to eat meat whenever possible. Oriental families have lived for generations with little meat in their dietary and have become accustomed to stretching the meat flavour by using small amounts in combination with vegetables or legumes or both in many hearty soup or stew dishes, stuffed vegetables or rice dishes. Grilled meats or kebabs are also popular.

Again, as with vegetables, the popular listing of meat dishes reads like an international cookbook: SAUERBRATEN and ROULADEN, CHOLENT (HAMIM or DEFINA), STEFADO, PUCHERO, BEEF STROGANOFF (the cream sauce is a "mock," creamed with a non-dairy creamer or blended with mayonnaise for a creamy taste and appearance), ROMANIAN KAR-NATZLACH, KLOPS (Dutch meatloaf), KIRSEH (Yemenite tripe dishes), WIENER SCHNITZEL, VITELLO ARROT OLATI (Italian rolled stuffed veal), PERSIAN JU-JU (stuffed lamb), KIBBE, MOUSSAKA, DOLMAS (SARMALI or MALFOUF) (stuffed grape leaves), and KEFTA or KEFTEDES (round meat-balls or hamburger).[13]

Poultry can be prepared in as many languages as well – flavoured with orange and honey, prepared as a curry, prepared with olives and pickled lemons in the Moroccan way, Tunisian chicken with SELERIAC (the Israeli type of root celery), chicken à la king ("cream" sauce made with egg yolks, chicken stock and flour), chicken pilau, chicken paprikash, and galantina di pollo (Italian boned and stuffed chicken). Turkey, geese and ducks, even quail and pigeons find a place on the menu. The giblets from all fowl are enjoyed in specialty dishes which make use of the gizzards, necks, hearts and livers. The large piece of skin from the neck of the fowl is often cut off separately and stuffed then roasted beside the bird; it is called by the Yiddish name, HELZEL.[13]

Fish too, are used in accordance with the traditional laws of Kashruth. Carp and tuna are the most-used fish and are taken from the Sea of Galilee, the Red Sea, the Mediterranean and also from what are popularly known as the "gefilte fish ponds" – the artificial ponds created on many of the farms for fish production. Only fish with scales and fins are used in traditional Jewish homes; eliminated are all sea foods and shellfish. Fish is a must as part of the Sabbath Eve dinner on Friday night, often in the form of pickled fish, or poached fish balls called GEFILTE FISH. But many methods and many different preparations are used to make fish dishes interesting. Besides carp and tuna, herrings in many preparations are great favourites, as well as bream, sole, sardines (fresh), grouper, red snapper, mackerel or drum fish, and PALAMIDA (little tuna).

While meat, poultry and fish are enjoyed when available, the real protein staples of the dietary aside from dairy foods are the legumes. Not only are they the ancient standbys of Arab and Bedouin meals, they are used widely in the contemporary Mid-East cuisine. Their popularity comes from the many ways they can be prepared as well as the fact that they are filling, satisfying and inexpensive.

Chick peas, also called NAHIT, HOUMOUS, BOB and HAMTZA, are used in many ways. They are even sold by street vendors and nibbled as salted peanuts. FELAFEL is made from ground, seasoned and cooked chick peas which are formed into balls and deep-fried. They are served with spicy hot sauces and vegetable shreds – often all tucked into the pocket of a PITA (Arab bread). PUL or PHUL, dried broad beans, are more popular than small white navy beans which are also used. Legumes (also lima beans, lentils of several varieties) may be served as an appetizer by mashing and serving as a well-seasoned dip. They also may be mashed and added to thicken soups and stews, served as a spiced side-dish for meats, or cooked and tossed in with salads. Israelis *never* eat greens alone as a salad: always as a mixture.[11]

Nor does the list of legume uses end there. Legumes are also used to make hearty soups – and often a meaty flavour and colour is obtained by browning shredded carrots in oil or using onions with their skins on.[11] Finally, legumes are often used together with cereals in combinations like beans and rice, lentils and BURGHUL. Soybeans are of great importance too. They are used to feed cattle and poultry, in the production of oils and margarine, and by law all breads must incorporate at least 2 per cent soya flour.[11]

Eggs are plentiful and widely used, with most Israelis consuming at least one egg a day and often two: one at breakfast and another as part of the lunch or supper meal. In homes for the aged and in institutions many dishes are prepared with eggs, so that consumption could be listed as one egg per day.[13] CHATCHOUKA, a whole egg poached and served in a hot sauce, and TETCHOUKA, the same ingredients but served as an omelet, are North African favourites. HAMIDAS, long-cooked browned eggs, are holiday favourites for Sephardic Jews because eggs symbolize the mystery of life; they also turn brown and flavourful when cooked in the Sabbath bean specialty, CHOLENT. Hard-cooked, soft, or scrambled, made into omelets or soufflés, or combined with many other foods, eggs form a staple part of the Israeli diet.

Breads and Cereals
It is easy to detect the origin of a family by watching to see which bread or cereal foods the members favour. Whether prepared in the homes or bought from street vendors or at bakeries, all form an important part of

the daily dietary. Varieties used include wheat, rye, rice, barley, oats, BURGHUL (coarse wheat), OREZON (fine and coarse whole wheat grits), cornmeal, noodles and pasta, KASHA (COUSEMET or buckwheat), and HIRSHE (DOCHAN, DURRA or millet). Between 50 and 60 per cent of the day's calories come from cereal foods.[11]

European light and dark breads and rolls, egg breads, bagels, rolls, MATZOHS (unleavened Passover bread) and PITA (Arab flat bread, hollow in the middle) are available everywhere.[14] Oriental Jews prefer BURGHUL and rice, while many Italians use cornmeal (POLENTA).[14] Cereals are used with milk for breakfast, cooked with meat, fish or vegetables, in soups, and often in desserts. For example, rice is often used as a kibbutz breakfast cereal by cooking with milk and cinnamon and eating with sugar and margarine; hospitals and Sephardim often cook a rice pudding instead of the bean CHOLENT for the Sabbath. (It is flavoured with egg and fried onions.) MOUCHALABEH is a popular Mid-East dessert of diluted milk thickened with rice flour and flavoured with rose water and spices then garnished with chopped nuts. FARINA is used as a thickener in cooking. It is also cooked then spread in a pan to cool and cut in cubes which may then be served as a soup garnish or breaded and fried then served with grated mild cheese or sprinkled with cinnamon sugar.[11] Oatmeal finds its way to the table as a cooked cereal, as MUESLI, in pancakes, cakes, cookies, breads and in meat mixtures and soups.[11]

International breads also include: ANBEISSEN STUTEN (Germany), KEYLITCH or CHALLAH (twisted egg bread), KHUBS and LAKHOACH (Yemenite), PITA (Middle East), KAYEK (Syria), CROISSANTS (France), ZEMEL or PAMPALIK (Russia), BOBKE (Polish), KRENTENKRANENBROOD (Dutch), and CHELSEA BUNS (England).[13]

Fats

Olive oil and sesame seed oil are most used for cooking, baking and as dressings for salads and pickles. Margarine is used in preference to butter because it is made *pareve* (that is, can be used both for meat and dairy dishes) and because it is less expensive. Butter is used when possible but never of course at the same meal with meat dishes.

TECHINA is the name for sesame seed oil, adding its delicate roasted seed flavour to many dishes. It is becoming very popular for any dish with legumes.[14]

Sweets and Snacks

There are many ways to satisfy a sweet tooth in Israel. Chocolate and candy factories produce tempting products, but the Israeli sweet tooth is not a strong one. In fact, many prefer sour or salted nibbles. Salted legumes, salted roasted seeds of all kinds such as melon and squash, pumpkin, sunflower and treats made of ground and roasted nuts and seeds such as HALVAH, are common wares of the street vendors. Fresh fruits and fresh fruit drinks and juices are popular. Candied nuts and many types of dried candied fruits, candied peels, and sweets made with seeds or nuts plus honey are popular too. MARZIPAN, a sweet made from ground almonds, can also be made from cereals such as oatmeal, farina and semolina. Turkish Delight or RAHAT EL HALKUM, flavoured with rose water, is a special sweet treat.

Seasonings
It would be impossible to take a group of seasonings and describe them as being typically Israeli. As yet, there is no one group of tastes that is predominant to the young land. To have some idea of the complexity, see "Ethnic Specialties" below.

Beverages
Heading the list of beverages, perhaps even before tea or coffee, is the special orange-flavoured citrus syrup made by many Israeli homemakers and kept on hand to be mixed with icy cold soda water for a refreshing beverage. This may be lightly spiced or flavoured with rose water, even a little wine.[13]

Coffee is the most popular hot beverage, but the number of ways of serving it is staggering. Here again, the cosmopolitan population of Israel demands that each specialty be available. Here one can find *capuccino*, instant coffee, *café au lait*, Turkish coffee, espresso. You can also have coffee with sugar, (varying amounts in each type), coffee with hot milk, coffee with cold milk, coffee with cream and coffee with whipped cream. If that does not satisfy then you can also have your coffee flavoured with ginger (Yemenite style), with hale or cardamom (Middle-Eastern), with chocolate (Italian) or simple American style.

Tea is also not a simple matter. Do you want it Russian style with a slice of lemon and a sugar cube? Moroccan style with mint? English style with milk and sugar? Finally, do you want your tea served in a glass or in a cup and saucer?

Israeli wines probably began with Noah, or even before. But in Israel the modern wine-making industry became established in the 1880s thanks to the generosity of the Baron Rothschild in both finances and cuttings from French vines. Beer is made and used as a beverage as well as in cooking, as are the many types of wines.[10,14]

Ethnic Specialties
Israel is too small a country and as yet too young to have regional specialties. However, because of the interesting mix of Jews from many countries of the world, food specialties not only exist, but many are preserved with great pride and taught to the younger generation. Some are beginning to take a special place in the emergence of an Israeli cuisine. While information and cookbooks abound on the foods of most

Asian and European countries – and the Jews from these countries have adapted all of these specialties with suitable changes for the "kosher kitchen" – the food specialties of the Oriental Jews are most intriguing, because little general information is known. Many of these minor groups are listed here; their food specialties can be traced back many hundreds of years. Unusual specialties from other groups are also included.

Special ethnic favourites for festivals are listed under "Special Occasions."

Afghanistan Jews

These Jews do not like soups or the flavour of sharp hot peppers. They often prepare meat dishes that include dried fruits cooked together. They enjoy a *pilau* of rice as a main dish, and favour onions, cinnamon and mild pepper as seasonings. Lamb and chicken are the favourite meats, LEBEN the beverage. Some specialty dishes include TASHKEBAB, tender lamb slices marinated in ARAK with salt and pepper, cinnamon and turmeric plus sliced onions. This prepared lamb is then placed on skewers alternately with tomatoes and onions and browned quickly on a grill. The cooking is finished in the same marinade.[11]

Most interesting is the SABBATH CHOLENDT. In order not to break the prohibition against working on the Sabbath (and cooking is working), a double boiler is used to prepare two hot meals. In the bottom pot is placed cut-up chicken and vegetables while in the upper pot fish, oil and a little water are set together. The double pot is simmered very slowly overnight to form the main meal of meat and vegetables and the evening meal of fish for the Sabbath.[11]

Another special dish is KONDY. This is a layered casserole with rice, meats and vegetables prepared with great attention to detail. Slightly cooked rice is mixed with egg and placed in the bottom of a pot to be topped with a layer of braised lamb and vegetables, then a further layer of plain pre-cooked rice. The whole mixture is slowly simmered or baked for one hour.

Other favourites include preserved sweet lemons: layers of sliced lemons and sugar served as a pickle; sugared rhubarb eaten boiled or raw; and tiny squash or pumpkins hollowed out and filled with a stuffing of meat, rice, mixed chopped vegetables, raisins, plums, cinnamon and turmeric then stewed or baked till tender.[11]

Arabs

Most Arabic families cling closely to traditional food customs. The nomadic Bedouins in the Negev depend largely on their own flocks for milk products and meats, and their crops for barley and other cereals. Dried fruits make up the balance of the dietary.[14] Most Arab farming in Israel is still based on the subsistence principle so that food produced is mostly for domestic consumption and perhaps enough extra for trade to buy a few other necessities. Crops are neither scientifically grown nor irrigated although many modern changes are occurring. Arabs have flocks of sheep and goats and cultivate crops of olives, wheat, barley, maize, millet, cucumbers, potatoes and other vegetables.[14]

Balkan Jews

This ethnic grouping includes those Jews from Romania, Bulgaria, Greece and Yugoslavia, most of whom speak Ladino (a mix of Hebrew and Spanish).[11] Definite elements of the great Greek cuisine are apparent in their preferences and specialties. They use yoghurt and avgolemono sauce, stuffed vegetables, goat cheese, thin sheets of *phyllo* pastry in many dishes, olives and spinach and legumes in many forms. Eggplant dishes abound, shredded pumpkin is enjoyed cooked, and there are many desserts rich with honey, sugar, syrups and nuts finished with whipped cream. Bulgarians make delicious vegetable croquettes, breaded and browned then simmered with lemon juice and sugar. Romanians enjoy a cornmeal pudding (MAMALIGA) baked and served with LEBENIA (similar to yoghurt), or fresh cottage cheese and butter (also called MALAI). Sweet red peppers or pimentos are a special pleasure and are called GAMBA, while a marinade of pickled pimentos with vinegar, honey, onions and spices is called GAMBA MARINADE.[11,14]

Bukharian Jews

Bukharians prepare Oriental foods with a special touch, using olives, rice and oil as staples, PITA as their bread and LEBEN or LEBENIA as their beverage. YACINI is a dish of combined pickled meats and boiled chicken served with *pilau* and salads of fresh and cooked vegetables. Bukharian *pilau* consists of rice cooked over a savoury bed of meats, carrots and raisins. BASCH is another rice dish of cubed meats, parsley and liver cooked and served with rice. HASAMOOSA is a complex flaky layered pastry leavened with yeast, rolled very thinly and filled either with a meat filling or a sweet almond mixture. Traditional holiday fare is fried fish dipped into a mixture of garlic, water, parsley and salt – served in a small dipping bowl at the table with thin crisp PITAS and LEBENIA.[11]

Central Asian Jews

These represent some of the underdeveloped Israeli communities because they had previously lived in remote areas and in some of the "darkest ghettoes of the Near East."[11] They prepare a dish of stuffed cabbage rolls similar to Russian style but often using lamb as the meat and tomato sauce as the seasoning. PASTLIKAS are small rounds of yeast dough topped with a filling that may be prepared from meats, cheese, spinach or other chopped vegetables, or eggplant well-seasoned. A brushing with egg and a sprinkle of sesame seeds precedes oven baking.[11] OROTO is the name given to a sliced cucumber salad tossed with olive oil and lemon juice and flavoured with both garlic and mint leaves.[11]

Cochin Jews of India

From the west coast of India and now largely "transplanted" to Israel, this small group eats typical East Indian fare, but conforming to traditional food laws. They use CARCUM (turmeric) instead of the costlier saffron, and many vegetable and fried dishes characterize their menu.[11]

Egyptian Jews

This group has brought many typical Egyptian dishes with them to Israel. They often fry fish then cook it with rice, and meats are *seldom* eaten alone but *always* in combination with vegetables or legumes. MOUSSAKA (from Greece) is a layered dish of eggplant, rice, and sometimes including chopped meat. BAMIA or OKRA is popularly cooked with a tomato sauce.[14]

Iraqi Jews

The largest emigration of Iraqi Jews to Israel occurred in 1948, creating another element in the Israeli food picture. They like to combine vegetables with meat, fish or rice and enjoy eating a large variety of foods including cheeses and LEBEN (which in Iraq was made from buffalo milk).[11] Although they are not fond of soups and usually serve them only when someone is ill, there is a bean soup that is more a stew than a soup. Oil and SAMNEH, the fat from the tail of sheep, is their favourite. RUBBEH is the national dish made from BURGHUL paste filled with chopped meats and nuts then fried or cooked. They enjoy a thick paste (similar to Indian DAL) made of puréed lentils, cumin and garlic with a touch of salt and pepper.[11] Curry blends are the favourite seasoning.[14] Others include cinnamon, cardamom, garlic, cloves, cumin, rosemary, orange blossom and rose water, CARCUM (turmeric) cayenne and salt and pepper. However, their food cannot be considered highly spiced.[11] Traditionally Thursday night supper is cheese, lentils and rice, for this is a traditional meatless day. Another favourite is a filled fried yeast pastry stuffed with lentil or meat paste. Among the staples are rice, burghul, semolina, chick peas, beans and lentils while TECHINA (sesame seed oil) is used on vegetables, meats and fish.[11]

Vegetables used include eggplant, BAMIA, sweet pumpkin preserves, vegetable marrow stewed and served with LEBEN or tomato sauce. Fresh dates are the most popular fruit; DIBS is a syrup made from fresh dates; unripe dates are preserved with sugar, lemon, cinnamon and cloves.

BURGHUL is used as in Lebanon and Syria. Made into KIBBEH, BAKED KIBBEH, filled and fried, the Iraqi touch is the addition of eggs and the steaming of the KIBBEH before frying to make the mixture lighter.[11]

Other Iraqi (as well as Lebanese and Syrian) specialties include MISHMISH, dried apricots sold in a firm block or as halved fruit and often cooked with meats; COUSA, zucchini; KIBBEH CHALAB, fried patties of mashed potatoes and rice, onions and ground chicken meat; and RECHEM, a mixture of chopped embryos (chicken egg yolks unlaid), lungs, giblets with seasoned rice used to stuff cleaned intestines, tripe or ovary sacs or vegetable leaves.[11] AGASI ADAMA are Camheen truffles, an underground fungi appearing like wrinkled potatoes but used and eaten like mushrooms.

Kurdistani Jews

This group enjoys drinking ARAK (potent anise-flavoured liquor) with MEZA (appetizers) of cooked sliced potatoes, hard eggs and chopped meat steamed in oil. They eat all the KIBBEE (BURGHUL) dishes, stuffed vegetables and leaf dishes and prefer a soup made from leeks and added rice. They enjoy, as a treat, MAMOUL, a slow-baked semolina cake flavoured with chopped nuts, cinnamon and rose water.[11]

North African: Moroccan, Tunisian, and Tripolitanian Jews

With an especially rich and intriguing cuisine, Oriental Jews bring these specialties to add to Israel's "pot." TAGINES, COUSCOUS, and special spices and aromas mark their exotic cookery. In some areas, a marked Italian influence in the preparation of pastas and pizza dishes is also noted. A TAGINE is a mixed stew of pulses, rice, or potatoes and other vegetables and may or may not contain meat or fish.[14] Pickled lemons, a staple of the cuisine, are prepared by layering lemons that have been cut in halves or quarters with red hot peppers and coarse salt and allowing them to stand about three weeks. They are to be seen in jars on the counters of restaurants everywhere in the Middle East.[11] The COUSCOUS is a basic staple prepared in many ways. One of these ways is to cook a variety of root vegetables under the perforated couscous pot fragrant with lemon, cumin, garlic, oil and paprika and after cooking forming a flavourful and colourful sauce over the COUSCOUS.

The Italian influence in Tripoli shows itself in the prolific use of garlic, tomatoes and tomato sauce. Desserts are not customary: fresh fruits, toasted seeds and nuts are the usual finale to a meal.[11]

SCHIKSUKA is a vegetable melange casserole finished by pouring over beaten eggs then serving when the eggs are set. CROUSHA is another vegetable dish made by frying leeks and onions in oil then adding a little water and fresh green peas and simmering till tender. MOUSSAKA is also popular in Tunisia and Tripoli as is ARROSTO, a stew of browned beef or lamb with vegetables added and then served with rice or COUSCOUS.[11]

Moroccan Jews never combine onions and garlic in the same dish; they prefer saffron to flavour and colour their rice, while the poor settle for turmeric. Favourite seasonings include cinnamon, cloves, marjoram, allspice, thyme and sharp red hot peppers. To wash it all down they favour green tea steeped with mint – a beverage as popular as coffee. HOUT CRAFS is a Moroccan dish of poached fish balls served with the broth in which a whole head of celery plus leaves have been simmered, giving it a fresh flavour. PHUL or FOOL is a dish of fried or deep-fried broad beans that are then simmered to tenderness. Popular too are many meat and fruit combinations – exotic by Western standards. Eggplants, leeks, onions and squash are widely used while dates, pomegranates and sesame seeds are probably the most popular fruits and seeds.

A favourite Moroccan dish after the Yom Kippur fast is a tagine of chickens, pickled lemons and olives, served with COUSCOUS.[11]

Persian (Iranian) Jews

Persian food is generally sharp but not greasy. Rice with meat forms the main dish for special occasions, while rice with legumes provides the everyday fare.[11] Many pickles are used and they are made with undiluted vinegar, turmeric, cumin and cinnamon bark. Between meal courses, they enjoy drinking strong alcoholic beverages or strong and very sweet tea flavoured with HAIL (cardamom). JOINDÉE is a typical dish of pounded meats, legumes, and vegetables formed into tiny balls and cooked in soup, stews, or in vegetable or legume casseroles.[11] A MOUSSAKA dish is layered sliced potatoes with a meat filling of ground meat, eggs and spinach all topped with beaten eggs.[16]

Sephardic Jews

Sephardic Jews have made their home in Palestine for centuries. They are for the most part the descendants from the large Jewish communities who made their homes in various areas round the Mediterranean after their forcible expulsion from Spain in 1492 (and some from Portugal at a later date). They settled not only in Palestine, but also in Italy, the Balkans, Egypt and Greece. They are distinct from the other Oriental Jewish communities because they speak Ladino, while others speak Arabic or the language of their native land.[11] The Jewish cuisine of these areas is of course largely a reflection of the general cuisine, but also features many Jewish specialties.

Among their many typical foods are the following specialties: BEREKES or PASTILIKES are meat, cheese or spinach-filled baked goods made with thin flaky *phyllo* pastry; KADROS are meat-stuffed artichoke hearts fried lightly to brown then simmered in lemon water and served with meat sauce; fried fish is also touched with lemon and frequently topped with crunchy pine nuts; HAMINDAS are eggs that have been hard-boiled in water containing onion skins so that they retain some of the brown colour; sharp pickles are an important part of the cuisine and are made from almost any vegetables including turnips, peppers, cabbage cucumbers and of course the ubiquitous pickled lemons, all with the indispensable ingredients of sharp vinegar and tiny hot peppers; MACHSHEE, a high point of Sephardic cookery (and an Israeli favourite), are carefully stuffed vegetables flour-dipped then fried in oil and arranged in a baking pan with lemon water and sometimes tomato sauce (*machshee* is an Arabic word representing a dish that has been loved in the Mediterranean area for centuries); garlic and lemon suffuses almost any dish except a sweet dessert; and when it comes to desserts, many pastries and cookies are honey-drenched, sprinkled with sesame seeds, and nibbled to the accompaniment of Turkish coffee.

Sephardic fish dishes also bring the lemon-garlic aroma and flavour in many versions of baked, stewed and fried fish dishes. Rice is frequently a part of many dishes, or may be cooked and served separately. KATCHEVAL is a mild cheese (similar to Italian cacciocavelli) used grated or sliced and breaded then fried or grilled as a light main dish. Still another dish is CHENAGEE, consisting of boiled chicken boned and cut up then baked in an egg custard with walnuts and served either hot or cold.

Served with mint tea or Turkish coffee, small cookies made with a rich dough and sesame seeds then drenched in a sweet syrup are frequent favourites. So too are date-filled cookies or rolls (AJVAH) and rich cookies called OOGIOT SUMSUM made from toasted ground sesame seeds.

South African Jews
Many Jews from South Africa are of Lithuanian origin. They like fried fish covered with a marinade (like ESCABECHE), and a flaked fish pie that consists of layers of flaked fish with crumbs and an egg-milk custard poured over and then baked. This baked fish pie is served with a sauce of sour cream mixed with anchovy paste and chives.[11]

Yemenite Jews
Coming from the southern tip of Saudi Arabia, an area called Yemen, these were the Jews airlifted (their transport to Israel on planes seemed to fulfill the ancient prophecy that they would return to their land "on the wings of an eagle") to Israel. They make up a very religious group of Jews who have always spoken Hebrew but have lived in a community unaccustomed to modern civilization.[11] They have distinct tastes and definite preferences. For example they do not eat cheese or drink milk in any form except for the Yemenites from Aden who eat a cooked clabbered milk called ZHUM. They use most foods in their natural, unprocessed state, prefer meats and use all parts of the animals. Their staple foods are meats, legumes, raw whole vegetables, and dried roasted nuts and seeds. Lemon and salt are used for pickling but not vinegar.

HILBE is a watery paste made from soaked *fenugreek* seeds ground and is seasoned with ZHUG, a fiery combination of garlic, cumin, coriander and dried hot spicy red or green peppers. HILBE with ZHUG is an ever-present staple used in soups, on breads, meats and vegetables – as indispensable on the Yemenite table as salt and pepper is on the Canadian. All leafy greens are used, but garlic, sharp, hot peppers, cumin, coriander, and cardamom are the staple seasonings. SEMNEH is butter clarified to keep well and containing garlic and sharp spices; other fats used are oils made from olives and seeds. ZHUM is the flour-thickened LEBEN made with garlic, salt, pepper and SEMNEH. This is served with ZHUG and mint.[11]

Many hearty soups are prepared: FTUT, a fat meat and vegetable soup to which torn PITA is added in the last five minutes is served with HILBE and ZHUG. Stews and soups are made almost daily for at least one meal and always contain meats and vegetables and often legumes. Tripe, lungs and brains are used in many dishes, and KEBABS of grilled meats are also popular. Marinated KEBANS of meat are called SHISHLICK and are alternated on skewers with tomatoes and onions.[16] All meat dishes, whether soups, stews or grilled, are well-seasoned.

Yemenite beverages display the same love of spicy flavours. Tea is prepared by boiling tea leaves with cinnamon or mint; coffee is made with ginger or cardamom; hot lemonade is served as a beverage "good for the ears"[11] and prepared with onions, ginger and honey. But ARAK is the national drink and KAT the leaves of a narcotic shrub that the Yemenites like either to chew or brew into a tea.[12]

Sabbath is special to the Yemenites as it is to all pious Jews. The morning meal is hot spicy tea served with KUBANEH, fragrant warm brown bread made with flour, yeast, water and SEMNEH. It is allowed to rise and then is placed in a tightly sealed, greased pan and baked very slowly overnight. For Sabbath afternoon a soft yeast dough will be baked into pancakes and eaten with HILBE; these are called LECHUCH. Other types of breads include HUBS or SALOUF, flat rounds of yeast dough baked on the sides of a pre-heated earth oven called a TABOON.[11]

Meal Patterns and Eating Customs

The emerging Israeli food pattern is one that makes imaginative use of plentiful local food products and adapts to the life-style of the different peoples and areas of the country. Already well-known and often emulated in Western brunches is what is known as the "Israeli breakfast." This was started in the communal dining rooms of the farming settlements. It includes a wide variety of fresh local vegetables, some served as "Ben-Gurion salad" and others made into various combinations of chopped and shredded vegetables mixed with different light dressings and including herring, fish, cheese, olives, and various cooked legumes. Eggs cooked in several ways, hot cooked cereals (oatmeal, cooked rice with cinnamon) and a variety of cheeses – cream cheese, cottage cheese, ALKERISH, KATOUSH, BRINDZA, SAFAD – breads, butter, fruit preserves, and honey provide a hearty and satisfying meal to start the day. Coffee, tea or leben is the morning beverage.

The mid-day dinner usually begins with an appetizer made of beans or vegetables – HOUMOUS TECHINA or CHOPPED EGGPLANT – followed by a hot meaty soup or a vegetarian soup. Israelis are great soup lovers and often the soup may be the most important part of the menu, notwithstanding the strong individual ethnic preferences. For example, many peoples of the Mid-East do not care for soups since most of their main dishes are juicy stews; those of Polish or Russian origin prefer meat-based soups but enjoy a meatless *borscht*; Yemenites may forego any course *except* the soup to which they always add bread and HILBE; Oriental Jews do not care for vegetable soups but prefer soups of legumes – and so it goes. One can only imagine the headaches of menu-planning in any large institution!

In general, jellied soups and those based on fish are not liked but the central European cold soups of fruit are well-liked. These include tangy soups made with dried fruits as well.[11] After the all-important soup comes the main dish of stewed meat or fish accompanied with either rice or potatoes and pickles. The dinner will be completed with fresh or stewed fruit or a simple pudding.

The evening supper is usually served between seven and eight o'clock, and is a light meal of an egg or cheese dish accompanied with a mixed vegetable salad, bread, margarine, honey and hot tea or coffee.

Tea breaks are usually taken in mid-morning about ten and again in the late afternoon about five. "Tea" may actually include tea, coffee, milk or a fruit drink served with simple sandwiches or cakes, or may even be a snack of fresh fruit. In the cities, people take frequent snacks of hot or cold beverages and the many nibbles offered by vendors: PITA, FELAFEL, pizza, salted and roasted nuts, seeds of every kind and fruits.

Hospitality and sharing is a way of life for the Israeli. Most especially is it considered a *mitzvah* (divine commandment, and thus a righteous deed) to extend hospitality to the stranger. Every effort is made to see that no stranger is left without a home or family to share a festive meal of the Sabbath or any other holiday. This hospitality is also extended to the stranger visiting a synagogue, for he is often given special honours during the services simply because he is a visitor.

Israeli eating customs are influenced by daily life-style, by the tradition of hospitality and also by the distinct customs that each ethnic group has brought from other lands.

Special Occasions
Israel's population is not only Jewish. Of the non-Jews, many are Muslims and a small minority are Christians. The smallest group of all are the Druses.[15] Religion and government are separate, but the Jewish holidays are celebrated nation-wide.

The seventh day of each week is a special occasion: *Shabbat*. Like all Jewish holidays, the *Shabbat* begins at sundown the evening before. Late Friday afternoon a hush falls over business and work areas, and throughout the cities of Israel, men and women can be seen hurrying home with a bouquet of fresh flowers for the *Shabbat* table. A white tablecloth and blessings over the Sabbath candles that are lit to usher in the day of rest precede the blessings spoken over the traditional *Kiddush* cup (of wine), and the two loaves of Sabbath bread, and then the eating of a peaceful dinner.

Traditionally, a small serving of some fish dish – gefilte fish, poached jellied fish or pickled fish – serves as the appetizer before hot soup. A chicken main dish is then served accompanied by cooked vegetables and a KUGEL. Dessert is usually fresh or stewed fruits followed by tea and small cakes. That is a typical Ashkenazic menu. Sephardic homes will reflect the foods more typical of many Mediterranean countries: fish with avgolemono sauce, chopped eggplant, roasted lamb, stuffed vegetables, rice and, to finish the meal, a honey-soaked cake or pastry nibbled with strong and sweet Turkish coffee.[17]

Since work of all types is prohibited on the *Shabbat*, and the day is devoted to prayer, spiritual study and family togetherness, cooking is done the day before. Hence the enormous popularity of slow-cooking casserole dishes usually based on legumes and called by various names: CHOLENT, CHOLENDT, HAMIN, DEFINA. These can be combined (often with a huge single dumpling in the centre or with eggs in the shell to bake to a soft brown) and then set either in the home oven or into a commercial baker's oven where the banked coals provide a slow even heat throughout the night. The next morning, after Sabbath morning services, the family can enjoy a filling hot meal. The Sabbath evening meal usually consists of cold fish dishes, bread and wine.

The youngest holiday celebrated in Israel is that of Independence Day, like all holidays falling on a different date each year as it is based on the Hebrew lunar calendar. Thus while independence occurred on May 14, 1948, the actual date of celebration may differ from year to year. Some Israelis spend the holiday promenading the city streets and stopping in at cafés for coffee and rich sweet pastries like DOBOS TORTE or a rum savarin with whipped cream; others celebrate with meals at home composed of FELAFEL and PITA, eggplant dishes, and breads with varieties of cottage cheese spreads. Dinners may include Israel's favourite meat, chicken, cooked with some citrus addition as for example orange wedges and honey.[13] Sephardic Jews will make HAMINDAS (24-hour cooked eggs, brownish in colour), while others may enjoy meals of herring and salads or poached jellied carp. Sesame seed and honey sweets as well as candied nuts and citron peels are nibbled by all.[13]

Other special occasions are those shared by Jews the world over. These include: Rosh Hashana (New Year's), Yom Kippur (Day of Atonement), Succoth (Feast of the Tabernacles, or Thanksgiving), Chanukah (Festival of Lights), Tu-Beshvat (Tree Planting), Purim, Passover, Lag B'omer, and Shavuoth (Feast of the Giving of the Law). These are celebrated in only slightly differing ways, depending on the country of origin and the types of foods traditionally available.

Rosh Hashana

Occurring in the early autumn, this is the traditional New Year's festival celebrated for one day in Israel and featuring foods to celebrate the hope of a sweet year. A hearty main meal of fish, appetizers, meats and honeyed vegetables (TZIMMES) is customary. Many sweet dishes of nuts, fresh fruits and dried candied nuts and fruits are served, as are special cakes and cookies that are rich with fruits, nuts and often honey. MANDELBROIT and LECKACH (honeycake) are traditional.[11]

Yom Kippur

The solemn ten-day period of prayer and introspection ushered in by Rosh Hashana is culminated in the solemn day of Yom Kippur. The day starts the evening before when each family partakes of a simple, mildly flavoured meal to be eaten before sundown. Foods are chosen that are not thirst-producing for this is the occasion when every Jewish person over the age of thirteen submits voluntarily to a 24-hour fasting period that is not even broken by so much as a sip of water. The entire day of Yom Kippur is filled with traditional synagogue services. Families are weary, thirsty and hungry from the ordeal and usually come home to a light, refreshing dairy meal.

The light chicken soup served in the traditional meal the evening before Yom Kippur is often afloat with meat-filled KREPLACH or KISONIM and the rest of the menu may include boiled chicken, mashed potatoes, a mixed green salad with lemon juice, and a dessert of quince or apple compote, a light sponge cake and tea. The meal after the fast may be a buffet of fish and pickled herring dishes, salads, breads, cakes and tea. Moroccan Jews traditionally break their fast with a TAGINE of chicken and olives; German Jews enjoy a chicken-rice dish; Italian Jews may serve a cold, stuffed turkey breast.[13,11]

Succoth

Many families build their own "booth" complete with a branch-covered ceiling open to the stars – for it is a *mitzvah* (divine commandment) to partake of at least one meal during this eight-day festival of thanksgiving in a *succah*. All the fresh harvested fruits of the season are enjoyed and are used to decorate both the *succah* and the festive table. Filled foods of all kinds like strudels, KREPLACH, and stuffed vegetables are traditional, as are sweets made with nuts, fruits and poppy seeds.

Chanukah

Occurring in the last month of the year, this eight-day festival commemorating the success of the Maccabbees in 165 B.C.E. when they united the Jewish people and restored the Temple, is celebrated by the lighting of candles in a progression from first to last night so that all eight candles brighten the holiday table on the final evening. Families play games with nuts and *dreidels* (small spinning tops), and everyone enjoys the special holiday foods.

For central European Jews the treat is the making and eating of stacks of crisp potato pancakes (LATKES) served with sour cream or applesauce. But for Jews from most other areas, the festive foods include some treats that are deep-fried in oil: Greek Jews serve LOUKOMADES, honey-drenched fried dumplings, and Persian Jews serve ZELEBIES made from a simple flour batter dribbled into hot oil then plunged into a pot of boiling honey. In Israel, too, all of these are served as well as many types of jam-filled doughnuts called POUNCHIKOT or SOUFGANIOT CHANUKAH and lightly dusted with sugar.[11] Fruits, nuts and sweet treats are served in every home and children are given small money gifts.

Tu-Beshvat

Occurring sometime in the month of February, this is the day for tree-planting. But throughout the world, even in areas where the wintry weather may not be conducive to tree planting, the fruits of trees and vines are enjoyed: fresh and dried fruits of all kinds as well as toasted and candied nuts. Sephardic Jews chant a special prayer in which many popular fruits are mentioned by name and it is customary to eat of each one: pomegranate, apple, nuts, carobs and mulberry.[6]

Purim

Amid parties, costumes, masks and carnivals, the festival of Purim, celebrating Jewish deliverance from the wicked Haman, is gaily celebrated. Poppyseed cakes and cookies, prune and poppyseed-filled HAMANTASHEN (three-cornered filled cookies) and three-cornered shaped BEREKES and KREPLACH are traditionally eaten to remember Haman's three-cornered hat. Greek and Italian Jews prepare a rich confection called MUSTATCHINONI or ESCRAVANIYA, with almonds and decorated with confetti sprinkles. Toasted and salted seeds are eagerly cracked and nibbled while handfuls of peppered chick peas are munched and everyone has a good time.[11,13]

Passover

This festival of freedom commemorating the Jewish exodus from Egypt is vividly celebrated in every Jewish home as though the event had just taken place. After a thorough housecleaning and the replacement of the daily dishes with special Passover utensils, the family sits down to a symbolically set table and members partake of the special foods. The service, led by the father, is called the *seder*. Throughout this eight-day festival no foods that are made with leaven may be eaten; in fact many families observe stringent food rules that may be traditional in their families because of local or regional rituals. The service and order of the *seder* meal are performed the world over, but one dish on the table may show the family's origin more than any other. This is the CHAROSET, a reddish mixture of fruit, nuts and wine eaten as a symbol of the bricks made by the Jewish slaves in Egypt. Israelis prepare their CHAROSET with chopped nuts, grated carrots instead of apples, orange juice and grated rind, honey and matzo meal with wine to bring it to the right consistency. Oriental Jews use a cooked mixture of dried fruits and nuts finely minced and seasoned with lemon, sugar and cinnamon. Yemenite Jews, always with a preference for the hot and spicy make theirs with chopped nuts and dried fruits, cayenne, sugar and ginger. Jews of the Western world prepare their CHAROSET with chopped apples, nuts, honey or sugar, cinnamon and wine.[11]

The most important symbolic food of the Passover festival is of course the unleavened bread or MATZOH. This is eaten not only in place of leavened bread, but it is also used in many dishes that are prepared specially for this festival. Matzoh meal, and matzoh cake meal (finer in texture) also form the basis for most cakes and cookies.

Lag B'Omer
The days between Passover and Shavuoth (festival of the Giving of the Law) are sadly counted as days of mourning in remembrance of the suffering that Jews in Palestine endured under the Romans. The thirty-third day, however, was set aside as Lag B'Omer to celebrate the harvest of barley. In Israel this is a day of weddings, picnics, dances and pilgrimages to the tomb of the great scholar Rabbi Simeon Bar Yohai, near the town of Safed. Candles and lamps are lit to the accompaniment of dancing and singing. It is customary to eat coloured eggs as a symbol of life and joy, also chick peas, FELAFEL and seasonal fruits and nuts. In some areas of Israel, bonfires also are lit in celebration.[7,11]

Shavuoth
Falling exactly seven weeks after Passover, the festival of Shavuoth is really a three-fold holiday celebrating the ripening of the first fruits, the harvesting of wheat, and the giving of the Torah to Moses on Mount Sinai. The festival is also celebrated by the serving and eating of the seven first fruits mentioned in the Torah: wheat, barley, grapes, figs, pomegranates, olives and dates. Traditional the world over among celebrating Jewry is the eating of dairy foods: cheesecakes, cheese-filled pastries of all types including strudels, knishes, blintzes, and kreplach.

But in Israel, once again, the country of origin is a factor in some traditionally different and interesting ways of celebrating this festive occasion. Aden Jews make special cakes of almonds, honey and coconut; Persian Jews serve a pudding of rice and dates; Yemenite Jews serve fried potato cakes; Kurdistani Jews prepare a meal of wheat ground in sour milk and rissoles of cheese and butter; Afghanistani Jews prepare butter-cooked rice and serve it with diluted yoghurt poured over top; Ladino-speaking Jews from Mid-Eastern communities prepare a huge seven-tiered egg bread (CHALLAH) filled with sweetmeats (fruits, nuts) to represent the seven weeks of counting Omer and the seven heavens to which it is believed Moses ascended on his death; the Sephardic bake SINAI CAKES.[11]

TWENTY-NINE

Italian

In 100 C.E., Pliny the Elder claimed Italy "mother of all nations with a mission to civilize mankind" and 1200 years later Dante, too, spoke of a politically united Italy that would have a "special place as the sacred garden of Christendom."[1] The universalism of Imperial Rome was one thing, but the sense of unity and mission collapsed with the Western Empire in the late 400s C.E.

Yet even if no other factor is considered, the profoundly civilizing influences of Italian kitchens and table manners touch almost everyone. Even a brief examination of Italian cuisine offers convincing evidence that Italy's mission of civilizing may have had its deepest impact on world gastronomy.

When the Romans conquered the Greeks in 197 C.E. they enlarged their empire and profoundly enriched their culture. The enrichment was in the form of arts and architecture, literature and philosophy. Greek became more than ever before the language of the literate and the language of international trade; so educated Romans, unlike the Greeks and unlike most early peoples, had to learn to use a second language.[2] Early Romans had learned to evaporate sea water to provide salt for their sheep and this skill became a profitable export to the Greeks in the south and the Etruscans in the north; in fact, the valuable salt exports increased with the expansion of the Roman Empire, but the language of trade was Greek.[3]

Despite the many tales of exotic, gargantuan Roman feasts, all classes of early Romans actually valued frugality and simplicity and nowhere were these values more evident than in their food customs.[2] Wheat, the staple food, was served at the early light meal called *jentaculum* in the form of wheat pancakes, biscuits or breads then served again at *cena* (the main meal) in the form of a boiled gruel or porridge. Milk, honey, olives and dates would accompany the main dish at either meal. Sometimes the wealthy would add GUSTATO or PROMULSIO – hors d'oeuvres of salads, radishes, mushrooms, eggs, oysters or sardines – to the basic typical meal, and desserts of honeyed cakes and fruits would complete the special meal.

While PULS or PULMENTUM was the staple porridge-like dish for all, early Romans also enjoyed cottage cheese, the use of iron kettles to boil their mutton, types of dumplings called GNOCCHI, even omelets and cheesecakes.[3] Some of the earliest Roman kitchens made knowing use of bakery molds, cutting knives and round chopping knives, cooking spoons and measuring spoons, mortar and pestle. Small portable brick ovens were used for keeping foods hot in the dining area; an arrangement of one pot inside another and set in hot water was used to keep other foods warm but not cooking. There can be little doubt that this latter technique was the forerunner of the French BAIN-MARIE and the Western "double-boiler."

Dishes chilled with snow, vessels treated with pitch to keep foods cool, inspectors to check the freshness of meats in butcher shops, commercial bakers and even commercially prepared food seasonings were all familiar. GARUM or LIQUAMEN was one such seasoning prepared from fish and salt; DEFRUTUM was a syrup made from wine and honey or grapes and honey; AGRODOLCE (said to have been developed by Apicius) was a sweet-sour sauce prepared in many ways.[2,3] Honey and vinegar were widely used but so was SILPHIUM or LASERPITIUM, a prized flavouring prepared from assafoetida.

By 200 C.E. all of these foods, seasonings and techniques were commonplace for the Romans. Gradually the commercial bakeries themselves became so widespread and dependable that all but the very poor relied on them for fresh daily baked goods. But those who could not afford to buy breads relied on the old gruels and porridges.[2] Small stones pressed into larger concave stones had probably represented the earliest forms of grinding, to be followed by mortar and pestle, but it was about 200 C.E. that a small handmill called a *mola versatilis* or *quern* came to be prized.

Apples were plentiful and popular but it took later conquests to bring the taste (and the plants) for cherry trees home from Asia. Apricots and peaches were brought from Armenia and Persia, melons from both Persia and areas of North Africa, and dates from Africa. Rome's returning Asiatic armies also brought back sophisticated ideas of seasoning and tales of Oriental dishes.[3,4]

By the 800s C.E., Islamic conquests began to influence European foods. The Saracens were said to have introduced spinach (the special ingredient in so many Florentine dishes) to Italy from its native Persia. Many unusual desserts were also introduced at this time but most notably

GELATI, the whole range of ice creams and sherbets that the Muslims had learned from the Persians and the East Indians.[3] There seems to be evidence that the earliest record of frozen desserts and ice or snow-chilled foods accrue to the Chinese.[5] Although the Arabs knew of sugar cultivation, they found it difficult to introduce successfully.[3]

In reciting all of the contributions to Roman cuisine, it must not be overlooked that the Romans introduced culinary ideas to other lands as well. From earliest times, the Greeks thought of the Romans as a wine-producing nation and learned from them many of the techniques of wine fermentation and processing as well as the drinking of wine diluted with water and often flavoured with honey.[2] Most of the known world had been content to dine on spit-roasted meats, but the Romans seem to have introduced the notion of boiling and stewing in kettles.[3] Various boiled greens (many considered weeds today) were commonly used in many lands, but the Romans brought with them the conviction that cabbage was worth cultivating since it contained medicinal properties. (Yet cabbage prepared in many ways – even fermented like sauerkraut – predates Roman times as it was known and used in early China.) In fact, Europe took the Roman's word that oysters were delicious and even set about cultivating them in many lands. Similarly, edible snails were introduced to European palates by the Romans and remain a French favourite today. It may have been the Roman belief in the efficacy of almonds as an aid to sobriety that was the forerunner of salted almonds as a cocktail snack in many parts of the world – especially Spain.[4] Central Europe's penchant for sausages in endless variety may have derived from the many types of spiced sausages, stuffed meats and fish that were common at the time of Apicius.[2]

In the era of the Crusades (around 1000 C.E.) some new culinary touches were introduced to Italy and some old ones revived. Indian salt was the name given to sugar, used at first as a condiment and later as a base for desserts and confections. Believed to have originated near Jerusalem and named for the Saracens, the Crusaders brought back buckwheat, called *sarracin* in French, *sarraceno* in Spanish and *saraceno* in Italian.[3] Use of many spices was revived and the use of the tangy lemon was reintroduced to replace the green grapes and other fruits that had been used both to flavour and to tenderize meats. The present-day CARCIOFI ALLA GIUDIA (literally "artichokes in the Jewish way") may have dated from the Crusades or from even earlier times when the Jews were brought back to Rome as slaves[4]; in any case the Italian enjoyment of CARCIOFO remains.

Encouraged by the meal styles they had enjoyed abroad, the Crusaders are also believed to have been responsible for the return of the meal pattern including appetizer, main course and dessert. The prevailing custom in the Middle East of serving foods on large heaped platters also found a place on many Italian tables.[3]

The question of the origin of PASTA seems to have no ready answer. Once again some of the earliest references to types of noodles seem to come from Chinese sources (wheat is the North China staple and noodles are the most popular form of preparation). Some believe that it was Marco Polo who brought dried noodles to Italy. Others believe that Italians were eating forms of PASTA before Marco Polo but its importance and use were limited. What cannot be argued is that the varieties of PASTA today are nowhere greater than in Italy.

The next most significant period in Italy's culinary history is that of the late 1400s and 1500s when her great cities were the merchant centres of the world and her gastronomic achievements had no competitors. The gluttony accredited to ancient Roman leaders had long given way to general simplicity and frugality, so much so that in many areas traditional favourites would have been lost to succeeding generations were it not for the monasteries that preserved the great recipes and encouraged their monks to interpret them with taste.[3] Sugar, coffee and ice cream were introduced to the rest of Europe via Venice together with many of the culinary details that had long been commonplace in Italian kitchens (stewing, frying, elaborate breads and baked goods and efficient utensils).

At the same time growing world explorations were bringing back to Europe New World products such as corn, red and green peppers, varieties of beans, turkeys and potatoes (of limited popularity in Italy). Most significantly, the *pomo d'oro* (golden apple) – the name given to the early tomato which was of a yellow variety – was lifted to gastronomic heights in Southern Italy's ubiquitous tomato sauces.[3] But there is also some evidence that original Italian tomatoes were started from seeds brought back from a missionary trip to China by Monk Serenio in the Middle Ages.[4]

While it may seem from the foregoing that food and food customs in Italy are the same throughout, this is not true. Nor are the Italians themselves homogeneous. But unfortunately the predominating Western view of Italy, Italian food and Italians is a blur of dark hair, emotional personalities and PASTA, tomato sauce, garlic and wine. In fact, the peoples of Italy developed from early migrations of tribes throughout Europe and even Asia and North Africa.[9] And while geography played some part in isolating areas from each other, much more important was the part played by the battles between the Popes and the Emperors – each courting towns and eventually favouring northern and central development of Italy as almost independent states. The fragmentation of the states left Italy vulnerable to powerful outside influences: French, Spanish and, later, Austrian. Most especially, Southern Italy, Sicily and Sardinia fell under Spanish control and exploitation for 250 years (from 1559 to the early 1800s), which resulted in great part in the poverty, pestilence, disease and famine relieved only by the great charities and hospitals run by religious orders.

The Spanish oppression of Southern Italy had many other effects as well. The debt-crushed peasantry rebelled with the growth of secret societies and the powerful emphasis of the family unit, both of which exist to this day.[1,6]

As recently as 1958, Edwin Banfield's study of Southern Italy confirmed the prevalent attitudes of "family first and family against everything else,"[1] and Luigi Barzini takes care to explain this same phenomenon by stating that mafioso (with a small "m") means ". . . a subtle art of promoting one's own interests without killing anyone," while Mafioso includes everything else.[6] Probably from the influence of the Saracens and their Muslim ideals of womanhood as well as the later influence of the Spanish, Southern Italians are possessively proud of their women, and consider honour a matter of life and death.[7] Also in keeping with Mediterranean influence, the South takes a leisurely view of punctuality, enjoys afternoon siestas, and spells happiness with the conviviality of boisterous friends and an open bottle of wine.

In 1713, Italy came under Austrian influence but was not isolated from the effects of the French Revolution. These events bound the Northern Italians in a *risorgimento* of culture, stressing the commonality of all of Italy's great cultural heritage and hoping for a political unity.[1] Even the proclamation of King Victor Emanuel of Piedmont as King of Italy in 1861 could neither allay the South's economic distress nor cement the cleavage of North and South.

Northern Italy remained strongly influenced culturally, economically and politically by Europe and later construction of railway tunnels in the mountains only increased this influence. The peoples themselves became diffused with Germans, French, Austrians and Slavs, gave their women considerable freedom, were too busy to consider siestas (nor did the climate warrant the rest periods), and cultivated conservative but elegant taste in everything from manners and clothing to food and wine.[7,8]

Home Life and Facilities

Most of Italian daily life from Roman times to today is spent in the streets and in the squares of cities, towns and villages.[2,10] Home was and is usually the place to eat dinner but the streets and squares represent Italian life. The squares (in ancient times and today) provide fountains and water wells, selling of wares and trading of gossip, a playground for the children and a place to see and be seen.[10]

The practicality of the early Roman kitchens with their cooking hearths, metal and earthenware pots and efficient range of utensils has already been discussed. In many areas all are in use today – even earthenware jars to store oil and wine. The older ways are more prevalent in rural and Southern areas, while the cities of the North design and produce ultra-modern appliances and kitchen designs that are not only used in wealthy Italian homes, but also exported to America.

The consideration of foods, facilities and food customs of ancient Roman times is not for historic interest alone: many parts of Italy and many Italian families still live in much the same way. In ancient times, the majority ate mostly wholewheat in many forms and vegetables while the wealthy ate the kinds of meals that have promulgated the legends of Roman banquets where "the wealthy ate till they vomited and often vomited in order to eat more."[2] The wealthy have long moved to an elegantly conservative pattern of eating and drinking but the poor still may be living in earthen huts with dirt floors and open fireplaces for warmth and for cooking. Their staple foods may well be plain bread and chicory[1] – not PASTA – or an oily sandwich of bread and olive oil with tomatoes and garlic.[7] PASTA may even be considered as a luxury food reserved for special occasions, while a thick vegetable soup-stew prepared when fresh greens are available may be a special meal. The poor seldom eat eggs because their sparsely fed chickens do not produce very many; some areas have no milk or cheese as cows are too expensive to keep. Yet even in areas where a sparse diet is familiar, the Italian spirit finds sustenance in enjoyment of life, music and wine. Those who cannot, emigrate.

Despite innumerable provincial variations and specialties, Italian cookery can be roughly divided into a dominance of milk, butter, rice and POLENTA (cornmeal) in the North; olive oil, wine, PASTA in the South; and a meeting-place for both areas in central Italy, particularly in Tuscany. Aside from these generalities, it is a difficult matter to discuss details of foods and food customs without specifying an area. This is more true of Italy than almost any other land. Interaction and exchanges between regions are recent; previously, lack of transportation and self-imposed pride and isolationism prevented communication. The familiar Italian "pasta-image" is well-founded, for most emigrants hail from Southern Italy, and most Italian restaurants in Canada and the United States are Neapolitan.[3,11]

The staple foods of Italy revolve around cereals, vegetables and cheeses. Breads and PASTA made from wheat, innumerable rice dishes and, in some areas, POLENTA made from corn are served at least once a day. Great varieties of vegetables are plentiful: staple root vegetables, fresh beans and peas, greens of many kinds, all types of squash, eggplant and zucchini, artichokes and asparagus. Each area produces cheese specialties and favourite ways of nibbling cheese – as appetizers or snacks, topping dishes, fillings, savoury fried foods, sauces and even sprinkled into soups. Fresh-dried bunches of herbs – parsley, borage, myrtle, rosemary, sage, oregano, and basil – are familiar in every kitchen, as are onions and garlic in varying proportions. Olive oil and butter are the favoured fats and the best olive oil is said to come from Lucca in Tuscany.[3] Rice (Italy is Europe's largest producer), vegetables and all types of PASTA are enjoyed *al dente*, that is chewy and not overcooked. Meats and products of the sea are enjoyed and cooked with imagination but are served in smaller amounts than is customary in other countries because they are both more expensive and less available. Fruits and cheese are a usual dessert when dessert is served; elaborate desserts are reserved for special occasions or restaurant dining.

Many regional wines of Italy are world-famous; others that are equally as good are not known simply because they do not travel well. Italy's high rate of alcohol consumption and low rate of alcoholism can be explained by many factors. Wine is considered a food and all children grow up accustomed to wine as part of a meal. The strong moral influence of the close-knit family structure and the national distaste for the state of drunkenness are powerful factors as well. While daily wine is commonplace, it should be stressed that wine always accompanies food, and the cosmopolitan sipping of the pre-dinner cocktail is practised only by very sophisticated Italians.[10]

Regional Specialties

Discussion of Italy's particularly important regional specialties will be divided into areas of the North, Central and Southern regions. The provinces of Piedmont, Lombardy, Veneto, and Emilio Romagna will be considered as North; Tuscany, Umbria-The Marches and Rome-Lazio as the Central; the Southern area will include the provinces and islands: Abruzzo-Molise, Naples-Campagna, Calabria-Lucania, Apulia, Sicily, Sardinia and Corsica.

Northern Italy

It is believed that the early merchants from Venice, Genoa and Florence were responsible for introducing exotic spices from the Orient.[12] Yet the pervading general preference in Northern foods is for subtle flavours with aromas of herbs rather than spices. Rice was introduced into Italy by the Spaniards in the 1400s and is used mainly as a first course where it "competes with the pasta."[13] Originally a distinction was made between rice dishes, where the rice was cooked first in water then seasoned, and RISOTTO, where the rice is cooked in hot oil or butter with seasonings then finished with a broth. Cold and colourful rice salads are also popular.[13]

PIEDMONT

White truffles, FONDUTA, game dishes, RISOTTO and enticingly sweet desserts are the famous specialties of the region. So insistent are the Piedmontese on the freshness of produce that most families use the fresh-picked seasonal vegetables and herbs from their own backyard gardens.[14] Many varieties of mushrooms are used and the special vegetables include CARDI, similar to an artichoke in flavour but resembling celery, and delicate asparagus.[12] Grapes, strawberries and small russet pears are grown throughout the area while cherries come from Pecetto or Ceresolo, and peaches from Casale. In the rice-growing areas, carp is raised in the water of the paddies and *tench* (a fish of the carp family) and frogs abound.[3] RANE DORATE is a specialty of skinned frogs, flour-dipped then fried in olive oil.[3] In mountain regions, wild goat, the white hare, wild boar and chamois await the hunter.

Pasta is used but rice is preferred and rich and satisfying dishes are made from POLENTA. Wild and cultivated herbs are used with a generous hand and, in this area, so is garlic. One of the famed dishes redolent of garlic is BAGNA CAUDA. A selection of fresh crisp vegetables like celery, cardoons, green peppers, etc., and GRISSINI are dipped into a hot pot of blended olive oil, butter, anchovies and garlic.[12] BAGNA CAUDA may be a first course – as rice, pasta or POLENTA usually are – or it may be the entire meal.

The area is also known for its production of fine cheeses: the spicy ROBIOLE D'ALBA, crusty TOMA VEJA and aged yellow FONTINA whose quick-melting properties are enjoyed in FONDATA or FONDUTA which is served over bread, rice or POLENTA.[3,12] Cream, milk and butter are found everywhere and used to add rich flavour and light texture whenever possible.[14]

Sweets and desserts are almost an art form: pastry shops resemble exclusive jewellery shops and the Piedmontese often enjoy leisurely snacks of pastries and tea. In mountain areas sugar is considered important to provide energy and calories – in case anyone needs an excuse to nibble candied chestnuts, macaroons, *caramelles, gianduiotti* (hazelnut chocolate) and *turcet*, the plain cookies baked in horseshoe shapes. Ladyfingers, anise cookies and the famed fried cookies known as CENCI or BUGIE delight every taste. Many sweet puddings and egg custards, especially ZABAGLIONE, a wine custard of Marsala and whipped eggs, are believed to have originated here. The long thin crisp bread sticks called GRISSINI are thought to have been created by a Turinese baker to tempt the flagging appetite of a young prince.

This region claims also to have invented Vermouth. Some of the finest red wines come from this region as well: *Barolo del Piemonte, Barbera, Grignolino, Friesa* (semi-sparkling with low alcohol content), *Gattinara* and *Dolce Della Langhe*. Sparkling wines include *Asti Spumante* (white) and *Muscato d'Asti* (sweetly sparkling). *Cortese* is the best of the local white wines served dry and chilled. Commonly a *digestivo* is offered after a meal: *Grappa del Piemonte, Genepy* (mountain herb liqueur), or *Acqua del Po*.[12,14]

LOMBARDY

The city of Milan, bustling and industrialized, dominates the plains of Lombardy. In the 1300s foods were sometimes gilded in a belief that gold was curative; the poor could not imitate this except by the use of saffron and the generous addition of golden butter to as many dishes as possible. This tradition is common in many Milanese dishes such as RISOTTO and COSTOLETTE ALLA MILANESE (butter-fried veal cutlets). Another famed dish is a version of MINESTRONE which includes toasted bread, poached eggs and a sprinkling of cheese with the soup poured over top.[14] BUSECA (tripe with white beans), VITELLO TONNATO (cold roasted veal served with tuna sauce) and OSSO BUCCO with RISOTTO (veal shanks braised then served with a GREMOLADA of minced garlic, parsley and lemon rind) are such beloved dishes that they are part of fine international cuisine and may be found in countless cookbooks.

PANETTONE, the richly sweet yeast cake eaten throughout Italy both for Christmas and Easter festivities, is believed to have been originated in Milan by a baker called Tony whose delighted customers then continued to ask for "panne Tony" (Tony's bread) – but other provinces claim it too. GORGONZOLA, the creamy-rich, blue-veined cheese also known worldwide, is the product of Lombardy. Many other cheeses are produced but are mostly used locally.

Lombardy wines include: *Cortese, Barbera, Montelio, Sasella,* and many others.

VENETO

The great staples of this province include POLENTA, RADICCHIO ROSSO (a reddish form of chicory or curly endive), rice, and fish of all kinds including the imported salt cod.

It was in Venice that the first sack of dried corn was believed to have been unloaded in Italy and certainly Venetians have retained their affection for it ever since. It was also Venice where the first fork and cloth serviette accompanied elegant dinners while the rest of the world ate with their fingers and wiped them on their clothes and anything else available.[14] The height of Venice's glory was in the 1400s: an elegant lady with the confidence and breeding that comes from 300 years of supremacy as a cultured city, intellectual centre, and merchant harbour to much of Europe.[15] Not surprisingly, her sophistication encouraged a cosmopolitan cuisine and, to this day, dishes such as sausages and sauerkraut, casseroles of salt cod, stews of offal, turkeys and geese are reminiscent of other European and Mediterranean lands.

Typically, too, the classic dishes of the region are prepared with loving precision. POLENTA may be served hot or cold, boiled, roasted, sliced and fried, layered with fish, cheeses, meats or vegetables into baked dishes, or served from a wooden slab or copper pan. Fish is cooked principally in one of three ways: poached in a broth, deep-fried in oil or grilled quickly over red-hot charcoal.[14] Although rice is widely used it is not prepared as in Lombardy. No saffron is used here nor is rice eaten by itself but it is cooked and served with a variety of other ingredients which may include meats, fish or seafoods, or even beans or raisins. Most famous is RISI E BISI, a famed first course of cooked rice with tiny green peas, grated cheese and bits of bacon or ham. Flat noodles accompany many meat dishes and may also be served with grated cheese as a first course. Game and all types of meats and sausages abound, and frequently it is the added grated cheese that distinguished Venetian dishes from those of Austria, Germany or Hungary. Cabbages, zucchini, fennel, squash of all types, potatoes (especially in the form of GNOCCHI) are all used in abundance together with tomatoes, peppers, onions and other common vegetables.

Some of the more exotic dishes of this region include SOPA COADA, a soup made of young pigeon squabs; ARROSTO DI MAIALE AL LATTE, browned pork flavoured with rosemary and garlic then stewed in milk, and CAPON A LA CANEVERA, capon stuffed with beef and guinea fowl meat then placed in a pig's bladder and sewn up with a bamboo pole as the vent – the bladder is discarded after boiling and the meat is cut for serving.[14]

EMILIO-ROMAGNA AND LIGURIA

The main city of Liguria on Italy's northwestern coast is Genoa. Often called the richest city in Italy, Genoa is also known for its conservative elegance and fine taste in everything from small cars to discerning food.[16] Basil grown in tiny pots on windowsills represents not only the wild weed that grows in every meadow, but also a beloved flavour. Genoa's traditional sauce PESTO is prepared from generous amounts of fresh green basil, pine nuts or walnuts, cheese and olive oil. Garlic may or may not be an ingredient in the puréed sauce that is served over pasta. Mortar and pestle traditionally pound the herb and nuts into a smooth fine paste, but electric blenders are also used.

Fish and vegetables are so popular that they blend together to form many of the most famous classic dishes of the area. One is BURRIDA, in which a variety of fish (*rospo* or frogfish, dogfish, mackerel, octopus, eels, etc.) is sautéed in a flavourful sauce of oil, garlic, parsley and tomatoes, then thickened with pounded walnuts, blended with white wine and finally served in its cooking pot with toasted bread. CIUPPIN is another fish soup but prepared with puréed mixed fish.

Liguria is also famed as the area where RAVIOLI was invented, where many tempting candies and sweets are prepared daily and where fine wines complement each meal.

SALAMI, MORTADELLA, BOLOGNA and ZAMPONI represent only a few of the famed sausages that prove the popularity and ingenuity of pork in the region of Emilio-Romagna. Parma is believed to be the area that originated PARMESAN cheese. Not only PARMESAN goes with pasta, but also the famed Bolognese sauce called RAGÙ prepared from a blend of well-cooked vegetables, mushrooms, and meats. The most famed pasta of the region are the many versions of TORTELLINI (ladies' navels). In general the cookery of the area is considered to be the "fattest" of Italy: rich and well-seasoned with spices and garlic.

Central Italian Provinces

TUSCANY

In the 1400s, which city dined first with a knife and a fork and dabbed elegantly with a napkin? Venice the Venetians, of course, claim but the Florentines claim Florence.[17] Also in the 1400s, not only was pasta and ravioli of many varieties commonly cooked, wines of many types were also enjoyed, and a favourite dish was FEGATELLI, a type of liver sausage.[17] Rules of behaviour and good manners were carefully listed in *Galateo* by Giovanni Della Casa. Among them were admonitions against eating noisily, burping or sniffing at food before eating. Furthermore drunkenness was considered repugnant (but the book noted that in Germany and France drunkenness was considered amusing if not manly). In the late 1400s, Florentine doctors were prescribing cabbage as a general cure – a panacea that was to be taken into many other lands.

The cuisine of Tuscany is noted for its classic simplicity and strict insistence on the finest and freshest of ingredients prepared with passion and artistry. While olive oil is important throughout Italy, in Tuscany only the finest from their own presses at Lucca can be considered.[14,18] The Florentine steak BISTECCA ALLA FIORENTINA is judged by the animal the meat came from, the perfect degree of heat for cooking, and the final flourish of a seasoning with salt and pepper and a brush of fine oil. Most meats are spit-roasted or grilled; vegetables are cooked with loving care, and in coastal areas fish gets the same kindly attention to detail.

FRITTO DEL MARE (a mixed plate of fried fish and seafood) and CACCIUCCO are two classics, the latter being a spicy fish stew inspired anew by each cook from the fish and seafood at hand. Pork, wild boar, guinea fowl, kid and hare take their turn on the grills and spits. Rice is widely used here too but in some specialties not known in other areas: RISO NERO, black rice prepared with cuttlefish ink, and RISOTTO ALLA TOSCANA that includes livers and kidneys.[14] Dried white (haricot) beans are a staple and are prepared in soups with ribbon noodles, as a main dish with sage, tomatoes and garlic, and sautéed with tomatoes and chunks of tunafish. FAGIOLI NEL FIASCO is a dish of beans cooked in a flask. Tuscany pastries and sweets are often distinguished by being prepared with chestnut flour. *Chianti brolio* is one of the great chianti wines.[3]

It should be noted that, throughout Italy but especially in Tuscany, recipes using beans often date from the Middle Ages or earlier.[13]

UMBRIA - THE MARSHES

This area is famed for its use of PORCHETTA (pork) cooked with fresh herbs, fine thread-like noodles called MACCHEROCINI, spit and oven-roasted meats, black truffles, and such a rich variety of fish that the local fishermen are reputed to be the best in Italy.[14] *Orvieto* and *Verdicchio*, the latter having a faint greenish cast, are considered to be among Italy's finest white wines. Versions of pizza are prepared here, but the garnishes are kneaded into the bread dough rather than sprinkled over the top as in southern areas. Chicken, turkey, geese, game birds and pigeons may be served when pork is not. But many versions of homey fish soups and fish stews served with garlic-rubbed bread also provide hearty meals.

ROME - LAZIO

While most of Italy balances its cooking between butter and olive oil as the favoured fat, Rome prefers matured pork fat called STRUTTO. In other ways Rome is different too: vegetables grown in the surrounding volcanic soil are said to have a special flavour and sheep, suckling lamb and suckling kid (slaughtered often when only weeks old) become specialty dishes. Romans think of themselves and their traditions with more seriousness than they would give to anything else. With a common saying, "Bread and water are fit for a dog," every home and every small restaurant proudly serves the very best, fully confident that their tradition truly is the best. With knowing skills the Romans do indeed select the best from north and south and create from it a distinctively Roman cuisine.

CROSTINI (toasted bread and cheese) takes on distinctive Roman flavour because it is made with Roman PROVATURA; SPAGHETTI ALL'AMATRICIANA is a spaghetti tossed with a delicate sauce of peeled and seeded tomatoes flavoured with onion and bacon; SUPPLI are cheese-flavoured croquettes filled with a mixture of northern rice, meats and dried mushrooms and STUFATINO is a Roman version of Milan's STUFATO (beef and tomatoes), but cooked in lard and garnished with cardoons. Tripe is beloved in many dishes throughout Italy, but Rome's version is cooked with either meat gravy or tomato sauce, then served with grated cheese touched with minced fresh mint.[14] CARCIOFI ALLA GIUDIA dates from ancient times and bases its tenderness on the quality of artichokes grown near Rome.

Roman cuisine also includes batter-fried squash flowers, stuffed zucchini, tomatoes, peppers and squashes; casseroles of simmered vegetables; fava beans and white beans served as thick soups or hearty casseroles with cheese or sausages – and if the fresh tenderness of young vegetables are not enough there is the haunting flavour of STRUTTO, the matured pork fat used in so many dishes and flavoured with sage, rosemary, garlic and anchovy paste.

Specialties of Rome include cheesecakes and filled pastries made from RICOTTA; fruit tarts prepared with VISCIOLE (sour cherry jam); tiny cookies shaped like beans (FAVI DOLCE) and crisp fritters.

Each of the many villages around Rome produces its own famed wines and most of the VINE DEI CASTELLI are white.

Southern Italian Provinces

Southern Italy is characterized by an inexpensive but hearty cuisine based on bread, together with milk and cheese, incredible variations of vegetable dishes and an unquenchable taste for very sweet confections and desserts. In some areas such as Calabria, meat is only used on special occasions and the mealtime beverage is mineral water.[3] Soups are often a mainstay of meals: fish and seafood soups in coastal regions and vegetable and pasta soups inland. Some pork and chicken may be used for meat but cattle are more important for their milk and cheese; offal forms inexpensive and nourishing meat-flavoured dishes.

NAPLES-CAMPAGNA

The Neapolitans who have made their homes in other lands also made famous their city's two great dishes: pizza and spaghetti. They also popularized POMMAROLA, the tomato sauce that graces pizza and most pasta dishes, so that for many in North America it comes as a surprise to hear about the great variety of foods throughout Italy. But it is not surprising that these simple foods have gained such popularity: they are easy to eat, tasty, satisfying and not expensive.

But Neapolitan food is not all pizza and spaghetti. For here is also an array of fish and seafood dishes that include octopus, clams, mussels, sea truffles and sea dates, eels, sea scorpion, shrimps and prawns, swordfish, dogfish and skate. These may be grilled, boiled or fried; served dressed with olive oil, garlic and tomatoes or capers and black olives; they may be simmered in savoury soup-stews or cooked and chilled then served in salads with lemon juice and olive oil.

Neapolitans love the idea that their foods and their lively temperament seem to symbolize Italy for much of the world. They treasure their traditional recipes as much as they enjoy indulging themselves in old songs and folk music, in ancient superstitions and modern pleasures. They enjoy eating on the run: tiny folded pizzas called LIBRETTI, snacks of fresh seafood and small containers with oysters and even small servings of vegetables that can be hurriedly enjoyed.

Many cheeses are used but MOZARELLA is the favourite for pizza. It is also used to top many vegetable dishes and in hot-fried cheese sandwiches such as MOZARELLA IN CARROZA. Other versions of mozarella-inspired foods include PANZAROTTI, pastry turnovers filled with several cheeses such as parmesan, mozarella and provolone then deep-fried to seal the melted cheese mixture within, and FRITTO DI MOZARELLA, squares of cheese, egg- and crumb-dipped then deep-fried and eaten while hot.[14]

While pasta of every description creates so many meals, this is not to say that rice and POLENTA have not reached the South. The famed SARTÙ DI RISO ALLA NAPOLETANA is a magnificent rice mold layered with cheese and meat-sauce, flavoured rice and tiny meatballs alternated with a filling of chicken livers, crumbled sausage meat and peas – plus more slices of mozzarella. The dish is baked then unmolded.[14] With similar Neapolitan flair, POLENTA finds itself sliced and layered with pork sausages, parmesan and pecorino cheeses and baked into a golden casserole called MIGLIACCIO NAPOLETANA. Whenever possible, Neapolitan dishes exhibit the same bursting exuberance as the people who cooked them – and those who happily eat them.

The first ice cream shops or GELATERIA are believed to have opened in the province of Tuscany in the 1500s, but the Southern Italians are believed responsible for the popularity of ice cream in North America.[7] SPUMONE is the specialty of Naples: a layered oval mold of several flavours of ice cream and sherbets with mixed fruits. But there are at least five distinct types of GELATI: GRANITE, a crystal-like sherbet usually flavoured either with lemon or coffee; GELATI, the familiar firm ice cream made with fruits, nuts, etc. in a rich creamy base; COPPE, several flavours of GELATI served in a dish and garnished with fruit, etc.; CASSATA, a decorative ice cream cake or mold layering several GELATI with whipped cream and fruits; and finally the SEMIFREDDI, a type of soft foamy ice cream that also comes in many flavours.[7] Most of these are usually served in dessert dishes with a topping of whipped cream and sometimes a liqueur as well.

But the GELATI do not satisfy every Neapolitan sweet tooth. Some desire to indulge themselves with the many crisply baked or deep-fried little pastries, honey-dipped and candy-sprinkled as well: ZEPPOLE or STRUFFOLI.

CALABRIA, LUCANIA, APULIA
Calabrian cookery is based mostly on pasta, many varieties of vegetables and cheese. Most coastal towns have their own specialties in fish dishes and these are usually types of fish soups which may be based on fish and/or seafood: BRODETTA, ZUPPA DI PESCE ALLA MARINARA and ZUPPA DI VONGOLE, using mussels, clams or VONGOLA, a shellfish similar to a snail.[3]

Tomatoes, artichokes and peppers find numerous expressions in filling dishes but none so often as eggplant. Spinach is another favourite but wild greens may also be used when available. Bread is so important and so revered that it is identified with Christ the Life Giver and often pieces of bread are offered to beggars rather than money. Bread doughs are leavened by saving a small piece from the previous batch; so entrenched is the tradition and reverence for bread baked at home that resistance to commercially baked bread can be understood.

While Naples-Campagna indulges itself with ancient symbols, rituals and superstitions sometimes with a "why not?" or a "just-in-case" attitude, here in the deep south, ancient customs, so closely intertwined with poverty and the ancestral history of conquests by the Turks, Greeks and others, have left a distinct mark on the inhabitants; time has stood still. Yet orchard groves, olive trees and lean cattle producing milk contribute at least to physical nourishment.

Pork is the most important meat, and pig-killing is a festive occasion fraught with tradition and great rejoicing. Local hams and fine pork sausages in many varieties, including CAPOCOLLO and PEZZENTE (made from sinews, livers and lungs), are well-flavoured with pepper and garlic. Lard is an imporant fat and the children love the crisp cracklings called FRITTOLI or CICCIOLI.[14] Sometimes chicken, kid or rabbits add variety to the menu as well.

Apulia's cuisine is similar but the inhabitants consider themselves the champion pasta eaters of Italy. They add cabbages, turnips, broccoli and cauliflower to their casseroles, soups and even sauces more often than others in Italy.[3,14] Vegetables, bread and pasta, with cheese in and on almost everything, is the staple diet but around the coastal areas there is also abundant fish and seafood and the oysters are considered special. Fish soups, stuffed shellfish, and squid stew are among the specialty dishes. Almonds are so abundant that there is believed to be an aroma of bitter almonds even in the local olive oil.[14] The specialty cheeses include CACIOCAVALLO, SCAMORZA, MOZARELLA, RICOTTA and PARMESAN. Apulian wines are known for their heavy-rich flavours and some are even used for blending with other Italian wines of lesser stature.

SICILY AND SARDINIA

These two islands represent an unspoiled tradition of what is believed to be the earliest Italian cuisine. The cuisine stems from many influences, especially the early Greeks who conquered Sicily and the early Phoenicians (Lebanese) who conquered Sardinia. It is a tradition dating back more than 2,000 years; the tradition of fine cuisine that touched the Romans and all of the Roman world.[3] But there is also a lengthy tradition of poverty, of feuding peasants and landlords, of insularism and a proclivity for traditional life-styles. Most notably, there is a difference in the personalities of the Sicilians and the Sardinians, the former being known for their explosive exuberance, the latter being similar to the Spaniards – quieter and more reserved.[3]

It is believed that the Saracens in the 800s C.E. introduced to Sicily a taste for sophisticated sweets such as the CASSATA, CANNOLI, and the crisp candied almonds thrown at the wedding couple for a "fruitful and sweet life." So famed are Sicily's sweets that monasteries still compete with treasured recipes of candies, confections and ice creams.[7] Their varieties of white and crusty bread and rolls include an unleavened bread that is enjoyed by dipping in oil and eating with saltfish. Fish of all kinds are important in the Sicilian dietary: salt fish, freshwater fish, seafood of all kinds and especially tuna and sardines each of which may appear in pasta dishes such as PASTA CON SARDE or PASTA CON LE SARDE, a layered pie of macaroni with a sardine sauce that includes fennel, anchovies, pine nuts and white raisins,[14] SAN VITO PIZZA, pizza dough topped with sardines and CACIOCAVALLO cheese, or SCACCIATA, a type of Sicilian bread pie where two rounds of dough are sandwiched with a filling of ham, anchovies, tomatoes and seasonings, then baked and served in wedges.

The list of Sicilian staples includes pasta and rice, fish of all types, meats in the form of meatballs and sausages, and a good variety of cheeses. Vegetables are important too: tomatoes, capers, olives, eggplant (MELANZANE), zucchini, cauliflower, artichokes and onions. Fennel, oregano, mint and sesame seeds highlight fresh natural flavours. Citrus fruits, cactus fruits and prickly pears, melons and fresh or dried figs are favourite snacks or desserts in season.[19] Grapes are enjoyed as a fresh fruit and also in the production of fine wines including Marsala, the richly-flavoured dessert wine used in making ZABAGLIONE, many fine white wines including Corvo and Etna, as well as muscatel wines.[14] Walnuts, almonds and hazelnuts are used in the many rich confections, cakes and ice-cream desserts. The abundance of pasta and breads, fruits and vegetables as well as cheese and wine make it no surprise that the typical country lunch is usually one of sausages, bread and cheese refreshed with local wine – a fine Sicilian meal.[3]

Sardinian meals are known to be heartier and more frequently use meats than do the meals in Sicily. Pit- or spit-roasted pig, lamb or kid braised over the smoking embers of natural woods add a special flavour to the Sardinian FÙRRIA FÙRRIA. Wild sheep, bears, many birds, wild boar and hare are usually prepared by boiling them first (to tenderize) with their innards, then flavoured by placing them in bags lined with myrtle leaves. Bread is more of a staple here than pasta and two types include PAN FRATTAU and CARASAU, thinly crisp and usually baked unleavened. PECORINO is Sardinia's best-known cheese. Sardinia's wines are unusual: Vernaccia, a richly flavoured amber wine redolent of orange blossoms and traditionally served with fish, and especially Malvasia, more popularly known as Malmsey and said to have come to Sardinia from Greece.[14]

Corsica
Politically, Corsica is a part of France, but her geography, history and language are linked inexorably with Italy. Most distinctively, Corsican cuisine is noted for its imaginative use of chestnuts which are used whole

or ground into a fine flour that forms a part of many types of dishes and adds special flavour. Even sausages and hams produced from crossbred pigs and boars are said to have a special taste based on the fact that chestnuts form an important part of the animal's food. The importance of chestnuts in the Corsican cuisine stems from the ingenuity of the peasants of the Middle Ages who decided to grow chestnuts instead of the grains that were so heavily taxed by foreign conquerors.[20]

Meal Patterns and Eating Customs

The influence of Roman gastronomy on the foods and customs of countless peoples is unquestionable. It was a sophisticated influence that included meat inspectors, bakeries, private caterers and even slave cooks.[2] Early meal patterns included two or sometimes three meals a day. *Jentaculum* or *Ietaculum* was a light breakfast based on bread or a type of pancake with cheese or honey and sometimes olives or dates including usually milk as a beverage.[2,9] *Prandium*, a type of lunch, was served infrequently but included eggs, fish or pork served with prepared vegetables or mushrooms and often fruit as dessert. Diluted wine was the meal's beverage and *mulsum* (honey-sweetened wine) was possibly an appetizer.[9]

The main and most important meal of the day was the evening meal, called *cena*. For many this meal was actually served in the late afternoon and for the average family it included a bowl of wheat porridge finished with milk and served with honey. For the wealthier, it began with appetizers called GUSTATO or PROMULSIO (salads, fresh vegetable relishes, oysters, sardines, olives, etc.) and proceeded through six or seven main dishes prepared from fish or meats with vegetables and served with white bread, *mulsum* and ending with sweets and seasonable fruits.[2,9] Occasionally the *cena* for the poor included vegetable soup and coarse bread.

By 200 B.C., the hour for the *cena* had gradually moved to the later part of the day obviating the need for what had come to be known as the *vesperna*, a light snack before bedtime.[2] The later *cena* became the practice as more and more people preferred to take a large meal after their daily public bath. Coinciding with the later *cena*, the *prandium* gained in importance. For many it was simply bread and cheese (similar to today's sandwich), but occasionally it may have been a more formal miniature meal similar to the *cena*. As a general rule, only slaves and young children did not recline while eating their meals.[9] Common practice in old Roman tradition was the silent offering of wheat, salt and wine to household gods at the conclusion of the *cena*.[2]

Modern day Italians in most urban areas have a wide choice of both location and menu for their meals. Cities boast simple or sophisticated *ristorante*, casual family-run *trattoria* featuring low-cost meals, or a choice of many *rosticceria* where a limited menu offers simple, inexpensive dishes and quick or stand-up service, and the *osteria* for quick light snacks. Innumerable street vendors, corner CAPPUCCINO and ESPRESSO cafés and pastry shops also eagerly offer sustenance to the passerby. Commonly throughout Italy a hot morning drink of tea, coffee or hot chocolate together with bread and jam or marmalade form the most typical breakfasts. Lunch and dinner (the former usually about one P.M. and the latter usually about 7:30 P.M. and later in Rome) are similar meals but may vary in the number of courses depending on status and occasion, and perhaps appetite. Seven courses may be distinctly delineated in the most formal meal: ANTIPASTO, a variety of small servings of appetizers; MINESTRA (soup) or ASCIUTTA which may include either RISOTTO or a pasta dish but in a small serving; PESCE, one of a number of fish or seafood dishes; CARNE, meat dishes usually served with separately selected CONTORNI or vegetables; FROMAGGIO, some form of cheese so important in any Italian meal; FRUTTA, selections from a platter of fresh fruits in season, and finally DOLCE, very sweet confections, pastries and desserts.[7]

Italians have some distinct preferences: they like their pasta *al dente* (chewy, not mushy), their rice tender and juicy with a sauce, and their tomatoes green unless specially ripened for sauces or specially requested as red.[10] Italians also think it important to select carefully the piece of fresh fruit they would like to eat, so touching, pinching and even sniffing for ripeness are all considered proper. Once Italians have finished eating, plates are immediately removed: it is almost a breach of etiquette both at home and in a restaurant to leave an obviously-finished plate in front of the diner.[10]

Special Occasions

Almost all of the people of Italy profess the Roman Catholic faith and according to many observers, the church comes second only to the family in daily importance.[7,10] From early infancy, through education and social services, festivities and special occasions, the church plays a meaningful and important role. Yet, like Italian foods, personalities and life-styles, there is great variation throughout the land and generalities are difficult. Probably each village and indeed each family have special festive favourites. Together with the specialty foods, most festive occasions begin with devotional prayers and end up with singing, dancing, wine-drinking and feasting.

Christmas is one of the most important holidays. In many regions the festivities begin with the setting up of miniature nativity scenes in the homes. Carolers visit from house to house, and the *zampognari* are the shepherds who descend into cities and villages playing ancient instruments such as flutes and *ciarmeddi* (bagpipes).[19,21]

Traditionally a twenty-four hour fast precedes Christmas Day, which generally means that no meats or meat products are eaten. Eels for Christmas Eve are a great favourite, but in many areas tuna, clams or squid with pasta may form the main dish or may be served as an accompaniment to CAPITONE (charcoal-grilled eels and bay leaves). Some may prefer FRITO MISTO DI VERDURE, an array of pre-cooked batter-fried vegetables.

The pre-Christmas tradition of meatless meals is climaxed with a display of treasured regional desserts, cookies and sweets, many made only at Christmastime, such as CULLURELLI, the sweet pastries from Calabria-Lucania made by deep-frying small balls of dough then serving hot with sugar; the traditional Neapolitan sweet called STRUFFOLI ALLA NAPOLITANA, made with tiny drops of fried dough bound in a rich honey syrup and garnished with tiny coloured candies; the special Christmas treat prepared in Abruzzo-Molise called CALCIUNI DI MOLISE, actually a type of sweet ravioli filled with a purée of chestnut and chocolate then fried and served with cinnamon sugar; and Bologna's favourite Christmas cake called CERTOSINA, a rich dark honey cake with bitter chocolate, fruits and nuts and the aroma of anise seeds and cinnamon. The Ferrara region of Emilio-Romagna boasts a rich chocolaty yeast cake delicately flavoured with lemon and almonds. It is eaten from before Christmas to Twelfth Night and is called PAMPEPATO DI CIOCCOLATO.[3.14]

Christmas trees are not a usual part of Italian festivites, but the treasured displays of the nativity scene are. Also typical almost throughout Italy is the rich egg-yolk yeast bread called PANETTONE which everyone enjoys with CAPPUCCINO or ESPRESSO coffee throughout the holiday time.[21] *Natale* (Christmas) is a time for family and friends and the day begins with coffee and the PANETTONE and often cups of ZABAGLIONE, the warm fluffy dessert made from whipped eggs and marsala wine. Dinner on Christmas Day is often a feast of the best the family can afford, sometimes following the traditional seven-course menu of homemade family specialties of antipastos, pastas, vegetable dishes, fish or seafood, with a traditional main course of stuffed roasted capons to be followed by brandied fruits, nuts, cookies, cakes and fine liqueurs.[3.19]

New Year's follows many local and familial traditions too. For Sicilians, on *Notte di Capo d'Anno*, the doors are opened to sweep out the old year and the windows are opened to let in the New Year. Plates of cut-up herring are enjoyed as a symbol of luck while lentils are a symbol of health and wealth and also the traditional staple of the poor.[19] Mistletoe is yet another symbol of luck. Money gifts (*strenna*) for the children and flowers sent for friends and relatives add excitement to the day. The traditional dinner is stuffed pig's legs and lentils, ZAMPONE DI MODENA.

In some areas, children receive gifts at Christmastime from the legendary *Befana*, the witch who travels on her broom in search of the Holy Child after hearing about the birth of Christ from the *zampognari* (shepherds). In other homes, children and family exchange gifts, and still others give only money gifts at New Year's.[19.21]

There are many other special days on the calendar but these vary from region to region, as do the customs and foods. December 13 is traditionally the Feast of Santa Lucia when CUCCIA, a mixture of wheat and chick peas, is eaten for each meal of the day. The Feast of St. Agatha is bright with parades and everyone enjoys nibbling on snacks of roasted seeds, nuts, beans and cookies made with almonds and pistachios. February 15 is the special day set for celebrating almond blossoms; sugar-coated almonds play an important role in many occasions such as weddings, anniversaries, graduations and baptismals, while chopped or ground almonds and nougat and marzipan confections sweeten and flavour many festive dessert plates.

Throughout Italy, March 19 is celebrated as the Feast of St. Joseph (San Guiseppe), the patron saint of hearth and home. In consideration for the poor, meatless feast tables are set up with fish and seafood, vegetable and cheese dishes and breads and fresh fruits. Most homes share this meatless day by serving appetizers of fruits, vegetables and olives such as orange slices, fennel and black olives. The main meal of the day may follow the appetizer with a soup then fish and vegetable dishes. Again, each area and family often prepares its own St. Joseph Day specialty dish.[14,19] BIGNE DE SAN GIUSEPPE, deep-fried beignets dusted with sugar, join the list of traditional sweets with fresh oranges and sweet yeast breads. Sicilians prepare SFINGE, crisp crullers with cheese filling.[19]

Pasqua (Easter) once again ushers in the familiar pattern of devotional prayers and gatherings of family and friends to feast together. Roasted whole suckling lambs, spring salads, eggs, roasted artichokes and FUGAZ-ZA DI PASQUA, an egg-rich yeast bread lightly flavoured with orange, vanilla, almond or lemon, replace MARITOZZI QUARESMALI, the light fruity buns that were eaten throughout Lent.[3,19]

Other festivals often retain more regional than national importance. For example Rome celebrates Midsummer Night or St. John's Eve with family gatherings where the traditional feast includes garlic-simmered snails touched with fresh mint and tomato.[3] May 9 and 10 are the special Sicilian dates for eating marzipan fruits (made from ground almond paste) and CUSCUSU, a dish patterned after the North African *couscous* but made with coarsely ground semolina and fish.[19] Many areas of Italy celebrate July's summer weather with day or week-long festivities that in-clude stewed snails and suckling roast pigs (PORCHETTA). In Sicily the first two weeks of August are known as *Ferragosto*, the Feast of the Madonna; streets are brightened with religious floats and parades and everywhere vendors sell grilled sausages and peppers, pizzas and POLPI (octopus) and in case anyone still feels hungry there are always some seeds, candies or nuts or delicious ice cream for cooling refreshment.[19]

On November 2, most Italians celebrate All Souls' Day, a time of feasting and a warm remembrance of dead loved ones. No one seems to know why anymore, but beans have long been symbolic of death and the souls of the departed, so it is not surprising that FAVE DOLCI (sweet al-mond cookies shaped like fava beans) are eaten especially on All Souls' Day.[14]

THIRTY

Japanese

The Japanese call their homeland Dai Nihon or Nippon, meaning "origin of the sun."[1] It is from this name that Japan has also been called "Land of the Rising Sun." It is an apt name. For in the short span of about one hundred years, Japan has shaken off the shackles of an ancient feudal system and hundreds of years of isolation from the rest of the world, united her people, elevated her standard of living and today proudly stands third in importance as a world industrial nation.

The four main islands that make up Japan – Hokkaido, Honshu, Shikoku and Kyushu – are 80 per cent mountainous. Picturesque lakes dot the mountain areas and small rivers water the rolling plains. Only 15 per cent of the land is arable but it is from this that diligent Japanese farmers coax rice and other grains, vegetables and a wide variety of fruits. From the surrounding seas come cold and warm currents and air masses that give Japan a climate that varies from short summers and severe winters in the north to torrential rains and whipping winds, hot days and humid nights in the south. But from the seas come also Japan's great harvest of fish, seafood and edible seaweed.[2]

Japan's first outside contact was with Korea in the early 300s C.E. Chinese industrial arts, crafts and learning found their way through Korea to Japan. Shintoism, Japan's indigenous cult of imperial and ancestor worship, existed side by side with Buddhism since the latter was introduced from India (through Korea and China) in 538 C.E.[3] Gradually the cult of ancestor worship blended with Buddhism and deeply affected many aspects of Japanese life. Appreciation of nature and a cultivation of simplicity and grace in everyday life influenced not only food and dress, but also literature and the arts.

Perhaps one of the most exquisite examples of the infusion of the blend of Buddhism and Shintoism into art and thence into everyday life is to be found in the Japanese art of *tsutsumu*.[4] This is the art of packaging, and includes everything from a farmer's quantity of eggs delicately laced in rice straw, to a gratuity that is not placed directly in the hand, but is wrapped in folds of delicate paper to resemble a flower. *Tsutsumu* represents utility as well as beauty and simplicity. Materials and colours for wrapping as well as the completed shapes delight the eye and symbolize the spiritual essence of nature.

In this same way, although Japan adopted crafts, arts, language, industries and even religion from other lands, she has given each an indelible Japanese stamp.

From the Chinese and Koreans the Japanese learned how to write by using Chinese ideograms but soon simplified and refined the complex characters (in the 700s during the Heian Period) into two native *kana* syllabaries: *katagana* and *hiragana*. The Japanese word *kana* means a symbol representing a syllable. This resulted in a flourishing of Japanese literature and learning previously unsurpassed.[1,3]

It was in the Meiji Period (1867 – 1912) that the next great advances occurred. With the government centred in the Emperor, Japan became unified for the first time and boldly stepped into expanding school systems and new industrial techniques based on Western patterns.[3,5] The Western influence in music and art, in transportation (steam engines and electric trolleys), lighting, household appliances, telephones and even Western-style skyscrapers was mostly apparent in the cities. The country areas continued their traditional ways, but not for long.

After a taste of territorial expansion – Japan for a time gained control of Okinawa, Formosa, Korea, Inner Mongolia, Southern Manchuria and several Pacific Islands – Japan laid down her arms in unconditional surrender on August 11, 1945. So began the American occupation. Once again Japan was to accept outside ideas, this time, those of democratic government, land reforms, franchise for women, and the demotion of Shintoism from state cult to minor sect. This latter meant that with the government no longer sponsoring Shintoism, the Emperor of Japan was no longer considered to be divine and no longer could the government impose religious education or activity on any Japanese citizen.[1,6]

By 1952, Japan had taken her place as one of the great industrialized societies of the world – and also shared in many of the problems that ensued. Yet it is surprising that although living and working conditions seem to parallel those of the Western world, differences remain. For although outward circumstances undergo rapid change, "the traditional aspects of the society are retained."[7]

This is worthy of closer examination because it reveals differences of thought and custom that are often incomprehensible to the occidental mind. In Japanese tradition, it is the group as a whole that matters: individuals are as important as the group they belong to. Further, traditional views maintain that only diligent hard work leads one to success: if one does not succeed in life it is simply because one has not worked hard enough.[7] These factors lead to intense familial and/or company loyalties as well as fierce competition. It often also leads to a lack of communication between fields or occupations because workers may belong to separate rival companies.

Japanese social life, too, differs from that of the Western world. There is a sharp distinction and division between social pleasures - enjoyment of friends, meals and entertainment - and the world of business, education or politics. Logical, philosophical, religious, business or even political discussions have no place when friends gather for a meal or a few drinks. "The ability to seek pleasure in a world that has no logic may appear as a kind of art in the eyes of foreigners."[7] But the ability to relax completely both mentally and physically in congenial sociability may explain, more than anything else, the traditional Japanese resistance to stress-related illnesses.

For those Japanese who emigrated, the story is only slightly different. Wherever they went - to Hawaii, the United States or Canada - the first emigrants left Japan for financial reasons. Their dream was to work hard, live frugally and then one day return to retire in their native Japan. But conditions frustrated their dreams.

It was these enclaves of frugal, hardworking Japanese - quietly retaining their language, dress, foods and traditions - that aroused the unwarranted indignation of their Western neighbours. Differences are seldom tolerated. But when it became evident that the dream of returning to their homeland was not going to be realized, their resistance to social change broke down. *Issei* (first generation Japanese in North America) sadly watched as the Western system of education proved to be one of the most important factors to change the traditional family patterns.[8] Schools emphasized individuality and the *nisei* and the *sansei* (second and third generations) wanted nothing more than to belong. Western dress and manners were readily adopted, and the Japanese language was lost by many. For most, assimilation was the rule and Japan-ness was evident only at meal times. The simplicity and symbolic qualities of Japanese foods and cookery could not be supplanted by Western ones. The separately savoured flavours of Japanese foods are as artistically presented as are the colourful and different dishes upon which they are served. Japanese still eat sparsely and with appreciation.

The traditional aspects so deeply a part of the people of Japan have not deterred her from becoming a bustling industrialized nation. They only somewhat deterred Western understanding and communication. But the rituals and beauty inherent in simplicity and restraint – so much a part of Japanese life and food customs – may prove a valuable lesson to be viewed in a new light by Westerners, just as the notion of separating daily work from daily leisure.

Home Life and Facilities

Present-day mass production of everything from electrical appliances to instant and even frozen foods has made the urban Japanese kitchen similar to any in the Western world. The main difference is size. Refrigeration and storage space are minimal for several reasons: the prevalence of small-size homes, the preference for foods purchased fresh daily, and the custom of entertaining guests outside the home.

But Japanese women are well-trained in the arts of the kitchen, in decoration, flower-arranging, poise and good manners. Many are graduates in home economics, belong to cooking clubs and love to watch food shows on T.V. But since most entertaining is done outside the home, and since very often the Japanese wife is not even sure if her husband will be home for the evening meal, most home cooking is of a much simpler nature than that found in restaurants. Yet the great care taken in the appearance and arrangement of both the table decor and the food itself is never neglected.[9]

Harmony and identity with nature is a constant theme.[12] Metal is used in cooking and cutting utensils out of necessity. But when it comes to wrapping foods – meats are often wrapped in large bamboo leaves – serving or eating foods, the elements of nature are preferred. Dishes and chopsticks are made of bamboo, ivory or lacquered woods. Soup spoons are not used: larger pieces of the soup are picked out with chopsticks and then the broth is sipped from the bowl. Every Japanese kitchen has a colourful collection of tea cups, soup and rice bowls, handled teacups and saucers (for Western coffee and tea), china plates, platters and tiny dishes of different shapes to be used for special dipping sauces. Chopstick rests made in a variety of materials and shapes complete the table collection. For decoration, many styles and colours of mats, cloths and vases for arrangements of blossoms, twigs and leaves add that special Japanese touch.

Kitchen utensils include a variety of sharp, strong knives and cleavers. Many have specific uses such as vegetable-cutting knives, fish knives, etc. The mortar and pestle is probably one of the oldest utensils and is used for grinding herbal medicines, tea leaves, and pounding rice for New Year's cakes. Other basics include a wooden spatula (rice paddle) to ladle rice, bamboo lattice mats for moulding SUSHI, sieves made of wood and horsehair, bamboo baskets for steaming, draining and straining, a tub for cooking rice, graters, ladles, pots and pans.

FOODS COMMONLY USED

The staples of the traditional Japanese diet are rice, fish and seafood, vegetables and tea. Although some meats were taken occasionally as medicine, and records show that the people often hunted and ate wild animals,[10] it was not until the American diplomat Townsend Harris' visit to Japan in 1856 that beef was considered a food.[11] After Emperor Meiji's enjoyment of beef became widely known, its popularity together with pork and chicken rose steadily. Today most main dishes are combinations of vegetables together with meat or seafood. Fruits in season are the usual desserts.

While the Japanese have borrowed from the foods and cookery techniques of Korea and China, there is no other cuisine in the world that can match the delicate artistry of the Japanese table. The Japanese cook is the artist, food his medium and the table its frame. The subtle influence of both Buddhism and Shintoism are felt and expressed in the simplicity and oneness with nature so evident in not only the food and its arrangement, but also the garnishes and eye-appealing combinations.

Milk and Milk Products
Although milk and milk products were known in Japan since ancient times, they have never been an important part of the diet.[10] More recently (since the American occupation after World War II) more milk is consumed but still not significantly. Perhaps in its place, the many products derived from soybeans are used. It should also be considered that broths made from simmering bones, and the eating of tender fish bones all add calcium and phosphorus to the diet.

Fruits and Vegetables
Japan's variable climate and the careful cultivation of the soil is responsible for a wide variety of fruits and vegetables enjoyed both in season and dried, salted, pickled and more recently frozen.

Fruits familiar to other temperate and subtropical areas are common. Many varieties of oranges form the staple fruit. Loquats, berries, persimmons, summer mandarins (NATSUMIKAN) and pear apples (NIJUSIKI) are among the favourites for simple refreshing desserts.

Japanese enjoy all available vegetables and vegetable, seed and bean sprouts and they enjoy them not only cooked by many methods such as stir-fried, steamed, boiled in soup but also as salads. Japanese salads are actually lightly cooked vegetables chilled and dressed with seasonings. Vegetables may also be salted or pickled and used as appetizers or separate courses – like the salads – to be served after the main course.

Yams and taro were introduced to Japan in ancient times and often form the staple food in mountainous areas as well as in times of famine when rice and grain crops have failed. Burdock, lotus roots, leeks, onions and white radish (DAIKON) are great favourites, but it would be difficult to find a vegetable not enjoyed. Several types of seaweed and many varieties of local mushrooms such as SHITAKE (tree mushrooms), SHORO, KOTAKE, SHIMEJI and HATSUDAKE are also used. TSUKEMONO is the name given to pickled vegetables, while SUNEMONO refers to vinegared vegetable dishes.

Meats and Alternates

Meats are available and used according to means. These include all varieties of cuts – including offal – of beef, pork, veal and lamb. Some poultry is used, as well as game meats as available. Japanese KOBE beef has gained a great reputation; it is beef fattened on beer shipped from the port of Kobe. Also famed and even more expensive is WADAKIN or MAT-SUZAKA beef raised in special dark sheds, fed on hot mash and even massaged regularly.

Although the precepts of Buddhism have been gently bent to permit meat eating, the Japanese still eat only small quantities; their fish intake is said to be five times that of Americans.[11] Unquestionably the abundant supply and the great variety of seafood from nearby waters has always and still does make the harvest from the sea the staple of the diet. Edible seaweeds, abalone, clams, squid, shrimp, prawns, oysters, cuttlefish, blowfish as well as salmon, cod, sardines, trout, herring and shark, tuna, flounder, sea bream (TAI) and bonito all find their way into delectable dishes.

In those areas distant from the sea, fish is most often prepared from dried or salted varieties.[10] In fact, it forms such an important part of all festive occasions that where marine food could not be obtained or afforded, seaweed or even salt was then substituted.

SASHIMI is a dish of sliced varieties of raw fish, arranged in a pattern on a plate and eaten by dipping into a sauce. Sometimes slices of raw chicken are also called SASHIMI and eaten in the same manner.[12] But most dramatic of all is the Japanese daring custom of eating raw blowfish called FUGU. FUGU-eating is dramatic because each year many people die from consuming raw portions of this fish (liver and ovaries are poisonous).[9]

Eggs are consumed in quantity often as appetizers in the form of fried egg yolk squares, boiled or pickled quail, duck or pigeon eggs, garnishes and square omelets.

Bean pastes are used as seasoning and as ingredients in desserts. For instance, RED BEAN CAKE is a type of candy made from agar-agar and red bean paste. But most widely used are the products made from soybeans which include SHOYU, a sweetish soy sauce made from wheat and barley, soybeans, salt and water; and MISO, mostly used for flavouring thick soups and made from fermented bean paste.

TOFU or soybean curd is so widely used in Japanese cuisine that it can safely be considered a staple. Its smooth, white custard-like texture and bland flavour make it an ideal ingredient. So versatile is it – it happily absorbs any other flavours – that restaurants in Japan take great pride in their TOFU dishes.

Chestnuts and GINKGO NUTS are enjoyed by themselves but more frequently in desserts and main dishes.

Breads and Cereals

Rice is the staple grain in Japan. But rice is more than food, it is also an indispensable symbol in Shinto religious ceremonies. It has always had a place of reverence and has sometimes been considered medicinal.[10] However, contrary to wide belief, rice is not the only grain of importance in the Japanese diet. Noodles are made from wheat or buckwheat flour and are so liked that they often form not only a main dish, but also a snack food. Rice may be eaten as a base for other foods, or it may be eaten from its own separate bowl. RED RICE is rice that has been cooked with the juice of red beans then served cold garnished with salt and black sesame seeds. But perhaps most popular is SUSHI, the rice sandwich. Basically, SUSHI is vinegared or sweet-and-sour cooked rice wrapped around colourful and flavourful food tidbits. There are three main types of SUSHI:

NIGIRI-ZUSHI: vinegared rice with raw or cooked fish, seafood or eggs garnished with grated horse radish (WASABI).

NORIMAKI-ZUSHI: Vinegared cooked rice and tiny tidbits of fish, seafood or meat and edible seaweed or laver rolled up like a jelly-roll then sliced into bite-size pieces.

CHIRASHI-ZUSHI: Complex SUSHI made from nine ingredients prepared in nine special steps. This is the most artful and complex of all.

SUSHI is eaten with the fingers, often as a snack, picnic food, or appetizer with swallows of tea in between. It is sold in shops and by street vendors. Many types exist, each with a specific name indicating the ingredients.

Japanese noodle dishes are very popular and may be served hot or cold. Noodles are served in one of two ways: KAKE, which means the cooked noodles are placed in a bowl and hot soup poured over; and MORI, which means the cold or hot cooked noodles are served on a bamboo plate and mouthfuls picked up with chopsticks and dipped into sauce before eating. SOBA means "fat" noodles, while UDON refers to thin noodles. Usually the name preceding either SOBA or UDON indicates the garnish. Buckwheat noodles (TOSHIKOSHISOBA) are considered good luck, are eaten on New Year's Eve and are considered an appropriate house gift, especially when wrapped in red paper and ribbon.[13] In eastern Japan buckwheat noodles are favoured, while wheat noodles are most popular in the west.

Besides rice and noodles made from wheat or buckwheat flour, barley and millet are also grown and used in Japan. Barley is also used to make a mild refreshing tea: roasted barley grains are brewed in a pot and served either hot or cold.

Fats
Little fat is used in food preparation as many dishes are eaten raw, pickled, steamed or boiled, barbecued or as soup. Few dishes are fried and this is mostly done in seed oil.

Sweets
Japanese are not sweet-eaters in the sense of consuming candies, cakes, pastries. However, much sugar is used in the seasoning of dishes rather than in actual sweet desserts. Sugar came into use in Japan in the late 1500s and has been an indispensable ingredient since then. Even the Japanese soy sauce called SHOYU is considerably sweeter than the Chinese version.[14] Japanese snacks are not sweets; most often they are snacks of skewered broiled meats, SUSHI or noodle dishes.

Seasonings
Since the goal of Japanese cuisine is to present foods with artful simplicity and natural beauty, seasonings are always subtle. Any flavour that is pronounced, such as horse radish or scallions, is most often added by the diner at the table so the powerful flavours do not override the delicate ones. It is also interesting to note that in Japanese cookery seasonings are added only one at a time and in strictly specified order – never all at once.

SHOYU, MISO, DASHI and AJI-NO-MOTO are the most-used seasonings. SHOYU is slightly sweetened soy sauce. Made from fermented bean paste, MISO is mostly used to flavour thick soups called MISOSHIRU. DASHI is clear base made from a broth of dried fish and dried seaweed; it can be purchased commercially prepared but is usually made at home. A small square of KOMBU (dried kelp) is placed in water and brought to a boil then removed. Shavings of KATSUOBUSHI (dried piece of bonito with green mildew on it) are then added and removed as soon as the broth returns to a full boil. The resulting liquid, seasoned with a dash of AJI-NO-MOTO (Japanese monosodium glutamate) is DASHI. Vinegar and sugar are widely used. SANSHO, a native pepper, and YUZU, citrus flavouring from peel, as well as sesame seeds (black and white), red peppers, hot mustard, horse radish, SHISO leaves and berries, ginger and occasional use of peanuts, ground walnuts, and GINKGO nuts round out the seasoning "shelf" of the Japanese kitchen.

Rice wine called SAKE and fortified rice wine called MIRIN or TOSO are often used in seasoning as well.[12]

Beverages

Tea is the number-one drink in Japan. Tea accompanies meals, is taken as a refreshment, and is the indispensable ingredient and symbol in the exquisite CHANOYU (tea ceremony). Green teas are favoured and there are many different types. MATCHA is the fine powdered green tea reserved especially for the CHANOYU, while GYOKURU (name meaning "gem-dew") is considered next to MATCHA. Other green teas include AOYAGI or AOYANAGI, SEN-CHA and BAN-CHA which are coarser, and HABU-CHA. KOMBU-CHA is a tea made from seaweed, while MUGI-CHA is a tea brewed from toasted wheat or barley grains and taken cold, especially in hot humid weather.

SAKE is made from fermented rice. This mild yeasty-flavoured wine is served warm in tiny cups accompanying meals. MIRIN is the type used in cooking; TOSO is for special occasions. SAKE contains about 15 per cent alcohol — most wines are about 10 per cent — so despite its gentle flavour it is potent. Beer is also enjoyed, usually brewed from inferior rice or sweet potatoes, called SOCHU. There is also a growing demand for scotch whisky.

Coffee has some popularity in Japan. Water is never drunk as such, milk very seldom.

Japanese Cooking Methods

Japanese homes or apartments have a serene simplicity and so does the cooking. Hidden behind sliding shutters are folding furnishings and decorations that can transform the atmosphere and even the use of one room. In the same way, one basic cooking method can make flavour differences in many different foods. Or reversed: one type of food cooked by many different methods will seem like a totally different dish. Again, a Japanese dining room with low table and soft cushions can be pushed to one side as mats, blankets and pillows transform the room into a bedroom. In the same way the TOKONOMO, which is a small alcove in the main room, is completely transformed by changing the wall hanging and the flower arrangement to give one a sense of another time or season. All of this is part of the complex artistry and creativity entwined with a oneness with nature that somehow in Japanese hands comes out looking so naturally simple.

There is great room for creativity in Japanese cooking. There is great joy in tasting something for the first time and a concentration of skills in producing an original dish or garnish. It is considered commonplace to repeat even what was a successful dish - one must always strive to improve. It is for this reason that Japanese cookbooks stress cooking methods rather than recipes, techniques rather than ingredients.

These are some of the basic methods:

TEMPURA or TENDON: In 1550, batter-dipped and fried shrimp was introduced to the Japanese by Portuguese traders.[15] The Portuguese did not eat meat on Catholic Ember Days (four times annually); these days came to be known as Quatuor Tempora and the fried shrimp that became the specialty was called TEMPURA.

TEMPURA now refers to the Japanese cooking method of coating cleaned cut or sliced foods in a light batter and frying quickly in a light vegetable oil. TENDON refers specifically to fried crustaceans. These foods so prepared are served with a base of rice or noodles plus sauces for dipping.

SAUCES: Aside from those sauces providing obviously contrasting flavours – for instance, SHOYU, hot mustard or grated horse radish – most sauces are made from the boiled stock of trimmings and entrails. Sauce is well-reduced then finished with a small amount of DASHI, SHOYU, grated fresh ginger root or horse radish.

SUSHI: This is discussed under "Breads and Cereals."

SASHIMI: Fresh ocean fish is best for this method of thinly sliced raw fish or chicken and sometimes raw lobster, shrimp or clams garnished with paper-thin slices of raw vegetables. They are eaten by dipping into a light sauce seasoned with SHOYU or horse radish. Sometimes SASHIMI is prepared by dipping the raw slices of fish or vegetables very briefly in boiling water before eating.[12]

FUGU SASHIMI: the highly-skilled preparation of raw blowfish. Since the liver and ovaries contain a lethal poison, incorrect handling or preparation could contaminate the meal. More than a hundred dead each year are mute testimony that this is a delicacy fraught with danger.

SOUPS: There are basically three types of soups:

SUIMONO: clear broths made from bits of meat, fish, bones, trimmings, entrails, skins, etc. These are strained and flavoured lightly with salt, SHOYU and DASHI.

MISOSHIRU: thicker and heavier soups made with the addition of MISO, fermented bean paste. Substantial soups that are more like chowders or thin stews and make a meal in themselves, these may be made from fish or chicken.

ZONI: a special soup made for New Year's, is a rich chicken broth with slivers of chicken meat but flavoured with Japanese herbs (NANAKUSA)and fish paste (KAMABOKO). Threads of lemon and spinach and sprinkles of SHOYU and DASHI complete the soup. To serve, ZONI is poured over specially made cakes called O-MOCHI.

SUKIYAKI: *Suki* means a plough and *Yaki* means roasted. This dish is cooked at the table in front of the diners, with the ingredients artfully sliced and arranged on a platter. SUKIYAKI is usually made with prime quality tender beef and an array of vegetables which may include onions, leeks, types of seaweed, carrots, radishes, squares of TOFU, SHIRATAKI (Japanese noodles), spinach, bean or bamboo shoots or sprouts, KONNYAKU (devil's foot squares), and MITSUBA (marsh parsley). The liquids to be added are water, SAKE and SHOYU. *Nabe* is the frying pan which is placed over an *hibach* or *hibachi*, an earthenware cooking pot heated with charcoal embers.

The cooking ritual begins with the sauces heating in the pan, then the meat slices are browned and finally the vegetables, pushing each to one side as they are cooked.

The meal is begun with a clear soup, SAKE or beer served throughout, rice served before or after the SUKIYAKI. Foreigners like to eat the rice with the sauces; to the Japanese this is unthinkable. Rice is revered and is savoured usually by itself. The meal concludes with fresh fruit and then tea.

Beef is the classic meat, but any other fish, meat or seafood and any vegetable variety may be used.

YAKITORI: Spit-roasted meats or foods grilled on tiny wooden skewers are prepared by this process. Often the meats are marinated first, basted with the marinade while roasting (MISO or DASHI-SHOYU marinade) and dipped in sauces while eating. Finely minced ginger or horse radish may enhance the flavours. TERIYAKI is one version using SHOYU and MIRIN as marinade.

NIMONO: This refers to boiled foods. This is also called one-pot cooking and may be done at the table or in the kitchen. Meats or seafood (in appropriate pieces) are boiled in the broth then removed and kept hot. Vegetables are then added and boiled till done, then removed. The cooked, slivered vegetables and sliced meats are well-drained, placed on a plate and served with a little broth as sauce.

MUSHIMONO: This is the classification that includes all steamed foods. There are three main methods:

1. Various ingredients are steamed in individual bowls and served in the same dishes.

2. Foods are steamed in one large platter or in layers of platters in a large steamer and then portioned out individually.

3. Prepared foods are arranged over hot coarse salt in a special earthenware (unglazed) dish called a *horoku*. The fresh foods placed on the scalding hot salt release their own moisture to steam-cook the foods. Dish is covered during cooking time.

DOBIN is a small teapot used for steaming single dishes.

CHAWAN-MUSHI: Classic dish of sliced chicken, shrimp, mushrooms with chestnuts or ginkgo nuts layered in individual dishes with an egg custard poured over. After steaming till set, the dishes are garnished with a sprinkle of lemon juice and lemon slivers.

ODAMAKI-MUSHI: Similar to above except that on the bottom is a layer of noodles which are topped with ham, sliced fish paste, then vegetable slices and finally the egg custard. A sprinkle of lemon juice sharpens the flavour before eating.

AGEMONO or KARAAGE style: *Kara* means "empty" and *age* "to fry." TENDON and TEMPURA are part of this style, although generally it refers to foods, lightly fried in a little oil, having been pre-dipped in cornstarch.

SALADS: Japanese "salads" are made from pre-cooked vegetables, meats, fish or seafoods, cooled and dressed and served as ZENSAI (appetizers), as side dishes or as small separate courses. The dressing is called AEMONO (or mixture). TSUKEMONO refers to pickled vegetables while SUNEMONO means vinegared dishes. These are usually eaten accompanied with many rounds of SAKE. Pickling is done with salt or salt and rice bran to aid fermentation.

Meal Patterns and Eating Customs

Many factors intrude on the strict maintenance of the traditional meals and customs of the Japanese, nonetheless there is an increasing Japanese pride together with the delight and curiosity of foreigners that is causing even NISEI (second generation Japanese) to turn to the traditions of their forefathers. Many Japanese have discarded *all* facets of their culture with the single exception of their food customs.

UMEBOSHI, a powerfully tart little red plum that so many Japanese pop into their mouths first thing in the morning, is one food that defies all the artful and delicate descriptions. It is not artful or delicate; it is potently sour and the punch it packs is intended to waken all but the dead. It clears heads and freshens mouths. Breakfast is either a hot rice bowl garnished with a raw beaten egg which cooks as it touches the hot rice, or NORI (dried laver), but most often a steaming bowl of MISOSHIRU, a thick nourishing soup made with fermented bean paste. Tea may be included.

Lunch is usually taken in restaurants, snack bars, or eaten from little lacquer boxes in the form of a picnic if the weather permits. The mother who is at home is most often alone for lunch and will frugally make her meal from leftover rice topped with tidbits from last evening's meal.

Dinner may frequently be enjoyed in a general or specialty restaurant in the company of relatives or special guests. If it is an evening when the husband is out with his friends, or if it is to be a family dinner at home, most likely the meal will be a boiled or steamed dish, accompanied with sake or beer, preceded by hot clear soup. After the main course, rice and pickles will be eaten. A dessert of fresh fruits will complete the meal.

Street vendors, snack bars and the temptation of delicious aromas from many types of restaurants make snacking a way of life. Almost anything cooked in any form can be purchased in small amounts for hasty nibbling.

Good manners have a special place in Japanese life and there are probably more words in the Japanese language indicating etiquette, humility and honour than there are in any other language. While men could enjoy themselves in a more uninhibited way, women were traditionally taught to be gracious, obedient, humbling and to make the household skills the centre of their life. Japanese women were never expected to be all things: one's wife should be an able homemaker and mother – scintillating conversation, musical ability and graceful dancing belonged to the realm of the geisha.

Whether in Japan or abroad, many Japanese cherish the time-honoured etiquette that surrounds hospitality and meals. Guests remove shoes and slip into tiny slippers before entering the home. Hot towels to refresh the hands and a cup of hot green tea are presented almost immediately. A traditional meal begins with the guest saying, "*Itadakamasu*" ("Now I will eat") and the host replies, with a small bow, "dozo," meaning "please go ahead." Meals conclude with the gracious, "*Gochiso-sama-deshita*" ("This has been a delicious dinner"). To which the host again ceremoniously replies, "*Arigato-Gozaimashita*," meaning "Many thanks."

Rice accompanies every traditional meal and it has specific rules based on the deep reverence for it as a food together with the awareness of the hard work that went into producing it. The rice bowl is always received or removed with both hands, and children are taught this very early. Since the rice bowl is placed at the left of the table setting, its cover should be removed also with the left hand and placed to the left of the bowl. Rice is never eaten all at once, but in separate mouthfuls between other foods and usually after the main course or dishes. Since after dinner tea is often served in the same bowl as the rice, one must never leave even one grain. However, if you wish more rice, a spoonful left in the bottom indicates this desire.

There are traditions surrounding the use of chopsticks too. They must be picked up with the right hand, using the left to arrange them comfortably. To take foods from a platter, the chopsticks are reversed, and when not in use they are to be laid one inch apart in parallel position on your own tray or placemat.

Since great skill is needed in making soups and broths, it is considered polite to praise the soup. To eat the tidbits from the soup bowl, the dish is lifted near the mouth and the pieces eaten with chopsticks. Finally the broth is sipped. In the process of the meal, hot foods are eaten first, then room temperature ones and finally chilled foods. Finally, as in most societies, it is considered thoughtful to wait for older persons to begin their meal before partaking. Since *sake* usually flows generously throughout a meal, it is sometimes good to know that the *sake* cup turned over is the polite way to say, "No more, thank you!"

But of all the Japanese traditions associated with food, CHANOYU, the Japanese tea ceremony, is the most profoundly significant. Although it was developed in the late 1400s by Murata Juko, it has been handed down through the generations almost unchanged. Most of the masters of this ceremony are men, but women are often taught the ritual as much for its beauty as for its profound effect on grace and poise, dignity and discipline. Every step of the ceremony itself, each movement and each utensil as well as one's clothes (which should be of quiet colours) and the little teahouse, the garden and the details of the room are all part of the experience. CHANOYU is strongly influenced by Zen Buddhism, "the aim of which is, in simplified terms, to purify one's soul by becoming one with nature."[16] The special powdered green tea called MATCHA is prepared and served in an atmosphere of serene simplicity with specially made foods called KAISEKI. This food too came under the Zen influence of simplicity and lightness and having the quality of harmony with nature. KAISEKI is thought to represent Japan's highest aesthetic form of food. CHANOYU is far from being a disappearing art: factories, many schools and clubs all have special classes in CHANOYU for its significance as one of Japan's most beautiful traditions is well-appreciated.

Although *nisei* (second generation Japanese) in Canada, Hawaii, and the U.S. mainland do still retain many traditions, for the most part they may be divided into three groups: traditionalists who have retained the Japanese eating customs but have added a few Western foods, for example breads, hamburgers and hotdogs (prepared with SHOYU): the second is the relatively acculturated group who prepare and eat traditional foods in decreasing frequency – this is the largest group; and finally those who have completely Westernized themselves even to changing their names, rejecting their heritage and intermarrying. Gradual increase in protein and fats and the switch to a Western style breakfast are the most notable changes.[8] While the gradual dietary changes have led to increased stature and life expectancy, they have also unfortunately increased the Japanese incidence of heart disease and dental caries.[8]

Special Occasions

The Japanese Constitution of 1946 guarantees religious freedom to all as well as separation of religion and state. Virtually all Japanese, except those converted to Christianity (numbering about 830,000) are regarded as Shintoists. But Shintoism, indigenous to Japan, is thought of more as a cult rather than a religion, and includes aspects of ancestor worship, faith healing, belief in spirits, and purification rites. Confucianism is regarded as a moral code rather than a religion. Thus, it is possible for a Japanese to intertwine not only Shintoism and Confucianism, but also Buddhism. The latter is the predominant religion of Japan's 104 million population and has more than 200 sects and denominations. It is not unusual for a Japanese person to follow Shinto rites for marriage and Buddhist rites for a funeral.[1,2,3]

Although modern in many ways, the Japanese mother takes great care to have the special symbolic foods that are traditional for each of the many festivities of the year: weddings, funerals, birthdays, visits to the shrines, Children's Day (May 5) and Girls' Day (March 3). November 23 is the memorial day for Kobo Daishi, the great Japanese teacher who united Shintoism and Buddhism in the late 700s under one doctrine called Ryobu Shinto.[17] The biggest festival, often lasting three or four days, is New Year's when families gather and meals of many courses of symbolic foods are enjoyed together with visits to the shrines.

Red is considered a joyous and lucky colour so it is found in abundance on festivals, whether in clothing, ribbons, decorations or foods. But most symbolic of all is rice. Most typical Japanese feast foods are MOCHI (rice cakes) and DANGO (dumplings made from rice flour, steamed or boiled then finished by broiling and eating with bean-jam, a sprinkling of soybean flour or sauce.)[10] SHITOGI is another ceremonial food made from powdered rice that is steamed or boiled. It is usually prepared as an offering rather than as a food.

Foods for holidays are always deliberately different in colour and flavour from those eaten the rest of the year. Red beans are popular and a sweet rice wine called *amazake* is served often. For the Girls' Day, also called "Doll Festival," MOCHI is made in diamond shapes coloured pink, pale green and white. The Boys' Festival Day (May 5) is celebrated with MOCHI wrapped in oak or bamboo leaves.[10]

But perhaps most interesting is the individual symbolism given to certain other foods. For example, lobsters are considered an indispensable part of the birthday celebration, the hump of the lobster suggesting the bent back of old age - thus it is hoped the person celebrating the birthday, by partaking of it, may also live to old age.

For New Year's customs and foods are so varied that often they differ from one family to another and certainly from region to region. A whole fish broiled in salt (TAI), sweet *sake*, red beans, MOCHI and many other dishes add to the merriment of the time.

THIRTY-ONE

Korean

Choson or Tai Han is the name the Koreans give to their beautiful mountainous country. The name means literally "Land of the Morning Calm," a name perhaps representing more hope than fact.

As a strategic land bridge between north Asia and the outside world, especially the islands of Japan, the mountainous peninsula of Korea traces its origin to a legend. According to this, it was Tangun the great divine being who descended from heaven and claimed leadership of the many Mongol tribes said to have inhabited the area more than 4,000 years ago.[1,2] Archeological findings confirm the presence of migratory Ural-Altaic tribes around the tenth century B.C.E. throughout the peninsula and in southern Manchuria as well.

The Land of the Morning Calm first faced invasions by the Han Dynasty of China which brought the introduction of bronze metal-working skills as well as the gradual division of the land into three kingdoms: Koguryo in southern Manchuria and northern Korea; Paekche around the basins of the Han River in central Korea; and Silla in the south of Korea. Chinese living styles, Buddhism and later Confucianism formed the foundations of Korean civilization.[3]

From 1392 to 1910, the Yi Dynasty in Korea took many steps to unify the people and the country. All government officials had to pass a national examination based on the Chinese classics, especially Confucianism; a phonetic alphabet of the Korean language was developed. This latter achievement and a much earlier one – the invention and use, before 1392, of what is believed to be the world's first metal type system (inaugurated with the printing of the Buddhist scripture, the *Tripitaka*

Koreana) – are credited by many as being two of the most important unifying features of the time. The phonetic alphabet was called *Hangeul* and its twenty-four precise letters were used in the publication of many precious books. This rich period of relative calm and great cultural achievement was broken in 1591 by Japanese invasions.[1,2]

In the past, although Korea had taken much from China, her "elder brother,"[4] the hundreds of years during which Korea experienced relative isolation helped to develop customs and distinctive ways of life that are uniquely Korean. So it was that although much suffering came with the Japanese occupation from sporadic conflicts after 1591, and for a long period between 1910 and 1945, another cultural layer was superimposed on the Korean foundation. While the walled towns and cities and the many Buddhist and Confucian temples suggested Chinese influence, it is equally obvious that modern-day Korea's many rapid transit and highway systems and even the electrical and telephone systems as well as new consumer habits resulting from mass production of cheap goods, the development of mines and factories and expanded seaports, all trace their origin from the western world via Japan.[3]

Although the Japanese can be credited with preserving the unity of Korea during their occupation, other results were not so favourable. It was both the increase in population and the pressures of politics that resulted in a large emigration of Koreans abroad. And with the Japanese withdrawal following World War II in 1945, the vacant administrative posts in government and executive positions in industry were left to be filled by untrained Koreans with the sad result of a period of economic corruption.[3]

About two-thirds of Korea's thirty million population live as peasants in the small villages that dot the countryside.[4] The ruling upper classes are mostly concentrated in the larger cities, some in the towns. Although the Koreans remain a closely knit community and are still struggling for independence as well as the basic concerns of human existence, the Land of the Morning Calm still cannot fully live up to its name. For the political events following the end of the Second World War allowed only the briefest period of jubilation. With the Russian occupation north of the 38th parallel, and the American occupation south of the 38th parallel, even the United Nations-sponsored election in 1948 did little to promote the hoped-for unity of the country.[2]

Presently, although North and South Korea seem to be on divergent ideological paths, many Koreans feel they will win the struggle for the restoration of their unique national culture, liberty, dignity and hope that their land of Choson will truly be the land of the Morning Calm.

Home Life and Facilities

There are strong contrasts between the home life of Koreans in farming villages and those who live and work in cities. The majority of Koreans live in farming villages, for even fishermen in seashore communities pursue some form of agriculture.[4] The villages are mostly democratic; each tending to be an almost independent social unit.

Many urban homes as well as almost all of those in the countryside follow traditional styles and decor. As the extended family grows, rooms and wings are added to the basic L-shape, U-shape or hollow square homes built of earth, clay wattle, brick or cement blocks. Old straw-thatched roofs are giving way to tiles, metal or plastic styles, but the heating system remains "age-old."[2,4] Under baked clay floors which are neatly covered with glazed paper, stone flues carry heat from either the kitchen or outside fire pits. Thus there is heat for cooking, hot water, and warmth for the occupants of the house as they sit on mats or sleep on quilted mattresses at night.

In the rural areas as well as many urban homes, the kitchen is the special domain of the woman. Pine branches may be used for fuel in the iron, stone or clay fire pits. Traditionally, three large globular iron pots of varying size are sunk into pits in the stove. The largest of these pots may be used for heating laundry water or cooking grass as food for oxen, the smaller ones for rice and other foods. An inverted dome of the iron pot is used as a griddle. Open shelves as well as at least one food cabinet are used for general storage, while foods needing storage in a cool place may be kept in the ground or in huge stone jars.[4] Trays for dining, baskets and brooms add to the decor of the kitchen together with the family's brass ladles hanging on the wall.

A special area of the traditional rural home is the outer porch or patio area, made with a floor of smoothened clay and often sheltered with a roof. This area is called the *matang*. Shoes are placed here before entering the home, but more important, it is here that old and young congregate to do odd jobs, talk and watch the children.[4] It is said that "he who does not know the *matang* will never understand Korea." In fact, for the men, the *matang* is the summer social area, while women prefer the kitchen or the tiny walled garden accessible from the kitchen entrance.

While sliding rice-paper panels within the homes are reminiscent of Japanese design, the influences of China are stronger. Borrowed from the Chinese is the village arrangement of homes clustered together around the courtyard. So too are the small market gardens near each home, the pine tree and bamboo groves surrounding the villages, and even the typical walls surrounding the towns.[3,4]

Upper-class Koreans living in the larger cities live in towering modern apartment buildings or western-style homes, many with modern appliances such as refrigerators, gas stoves and piped-in hot water.[2]

Homes as well as family life are making gradual changes. Father and son still form the primary family relationship, but the large extended family living in one home unit is gradually giving way to the nuclear family consisting only of father, mother and children.

Yet respect for elders and ancestor worship are said to be almost as deeply inculcated in the Korean as are the fundamental Confucian values. Among these is the belief that "a good life depends on knowledge and observance of proper behaviour between one individual and another."[4] This is outlined in the five Confucian categories: parent and child (especially father and son), king and minister, husband and wife, elder and younger brother, and between friends.

These fundamental traditions persist even among those Koreans who profess the Christian faith. First Chinese, then Japanese and more recently Russian and American cultures, religions and life-styles have all been superimposed on traditional Korean ways, but they do not replace them.[4]

Following this age-old pattern it is not difficult to understand that even if the modern-day Korean woman works outside her home, the likelihood is strong that within the family she is the "inside master" while her husband is the "outside master." That is, while the Korean family may live in a modern multi-storey apartment building and enjoy modern conveniences, a scratch on the surface will reveal ancient codes and beliefs.

FOODS COMMONLY USED

The foods that are the daily staples reflect the produce of agriculture: rice, barley, and many varieties of beans, cabbages, potatoes and squash. Pear and persimmon trees are most common, but peaches, chestnuts and walnuts are also enjoyed. While the Chinese introduced market gardening and irrigation methods, the Japanese influence was greater in the increasing yields of the fishing industry and it is believed that the Japanese introduced the culture of maize and tobacco.

Rice and rice dishes – that is, rice mixed with barley, beans and potatoes – head the list of staple Korean foods. Two Korean specialties include the brined, pickled and spiced KIMCH'I and the tea called SUNGYUNG which is made by throwing cold water on the burned rice or barley at the bottom of the pot. This latter is served as a beverage at the conclusion of the meal.

Koreans enjoy soups immensely and show their appreciation by slurping which is accepted etiquette.[4,5] Many Chinese and Japanese dishes find a place together with these distinctly Korean specialties, while barbecued and roasted meats and many intricate dishes add to the great variety. Chinese cuisine is still the richest and most varied, Japanese the sweetest, and Korean tastes include both, yet again with special touches that make it different, like SINSUN-LO, the Korean "hot pot."

Milk and Milk Products

As in China and Japan, the use of milk, milk products such as cheeses and butter and cultured milk products are not a part of the Korean menu.

Fruits and Vegetables

The persimmon and the Chinese pear are the most common fruits. However, fruits are not a staple part of the menu, nor are they served with any frequency. In city homes or in upper-class families, fruits may be part of a snack or a treat offered to guests. When strips of raw meat are served (after marinating in garlic and sesame seed oil) it is customary to accompany the dish with thin slices of Chinese pear.[6]

Vegetables offer important nutrients and variety to the diet. Many types and varieties of vegetables are grown and prepared in a variety of ways: white potatoes, sweet potatoes, pumpkin, many squashes, onions, leeks, Chinese cabbage, turnips, red and green peppers, DAIKON (Oriental radish), many types of mushrooms, cucumbers, garlic and many types of beans (red beans, green beans, soybeans and pea beans).

Unquestionably the most important Korean vegetable dish present at every meal is KIMCH'I. There are almost endless combinations but the general categories include DAIKON KIMCH'I made in large cut, small cut, salty, very salty, pickled and summer; CABBAGE KIMCH'I made with shredded Chinese or round cabbage; and CUCUMBER KIMCH'I. This Korean national dish is made by layering cut vegetables with varying amounts of salt and onions and allowing it to ferment for a short time. After rinsing, the prepared vegetables are seasoned with peppery spices, garlic, leeks and ginseng. A great variety of other special ingredients may be added to create the KIMCH'I specialty of the household, such as dried or fresh shrimp, fish or other seafood, pine-nuts, meats, chestnuts, pears or apples.[1,6]

In some households, KIMCH'I and rice may be the entire meal. Huge earthen jars are used to store the KIMCH'I and these are placed either underground or in cool places during the summer.

Cucumbers and eggplants are greatly favoured and are prepared in a variety of ways: stuffed, fresh, cooked, pickled, steamed, roasted, or as a salad with vinegar.

More than 1,000 varieties of seaweed or laver are found around the shores of both Korea and Japan. Edible seaweed is called *nori* in Japan and *kim* in Korea. It is popularly served by dipping in sesame seed oil and soy sauce then toasting. It can also be toasted then crushed and mixed with soy, sugar, sesame seed oil and red pepper. Another way is to cut into small pieces, paint with rice powder and seasonings cooked together, then dust with sesame seeds, sun-dry, and finally fry.

Other vegetables in the category of greens are parsley leaves, spinach, bean sprouts, lettuce, celery, bamboo shoots and even carrots. A delightful "lettuce lunch" called SANG-CHI-SAM is prepared by washing fresh green lettuce leaves (a few drops of sesame oil in the last rinse water makes the leaves shine). The leaves are arranged on one platter, and various tidbits such as varieties of seafood, bean paste, slivered meats, KIMCH'I (many types) and other greens are arranged on other platters. Diners choose their fillings, roll up their lettuce leaves and eat. This dish is often served with soup.[6]

An important ingredient and condiment is hot pepper mash made from sun-dried red peppers. Seeds are knocked off (they add bitterness) and the peppers are pounded into powder. The resulting powder is then mixed with soy sauce, sticky rice and seasonings of onions, leeks and spices.[4] This may be eaten as a side dish, condiment with other foods, or in soups.

Finally, proper distinction must be given to the soybean, one of the most ingeniously used crops in China, Japan, Korea and southeast Asis. Arising from using the dried beans as any other bean (mixed with rice or vegetables), six distinctive uses are made. Soybeans may be used in soy sauce; as soybean mash; as raw beans that are toasted in an iron pot then ground up and used as a garnish over rice cakes or plain rice (children enjoy eating the toasted coarser bits not used in the toasted meal); sprouted into soybean sprouts to be eaten lightly cooked as a vegetable; prepared into TU BU or soybean curd.

TU BU is sometimes called "Oriental cheese" because of its creamy white appearance and smooth spongy texture. It is prepared by grinding soaked soybeans with water. The liquid is strained, boiled and eaten as is or it may be strained through a hemp bag into a shallow bowl; the curds left in the bag form a firm cake which may be cut, dipped in soy sauce or else fried in sesame seed oil and eaten. Oil can also be made from the soybeans, but it is not commonly used or prepared.

Soy sauce can hardly be considered a vegetable, but since it is prepared from the utilitarian soybean, its preparation is mentioned here. Commercially prepared sauce of course is widely available, but many households in Korea still prepare their own. Prepared in the fall of the year, the boiled and pounded soybeans are molded into a cone shape and set to dry hard. Then they are wrapped with rice straw, hung from ceilings and allowed to ferment for several weeks. (Such fermented cones may be winter-stored in huge rice straw bags kept in a cool place.)

In the spring, bits of the cone are broken into a water-filled jar to which is added salt, spices, red peppers and a few charcoal lumps. This is left in the sun a few days until the molded soybean clumps float on top and the resulting liquid turns black. The final step is the ladling out of the black liquid which is then boiled to become soy sauce. The remaining contents of the jar are used as soybean mash.[4]

Meats and Alternates
In many households, meat and fish are considered dishes for special occa-

sions. Pork, chicken, fish and many types of seafood are enjoyed when available. Fish is probably more plentiful than meats, though all rural households maintain a few pigs and chickens. Bits of fish or meat may be used in the preparation of KIMCH'I, soups, in casseroles and other dishes where the combination of grains and vegetables stretches the flavour of the more expensive meats and fish. Marinated dried beef is a favourite for appetizers; some may be toasted before serving. Raw beef strips are enjoyed after marinating in garlic and sesame oil, served with slices of raw pear.

Charcoal fires are frequently used for barbecues. Strips of chicken or beef are marinated in mixtures of ground sesame seeds, sugar, soy sauce, minced garlic and green onion with a little sesame oil added near the end of marinating.

Eggs are used as available. They are scrambled, formed into small pancakes with vegetables or KIMCHI'I, or made into steamed custards generally eaten for breakfast and, finally, sometimes as soup garnishes.

The tiny Korean kitchens make ingenious use of their facilities: fish or meats are usually grilled over hot coals in a little pot stove; a cook may scramble eggs and add a few other ingredients and set the little filled bowls to steam over the rice in the rice pot; frying can be accomplished by using the top of the iron pot upside down; finally, great varieties of soups are begun with the simple browning of tiny bits of meat or seafood in the bottom of a pot, followed by a sprinkling of soy sauce or other seasonings and the adding of water to make a basic broth.

Foods from the sea include sea cucumbers, oysters, crab, cuttlefish, cod, herring, white bait (BAINGO), sea bream (plentiful and eaten with vinegar soy sauce), clams, crab, shrimp and jellyfish.

Pine nuts, chestnuts and walnuts are also used and must be considered for their texture and flavour as well as being a protein source. KOCHUJAN, which is a seasoned red pepper bean paste, may be mixed with minced pine nuts, green onions and sesame seeds to form a popular condiment used with pickled cucumbers and vinegar soy sauce. Many other dishes use pine nuts collected from the five-needled pine tree whose nuts are thought to have the essence of longevity.[6]

Finally, two exotic foods enjoyed by the Koreans are crickets and silkworms. Crickets are boiled whole then mixed with soy sauce usually as a special dish for babies and children in the autumn (said to prevent drooling) but also considered as an upper-class delicacy for city people. Children also enjoy boiled silkworms when available.[4]

Breads and Cereals
Koreans do not generally eat breads as known in the Western world. Rice is the staple and most important food. As a rule the rice is washed four times before cooking. The first rinse water is given to the pigs, the second

may be used in the soup pot. Distinct personal preferences exist about exactly how much water to use for cooking the rice and the exact degree of hardness or softness desired. Rice accompanies every meal and often only rice with KIMCH'I may comprise the entire meal. Rice may be served plain or mixed together with barley, cubed potatoes, sorghum, millet or a dish of rice, barley and potatoes.

Rice flour is used in making special-occasion cookies, steamed dumplings and for the very special TUK-KUK or New Year's rice cake soup. For the rice cakes, the rice flour is steamed then kneaded.

Barley is the next most important grain. It is grown in between the season for the rice crops and is considered important especially in times when rice is scarce. Since it takes a long time to cook, it is often boiled separately first and is always served combined with other foods. It is considered a "low-level food" but nonetheless important.[1]

Although corn is grown in some areas, it is not used as a grain. It is considered more of a children's food and is cooked by steaming the ears of corn on top of the rice pot. Smallest children and babies are given cooked corn or white potato to gnaw on when hungry.

The buckwheat grown in Korean fields is widely enjoyed in the form of buckwheat noodles. In fact, noodles are frequently homemade from a dough of buckwheat flour, salt, rice flour or cornstarch and water. The stiff dough is then pressed through a Korean noodle cutter placed over a pan of boiling water. Noodles are called MYUN. Noodles are considered a lunch dish, whether served hot or cold. NAING-MYUN is a cold plate of cooked buckwheat noodles served with a garnish of chopped KIMCH'I, strips of beef or chicken and sliced pear and sliced hard egg; chilled broth is poured over. A similar dish served hot and said to be a favourite of the masses – especially enjoyed by men as they eat sitting cross-legged – is JAING-BAN. The heated meat and condiments are enjoyed with wine, the noodles are eaten last and the entire platter is kept hot over small fire pots placed on the low tables.[6]

Fats
Sesame seed oil is used both for cooking and frying. Frequently the flavourful oil – reminiscent of toasted sesame seeds – is also used to give a sheen to washed greens or roasted (grilled) meats.

Other fats consumed would include those contained in pork crackling and chicken skin and in the actual meats themselves.

Sweets and Snacks
Considering that a small Korean child is commonly given a cooked potato or a steamed cob of corn to gnaw on as a snack between meals, as opposed to the early Western introduction of sweet cookies and sweetened desserts, it can be seen that the Korean sweet tooth is an insignificant one.

Desserts are not part of traditional Korean meals but they are served when special guests come and also for holiday and feast occasions. CHUN-KWA is the name given to a variety of candy-coated thinly sliced vegetables; the prepared vegetables are dipped into a syrup then allowed to cool and harden. Many types of dried fruits – sometimes candied – are also enjoyed. Steamed and kneaded glutinous rice can be made into many types of small cookies and pastries often flavoured with honey and nuts. Some are even sun-dried then deep-fried. KAI-YUT are sesame seed candies and a candy favourite made from glutinous rice powder, chestnuts, honey, dates and cinnamon is called "flower paste" or JU-AK. JU-AK is shaped and fried in sesame oil then sprinkled lightly with sugar.

Pine cakes or SONG-PYUN are specially festive and often used as offerings to the spirits of ancestors. They are made with rice powder dough pressed into small cup shapes then filled with red beans, chestnuts and raisin mixture. The unusual flavour comes from steaming them together with fresh pine needles.[6] Another festive favourite is KYUNG-DAN, sweet dumplings which are also prepared from glutinous rice powder dough. Red bean paste and chestnut paste are popped into the centre then rolled in a ball which is finally coated with yellow bean powder or very finely chopped walnuts or dates.

It is interesting that although many of these festive and dessert specialties are considered to be sweets, many are also considered medicinal because of their content of nutritious ingredients such as honey, raisins, etc.[6]

Sometimes fruits are poached in a light syrup and flavoured with ginger root. Such a dessert is SU-JUN-WA, made from persimmons.

The traditional children's treat, particularly in rural areas at New Year's, is YOT. This is ritually prepared from ground barley powder mixed in a ratio of one-to-three parts of boiled rice, then heated carefully with water (overheating makes it bitter). The thick part is gradually spooned off and the remaining liquid is allowed to boil until it thickens into a rich syrup. This is much enjoyed by dipping rice cakes into it.[4]

Seasonings

The flavour of sesame seeds is characteristic of Korean cooking because sesame seed oil is the preferred fat, and sesame seeds are used in many dishes. Garlic, green onions, ginger root, pine nuts and monosodium glutamate are all used generously. Pears and pear juice are often used both as seasoning and as condiment. Soy sauce, vinegar soy sauce (a combination of two parts soy sauce, one part vinegar and monosodium glutamate) and KOCHUJAN are the condiments. The latter is a red pepper and bean paste made from a blend of soy sauce, bean paste, and powdered red peppers in equal parts. Another condiment is prepared from a base of KOCHUJAN with minced green onions, crushed pine nuts, and sesame seeds. This pine-nut condiment is served with pickled cucumbers.[6]

Beverages

Water is an anytime drink. Well water is considered superior but spring waters are considered to have a medicinal value. In wintertime (November to February) hot water is sometimes taken with lunch.

It was the Japanese who introduced tea as a beverage in the cities and towns, but it is almost nonexistent in the villages. SUNGYUNG completes every meal: the colour and flavour are derived by pouring hot water over the charred rice or barley in the bottom of the pot.[4]

There is a great fondness for wine and spirits although at all times drunkenness is considered very offensive while an inebriated woman is simply intolerable. However, there are great leeways in regard to what is considered drunkenness. One old village saying insists that a man may not be considered drunk so long as he can still move an arm. . . .[4] T'AKJU is a light wine having an alcohol content of about 10 per cent, a bit stronger than beer. YAKJU is a stronger version of T'AKJU with about 15 per cent alcohol content and is considered medicinal, as are many other good things. SOJU ("burning wine") is a spirit so named because of its effect and probably because of its 25 per cent alcohol content.

OMIJA-WHA-CHAI is a refreshing beverage made either in the home or commercially. It is a seasonable drink prepared from fresh or dried fruit, parts of tart or sour flowers and is sweetened with honey or sugar.[6] SHIK-HE is another sweetened drink, prepared from fermented rice and sugar and lightly flavoured with citron.

Meal Patterns and Eating Customs

Koreans disagree whether breakfast or supper is the main meal of the day. Generally breakfast is more important in the country, while supper is the main meal in the city. Considering the work patterns, this emphasis can be understood. Since rice and KIMCH'I is present at every meal, the additions of soup, meat or fish and vegetable dishes and more probably, the amount and number of courses would signify which is the most important meal of the day. Many Koreans prefer rice for breakfast and supper, while a noodle dish with meat or fish and vegetables and sometimes soup provides a satisfying lunch.

Meals are usually taken while the family and guests sit cross-legged around a floor mat upon which are placed separate low-legged trays with the foods for each diner. Sometimes foods are arranged banquet or buffet style and each diner takes his or her portion to eat with rice.

Ladles made from gourds as well as crafted ladles from brass are used for spooning out foods, but brass chopsticks and spoons are used for dining. Rice, soup and KIMCH'I may be eaten with the aid of spoons; liquid soup, KIMCH'I juice and wine can also be loudly and appreciatively sucked from bowls. The etiquette of chopsticks demands that they be held close to bowl and mouth. Further, they should always be held close to the top ends for it is said that those who hold their chopsticks near the working end will have a bad wife.[4] It is considered bad taste to make a scratching sound with chopsticks or spoons against the food bowls.

It is expected that liquor will be served at funerals, weddings, sixty-first birthdays (61 being considered a significant age), at any old man's birthday, at all ceremonial festivals and also "when the co-op workers go to the rice fields."[4] Wine is poured graciously into a bowl and passed around, while the men sit on their heels and sip. The largest wine bowl (about 4") is for T'AKJU, YAKJU is served in a smaller one while the potent SOJU is presented in a tiny winecup. The many forms of KIMCH'I are nibbled in between sips of the wine as an hors d'oeuvre.[4]

Both men and women enjoy pipe tobacco at any time. In the cities and towns people enjoy smoking cigarettes, but these are too expensive for most villagers who simply grow and dry their own tobacco suited more to pipe smoking.[4]

Children are nursed till about two years of age but in the villages it is not uncommon to see even six-year-olds occasionally nursing. This is no embarrassment to either. Weaning is accomplished by the simple expedient of dabbing the nipples with pepper. Children are fed whenever they cry. As the child becomes older he may be given a corn cob to nibble or a cooked potato or even a DAIKON soaked briefly in salt water.

Social life in the villages centres on the *matang*, and guests are always welcomed. The only exception to this is the few days after childbirth when it is understood the family would prefer to be alone. Men enjoy eating their meals together and gathering for wine and a pipe of tobacco. Women prefer to gather in the kitchen or in their garden areas. In the cities, many fine restaurants abound and men enjoy bars, cafés and night clubs. Upper-class men enjoy the company of *kisaeng* (female entertainers like the *geishas* of Japan), while the upper-class women for the most part live a secluded and isolated life spending their free time sewing and embroidering when the details of managing the home are completed. However, Korean cities like large cities everywhere are changing with the pressures of modern society and more and more women are venturing into the business and professional world.

Special Occasions

The religion of Koreans is similar in pattern to their culture: a gently layered religion. That is to say, although many are Christians today, the Christianity does not dispose of but somehow rests amiably with the traditional "layers" of Buddhism, Confucianism, spirit worship and animism.[3,4]

Special occasions may be divided into those concerning family rites and those which are widely celebrated holidays. The first and the sixty-first birthdays are considered the most important and the most festive.

The child's first birthday is celebrated by dressing the youngster in bright colours and treating him to rice cakes, cookies and fruits. The whole family delights in the ceremony where the child is placed in the midst of symbols representing possible future careers and everyone enjoys predicting which one the child will grasp. For example, should he grasp a coin, it is believed he will be a business man.[2] The sixty-first birthday, especially of a man, is greeted with festive foods and much wine and rejoicing; this is called *hwangab*.

Traditional weddings and funerals have recently been much simplified. Elaborate processions, numerous guests (or professional wailers and mourners) and huge presentations of food and wine have been reduced to simple meaningful rituals more in accord with the times. Weddings are most often performed amidst flowers and music in special wedding halls. There is still a treasured tradition that requires parental approval of the match before the wedding, and sometimes even the astute services of a matchmaker.[1,2]

On New Year's Day (usually in February on the lunar calendar) families surround the ancestral shrine in the home of the eldest son with plates of fruits and cookies, rice cakes and "sweet wine" (a non-alcoholic mix of liquid YOT with the residue previously spooned off.[4] Everyone dresses in his or her best clothes and pays respect by bowing to the elders in the family. Small treats of foods and gifts of money are given to the children. Families and close friends visit one another; those in mourning may receive visitors but do not pay calls.[2]

BIBIM-BAB is a specialty dish often prepared for festive nights and New Year's. A variety of mixed fresh and dried vegetables are all individually cooked and carefully shredded together with a beef and egg pancake; each of the ingredients is artistically arranged on a rice bowl and is mixed just before eating. This colourful and substantial dish becomes a meal with soup and KIMCH'I.[6]

On special occasions as always, Korean children are taught to drop their eyes to show respect, and always cup both hands when receiving any gift, sweet, or special treat. (Koreans stare into each other's eyes only in anger).[4] While festive occasions are times of happy chatter, there is always a hush when the trays of foods are served, for Koreans prefer to give their attention to the food at hand rather than to converse while eating.

In Korea most traditional holidays are based on the seasonal farming cycle and the dates are from the lunar calendar. In the villages these festive days are observed as in olden times but in the towns and cities and amongst emigrant Koreans, the observance of the holidays varies greatly. Some will prepare the festive foods out of nostalgia and enjoy them with family and close friends, others will retain the ancient traditions of ancestor tributes, while many take the occasion as a day of rest or partying.[2] There are few Korean homes, however, that do not keep a traditional lunar calendar with the special occasions clearly marked.

The fifteenth day of the first month on the lunar calendar is celebrated with singing and dancing and wrestling contests (*ssirum*). This is called *Taeborum* or *Dongsin-je*.[1,2] The first full moon of the new year is called *Dal-magi* or *Talmaji* and is celebrated by torch-light parades to the highest hill in the area to view the moon clearly while huge bonfires are lit expressing hopes for fruitful crops, long life and the good things of life.

Cold Food Day or *Hansik* is celebrated approximately 105 days after the winter solstice. People offer tributes of wine and cold foods near the graves of their ancestors; later, the foods and wine are eaten by the family in picnic style.[1,2] In some areas the festival is marked by tree planting. Later in the same month some homes mark Buddha's birthday by processions, banners and lanterns; some shrines and homes are specially decorated as well.

Tano is a day of sports events, including wrestling for the men and contests of see-sawing for the women and swinging for the children. It is celebrated on the fifth day of the fifth lunar month. Those who are too old to participate content themselves with watching and musing on the strength they had when they were younger.

The day of the full moon in the eighth month brings the beautiful harvest festival of thanksgiving called *Chusok*. Foods and wine are offered at the ancestral shrines. Celebrations include feasting, dancing, village bands and much rice wine. One need not be in the countryside to enjoy and treasure the abundance of this festival, for it is celebrated everywhere.

During the traditional period of the winter solstice, women cook and sew while men enjoy a respite from the hard work of the fields. On *Dongji*, the day of the winter solstice, foods are prepared with red beans both in JUK (porridges of rice) and in KUK (soups). Special sweet cakes made with glutinous rice also mark the day.

Korean Christians mark Christmas in quiet family gatherings. Many attend church services. For those living in Korea, this season is their winter, so Koreans enjoy a "white Christmas" too.[1]

Special and ceremonial dishes include the following: roasted chicken; oysters, sea cucumbers; soups of beef, pork and seaweed; grilled pork, fish or beef dishes; fried eggs with pumpkin or dryfish; fried bean curd; tiny boiled bean sprouts or Chinese "flower bell"; steamed rice cakes; glutinous rice cakes; *kimch'i*; pumpkin, flour-dipped and fried; *yot*; white rice; sweet wine, and varieties of wine spirits.[4]

THIRTY-TWO

Latin American: Argentinian and Uruguayan, Brazilian, Chilean, Colombian and Venezuelan, Peruvian

For the adventurous Spanish explorers and navigators who first touched western lands, new lands to conquer were the lesser goals; hope of riches was the driving force that pushed them through uncharted waters, steamy jungles, and over defiant mountains.

But the Spaniards were in fact not the first. Many centuries before them, tribes of Indians had migrated from north to south, settling in areas along the way, adapting themselves to their surroundings and even building temples and cities of incredible grandeur. They staked out their territories, in many cases set up complex systems of government and systematically cultivated a number of crops. These included many varieties of beans, the whole family of squashes and pumpkin, sweet and white potatoes, tomatoes, and hot chili peppers, and tobacco. Pineapples, papayas, bananas, coconuts and many varieties of corn found many uses. In ancient *Tenochtitlán* (Mexico), corn was revered as a deity. Chocolate from cacao and vanilla from leathery brown pods were also cultivated and used by many Indian tribes.

How could the Spaniards have known that the gold they sought would be so tainted with blood? Or that the countries they fought to establish would in later years suffer still more bloodshed in fighting for their independence? And how could they have known that the cargoes of foodstuffs and plants that they would bring back to the European continent would spread to many countries and effect far more profound and lasting consequences than gold?

In a similar way, the many peoples, herds of cattle, swine and sheep, and the many plants that would migrate to South America would change the topography, the life-style and even the food habits of the inhabitants. For the Europeans brought with them the culture of wheat and rice and the taste for domesticated meats such as beef, lamb and chicken and the use of fats in cookery. Onions and garlic added piquancy to the bland and the hot flavours of indigenous herbs and peppers. A quickly spreading taste for sugary sweets was another introduction from the Old World.

Perhaps one of the most important products introduced to the New World was coffee. Coffee was said to have been discovered in the ancient Arab world, and took hold in Europe in the 1700s. But it owes its introduction to the Western Hemisphere to a Frenchman, Gabriel Mathieu Desclieux, who brought a cutting of the coffee plant to the French-owned island of Martinique in the West Indies in the 1700s.[1,2] It was from there that other cuttings were taken to French Guiana and from there to Brazil.[2] Today it is Brazil and Colombia who lead world coffee production.[1,2]

Early food patterns in Central and South America before the arrival of the Europeans still form an important part of the basic food patterns of today. The early subsistence foods of corn and beans in fact are the same subsistence foods in Mesoamerica today. The preparation of the corn itself involved a limewater soaking (incidentally adding valuable minerals to the diet), then a crushing and grinding to prepare the MASA HARINA used to form the flat corn cakes called TORTILLAS.[3] This is the core staple of Mexican food, while simply crushed corn forms the modern-day Panama staple.

In the mountainous Andes area, corn is more commonly eaten green (both in early times and now), supplementing the indigenous potato and other tubers such as OCA, ULLUCO, and MASHWA. Grain, such as the Andean grain called QUINOA, is also a staple.[3]

The agricultural Indians along the Atlantic coast, in the Caribbean and in the northern part of South America survived by hunting and fishing and by cultivating a poisonous bitter plant called MANIOC. There are many varieties of this tuberous plant, called sweet CASSAVA in North America and YUCA in South America. But it was the bitter and poisonous MANIOC that the Indians somehow not only discovered how to eat and prepare, but most important, how to process to remove the poisonous quality of the juice. They did this by patiently grating the pulp and allowing it to hang in a mesh basket till all the juice dripped through. By boiling the juice they were able to make it into a palatable sauce. By toasting the dried pulp they formed MANIOC MEAL or *farinha de mandioca*. Modern Brazilians still enjoy the absorbing quality of the meal and sprinkle it liberally on almost any juicy food. Today in Brazil the processing of MANIOC is of course commercialized; the rest of the world enjoys it too in the form of tiny pellets called tapioca.[4]

The Spanish conquests of the 1500s brought the complete destruction of many tribes and ancient civilizations. But they also added wheat and rice to the diets, and introduced the use of fats in cookery, particularly sautéeing and frying. The cattle, swine and fowl that the Spaniards managed to bring on their sailing vessels became the initiators of domestic herds of cattle, swine and flocks of chickens and ducks. It was not long before large quantities of meats became readily available and an important part of the Latin American dietary. Before this, only those meats from successful hunting were a part of meals and in many areas, such as Mesoamerica, wild game was often reserved for royalty and seldom became a part of the daily meals of ordinary people.[3]

In fact, a sad commentary on the "modern diet" may be that it has moved too far from the basic nutritious diet of the native Indians, and the wealthier classes may in many cases have a poorer dietary, too heavy in sweets, fats and breads.[3]

The effect on the diet of the native peoples in the Andean Highlands was negligible as they had little contact with the Europeans. However, one of the most notable shifts in consumption for the lowland peoples was the introduction and acceptance of rice as a staple in areas as far distant as the Panama to many of the lower jungle areas of the entire Andean range.[3] But the general trend throughout Central and South America, aside from the foods mentioned, was the impressive use and adaptation of the range of indigenous staples by the new European population.[3]

Although the Amazon flood plain has a strong potential for growing rice, it is still mainly a MANIOC-corn-beans area, following the aboriginal patterns. In fact the areas where heavy meat-eating becomes the pattern together with areas where wheat, milk and rice consumption has taken over are clearly those areas where the native Indian population is diminished or no longer exists and urbanization has taken over.[3]

In South America as elsewhere, home life and the facilities for preparing, serving and storing foods vary according to class prestige, economic ability, local customs and taboos. Obvious differences in family relationships and household facilities must exist between the *gauchos* of the Pampas and the Andean herders, between the native Indians in remote jungle areas and the sophisticated urban population of the large cities.

The vast size of South America with its varying climates and topography and differing ethnic populations makes generalizations difficult. But some food items are common to most countries, and the diligent cultivation by native Indians is responsible for the enjoyment of so many of these foods and products in almost every country of the world: chocolate and vanilla, pineapples, bananas, squashes, potatoes and pumpkins, tobacco, tomatoes, and hot chili peppers. These indigenous foods gradually blended with those introduced by the Europeans: rice, wheat, milk and cheeses, garlic and onions, coffee, sugar and rum.

Because of the introduction of domesticated animals and fowl, a much greater increase in meat consumption also occurred.

The very old staples of corn, beans and manioc are still the subsistent foods for millions of Latin Americans, while high in the Andes, native Indians still survive on the staples of potatoes, quinoa flour and dried llama meat as did their forefathers before them.[3,4] In coastal and river areas fish and seafood forms an important part of the diet while the grassy Pampas provides a diet high in beef for those of the area. Urban populations in any country enjoy the indigenous staples together with European staples and blend them into different cuisines. These are discussed under "Regional Specialties."

Rum (prepared from sugar cane) and coffee are the most widespread beverages, although some areas produce grapes for wine production. MATÉ and various fruit juice punches and soft drinks are important too.

Argentinian and Uruguayan

Argentina and Uruguay share many similarities in history, climate, people, food production and food customs. The gentle temperate climate, the rolling grassy Pampas, and the many river systems attracted increasing numbers of hardy and adventurous Spanish settlers bringing with them their cattle and sheep, horses and hogs. Settlers enjoyed the natural beauties of the area, but natural growth and productivity was marred in subsequent years by battles for independence from Spain.[5] Still weakened from battles with Spain, the Portuguese in Brazil took advantage of Uruguay's weakness and annexed the "Banda Oriental," as the area was called. Argentina's unrest centred on freedom from Spanish rule and this was attained in 1835, while Uruguay was granted independence only a few years earlier in 1828. Civil wars and political and economic unrest plagued both countries for the next hundred years, nor are they at peace yet.

Both Argentina and Uruguay have very high literacy levels among their predominantly European populations. Most claim Spanish or Italian heritage, but others include French, German, Russian and Turkish in Argentina, while Uruguay's citizens claim aside from Spanish and Italian also Brazilian and Argentinian as well as French heritages. Uruguay is particularly proud to be the only nation in the Western hemisphere where all levels of education from public school to post-graduate work are free.[5] In both countries the official language is Spanish and the predominant religion is Roman Catholic.

Fathers in both countries typically work on a ranch or in some area of the food-processing industries. Most women tend to occupy themselves with caring for the home and family.[6,7] Family life is of great importance and the saying "*Mi casa es su casa*" is meant in the warmest sense of rich and generous hospitality. Entertaining in one's home is preferred although casual meetings in cafés and inns are as much enjoyed as in Spain or Italy. Gatherings of friends and guests are always loud and lusty with comparative quiet only coming while everyone eats.

FOODS COMMONLY USED

Quantities of milk and varieties of cheeses are produced in both Argentina and Uruguay but both these products are used mostly in cooking. Cheeses and fruits are a part of dessert selections among the upper classes. The favourite meat of the Argentinians is beef and for the *gauchos* it is also their sole staple, washed down with YERBA MATÉ. Uruguayans also add mutton and lamb, while in both countries outdoor grilling of meats provides the favourite cooking method. ASADO (outdoor roasted meats), MATAMBRE (rolled stuffed meat served in colourful slices) and EMPANADAS, meat-stuffed pastries of Spanish origin, are great favourites too. Fish, eggs, and legumes are available but are less commonly used. Vegetable staples include the many varieties of both squash and potatoes as well as corn and pumpkin. They form the basis of many soups and stews and are used by all classes. Fruits are mostly enjoyed by the upper-class urbanites as are certain vegetables and salad greens. But all have a penchant for richly-sweet desserts and pastries as well as well-sweetened beverages such as the YERBA MATÉ, coffee or fresh fruit punches. Rum and many fine local wines as well as strongly-brewed coffee add to refreshment.

Milk and Milk Products
The Argentine dairy cattle, Holando Argentino and Jersey breeds, produce quantities of fresh milk used in similar ways as in North America.[9] Urban populations consume some fresh milk but most is used in custards, FLANS and puddings, such as rice puddings, where the cereal is cooked in milk. Many varieties of cheeses are produced similar in appearance and flavour to the prized European ones. In Argentine mountain areas cheeses are made from goat's milk; other areas produce fine cheeses from sheep's milk.[8] Grated and sliced cheeses are used in many dishes such as soups, casseroles, pasta dishes, and for dessert with fresh local fruits.[9]

Fruits and Vegetables
Fruits, fruit desserts, and fruit jams are widely used, but mostly in urban areas and among the upper classes. Many varieties of apples and pears,

quinces, peaches, and apricots, cherries and grapes as well as bananas, coconuts, pineapples and other tropical and semi-tropical fruits are available. The varying soils and climates are suited to different types of fruit cultivation.[9] Many types of preserves and jams form a part of breakfast with breads and a beverage, while fresh fruits are more likely to be a part of desserts at lunch or dinner. Typical of Argentina is a dessert of cheese served with a jam made from quince or sweet potatoes.[9]

Pumpkins and many types of squashes, sweet potatoes, and mealy white potatoes and corn are the principal vegetables used. Salad greens and other vegetables are mostly used in urban areas. *Gauchos* seldom eat either fruit or vegetables, surviving mainly on large quantities of roasted or boiled beef and YERBA MATÉ, the tea-like beverage sipped from a silver straw, called a BOMBILLA, placed in a gourd.[4]

Both squashes and corn are used in many interesting ways. Squash soup, squash fritters, baked squash puddings, and chunks of squash in stews such as CARBONADA CRIOLLA add colour and rich smooth flavour. In the CARBONADA, the rich beef stew is served in a hollowed out squash shell. In other dishes the chunks of squash are allowed to cook till they disintegrate into a thick golden mass, enriching the sauce by colouring and thickening it.

Corn is used imaginatively as well. Small chunks of corn are cooked together with beef and other vegetables in the CARBONADA, but grated green corn also forms the most important ingredient in HUMITAS, a spiced mixture of grated corn served as a side dish, or the mixture may be spooned into cornhusks called CHALAS then wrapped, tied and steamed. The HUMITAS EN CHALA are prepared exactly as they were hundreds of years before by the ancient Aztecs; the Mexicans call them TAMALES.[4,9] Cornflour cakes, buns and puddings abound in many variations. CHUCHOCA is the name given to maize toasted on hot coals, TIMBALES DE POLENTA betray the Italian name for corn (POLENTA) and refer to a type of cornmeal porridge, while MAZAMORRA is the name given to sugar-sweetened maize cooked in milk.[9]

Meats and Alternates

The favourite meat of the Argentine is beef. Huge quantities are consumed and it is not uncommon for beef to appear in each meal of the day. Uruguayans also enjoy sheep and lamb. In both countries, open air grills called *parrilla* are so commonly used to prepare ASADO (roasted meat) that it is said the tantalizing smell of meats roasting over wood fires may be called "the national aroma."[4]

Probably it is the *gauchos* (cowboys) of the Pampas who introduced the ASADO CON CUERO, meats in their natural state, that is with hide and hair intact, roasted over open wood fires.[9] Huge sides of beef, lamb, kid and sometimes pork may be cooked by this method. On smaller grills, together with meat chunks, many parts of the animal are grilled also in their natural state: chunks of intestine, liver, etc., all become part of the ASADA.

The Argentine appetite for meat can be noted in two popular appetizer dishes that often precede a hearty meal: MATAMBRE and EMPANADAS. MATAMBRE is a prepared piece of flank that is rolled up and stuffed with attractively arranged vegetables. After moist roasting or steaming, the roll is sliced and served hot or cold. EMPANADAS, from Spain, are half-moons of pastry well-filled with meats, olives and raisins. Pitchers of wines and assorted fruit punches wash down the appetizers and stave off hunger while the diners await the ASADA.[4]

Fresh fish and many varieties of seafood are available but do not form nearly as important a part of the diet as do the meats. Eggs are poached or fried and often top steaks or chops as a garnish. Eggs are also part of the caramelized FLAN that is a frequent dessert. Beans and nuts are not a widely used form of protein, although nuts may be used as snacks or ingredients in desserts and confections.

Breads and Cereals
A wide variety of breads, buns and rolls prepared from wheat, rye and cornflour is served at most meals. Bread is especially important for breakfast when it is usually served with butter and jams. Corn and rice become part of many dishes as well.

Fats
Beef fat, butter, and olive oil are used in cooking, baking and salads.

Sweets
Much sugar is taken in coffee, sugar-sweetened fruit punches and soft drinks, which are favoured beverages. Jams are a part of every breakfast. Many types of FLANS, custards and sweet puddings as well as confections made of fruit pastes, ground seeds (squash seeds, for instance) and nuts heavily sweetened and coloured may be seen often for desserts or on special festive occasions. As in Spain and Portugal, many convents are famed for the sweet confections and special-occasion cakes they prepare. DULCE DE LECHE is a thick, jam-like sweet that is prepared from the slow-cooking of milk and sugar.

Seasonings
In most of South America, onions, garlic and tiny hot peppers are the predominant seasonings used. Mostly the fresh natural flavours of fresh produce and ingredients prevail. Chocolate, sugar and vanilla are used in desserts as are the tangy flavours of fresh citrus juices or the grating of their rinds.

Beverages

Argentina and Uruguay produce sufficient quantities of grapes to produce some fine local wines, both white and red. Coffee is a favourite beverage but is taken so sweet that often even the beans are roasted with sugar. MATÉ is drunk mostly by country people who still brew a tea from the dried leaves of a holly tree. The liquid is steeped and drunk from a small gourd, by sipping through a BOMBILLA which has a rounded, sieve-type base which acts to strain the leaves.[4] YERBA MATÉ is popular in Argentina, Paraguay and parts of Chile and Brazil.

Brazilian

Brazil, occupying nearly half the continent, is the fifth largest country in the world.[10] The climate varies from tropical to sub-temperate and ranges over a topography that includes the highlands of the Brazilian Plateau to the Amazon River Basin, largely an uncharted area of flood plains and tropical rain forests. Despite the fact that only about one-fortieth of the land available for agriculture is actually cultivated, it is from these lands that Brazil supplies two-fifths of the world's coffee, is a leading producer of bananas and castor beans, takes second place in world production of cacao, corn and oranges, and third place in sugar and tobacco production.[10] Crops of rice and edible dried beans as well as thriving fishing and livestock industries add to the nation's table and general economy.

Brazil differs from every other country in South America. More than 60 per cent of the population is of European origin and Portuguese is the official language rather than Spanish which is common elsewhere. To the staple indigenous foods of beans and manioc, the Portuguese added the use of wine in cooking and as a beverage. They also added the many fish dishes for which the Portuguese are famed, especially those including BACALHAO or salt cod. The Portuguese added their COSIDAS (stews) and, most importantly, elevated the humble FEIJOADA of Portugal into an elaborate national buffet meal of Brazil still called by the same name, FEIJOADA COMPLETA.

Another important and different influence on the cultural development of Brazil was the importation of slaves from West Africa. Far from being absorbed, the slaves not only retained their own cultural traditions, taboos and food customs, they successfully made them a part of Brazil.[11] To the basic African food crops of bananas, coconuts, yams, okra, and many beans, spices and the small hot pepper called MALAGUETA, the Africans added the native corn, beans, and MANIOC. DENDÊ OIL, so characteristic of West African cooking and noted especially for the dense yellowish colour it adds to so many dishes, is extracted from an African palm. The negro slaves quickly became favoured cooks and wherever they cooked they also brought with them their basic utensils: mortar and pestle, gourds that were fashioned into bowls, measures, scoops and cooking utensils; grinding stones used to crush corn, beans or rice and earthenware or clay cooking utensils and wooden spoons. Many of these utensils were felt to have special magic properties and others related to certain taboos.

The rice originally brought by the Spaniards, and much favoured by the Portuguese, quickly became a staple food. In Brazil, the combination of black beans and white rice sprinkled with manioc meal is eaten at least once a day and often twice by every class of people, and is considered so basic that few salads or vegetables are served.[11] Black beans and rice are looked upon in the same way as bread on the table in many other countries. In fact it is known that servants and workers will not remain in a place where beans, rice and manioc are not part of the meals.[11]

Cozinha Baiana or Bahian Cuisine is the name given to the distinctive contributions of Brazil's African population.[12] The Bahian kitchen staples include *dendê* oil, coconut milk, fresh coriander, dried shrimps, sweet red or green peppers, ground almonds or peanuts. The hot pepper sauce made from crushed *malagueta* peppers in *dendê* oil is always on the table, as salt and pepper graces North American tables. Because sugar was often a luxury in Europe, the Negro slaves in charge of Brazilian kitchens used it lavishly to flavour many dishes and produce many intriguing sweet desserts to the delight of the Portuguese.[13] Bahia represents the area near the port of Salvador where the Negro slaves were first brought to Brazil.

But there are more than three basic influences upon the culture and food customs of Brazil. The native Indians, the Portuguese and the Negroes all have played their part, but so have the other immigrants. Germans, Italians and Japanese have all brought with them food favourites that have gradually become a part of the general cuisine. Evidence of the French cuisine is also a part of the Brazilian blend.[11]

FOODS COMMONLY USED

The staples of Brazilian cuisine are rice, black beans and manioc meal. To these may be added, according to income, location and class, the Portugese contributions of codfish dishes and other fish preparations, stews called *cosidas*, and the use of wine as a beverage and in cooking. Negroes from West Africa brought the tastes for *dendê* oil and hot *malagueta* peppers, condiments and sauces, coconut and coconut milk, dried shrimps and ground nuts (usually peanuts). These form an interesting cuisine when native fruits, grains and vegetables are added. Wine, YERBA MATÉ, and coffee are the favourite beverages.

Milk and Milk Products

Milk as a beverage is seldom used but much milk is consumed in custard-type desserts such as the Portuguese PUDIM FLAN, the caramelized baked custard so much loved in Spanish-speaking countries as well. Many varieties of cheeses are used with pastas, in creamy cheese sauces for vegetables and sometimes with fruits for desserts.

Fruits and Vegetables

Coconut and coconut milk are basic staples used in many dishes. Bananas and oranges are favourite fruits. Fruits familiar to North Americans are widely available together with persimmons introduced by the Japanese, fresh figs, pomegranates, melons of many types, breadfruit, citrus fruits, quinces and more than twenty-six tropical fruits unknown to North Americans.[11] Fruits are combined in salads with fresh vegetables, and sometimes fruits are a part of casseroles with meats and vegetables.

Palm hearts, avocados and artichokes are great favourites; stuffed avocados are often part of a buffet meal. MANIOC, the Brazilian favourite prepared as a flour from the tuberous root, was one of the ancient Indian crops together with corn and sweet potatoes. TAMALES or HUMITAS, that is a seasoned corn mixture wrapped and steamed in corn husks or banana leaves, is made in both Mexico and Brazil.[4] Salads and vegetables simply cooked by themselves are not popular in Brazil, but their use is increasing.[11] The Afro-Brazilians favour greens that take to long cooking, especially TAIOBA (also called "elephant's ears"), collards, okra and cabbage. The Japanese, especially around São Paulo, have been responsible for an increase in vegetable consumption through the produce of their truck gardens: asparagus, broccoli, beets, carrots, lettuce, leeks, scallions, parsnips, radishes, cucumbers, cauliflower, etc.

The *salus* is a special container lined in a black substance containing powerful germicides. All vegetables to be eaten raw are placed in the *salus* for one hour before serving.[11]

There is also a favoured place on the menu for the many squashes, gourds, pumpkin, chayotes and the many types of yams such as *cará* and *inhamé*.

Meats and Alternates

As in Argentina, beef is the most important meat eaten in Brazil. Some veal, pork and chicken are also used as available and where the budget permits. CHARQUE is a popular form of beef, especially with the working classes. Strips of beef are sun-dried while being brushed with a solution of salt and water. Brazilian labourers in the north and northeast areas live on black beans, rice, manioc and CHARQUE (also called CARNE SÊCA).[11] Southern labourers depend more on freshly barbecued meats (meat is more plentiful in the south), MANIOC, and *maté*, the popular beverage. CHURRASCO is the name for barbecue; most barbecued meats are prepared simply by grilling over a fire with the occasional salt-water brushing for flavour. *Gauchos* make their staple meal of the grilled meat dipped in manioc then washed down with MATÉ.

Beans are the third great staple food of Brazil, together with rice and manioc. Brazilians produce many types of beans but prefer the tiny black beans. Their great national and festive dish, FEIJOADA COMPLETA, is based on black beans; the name is taken from the Portuguese word for beans, *feijao*. Basic preparation involves cooking the beans till they are soft. A portion is removed and mashed with lard, chopped onion and minced garlic; returned to the bean pot this forms a flavourful smooth sauce to bathe the rest of the beans. TUTU DE FEIJÃO is the basic bean dish with manioc added to thicken it. Sometimes the beans are cooked with meat and sometimes with coconut milk.[4]

To the Brazilian family to whom the three staples are daily fare, the table setting is routine: a plate of prepared beans is garnished with a mound of cooked rice; there will be a shaker of hot pepper sauce and another of the fine grainy manioc. The manioc is similar to the North American farina and, sprinkled on the juicy beans, absorbs the moisture and flavours and adds the final filling touch.[4,11]

Many types of fish and seafood are used but two are outstanding in Brazilian cuisine: BACALHAO or dried salt cod and the dried shrimps so much a part of Afro-Brazilian cuisine. BACALHAO dishes are of Portuguese influence, while the dried shrimp strong in flavour show up in sauces like NAGÒ, a blend of dried shrimp, lemon juice, cooked and sliced okra, and *malagueta* peppers, served as a condiment with stews. MO-QUECA, originally a meat or shrimp mixture seasoned with *dendê* oil and coconut milk then packed in banana leaves to steam, has more recently been prepared in a pot then served with rice that has been cooked in coconut milk. ACARAJÉ is a puffy deep-fried dumpling made from the dried shrimp and mashed bean paste.[4,11] CARURÚ, the traditional stew of Bahia, incorporates fresh shrimp, sliced okra, shredded coconut all thickened with manioc then flavoured with *dendê* oil and crushed peanuts at the end – a blend of Brazil and Africa.

The Portuguese have never given up their taste for very sweet and often intricate desserts, many of which are made with incredible numbers of egg yolks or egg whites. It takes a skilful cook to prepare the FIOS DE OVOS, threads of egg yolks cooked in sugar syrup. These may be eaten as part of a dessert or may be used as a garnish for many other dishes.[11]

Brazilians enjoy soups especially for lunch. Most of these are rich hearty preparations thick with beans or rice and often containing many vegetables such as corn, yams, squash or pumpkin. One regional soup features peanuts and rice cooked in small cakes then served in bowls with a rich broth poured over.[11]

Peanuts have a small but special place in the Brazilian cusine. They are grown in Brazil and the Afro-Brazilians are familiar with their use in sauces (either crushed or chopped), for in Africa, where they are called groundnuts, they are widely used.

Breads and Cereals

Since wheat production is low in Brazil, wheat breads, made mostly in the cities, are prepared from imported wheat. Most common type of bread is similar to the long crusty white French loaf and is called PÃO FRANCÊS, with the smallest variety called BISNAGA. Many other types of breads are available as well as rolls, twisted breads, breads rich with milk and eggs like CUCA, which, with its topping of heavy cinnamon sugar and butter, is more of a coffeecake than a bread.[11] The name BROA is applied to any breads made with corn meal, and originates from the Portuguese bread of the same name.

Most Brazilians, however, do not eat breads in the European or North American sense. Their daily "bread" is the MANIOC so generously sprinkled on all dishes from a shaker called a FARINHEIRA.[11]

Rice is another basic staple cereal. Brazilian rice is well-seasoned and cooked light and fluffy. The rice is first tossed in a pan with fat or oil plus any desired seasonings. When all the grains are coated, the liquid for cooking is added. This may be water, broth, or often coconut milk. Desserts are prepared by cooking rice in milk and adding sugar, eggs, and sometimes raisins and nuts.

Probably the great variety of breads in the cities of Brazil, and the great variety of desserts and types of puddings and cakes, are due to the many types of flours available. Rice flour, cornmeal and cornflour, manioc meal as well as many types of wheat flours all add variety. Tapioca, hominy and crushed rice also thicken many desserts. The poor make porridges and a type of bread from the FARINHA DE MANDIOCA.

Cereal grains and flours form the basis of many special Brazilian dishes. FAROFA is the soft porridge-like dish made by cooking toasted manioc meal in water and butter. Many added ingredients can change it into different dishes that can be used as stuffings, side dishes to meats or fish, or into a small meal in itself. PIRAÔ is a bland molded pudding made very simply from corn starch, crushed rice or rice starch flour. Unmolded and served on a platter, it is used as a bland foil to spicy dishes of meats or fish.

Fats

Dendê oil is the most typical Brazilian fat. But beef fat, olive oil and butter are widely used as well. Lard is used in the flavouring of bean dishes and often for deep-fat frying.

Sweets

Brazilian "snacks" include hotdogs, hamburgers and wedges of hot pizza. Brazilian desserts are very sweet puddings, cakes, custards and the classic

PUDIM FLAN. They also enjoy DOCE DE LEITE, the thick caramel-like sweet made from slow-simmered milk and sugar. Gelatin desserts and many kinds of pudding mixes are also popular. Fantastic confection and candy creations and many special-occasion cakes are prepared by cooks in wealthy homes, and many convents finance schools by selling the exquisite sugar creations of their artistic nuns. These are especially famous in the area of Pernambuco which happens to be the area of highest sugar production in Brazil.[11]

The only similarity between the specialty dish called CUZCUZ and the North African COUSCOUS is that they are both steamed in colander-type pots set over boiling water. The CUZCUZ of northern Brazil differs from the CUZCUZEIRO made in the southern part. The northern version is a sweet dessert like a steamed cake made from starchy flour such as rice flour, cornstarch, corn or manioc flours flavoured with coconut milk, grated coconut and sugar. The southern version is not a sweet at all but a showy main dish where the starchy flour is mixed with meats, fowl or fish and well-seasoned and garnished like a steamed savoury pudding.[4,11]

Seasonings

Brazilian seasonings are usually thought of in terms of mixtures or sauces that are distinctively either African or Portuguese in origin. The native Indians ate their foods in simple natural flavours.

RÉFOGAR is the Portuguese art of marinating, or the technique used to cook almost any meat, seafood, fowl or vegetable by first sautéeing in a mixture of fat, onions, garlic, peppers, tomatoes, herbs and seasonings. Then the appropriate liquid is added and the cooking completed as desired.[13] The very simplest Portuguese RÉFOGAR consists of marinating the food in wine then cooking.[11]

TEMPÊRO literally means seasoning. Typical Brazilian TEMPÊRO is a blend of onions, garlic, parsley and tomatoes. The typical Afro-Brazilian TEMPÊRO is a blend of *dendê* oil, coconut milk and *malagueta* peppers.

Four typical sauces accompany all Afro-inspired dishes:

ACARJÉ SAUCE: a blend of *dendê* oil, onions, ginger, dried shrimp, and *malagueta* peppers.

PEPPER and LEMON SAUCE: hot peppers, lemon juice, salt *dendê* oil, garlic and onions. (Considered most popular.)

DENDÊ OIL and VINEGAR: a simple vinaigrette used for fish and seafood.

NAGÔ SAUCE: Served with stews, this sauce is a blend of *dendê* oil, lemon juice, dried ground shrimp and cooked sliced okra.

Beverages

Sweetened coffee served with milk begins the day for most Brazilians. Other meals are always concluded with a demitasse of coffee, and the same little demitasses of strong sweet coffee are part of meetings, chats, breaks and probably twenty other excuses to account for the average Brazilian intake (at least in urban areas) of twelve to twenty-four demitasses in a day.[11] Most popular method of preparing coffee is by the filter method. Without *cafezinho* what would a Brazilian do?

Probably the next favourite beverage would be GUARANÁ, a soft drink based on the flavouring extracted from a shrub of the same name. Innumerable fruit punches could also quench thirst and accompany snacks and meals as could wines for the sophisticated and *maté* for the *gauchos* or cowboys who claim that *maté* reduces hunger pangs and fatigue.[11] The fiery white CACHAÇA mixed with sugar and lemon juice may be downed between courses of the festive FEIJOADA COMPLETA. But its potency is only for the experienced few.[4]

Meal Patterns and Eating Customs

Brazilian cookery has a healthy helping of Afro-folklore and superstitions that have become a part of the kitchen. Perhaps with the attitude of "Why take a chance?" or simply because in many European homes the cook was of West African descent, many rituals and customs are a part of the daily meal preparation. Corn is believed to possess special virtues, beans are only considered good if cooked in a clay or earthenware pot, and special dishes based on vegetables and with minimal seasoning are often prepared as offerings to the gods.[4,14]

The early *dona de casa* (Brazilian housewife) was of pampered Portuguese background and only too pleased to hand over the tedious and skilled details of cookery to the black slaves. The West African women were not only skilled, they were pleased to find many familiar ingredients, and enjoyed the challenge of combining familiar old sauces and ingredients with the new meats, fruits, vegetables and sugar. It was they to whom most of the credit for the ingenious Brazilian cuisine must go.

The wealthy Brazilian middle-class families follow French meal-planning and service, and their menus are often a cosmopolitan blend of cuisines. Coffee is a symbol of hospitality at all times and always concludes a lunch or dinner.

Breakfast in most of South America is a simple affair usually consisting of strong, sweet coffee with hot milk and a variety of breads and rolls served with butter and jams.[11] Lunch is usually the heaviest meal of the day, featuring five or six courses usually including soup. The hot lunch is the rule whether taken at home or in a restaurant. Sandwiches are only served in small forms for appetizers or for teas; American-style hamburgers, hotdogs and pizza wedges are more likely to be nibbled as between-meal snacks. Wednesday and Saturday lunches as well as any festive occasions are the traditional times to serve FEIJOADA COMPLETA.

Almoço is the name for lunch, while *lanche* means an afternoon snack usually consisting of a beverage plus cookies or cakes. Formal teas are still a popular social event and the array of fancy pastries and cakes adequately illustrate the Brazilian love of sweets.[11]

Special Occasions

Most special occasions are marked by an elaborate presentation of the FEIJOADA COMPLETA, preceded by appetizers of EMPANADAS in small shapes either baked or fried and filled with mixtures of meats, raisins and seasonings. Family occasions may be marked by a huge cook-out and much drinking.

Christmas dinner is centred around a huge roast turkey with many side dishes or a roast suckling pig. Easter features some dish based on the dried salt cod, BACALHAO. But both occasions would be incomplete without a course of RABANADOS. This is a rich dish of crusty white French bread dipped in a mixture of eggs and port wine then fried in butter and served with generous dustings of cinnamon sugar and much coffee.

St. John's Day, June 24, is celebrated everywhere by preparing and eating dishes made with pumpkin or corn. In Bahia, the traditional sweet pudding of hominy and cinnamon is called MUNGUNZÁ. It can be prepared as a creamy pudding of hominy cooked in milk and well-flavoured with cinnamon and cloves, crushed roasted peanuts and rose flower water, or it may be made very thick and served in pieces.[11]

Chilean

South America has many unique characteristics. The Andes mountain range is the longest in the world, running 20,000 miles. The driest region in the world is the Atacama Desert of northern Chile. And Chile itself has a Pacific coastline of 2,600 miles, making it the longest country in the world in a north-south direction. The Andes mountains that rise like a wall between Chile and her neighbours are the reason for her relatively calm history and the fact that monkeys, jaguars and poisonous snakes do not mar her tranquillity.[15] It is in the Central Valley, with its temperate climate, that Chile grows her crops of grapes for wine, and all the familiar temperate-climate fruits as well as wheat, potatoes, corn, oats, rice and legumes such as chick peas, beans and lentils. Sheep, cattle and pigs graze on some of the lands but only about 25 per cent of the Chilean population is involved in any aspect of agriculture. More than 60 per cent is urban and many are involved either in the huge fishing industry or the copper of which Chile is said to have the largest deposits in the world.[15]

The Chilean settlers in the northern part of the country are mainly native Chileans while settlers in the south are immigrants, predominantly Germans. The original Indian descendants live in southern reservations and are all called simply the Auracanians, but are actually the remnants of many tribes. The majority of Chileans are a homogeneous group of Mestizos, that is a mixture of Spanish and aboriginal peoples.[16] Only the land shows great diversity from snow-tipped mountains to arid deserts and areas of rich agricultural yield.

From a slow and bloody beginning – the early Spanish settlers fought almost continually with the powerful Auracanian Indians – Chile has emerged from the colonial stage with many firsts. It was the first country in South America with the material signs of progress: railways, steamships, and telegraphs as well as one of the largest navies.[16] Some say the Chilean's calm and energetic personality is due to the temperate climate, while others trace it to the "Nordic stock" – from the many Germans, British, Irish and Scandinavians who were among the early settlers.[16]

Chileans enjoy large generous meals with many courses and enjoy beef as much as their Argentine neighbours, except that there is more seafood available than meats and fowl. In kitchens that are often painted a deep blue to keep away flies, Chilean cooks prepare their CAZUELAS or CURANTOS.[17] Preceded by appetizers, the CAZUELA is a rich rice-vegetable soup well-filled with chunks of meats or fish. Its origin is said to be from the pork stews of Milan called *cassolas*; these were brought to Chile by the *conquistadores* who had fought in Italy.[17] CURANTO is also called Chilean stew and is a slow oven-baked casserole of alternating layers of many different types of meats and sausages with shredded cabbage and seasonings. ALBONDIGAS, poached meatballs, EMPANADAS, the half-moon filled pastries, and SOPAIPILLAS, the fritters made with yams or pumpkins and served with brown sugar syrup, all hint of their Spanish background.

Chileans begin their day with a light breakfast of buttered rolls and coffee with sugar and boiled milk. Lunch will feature appetizers, a CAZUELA, a vegetable or fish course, a course based on legumes or pastas, a steak with french-fried potatoes, all served with any of the number of fine Chilean wines and followed by desserts in the Spanish manner (more than one and very sweet) or fresh fruits and finally coffee. Afternoon tea is common and consists of a brew of tea blended with *maté* and served with boiled milk and sugar. A variety of tiny sandwiches and pastries and an array of rich layered cakes will also be served. By eight in the evening, the average Chilean is ready for his dinner. A clear or cream soup will be followed by a fish course, then a meat course with a salad and finally a light dessert and coffee.[17]

Chilean bread is usually a long white crusty loaf resembling the long French bread stick, but many other varieties are made as well. Corn is used abundantly, and is given an imaginative range of tastes by being used in many forms from green to very ripe, each stage giving unique flavour to dishes. PASTEL DE CHOCLO is a classic Chilean dish rather like a meat pie with a topping of fresh ground corn baked to a custard rather than a pie crust. This is served in a large casserole or individual earthenware ones.[4] Beans in many varieties are used as abundantly as corn, because both grow in the country and are readily available.

Chilean cuisine features two unique sauces used for flavouring. Heating garlic and paprika in fat produces a warm, rich colour and fine flavour that is sometimes pepped up with AJI, those small fiery hot peppers. This sauce, either bland or peppery, is called COLOR. PEBRE is a more complex sauce of onions, garlic vinegar and olive oil plus chili and coriander. Like COLOR, PEBRE may also be zipped up with the addition of the hot AJI peppers. Both sauces and their variations are household standards much as salt, pepper, and ketchup are in North America.[4]

Colombian and Venezuelan

Both Colombia and Venezuela were explored and settled by Spaniards. Since the few local Indian tribes in the area proved primitive and unresisting to the Spanish conquest, the Spaniards found that their search for gold was far more hampered by the tangle of jungle and pestilence-ridden rivers.[4] But beyond the jungle-rimmed ocean fronts, they were surprised to discover temperate and pleasant valley areas, plateaus with jungle tropics on the one side and high mountains on the other. For many hundreds of years these early settlers created their own life-styles, almost completely isolated from the rest of the world, while honing the arts of agriculture and cuisine and making the most of land, climate and skills. Corn, many kinds of potatoes, yuca (sweet cassava), avocados, green bananas, plantains and beans became the staples of their kitchen together with whatever fresh tropical fruits the jungles below them yielded. Lean, grass-fed cattle, hogs and chickens multiplied and provided variety for the table as well as the many types of seafood that could be caught or brought in.

From the early Spanish and Indian beginnings, the lands now possess rich oil reserves in Venezuela while Colombia is famous as the world's second producer of fine coffee. Many cereal grains and vegetables, sugar cane, rice, and bananas as well as coconuts, pineapples, peanuts and cacao today more than round out the foodstuffs for a varied table.[18]

Because of the low rate of immigration, the population is fairly homogeneous, being predominantly a mix of Spanish, Indian and some Negro ancestry, almost all Roman Catholic and Spanish-speaking.

The jungle peoples of Colombia and Venezuela are either strongly Indian or African and live on a subsistence level with yuca, plantains, corn and beans as their diet mainstays. The diet is occasionally supplemented with any animals or birds they can hunt and, at certain times of the year, with varieties of ants which are considered a delicacy.[4] The rest of the population dine on some exotic tropical animals and birds occasionally too, but their mainstays are not much different from those used by the rest of South America.

Beef, veal, pork and chicken are usually prepared by cooking slowly in a sauce that is well-seasoned and often sparked with chunks of vegetables such as white and sweet potatoes, yuca (cassava), plantain, and squash. One such typical Colombian dish is SANCOCHO ESPECIAL. When the richly flavoured stew is cooked, the savoury broth is served from a tureen and the meat and colourful vegetables (plus chunks of corn on the cob) are served from an attractively arranged platter. Okra is another vegetable that is used in many stew and soup dishes. Avocado lends its smoothness to sauces, dips and soups. Coconut, grated coconut and coconut milk flavour many dishes and desserts: PATO CON COCO is duck in a coconut sauce, while ARROZ CON COCO Y PASAS is a side dish of rice and raisins cooked in coconut milk.[19] Potatoes, yuca and plantain are often served as crispy nibbles or snacks by slicing them thinly then deep-frying to form chips.

It is no surprise that in Colombia, a country that grows both coffee and sugar cane, there would be many delightful recipes for drinks featuring coffee well-flavoured with rum. The people of both countries enjoy many demitasses of coffee throughout the day and always to end a meal.

Peruvian

In a land where mountains, jungles and gorges make transportation and communication difficult, the llama is an eminently sensible and reliable beast of burden. The Indians pursue a simple life. Many are shepherds, while others reap crops of corn, potatoes, barley, manioc, beans and QUINA (Peruvian wheat). The sheep help to alleviate the perennial shortage of meat, while their wool is important for the Peruvian textile industry. Sugar, rice and coffee are important crops as well.

Like most other South American countries, Peru has witnessed a turbulent history. It began with the Spaniards who were attracted by the legends of gold and silver said to be in the area, then remained to rule oppressively over the Incas who had for so long lived with a theocratic government of their own.[20] For 200 years discontent rumbled and finally exploded into an Indian revolt in 1780 which was crushed but led in subsequent years by revolts of Creoles (those of Spanish descent born in America) who resented the Spanish aristocracy's exploitation.[20] In almost every country of South America it was these revolts that led finally to the independence of each country, with Peru being one of the last, in 1821.

The early Incas lived quite well on crops of corn, beans, various roots, jungle fruits and fish. The Creole cuisine that later evolved from a mixture of ancient Indian customs and traditions brought by the Spaniards is said to be one of the best in South America.[4] The Creole cuisine of the coastal areas reflects the greater abundance and variety of foods that are available, while that of the mountain areas unfortunately reflects poverty and hungry times.

In the worst of times, potatoes serve as the mountain staple. They are eaten simply boiled, sometimes with a hot AJI pepper sauce, and in better times they are served with a cheese and milk sauce (a side dish on the tables of wealthier coastal Peruvians). PAPAS A LA HUANCAINA is a dish that combines the good yellow potatoes of the Indians with the cheese of the Spaniards. CUY or South American cavy is said to be the ancestor of the guinea pig and is widely used both in the coastal and mountain cuisines. The flavour and texture is said to resemble rabbit and many interesting grilled and stewed dishes are made from it.[4,21]

The festive occasion in almost any Andean area demands the careful preparation of a PACHAMANCA. A deep pit is dug to form the basis for the earth oven which is then filled with wood and straw and topped with rocks. After the wood has burned and the rocks are red hot, moist green leaves form a base for all the good foods – whole young pigs or goats, casseroles or rice, many types of potatoes and vegetables – all to be eaten many hours later when well-cooked, together with drinking and dancing.[4]

Coastal Peruvian cuisine reflects the wealthy homes, well-staffed kitchens and the heritage of their owners. Spanish dishes prevail, but certain Peruvian specialties are valued too. Grilled cubed heart on small skewers are called ANTICUCHOS, much enjoyed as street snacks or appetizers in large homes. Fried fish slices and the pickled raw fish called CEVICHE (also popular in Mexico) may also be served to start an ample meal. Shrimps and scallops in many forms may also be offered as appetizers, the scallops often served raw with sauces.[4] A hearty soup with several kinds of meat, wheat, rice and many vegetables usually follows. Only the broth is served to the guests; servants eat the boiled parts of the soup. Another soup similar to a fish chowder is called CHUPE and still other soups become the whole meal with the broth served first, then other ingredients attractively arranged and served with a variety of peppery and spiced sauces afterwards.[4,21]

The main course of meat may come to the table as stews, roasts or in a heap of fine shreds. This latter technique of serving boiled, tough meat makes it easier to chew and more attractive in appearance. It is also a common technique in Mexico.

Peanuts, believed to be originally from South America (peanuts have been found in ancient pre-Inca tombs)[4] are widely used, mostly crushed and as a flavour in sauces. Some recipes use boiled peanuts, in which case they have little flavour but add a mealy texture.

Bananas are widely used also. When green they are thinly sliced and fried to form appetizer chips. The people of Ecuador, which produces huge banana crops, frequently use mashed bananas simply mixed with flour and other ingredients to create a great variety of breads and pastries. Sautéed bananas is one of the simplest desserts in Central and South America and almost as popular as the PUDIM FLAN. Slit, peeled bananas are warmed and coated in a sauce of butter and brown sugar then flambéed with rum and/or brandy. Served as they are, or with ice cream or whipped cream, they make a delighful ending for any South American meal.

THIRTY-THREE

Lebanese and Syrian

In the area of the Middle East known as the Fertile Crescent, where the summers are dusty and hot and the winters cool and rainy, lie the four Arabic nations of Iraq, Jordan, Lebanon and Syria. They share a common heritage, many common problems and a very similar cuisine.

It is difficult to believe that in the parched hills north of Iraq lies an area that is believed to be the home of modern agriculture. Here primitive peoples are said to have first tamed sheep, grown wild wheat and even cultivated fruits. The sheep were used for wool, milk, meat and as a source of fat. The wild wheat, carefully nurtured, formed the basis of early man's existence. It was used in the form of porridges, gruels and assorted types of simple breads baked on stones from coarse flour and water mixtures. Craggy olive trees were first cultivated for their oil but it was not long before the fruit was also appreciated as a food: green olives, ripe black olives and olives that were cured in oil or vinegar or enjoyed with spices. Even the pruned olive branches could be used as fuel or carved to form implements. Grapes were enjoyed as a fresh fruit and fermented to form wines. The delicately luscious fresh figs were enjoyed at first only in local areas where they grew, but when sun-drying was used to preserve them, they became a favoured fruit in many other areas.[1,2]

Today in Iraq, the same ancient foods form the dietary staples. Every part of the sheep is enjoyed: meats are roasted, offal simmered in broths made from cracked bones; milk is used for cheeses and fat from the fat-tailed sheep is used in cookery. TURSHI, a mix of pickled vegetables, accompanies a usual meal of broth, wheat bread and select bits of sheep such as the tongue, sheep's head or stomach. Olives are a staple and frequent food; grapes and figs too. The Tigris and Euphrates Rivers yield fish that require only the simplest of broiling and seasoning to make a memorable meal.

The Hashemite Kingdom of Jordan is also part of the Fertile Crescent where, because of present arid conditions, the once-fertile area now only barely supports camels, sheep, goats and cattle. Today, as in many other Arab countries, special cultivation of legumes such as beans and lentils, vegetables such as okra, eggplant and varieties of pumpkins and squashes, and fruits such as citrus and bananas all add to the daily dietary.

The Fertile Crescent was so-named not only because this was the area believed to be the start of agricultural and pastoral occupations, but also because in ancient history it was a "mentally fertile" area as well. About 1700 B.C.E. Syria itself was the home of an advanced culture, much affected by the complex systems of law and religion and even the art of writing believed to have developed very early in the ancient Iraqi area of Mesopotamia.[2]

It is this same area that attracted waves of conquerors throughout history, each bringing their own cultures and each leaving behind some indelible mark on the peoples of those lands. Attacks by Assyrians and Chaldeans were soon forgotten when Syria, Jordan (then part of Palestine), Iraq and Lebanon (then part of Phoenicia) were all melded as part of Alexander the Great's empire in 332 B.C.E.[3] Hellenistic culture and customs touched everything from the architecture of the cities to the food on the tables: MEZE, assorted small appetizers taken with ARAK (similar to OUZO); tart egg-lemon sauces and rice-stuffed vegetables; even the sweetly-rich phyllo pastries.

The Roman Empire and then the Byzantine Empire each held their place for a time in the affairs of the Fertile Crescent. But the greatest influence of all was to come in 636 C.E. when the Muhammedans conquered Syria from the Byzantine Empire and established Damascus as the centre of the Muslim Caliphate. With the spread of Islam came the practice of the Laws of the Koran which included Friday as the day of rest, prescribed hours of daily prayer, man's acquisition of as many as four wives and their carefully secluded position within the home, and the dietary laws proscribing wine and pork. The entire area is still predominantly Muslim today, but this has not brought the end of wars or hardship.

Yet another empire was rising, and it was to be so powerful that its grip over this coveted area would last for 400 years. In 1516 C.E., the Fertile Crescent fell to the Turkish Ottoman Empire.

The Lebanon of today traces its ancestry to the ancient merchants and seafarers known as the Phoenicians. It is an ancestry that still boldly characterizes the Lebanese penchant for travel and for business. Although frequently listed as "Syrian" in foreign immigration files, a more careful study shows that 95 per cent of the emigrants from the Near East to other parts of the world are in fact from Lebanon.[4] Beirut, the capital of Lebanon, is also known as "the Paris of the Middle East." Beirut has earned this title not only as a cosmopolitan city of culture and entertainment, but also as a vital commercial and banking centre and one of the most important seaports of the area.

Lebanese have emigrated from their homeland partly because of their adventurous spirit but also because of poverty and persecution. The largest flood of emigration occurred after 1860, a date marking one of the worst religious persecutions which sent Christian Lebanese to any part of the world where they could find religious freedom. The majority settled into business or professional activities, but most have retained their fluent Arabic, their native celebrations and customs, their deep devotion to the church and their food specialties.[4]

Because France had occupied both Lebanon and Syria during World War I, she was given a mandate over both countries by the League of Nations. In 1920, therefore, Lebanon became officially "detached" from Syria but actually did not attain independence until 1943. Both Lebanon and Syria simmered with hostility under the French rule which lasted twenty years and was disrupted by British intervention in 1943. By 1946 Syria, too, gained independence. To this day, not only Arabic but French and English are fluently spoken by the educated upper class of both countries.[2,3]

Life moves more slowly in Syria than in Lebanon. Most of Syria's population is concentrated in the coastal region and the cities; few live in the vast Syrian desert.

Lebanon's population is almost equally divided between Druses and Christians. The Druses are a religious sect considered to be an outgrowth of Islam but with both Judaic and Christian ideals.

Syria's population is overwhelmingly Muslim with the next largest group being Bedouins, then small groups of Druses and still fewer Jews.[3]

Agriculture and animal husbandry provide the main occupations for 75 per cent of Syria's population. Lebanon is one of the few countries in the whole area whose gross national product is not from agriculture but from commerce. This accounts for the different pace of life and life-style. In fact, it is the only Arab country with a predominance of Christians.

The nomadic Bedouin tribes are principally the inhabitants of the desert and there are approximately 300,000 tribes in this area. They profess the faith of Islam, but such is the power of the sheiks of various tribes that they grant themselves some latitudes in interpretation of the faith. They may be divided into three broad groups: "Bedouins of the Camel," "Bedouins of the Sheep," and "Settled Tribes."

The first group are truly nomadic and roam the driest desert areas. Their tents, their clothing and even their food is derived almost entirely from camels, for they use the camel hair for cloth and the milk and meat for food. Dates are also important in their dietary; anything else they may require is bartered.

The "Bedouins of the Sheep" are less nomadic and tend to live nearer large cities. Wool from their sheep is used in making tents and clothing and the sheep also supply milk and meat. This diet may be supplemented with bartered rice and some local vegetables. Honey, locusts and lizards may also form a part of their food.[3,6]

The "Settled Tribes" follow general agricultural pursuits and in many cases have adapted themselves into the customs of the areas.

The many peoples who inhabit the Fertile Crescent share a common heritage of historic conquerors all of whom were intensely aware of the strategic value of this crossroads location. The people share, too, the common problems of poverty and illiteracy, as well as periodic political and religious upheavals. But hope for the future lies in the warm and unstinting sense of hospitality that is also common to all these peoples. The open door and the dual symbols of the fig tree and the olive branch bespeak the hope of peace and plenty for all.

Home Life and Facilities

The peoples of Syria and Lebanon share with this entire area of the Middle East a complexity of contrasts. It is impossible to paint a picture of "average." There is no average life-style, only contrasting extremes. The wealthy lead an entirely different life-style from the poor; the nomads differ greatly from those who are settled in groups. All share the gracious and generous display of hospitality, the typical Mediterranean sense of time, and a pride in food traditions.

Even the humblest shopkeeper will take time to converse and offer tiny cups of sweetened tea or coffee before conducting business; Bedouins will invite passing strangers to dine with them; and hospitality in private homes invariably offers a buffet of local delicacies. It is not unheard of that the poorest widow may slaughter her only goat to present a meal for a visitor. One can then only imagine the sumptuous repast presented by the wealthy.

The Mediterranean "sense of time," although often suggested by the saying "If Allah wills it," really has little to do with the Muslim faith. Mealtimes, social and business engagements and even international appointments may be delayed hours or even days much to the chagrin of punctual foreigners. Every minute seems to count to the bustling Westerner: but the Middle East people move about their daily affairs with a sense of eternal time. What is not done today will be surely accomplished tomorrow, if Allah wills it.

Perhaps as an extension of hospitality, larger cities - especially Beirut and Lebanon - all offer foods for the homesick tourist; anything from English fish and chips to Japanese saki may be found in suitable restaurants catering to these desires.[7] But in every home it is likely that traditional dishes and local specialties hold the spotlight. Small appliances and kitchen gadgets can never gain great popularity where the hands of many servants are still readily available; but those who can afford them enjoy the use of small refrigerators. With only few exceptions, most women make their homes the centre of their interests, supervising children and cookery with the aid of as many servants as they can afford.[2] In rural areas, the women add many agricultural tasks and care of animals to their daily work routine.

FOODS COMMONLY USED

There is no difference in the basic cuisine of the Syrian or Lebanese kitchen. The staple foods for both include wheat which is used for many types of breads and the popular BURGHUL as well as rice which is the basis of many dishes; LEBAN, yoghurt and MADZOON are all forms of cultured (soured) milk served at any meal and eaten with bread, pilafs, meats or fruits. Olives are the most useful and widely planted fruit; tropical and semi-tropical fruits are eaten seasonally as available and according to means. Eggplant, tomatoes, onions and potatoes head the list of vegetables most widely available but in many areas wild greens also supplement the diet. Aside from milk and local cheeses, legumes are the most widely used protein source in the form of many varieties of peas, beans and lentils used as soups and stews. The favourite meat is lamb eaten several times a week by those who can afford it and only on special occasions by the poor. The use of many exotic herbs and spices, especially garlic and cinnamon, are common; while olive oil adds its richness to many dishes.

In considering the foods commonly used by both groups, the climate, topography and agricultural systems cannot be overlooked. The varied topography and climate of Lebanon as well as its advanced technology and the fact that it is the most Westernized of all Arab countries are all factors that contribute to the important fact that while the staples are the same, the Lebanese diet invariably includes more quantity, quality and variety than does the average Syrian diet.[6] Both the Syrian herdsmen and the agriculturalists tend to work on a subsistence basis; that is, they plant or herd only enough to supply their own needs and contribute little to local markets. Combine this subsistence philosophy with the limited rainfall and primitive farming and pastoral techniques and the limitations of the Syrian diet can be readily seen.[6]

Milk and Milk Products

Necessity and availability dictate food customs. Thus it is not surprising that the combination of dry hot climate and the lack of storage and transportation facilities all combine to make the use of soured milk products most practical. Milk is used from whatever is locally available: sheep, goats, cows or camels. Soured or fermented milk produces yoghurt, LEBAN and MADZOON. LABNEH is a delicate fresh cheese prepared in most homes simply by allowing yoghurt to drip overnight in a cloth bag. Some locally made cheeses are preserved in salt brine or olive oil.

Fresh fluid milk is not popular. Pasteurization of milk is available in some of the larger cities only, otherwise fresh milk may be sold locally in small quantities. But unhygienic handling is common and often the milk may be skimmed or adulterated with the addition of water.[6] Sometimes boiled milk with bread may form a breakfast dish.[9]

Fruits and Vegetables

The fruit of the vine, grapes, and the olive tree are important additions to almost everyone's table. Wine is not used by observant Muslims but fresh grapes of every variety are eaten in season and dried as raisins or used to make a type of molasses.[6] Olives are eaten green or ripe and in many forms including spiced, oiled, brined and vinegared. Melons and citrus fruits, stone fruits such as peaches, cherries and apricots as well as dates and figs, quinces, pomegranates, apples and plums are all enjoyed seasonally, locally and as the budget permits. AARAK, a national drink in Lebanon, is distilled from grape alcohol. Dried figs, dates and raisins are also enjoyed but KAMARADINE, a form of dried apricots pressed into sheets, is especially popular.[6,8]

Middle East housewives often have their own small vegetable gardens where fresh beans, cabbage, scallions, cucumbers, tomatoes, squashes, okra and even their own onions and garlic may be grown.[8] The eggplant is a special favourite. Vegetables may be cooked, puréed and blended with garlic and olive oil to be used as an appetizer dip with bread. Stuffed vegetables, well-spiced and vinegared pickled vegetables as well as salads of fresh vegetables dressed with lemon juice, olive oil and fresh black pepper – all are enjoyed and used when available. When available, a side plate of cucumbers, fresh onions and olives is a common sight at most meals.

Meats and Alternates

More than any other food, meat takes on class distinctions. The rural poor rarely if ever eat meat and then it is usually an old animal about to die anyway, or on a special occasion warranting the slaughter for food. The favourite Syrian and Lebanese meat is lamb – and nothing is wasted. Offal and bones lend their meaty flavour to many dishes while other parts of lamb may be roasted whole or skewered for KABABS and frequently used as ground lamb in the national dish of KIBBE (ground lamb and BURGHUL) or in the many PILAFS (rice dishes) and stuffed vegetables. Chicken and beef are also used. Except for lamb (which is slaughtered very young and therefore tender) most other meats used by the Syrians and Lebanese require either marinating or slow moist cooking for tenderness as cattle and poultry tend to be lean and tough.

All legumes have an important place in the diet. Soups made of orange or brown lentils, chick peas, dried beans of many varieties as well as vegetable and bean stews are all well-liked and may form the main dish or at least an important part of the meal. Legume dishes may be enjoyed at any meal (even breakfast) and are served warm or cold.[8,10]

Fish is usually prepared in a complex way: browned fish pieces heavily seasoned with cayenne and garlic then simmered in a broth and served chilled (YAKHNIT SAMAK EL HARRAH); sautéed onions and pine nuts tossed with cooked rice and saffron then served with olive-oil fried fish (RIZ BI SAMAK); or the classic SAMAK TAHINI, an elaborately baked fish served with a sauce of sesame seed oil and lemon juice. In Syria this dish is liberally touched with onion while in Lebanon the same dish is preferred liberally flavoured with garlic.

Eggs are not plentiful but are enjoyed scrambled, sometimes lightly flavoured with powdered cumin seed for breakfast.

Although minimum food preservation techniques are used, especially in rural areas, the fat-tailed sheep do provide important winter food for many. The mutton is heavily salted and rolled in its own fat for later use.[8]

Almonds, walnuts and pistachios are widely grown and used in desserts, pastries, rice dishes and eaten roasted and salted as nibbles.

Breads and Cereals

Bread is unquestionably the "staff of life" and the basis of every meal. For the poor it may often be the only food augmented at times by olives and some form of soured milk. Wheat breads in many varieties are the favourite but breads made from corn, barley or millet – sometimes in varying quantities with wheat flour – are used by the rural poor. The exact type of bread depends on locality and income.[6]

Wheat that has been boiled, dried and cracked into fine, medium and coarse grains is called BURGHUL in Arabic, while BULGUR is the common Western name.[10] This versatile nourishing grain forms the basis for several classic dishes:

KIBBE: lean lamb meat is pounded to a smooth paste and combined with BURGHUL, seasoned with garlic and cinnamon, layered in a pan and oven-baked. Served with melted butter poured over and cut in diamond shapes. This is called KIBBE BIL SINEEYAH. Raw KIBBE mixture is called KIBBE NEYEE. The same mixture shaped into ovals, hollowed out with one finger and stuffed with ground lamb and pine nuts then fried in hot butter is called KRAS MIHSHEE. In whatever shape, cooked or raw, BURGHUL and lamb make KIBBE the classic dish of Syria and Lebanon.

TABOULEH or TABOOLEY: soaked BULGHUR is drained and tossed with fresh minced parsley and other greens and flavoured tartly with fresh lemon juice. A favourite salad and appetizer.

Rice is the next commonly used cereal. Many varieties are used: polished, unpolished and brown. All find their way into aromatic mixtures for stuffed vegetables (often with ground lamb and pine nuts) or moulded into PILAFS.

Fats

The most widely used fats are olive oil and clarified butter. The latter is made from sheep or goats' milk and is commonly called either GHEE or SAMNEH. Clear golden olive oil is used both in cooking and frequently as a final shimmering touch to puréed vegetables, PILAFS, cold cooked vegetables or bean dishes.

Sweets

Throughout most of the Middle East, sweets are very sweet. Confections of seeds and nuts, fruit drinks and even tea and coffee are heavily sugared, and pastries are layered and drenched in honey or sugar syrups. These treats are taken at the end of meals or as mid-afternoon or evening snacks, sometimes with seasonal fruits. The poor seldom taste such luxuries, their treat being the sweetened tea or coffee or the occasional use of dried fruits, most likely dates, when available.[6] For many villagers DIBS, a molasses made from fruits, is an important sweetener.[6]

Seasonings

Spices are the great deceivers; in places where foods are simple the arts of seasoning reach great heights in order to deceive the body that a great meal has been eaten. Syria and Lebanon are no exception. SFEEHA, those peppery little meat pies which are a specialty of Syrian homemakers, can be made of fine ground lamb and pastry or a highly spiced filling of legumes. KISHIK, a fine powder made from LEBAN, flour and spices, is used for adding flavour to soups and even some egg dishes; sometimes it may form a soup simply by adding water. TARATOUR is a classic sauce made from sesame seed oil and lemon juice often zipped up with garlic, and used for many dishes, especially fish, or simply as a dip for bread. ZAHTER is a blend of thyme and sumac and is used to season breads.

Cinnamon, coriander and mint, olive oil, yoghurt and lemon juice. Scarcely a dish can be prepared without at least one. But even more common is the pungency of onions and garlic and the peppery hotnesss of fresh ground black and white peppers and cayenne. Syrians tend to favour onions, while the Lebanese show a preference for garlic.

Toasted nuts and seeds spread their rich flavour through many dishes, while crushed nuts and seeds, syrup and honey and flavours from rose water and orange flower water as well as anise lend an exotic touch to desserts and pastries.

Beverages

NBEETH (wine) is enjoyed by the Christians. AARAK, an anise-flavoured liquor, is enjoyed by many as an appetizer with the varied MEZES, dozens of small morsels of pickled and spiced vegetables and olives, salted and roasted nuts, legumes and seeds, purées of spiced garlic-rich seeds and vegetables and many other tidbits. Many drinks made from mixtures of fruit juices or fruit syrups (such as rose petal syrup) blended with plain or sparkling bottled water as well as locally made beers are all popular refreshers.

Sweetened tea spiced with cinnamon or flavoured with mint is called SHAI (note similarity to Chinese name CH'AI) but the most honoured beverage of all and the symbol of hospitality is KAHWAH, coffee.

Yet in countries where water is at such a premium, a humble drink of plain water is highly esteemed and often will be seen taken from a BREEK, a special water jug. The art of pouring water from the BREEK's spout into the mouth without either touching or spilling takes practice.

Meal Patterns and Eating Customs

Arab peoples have a deep respect for elders and family. Early risers love to stroll through their walled gardens or go out at a very early hour to take coffee and fruit with friends or relatives – even before breakfast. Bread, cheese and olives can make a meal anytime, and for the *fellaheen* probably do. For others, freshly prepared coffee will be accompanied with wheat bread and fresh cheese, olives and perhaps eggs scrambled with ZAHTER. A serving of fresh seasonal fruit such as melon or ripe figs may conclude the FUTOOR (breakfast).

The main noon meal, GATHA, is often the largest of the day unless guests are expected for the evening meal which is usually taken at sundown. GATHA may consist of one or two filling dishes, dessert and coffee. In wealthier homes many courses are served, preceded by AARAK and MEZES. There is never any problem of leftovers as these become the food for servants. ASHA is the name given to the customary light meal at sundown. It consists of salads, bread, cheese, vegetable stews or vegetable PILAFS.

In traditional Muslim homes and in the Bedouin tent, an ordered ritual of hospitality is followed. It matters little whether the meal offered is only bread and cheese or a few dates or the Bedouin festive fare of MANSAF (shredded cooked lamb heaped on a mound of cooked rice with soured milk poured over all) and SHRAK, the thin layers of wheat bread baked on a dome, or a many-course display of KABABS, KIBBE, TABOULEH, stuffed grape leaves and cabbage leaves, rice-stuffed young zucchini and tomatoes. Whatever the main meal, it will be preceded with ceremonial handwashing and prayers of grace. Frequently the host will stand apart and enjoy watching his family and guests enjoy the meal, eating only with three fingers of the right hand; sometimes he will join the feast. Traditionally only men eat together and only men servants wait upon them. After they have completed their meal, with belt-loosening, lip-smacking and even a few belches of satisfaction, the leftovers are removed and eaten in another area by the men servants. What they leave becomes the meal for women and children.[2]

Traditional Syrian and Lebanese meals are served on carpeted floors decked with white cloths and surrounded with many plump pillows for the comfort of the diners. More modern homes provide tables and chairs but still enjoy settling into soft pillows after dinner for the *narghile* (water-pipe) and coffee and the inevitable platter of BAKLAVA.

Christian homes follow some of the above traditions, except that women are a part of the meal with the men. For both Christians and Muslims, many small dishes of assorted appetizers and many rounds of AARAK, usually diluted with water to a milky white, precede the main meal.

Special Occasions

Syrians are mostly of the Muslim faith, while the Lebanese are made up of almost 52 per cent Christians (Maronites, Greek Orthodox and Greek Catholic) and the remainder predominantly Muhammedans, mostly Druses.[3,6] The creed of the Druses is basically Muslim with some elements of Judaic-Christian principles.

Since legendary hospitality is an everyday matter among the Arab peoples, as is the elevation of simple ingredients to gastronomic creations, the gracious manners and display of special foods for special occasions know no limits – except perhaps the pocketbook of the host. Days of preparation precede any feast or happy family occasion: lamb, kid or camel are ritually slaughtered and knowing hands prepare the classic dishes, such as:

SYRIAN SFEEHA: peppery hot little meat pies made with thin yeast dough.

HUUMUS BI TAHINI: puréed chick peas brightly seasoned and blended with sesame seed paste (TAHINI), garlic and lemon juice. This smooth mix is spread flat on platters and swirled with a decoration of olive oil and sprinkled pine nuts or parsley (coriander).

KIBBE BIS SINEEYAH or SAYNIYYI: bulghur and finely minced lamb seasoned with spice (cinnamon, allspice, pepper) and layered in a pan, drizzled with olive oil and or melted butter, marked into diamonds and baked.

KIBBE NAHYEH: same mixture as above but served raw in a mound on a platter to be eaten with broken pieces of bread.

TABOULEH: a tangy fresh salad made of soaked, drained bulghur tossed with chopped vegetables such as parsley, onions, tomatoes, etc. All tartly flavoured with lemon juice.

BABA GHANOUJ: smooth smoke-flavoured purée of cooked eggplant (charring of the skin gives smoky taste), minced garlic olive oil and lemon juice. Eaten with pieces of bread.

DOLMAHS: the wrapping may be any green leaves: chard, spinach, grape leaves, cabbage. The filling will likely be a blend of cooked rice, pine nuts, cinnamon and ground lamb.

LUBIA BISHMI: a slow-simmered stew of lamb (kid or camel) with tomatoes and green beans. Served with a rice PILAF of saffron, rice, pine nuts, melted butter and/or yoghurt.

The above list represents only the classic festive dishes of the Syrian-Lebanese cuisine. There are many other lesser dishes. Besides the tidbits that have been previously mentioned and many that may come to mind, there are many exotic specialties such as miniature SFEEHA, pickled grapes, pickled tomatoes, pickled walnuts, pickled eggplant, spicy vegetable or legume purées to be scooped up with broken bread, and many variations of the BOUREK or BOREK which are tiny rolls or triangles of butter-drenched PHYLLO pastry filled with cheese, meat or vegetable mixtures.

That is still not the end. To complete the picture, the leisurely ending of the feast would be KAHWAH, tiny cups of Arabian coffee enjoyed with the passing around of the *narghile* and interrupted only by conversation and a few platters of BAKLAVA.[10,11,12]

The sweetness of weddings is emphasized by a series of festivities preceding the special day. Guests are served trays of sweet pastries, nuts, confections and KAHWAH. Candy-coated almonds are a special symbol of a sweet and prosperous life.[8] The wedding feast itself would feature all the traditional dishes with kid and lamb forming the main festive dishes.

For Christians, Lent marks the beginning of a pensive period of fasting and abstinence, but it is introduced with festivities featuring games, dancing and costumes. *Marfeh* is the name given to the preceding two weeks: the first is a week of meat-fare dishes followed by a week of cheese-fare dishes. Meat and cheese, indeed all foods of animal origin, will not be eaten again by the Orthodox Christians until Easter itself.[8] The forty somber days of Lent as observed by the pious Christians follow a dietary pattern of mostly cold foods made from olive oil, legumes, vegetables, grains and breads. These same fast-day foods are also served at other fast days during the year:

JANUARY 5, Eve of Epiphany;
JUNE 29, Fast of the Holy Apostles for one week from All Saints' Sunday
     to the Feast Day of the Holy Apostles (June 29);
AUG. 1-15, Fast of Theotokas;
AUG. 29, Fast of the Beheading of St. John the Baptist;
SEPT. 14, The Elevation of the Holy Cross;
NOV. 15-25, Fast before Christmas.

It should be noted that many strictly observant Orthodox Christians
also maintain a year-long fast on Wednesdays and Fridays of each week.
The Wednesday fast is said to be in memory of the betrayal of Christ,
while the traditional Friday fast is in memory of Christ's death on the
cross.[8] The very elderly, those who are sick and young people under the
age of twenty-one do not follow the fasts.

Easter is one of the most important occasions on the calendar of Christians and the colourful ceremonies are concluded with the eating of eggs
to break the abstentions of the previous weeks. With joyous gatherings,
the festival is ended with the classic dishes of feasting.

But not all the Christian religious occasions are ones of penitence and
fasting. There are also twelve special feast days, some with specific foods
to mark them, and all with as many classic festive dishes as the family can
afford. Some of these include:

MAR. 25, Annunciation of the Virgin Mary, when seafoods are eaten;
AUG. 6, Transfiguration of Christ, when a special fish (SAMAK) meal is
     served;
AUG. 15, Assumption of Mary;
DEC. 4, St. Barbera, when IYUOK, a traditional yellow barley pudding
     is served.
JAN. 6, Feast of Epiphany, the oldest and one of the most important
     feast days. The day is spent in prayer and church services fol-
     lowed by the priests visiting homes to bless every corner of each
     room with prayers and holy water. AWAM and ZALABEE (round
     and ring-shaped fritters and doughnuts made from sweet yeast
     dough and sprinkled with sugar) are served to family and guests.

Christian funeral rites also follow traditional patterns. Before the
burial of the deceased, family and friends gather together and each in
turn says a few words about the departed.[4] Forty days after the death and
again on the first anniversary, an ancient tradition is followed in the
preparation, blessing and serving of a cooked wheat dish. A mound of
cooked wheat, spices, raisins and nuts is symbolically decorated to reaf-
firm faith and the "sweetness of everlasting life."[8]

Similarly, Muslim feast days and family occasions display as many of
the classic festive dishes as can be afforded by the household. As a part of
their faith, Muslims are cautioned at all times to eat foods for health and

survival and never to over-indulge.[13] The important annual fast takes place for the entire ninth lunar month: *Ramadan*. During the entire daylight hours of this month a total abstinence of all food and drink is observed by the faithful; food and drink are only taken before sunrise or after sundown. The fasting ends with a great feast on the first day of the next month: *Bairam*. Those who are ill, or for some other reasons unable to fast during *Ramadan*, traditionally make up those fast days at some other time.[14]

THIRTY-FOUR

Maltese

Homer called it "the navel of the sea" and most maps show Malta as a dot in the Mediterranean between Sicily and the north African coast of Tunisia. Actually, Malta is an archipelago of several islands, the three largest and inhabited ones being Malta, Comino (named for the abundance of wild, fragrant cumin-seed plants) and Gozo. And history has considered Malta more than a mere dot on the map. The strategic location and the sheltered harbours lured so many great maritime powers that it is impossible to dismiss either Malta or the Maltese people as insignificant.

The Maltese people are believed to be descended from adventurous settlers from Sicily who made their home on the islands more than 6,000 years ago.[1] Excavations of animal remains reveal that Malta may once have been connected to Sicily: the animal remains are of European origin, not African.[2] There is no doubt however, about the later succession of occupations by the Phoenicians, Greeks, Carthaginians, and Romans. It was during the Roman occupation in 60 C.E. that the ship carrying St. Paul to his trial in Rome was said to have been wrecked on Malta's shores.[1,2] Deeply impressed by the warmth and hospitality of the Maltese people, St. Paul was apparently equally impressive to them, for it is from that date that the Islands were converted to Christianity. Now, with almost 100 per cent of the population being Roman Catholic, Malta is often described as being "more Catholic than the Pope."[3]

Byzantine conquest followed the Romans, but it was the subsequent domination of the Arabs, who held Malta from 800-1000 C.E., that left deep imprints on Malta's architecture and language. Present-day Maltese is an Arabic dialect strongly flavoured with the later addition of Italian, Spanish, French and even English words. It is the only Semitic language written in the Latin alphabet.[3]

The long line of conquerors did not end with the Arabs. Normans and Spaniards took their turn at the strategic islands, but it was the Knights of Saint John who were to leave the next lasting marks upon the Maltese.

It was King Charles V, Emperor of the Holy Roman Empire and King of Spain, who "rented" Malta to the Knights of the Order of Saint John of Jerusalem after the Turks had driven them from Rhodes. The "rent" took the form of an annual tribute of one falcon – thus the legendary but mystical importance of the "Maltese Falcon" dating from 1530 and immortalized much later in Dashiel Hammett's novel of the same name. Both the falcon and the Knights' eight-pointed cross (the Maltese Cross) remain today as Maltese symbols. Lesser known but of more importance are the many hospitals and charitable organizations that the Knights left behind in Malta and which continue in operation to this day.[3]

Although the Knights of the Order of Saint John were able to help the Maltese withstand a powerful Turkish siege, their rule collapsed in 1798 without a shot being fired. It is believed that Napoleon seized Malta for France with the secret aid of some of the Knights.[3] Nonetheless, French rule was only a brief two years, and was brought to an abrupt end by a Maltese revolt aided by the British. In 1814, the Treaty of Paris officially gave Malta to the British and the 150-year British rule was to leave its indelible mark. Although the British preferred to retain their own traditions, the Maltese cheerfully adapted the habit of "elevenses" and four o'clock tea, bright red postboxes, helpful policemen and driving their cars on the left. They even developed a taste for beer.[3]

Despite the long, tiresome hold of so many conquerors, the Maltese have stubbornly retained their distinctive language, their Roman Catholicism, their many traditions and festivals and their national flag. In 1964 they achieved their independence, and in 1974 the international status of a republic.[1]

They have also retained something else. In spite of those successive dominations by so many foreign powers and in spite of the density of population on the tiny islands, the Maltese are known for their courtesy and good humour and they are never too busy to take a stroll or chat with friends. Perhaps these are the very qualities that enabled them to endure even such relentless hardships as the incessant bombing raids in World War II. So incredible was the courage of this tiny nation of approximately 300,000 people living on 122 square miles, that in 1942 King George VI awarded the nation the George Cross for "heroism and devotion" and in 1943 President F. D. Roosevelt of the U.S. also presented the nation a special citation.[1]

Perhaps the sunny disposition of the Maltese people comes from the moderate Mediterranean climate that basks the islands for most of the year in a pleasant warmth. Two winds occasionally disturb the tranquility of climate: the hot *sirocco* blowing during August and September, and the *gregale*, a sharp northeasterly that can whip the sea to a froth and cause fishing problems.

The climate also helps the scanty topsoil to coax forth enough potatoes and onions for export, but of the other vegetables, fruits, wheat and barley, only enough for local use are grown. Goats are still used for meat and milk but are mostly supplanted by the sheep (lamb and mutton) and the dairy farms of cows introduced by the British to supply cream, milk and butter.[3] The main sustenance comes from the sea. Even with skill and ingenuity, almost 80 per cent of Malta's food needs must be imported.[3]

Retaining their identity and cheerful disposition despite a lengthy list of conquerors is a tribute to such a tiny, vulnerable nation, and so is their legendary hospitality. Out of a desire to please others, it is actually easier to find cosmopolitan restaurants in Malta than it is to find local cuisine, but the increase in tourism and increasing pride in "things Maltese" is changing this.

Malta may be small in population and size but her people are content to stay put; travelling three to ten miles is considered a considerable distance and a family living only a few miles from the sea may actually visit the seashore only once or twice in a lifetime.[3] Further, size has nothing to do with the ability to distinguish "local" customs and even varying dialects of Maltese.

Most interesting and notable example of the Maltese view of native differences are the Gozitans. These inhabitants of the island of Gozo are viewed by the other Maltese as "the Scotsmen of our islands"; thrifty, industrious and plain speaking, the Gozitans can be singled out as leaders in business and church. The island of Gozo is said to be the most fertile because of the persistent and patient toil of her people. And there is a saying that if a fisherman brought in a record catch, he was probably a Gozitan.[3]

Home Life and Facilities
Density of population brings with it both noise and a lack of privacy. Neither of these bothers the Maltese. Only in his own home does he treasure quiet and privacy; once outside he literally basks in the crush of cars and people and the cadenza of horns, noisy talk and church bells. The Maltese has an extended home; the city streets are part of his living room and he is friendly and gracious to everyone he meets (the Maltese have a phenomenal memory for names and faces). The church is his second home, a place for help and prayer, thanksgiving and consolation.

Maltese cooking and hospitality is probably best symbolized by Maltese bread and white fresh RIKOTTA cheese. Simple and honest, they are a part of almost every meal, and form the edible centrepiece of the table. They are not only sustaining in themselves but also represent a blend of flavours and textures that would cause a Maltese mouth to water anywhere in the world. The crusty white sourdough bread shaped in a gentle golden oval, eaten with creamy mild RIKOTTA cheese, may form the appetizer, the main dish or merely a side dish of any meal. Add a glass of Maltese wine and you have the quintessence of hospitality.

The delicious aromas that pour forth from Maltese kitchens belie their tiny size. Sideboards and open shelves store groceries and utensils, while a small refrigerator will hold perishables. Maltese prefer fresh seasonal fruits and vegetables and prefer to shop daily in nearby stores for their needs. Although supermarkets and a wide range of prepared mixes are slowly changing old ways, the pot of soup simmering on the small petrol stove is so much a part of the meal pattern (and the aroma of Malta) it is difficult to visualize it being pre-empted by a cold sandwich for lunch. Freezers for the home and small kitchen appliances such as blenders, pressure cookers, etc., are not common in Malta.[4] Baking is usually done in commercial communal ovens, carefully watched over by the local baker.[5]

FOODS COMMONLY USED

The foods of the Maltese table are simple and satisfying. Unquestionably, many favourite dishes can trace their origins to foods introduced by historic invaders: Greeks, Romans, Arabs, French and British. The latter left a taste for beer, mutton, lamb, turkey, Christmas pudding, and probably also the custom of a "roasted joint with potatoes" for Sunday dinner.[5] Crunchy Maltese sourdough bread and RIKOTTA cheese are certainly staples but these are well-rounded with hearty soups, stews and pasta dishes that deftly spin out the flavours of meats and fish. Vegetables are preferred cooked; salads are few and usually seasonal. Local fruits are relished as snacks or desserts but are expensive. Wine is the commonest beverage and knows no age limit.

Milk and Milk Products

With fresh milk for drinking, canned milk for tea and coffee, and the daily use of cheese with bread or as part of a sauce or casserole (pasta dish) milk is obviously high on the list of priorities. The famed PASTIZZI or Maltese cheesecakes may be large or tiny and although usually made with puff pastry and a filling of RIKOTTA, they still retain the same name when they are made with anchovies or even peas and onions. So popular are the PASTIZZI that they are available everywhere in bars and coffee-shops and commonly form a mid-morning snack with tall glasses of tea or coffee.[5] Many varieties of hard or aged cheese are used, shredded or grated to add flavour in rice or pasta dishes. GBEJNIET are the small fresh cheeses made by farmers' wives and sold fresh, dried or peppered, and preserved in olive oil and vinegar.[5]

Fruits and Vegetables

If you want someone from Malta to become nostalgic, just mention prickly pears. These are by no means the only native fruit – just the favourite. Also included and eaten mostly fresh and juicy are pampamousse, small round watermelons, dates and figs, oranges and apples and many small berries. Most home gardens grow their own pampamousse and grapes. Fresh fruits are the usual dessert.

Vegetables are more than a garnish or accompaniment; they are cooked in a variety of ways and often form the main dish of a supper. From the Greeks the Maltese adapted a number of stuffed vegetable dishes; from the French they adapted the method of "refreshing" – a brief boiling of the fresh vegetables then a dunking in cold water, thus retaining both colour and texture.[5] Favourite vegetables include pumpkin (ripened on Malta's flat rooftops), aubergines and courgettes (eggplants and zucchini), broad beans and artichokes. Many varieties of squashes and gourds, leafy greens, cabbage and cauliflower and of course potatoes and onions are cooked in satisfying and imaginative ways. These include not only the stuffed vegetable recipes already mentioned but also breading and frying, layering in casseroles, baking as a filling in crispy pastry pies, as patties and fritters and even as steamed, molded puddings to be served with cheese and béchamel sauce.

Meats and Alternates

In a Maltese cookbook, the recipes for fish will likely come before the recipes for meats. Not only are there many varieties of fresh fish and seafood and dozens of ways to prepare and serve them, but even with the lifting of the ban of meat on Fridays, most Maltese prefer to make Friday a fish day. Many others also abstain from meats on Wednesdays.[5]

Most famed is the LAMPUKA, also called DORADO or DOLPHINFISH, closely followed by varieties of mackerel, tunny fish, mullet, bass, grouper and many more. *Lampuka* is poached, baked, fried, stewed or made into fish soup. In the meal-in-a-dish, TORTA TAL-LAMPUKA, between two layers of pastry is placed a combination of *lampuka* and a sauce of vegetable chunks surprisingly flavoured with olives, sultanas and walnuts. Salt cod, cuttlefish, turtle, snails, sea-urchins (RIZZI), and ARTIKLI are also enjoyed.

Meat in any quantity is usually reserved for a Sunday or festive dinner with the best and largest cut going to father, the head of the household. The rest of the family will round out their meal with potatoes and other vegetable dishes, bread and cheese. Maltese homemakers value meats and nothing is ever wasted. Not only are bits of meats and bones used to flavour casseroles, stuffed vegetables and soups, but there is also a long list of appetizing dishes prepared from offal, including tripe, brains, liver and tongue. ZALZETT TA' MALTA (Malta sausages) are composed of a mixture of fat and lean pork seasoned with garlic and coriander and stuffed into pork intestines and hung for two to three days. Beef and pork, lamb and rabbit, chicken, and game birds add variety to the menu.

Eggs and legumes are not a special part of the Maltese menu. Eggs are used occasionally as a light meal or snack but most often as an ingredient in other dishes. Dried legumes are seldom used except for the large brown lentils which are popular in SOPPA TAL-GHAZZ, a thick lentil soup simmered with vegetables and pig's feet.[5]

Breads and Cereals

Bread and pasta, the staples of the Maltese diet, are both prepared from wheat. But the Malta bread is memorable because it is baked from a sourdough starter which gives it a particular flavour and coarse texture. The crispy crust is enhanced by the traditional baking of the bread on the floor of the oven rather than on a pan. This is the bread that is not only part of every Maltese meal, it is also the main dish for lunch or even a light supper when hollowed out and stuffed with tomatoes, anchovies and cheese and dribbled with olive oil. Rubbed with a pungent clove of fresh garlic and sprinkled with salt and olive oil, Malta bread makes a quick savoury snack. And every Maltese is familiar with ĦOBZ BIZ-ZEJT, thick slices of bread rubbed with fresh tomatoes, sprinkled with olive oil, salt and pepper, then topped with any combination of sliced onions, garlic, herbs, capers, olives or anchovies. This quick snack satisfies workmen's appetites for lunch, children for "elevenses" (mid-morning snack) and whole families as an easy light supper served with local wine.[5] GALLETTI, KRUSTINI and BISKUTELLI are small breads sometimes made at home.

Pasta dishes abound, but most are complex. TIMPANA is really a version of a similar Sicilian dish where puff pastry forms the outside layer of a centre filled with layered cooked macaroni, bits of brain, liver and pork seasoned with tomato paste, parmesan and onion. Carefully baked, the dish is unmolded and served in slices. (Today TIMPANA is a main dish; in previous times it was merely an appetizer.) RAVJUL (ravioli), and many types of pasta cooked to perfection and topped with delicate sauces of cheese, vegetables or fish are a part of every Maltese menu.

Close in importance to both bread and pasta is rice. Rice is used in stuffings for meats and vegetables and in many dishes in the same way as pasta. One of the classic Maltese dishes is ROSS FIL-FORN, literally "baked rice." It is made from a mixture of ground meat, seasonings, raw beaten eggs and tomato paste blended with stock or water and raw rice. The whole mixture is slowly baked in the oven to a golden crustiness.[6]

It should be noted that while few Maltese cooks bother to bake their own bread, it would be difficult to find one who was not an expert maker of light flaky puff pastry, and who did not possess an old treasured family recipe for filling PASTIZZI.

Fats
Maltese use many fats for cooking, baking and as a spread. Lard, margarine and salt butter are used widely for cooking and baking. Margarine is used at the table but RIKOTTA cheese is the favourite spread. Olive oil and a variety of vegetable and seed oils are also used.

Sweets and Snacks
As has already been noted, the popular Maltese dessert is usually fresh fruit and sometimes cheese. Sweets in the form of pastries, candies and rich desserts are usually reserved for special occasions and most often purchased from the confectioners rather than prepared at home. A listing of specialty sweet dishes sounds like an international roll call of sweetmeats for it includes the favourites known in many other lands: chestnut fillings, almond, chocolate and nougat, sesame seeds, dates and treacle, trifles and steamed puddings, pine nuts and crunchy meringues. (See also "Special Occasions.")

Seasonings
Maltese food may be simple and hearty but it is seldom subtle. Strong flavours are enjoyed and these often include the pungency of garlic and onions cut with the bright acidity of tomatoes. In fact one of the most basic seasonings is actually an all-purpose sauce of fried onions, garlic and tomato paste known as TOQLIJA. Freshly ground pepper, spicy hot curry blends and fresh aromatic herbs are all used with a generous hand.

Beverages
Beer was introduced by the British, but local wines are still the favourite accompaniment for the evening meal. Coffee and tea with canned milk is taken by adults for breakfast and lunch, for "tea" at four and for "elevenses" in mid-morning. Children drink milk except for the evening meal when they will often have a glass of wine.

Meal Patterns and Eating Customs
Maltese restaurants, snack bars, coffee shops and vendors satisfy the taste whims of most tourists, but the Maltese prefers to eat hearty, simple, and well-flavoured food at home.

Breakfast for most is a small light meal of bread and cheese, honey and ham accompanied by coffee and milk. If that seems a light beginning for the day, a snack of tea or coffee and PASTIZZI around eleven will hold any Maltese till lunch-time.

Maltese homemakers begin early in the morning to prepare the ingredients and simmer their soups over small petrol stoves. Soup for lunch is a tradition broken only by the labourer who cannot get home for lunch. Then a bundle of ḤOBZ BIZ-ZEJT (bread rubbed with tomatoes, flavoured with oil and seasonings and topped with garlic, sliced onions and herbs) and a glass of wine will ease his hunger till the evening when he will enjoy a hot meal – probably a pasta dish or a meat and vegetable stew.

Housewives, businessmen, labourers and children all stop their day's routine for a short break at four for tea and small cookies. The tea break is especially important for those who customarily take their evening meal between nine and ten. Villagers usually have a light evening meal around seven.

Regardless of the meal, in Malta men are served first, most, and usually the choicest portions. But Maltese meal service is generally pleasantly casual; enjoying food takes precedence over formal manners. Thus there are no frowns when succulent bones are eaten with the fingers.

Special Occasions

Together with special family occasions such as weddings, christenings, birthdays and funerals, the Maltese calendar includes Roman Catholic festivals, national holidays and many local *festas*. It would be difficult to spot a time of year when nothing exciting is happening.

Special occasions are the time for specific sweet treats more than special main dishes. They are made extra-special because they are served or prepared only for specific festivals. Some of these include the following:[1,5]

CHRISTMAS: Roast stuffed turkey and steamed plum puddings are the Christmas specialties. The Christmas pudding is usually made near the beginning of November then soaked with rum each following Sunday till the festive day.

Hot chestnut soup (MBULJUTA), flavoured with cocoa and tangerine peel, and specially baked treacle rings (QAGHAQ TAL-GHASEL) are also made. The latter is a white pastry filled with a rich treacle and semolina filling and shaped to form a round "sausage." Small slits in the white pastry reveal the rich filling beneath.

CARNIVAL: Loud bands, winding parades and costumed figures mark the three- to seven-day celebrations preceding Lent. PRINJOLATA, a rich pine-nut cake, almond chunks and QUBBAJT (nougat) are the special sweets.

LENT: Lenten restrictions have been considerably relaxed. Usually no meat is eaten, but dairy products and fats are now allowed. KWAREZIMAL, a Lenten cake containing no eggs or fat but made from minced almonds and flour, sugar and citrus flavouring, is still a tradition.

EASTER: It wouldn't be Easter without FIGOLLI: human and animal shapes cut from sugar-cookie dough and filled with almond paste and brightly decorated with coloured icing. Too good to save only for Easter and often made at other times are the tiny RIKOTTA-filled tartlets called QASSATAT.

BISKUTTINI TAL-MAGHMUDIJA or "christening biscuits" are rich cookies shaped into rounds or oblongs. BISKUTTINI TAL-LEWZ are delicately crisp almond meringues. Both are specialties of all christenings and most family gatherings and *festas*. But no Maltese birthday would be complete without XKUNVAT, fried twisted strips of rich pastry flavoured with orange-flower water and served in a golden crispy pile dribbled with Maltese honey (thyme-flavoured) and coloured "shot" (tiny pinheads of coloured candies used for cake decoration).

THIRTY-FIVE

Mexican

To millions of Mexicans and tourists alike, Mexico usually means Mexico City. That thriving metropolis carries her more than 640 years with dignity, charm, and a great deal of sophistication as she cradles more than 8,000,000 people on her plateau situated about 7,300 feet above sea level.

Mexico had a highly intelligent and predominantly agricultural civilization thousands of years ago when the rest of the world was in its infancy. It is believed that the original Indian tribes – Olmecs, Toltecs, Mayans and Aztecs – who made up her population originally came from Asia across the Bering Strait to settle in the land and develop the crops from which the world now derives almost half of its food supply.[2,6,7] These include corn, beans, potatoes, tomatoes, chocolate, eggplants, avocados, many varieties of squash, vanilla and chilies.

In 1523 Hernando Cortés came to Mexico from Spain; and, because Montezuma believed him to be a former god returned to life, Cortés was able to conquer the land with little resistance. In return for all the Mexican foods which the Spaniards subsequently introduced to Europe, they left behind in Mexico much of their influence. Spanish architecture, the Spanish language, the Roman Catholic religion as well as the Spanish foods: rice and wheat, oil and wine, olives, cinnamon, cloves, peaches and apricots, and the breeding of cattle which added beef, butter and cheese to the Indian cuisine. All were widely accepted and embedded themselves deeply into Mexican culture.

The brief rule of the Viennese Maximilian, and his wife Carlotta, spread a wave of European manners and customs as well as the influence of French, Austrian and Italian cookery (SOPA SECA, which is similar to a southern Italian pasta dish, is an example). But with the reinstatement of the Indian, Benito Juarez, as leader in 1910, Spanish and other influences were somewhat mitigated and once again Indian culture came to the fore. To this day it is the ancient Indian culture that has predominant influence, although the language is still Spanish – the Mexican Spanish varying somewhat from the classic Castillian Spanish – and the predominant religion is still Roman Catholic.

Contrary to popular belief, all Mexican food is not spicy hot. This is not to say that Mexicans don't take good-natured delight in watching a *tourista* attempt to eat some of their fiery dishes. What could be funnier than the involuntary tears shed by a novice sampling a *piquante* dish?

While Mexicans pride themselves on their supposed immunity to the many varieties of fiery chilies, the range of their dishes and the subtle seasonings commonly used are very wide indeed and go back several thousand years in history.[3] Specialties can be found in every province and region of Mexico, and the techniques are handed down from mother to daughter with pride and meticulous attention to detail. Here are a few:

MOLE POBLANO – from Puebla (a spicy sauce made with bitter chocolate);

TAMALES – from Oaxaca (meat filling steamed in corn husks);

BUNUELOS – from Oaxaca (crispy fritters soaked in syrup);

BANANA DISHES AND STEWED TURTLE – from Tabasco;

BARBACOA – from Mexico province (meat packed in the fleshy maguey leaves and buried in a pit with hot coals);

CEVICHE ACAPULCO – from Guerrero (raw fish marinated in lime juice, well-seasoned and served cold);

BEEF AND BEEF DISHES – from Sonora.[2,3]

But time is the best cooking pot, and although Mexican cuisine and food habits are a blend of Indian, Spanish and other European influences, it is the native Mexican ingredients adapted over thousands of years that have given Mexican food immense variety and a unique quality all its own.

Home Life and Cooking Facilities
Many primitive but very practical cooking utensils are still widely used in Mexico. These include:

CAZUELAS: earthenware casseroles;

OLLAS: earthenware jugs;

COMAL: round iron or earthenware baking sheet used to cook tortillas;

METATE: three-legged oblong stone base used with a cylindrical stone called a *metlapil*[3] to grind corn or chocolate.

And while most women can pat a tortilla to paper-thinness – a considerable skill – with just their hands, the use of a tortilla press is common, and store-bought tortillas are inexpensive and increasingly popular.[4] The tortilla is the staple pancake-like bread, used by every class and present at every meal. It can be used in many ways in a great variety of dishes, and also as a plate or utensil to scoop up and eat other foods.

Most modern Mexican kitchens consider the electric blender a necessity to purée sauces and grind spice mixtures and pastes to the right consistency, for those techniques are the most exacting and time-consuming in the Mexican kitchen.

It should be pointed out that although there exists in Mexico today a poor lower class and a wealthy upper class, the white-collar middle class is expanding rapidly thanks to newer and better schooling and living conditions. Annually more and more of Mexico's citizens are enjoying the benefits of these good living and working conditions. And while the poorer and suburban people make excellent use of the many primitive yet practical utensils, the kitchens of the middle and upper classes would rival any in Canada or the U.S., but with one exception: it is rare that the lady of the house is also the cook.

Since many fine markets with fresh produce abound, food storage is really not a problem as most families prefer to buy their foods fresh for each day. In some homes this may even include a fresh daily supply of TORTILLAS. Refrigerators are common in the middle- and upper-class homes, as are various small electrical appliances, especially blenders. But freezers are not widely used. Lower-class homes rely on earthenware vessels to keep foods cool as needed.

FOODS COMMONLY USED

The staples of the Mexican diet are:

FRIJOLES: beans of many varieties but most commonly the small black beans which are usually well-cooked then mashed with lard and reheated before eating;

TORTILLAS: flat, pancake-like bread made from specially ground corn meal called MASA HARINA. High in calcium content since it is made with lime water;

CHILIES: as many as ninety-two varieties are available,[4] each varying both in hotness and flavour;

CHORIZO: a fresh sausage made from pork and seasonings;

TOMATOES and ONIONS

These staples are popular with every class level and are present in every day's meals. In fact, there is seldom a meal that does not have TORTILLAS and FRIJOLES on the table. Canned milk is favoured over fresh, and mild cheeses are used mostly as a grated garnish to other dishes. Fish and seafood are plentiful especially in coastal areas. Fresh fruits and many seeds and nuts are used for snacking. Dried or candied fruits (and sometimes candied vegetables such as pumpkin or squash) are favoured treats but many prefer the taste of salted foods or spicy ones rather than sweet. There is a knowing hand with many types of seasoning and these are usually according to local tastes. Soft drinks and local beers are popular as well as tea, coffee and hot chocolate. In cosmopolitan Mexico City can be found restaurants featuring foods of many lands, as well as local traditional favourites.

Milk and Milk Products
Fresh milk is available but is not widely used. Canned evaporated and sweetened condensed milks are popular, perhaps because they keep better. These are used in beverages and especially to make the dessert FLAN. Mild cheeses are usually used grated as a topping or garnish to other foods.

Fruits and Vegetables
There is a year-round availability of fresh fruits and vegetables both for meal preparation and also sold on the streets and roadsides by vendors for impulsive snacking. Corn and many types of squash and pumpkin are used most widely, but other vegetables include peas, onions, tomatoes (both red and green types), JICAMA (bland, with an apple-like crispness), cactus leaves, beets, potatoes, squash blossoms, lettuce, radishes, NOPALES (prickly pear leaves), garlic and peppers. Many vegetable dishes take much preparation time and involve the intricate assembly of stuffed vegetables with sauces also prepared from vegetables, often with a tomato base. Both red and green tomatoes are used frequently for dipping and garnishing sauces and many vegetables are used for soups. Fresh salads of either fruits or vegetables are used mostly by upper classes.

Fruits include a wide and colourful range of tropical and subtropical varieties such as pineapples, bananas, avocados, strawberries, pomegranates, oranges, mangoes, papayas, coconuts, quince, cherimoyas and apples. Limes are almost everywhere and appear often as a plate garnish and to heighten the flavour of spice mixtures. Bananas are enjoyed baked for dessert, but most other fruits are eaten more often as a fresh snack purchased from vendors.

Meats and Alternates
Meat is too expensive for many tables, but pork and pork products including sausages and offal head the list of favourites. Goat, beef, chicken, lamb, turkey, turtle and veal are also used. Fish and seafood are plentiful in coastal regions, including the *huachinango* (red snapper) and *camarones* (shrimp).

Beans are used daily, mostly as FRIJOLES or FRIJOLES REFRITOS (refried) and eaten as a side dish with TORTILLAS or other foods, or combined as fillings to other dishes. Nuts are enjoyed as snacks or sometimes finely ground and used to thicken sauces. As a snack they are preferred well-salted, toasted and often dusted with spicy-hot chilies. CACAHUATES (peanuts) are abundant, but walnuts, cashews and pistachios are also used. The toasted and sometimes well-seasoned seeds from pumpkins and varieties of squash may be crushed and used in cooking or nibbled as a snack.

Breads and Cereals
TORTILLAS made from MASA HARINA are the ubiquitous staple for every table at every meal, either made by hand or purchased fresh daily. BOLILLAS are also very popular, especially in the cities. These are oval-shaped white rolls with a chewy crust, said to be baked hourly around the clock and made from wheat flour. There is some limited use of dry breakfast cereals in middle- and upper-class homes.

Fats
Lard is the most widely used fat for cooking, baking and deep-fat frying. There is a limited use of oils. Some margarine is used and some butter, mostly as a table spread (for BOLILLAS) or in specialty baking.

Sweets and Snacks
The favourite sweet of all ages is candied or dried fruits, especially candied squash, candied sweet potato and pumpkin. Tamarind is another favourite. Chocolates and candies are expensive, and many prefer tangy, salty or spicy flavours to sweet. The favourite Mexican dessert of Spanish influence is the FLAN, a slow-baked custard of eggs and condensed or evaporated milk, glazed with sugar and often flavoured with vanilla or coconut. Very young children also enjoy nibbling on sugar cane when it is available. Fresh sliced fruits such as pineapple or JICAMA are often eaten as a snack first by dipping into little dishes of spicy hot sauces or bowls of blended dry seasonings.

Seasonings
There is a wide and general use of many seasonings, especially in particular areas. These include skilful blends of varieties of chilies, as well as cinnamon, cloves, vanilla, chocolate, nuts, coconut, limes, oranges, garlic and onions, capers and many fresh Mexican herbs such as *cillantro* (like Chinese parsley), *epazote*, mint, marjoram and sage. Red tomatoes and small green ones are used so frequently that they must be considered a seasoning as well. Limes are used freely everywhere as juice, seasoning and garnish.

Beverages

Soft drinks are popular and inexpensive. Tea, coffee and hot chocolate are used according to taste. Excellent local beer is made, an increasingly high quality selection of wines and even brandy made in different areas. Pulque, fermented cactus juice, is an old favourite. Tequila, the national potent drink made from cactus, is traditionally enjoyed straight, first with a lick of salt and after with a squirt of fresh lime.

Meal Patterns and Eating Customs

Desayuno is breakfast in Mexico and, as in many other places, it is eaten early and is usually a light meal. For the countryside farmer or the worker in Mexico City, the first meal may be TORTILLAS with FRIJOLES REFRITOS, sprinkled with mild grated cheese and washed down with hot chocolate or CAFE CON LECHE (coffee with milk). For the city person, the TORTILLAS may be replaced with fresh BOLILLAS or other breads, the hot drink will be the same, but the morning paper may be the accompaniment. Where time and money are no problem, a more leisurely *desayuno* may include fresh fruits, eggs (HUEVOS RANCHEROS), TORTILLAS and FRIJOLES REFRITOS garnished with grated cheese and a few wedges of fresh avocado, together with *cafe con leche* or hot chocolate.

The main meal of the day is usually the *comida* lasting a leisurely two or three hours (which may include a rest time), from 2:00 to 5:00 P.M. Most people try to take this meal at home with their family.

The Mexicans also have a name for a special lunch about 11:00 A.M. which they call *almuerzo*. This meal usually consists of one filling dish such as SOPA SECA or something based on TORTILLAS such as TACOS or ENCHILADAS. But if *almuerzo* is taken, then the *comida* would be correspondingly a lighter meal.

And if either the *almuerzo* or the *comida* left some hunger pangs, there is a type of "sweet break" in the late afternoon that usually consists of sweet rolls or small pastries with coffee or chocolate and this is called *merienda*.

In spite of the many "official" meals, snacking is a national pastime and many vendors on city streets and along the highways make their living by carefully preparing fresh sliced fruits, fruit drinks like HORCHATA, candied fruits and vegetables, salted and spiced nuts and seeds.

On special occasions, many villages have their own local sweet bakeries and small confections that are prepared in the homes then offered for sale to passers-by. Some of the oldest traditional sweets and baked goods were prepared by nuns in the convents for special holidays. Within minutes a small stand can be set up to make fresh TORTILLAS and varieties of fillings and bottles of hot spicy sauces to be used to taste. Other stands are specially constructed to bake bananas where they are served hot with a sprinkle of sugar and a dribble of canned milk. CHICARRONES (pork cracklings), fried TACO chips and crispy-fried cookies all beckon the appetite of anyone walking by.

The evening meal is called the *cena*. In the rural areas this would, like the other meals, be based on the staples of TORTILLAS and FRIJOLES and may include a CAZUELA of vegetables, seasoned with garlic, onions, tomatoes and chilies. This evening meal is taken very late in the city, eight to ten being a usual time. But this meal would not be a heavy one unless the family is dining out or there is a special occasion. Much entertaining is done out of the home, especially in the city. Home parties are likely to be buffet style.

Special Occasions

The predominant religion in Mexico is Roman Catholic. But together with Christmas and Easter, many other typical Mexican festivals are observed and many of these are peculiar only to a province or town. Festivals are generally characterized with local costumes, street dancing and vendors busily selling sweet cakes and confections for the occasion. Among those occasions celebrated nationally are:

JAN. 1: New Year's Eve and New Year's Day, celebrated with parties, restaurant dinners, festive meals.

JAN. 6: *Fiesta de los Santos Reyes* (the Coming of the Kings). Costumed wise-men roam the streets and give candies and treats to the children; in homes there is gift giving. Traditional *rosca de reyes*, a ring-shaped bread decorated with candied fruits, is eaten. Somewhere in the bread is hidden a tiny figurine, and the finder is obliged to make a party for all on February 2.[3]

SHROVE TUESDAY AND EASTER WEEK: Most businesses and schools take this week (and Christmas week) as annual holidays. This time is characterized by visits to families, church services and pilgrimages to shrines. Each locale has specialty cookies, cakes and confections sold by vendors.

MAR. 21: Birth of Benito Juarez.

NOV. 1 AND 2: All Saints' and All Souls' days. Families visit the graves and leave offerings of *zempazulchitl*, bright fragrant flowers similar to marigolds, as well as specially baked bread called *pan de muerto*. These round breads, decorated with crossbones and teardrops and sprinkled with pink sugar, are baked and eaten by all classes days before the solemn occasion.

NOV. 20: Anniversary of the 1910 Revolution, restoring Juarez to power.

DEC. 16-25: The happy time of the *posadas*, colourful parties with candy-filled *pinatas*, games for all, and a table laden with buffet dishes – the best the family can offer. *Ensalada de noche buena* is the Christmas Eve specialty: a huge salad of chopped fruits, crunchy peanuts and red beets all lightly flavoured with sugar and vinegar.[3]

Every festival, small or large, brings out regional and local specialties, alcoholic and fruit beverages, bright costumes and communal dancing. Small rich sweets, some specially wrapped in papers, candied fruits and hot spiced snacks provide the refreshment and energy for the celebrants.

THIRTY-SIX

Moroccan

Morocco nestles on the northwest coast of Africa bordering the shores of the Atlantic Ocean and the Mediterranean Sea and with a finger of land pointing northward to Spain. It is said to have the broadest plains and highest mountains in all of Africa. There are great extremes of climate and temperature between the coastal areas and the tips of the Atlas Mountains where snow is not uncommon year around.[2]

Crops of barley, wheat and corn flourish on the 10 per cent of the land that is arable. Many varieties of dates are grown and ancient olive trees and gnarled grape vines add to the Moroccan larder together with the fruit trees, especially the fragrant almond. Sheep and goats form the largest livestock herds although there are cattle as well. As in most of North Africa and the Middle East, meat is usually in short supply and fish is consumed mainly in areas where caught because of limited storage facilities.[3]

Long referred to as "Moors," the people of Morocco are actually a mix of Berber, Arab and Negro peoples. The 800-year occupation of Spain by Arabs and Moors (from the seventh to the fifteenth centuries C.E.) probably established the term Moors because most Christians at that time referred to all Muslims as "Moors."[4] The Berbers were the first-known inhabitants of Morocco and even today make up more than 75 per cent of its population. These non-Arabic tribes inhabiting many parts of North Africa are a lean, hardy people, white to dark brown in colouring. They belong to more than 200 separate groups each with distinctive customs and dialects. They live by herding sheep, goats and cattle and increasingly work as crop-raising farmers.[5] Their individualism and fierce independence can be illustrated by two facts: their adoption of both Islam and Judaism[6,7] did not replace but added to their former beliefs and traditions[6,7]; and the continued agitation of the Berber tribes against the French occupation of Morocco actually led to the Moroccan independence of 1956.[5]

The fact that almost 80 per cent of the Moroccan population is illiterate[3] can be misleading. For it must be understood that most of the Berber dialects do not have a written form, knowledge having been carefully transmitted verbally to succeeding generations. However, these peoples have a great appetite for education and Arabic and French are commonly taught in the increasing number of schools springing up even in rural and mountain areas.[7]

Despite successive foreign conquest by Phoenicians, Carthaginians, Romans and Byzantines, the Berbers stoutly maintained their early life-styles. It was the sweeping Arab conquest in 682 C.E. that left the deepest mark. The entire population with the exception of the few Christians and the Jewish settlers in the larger cities all intermarried and adopted Islam but never really replaced their own ancient Berber traditions. Even now, of all the many sects of Islam the Berber brand is one of the loosest and varies from tribe to tribe.

In fact, the Berbers had a profound effect on the Arabs. The rituals of serving and eating foods as well as many classic dishes are definitely traced to Berber origin. These include the eating of foods with only three fingers of the right hand; however, the ceremonial handwashing that precedes the meal seems to be of Jewish rather than Arabic or Berber origin. It must be remembered that many principles of the Muslim faith and practice were in fact founded in Judaism.[6] The classic dish of COUSCOUS – national dish of the entire Maghreb which includes Morocco, Tunisia, Libya and Algeria – is also enjoyed in Egypt and other Mid-East countries. MECHOUI (succulent roast lamb), with its many variations, is found all around the Mediterranean. BISTEEYA or PASTILLA, the whisper-thin pastry layers shaped in an eighteen- to twenty-inch pie enclosing curdled eggs and pigeon meat, closely resembles the spring roll pastries of China. The TAGINE, prepared and served in an earthenware dome-shaped dish, is the classic of all stews.[9,10]

Berber traditions are deeply steeped in the supernatural. Arabs, Berbers and even many Jews profoundly believe in the power of the colour of blue to ward off evil spirits; it would be impossible to count the doorways and even the windows that are painted blue in Morocco and in many other areas of North Africa and the Middle East. And it is attributed to a mysterious supernatural power called *kimia* that lowly but faithful peasants are able to survive despite only subsistent levels of food – often only scant quantities of bread dipped in oil. Satiety is said to be attained more by faith than by food.[9]

"What isn't known can't be stolen. . . ." Who can say whether this ancient saying was born out of folklore or the reality of prevalent thieves? Nonetheless in Morocco perhaps more than any other area of North Africa the cloak of secrecy and the characteristic of self-debasing modesty exist side by side with scenes of secluded walled courtyards, hidden blue doorways, women clad in *burkas* (head-to-toe enveloping cloth "veils") and *djellaba*-clad men together with vendors of amulets, potions and formulas all guaranteed to ward off the evil eye. Great wealth and lovely women, like other treasured Moroccan possessions, are never displayed openly. Even the great cuisine of Morocco is seldom tasted in public places but is reserved for the hospitality of the home. Such is the Moroccan world: a curious blend of faith and superstition, lore and legend, Arab, Berber, Negro and Jew all touched by history and ancient customs, yet secretive.

Home Life and Facilities

Just as it is impossible to make sweeping generalizations about the 200 distinctive Berber groups, so is it impossible to speak of the average Moroccan home. The great gap between rich and poor defies comparisons. How can one even speak in the same breath of the life and style of a nomadic Berber tribe of goat herders and a palatial servant-filled home of a Moroccan family serving a thirty-plate *diffa* (banquet)? Yet both are valid examples of Moroccan life.

But some things are the same. Everywhere it is the women who cook. Everywhere classic Arabian hospitality climaxes itself in the philosophy of *shaban*: abundance of satisfaction characterized by heaping plates of the best the household can offer. For even the lowliest of peasants *shaban* can be achieved if one has sufficient *kimia*. The Moroccan legends of endless exotic dishes preceded by long flowery speeches may not seem so lavish if one remembers that the arts of speech and the arts of the cuisine have been carefully cultivated for centuries and just as carefully handed down from mother to daughter. It also helps to bear in mind that many of these culinary wonders are actually prepared from the simplest and least expensive of ingredients. They require however, the agility of many knowing hands – of which there is no shortage in Morocco.

Food preparation begins with the daily shopping for the freshest available ingredients found in the SOUKS (market places) or sold by vendors sometimes from house to house. Everyone has a favourite source of fine spices, fresh vegetables and fruits.

Despite the incredible quantity and endless variety of Moroccan food, the utensils needed in the kitchen are few. They include the mortar and pestle for grinding and pounding seasonings, a *couscousière* (a two-layered pot for cooking stew in the bottom and the COUSCOUS in the perforated top), several pots and pans of universal design, earthenware *tagine slaouis* (their conical tops may be heaped with charcoal embers to simulate baking or for long slow simmering), shiny copper *taouas* (casseroles), a range of knives and a small charcoal stove. If large amounts of food are to be prepared, neighbourhood ovens are used.[9]

Not evident in Moroccan kitchens are measuring utensils and electrical appliances. Like loving dedicated cooks throughout the world (only maybe more so in Morocco) amounts of ingredients are measured by experience, tasted knowingly and seasoned deftly with shakes of this and pinches of that. Small wonder that Moroccan girls begin their training in the culinary arts very early. Electrical power is being increasingly produced from the many rivers but is still considered a luxury and is not widely available. For this reason, perishables are bought daily rather than being stored.

The accomplished Moroccan cook will also have the following utensils for specialty dishes:[9]

GDRA DIL TRID: earthenware dome used to stretch the thin pastry for TRID (similar to BISTEEYA);

TOBSIL: similar to above, except this utensil is placed over heat or over boiling water and is used to make the WARKA (pastry for BISTEEYA);

M'GHAZEL: silver or brass skewers for meat and vegetable tidbits or meatballs (KEFTA);

GSAA: large wooden or earthenware kneading trough for bread dough (easier than a board).

Included also would be a variety of brass, copper or silver trays for serving, ornate teapot and sets of glasses for tea-serving, and small decorated kettles and basins for pouring perfumed waters in the hand-washing ritual.

For rural Berber women, the arts of cookery are somewhat simplified. Both breads and main dishes are cooked over open fires with few utensils. Yet the serving of foods, though not as elaborate as a *diffa*, may be nonetheless gracious. Low tables are placed before the diners and the customary heaped platters are eaten with three fingers, while the frequent trays of sweet tea or spiced coffee are just as much enjoyed as in the palatial city homes.

FOODS COMMONLY USED

A variety of cultures have reached into Moroccan kitchens. Spanish chick peas, Arabian spices, Portuguese fish dishes (especially in the coastal city of Essaouira) and African and Senegalese spicy sauces all take their places with the ancient Berber dishes of COUSCOUS, TAGINE, BISTEEYA and MECHOUI and make artful use of local barley and wheat for breads and pastries, dates, olives and almonds and seasonal fruits and vegetables. Grains and vegetables form the dietary staples: the larger the household the smaller the meat consumption.[3] The commonest beverage is hot sweetened mint green tea sipped from small glasses. From the British the Moroccans learned "tea-dunking"[9] and the country was a French protectorate for so long (1912-1956) that it is inevitable to find Gallic touches, especially in upper-class homes.

Milk and Milk Products

Fresh milk consumption is considered to be low, but for good reasons. As in other areas of North Africa and the Mid-East, transportation and storage facilities make it difficult to distribute perishables such as fresh milk.

Whether out of taste or out of necessity, LEBEN is a favoured beverage. It is similar to buttermilk except that the natural milk from which the butter is churned is first allowed to ferment in an earthen jug. The low-fat LEBEN is widely used especially by lower-income groups, cream and natural full milk being used sparingly by upper classes.[3] Served cool or slightly chilled, RAIPE is a type of thickened milk dish eaten as a refreshment. The milk is warmed then thickened with the addition of the pulverized powder from dried wild Moroccan artichoke hearts.[9]

Fruits and Vegetables

It was the Moors who introduced the fragrant almond, peach and apricot trees and the bittersweet "Seville" oranges to Spain. They merely introduced luscious fruits with which they were already familiar. In season, grapes, figs, dates and many varieties of melon are readily available even to the poor. Many varieties of olives are used in cooked dishes and salads. Green cracked olives are usually brine-cured and may be flavoured with lemon, spices or garlic, the seasonings depending on the bitterness. Ripe olives, which may be any colour from green to tan or purple, are usually preserved in a mix of olive oil, a little salt and lemon juice. Shrivelled ripe black olives are either salt-cured or packed with the hot sauce called HRISA or HARISSA.[9]

Dates are a staple everywhere in North Africa, but in one oasis alone – Erfoud – more than thirty varieties are grown. Dates may be nibbled as a dried fruit but they are also used to stuff fish, in combination with lamb, and also in vegetable dishes as well as desserts and sweets.[9]

Main meals are concluded with platters of fresh fruits and assorted nuts. When fresh fruits are out of season, dried fruits take their place. Dishes of assorted nuts and dried fruits are common snacks at any time.

There are times in Moroccan cuisine when the line between fruit and vegetable is not so clearly delineated as in the Western world. For example, jams and sweet preserves are frequently prepared from vegetables such as types of squash or tomatoes. Fruits as well as vegetables lend their aroma and flavour to many a TAGINE. The smooth texture and tangy pickled flavour of preserved lemons are indispensable to Moroccan cuisine. Most are preserved in salt and lemon juice; Moroccan Jews preserve their lemons with the addition of olive oil.[9] It is not uncommon to present a whole fish stuffed with one or more dried fruits, for instance a shad stuffed with dates. Fruits and vegetables are happy mates in salads too.

Basic vegetables and staples in almost every household include onions, tomatoes, turnips (widely used in cooking, salads and also as a preserve[10]), carrots and many varieties of squash and pumpkin.[3] Quinces may also be used fresh or preserved. Other basics are okra, zucchini, artichokes, green peppers, eggplants, string beans, sweet potatoes, cabbage, cauliflower, and many other common vegetables. Wild white truffles, wild cardoons and wild artichokes also add their special flavours when picked in season.

Meats and Alternates

Even though the consumption of meat is low by Western standards, small amounts of meats are used so artfully in cookery that their flavours permeate many dishes. The TAGINE, the classic Moroccan stew, can be made from any combination of meat, legumes, fruits, vegetables and even grains. In fact it seems if a mixture is cooked in the TAGINE cone-shaped casserole it is therefore a TAGINE, ingredients notwithstanding.

Lamb and kid head the list of favoured meats and are the most plentiful. Mutton and beef are also used and it goes without saying that no part of the animal is ever wasted; heads and innards are regarded as special treats. For festive occasions, lamb is most sought after, kid second in favour and the poor may have to be satisfied with chicken or pigeon meat.

Moroccans cook their meats as part of a TAGINE (with literally endless combinations of fruits, vegetables and spices), grilled as MECHOUI, or sometimes made into sausages (usually from innards). Any odd bits and pieces are usually finely ground and richly spiced to form KEFTA, which refers to any ground meat mixture. KEFTA may have many variations; it may be shaped like finger sausages and skewer-grilled, formed into meatballs as part of a TAGINE, or stuffed into vegetables or fruits.

In coastal areas where fish is more often used, imaginative cookery adds ginger, cinnamon, sugar, sweet butter as well as incredible combinations of fresh or dried fruits and nuts. There are TAGINES of fish and seafood, baked fish dishes, poached fish dishes and a great variety of tiny fluffy fish balls served with many accompaniments of seasoned sauces, fruits or vegetables. The only combination that is wrong is the one that doesn't taste good!

Special mention must be made of the preserved meat called CHELE or KHELEA. This sun-dried, salted and spice-preserved beef is similar to the Romanian PASTRAMA (which is also smoked) and the Greek or Turkish BASTOURMA. The sun-dried beef is cooked in boiling olive oil and water, then stored in the fat until used.

Eggs are widely used but often prepared differently than in the Western world. Street vendors hawk hard-boiled eggs and serve them with cumin-flavoured salt for dipping. The Tunisian BRIK – a triangle of crisp thin pastry enfolding a raw egg which is quickly fried and eaten immediately – is also a favourite, whether as a street snack or part of a home meal. Saffron-tinted hard eggs may garnish TAGINES or other platters. Eggs beaten with lemon juice and cooked into soft curds are a part of the famed BISTEEYA. Eggs may be poached in a flavourful tomato sauce with tiny KEFTA or set into a SEFIRNA, a casserole of meat and legumes baked overnight. The SEFIRNA is related to the Spanish OLLA PODRIDA or ADAFINA, a dish based on long-cooked beef, vegetables, legumes and whole eggs in the shell. ADAFINA (Spanish), SEFIRNA (Moroccan) and the central European CHOLLENT are all believed to be derived from ancient Jewish dishes. This meal-in-a-dish set to bake in banked ovens before the Sabbath could be eaten as a hot meal on the Sabbath without violating the commandment against work.[9,11] The long slow cooking of the eggs in the casserole leaves them with tanned whites and mellow creamy yolks.

Nuts are so widely used in Moroccan cookery that they must be viewed as a source of valuable protein. Almonds are most frequently used in whole blanched form, chopped, and often as almond paste. Nuts are also used in desserts and pastries and not uncommonly in many meat and fish dishes.

Breads and Cereals

Bread is the essential of every meal. For the very poor the whole meal may be only bread, sometimes dipped into olive oil. The classic Moroccan bread is shaped into absorbent, chewy oval discs, made from a mixture of whole wheat and unbleached white flour and faintly seasoned with aniseed.

Bread is much more than a meal accompaniment. Bread is viewed respectfully in deep recognition of its ability to satisfy hunger, and as a gift from God. A piece of bread inadvertently dropped may be kissed and blessed as it is carefully retrieved. Broken pieces of bread become eating utensils as they scoop up moist foods and soak up tasty juices and sauces. Community bakers pride themselves on recognizing each family's special symbol stamped on their breads, for breads are made with loving attention in private homes then toted on trays to be baked in the communal ovens.[9,12]

Moroccan diets can be described as "classic antique Mediterranean" because grains and oil form the basis. Wheat and barley are the principal cereals and are used to make a great variety of breads. European-type white bread is increasing in popularity.[3]

After weaning, the child's principal food is sweet tea and grains in the form of rice, corn, semolina, breads and pasta.[3]

Despite the importance of bread, no other food can compare in variety of preparation and importance to the legendary COUSCOUS. Of undisputed Berber origin, this incomparable dish may be called by various names, contain infinite varieties of ingredients and seasonings, and may be made from wheat, corn, barley, millet, green wheat, green barley shoots or sprouts and even rice, tapioca or bread crumbs.[9] Named SEKSU by Moroccans, it may also be called SIKUK, SKSU, UTSU, TA'AM, and even KOUSKI as in Tunisia. The principle is the same. Dry floury grains are dribbled with water and rubbed to form tiny pellets. These are carefully steamed with no cover over a perforated pot set upon a bubbling stew. The small pellets swell with moisture and absorb some of the flavours of the broth. Often two steamings are required to get the proper consistency of separate fluffy and tender granules. Frequently a light sprinkling of oil or SMEN is added.

COUSCOUS may be served upon one large platter, with meat, fruits, vegetables and well-seasoned sauce heaped over the grain base. Or, as in the French or Algerian version, each part of the COUSCOUS may be served on separate plates. COUSCOUS may be savoury or sweet, and is usually served as a luncheon meal or at the very end of a *diffa* (banquet) solely for the purpose of achieving *shaban*, total satisfaction.

Fats

Many Moroccans use large amounts of oil in cooking and often a swirl of oil is added as a garnish to complete a dish. Oily sauces are frequent. Because it does not cloud and retains a shiny appearance, olive oil is used in many salads and cold dishes while vegetable oils or peanut oil is favoured for cooking. Oil extracted from the nuts of the argan tree is used in the southwest region. A mix of honey, crushed almonds and oil is called AMALOU and is popularly used on breads. When AMALOU is mixed with more honey and wheat germ it makes a kind of breakfast gruel called ZEMATUR.[9]

SMEN is a type of clarified butter widely used to flavour soups and COUSCOUS. Sometimes it is flavoured with herbs and often it is fermented and stored. The strong smell and pungent flavour of SMEN is not too widely appreciated except by Moroccans.

Sweets and Snacks

Many sweet pastries, chewy nougat-type candies, sugared dried fruits and spicy sweet COUSCOUS as well as sugared fried pastries are readily available. But probably more sugar is consumed in the endless cups of heavily sweetened green tea scented with mint than in any other form.

The traditional dessert to end a meal is inevitably an array of available fresh fruits and nuts. Dried fruits may replace the fresh. Moroccans will likely enjoy their sweetly rich pastries at the start of a special-occasion meal such as at a wedding or circumcision and especially during the month of Ramadan where the meal after sundown is often begun with sweet cakes called SHEBBAKIA or MAHALKRA hungrily downed together with bowls of spicy HARIRA soup.

Seasonings

Basically, Moroccan food has humble beginnings; it is the artistry of careful preparation and complex seasoning that set it apart. Spices are used not only in foods but also in perfumes, medicines and even magical potions with mysterious powers. Spices are not used to mask flavours; they are used with discretion and knowledge to enhance, to tantalize and to blend. Each cook measures with her nose, her fingers and her eye but never by actual measurement. These are the skills that are passed from generation to generation. So is the knowledge of exactly which *souk* (market) and which merchant has the best seasonings.

Salt and pepper are basic. But to the Moroccan cook ten basic seasonings are always at hand: black pepper and cayenne, cumin (subtler than caraway) and saffron, ginger and turmeric, paprika and cinnamon as well as sesame seeds and aniseeds. This is by no means the end to the list, for allspice, cloves and gum arabic (MKSA) as well as cardamom, coriander seeds, and many others too exotic for most Western tastes subtly season many foods.

Much like the many varied blends of curries (KARI) in India, Morocco too has its prized blends of seasonings called RAS EL HANOUT. These blends may contain almost anything including alleged aphrodisiacs such as ash berries, Spanish fly and monk's pepper;[9] they are purchased in prepared amounts or created in special blends by individual experts.

CHARMOULA is one example of a highly seasoned sauce made with a blend of herbs and strongly flavoured with crushed fresh garlic, cayenne and lemon juice. CHARMOULA is used mainly as a marinade for fish but other blends of seasonings may be specially prepared for soups and sauces.

Fresh mint or spearmint is used with steeped green tea while other fresh or dried herbs take their place with spices to enliven foods: green parsley or green coriander leaves, oregano, basil, grey verbena and ZA'ATAR, a much-used herb similar in aroma and flavour to thyme and oregano.

Rose water and orange flower water are used often in sweets and pastries and sometimes in the water used for ceremonial handwashing. Many dried herbs and even dried flowers and buds are used in mixing special medicinal potions and herbal teas.

A truly hot spiced relish made from crushed fresh garlic, chili peppers, salt and olive oil is similar to the Indonesian SAMBAL OELEK and is called

HARISSA. This hot condiment may be used as a dip or added judiciously to soups and sauces.

Beverages

Tiny decorated glasses of green tea served hot, sweet and flavoured with fresh spearmint are the classic Moroccan beverage. Countless glasses are enjoyed every day at any time. But coffee is a favoured beverage too and helps many a Moroccan to begin the day. Coffee may be served black and sweet – it may also carry the surprise of a blend of sweet and peppery spices. Carbonated beverages are gaining in popularity but sweetened fruit drinks made from local produce and sometimes from crushed nuts are enjoyed as refreshers; these are called SHARBAT. Cool LEBEN, similar to buttermilk, is also a frequent thirst-quencher.

Street vendors sell plain water, fruit juices and even SHARBAT. Water is also the usual mealtime beverage accompanied by the main dishes with green tea following the meal. In rich homes, it is not unusual for the mealtime beverage of water to be lightly perfumed with the subtle addition of orange flower water, rose petal syrup or other aromatic concentrates.

The prohibitions against alcoholic beverages that stem from Islamic traditions are kept to varying degrees. No such prohibitions exist in Jewish homes and many Jewish kitchens are known for their homemade wines and fruit brandies prepared from ancient recipes and distilled from a great variety of fresh fruits.[9]

Meal Patterns and Eating Customs

Moroccans commonly awake to the nose-tickling aroma of freshly brewed coffee. Tiny cups of coffee may be served black, heavily sweetened or delicately spiced depending on the home and the location. Breakfast is not an important meal; the important meal of the day is usually the midday meal. Usually more than one set of talented hands prepare the noon meal from the freshest ingredients available and everything from grinding spices in mortar and pestle (or, if fortunate, in an electric blender) to cutting meats, trimming and chopping vegetables, scaling fish and washing and preparing fruits – everything will be done in the four to five hours preceding that meal.

The main meal of the day may begin with three tiny glasses of sweet green tea; or, in the south, with a plate of fresh dates and a bowl of milk; or, in the countryside, with plain biscuits, honey and SMEN. More cosmopolitan areas may begin a meal with rounds of drinks and platters of appetizers such as miniature meat balls or fish balls or tiny stuffed crisp pastries (BRAIWATS). Moroccan salads, usually a mix of spiced and sometimes sweetened vegetables which have been cooked and chilled, may be one of the many dishes or may introduce the meal much as Italian ANTIPASTI.

Dining is almost always communal, the meal being on platters in the centre of the table with diners helping themselves. The food is always eaten with the first three fingers of the right hand. Only soups and sometimes COUSCOUS (traditionally served at the end of a banquet and as the main course only in family meals) may be eaten from spoons. Adept fingers form foods into small balls, dip them with a calculated swirl into the savoury sauces and pop them into waiting mouths.

Festive occasions are not the only time when hospitality and a great show of abundance is important. Heaped platters and full stomachs are always the goal. But even when the platters are whisked away, hungry mouths will take care of the leftovers: nothing is ever wasted. To a Moroccan the great show of abundance is a matter of deep pride and is essential for any feast and for any guests. It is not, however, the dictum of restaurants.

Meals are always preceded and ended with ceremonial handwashing. This may be done humbly and simply or with great elaborate gestures and appropriate gracious words accompanied by elegant towels and perfumed water. Just as commonly, the custom of tea drinking – a minimum of three tiny glasses – often also precedes and concludes important meals.

The importance of the one midday meal can be understood when one realizes the great prevalence of vendors, *souks*, tiny shops and restaurants offering drinks and snacks at any time of day. Seldom is any work done or business discussed without a customary drinking of tea and often the offering of snacks. Thus the Moroccan is not so concerned with food upon awakening, nor is the evening meal of great importance; there has been a hearty meal at noon and many tidbits and sips throughout the day.

Special Occasions
Religious holidays, family occasions and guests all call forth gracious hospitality and an abundance of the best of foods. To mark the sweetness of the occasion it is not unusual that the festive banquet begin with rounds of sweet pastries accompanied with glasses of sweet green mint tea. Eventually, many courses and dishes later, the DIFFA will likely end in the way it began: with sweetness as the theme.

For those Moroccans of the Muslim faith, the month of Ramadan, calling as it does for complete abstinence from food and drink through the daylight hours, is ended each day at sundown with the serving of the soup called HARIRA. This is a thick soup of meats and legumes flavoured richly with vegetables, lemon, turmeric or saffron, cinnamon and ginger and thickened with a fermented, slightly musty flour-water mixture called TEDOUIRA or sometimes with a clean tangy mixture of beaten eggs and lemon juice. This hearty soup is accompanied with MAHALKRA or SHEBBAKIA, pastries cooked in boiling honey. Platters of fresh dates, fruits and coffee or milk complete the ceremonial meal.

THIRTY-SEVEN

New Zealanders

It is almost as though it were the last place created. For carefully arranged on two main islands it seems that nature's awesome creations display themselves solely for the delight of man. Here is everything: snow-tipped mountains piercing the clouds, emerald green pasture lands dotted with sheep, glacial lakes spilling into waterfalls, and sunny beaches splashed with blue waters. Small scrubbed cities nestled into hillsides, a few bustling hustling cities where the main business gets done, and then miles and miles of peaceful but rugged natural beauty to calm the mind and quench the soul with serenity. But most of the world thinks of New Zealand as a far-away place where people drink tea at four and spend the rest of their time tending sheep. No doubt this is the image deliberately perpetuated by the nearly three million New Zealanders who are fully aware of their good life, beautiful land and benevolent climate.

If New Zealanders have a reputation for pride, it is for good reason. Although they cannot take credit for the beautiful land or for the benevolent climate, they can take credit for creating a society where pollution, poverty, malnutrition, racism and unemployment are almost non-existent. This is not to say that life for the New Zealanders was always idyllic. There had to be friction between two peoples of such diverse philosophies: the Maoris and the English.

Well-preserved legends tell of the seven canoes in the Great Migration that brought the first Maoris in 1350 C.E. to the islands of New Zealand. They quickly disposed of a small population of simple people known today as the "moa-hunters"; those they favoured they married, the others they ate. Surviving on the many indigenous birds and planting their own crops, the Maoris soon expanded into many powerful tribes.

Today most of the prominent Maori families trace their origin to these early adventurers who worked with bone and stone and created a highly developed culture that survived untouched for about 300 years. Then, in December 1642, the Dutch explorer Abel Janszoon Tasman arrived. His visit was brief. A skirmish resulting in the deaths of several of his men convinced him to return to sea. More than a hundred years later, in 1770, Captain James Cook carefully charted the coasts of both islands and the European influx began.[1]

The first Europeans to create settlements were missionaries bent on saving souls and fishermen bent on hunting whales. The established Maori population did not take kindly to all of this and sporadic fighting ensued. The Treaty of Waitangi in 1840 gave Great Britain sovereignty over the islands but guaranteed the Maoris right to their lands. English colonization was slow, and occasional uprisings and disagreements between the European and native populations did little to encourage peaceful growth of the new nation. But a gold rush in 1865 brought a swell of immigrants who later settled into farming pursuits when the gold fever exhausted itself. Production of mutton and lamb quickly exceeded local needs and the introduction in 1882 of refrigerated ships gave impetus to the production of fresh meat, stimulating both the intensity of farming and the flow of immigrants.

Light industries based on food and forest products, clothing and light machinery together with the small population probably account for New Zealand's lack of pollution problems. Although the sheep outnumber the people by twenty to one, farming only absorbs about 12 per cent of the population. At its worst, the unemployment level reached less than 1 per cent.[2] Likely it is a combination of climate and agricultural efficiency that accounts for the abundance of meats and dairy products and a year-round selection of fruits and vegetables that places nourishing foods on every table. Nurses and health-care information are available from a system of 109 branches and 566 sub-branches of medical offices that one way or another place health services into every New Zealand home. Privately sponsored by the Plunket Society and begun in 1907,[3] this health-care system was also responsible for the development of the "New Zealand Whole Milk Biscuit," actually a high-protein dietary supplement in the form of a cookie (biscuit) especially created for children.

That the easy-going nature of the Polynesian Maoris can exist side-by-side with the work-oriented English (or Pakehas as they are called in New Zealand) is a tribute to both peoples. More than 90 per cent of the Kiwis (New Zealanders) are of British descent, with about 7 per cent of Polynesian Maori origin and the rest small groups of mixed European and Asian descent.[4] Working in all types of industries and professions, the Maoris have adapted themselves into the mainstream of New Zealand society.

Nonetheless, their cultural differences are often apparent to the Pakehas, and attempts to understand and explain these differences have resulted in the publication of a pamphlet entitled *Understanding Polynesians*, by Margaret Lee.[5]

A phenomenon called *musu* is often apparent among the Maoris, as it is among other South Pacific and even African groups. It is characterized by a deadpan expression and monosyllabic speech and is said to be caused by a combination of fear, shame and perhaps a sense of unjust accusation. The intervention of a trusted person who speaks the language will usually calm the afflicted Maori. Regarding all property as communal and seeing no wrong in "borrowing" something he desires is another Maori cultural trait that has frequently caused misunderstandings.

But in the fabric that has built the New Zealand nation, the interweaving of the Maori spirit of nature and the Pakehas' ethic of work and order have combined to produce a proud and pioneering people in a fresh clean land of boundless beauty, in a climate that is never too hot and never too cool and where no one needs to pray for rain.

Home Life and Facilities

Abundant water power produces hydro-electric power widely used in industries and homes. About 82 per cent of New Zealanders cook by electricity while only 11 per cent use gas.[2] They enjoy the use of a wide range of electrical appliances including refrigerators, freezers and small kitchen appliances.

The ability to bake has always been a criterion for the New Zealand homemaker, but today many other factors influence her cookery skills. These include widespread travel and communications, increasing sophistication of restaurants, the burgeoning New Zealand wine industry and the influence of other ethnic groups: Chinese, East Indian, Pacific Islanders and the Dutch. Curiosity and pleasure in discovering new foods and food combinations have stimulated not only interest in cooking other than British, but also interest in acquiring unusual cooking utensils, recipes and menu patterns. Previously, a simple cook top and an oven produced the typical Pakeha dinner of roasted meat and roasted vegetables topped off with a creamy fruit dessert. But today, skewers for shish-kabob, woks for Chinese dishes, and casseroles for moussakas and electric blenders to create curry combinations are all a part of the New Zealand kitchen.[6]

While being eager to taste and adapt new food ideas, the Kiwis are also wise enough to retain at least one cooking tradition that has not only stood the test of time, but has proven to be a practical modern innovation as well. From earliest times, the Maoris cooked their main meal of the day in an earth oven which they called an UMU or HANGI. A pit would be dug and a wood fire kindled in the bottom. As the fire progressed, smooth stones would be placed on top. By scraping out the fire's ashes, and retaining the red-hot stones in the pit, the Maoris created a well-insulated oven. Over the heated stones they placed joints of meat, leaf-wrapped fish and seafood and finally placed KUMARA (sweet potatoes) or other vegetables on top. Liberally sprinkled water created steam, and woven mats placed on top sealed in the heat and moisture. After a period of undisturbed cooking time, a well-cooked tasty meal of meat, fish and vegetables could be enjoyed by a large number of people. Today, many a large outdoor party, sports club gathering or family picnic is highlighted with a feast made in a HANGI.[6,7]

Except for certain isolated areas, food storage has never been a problem in New Zealand. This is because of the combination of efficient agricultural methods and the variations from temperate to sub-tropical climates which allow for an almost continuous supply of fresh fruits, vegetables and grains as well as meats and dairy products. Refrigerators and freezers are widely used and most Kiwis also enjoy convenience foods, delicatessen specialties, and a range of imported foods as well.

FOODS COMMONLY USED

The basic food preferences and meal patterns of New Zealand are British. A great variety of home-baked scones, biscuits, quick breads and cakes are visible at most meals and whenever tea is served – which means often. Lamb is the favoured meat and careful distinctions are made in regard to the age of the lamb, mutton being favoured only by the staunchest Englishman. Abundance of local fish and seafood and a plentiful supply of a variety of fresh fruits and vegetables all make the New Zealand diet a good one.

Milk and Milk Products
Milk is taken by most children at most meals in the form of fresh whole milk. Where considered necessary, toddlers are provided with the "New Zealand Whole Milk Biscuit," a cookie enriched with protein in the form of skim milk powder. Most adults take some milk in tea, soups and creamy desserts. The use of skim milk, powdered skim milk, yoghurt and cottage cheese is still limited although increasing in popularity. Many varieties of cheeses are available but not widely used.

Fruits and Vegetables
Produce is mainly grown on the North Island where the climate varies from temperate to sub-tropical, allowing for an almost continuous growing period. Imported, frozen and canned fruits and vegetables are also used. Fruits include apples, pears, varieties of berries, plums, peaches, apricots, nectarine, cherries. The more exotic fruits include *feijoas,*

tamarillo (tree tomato), *kiwi* (Chinese gooseberry), passionfruit and pineapple. Pumpkin and sweet potatoes are the staple vegetables but many other common vegetables and salad greens are also used.

Meats and Alternates
Lamb is the number-one meat in New Zealand almost to the exclusion of beef, pork and poultry. Distinction is made in the age of the lamb: the youngest and tenderest is called spring lamb and is aged from twelve to eighteen weeks; weaned lamb is aged from four and one-half to nine months old. Hogget is the deeper pink-fleshed lamb butchered from nine to twenty months. Young mutton is the next classification and includes lamb from twenty months to two years. Mature mutton is strong in flavour, deep red in flesh colour with brittle white fat, and for this the sheep are butchered from two to five years old. Most common method of cooking is oven-roasting with prepared vegetables being added near the end of the cooking time. More recently lamb has been used more imaginatively in a variety of international dishes.[6,8] Popular fish include trout, cod, red snapper, groper, *terekihi*, John Dory, flounder and tuna, with whitebait considered a special delicacy. Oysters, mussels and eels are widely used. *Tohera* is a native bivalve considered a delicacy but not always available. Crayfish, similar to lobsters, are enjoyed and crayfish tails are exported. Fish is eaten in quantity, often as an ingredient in other dishes, sometimes as a garnish or side dish. Legumes are seldom used except for special dishes.

Breads and Cereals
New Zealand is almost self-sufficient in wheat production. Few whole grain breads or cereals are consumed; white wheat flour is favoured. Oats as a baking ingredient and hot breakfast porridge is used occasionally. But there is increasing emphasis on "health foods" with the resulting interest in whole grains and varieties of different grains, including wheat germ. "Tea breads" or quick breads, biscuits, scones and cakes are served whenever tea is poured and often are a regular part of most meals as well.

Fats
New Zealand butter and cream are of fine quality and widely used. Butter, lard, cooking oil and salt pork are all used in cooking.

Sweets and Snacks
Much sugar is consumed in the form of sweetened tea, sweet pastries and candies as well as preserves such as jams, jellies and marmalades.

Seasonings
With traditional British restraint in seasoning, Kiwis have used little more than salt, pepper and onions. However, more current interest and stimu-

lation in imaginative cooking has brought an increase in both seasonings and condiments, although bland flavours still prevail.

Beverages
Tea is the favoured beverage for every meal and as a mid-morning snack usually with biscuits or breads. Tea is traditionally taken with milk and sugar. Local wines are appearing more frequently in homes and restaurants, and beer is a favourite for quick lunches and outdoor parties.

Meal Patterns and Eating Customs
The pattern of three meals a day is slowly making inroads into the long-cherished tradition of six meals: breakfast, morning tea, lunch, afternoon tea, dinner and supper (although often afternoon tea and dinner may be one and the same). The factors that are creating the changes in New Zealand are similar to those found almost world wide: increased food costs, more married women joining the work force, concern about obesity and a distinct increase in nutrition awareness. Although morning and afternoon tea breaks are still widely observed both at home and at work, meals are becoming lighter and more varied. In spite of all of these factors, British influence still predominates in most meals and the way in which they are served.

Substantial breakfasts, small lunches and meat-and-vegetable dinners are punctuated by tea breaks. Ice and ice water are seldom seen although beer is usually served chilled. Most table service is on the formal side with a special knife always set for the sole purpose of buttering one's bread. And British as well as New Zealanders still frown on the habit of resting one's knife on the dinner plate; the main course is to be eaten throughout with knife and fork. Further, New Zealanders have no qualms about placing a spoonful of chilled salad on their main dinner plate right beside the roast and hot vegetables.[10]

Special Occasions
The New Zealand population is predominantly Christian with about 80 per cent of the people being members of one of four denominations: Church of England, Roman Catholic, Methodist and Presbyterian. Ratana and Ringatu are the two main Maori sects, though many Maoris are Christian. Close to 4,000 New Zealanders are of the Jewish faith.

Although Christmas and Easter are celebrated with family gatherings, there is little question that the avidly sports-minded Kiwis generate more excitement over "rice dyes" (that's Race Days, of course) and the accompanying outdoor picnics or HANGIS (pit-cooked meals) than over any religious oriented occasions. Foods vary little from the daily fare except that Sunday dinner is almost invariably roast lamb and roasted vegetables with trifle or PAVLOVA for dessert. Festive days may include meals that are more leisurely but differ little in content.

THIRTY-EIGHT

Norwegian

There is more to Norway and Norwegians than meets the eye. Outwardly the country is the most sparsely populated in all of Europe with less than 25 per cent of the land inhabited and more than 75 per cent of it a vast stillness of barren mountain ranges. Outwardly Norwegians seem to be a literate, calm and homogeneous people, conformity seeming to be the key to their way of life.[1,2]

Yet the Norwegians were the first in Europe to recognize the potential of water-powered electricity and in 1891 installed in northern Hammerfest the first hydro-electric plant in all of Europe – while the rest of Europe lit their candles and kerosene lamps. As early as the 700s, while the rest of civilization was still yawning, Norwegian Viking ships set out to far-off coasts of the Arab world and even North America, to explore, to trade and to plunder. Stone Age carvings visible throughout Norway on mountainsides and rocky strata are said to be more than 4,000 years old and depict a vivid way of life with images of the sea and the land and even well-posed skiers.[3]

Even today with little more than 3 per cent of the land arable, Norway has an efficient mechanized system of agriculture and a bustling industry in forestry and fishing products while her merchant shipping fleet is the third largest in the world. And while much of the rest of the industrialized world concerns itself with problems of pollution, Norway exports an increasingly prized resource: pure spring water.[3]

While Norwegians freely admit to being hooked on sports and physical fitness and being avid readers – there are said to be three times as many daily newspapers in Oslo as in New York – they also admit that alcoholism is one of their oldest problems.[3] And while they enjoy parties after skiing, skating, sailing or mountain climbing, there is sure to be at least one guest abstaining from alcoholic drinks so that he may drive the others home. For in Norway impaired driving carries the stiff penalty of twenty-one days in jail and this is strictly enforced.[2] Special government stores dispense alcohol at high prices and close for weekends. Perhaps it is a spark of the old Viking fire that accounts for the Norwegians openly adhering to the letter of the law, while most of them quietly make good use of a still hidden in the cellar![3]

And while 96 per cent of the population profess to the Lutheran faith, complete with the celebration of Christmas, Easter, confirmation ceremonies and parties on the fifteenth birthday, examples of still older beliefs are much in evidence. Dotted throughout the rugged countryside are gnarled and grotesque rock formations which the Norwegians – only slightly hesitantly and more than half-jokingly – will tell you are fossilized trolls. Many inexplicable events are quietly attributed to the varying dispositions of the mischievous trolls inhabiting the rocks and trees throughout Norway and there are few who would dismiss their existence completely. And there is scarcely a Norwegian family who would not set out a plate brimful of creamy RØMMEGRØT for Julenisse, the Christmas gnomes dressed in red caps and white beards. With a full belly on Christmas Eve, they are not so likely to play tricks on the family the rest of the year. . . .

The Norwegian's apparent contradiction between his inner and outer self is an ancient trait. While daring and violence seemed to characterize the Viking abroad, at home he organized *things* – special meeting places where village grievances and disputes could be heard and settled. This surprisingly democratic system was in existence before the 600s.[3] And while the Viking held the belief that to fall in battle meant a place in Valhalla with Odin in the afterlife, he also clung to a firm belief in *ragnarok*, "the final confrontation between Good and Evil," and the accounting of man's deeds.

But it is history as well as ancient cultures that have molded the Norwegian life-style. The flamboyant era of the Vikings ended in 1066 followed by almost 500 years of internal strife, domination by Sweden and Denmark in ill-fated unions and finally the Black Plague which decimated the population. Pressure from the German Hanseatic League controlled Norwegian trade for almost 200 years, while the Danes ruled and taxed the people and spread the Lutheran faith.[3] Finally, towards the end of the 1700s, with her population increased, her economy strengthened, and a resurgence in rich peasant art awakening, Norway adopted English manners and culture and stepped towards independence.

Although the democratic constitution was signed on May 17, 1814, it is still celebrated today with children's parades and a buoyant sense of freedom as though "the ink were still wet on the paper."[3]

Wherever Norwegians have emigrated they have adapted themselves quietly into the community, retaining their Lutheran faith and their love of sports, everywhere their calm natures and gentle strength pervading their life style. Unquestionably their long historic struggle with the elements of nature and their life in a vast quiet country have left them with a deep sensitivity to the concerns of others as well as a personal need for solitude.

Cooking Facilities

Although Norwegians treasure their solitude and their privacy, this is not to say that they do not enjoy social occasions. In the rural areas social occasions are often combined with co-operative efforts concerned with smoking, pickling, salting and preserving meats and fish, preserving berries and other fruits, and communal baking of huge batches of FLAT-BROD, enough for a whole season. The dimpled crispy round bread keeps well and is the perfect accompaniment to the many cheeses made over the summer months when the sheep and goat's milk is at its richest.

Although refrigerators and freezers are made use of almost everywhere, traditional foods and implements still have an important place in the Norwegian *kjokken* (kitchen). Even many large restaurants and modern homes still proudly use the intricately carved wooden butter molds that were in use hundreds of years ago.

Agriculture is fully mechanized, but the Norwegian farmer still keeps a few cream-coloured Westland "fjord ponies," more out of nostalgia than need. And dotted over the landscape are the *stabburs*, two-floor storehouses reminiscent of a time before electricity and freezers, yet still much in use. The main floor is used to store grains, apples and pears, home preserves, pickles and root vegetables. And the sweet and musty food smells mingle with the heady aromas of fermenting beer and wine and waft upward to the second storey which is used as a guest house and where the Norwegian family proudly keep some of their best possessions. Travel throughout the more remote areas is still often difficult, and guests are always welcomed and expected to stay at least overnight. Also reminiscent of former times are *saeters*, the tiny cabins perched precariously on craggy ledges. In summer months the women of the household would often spend weeks at a time busily collecting, churning and aging the creamy milk from sheep and goats into a variety of cheeses. Today most of the cheese making is carried out commercially in factories and the picturesque *saeter* is treasured as a summer cottage by the solitude-hungry urban Norwegian.

FOODS COMMONLY USED

Although ice-cream vendors commonly hawk their wares at ski matches and shows throughout the winter, in other respects Norwegians are uncommonly conservative not only in foods but also in food preparation. This is not to say that Norwegian food is bland. It is not. Rather, care is taken to preserve the natural sea or earthy flavours inherent in all fresh foods. Freshly caught fish (often still alive), fresh meats, young vegetables and seasonal fruits are all enjoyed with a minimum of fripperies: simply boiled or gently stewed and served with their own freshness and flavour intact.

Robust, pungent and heartier tastes are evident in the many fermented, cured, pickled and salted dishes that appear on the Norwegian table; fermented fish (especially trout, called *rakor-ret*) and smoked, cured meats, pickled herrings, pickled and salted vegetables and tangy salads all take their place with aged cheeses and sour, crisp, whole-grained breads. So much are natural flavours relished that often dishes – soups, stews and desserts – are seasoned only with salt or sweetened with sugar. Milk and milk products are enjoyed daily and sour cream is as important an ingredient in many dishes as salt. Though fruits and vegetables have only a short growing season, they seem to make up in quality and flavour what they lack in variety. Self-sufficient in meat (domestic and game), dairy products and vegetables (basis), Norway imports most of her grain needs, fruits and some vegetables.

Milk and Milk Products

Glasses of cold milk, sour milk and buttermilk are enjoyed by all ages at all meals and often as a refreshment. Many varieties of cheeses, mostly made from sheep and goat's milk, range from creamy and sweet in flavour to the powerful GAMMEL OST, a cheese so aged and odiferous that it is always kept on its own covered plate.

Most commonly used is the caramel-coloured sweetish-flavoured goat cheese appearing at almost every meal and often blended with a *roux*, and flavoured with currant jelly to make a sauce for meats. A Norwegian kitchen is never without a supply of sour cream, for this is used to flavour fruits, vegetables, stews, soups and is an important ingredient in pancakes, waffles and baked goods. Even RØMMEGRØT, the traditional ending to a meal and an indispensable dish at a country weddings, is made basically from flour-thickened sour cream and served with a dribble of clear melted butter and a drift of cinnamon and crunchy brown sugar.

Fruits and Vegetables

Apples, pears and plums are the staple fruits, with some apricots and peaches being grown at Sjoholt. But when the wild berries ripen, almost half the population declares a holiday from work to attend to the urgent business of picking berries: lingonberries, cloudberries, blueberries, cranberries and tiny wild strawberries. What cannot be eaten in short order is preserved in freezers or packed in jars as sweet preserves to be enjoyed all winter. Fruits, especially the variety of sweet and tart berries, are enjoyed sometimes slightly thickened and sweetened into puddings, enfolded into pancakes, layered in cakes, sprinkled into waffle batter and frequently as a side dish with roasted meats and game.

Norwegians enjoy all the commonly stored winter vegetables such as cabbages and potatoes, beets and carrots. But they especially savour young fresh vegetables in season, serving them simply boiled and lightly flavoured with fresh butter, sour cream and dill. Freshly made sauerkraut still crisp and crunchy with caraway seeds, wilted cucumber salads and bright tart pickled beets are year-round favourites.

Meats and Alternates

Norwegians enjoy many meats, especially lamb and mutton, either fresh or salted, dried, smoked and eaten hot or cold. Pork (ham, bacon, salt pork and sausages) beef and veal and geese and ducks appear less often on the menu.

Even more than lamb and mutton, Norwegians love fish. The almost endless varieties of fresh fish – salmon, trout, mackerel, flounder, herring, eel, turbot, halibut and cod as well as shrimp and crayfish – are matched by the almost endless methods of preparation – salting, smoking, drying, marinating, poaching. The early simple but hot dinner favoured by the Norwegians is most likely to be poached fresh fish with a mustard or horse radish sauce accompanied by boiled vegetables, or a simple mutton and vegetable stew like FAAR I KAAL. There is surely no shortage of protein, for meats and fish may be consumed not only for dinner but often are a part of a sandwich lunch and frequently are consumed together with cereals and eggs as part of *frokost*, the ample Norwegian breakfast. Legumes are not widely used, except the dried peas so popular for soup. Almonds and almond paste are usual bakery ingredients.

Breads and Cereals

A great variety of breads and rolls – crisp, dried, chewy, crusty, even soft and light – make their appearance at almost every meal. Most popular is the crisp dimpled circle of rye bread called FLATBROD which is still made in huge quantities, often as a communal effort. Norwegian women take great pride in their baking and, even though guests may drop in unexpectedly, there will always be crispy cookies and at least one cake to accompany the inevitable good coffee. Cooked and cold cereals are also very much a part of the popular *frokost* which also includes cheeses, meats and fish. The Norwegians are firm converts to a hearty breakfast.

Fats
Butter is not only a cooking fat and a spread, it is also used as a flavouring and an ingredient in almost every dish. Cheeses, milks, cream and sour cream are all rich in butterfat and skimmed milk is considered suitable for anything but humans. Smaller amounts of other fats such as rendered duck or goose fat, salt pork and lard are also used in cooking.

Sweets and Snacks
The Norwegian preference is not for sweets, but an undeniable sweet tooth does exist. Although candies are eaten as well as cakes and pastries, they are seldom richly iced or syrupy. Most baked goods are only slightly sweet and coffee is usually preferred strong and black.

Seasonings
Natural flavours predominate in the Norwegian cuisine, but there is a definite predilection for salted foods. Salty cheeses, salted and pickled vegetables, salt-cured meats and fish are a daily part of the diet. Only moderate amounts of other seasonings are used: bay leaves, peppercorns, mustard, horse radish, dill, thyme, and of course butter and sour cream are liberally used.

Beverages
The general Scandinavian custom of *skaal* is as prevalent in Norway as it is in Sweden and Denmark: the raised glass of chilled AQUAVIT, the firm meeting of eyes followed by a decisive gulp and then the triumphant raising of the emptied glass and the final meeting of the eyes. Frequently this is followed by chasers of beer and most often the whole ritual precedes a meal and is carried on throughout the dining. The final bottomless cups of coffee are perhaps a token attempt at sobriety. It is difficult to say for which of these beverages the Norwegian has the greatest capacity. Suffice it to say that all are consumed in Norway by Norwegians in quantities unrivalled in North America.

Meal Patterns and Eating Customs
So keen on sports and the outdoor life are the Norwegians that it seems they rise deliberately early to have time to fortify themselves with a heroic breakfast selected at will from a KOLTBORD. This would consist of an assortment of cold roasted and cured meats and sausages, eggs, ham, bacon, hot and cold cereals, a selection of mild to strong cheeses, crisp and soft rye and wheat breads, fresh butter and several fruit preserves as well as fruit juices and fruits and coffee.

Then they are off to the day's activities. Schools and work begin very early but they also end early in the day, and most are homeward bound to eat a simple early dinner around 4:00 P.M. Throughout the day, small snacks of coffee, pastries or bread and butter and cheese may suffice to replenish and nourish; sometimes lunch is an abbreviated form of the breakfast KOLTBORD: open-face sandwiches with coffee or beer.

Aside from breakfast, there is little doubt that food and its preparation are never really as important in the Norwegian mind as having time to ski or skate, sail or mountain-climb. The 4:00 P.M. dinner is always a hot though simple meal, sometimes a hearty soup and a filling dessert of waffles or pancakes with fruit, other times a fish soup and poached fish with boiled vegetables. At least once every week FAAR I KAAL, a simple but substantial casserole of wedged cabbage and mutton, is served.

Of course sometimes occasion demands a more leisurely and lengthy dinner. Then, whether at home or in a restaurant, the three- or four-hour meal will be frequently punctuated with *skaal* as well as convivial conversation and laughter. Later in the evening, a small version of the KOLTBORD will again make an appearance just as a "snack" to beckon sleep.

Norwegians are fond of flowers. Even though they may be expensive, they always grace a special dinner table and the best restaurants will always have at least one fresh flower in a vase at each table.

Perhaps because of the isolation of many villages or perhaps just because of the Norwegian natural love for people, it is impossible to visit a Norwegian home and leave without at least having had coffee and cookies or cake. Usually a visitor will be expected to partake in the next meal with the family. Traditionally in Norway wedding or confirmation guests are expected to stay for a few days: they may sleep over at a neighbour's but they will take all their meals with the host family, the food and drink mingling happily with songs, speeches and dancing.

Blending with their love for natural flavours and their appreciation of life, Norwegians take more than ordinary delight in seasonal foods. Skipping school and work to pick the ripening berries is a pastime enjoyed just as much as gorging oneself on prawns. Both seasons are so precious and so short that meals of berries or prawns are an unabashed national pastime. Even the fishermen must stagger their summer holidays so that no one will be denied the classic meals of prawns accompanied by crusty fresh bread with sweet butter and homemade mayonnaise with pauses only long enough for swallows of chill white wine. In fact, bags of cooked prawns are bought from street vendors and munched like peanuts.

Firm about the food traditions of their own land, Norwegians are not much concerned about breaking so-called rules of eating and drinking. The order of courses in a meal is not of great urgency: if the main dish is ready first, it will be eaten first and the fish course may follow later. A fish soup may precede a main course of fish that may be garnished with a shrimp sauce: the duplication matters little. Frequently a robust red wine is served with a main course of poached cod and mustard sauce – though unorthodox. the combination is delicious!

Special Occasions

The Norwegians were the last of the Teutonic tribes to set aside their beliefs in Odin and Thor and the glorious afterlife in Valhalla, the warrior's final reward. This was followed by almost 500 years of Catholicism which in turn was suppressed in favour of Evangelical Lutheranism. Although the Norwegians are almost 96 per cent Lutherans and devoutly celebrate Christmas, Easter and confirmation at the age of fifteen, they are not avid churchgoers, nor have they completely relinquished their respect for the heavenly bodies (they celebrate Midsummer's Eve in honour of *solsnu*, the turn of the sun). The Christmas troll Julenisse has a definite place in Christmas celebrations and Easter is as much celebrated for its religious connotation as for the fact that it marks the beginning of the annual mountain-trekking.

There is a growing difference between urban and rural dwellers in the way everything from weddings to funerals is celebrated. Because most inhabited areas are generally isolated from each other in the countryside, lengthy and often difficult travelling conditions make it more practical for guests or visitors to stay at least overnight. This necessitates extensive cooking preparations and even the sharing of neighbour's accommodations. In contrast, urban dwellers are less gregarious, emotionally colder, and tend to put forth less effort than their more traditionally minded country people.

This situation is probably most evident in funerals. The death of a villager will be mourned by the entire area with all flags at half mast and all the area people coming out to attend the services, gathering afterwards to share sandwiches and coffee. In the cities cremation is popular and this together with the custom of hiring not only a preacher but also professional hymn singers and even mourners makes for a brief cold ceremony. After a city funeral only the immediate family gather quietly for GRAVMAT (grave food) and GRAVOL (grave beer).

Similarly many villages are not only retaining but in many cases reviving age-old traditions for weddings. In the village of Voss, Saturday is the day for weddings with a traditional wedding cake made of towering layers of almond rings decorated with tiny Norwegian flags, sugary flowers, miniature crackers all topped with a tiny bride and groom. In Hardanger, a bridal outfit would be incomplete without an heirloom gold or silver crown (if necessary rented from the village goldsmith). Everywhere in the rural areas, weddings are events of many days' duration, often going through the night, with courses of coffee and sandwiches or sometimes hearty soups and nibbles of cheeses and thinly sliced sausages to periodically revive the merrymakers. City weddings are more brief, more and more becoming merely a one-day affair, but most still retaining the traditional wedding cake.

Birthdays are special in Norway, the most important being the fifteenth. This is Confirmation Day, and preparation is taken seriously with all the candidates preparing themselves both in knowledge of the church as well as in new clothes. The confirmation service is announced with special invitations, the candidates appearing at the service in long white gowns covering their new clothes as they nervously answer questions on their teaching before a hushed audience. The tenseness of the services is broken with lavish gifts, flower-decked tables and hours of singing, eating (an enlarged *frokost*) and drinking.

While confirmation is an undeniable highlight on the birthday register, so is the fortieth, fiftieth, and sixieth. In fact, these special birthdays are celebrated with beautiful gifts, flowers and special cakes. At the age of seventy the occasion is considered so important that photos of septuagenarians appear regularly in local papers, and women who reach one hundred years of age are sent a special birthday cake by a Norwegian women's magazine.

From noon on Christmas Eve, Norwegian shops close and exactly at 5:00 P.M. church bells throughout the country herald the holiday. But weeks before the bustle of holiday baking, slaughtering of animals and curing meats and the preparation of LUTEFISK as well as the sending of typical Norwegian Christmas cards – a jolly picture of Julenisse gobbling his plate of RØMMEGRØT – leave little doubt of the coming occasion. In areas of the west coast of Norway the Viking tradition of serving dried salted lamb at this time is still enjoyed while in most of the eastern areas traditional roast pork together with LUTEFISK and a delectable display of fruits, nuts and bakery highlight the Christmas menu.

While there may be a difference in menu, other traditions are uniform throughout the country. Everywhere animals are given a special treat on Christmas Eve in the belief that they shared in the holy event in the stable on the special Eve; Norwegian cows get a special treat of salted herring. After the Christmas Eve dinner carols are sung around the Christmas tree which is aglow with white candles or white lights. Then the exchanging of gifts ends the evening. Christmas Day is a quiet family day; the rounds of parties begin the following day.

JULEBORD is the special name given to the groaning table of Chistmas delicacies whether at home or in a restaurant. The display will include the finest specialties of the country: whole poached cod, whole smoked salmon, glazed roasted ducks and roasted pork stuffed with prunes and apples. By January, Oslo has only eight hours of daylight, but the JULEBORD and the white lights of Christmas as well as the parties and *skaal* make all oblivious to the outside gloom.

Lent and Easter are observed more casually by Norwegians. Easter Sunday services are followed by a hearty but brief dinner for traditionally this is the day the mountain-climbing begins.

Baptisms and birthdays, Christmas and Easter all compete on the festive calendar with ancient holidays closely related with the changing seasons, seasonal activities and the enjoyment of fresh seasonal foods. The threads of paganism and even superstition that persist into the culture of the modern-day Norwegian, and indeed most Scandinavians, seem to be no more contradictory than their delight in parties and their craving for solitude.

THIRTY-NINE

Polish

Her neighbours invaded her, fought with her, divided her into pieces and for a time even erased her name from the map of Europe. Over a period of about 400 years, from the 1300s to the late 1700s, intermittent wars with Sweden, Russia, Turkey and Germany continually changed the borders of Poland until she was swallowed up and divided into Russia, Prussia and part of the Austro-Hungarian empire and finally disappeared. At least her name disappeared, but the western Slavs known as "Polanians" or "dwellers of the plains"[1] clung tenaciously to their own traditions and held fast to their beloved church. And, despite the influence of three foreign masters at one time for a period of more than one hundred years, the Polish spirit proved indestructible.

Under the subsequent oppressions of the 1800s, the parts of Poland under Prussia and Austria did not fare as badly as those under Russia. These latter areas were subjected to forced Russification which included sharp restrictions in the use of the Polish language and even in the attendance of religious services. Feudal land systems prevailed widely and so did illiteracy. And while the princes and the aristocracy dined at sumptuous banquets, the labouring peasants survived on cabbage and potatoes and their deep religious faith.

These difficult times witnessed many Polish uprisings, and following each unsuccessful attempt waves of soldiers, political refugees, and peasants made their way to North America.[1] With the outbreak of World War I Poles conscripted into both the Russian and the German army resulted in Pole fighting against Pole.

But on November 3, 1918, Poland accomplished a miraculous resurrection and proclaimed the Republic of Poland. Establishment of the republic was only the beginning. Poland hoped also to regain her lost territories and these hopes led again to conflicts, mainly with Russia. In the ensuing years, problems with minority groups, financial crises and government turmoil all added to the difficulties and the weakening of Poland. These problems culminated in 1939 with the Third Reich's sweep of Poland and the beginning of World War II.

This history of repeated conquest and subjugation resulted in a draining of the spirit of the people, of natural resources and of the arable lands (arable land requiring great quantities of costly fertilizer).[2] It also served to intensify family relationships and the enjoyment of special occasions. Many ancient pagan rituals blend with religious ceremonies and festive celebrations that all demand a great flurry of fine cooking and baking, decorations and party clothes. Poles, in common with all Slavs, love to have a party, enjoy wearing their best clothes and sharing an abundance of food and drink in parties that often last several days.[3]

While it is inevitable that the turbulent history of conquerors and oppressions should have affected Polish life, traditions and cuisine, it is also interesting that two royal romances, an influx of refugees and a brief rule by a French dandy also affected the Polish culinary arts. In the early 1300s, the love Casimir III bore for Esterka, a Jewess, resulted in Poland's welcoming of Jewish refugees from all the oppressed areas of Europe, particularly western Germany.[4,5] The introduction into Polish cuisine of potato puddings (KUGELIS) from Lithuania, honeycakes (PIERNIK) and sweet and sour dishes like the classic jellied carp with raisins and almonds from Germany are all attributed to Jewish influence.[4,6]

Two hundred years later when the Polish King Sigismund I wed Italy's Queen Bona Sforza, Poland not only gained a queen but also a retinue of Italian chefs. They introduced pastas, pastries and ice-cream desserts. Italian gardeners cultivated many vegetables new to the Poles, including tomatoes.[7] And it was the son of Catharine de Medici and Henry II of France – Henry III – who briefly ruled Poland in the late 1500s and left as probably the only redeeming aspect of his rule, a Polish appreciation for sauces and mayonnaise.

Also entrenched in the Polish cuisine are evidences of Russian, German and Austrian culinary arts. Sour cream and dill, baked grains (KASZA in Poland, KASHA in Russia), cabbage soups and beet soups, ZAKASKI and VODKA are all as familiar in Poland as they are in Russia. Sausage-making, a taste for sweet and sour foods, and specialty potato dishes can all be traced as favourites in Germany as well. And the influence of the far-flung Austro-Hungarian empire (before 1918) was no doubt responsible in large part for the Polish predilection for paprika from Hungary, dumplings and bread-crumb sauces from the Czechs, and strudels, tortes and other delectable bakery from Austria.

The ingenuity of the Polish peasant women combined the produce of their own land with the tastes that history meted out to them from other countries and developed the great classics of Polish cuisine. These include:

BIGOS: a hunter's stew of layered cabbage or sauerkraut, mixed meats, game and sausage;

CHOLODNIK: a cold beet and sour cream soup garnished with sliced fresh vegetables and shrimp;

PIEROGI or PIEROZKI: boiled dumplings made of filled noodle pastry;

BABKA: a rich delicate yeast cake of eggs and dried fruits, special for Easter; and

PIECZONY SCHAB: roast pork loin.

Home Life and Facilities

For the most part, in cities, only the most privileged can afford modern appliances for the kitchen. Country kitchens have changed little in hundreds of years: enamelware and cast-iron cooking pots, wooden implements for stirring and pounding, heavy rolling pins for doughs, mortar and pestle for crushing and blending and sturdy, well-scrubbed wooden tables. All utensils and furnishings have been time-tested and in many cases used for many generations.

Food storage poses little problem for city dwellers: in good times and bad, preference is for foods freshly purchased. Age-old methods of food preservation still prevail in rural areas: brining of vegetables, salting of fish, drying of wild mushrooms and garlic and large quantities of home-preserved fruits and jams all carefully stored in cellars or kitchen shelves are the pride of every peasant household.

FOODS COMMONLY USED

The food tastes of conquerors and the ingenuity of the Poles in hard times is still evidenced in the general taste for hearty substantial dishes based on local produce. The staples of the Polish diet are the home-grown grains, basic vegetables (beets, potatoes and cabbages) that store well, and the many smoked and cured meats and sausages prepared from pork.

Among dairy products a preference is shown for sour cream and soured milk. Simple pot cheese is prepared and served in many satisfying ways to make complete meals.

The rich flavour of abundant wild mushrooms appears in many thick soups and stews, and few homes are without their own barrels of sauerkraut which is used in many ways. The Polish taste for sweets is evident in their honeycakes and fine baked goods, and is characterized in a definite touch of sweetness in soups, fish dishes, and even salads made with vinegar and a generous taste of sugar. The flavours of dill, garlic, paprika and sour cream are laced through many dishes, while the baked goods are redolent with honey, raisins and almonds. Beer and coffee are not as frequently taken as vodka and tea.

Milk and Milk Products

Fresh whole milk is used mainly by children with the adults preferring soured milk or buttermilk. Sour cream is widely used as an ingredient, as a dressing or a sauce, blended into soups, gravies and as a side dish. Cheeses are available, but the bland smooth flavour of pot or cottage cheese is preferred both as a spread and in many cooked dishes.

Fruits and Vegetables

Some fresh fruits and vegetables are eaten in season, but Poles enjoy fruits in the form of compotes and stews and they like their vegetables either well-cooked or pickled. Plums, apples and pears are the most readily available fruits and these are used as compotes, thick richly sweet preserves, fillings for cakes and yeast bakeries, and even served as condiments with meats for a sweet-sour flavour (but mostly sweet). Vegetables favoured are potatoes, red and green and savoy cabbages, beets, kohlrabi, and smaller quantities of carrots, peas and beans. Wild mushrooms are used both fresh or dried in many dishes. Both mushrooms and sauerkraut are used not only alone, but in so many other dishes they can also be considered as a flavouring.

Meats and Alternates

Poles favour their meats well-cooked, tender and juicy and with accompanying sauces or gravies. Broiling or dry roasting are not a part of their culinary practices. Pork and beef are the favourites but chickens, ducks, turkeys, game fowl and game animals are eaten when available.

Except for herring in many different forms and occasional baked or poached pike or carp, the Poles seldom eat fish or seafood. Eggs are used generously in baking and in cooking; occasionally as main dish omelets, more frequently as appetizers. Legumes are not widely used at all. Nuts, especially almonds, find a place in baking or as a garnish.

Breads and Cereals

Rye, wheat, buckwheat, barley and oats are grown in quantity. Wheat flour is used in all bakery but rye flour is preferred for breads. Barley and buckwheat are used almost daily as stuffings, fillings, in soups or as side dishes to meat and vegetables. This type of side dish is called KASZA. Rye bread is a staple at all meals especially in the country, but potatoes often supplant bread at a meal, especially at dinner.[3]

No crumb of bread is ever wasted. POLONAISE SAUCE, famed in many other lands besides Poland, is actually not a sauce in the usual sense, but a toasted mixture of crumbs browned in butter. Cooked vegetables, especially green beans and cauliflower, benefit from this flavour. Bread crumbs also form the basic ingredient for poached dumplings served either with meats or with a fruit sauce or sour cream as a dessert. Many fine cakes are made from light mixtures of separated and beaten eggs together with fine bread crumbs and ground nuts.

Fats
Butter is favoured for cooking and baking and as a spread. Lard, salt pork and bacon fat, rendered chicken, goose or duck fat are also used. Vegetable oils and margarine are used only sparingly.

Sweets and Snacks
Poles have an insatiable sweet tooth that encompasses a great array of fine baked goods and pastries, tortes, strudels, MAZURKAS, etc. They also enjoy munching raisins and almonds together as a treat. There is a general use of much sugar in beverages, and honey in cakes and drinks. Polish dishes that are purportedly "sweet and sour" are always very sweet with only a hint of the sour. An added sprinkle of sugar is felt to enhance everything from soups and meat dishes to pickles and fish specialties.

Seasonings
Favourite Polish seasonings are sour cream, dill, garlic, paprika and dried or fresh wild mushrooms. Horse radish is used alone or in combination with finely grated beets as a sauce for fish. Lemons and the fermented juices from grains and pickled vegetables are used for tartness, always tempered with sugar or honey.

Beverages
Tea is the most common beverage, served clear or with lemon and sugar. Coffee is generally only served after a more formal meal and then it is served strong and black or with sugar. Beer served in small glasses may accompany meals; wine is used only by the more affluent or "more refined."[3] Polish vodka is believed to be the finest, even by Russian standards; it is made from grains or potatoes and is taken straight with appetizers (ZAKASKI). In recent years it has been consumed by rich and poor alike in such quantity as to constitute somewhat of a problem.[2] KRUPNIK is a fine liqueur prepared from honey, spices and vodka.

Meal Patterns and Eating Customs
Polish women take great pride in their culinary abilities; even daily foods are prepared with loving care. Festive foods are often simply the daily fare in larger quantity, because (so-called) daily fare is of classic quality.

Polish meal patterns are similar to both Ukrainian and Russian in that soups, grains in the form of breads or KASZA, and vegetables (mostly cabbage and potatoes) are really the mainstays of the diet. Before tea and coffee became popular beverages, it was customary to start the day with a hot filling bowl of soup accompanied by dark bread.[3] More recently, tea or coffee plus breads and preserves start the day's meals.

The noon meal is most often taken in state institutions or factory cafeterias and most often includes filling soups based on grains and vegetables, accompanied by bread and beer. The evening meal may be similar, but if guests are expected or the occasion is special, then the dinner will be preceded by an array of pickled appetizers, stuffed cabbage rolls (GOLABKI), and salted and pickled fish dishes all accompanied by vodka. Soup, braised or stewed meat with cooked vegetables, and stewed fruits or home-baked or purchased pastries will complete the meal. Also enjoyed are light suppers consisting of sweet fruit soups made from seasonal berries or fruits, or light vegetable soups. A filling dessert completes the meal. These desserts may be fruit dumplings with sour cream, rice dishes, pancakes (NALESNIKI), puddings, or most often cooked noodles sprinkled with cheese, poppyseeds or chopped nuts and sugar.

Poles are hearty eaters, and foods are always enjoyed in large servings. Most meals are served family style with everyone helping himself.

Special Occasions

The largest majority of Poles are members of the Roman Catholic Church. An estimated three million out of the total population of over 35 million were of the Jewish faith before 1931, but this group were almost all victims of Nazi annihilation before and during World War II. Very small groups of Poles are members of the Orthodox Church and of some Protestant denominations.

Poland being a Christian country, Christmas and Easter are still occasions for lavish preparations of feasts, singing and dancing and family gatherings. A day of abstention from meat is culminated in a sombre and ritualistic dinner (called the Vigilia) on Christmas Eve. The meal contains no meat dishes and opens with the ceremony of bread-breaking; the mother holds in her hand a white communion wafer – symbol of love, forgiveness and friendship – and all at the table share it. An old tradition of a sheaf of wheat or a bit of hay sprinkled under the white tablecloth is still carried on in many homes today as a remembrance both of the agricultural blessings and the holy manger.

Some still carry on the tradition of twelve meatless dishes served in remembrance of the twelve apostles: three types of soups, three different fish dishes (one of which is sure to be jellied sweet and sour carp slices), three side dishes of grains or vegetables or noodles, and finally three desserts. Each of the diners helps himself to at least one serving of each dish. And out of Poland's pagan past, there will surely be at least one dish with poppyseeds to symbolize the peaceful sleep of the dead. Another dish will be sure to contain honey to provide a year of sweet content for all.

Christmas Day is one of quiet family togetherness. Even the mother of the house enjoys peace and rest, for all of the cooking and baking has been done in the frenzied days before. On this special day the family will enjoy a buffet of cold meats: sliced ham and chicken, salads made with potatoes, pickles or sauerkraut, delicious pastries and finally coffee. And what better way to combine all the leftovers than in a hunter's stew (BIGOS) to be served the next day.

To the Poles, a party is always a reason to dress up, and at no time is this more meaningful than on New Year's Eve. Candy, flowers and wine are brought by the guests, and the evening's food will include an impressive diversity of ZAKASKI, hot and cold meat dishes, pickled salads and vegetables, BIGOS, and finally dessert pastries, liqueurs, coffee and of course vodka.

Members of the predominantly Catholic population observe Easter with deep devotion. The fast period of Lent is usualy observed with two to three meatless days a week; meals on these days consist of pasta or noodle dishes or a main course of cold fish, poached, baked or pickled.

The final week of Lent includes many special prayer services at church and a frenzy of cleaning and painting in the homes. Special baking and cooking for the Easter luncheon increase the anticipation of the Holy weekend. Good Friday is traditionally spent visiting the church displays of Christ in a tomb, surrounded by floral displays, bathed in coloured lights and guarded by groups of specially costumed children. A humble dinner of vegetable or barley soup followed by bread and herring or potatoes and the decorating of Easter eggs completes the day's activities.

The large traditional buffet table for the Easter Sunday luncheon is arrayed with the finest foods of the year: cold sliced Polish ham, roasted pig, beef or veal, pickled salads and relishes and CWIKLA (traditional Easter relish of grated beets and horse radish). Sliced BABKA, fingers of MAZURKA, tortes and cakes with nuts, fruits and poppyseeds will be served for dessert with vodka or liqueurs. But before the Easter meal is enjoyed with family and guests, a special food basket containing hard-boiled eggs, salt, butter, sausages and sliced BABKA, will be taken to church for blessing. The Easter table itself will not be considered complete unless a display of painted eggs shares the centre of the table with a molded lamb (a symbol of Christ) made of sugar and candies.

Easter Monday is a restful day, the quiet broken only by a meal of BIGOS and often a surprise dousing of cold water – a bit of traditional fun which is considered good luck and called *smigus* or *dyngus*.

FORTY

Portuguese

Why are the Portuguese so similar to the Spanish and yet so distinctly different? Portugal and Spain share what was once considered the Iberian Peninsula, and the Portuguese themselves are an ethnic mix of Iberian and Moorish elements as are the Spanish. Yet a range of jagged mountains isolates Portugal and causes her to turn inward on herself.

The Portuguese express their difference in many ways. There is the exuberant burst of song and dance that seems to be a part of any group of working Portuguese. Many writers describe the favourite foods and drinks of the Portuguese not merely as "favourites" but as "obsessions," "passions," or even "manias." This innate intensity of feeling is a part of every Portuguese. A cup of coffee or a glass of wine can become that obsession. Any one of the several hundred dishes made with salt cod (BACALAO) may well be described as a passion. And the Portuguese delight in rich sweets does indeed border on a mania.

The same intensity of feelings appears again and again. The Portuguese ability to lose oneself temporarily in melancholia is called *saudade* and periodically surfaces especially when in the atmosphere of a candle-lit café and the soulful *fado* songs. The national love for artifice, ornament and colour satisfies itself in the Portuguese bullfight, religious parades and festivities and even in architecture - especially that of the Manueline period.

On only two subjects does a Portuguese ever show the slightest signs of nonchalance or vagueness. These are the subjects of time and distance. After all, what does time matter or even distance so long as one is enjoying oneself?

Until the Middle Ages, Portugal and Spain did indeed share their destiny as part of the Iberian Peninsula. So it is not surprising that the Portuguese language bears many similarities to the Spanish and this is especially noted in the Spanish dialect in the provinces of Galicia and Asturias. Portuguese dishes bear a distinct resemblance to many Spanish ones but veer off in combinations that the Spaniards would never dare.

The Portuguese are still influenced daily by Spanish customs such as the formalities observed in addressing strangers, the tendency to flamboyancy in the use of adjectives, and the rigid codes involving the dating and chaperoning of daughters. In Portugal as in Spain the main festivities of the year centre around family and church, with each locale devoting special festivities and rites to local legends and saints.

Probably the earliest traders to touch and influence Portugal were the Phoenicians who brought with them the roots and twigs that stand to this day as craggy olive trees and rows upon rows of sprawling vineyards over the entire Iberian Peninsula.[2] In the eighth century C.E. the Moorish Muslims swept northward from Morocco introducing rice culture, sugar plantations and groves of lemon, almond and fig trees as well as the persistent "mania" for rich sweet desserts.[2] For the next several hundred years the land of Portugal was so often a part of Spain in many see-saw battles, that Spanish tastes, traditions and customs melted into Portuguese.[3]

Portugal's Golden Age of the 1400s and 1500s was preceded by a period of calamities. In 1346 a massive earthquake erupted in Lisbon. Two years later plague ravaged the country and it was said that "six bodies were buried in every grave." A heatwave in 1354 scorched crops and killed cattle.[4] Spain was gripped with the evils of the Inquisition while tales of monsters in the seas and the flatness of the world were told and retold.

Yet from the calamities, evils and superstitions of the times, one man dared to set a different pace and launched Portugal as one of the great world powers. With the intensity so typical of his people, Prince Henry – son of King Joao I and later to be known simply as Henry the Navigator – set up a planned system of navigation, dispelled the fantasies of the times with scientific facts, and launched a sailing craft called the caravel. The caravel won such a reputation for reliability that for several hundred years it was believed only a Portuguese-built ship could navigate African waters successfully.[4] Inspired and encouraged by Henry the Navigator, Portuguese adventurers and explorers relentlessly pursued the search for new routes and discovered the Madeiras and the Azores, acquired parts of Morocco and Africa, and under Bartholomeu Dias opened a sea route to the Orient in 1487.[3]

Portuguese daring and expertise of the seas shine in names that are legends today: Vasco da Gama, Cabral, Magellan. The Portuguese were among the first to visit Labrador (which they mistook for a part of Greenland) and named it after a captain who was called "Lavrador," meaning "farmer."[4] It was they who brought back tales of seas so laden with fish that the ships could scarcely move. To this day the "beef of the sea" are the great catches of fresh cod later to be salted and dried in Portugal and cooked in hundreds of dishes. The BACALAO, one of Portugal's passions, is still found but in diminishing quantities in the North Atlantic seas.

Portuguese explorers revolutionized the taste buds and markets of Europe. They brought back gold and diamonds from Brazil as well as pineapples, corn, potatoes, squash, pumpkin, tomatoes and beans of many types. From African ports they loaded their ships with yams, cocoa and vanilla pods.[2] Vasco da Gama's crews – at least those who survived the scourge of scurvy – became rich beyond dreams. The black pepper they brought back from India is said to have alone financed churches, monasteries and street-widening and made Manuel I one of Portugal's richest kings. With the pepper selling at more than sixty times its cost, Lisbon became a commercial centre, one that could well afford the flamboyant ornate architecture that came to be called "Manueline."

The audacity of Portugal's seafaring adventurers and the merchandizing skills of the Jews who had fled to Portugal to escape the Spanish Inquisition were said to be factors quickly leading Lisbon to the title of the world's leading commercial capital. But the Inquisition spilled over Portugal's borders and Manuel was forced to threaten to expel the Jews unless they were willing to change their faith and become *conversos*.[4]

Portugal lost much of its vital merchandizing middle class when many Jews left Lisbon. Portugal was further weakened in the 1500s with the growth of French, Danish, Dutch, Swedish and English fleets, who "cut their slices of East India cake and New World pie,"[4] effectively breaking the Portuguese monopoly of the seas. Only the areas of Africa and Brazil were left open to Portuguese traders who once again revolutionized European tastes and social life with the gradual introduction of a new beverage called coffee and a new institution called the coffee house.

Despite Portugal's decline as a world power in the late 1500s, her successful diplomatic trade with China cannot be overlooked. Of all the world sea powers, the Portuguese were the first to reach China, to settle in Macao, and to set up a viable volume of trade that lasted unchallenged for more than 300 years. Elegant Chinese goods of porcelain, lacquer and silks were traded for silver and furs from North America and sandalwood from the Hawaiian Islands.[5] From China came oranges, limes, peaches, walnuts and coriander.[2] And, while the Portuguese passion for wine and coffee continues unabated to this day, there is still a place for tea on the Portuguese menu. Originating from her trade with China, the Portuguese call tea "CHÁ" a name hauntingly reminiscent of its origin, for the Chinese call their tea *Ch'a*.[6]

Portugal may have declined as a world power in the annals of history, but the products she brought back and the instigation of sea adventure that she nurtured still deeply affect the tables of the world and are still reflected in the agriculture and cuisine of her own land. Today Portugal is almost self-sufficient in grains, fruits and vegetables. But despite a rich harvest of fresh fish and seafood, the Portuguese still passionately manage to consume salted and dried cod at the rate of 100 pounds per person per year.[2] Northern Portugal's language and cuisine still reflect the tastes and ties of Brazil from fine coffee to *piri-piri*, that fiery little hot pepper that becomes a favoured seasoning for fowl or seafood when ground and blended with oil.[2] And Southern Portugal's Algarve district still leans heavily on the favourites of Moorish cuisine: almonds in so many dishes and as a sweetmeat, and crusty whole wheat bread to mop up sauces in the Moroccan style.[7]

Said to be prepared in at least 365 different ways (one for each day of the year), BACALAO was first introduced into Portugal in the early 1400s as a result of barter with the English. English fishermen gathered huge catches of cod off the Grand Banks of Newfoundland, salting and drying the fish for preservation. With little market for the cod in Great Britain, the English tried elsewhere and so began to barter with the Portuguese – a coarse red Portuguese wine for dried salted cod. The English called the wine "Red Portugal." This early trade formed the basis for strong English-Portuguese ties and is known to this day, some 500 years later, as the Port Wine trade.[2]

There is a story of the sons of a Liverpool wine merchant who journeyed to Portugal to select their wines firsthand and decided to add a "dollop of brandy" to the kegs to fortify the wine for its journey to England. The fortified wine is said to be the origin of port wine. There may be some debate about the story but there is no debating the English taste for port wine. The Methuen government in 1703 agreed to allow Portuguese wine to enter England at a lower tariff than French wines in exchange for Portuguese importation of English wools.[3,4]

In 1756, Prime Minister Pombal laid down strict rules in regard to the growth and production policies of port wine. These policies form the basis of the rules today. During the next 200 years, Portugal was to suffer through the Napoleonic Wars, which left the Portuguese with a taste for French furniture and French silver; through Brazil's formation of an autonomous republic in 1889, but with no diminution of the Portuguese passion for coffee; and through the grim years between 1910 and 1926 when it is said that the Portuguese "averaged one revolution and three governments a year."[4] Yet the Portuguese port wine trade was still so important after 200 years that it was considered Portugal's sole stable institution when Dr. Salazar took the job of prime minister in 1932 and ruled for 36 years.

Yet beneath the rumblings and political upheavals, the Portuguese people have remained steadfastly absorbed with undiminished feelings for the intensity of life itself, and with their passions, obsessions and manias for food and drink, and for work and play.

Home Life and Facilities
Portuguese family life follows traditional patterns and in many rural areas regional costumes are much in evidence. Discipline of children and courtship all follow strict patterns. These factors result in adjustment problems when Portuguese emigrate to Canada and the United States.[9] The father is the household head, but Portuguese women frequently work side by side with their husbands in agriculture, fishing or factories. In fact, many work activities are considered family affairs and after the work of shucking corn, beating trees for olives, or picking grapes is completed a family picnic ending with singing and dancing is more the rule than the exception.[10]

It is typical of Portugal that modern methods are only implemented where traditional ones are no longer feasible. If the old method works, why toss it out? In the fields ancient agricultural techniques are practised side by side with modern mechanization.[10]

This is true too of the Portuguese kitchen. Since three-quarters of the people are engaged in agricultural pursuits,[10] the country home and kitchens dominate the Portuguese way of life. Self-sufficiency is a matter of great pride. Many types of homemade pork sausages, sausage-like strings of lard, barrels of salted bacon flavoured with bay leaf and garlic, and of course a good supply of home-made wines, stores of fruits, vegetables and grains stock the pantries and cool storage areas of the Portuguese home.[10]

Many communities share a huge cement and stone oven where breads and confections may be baked. Kitchens glow with tiled floors and walls and often tiled cooking areas. Few electrical appliances are used as traditional mortar and pestle, hand coffee-grinders and strong arms prefer to do the blending, crushing, chopping, mixing and beating of kitchen chores.

Southern Portugal reflects many dishes of the Spanish cuisine such as *gaspacho*, the cold vegetable soup, *pudim flan*, the sweet caramel custard, and many dishes that are cooked all in one pot by steaming. The *cataplana* is used especially in the Algarve, the southernmost province of Portugal. Two rounded lids are clamped tightly together, cooking food on the stove top like a type of pressure-cooker and giving any food combinations a moist freshness of flavour.[1,7]

FOODS COMMONLY USED

Cooking in Portugal is hearty, simple and distinctively regional.

The penchant for fresh ingredients simply prepared is as important in Portugal as it is in Spain. But the Portuguese delight in unusual combinations such as seafood and pork in the same dish, and take pleasure in a stronger use of garlic and the frequent surprise of a stinging hot sauce made with the Brazilian fiery peppers called *piri-piri*.

Dishes of pork, seafoods of all kinds – especially the beloved dried salt cod called BACALAO – form the main dishes together with any variety of available vegetables and greens. Every meal is accompanied with bread, whether it is the cornmeal bread called BROA in Northern Portugal, or the many types of wheat breads in the south. Rice, widely used as a base for other foods, appears well-sugared in many dessert dishes. Rich sweets in the forms of puddings, baked custards, imaginative confections and pastries are the specialties of many monasteries and special pastry shops. Each region is proud of its own sweet delights.

Portuguese red wine is abundant and considered so superior to the white, that it is consumed with every dish, even fish. In fact drinking red wine with fish dishes is considered to be a tradition in the Algarve.[7] But the drinking of red wine in no way diminishes the Portuguese love for good coffee which appears after meals and frequently accompanies the many tempting sweets.

Milk and Milk Products
Cows and ewes supply milk which is used more to produce the many varieties of local cheeses than as a beverage. Five- and six-course meals are not uncommon in Portugal, especially in the north where hearty eaters abound in the cooler, moister weather. Some form of white soft or mild local cheese appears either before or with the fruit course.[11] QUEIJO DO ALENTEJO and SERRA are two popular soft cheeses made from ewe's milk. They are especially good with apples and walnuts and washed down with a velvety red wine like DÃO.[2] Other good cheeses include: QUEIJO DA SERPA and QUEIJO DA AZEITÃO.[4] FLAMENGO is a cheese often proffered to tourists; it is similar to a GOUDA but considered not as good as other local cheeses.[4]

Fruits and Vegetables
Most of the fruits of Portugal come from area orchards and vineyards and are enjoyed in season: oranges, apples, figs, melons, limes, peaches. Imported fruits such as pineapples and bananas also form an important part of the fruit intake. Monks in the 1300s are credited with teaching the peasants the arts of fruit-growing.[4] Fruits, enjoyed in their fresh ripe state, are often eaten with cheese as a meal course before the sweet

desserts. The famed plums of Elvas are eaten liqueured and iced or fresh.[8]

Portuguese vegetables are enjoyed garden-fresh frequently as soup or casserole ingredients but seldom over-cooked.[4] Turnip greens are a great favourite as is the strongly-flavoured kale, the principal ingredient in the northern specialty, CALDO VERDE. This is the national soup, made from potatoes and finely-shredded kale or other greens, well-flavoured with pork sausages (LINGUIÇA or CHOURIÇO) and garlic. Fresh coriander with its clean parsley-like flavour is used in so many dishes that it can almost be regarded more as a food than as a seasoning.[1]

Potatoes belong at the top of the list of favourite vegetables. They are used in soups and stew-type dishes with either meat, fish or seafood and they are a part of almost every dinner or supper. So fond are the Portuguese of their potatoes, that potatoes often appear beside rice as the second starchy food of the meal.[1]

The Portuguese enjoy a wide variety of vegetables but prefer them in the cooked form rather than fresh in salads. Many soups are made predominantly with vegetables and flavoured with garlic browned in olive oil and the pungent garlic sausages of which there are so many types.

Garlic and onions, scallions and leeks are a large part of the cuisine. And the ancient olive trees deserve special mention. Olives are used in cooking, adding their colour and flavour to many dishes. They are enjoyed brined, pickled, black or green.

Meats and Alternates

Porco (pork) is the staple meat of the Portuguese table. Nothing is wasted; trimmings and odd pieces as well as fat and offal are used in the many varieties of sausages, some spicy and some mild but almost all pungently flavoured with garlic. PRESUNTO is the name given to smoked hams while PAIO is salted, smoked and spiced pork tenderloin. The spicy casserole called PORCO CON AMÈIJOAS is only one of many combining stewed or braised pork with some form of seafood, in this case cockles.

Some beef is used but it is leaner and tougher than that found in North America, for the most part requiring slow moist cooking or else held in marinades to tenderize before grilling. Chickens, ducks and game are also used when available. Meat of young animals is favoured; veal, lamb, kid, suckling pig.

So important is fish in the Portuguese dietary, that at least one meal a day will be based on a fish dish, and even if meat happens to be the main dish of the meal, it will be preceded by both soup and a fish course. In June, the sardine season, almost everyone grills sardines out of doors on small charcoal-heated braziers. Lampreys have the height of their season in March and these are used mainly in stews. It should be noted that grilled fish is the one dish that is often accompanied with a salad of freshly-sliced tomatoes and onion rings. Herring, cod, salmon and trout are plentiful as are every variety of shellfish and seafood.

Beans are served frequently, especially in stews and casserole-type dishes. DOBRADA is a hearty peasant dish of tripe and beans. Incidentally, the natives of Oporto are so noted for their love of tripe and the many ways of preparing it, they are often called *Tripeiros* or "tripe-eaters."[2]

While chicken meat may not be so important, chicken eggs certainly are. Where would all the lusciously sweet yolk-rich desserts, the airy-light sponge cakes and delicate meringue confections with exotic names like "nuns' nipples" and "nuns' breasts" be without eggs? Hardly a sweet rice pudding or the ubiquitous PUDIM FLAN (caramel custard) could possibly exist without eggs. Aside from the multitude of sweetmeats and confections that are based on eggs, it is also possible to see eggs served hard-cooked or poached as colourful garnishes to other dishes like fish casseroles or cod-fish cakes. TORTILHA is the name for omelet and the omelet, aside from eggs, may also contain a satisfying portion of onions, potatoes, other vegetables and a garnish of spicy sausage.[12]

The trees in Portugal offer many things: fruits for eating, pine boughs to add aroma to the bake ovens, cork for wine bottles, olives for eating and making oil, and, last but not least, almonds, walnuts and chestnuts, nuts for roasting, munching, salting, sugaring and making into cakes and pastries. Almonds are especially plentiful in the southern Algarve district.

Breads and Cereals
The basket of fresh bread is probably the first thing that is put on any Portuguese table for any meal. If the meal is breakfast, then the local bread – whether made from cornmeal or cornflour, rye flour or coarse, nutty whole-wheat flour – will be accompanied with fresh butter, sweet preserves and, depending on the area, either hot tea or coffee.

The slightly sweet heavy bread made from the flour of maize is the bread of Northern Portugal and is called BROA. Crusty and warm, it is particularly good served with CALDO VERDE, the national soup of greens and potatoes.

Crusty breads of rye or whole wheat flour are more popular in the mid and southern regions where they are commonly used in the Moroccan way to mop up gravies, juices and sauces from meat or seafood dishes. Breads are only taken from the table when the desserts are brought out.

The Moors brought rice cultivation to Portugal, and rice is much used in many savoury and sweet dishes. It seems that the Portuguese cannot decide if they prefer rice or potatoes, so commonly are both served on the same plate.

Fats
Fats are consumed in many forms. Fatty sausages made mainly from pork

and lard, the fat contained in egg yolks and used so widely in desserts and confections, but most of all from olive oil. Portuguese olive oil, called AZEITE, is produced for domestic consumption and is rarely exported. AZEITE is the principal cooking fat and is also used by the canners of anchovies and sardines. The characteristically strong colour and flavour of the Portuguese olive oil is due to the processing. Olives are allowed to remain in the field from two to ten days before pressings and are deliberately run through hot water to bring out the strength of flavour and depth of colour. In other countries pains are taken to rush the fresh olives for pressing and to pass them through cold water to give a product light in both flavour and colour.[11]

Sweets and Snacks

Only the sweets of Iran, Turkey, Greece and Morocco can vie with the confections, pastries, puddings, cakes and other desserts of Portugal for honey-rich syrupy sweetness. It is not difficult to see that Portuguese sweets must have originated with the Moorish occupation, but the Portuguese have gone further with the addition of egg yolks and feathery light meringues to create a confectioner's heaven of desserts. Each small village proudly displays at least one fancy pastry shop and most villages even have their own specialties for the sweet tooth.

From olden times, the nuns in monasteries were famed for their exquisitely wrought sweets rich in sugar, eggs, vanilla, chocolate and almonds. Tinted sugar and almond paste molded sweets are called MAÇAPÁO or marzipan.[1] Similar sweets may be shaped like tiny sausages, fish, shellfish, fruits or vegetables and some are more suggestive with shapes and names like "nun's kisses," "nun's nipples" and "nun's breasts." At least one place, Amarante, is famed for its phallic-shaped brioches, probably survivors of ancient fertility rites common in many European areas and now melded into religious festivals.[8]

Seasonings

Staple seasonings include garlic, coarse sea salt, lemon juice and wedges, and the generous use of fresh or freshly dried herbs such as mint, coriander and parsley. AZEITE, the Portuguese olive oil, must also be considered a national seasoning for the special flavour it imparts to many dishes. Fresh eggs, fresh butter and vanilla together with grated lemon or orange rinds are the favourite flavourings of bakery and desserts but almonds must take an important place too. Curry blends also find a place, hearkening to Portugal's ties with India.

Beverages

With wine appearing at every meal except breakfast, there can be little doubt as to Portugal's favourite beverage. Yet, many writers speak of Portugal's passion for coffee too. And some areas favour tea over coffee as the beverage both for breakfast, after meals and with the many sweets taken as snacks or between-meal treats.

More than 240,000 people in Portugal are permanently engaged in some aspect of wine-growing or processing, while more than 1.25 million depend directly on the wine trade for their income.[4] These are startling figures considering Portugal's size. The variety of her wines usually startles outsiders as well. The world is familiar with port and Madeira but many should familiarize themselves with the varieties of port: vintage port, crusted port, wood port, vintage tawny and the lesser known white port made from white grapes to produce a fine dry aperitif which is excellent when chilled.[4] Similarly, Madeira wine is infrequently known in all its varieties from the dry aperitif sercial Madeira to the light dry verdelho, good also as an aperitif or with a first course. The bual Madeira is considered to be in the middle range, rich but versatile, while the well-known richly full malmsey Madeira is best served as a sipping wine or with dessert.[13]

The vinho verdes of the northern Minho province (named from the grape) are zesty wines that come in either red or white. Aromatic whites are produced in Obidos while the whites of Alcobaça and Bucelas are richly golden, reminiscent of fine Rhine wines. The grapes of the Duoro are used mainly for the production of a popular red table wine called consumo. About one-quarter of the grape production is used for port wine. The muscatel grapes of Azeitao produce a sweet dessert wine whose flavour is heightened with the addition of fresh muscat skins giving it the perfume of fresh fruit.[4]

Lisboans enjoy the many wines as well as tea and coffee but in Lisbon more than anywhere else in Portugal, foamy beer is also enjoyed especially in the *cervejarias* (beer parlours) where the beer is accompanied by steaming plates of fresh fish or seafood specialties.[1]

Meal Patterns and Eating Customs

"Few people feel more deeply about their native land, their childhood, or their food and drink than the Portuguese."[4] They bring to their meals the same intensity as they bring to every other aspect of their lives. There is no philosophizing about food or drink as there is with the French, nor is there a plethora of cookbooks in Portugal. Portuguese prepare their food with simple dignity, making the most of nature's rich gifts and in the same humble way they eat quietly and appreciatively. Food is important and meals are generous but food is never glorified or categorized.

Dinners and suppers frequently run to five- or six-course menus and these include soup, fish, meat and vegetables with rice and potatoes, cheese, fruits, and a choice of sweet desserts of which at least two must be taken in order not to cause offence.[4] Meals are usually leisurely with dinner from 1:00 to 3:00 P.M. and the evening supper sometime between 8:00 and 10:00 but not as late as the Spanish. The Portuguese enjoy eating meals with their children and the latter are not only included in the adult conversation, they also join their parents in drinking wine as freely as water.

Though dinner and supper are often filling meals, the typical Portuguese breakfast is simple and light, usually consisting of a hot beverage like tea or coffee and a variety of fresh breads and rolls to be eaten with honey, jams and butter.

Special Occasions
The predominant religion of Portugal is Roman Catholic.

Every town has its special legends, saints and festivities concerning every aspect of the seasons, the land, family occasions and religion. In fine weather almost anything becomes excuse enough for a family outing that probably includes relatives, neighbours and ample provisions of fresh breads, cheeses, cured hams, cold roasted chickens, boned and stuffed suckling pigs, salted herrings and of course huge wicker covered jugs of fine homemade or local wines.[10]

Everything wild in Portugal is usually called "brave" or "royal" so a gathering that later turns into a party but is ostensibly for the purpose of branding young bulls may be called "*festa brava*"; while a dish of wild duck may be called *pato real*, recalling the days when all wild game was strictly for royalty to enjoy. It is well to remember that the Portuguese *brava* does not mean "brave" but "wild." Sometimes Portuguese may refer in faltering English to a young girl as being "brave" when they really mean that her dress and manner indicate her to be "wild" – at least by Portuguese standards which tend to be conservative.

Any part of outdoor work that requires several hands is also turned into a special occasion. Gathering olives, grapes, shucking fresh corn, treading grapes for wine, in fact most rural jobs that others may consider simply as work, the Portuguese turn into a pleasure by working and singing, enjoying a meal of perhaps BROA and CALDO VERDE, then finishing with extra wine, sweets and much music and dance.[10] An example of this is the *esfolhada*, the party for corn shucking. With everyone in best clothes, the work proceeds seriously enough until someone finds a cob of red corn and then the fun begins: the lucky holder of the red cob gets to kiss all the ladies present, or vice-versa. Incidentally, corn is an important crop in Portugal, but not just for reasons of fun or food. The thinnings are fed to the cattle, coarsest stalks are used to bed cattle while others are torn into fine strips and used to stuff mattresses and pillows. The emptied cobs are saved and dried to use as fuel.[10]

In the summer months, especially in the north, there is an almost continuous round of fairs and special pilgrimages called *romarios*. Church services and processions are interspersed with feasting, singing and dancing, ornate decorations and often fireworks.

One of the more interesting festivals, the Feast of Tabuleiros, is held every three to five years in the town of Tomar. Girls march in processions with huge layered headdresses made of loaves of bread decorated with wheat sheaves, flowers and ribbons. The clergy follow bearing richly decorated silver crowns on small black pillows and several young bullocks bring up the end. Later the cattle are slaughtered and portions of meat and breads from the headdresses are distributed to the poor of the area.

Country fairs sell everything from pottery and ribbons to boots and donkeys, but the most celebrated of all is the Feast of St. Martin held in mid-November in Golega. It is a horse fair and a national occasion, a spectacle of Lisbon *sociedade*, visiting dignitaries and royalty, army horsemen, *cavalheiros* who fight the bulls on horseback, and the great horsebreeders of Ribatejo and Alentejo, all dressed in their special attire of trim grey jacket and trousers and the wide grey flat-brimmed hats. Each group dresses in its finest, with the horses prancing in their best manner and everyone there to see everyone else. Nearby dining rooms are ready with fine foods and wine always on tap.

All Saints' Day, Nov. 1, always brings with it memories of that same day in 1755 when almost three-quarters of Lisbon crumbled in a brief but violent earthquake. Then as now it is a solemn day set aside for quiet church services and memorials of all who died. After services, street vendors sell *broas dos santos*, saints' cakes and other sweets, a brief reminder of the sweeter side of life.[1,10]

FORTY-ONE

Romanian

The Romanian is a study in contrasts. Like the Romanian climate which is icily cold in winter and fiercely hot in summer, the Romanian can be consumed with melancholy listening to the *doine* (poignant country songs of love and longing) or elevated to a passionate frenzy while dancing the *hora* or the *colusari*. Gypsy violins can make him cry but the sound of flutes and *nai* (pan-pipes) or *cimpoi* (bagpipes) will evoke songs and laughter. He likes his tea very weak and his coffee very strong, his pickles very hot and his desserts very sweet. Like the powerful wind called the *Crivetz*, which whips up the snow in the winter and drives the yellow dust in the summer, the Romanian soul is alternately gay and animated or sad and despaired – but seldom dull.

Aside from these extremes of temperament and taste, the two-thirds of the Romanian population engaged in agriculture do show a form of moderation when it comes to their work. The rich fertile lowlands and the Wallachian Plains yield bounteous crops with little effort and for centuries the people contented themselves with their own needs and little more.[1] Currently the Communist regime has attempted to impose standards and quotas of production similar to those in other Soviet republics. Gradually – though unofficially – the independent will and the passionate easy-going nature of the rural Romanian has made itself felt and more and more the production of the lands is being left in the hands of the farmers.[1,2]

Probably it is those same fertile pastures, orchards, vineyards and fields of grain that enticed the Roman conquerors about 100 C.E. In exchange for the grain and the gold that they took from the land, they built bridges and roads; but more important they built the beginnings of an identity and left a language and a culture that is proudly preserved to this day.[3] The strength of the Roman cultural identity can be better appreciated when one realizes that Romania was and still is almost surrounded by Slavic peoples and even counts within her own population more than a dozen ethnic groups.[1,3] Despite this, more than 85 per cent of the population speak Romanian, which is closely related to the other Romance languages of Latin, Spanish, French and Italian. Further, their homogeneity is displayed not only in their almost universal temperament and tastes but also in their religion, for more than 85 per cent of the population are members of the Romanian Orthodox Church.[3]

Romania today is composed of the areas of Transylvania, Banat, Wallachia and Moldavia, with the Transylvania Alps and parts of the Carpathian Mountains forming her interior. In former times, Bucovina and Bessarabia were also a part of Romania – but never all these areas at one time. Because of the tug-of-war for her lands, parts of Romania developed differently, being strongly influenced by the invaders. For example, Transylvania, originally a Romanian province, before 1000 C.E. became a Hungarian province but in the 1200s was settled by German colonists adding to the population of Romanians, Hungarians and Szecklers (of non-Hungarian origin). At this time Hungarian domination spread to most of Romania and the original Romanian population was kept in ignorance and subservience for a period lasting almost 800 years.[3]

In the 1400s the Turks conquered Moldavia and Wallachia and placed Greeks on the thrones. In the late 1600s a contest of power between Austria and the Ottoman Empire further suppressed the Romanians and added Hungarian peasants to the oppression.

By the late 1700s Russia joined the battle for Romania's lands and by 1812 Bessarabia became Russian. But a surge of Romanian nationalism resulted in the creation of Romania as an independent kingdom in 1881, and rather than wars, she attempted treaties with Russia and the Austro-Hungarian Empire and gained some internal stability.

In the powerful desire to throw off their subservient yokes and gain independence, the Moldavian peasants began a surge of anti-Semitism that later became government policy and led in the early 1900s to a mass exodus of Romania's Jews.[4]

Towards the end of the First World War, Romania's siding with the Allies gained her more territory at one time than she had previously ever known. Back into her fold came Transylvania, Bucovina, most of Banat and Bessarabia. In the wake of this good fortune, Romania rescinded the anti-Semitic policies and attempted much-needed land-reform policies. This too was short-lived and growing political pressures and Fascist sympathies led again to Jewish repression, censorship and alignment with the Germans during the Second World War.[4] By 1944, Russian armies swept into Bessarabia and Bucovina and deep into Romanian territory to secure her surrender. The gradual spread of Communism began, as did the shift from a basically agricultural economy to a more industrialized one.

Because of this repressive history of Romania, it is all the more intriguing that she has retained her ancient Roman cultural identity and language – even the Orthodox religion. With the many territorial exchanges, foreign rulers and despite the sufferings of her people, Romania mirrors her history in her cuisine but not in her identity. From the many peoples of Yugoslavia came the SARMALES and GHIVECIU, from Hungary the TOKANY, GULYAS and PAPRIKASH, from Austria the STRUDELS, TORTES, and WIENER SCHNITZEL, from Turkey the PILAFS, BAKLAVA, HALVA, DOLMAS and strong Turkish coffee, and finally from Russia the taste for soured soups, BLINI and a variety of dark breads made from rye and coarse wheat flours. The German love of potatoes predominates still in some areas over the inherent Romanian love of MAMALIGA, Romania's staple "bread of gold" made from cornmeal.

Aside from cuisine, one other Slavic tradition has become important in Romania. This is the reverence for wheat as the symbol of life. A part of the Romanian Orthodox funeral service is the blessing of a plate of mounded wheat sprinkled with sugar, raisins and nuts. This is similar to the Ukrainian KUTYA, the Russian KUTIJA and the Serbian KOLJIVO or ZITO.[3]

Although Romanians are noted for extremes in temperament and taste, diversity in history and cuisine, some things have remained comparatively consistent. Although the women are stepping more and more into full-time jobs away from their homes, they still retain their age-old respect for their menfolk; the Romanian man comes first. And although Romanians are devotedly religious, they have embraced Christianity in addition to – not instead of – paganistic rites and superstitions.

All share one other characteristic: they believe firmly that old age is simply a disease, not an inevitability. Health spas, mineral baths, drinking waters, the assiduous application of herbs and sometimes even a spell or two are believed to do the trick. From infancy to adulthood the taking of special waters, teas and herbal brews are as much a staple as their beloved MAMALIGA. Hence too the serious devotion paid to the skills of the kitchen by all Romanian women: what can be more important than food and herbs?

Home Life and Facilities
Romanian homes are brightly decorated with wall hangings, curtains, coverlets and tablecloths of richly intricate embroideries. Displays of folk pottery and carved wooden objects attest to an artistic people who are seldom idle with their hands. Even much of the furniture is handmade and beautifully carved and finished.

The centre of most homes, whether rural or urban, is the kitchen. This same room is not only the largest in the house, it is also the living room, the dining room and the children's bedroom. One other small room will be the parents' bedroom and a still smaller one will be the food storage room or the pantry. A large wood-burning stove with ovens, cooktop and open hearth will be centred against one wall of the kitchen's whitewashed interior. Not only do all the good foods come from here, but so does the heat.

Colourful earthenware dishes, mixing bowls and casseroles for baking the many popular vegetable stews are basics of the kitchen as are the heavy cast-iron pots for soups and cooktop stews like GULYAS and TOKANY. But most important are the utensils involved in the preparation of MAMALIGA. This thick cornmeal porridge that is almost all things to a Romanian is so special it is cooked in a special cast-iron pot called a CEAUN and stirred with a carved wooden stick called a FACALET. Finally, it is turned out on to its own wooden board to cool and is cut with a special string into hearty wedges. That is, if it is not prepared to be eaten in one of countless other ways.

Romanians prefer fresh fruits and vegetables, each in its own season. But the pantry area does hold cabbages and root vegetables that can take storage: those vegetables that are more perishable are sometimes preserved for winter use by being wrapped in leaves and buried in an earthen pit. Mostly, however, seasonal fruits will be preserved as jams, fruit butters to be used for pastry fillings, dried, or cooked in heavy syrup to produce DULCEATA, thick sweet preserves of whole or sliced fruits or berries eaten with a spoon between sips of icy cold water and finally washed down with strong Turkish coffee. Cabbage may also be stored as barrels of sauerkraut; other vegetables will be preserved for winter and year around use as spicy hot, sweet or sour pickles.[2,3]

FOODS COMMONLY USED

The single most important staple of the Romanian diet is MAMALIGA (the name being of Turkish origin from *mama*, meaning food). Many peasants have survived almost solely on this cornmeal porridge while even the upper classes make it almost a daily part of the menu. Romanians are also fond of spicy and tangy appetizers, cheeses, sour soups, stews of vegetables and meat, grilled and roasted meats and fish as well as sweet desserts and pastries. All of this is enjoyed with good wine, potent plum brandy (TUICA), thick Turkish coffee and sometimes weak tea. Simple or complex, Romanian foods all have distinctive flavours, and as in everything else, contrasts of flavours are much enjoyed.

Milk and Milk Products

Yoghurt, soured milk and cottage cheese head the list of dairy products for these are not only eaten by themselves but enjoyed as parts of many other dishes. Sweet cream is widely used as whipped cream in pastries and sour cream finds a place in many Hungarian and Slavic-inspired dishes.

Even when other protein sources such as meat and fish may be scarce or expensive, cheese is consumed at least once daily and often more. Most cheese are made from sheep or goat's milk and include the KASHKAVAL, a firm yellow cheese, and BRINZA, a soft creamy cheese. Together with the fresh cottage cheese, all cheeses are eaten as they are with breads, with MAMALIGA, atop casseroles, or enfolded in cakes and dumplings, yeast doughs and CLATITE (thin crêpes). Some sharp and flavourful cheeses are eaten as an appetizer with TUICA and black olives.

Fruits and Vegetables

The climate and fertile lands produce an abundance of quality fruits: peaches, apricots, pears, apples, plums, cherries, grapes and many varieties of melons and berries. In season these are eaten fresh or as a compote. Some fruits are dried, others made into fruit butters and jams and the famed DULCEATA.

Many varieties of vegetables are available and are eaten in quantity and variety commensurate with the pocketbook. The staples are cabbage and potatoes as well as the usual root vegetables. In season, many vegetables such as tomatoes, cucumbers, radishes and scallions are all eaten raw as a side dish. Cabbage may be stored as sauerkraut, and peppers, cucumbers, etc., will be made into spicy pickles. Eggplant is one of the more popular vegetables because of its versatility as an appetizer. *Vinete tocate* is a vegetable stuffed with meat and rice or as the important part of MUSACA.

The uses and nutritional values of vegetables are well appreciated by the Romanians. Infants are fed finely puréed vegetables as one of their first solid foods. The cultivation of herbs both for flavouring and for medicinal purposes is widely pursued. Vegetables in colourful profusions are munched raw, nibbled as appetizers, enjoyed as raw or cooked salads, may be stuffed, pickled, wrapped, layered, stewed or simmered in hearty soups. At the very least, most vegetables will be accorded the "simple" Romanian treatment of being chopped, shredded or diced then tossed with lard and browned onions with just a little water. They are then cooked till tender, sloshed with sour cream or yoghurt and blended with a little vinegar just before serving. Finally, most Romanian sauces are really just a purée of vegetables blended with oil.[1.6] One way or another, everyone in Romania gets their vegetables.

Meats and Alternates

Pork and veal are the favourite meats and there is no part of the animal that is not used. Meats are grilled or roasted but most often are a part of mainly vegetable soups and stews. One of the favourite snacks is MITITEI, sausage-like fingers of highly seasoned ground meat grilled over an open fire and served with sour cabbage, hot pickles and dark bread. Often tidbits of variety meats and offal are grilled too such as heart, liver, kidney, lungs, brain or udder. Some chickens, ducks and game birds are occasionally used, but chicken and egg production is low, chickens are often tough, egg production scanty and therefore too often scarce or expensive.[1]

From the Black Sea coast, the Danube River and countless smaller rivers and lakes comes quite a good supply of fish. Sturgeon, trout, carp, pike, perch and bream are baked or grilled and often made into soups or stews. Sturgeon roe (caviar) is expensive, but carp roe is often prepared by mashing and blending into a thick sauce with olive oil. This appetizer is called ICRE and may be a part of the appetizer assortment together with salted olives and tangy cheese.

Beans are used quite often in soups, salads, or casseroles.

Breads and Cereals

Corn, wheat, oats, buckwheat, rye, barley and rice are all grown in Romania but nothing exceeds cornmeal in popularity. From this is made MAMALIGA. Its versatility equals the pasta, rice or potato staples of other peoples, and even the most affluent Romanian must succumb at least occasionally to a meal based on MAMALIGA. This is not difficult to enjoy, for MAMALIGA in its bland sweetness seems the perfect foil for meats and gravies, cottage cheese, yoghurt, butter or sour cream, various vegetable sauces or simply a mound of browned mushrooms or onions. Cold, it can be sliced into wedges and eaten as a bread or sliced thinly and dipped in egg and breaded and fried in squares, layered into vegetable and/or meat casseroles or served in the bottom of a soup plate. Sometimes MAMALIGA is the companion to fried or scrambled eggs, or even just sauerkraut or pickles. With MAMALIGA who can be hungry?

Wheat flours are processed in various stages of refinement and used for the many pastries, cakes, tortes and desserts so beloved by the Romanians. If MAMALIGA is not on the table, it is certain there will be an assortment of dark and sour rye breads or crusty coarse whole wheat breads to accompany the meal. Rice and barley are used in soups and stews, in stuffed vegetables and as a base for meat and gravy dishes.

Fats

Lard, butter, olive oil and sunflower seed oil are used in cooking and baking. The latter two also serve as salad dressings.

Sweets

Romanians are fond of sweets and they like their sweets very sweet, perhaps as an antidote to the hot peppers.

DULCEATA (fruits preserved in heavy syrup) and sweet thick Turkish coffee plus the whole range of rich tortes, layer cakes, filled cakes, honey and syrup-drenched Turkish pastries, sticky-rich dried fruits, strudels filled with fruits, nuts, poppy seeds . . . the list is endless. Chocolates in every form, plain or filled, are a specially treasured treat. Failing chocolates, Romanians will munch happily on raisins.

Seasonings

As in other parts of the Romanian cuisine, the intertwining of Slavic and Oriental tastes is seen. Olive oil, sour cream, onions and leeks, garlic, black olives (MASLINE), paprika, wine and a wide range of herbs are used not just for flavour but for their other properties as well. Babies enjoy sucking sprigs of sassafras tied to their wrists. Parsley and garlic are believed to purify the blood, yoghurt to aid digestion and caraway to be a mild laxative.

In order to prepare the many sour soups that are a frequent part of the menu, fermented grains, fruits, beer or vinegar is used.

Beverages

Romania's vineyards produce a variety of good local wines enjoyed with dinner and supper and often in between especially when mixed with soda water as a *shpritz*. Most popular aperitif is the clear plum brandy called TUICA or TZUICA enjoyed straight but always with appetizers such as ICRE, VINETE TOCATE, MASLINE, MITITEI, tiny hot peppers, pickles or sharp cheeses. MUST is an autumnal beverage of lightly fermented grape juice.

On the sober side, clabbered milk called LAPTE BATUT is often a part of breakfast with breads or rolls (croissant or brioche) or even MAMALIGA. Sweetened soft drinks and cola are increasingly available, and fruit drinks called nectars are also enjoyed.[17]

Romanians often take holidays at spas featuring mineral baths and mineral waters, as if on a quest for the fountain of youth.

Turkish coffee, tea and herbal teas are also taken.

Meal Patterns and Eating Customs

Breakfast may of necessity have to be only MAMALIGA and yoghurt or clabbered milk, but Romanians prefer a hearty breakfast including soft-boiled eggs or omelets, sliced ham and sausages, cheeses and dark bread. Lunch or dinner is considered the biggest meal of the day and may be anytime between one and four P.M. It usually begins with a GUSTARE or "taste" of cheeses, olives, scallions and TUICA, then on to soup, followed by a good stew of meat or fish with vegetables, a dessert of fruit or pastries or CLATITE (rolled thin pancakes). This is accompanied by wine and completed with Turkish coffee. The evening meal will be lighter and taken around nine. It is usually made up of leftovers from dinner, noodle or dumpling dishes or something based on MAMALIGA (cottage cheese and butter atop a plate of MAMALIGA for instance). Large servings are the rule.[2]

Casual visitors are always offered a tray with DULCEATA, cold water and tiny cups of Turkish coffee. The procedure is to take small spoonfuls of DULCEATA followed by sips of water. Turkish coffee completes the ritual. In some areas the offering of the second cup of coffee means that the visit is over and it is time to leave.[5]

Meals at home tend to be not only generous in portions, but simple and hearty. The many-course meal is a rarity except in affluent homes or in restaurants. There is little home life in the cities, because of the congested and sparse living quarters, so people enjoy the evening stroll (like the *korzo* of Yugoslavia and the *paseo* of Spain) with a stop for drinks, snacks and gossip. Meals in restaurants feature fine quality beef and all of the complex dishes that require skilled preparations: CIORBAS, TOCANAS, GHIVETCU, TORTES, STRUDELS and other specialties. Coffee houses serve tea and coffee but mostly aperitifs with appetizer plates of olives, pickles and cheese.

Street vendors sell fresh fruits in season, dried fruit snacks, and the Romanian specialty: MITITEI.

Special Occasions

Over 85 per cent of the population is Romanian Orthodox. Very small minorities of Roman Catholics, Protestants and Jews make up the remainder. The Romanian calendar burgeons with fast days and feast days, lucky days and unlucky days, rites for spring and rites for winter, shepherd milking festivals, harvest and seeding festivals, wine festivals and festivals for the invocation of rain. All have traditional songs and dances and often costumes and much wine and good food.

Funeral customs exemplify many ancient pagan rites, beliefs and symbols: dirges and funeral songs are played, special dawn ceremonies are held, and many don special masks while keeping the vigil with the corpse. In the church service, the priest blesses a special plate of cooked grain, nuts and sugar in memory of the dead.

Weddings are gay, colourful and bursting with exuberant song and dance. One of the oldest country wedding traditions is the amusing fertility rite of "the song of the hen." Feasting and good times may continue more than one day.[2]

In Wallachia, Gypsy children parade in green-leaved costumes, knocking at each house, singing, dancing and being splashed with water by the villagers. This *paparude* is intended to invoke rain and is usually performed in the spring or during a drought.[3] More water-throwing accompanies June 24, St. John's Day , when little girls dress in costumes and hats decorated with ears of corn, singing, dancing and uttering occasional shrieks destined to reach the ears of some unknown corn god . . . another ancient tradition.

Christmas is celebrated more quietly with carolling and good food. But the stress on agricultural themes can be seen again in the fact that in many villages New Year's is celebrated by carrying a decorated plough from house to house accompanied with songs to ensure the next year's good crops.[3]

FORTY-TWO

Russian

Nobody can find more excuses for eating than the Russian. The generous, gregarious Slav spirit can make a party with only one herring and a bottle of homemade vodka. Even the greyest, most depressing day will be greeted by the Russian with a gathering of chairs to the table and comments like, "It's a good day for eating." And the visitor who protests the endless flow of food and the pressing of drinks is reminded that "God created everything in pairs," a rough translation being, "How can you eat just one?"

Religious feast days and fast days, saint days and name days all are further excuses for the Russian creative ingenuity to produce a veritable flood of culinary delights for which it is said the Russian soul pines when away from home. So closely intertwined are food and happiness that it is even rumoured that concert artists travelling abroad bring with them a special delegation whose sole task it is to locate and provide black bread, BORSCH, vodka and perhaps with luck even KASHA.

In 1875, John Murray commented in *A Handbook from Travellers in Russia* that "hospitality is still . . . one of the chief virtues of the Russian people."[1] One hundred years later hospitality – whether it be the traditional welcome of bread and salt, a sumptuous dinner beginning with ZAKUSKY, or even the offering of a glass of tea with lemon and sugar cubes – still characterizes the generous sharing spirit of the Russian. Whatever is offered will be accompanied by excited talk, which will sometimes lapse into soulful songs and the melodic strumming of the balalaika, and the guest will be left with an aura of hearty warmth and conviviality.

The passion with which the Russian describes (often in beloved diminutives), cooks, and serves his food may have its roots in the many long and painful periods of suffering endured over their almost 2,000-year history. The pleasures of guests were never frequent pleasures for a people who were often isolated not only by miles and transportation difficulties but also by long and severe winters. And food itself could never be taken for granted by a people who still retain memories of the great famines of the 1100s and 1200s when straw and bark were soup ingredients and when more than one family survived only by resorting to cannibalism.[1] Nor can the stinging memories of hundreds of years of oppressive rule by callous royalty (with few exceptions) more concerned with territorial acquisition and sumptuous banquets and extravaganzas than with the tortured, starving and illiterate serfs be quickly erased. To have food and drink and to share these with family and friends – these simple pleasures have been elevated to artistry unequalled elsewhere, perhaps because their passionate appreciation is not equalled elsewhere.

Spilling over two continents with its more than 240 million people spread over fifteen republics, the Soviet Union was formed after the Russian Revolution of 1917. It embraces more than 170 ethnic groups speaking predominantly Russian but also almost 200 other languages and dialects.[3,4] The largest group of these are the Slavs making up Great Russia and Little Russia or the Ukraine. Others include the Turko-Tatar, the Japhetic peoples of the Caucasus, the northern people mainly in the Baltic states of Finno-Ugric origin, as well as much smaller groups of Jews, Greeks, Bulgarians, Koreans, Chinese and others.

What is perhaps most interesting is that despite a history of migrations, wars and fluctuating borders not only each of the republics, but frequently each of the ethnic groups clung to individual food customs. Further, much of what we consider today as Russian cuisine can be traced to influences of the early Slavic paganism. The reverence for bread and water is an example. The Russian Orthodox Church's proclamation of Wednesdays and Fridays as meatless days leads to the inclusion of more fish and imaginative flour-based dishes. The adoption of tea and noodles and dumplings from China, wine from the Greeks, pastas from the Italians and sauerkraut and sausages from the Germans has greatly enriched the Russian cuisine.[2,5,10]

The basis of the Slav cuisine is grain. Rye bread and KVASS, a fermented slightly alcoholic beverage made from rye, are important in the north; wheat flour and wheat breads predominate in the south, while corn is the staple in the southwest. From the dawn of the Russian Empire under the rule of the Scandinavian chief Rurik, breads and meats were the staple foods. They were plainly cooked and plainly eaten with dried or fresh fruits such as apples and pears forming desserts, and salted or seasonal vegetables adding some variety.[1]

From this period of Scandinavian influence comes the Russian ZAKUSKY, an array of assorted appetizer foods adapted from the Swedish smorgasbord and now an integral part of the evening meal.[5] The conversion of Vladimir the Great (980-1015) to Greek Orthodox Christianity and its subsequent acceptance by the people through the slightly differing Russian Orthodox Church[3] led to taboos regarding the eating of wild animals and the eating of meats with blood. Further, the meatless fast days as well as Lent led to the increased used of fish, dairy products and vegetable oils.

But perhaps most influential of all was Peter the Great (1672-1725) who attempted to "westernize" the semi-Oriental society of his country. He stimulated the organization of the military, increased industrialization, acquired territory and supremacy in the Baltic, and brought home from his travels chefs, artisans, officers and boatbuilders. It was these latter who introduced French soups and sauces, Italian pastas, pastries and ice cream, German sausages and sauerkraut. But it was the Russians themselves who added their own touches of mushrooms and sour cream, dill and brined vegetables.

Today, with increased production, improved transportation and exciting imports from neighbouring republics, the Greater Russian diet often includes exotic Caucasian and Central Asian fruits, Siberian canned gamed meats, a greater variety of vegetables from the Ukraine and cakes and sweets from the Baltics.[2] Nonetheless, the "soul food" of Great Russia continues to be cabbage, beets and BORSCH, black bread and KASHA and what is life without vodka to wash it down?

Home Life and Facilities

The centre of the traditional Russian kitchen is a remarkable range called the PLEETA. Remarkable because it not only often provides the heat for most of the house, serves as a warm bed at night (with a mattress on top) for the maid, but also cooks meals and bakes foods in either one of two ovens: a slow oven and a fast oven.[8] Further, an area near the ovens is perfect for broiling SHASHLYK, while a covered hole in the chimney carries the charcoal fumes away from the heating samovar. This latter could be described as the second most important piece of equipment in the Russian kitchen for the huge polished samovar is used to heat water for tea, and unquestionably tea has a special place in the Russian home.

Upon the heavy PLEETA can be found an array of practical cooking utensils, almost all of cast iron. These include pots, skillets, and the special griddle, which is actually a series of round "nests" all in one piece, used for preparing BLINI. Of special importance is the earthenware pot used especially for baking KASHA. Characteristically there are no individual-sized baking or cooking dishes because limiting anyone's food is contrary to Russian thinking. A big wooden table for working, wooden mixing bowls and a set of scales complete the important items for cooking and baking.[2,8]

In the country areas of modern-day Russia, the traditional kitchen and utensils are still used. But many people living in urban apartments have little time to fuss over cooking. They prepare simpler meals in smaller kitchens.

Traditionally, home preserves of fruits and jams and barrels of pickled vegetables and cured meats all formed a part of the family's winter supply. More and more, foods are purchased on an almost day-to-day basis as city dwellings have little storage space and refrigerators are costly. In fact very few electrical appliances or gadgets are used which means that water boiling, puréeing, etc., are all done by hand as needed rather than by electric kettles, juicers and blenders.

FOODS COMMONLY USED

The staples of Great Russia are few but are prepared in many classic variations that form a hearty and filling repertoire of cookery. Basic grains include dark whole-grained rye breads, coarse wheat breads, and the all-encompassing KASHA which usually refers to whole fluffy grains of buckwheat but may also be used to refer to barley, corn or millet.

Basic year-round vegetables such as cabbage, potatoes, beets and mushrooms appear in the guise of thick soups, tart and tangy pickles, well-cooked casseroles or encased in satisfying envelopes of chewy noodle doughs, flaky buttery pastries or airy yeast doughs. Liberally laced through the grains and vegetables are generous servings of soured milk, cream, sour cream and especially butter. Beef, game and fish, like fresh salad vegetables, are enjoyed when available.

Fruits are relished but are most commonly used in some cooked form. To the Russian, such hearty natural foods require little seasoning except perhaps dill and garlic, sugar, sour (acid) crystals and usually a little more butter. There are many fermented drinks, soured milk drinks and fruit drinks but tea and vodka are the most important. Tea is elevated to an important social ritual with the samovar, while any gathering is an excuse for endless toasts with vodka.

Milk and Milk Products

SMETANA (sour cream) is an indispensable staple. Too many dishes would be unthinkable and uneatable without a topping of SMETANA. Whole cow's milk, mare's milk and fresh cream are widely used in many dishes and as beverages but usually well-cooked. Sour milk in many forms, pot cheese and cottage cheese, baked milk or KAIMEK and many varieties of excellent local cheeses are used abundantly.

Fruits and Vegetables
The most available fruits are those that can survive the generally extreme climate, or are imported: apples, pears, cherries, plums, cranberries and lingonberries. Other berries such as raspberries, strawberries, currants, gooseberries, blackberries and huckleberries are eaten with relish when they can be obtained. Some fruits are enjoyed fresh, others are preserved or prepared as stews, compotes or the puréed fruit dessert served everywhere called KISSEL. Fruits are also used well-sweetened as fillings for dumplings, as fruit sauces, or served as a "spoon-sweet" to be taken with tea.

Most-used vegetables include cabbage, potatoes, beets, onions, black-skinned radish (REDISKA), carrots, turnips, squash. Enjoyed but used less frequently are green beans, green peas, cauliflower, eggplant, spinach, sorrel and pumpkin. The greens are used in soups, and the less-used vegetables are considered a special garnish to other dishes. Cucumbers are avidly enjoyed fresh with salt to form a type of fresh salad-pickle, or brined to form pickles that will be used all winter. Home-made barrels of sauerkraut (sometimes with fermented apples) are used all year round in many ways too. Mostly the vegetables are used well-cooked in soups, used as fillings or served pickled. When served cold as salads, they have been cooked first then chilled and chopped or sliced and served with sour cream or mayonnaise. Russian salads are never green leafy mixtures, and seldom include raw vegetables.

Citrus fruits are not in abundant supply, but very thin slices of lemon are a special treat with hot tea.

Meats and Alternates
Beef, veal, pork and mutton head the list of meats. Most chickens are tough unless they are capons; geese, ducks and turkeys as well as game birds, deer and hare are used when possible.

Fish is eaten fresh, salted or smoked. Salmon, herring, crayfish and caviar from sturgeon are considered special delicacies.

Soft-cooked or scrambled eggs are beaten occasionally for breakfast. But most eggs are consumed as garnishes, appetizers (pickled, stuffed, chopped), in meat mixtures, and as fillings for BLINI, doughs, dumplings and other baked goods. Legumes are not widely used except in some regions and occasionally in soups. Except in the republics, especially Georgia, nuts are only used in baking or as an occasional confection.

Breads and Cereals
Dark and heavy whole-grain rye breads, coarse firm wheat breads and the ubiquitous casserole of KASHA (usually buckwheat) are the most firmly

entrenched Russian staples. But there are enough shapes and types of breads and rolls – KULITCH, KRENDEL and BAGEL – to make even a diet solely of breads an interesting one. Add to this the hearty list of large and small pancakes, KULEBIAKA, noodle dough and yeast dough dumplings that may be baked, boiled or fried and filled with anything from chopped cabbage to meats, to mushrooms or fruits, then one can see the importance and variety of grains. Further, every kitchen and countless bakeries produce sweet cakes, tortes, rolls, pastries and fruited yeast doughs (KULITCH) that daily find a place on the Russian menu, if only as an accompaniment to tea.

Bread itself is so appreciated that it is a featured part of church blessings. Bread and salt are the traditional symbols of welcome.

Fats
To a Russian, no dish ever contains quite enough butter. Butter is used during cooking, after cooking and more is added during eating. Sunflower oil or peanut oil are used for some dishes.

Sweets and Snacks
Ice cream, available from street vendors or in ice cream parlours, is a frequent snack. Snacks of toasted sunflower, pumpkin and squash seeds as well as many candied fruits are munched frequently. Chocolates or candies are special-occasion treats and not used as often as sweets in other forms. Rich baked desserts are enjoyed whenever possible and for any excuse (one never drinks without eating). But it is more common to sip one's tea with a sugar cube held between the teeth for maximum sweetness or to enjoy a small saucer of sweet rich fruit preserves, a spoonful at a time, with hot tea.

Seasonings
The main seasonings include dill, onion, sour cream, sour crystals (citric or acetic acid crystals), the fermented juices from sauerkraut or pickles, sugar and salt, butter, parsley (coriander) and many types of dried or fresh mushrooms. Foods are generally not highly seasoned; the predominant flavours are either buttery and creamy or a blend of sweet and sour. There is a frequent use of equal measures of both sugar and salt to heighten flavour.

Beverages
Tea and vodka rank as the great Russian beverages. Tea is always served very weak. KVASS, a fermented drink made from black bread, sugar and yeast, is said to be the drink of the Russian peasants.[1] KUMISS or KOUMISS is an ancient Tatar drink said to have legendary nutritive and restorative powers. It is made from mare's milk that has been fermented in wooden tubs or horse skins. It is drunk mainly in the Central Asian Kirghiz

region. Other fermented beverages include pear and raspberry liqueurs, cider, beer and MED (similar to mead). Soured or clabbered milk and whole milk are also enjoyed as beverages.

Regional Staples and Specialties of the U.S.S.R.
(See also individual chapters: Ukrainian, Polish, Lithuanian, Czechoslovakian, Latvian, Estonian, Byelorussian, Armenian.)

Armenia
Here the cuisine is mostly in the Turkish style: a highly refined and varied dietary including Near-Eastern specialties of stuffed vegetables, sweet rich desserts made with phyllo pastry, and a wide range of seasonings. Staples include flat unleavened wheat bread, lamb and chicken, yoghurt and cheeses made from sheep's and goat's milk plus a wide variety of fruits and vegetables. Wines, yoghurt, coffee (Turkish style) and RAKI (clear anise-flavoured brandy) are the favoured beverages.

Azerbaidzhan
Lamb, rice and yoghurt predominate the cuisine while soups and stews are the favoured forms of cooking. A custard of eggs sprinkled liberally with fresh green herbs forms the final garnish to many dishes and exotic seasonings include saffron, cinnamon, pomegranate seeds and the dried powder of plums and barberry.[5] Other Central Asian dishes include PILAFS (a base of seasoned rice served with meat or fish together with vegetables or fruits), and SHASHLYK (skewered broiled meats).[6] KYURDYUK, the fat rendered from fat-tailed sheep, is used liberally both in cooking and as a final flavour fillip (like a dab of butter). The KEUFTA or meatballs are astonishing in size, many weighing several pounds, sometimes cooked with a whole chicken inside. But it is PITI, the Azerbaidzhan thick lamb soup served in earthenware bowls that is considered the outstanding specialty. Generally, a preference for tart and sour flavours predominates, an example being DOVGA, a thick soup of yoghurt, rice and greens served as dessert.

Baltic Republics: Latvia, Lithuania, Estonia
These three republics feature a combination of German, Slavic and Scandinavian influences in their cuisine together with some local touches. They all favour the use of sour milk and sour cream. Their famed winter salads are delicious combinations of pickled vegetables, sour cream and meat or fish, often flavoured with raw onions and caraway. Abundant fish and pork, potatoes and black bread together with pickled cabbage, cucumbers, beets and dairy products form the dietary staples. Favoured seasonings include caraway, allspice, dill, bayleaves and parsley. Both Latvia and Estonia are famed for their pastry shops featuring elaborate cakes and layered pastries introduced by French chefs long ago.

Byelorussia

Pork and fish, cabbage, potatoes and mushrooms form the staples. Many specialties are similar to those in Polish, Russian and Lithuanian cookery but the favoured preserved beet greens add a special Byelorussian touch to borsch and other dishes.

Caucasus

Eastern Mediterranean cuisine predominates here with rice as the staple, along with stuffed vegetables, yoghurt both as beverage and ingredient, and great variety in fruits and vegetables. Lamb is the favoured meat, lamb fat is preferred for cooking, olive oil is used for salads and stuffed vegetables, while butter is used only occasionally in baking.

Their unleavened wheat bread is made only with flour and water. Onions and garlic are much beloved; walnuts and pine nuts are pounded into sauces or used in dishes and fillings; while the exotic fragrance of rose water, cumin, mint and coriander flavour many other dishes.

Central Asia

A huge area in large part consisting of a dried-up sea basin whose plateaus and deserts are visited with extremes of climate, the Soviet Central Asian republics include Turkmen and Uzbek, Tadzhik and Kirghiz and the Kazakh republic north of those.[7]

Nomads still roam the lands with herds of horses and camels, goats and sheep, yaks and cattle and live primarily on cheeses, lamb, mutton and horsemeat. Their beverages include green tea and the fermented mare's milk called KUMISS. When meats and rice are available, they are cooked usually by steaming in a sheepskin pouch that is lowered into a pit of hot coals then banked with earth or sand. Open fires are used for broiling skewered meats and heating water for tea.[5]

The rest of Central Asian cuisine is similar to Azerbaidzhan cookery with few exceptions. These include the use of sauces made of crushed garlic and broth and crushed garlic and yoghurt to be poured over meats, general use of carrots in most Uzbek dishes, and the popularity of stuffed steamed dumplings of which MANTY is the most famous. Pilafs are the most popular rice dishes while many types of flat almost unleavened breads accompany most meals.

Other than the nomads, the peoples of Central Asia live in permanent homes and consequently have a wider variety of cooking utensils and techniques which include chopping foods into small morsels and cooking by stir-frying; steaming foods in a type of double boiler; and cooking foods by dipping into a Mongolian hot pot where the food morsels are eaten first and the broth served later. Staple vegetables include pumpkin, onions and turnips and more recently tomatoes and potatoes. Fresh green herbs, spicy hot peppers, onions and garlic all add zest to what is basically a well-balanced diet of meats, milk and cheeses, seasonal fruits (or preserved fruit syrups) and vegetables.

Central Asian dishes include:

BOZBASH: a thick Azerbaidzh mutton and vegetable soup.
CHIKHIRTMA: a chicken or lamb soup finished with beaten yolks and
    lemon juice.
CHUP OSHI: an Uzbek dish of tossed cooked noodles, fried onions and
    sour milk.
DYUSHBARA or BYUSHPERE: the Caucasian form of dumplings.
PALOV: the Uzbek name for pilaf.

Georgia

One cannot think of Georgian cuisine without thinking of walnuts.
Pounded into a paste and combined with garlic and fiery hot peppers,
walnuts make a sauce that is used to flavour and garnish many dishes.

But that is not all. Walnut oil is used in cooking, walnuts are made into
candied treats and chopped walnuts are a nutritious ingredient in stews,
soups and appetizers. Corn and many varieties of beans as well as soured
milks (sheep, buffalo) and curds form the staples but in good times there
is also an abundance of stone fruits eaten fresh and dried and used as
syrups, sauces, preserves and even in soups.

Fresh green herbs are often eaten out of the hand as snacks or liberally
used in the form of garnishes, salads or seasonings. Eggplants, pumpkins,
squash, cucumbers, radishes, onions and scallions precede most meals of
which a plate of beans is usually a part together with stewed or roasted
lamb, kid or fowl.

Georgians enjoy wines but are not big sweet eaters. A great variety of
bread from the thin crisp LAVASHI to the heavy cornbread called TCHADI
or MCHADI as well as the elliptical PURI baked from whole grain wheat
and leavened with sour dough starter is a part of all meals.[2,5,6.]
Some Georgian specialties are:

TCHADI or MCHADI: a coarse heavy bread of cornmeal often baked
    with a layer of cheese or onions in the middle.
LOBIO: a cold appetizer dish of cooked beans dressed with SATSIVI, one
    of the walnut sauces, or a sauce of pomegranate seeds and juice.
KHADJA PURI: a dessert of hot bread filled with cheese.
CHICKEN TABACA: young chickens split, flattened, butter-browned,
    and served with pickled vegetables.

Ukraine

With good reason the Ukraine is called the "Bread Basket of Europe," for
this area produces wheat, rye and corn in quantity and in fine quality.
Together with the production of the grain fields and the skills and artistry
of her cooks, the Ukraine (also called Little Russia) is said to produce over
sixty-five varieties of breads as well as many delicious dumplings, cakes,
pies and rolls. Generally Slavic cookery predominates with the styles being

closer to the Russian in the East Ukraine and to the Polish and Czech in the far west.[5] Corn and beets are the staples in the west, while potatoes and cabbage are more favoured in the other areas. Generally the Ukrainians use more garlic than the Russians, eat a greater variety of vegetables and together with their fine breads and dairy products favour lamb and pork.

Ukrainians are generally credited with introducing BORSCH, that Russian favourite, a soup of cabbage, beets and potatoes and rich in meats. Other specialties include the following:

VARENIKY: boiled dumplings filled with cheese (or other fillings), covered with noodle dough and served with melted butter, sour cream or preserves.

BORSHCHOK: the hearty western Ukrainian borsch containing more beets than other vegetables.

UKRAINIAN SHASHLYK: most often a variety of broiled skewered meats.

Meal Patterns and Eating Customs

The Russian day begins with a light breakfast of breads and tea and occasionally an egg or two fried or boiled. Lunch is usually a light meal, usually a hot meat or fish dish and often a PIROG (type of pie). Even more frequently for a family lunch the main attraction would be a huge pot of KASHA and a pitcher of milk with perhaps a fish or pot cheese dish for variety. A simple milk pudding or stewed fruit would finish the meal.[1,8]

Since breakfast is small, snacks in the morning rare, and lunch generally a humble light meal, the true Slav spirit (obviously not in full bloom till later in the day) really appears with dinner. *Obed* or dinner may begin anytime from three to five P.M. and though seldom punctual always begins with ZAKUSKY plus vodka. The ZAKUSKY appetizer may be as simple as a plate of salt herring or IKRA (chopped eggplant) or as elaborate as an array of fish and pickled vegetable dishes as well as one or two hot dishes. Small or large, the ZAKUSKIES are all eased down with many toasts of vodka and then the meal begins with hearty soup and probably PIROSHKI followed by meat, fish or game birds, a vegetable and whatever elaborate desserts the hostess can conjure.

For a typical dinner, family and guest will sit down to a table set with a centrepiece of crystal or cut glass filled with fruit, and at each setting will be a small top plate for the appetizers and a larger plate below for the main dish. Soup is always served from a tureen into ample soup plates, and all the dishes that follow will be arranged on platters or in serving bowls. There is no place in the Russian kitchen or on the Russian table for "individual servings," for in the Slav idiom a serving is not only what a person wishes to eat, but the hope is always engendered that he can be coaxed into "just a little more." It would therefore be an insult to have even provoked the suspicion that the food had been measured at all.

Meats are always carved in the kitchen or on a discreet side table, and heaping dishes are the sign of generous hospitality. While the hostess always sits at the head of the table, the host sits wherever he pleases. But both share in the responsibility to urge their family and guests to enjoy, that is – eat.[1,2,8]

The vodka that was downed from one-ounce glasses following appropriate toasts during the sampling of the ZAKUSKIES is continued in a steady flow throughout the meal. All drink when toasts are made, for to decline is considered unfriendly. Though wine sometimes accompanies meals among more cosmopolitan families, it is generally regarded somewhat with suspicion and gulped down like a soft drink.[1]

Meals end with many warm thanks to the host and hostess whose warm reply of *"yeshte na zdorovie"* – "eat and have good health"[8] – congenially sums up the entire meal. Another ritual of delightful warmth and courtesy is the traditional welcome to guests or newlyweds: *"chleb ee sol."* The visitors are welcomed with these words which mean "bread and salt" and are presented with a freshly baked loaf of bread and a mound of salt as they enter the home. They must cut a slice and dip it in salt before eating. The beautiful symbolism indicates that the guests are welcome to share whatever the household can offer, and expresses the hope that there will always be at least bread and salt, the necessities of life.

Though life today in Russia is often more hectic and there is little opportunity to practise time-honoured traditions, the customs associated with foods are still honoured. But perhaps the most pleasurable tradition of all is the fourth meal of the day – *vechernyi t'chai* – that intimate get-together of friends and family around the samovar. Over glasses and cups of tea – all scalding hot – and between hearty bites of breads, meats and cheeses and finally a torte or two, the talk is as continuous as the tea and sometimes as hot. There is a choice of thin lemon slices, sometimes apple slices, and always sweet preserves to enjoy with clear weak tea and cubes of sugar to suck. It is believed this practice of fruit or preserves added to tea was adopted from the ancient Chinese caravanserais.[1,8] Glasses for tea-drinking are favoured by the men and usually the glasses are set into ornate straw or metal holders. But it is not unusual to see tea being sipped while the glass is held casually between thumb and third finger, the thumb resting on the upper rim and the third finger acting as the bottom stand. It would be a good bet that unaccustomed hands could scarcely touch the glass even after it was emptied. Women prefer to take their tea from cups and both men and women like to have a small cut glass side dish from which to spoon up their preserves.

Even in the most modest of dwellings it is likely that a gleaming samovar will be one of the proudest possessions. Contrary to some notions, the samovar does not dispense tea from its spout. It is a large chamber heated by a central chimney containing charcoal embers and its sole purpose is to boil and dispense water. The embers are dropped in the chimney after the water is poured in the surrounding section. The top of the samovar is then connected to that special section of the PLEETA (kitchen stove) in order to draw off the charcoal fumes. A strong essence of good tea is brewed in a small pot. When the water is boiling, the small pot of tea is placed on top of the samovar and the whole thing is transported from the kitchen to the dining room and placed at the right side of the hostess. To serve tea, a small amount of the strong essence is poured into the bottom of the cup or glass which is then filled with boiling water from the tap of the samovar. A lemon slice is floated on top, sugar cubes or preserves are placed on the tiny side dishes. And though a tray of vodka and perhaps a few liqueurs may be visible during the evening tea, unquestionably it is the samovar and the good talk that highlight the *vechernyi t'chai*.

Special Occasions

The predominant faith of the U.S.S.R. is represented by the Russian Orthodox Church founded by Vladimir the Great in C.E. 988 as an offspring from the Greek (Byzantine) Orthodox Church.[11] The main difference betwen the two is the translation of the service in the Russian Orthodox Church into what was known as Church Slavonic. Other Christian religious groups include Baptist, Lutheran and Roman Catholic, the latter being found mainly in Lithuania and the extreme westerly regions of the Soviet Union. Islam is the predominant religion in the Central Asian republics, while almost two million Jews live mostly in the larger cities.[3]

In 1918, the Soviet government nationalized all properties of religious groups and disestablished the Russian Orthodox state church. Since 1936 the constitution has stated that "Soviet citizens are granted freedom of religious worship and antireligious propaganda . . ."[3] though in practice the churches have become more like museums, seasonal and national holidays are replacing those with religious connotation, and overt atheism seems the rule.[2,3]

Yet the highlight of the Russian calendar is Easter. It is a day kept by all with a Slavic heart whether out of nostalgia, faith or simply because it is so good to have a celebration to welcome the long-awaited spring.

Traditionally the festival begins during still-wintry days with a week long festival called *Maslyanitsa*, a gay time of carnivals, parties and above all contests of BLINI-eating. Slathered with melted butter and dollops of sour cream, jam, sliced smoked fish or herring, BLINI are consumed in gargantuan quantities. Following this gaiety and gorging of the "Butter Festival" are the forty days of Lent which the Orthodox Russian observes with a strict diet of vegetables, vegetable oils and grains. This strict period is sometimes softened by a preceding week of the "Little Fast" in which dairy products and fish are permitted, but no meat.[1,2,8] After the Little Fast and the Great Fast, Easter is celebrated with midnight mass, a service beginning with each worshipper carrying glowing tapers and ending with the victorious cries of "Christ is risen!"

With gay hearts the worshippers hurry home to festive tables laden with the preparations of previous days: ham baked in rye dough, pâtés, salads of beef herring and sour cream, PIROGI, MAZURKA and gaudy decorated eggs. But the highlight of the rich meal is the towering rich fruited bread called KULITCH served side by side on a special plate with the creamy smooth PASCHA, rich cream cheese molded with fruit and nuts.

In modern times the traditional Easter feasts and fasts and worship services are celebrated mostly by those Slavs living in other countries. In the Soviet, the *Maslyanitsa* is reduced to rounds of BLINI parties in villages or private homes. Few fast, and those who attend services probably do so more out of nostalgia than faith. Nonetheless the Easter buffet of good foods is still ruled by the KULITCH and PASCHA.

Although Russians adore any excuse for a party such as birthdays, anniversaries, name days, weddings, picnics, seasons, national holidays, the beginning of Lent, Easter and Christmas, very often the gathering of friends and family and the spirit of conviviality overrides the need for special foods. If it is a gathering then it is a party!

The other Russian holiday that is being liberated from its religious connotation (at least in the Soviet Union) is Christmas. This occurs on January 6 with a big celebration featuring Grandfather Frost (the hero) and Baba Yaga (the villain) engaging in nationalist type plays, songs and dances. The victory of Grandfather Frost (with the help of the Young Pioneers), the sharing of gifts and candies and the lighting of an enormous Christmas tree culminate the celebration. This festival is now called New Year's.[12]

The traditional Christmas was always a quiet family festival and Orthodox Russians fasted (abstained from meats) for six weeks before. The traditional Christmas Eve dish was KUTIJA, a mixture of boiled grains mixed with sugar, honey, nuts and raisins. This dish has ancient symbolic meaning, is prepared with slight variations (whole wheat grains or rice), is always served at Christmas Eve and also from a larger platter to all mourners at an Orthodox funeral. Traditional Orthodox Christmas is called *Rozjedestvo*.[1,2,8] The Christmas Day family almost always includes a roast goose garnished with baked apples and preceded by ZAKUSKY.

Other occasions on the Russian calendar also demand traditional foods. An example would be Name Day or *Iminine*. Orthodox Russians are named after saints and the Name Day is also the day of the patron saint. It is celebrated with PIROGI, KRENDEL and steaming hot chocolate served somewhere between the vodka and the ZAKUSKY.[1,2]

Weddings (*Svadisa*) are traditionally solemnized with a church service, the entire congregation standing for the service. Weddings often take place on Sundays since fast days, Tuesdays, Thursdays and Saturdays are forbidden according to tradition for weddings. The "Happiness Cake," a rich yeast dough baked in a large round pan and topped with a small container of salt, symbolizes the bread and salt ceremony of welcome. Bride and groom have some first, then it is shared with the guests. Banquet foods, champagne and vodka follow.

Picnics are a favoured pastime and any collection of ZAKUSKY foods together with vodka and meat for SHASHLYK are deemed suitable for enjoying in the outdoors.

FORTY-THREE

Scottish

A small, rocky country of streams and lakes, with a moderately cool climate, and proud, vigorous inhabitants, Scotland is also known for shortbread, marmalade and Scotch whisky. Though about five million folk make their homes in the Highlands, Lowlands and Uplands, it could almost be said that one of Scotland's principal exports is people; an estimated twenty million Scots have emigrated to other countries.[1]

They have carried with them their kilts and their pipes, their brogue and their oats to whatever wee corner of the world they decided to call home. And several times a year they gather for their Scottish Games – a day of Highland flings and sword dancing, tug of war and the flinging of the mighty caber all to the stirring wail of the kilted bands. For each time Scottish souls are stirred by the foot-tapping rhythms and Scottish eyes mist as "Scotland the Brave" fills the air. And though they may be heard to call themselves "Scotch and proud of it," they'd rather you refer to them as Scots and their fine smoky whisky as Scotch.

Early accounts show a predominance of oats, barley and dairy products as the mainstay of both urban and rural diets in Scotland.[3] Although sheep and black Angus cattle were raised, they were mainly for export rather than local consumption. The general porridge and milk diet was supplemented with kale or cabbage. Small amounts of fish were used in coastal areas and occasionally some meats in the interior.

By the 1800s the rapid growing of urban areas in Scotland became the impetus for agricultural improvement and diversification. There was a sharp increase in the use of wheat bread, meats in broths and stews, and wider acceptance and use of potatoes. This soon made barley and oats a minor part of the daily fare except in the more remote agricultural settlements where economic factors still limited the variety of the diet.

Although people generally ate what was available and what they could afford, good food simply prepared is still the keynote in Scotland. Scots have never been keen on seasonings, sauces or exotic mixtures of foods.[1]

The earliest influences on the Celtic and Gaelic traditions of Scotland were English. But English influence gradually threatened to become English control. In 1295 John de Baliol, King of Scotland, formed an alliance with France, making England the common foe. This alliance lasted several hundred years and through many successions of kings. To this day many Gaelic food names can be traced from the original French name: flam from *flan*; tartan purry from *tarte-en-purée*; kickshaw, *quelque chose*; stovies, *à l'etuvée*; and jigget, *gigot*[1,5]

Yet Scottish food retains the individuality of its people. To this day Scottish foods preserve their simplicity while retaining the most delightfully endearing names – even if some of the sources are long forgotten.

Home Life and Facilities

Simplicity and practicality, so much a part of the Scottish diet, is also a part of the Scottish kitchen. Utensils are sturdy and useful rather than ornamental and many pieces of kitchenware (as well as recipes) have been handed from mother to daughter. There are few gadgets, fewer luxury-type electrical appliances and a more limited spice shelf than may be found in typical Canadian kitchens. Refrigerators generally are smaller because cold pantries are frequently found as an adjunct to the Scottish kitchen, pantries being practical for food storage in a moderately cool climate.

Grease-proof paper is still widely used for baking pans, iron griddles are still favoured for scones and bannocks, and carved thistle presses are still used to shape the traditional Scottish shortbread. But other traditional utensils are declining in general usage. These include the SPURTLE, a stick with a thistle-shaped handle used for stirring porridge; and an ASHETE, the traditional oval- or rectangular-shaped and enamelled baking dishes with high sides to support a pastry crust.[6]

FOODS COMMONLY USED

Hearty soups, fish dishes and a great variety of quick breads and cakes (leavened with soda or baking powder rather than yeast) are the staples in a Scottish kitchen. Fish may be considered one of the most important staples, but milk and milk products are also used in abundance. Fruits are used mainly in season and in the form of jellies, preserves, and marmalades rather than fresh fruits

to satisfy the Scottish sweet tooth. Garden vegetables are popular but kale and seaweed, cabbage and potatoes are the favourites. Thistle leaves may be used as a food but usually only in times of necessity.

Canadians tend to think of oatmeal as a breakfast cereal and perhaps occasionally as a component of breads and cookies. But the Scottish use of oatmeal has stimulated an astonishing array of recipes including beverages, soups, meat and fish dishes, puddings, dumplings, stuffings and many desserts and baked goods. There is even a popular cheese which is sold coated in oatmeal.

Though Scottish food may be prepared with a minimum of seasonings and a maximum of cooking, it is nonetheless substantial and filling.

Milk and Milk Products

Milk, cream and butter is widely and generously used. Cheeses in great variety are assuming increasing importance in the Scottish diet.[5] Some types commonly used:

CAITHNESS: a soft cheese aged sixty days.

CABOC: a log-shaped, soft, buttery cheese rolled in fine oatmeal and traditionally served with BAPS.

RAASEY CHEESE: a thick, cooked mixture of milk, eggs and cheese served on toast.

RAREBIT: a thick sauce of melted cheese with beer or ale, seasoned with mustard and served on toast.

HATTIT KIT: the Scottish version of cream cheese, often molded and served with fresh fruits and cream (French food buffs will note its similarity to *coeur-à-la-crème*).

Fruits and Vegetables

Fresh fruits and vegetables are usually served in season and are often prepared with milk, butter or cream. Staples for winter use include kale, seaweed, cabbage and potatoes. Canned peas are often a garnish. Fruits are consumed as preserves, sweetened desserts or in baked goods. Scots by tradition are not large vegetable eaters nor do they usually consume any great quantity of fresh vegetables or green fresh salads. Typical fruits include apples, plums, and many types of berries. To the staple vegetables listed above may be added turnips (NEEPS), leeks, onions, tomatoes and parsnips.

Meats and Alternates

Fish and, more recently, beef are the favoured protein foods. Extended practical use of offal (heart, liver, kidneys, tripe, etc.) and economical cuts of meat are favoured. Usual methods of cooking include meaty soups, stews or meat pies and broths. When the budget permits, beef, veal and mutton are used most, with chicken and pork products less favoured. The exception is bacon which is used often and frequently lends its smoky flavour to many economical dishes or light suppers. In some areas wild fowl and game are used. Fish is preferred over other seafood (see "Meal Patterns"). Favoured fish include salmon, trout, cod, haddock, kippers and herring. There is some consumption of mussels, oysters, crab, winkles, and shrimp.

Eggs are mostly used as an ingredient in other dishes or prepared as a light supper. Legumes are used only occasionally in some soups.

Breads and Cereals

Oatmeal is no longer the leading item in the Scottish diet.[3] Nonetheless it is still the most important grain cereal used. A perusal of the food glossary will show a few of the ingenious variations, including use as a thickening and coating agent; as a breakfast cereal; toasted, baked, griddled, boiled or fried; as part of soups, beverages, desserts, dumplings, cookies and meat mixtures. Scottish oatmeal is used in the fine ground form rather than as rolled flakes.

Each Scottish cook takes pride in the authenticity of traditional family recipes for breads, cakes, biscuits and shortbreads. Most are made from wheat flour, very few use yeast as a leavening agent and all are characterized by their delicate natural flavours.

Fats

Butter, margarine, lard and suet prevail as the favoured fats in cooking and baking. Oil is seldom if ever used. Fats are also consumed in the form of buttery cheese and cream.

Sweets and Snacks

Candies, especially butterscotch, taffy, and hard sugar candies, are frequent treats, found in many pockets and often used to reward children. Jellies, jams, marmalades and preserves such as fruit butters are on the table daily. Quick tea breads, plain un-iced cakes and crisp plain cookies (BISCUITS) are consumed in large enough quantities to form a significant part of the diet.

Seasonings

The Scottish spice shelf is one of the smallest in the world. Salt and pepper are used but seldom are other spices or any herbs called for. Onions add their flavour to many dishes, and butter and oats are used with such frequency that they could also be considered as typical flavours. Ginger is the spice most used in baking, if at all. The pure natural flavours of fresh ingredients are preferred to the addition of any spices or herbs or anything that may mask those natural tastes.

Beverages

It has been said that Scotch whisky is the staple beverage of Scotland, and there's scarcely an individual who won't stoutly defend the attributes of his favourite brand. But a fair amount of beer and some imported wines are also consumed.

Tea is the favoured beverage for breakfast and as a refreshing break. This is usually accompanied by at least a few of the famed tea breads and cakes for it wouldn't do to have tea alone. At its simplest, tea will at least be accompanied by bread, butter and preserves.

Meal Patterns and Eating Customs

It has been said that the best Scottish meals are breakfast and tea.[5] But those who have enjoyed fine black Angus beef or rich Scottish salmon may well have a quarrel. And though there has long been a Scottish superstition (especially in the north) against shellfish and seafood as "the lice of the sea," many Scots do enjoy locally caught shrimps, mussels, winkles, crab and lobster. But those persisting in the old beliefs hold that salmon, cod, haddock or herring can't be beat for a fine meal.

Generally Scots prefer a few simple good dishes for a meal rather than many courses and elaborate service. What they lose in variations they make up in hearty servings. Scottish hospitality is legendary: no one leaves a table hungry no matter how simple the fare.

A Scottish breakfast will likely include oatmeal porridge made from finely milled, unrolled oats and served with cool milk or cream. Traditionally each spoon of hot porridge is dipped in milk to cool it. Toast with butter, preserves and a cup of tea complete the meal. More elaborate breakfasts may include a fish dish, bacon, and tea breads.

The noon dinner often consists of a hearty meat and vegetable soup, a dessert of steamed pudding, custard or baked bread pudding and tea.

Often the highlight of the day will be the tea served in the late afternoon about 5:30.[7] Here will be the display of breads and cakes, preserves and marmalades that Scotland is famed for: BAPS, BANNOCKS, SCONES, TARTS and BUNS all served with strong tea, milk and sugar. Chops or sausages with eggs or a favoured dish of sole, kippers or salmon may accompany the tea.

Perhaps because the late-afternoon tea is so special, the evening meal is usually light and includes only one course: either sausages, bacon, chops with eggs and a garnish of peas or a mashed vegetable combination dish served with a glass of buttermilk. In humbler homes, the evening supper may be just a bowl of hot porridge made of oats or barley and served with milk.

Special Occasions

The Presbyterian Church of Scotland has more than a million followers.

The Roman Catholic Church is second in importance with other denominations following in much lesser numbers.[4]

Christmas in Scotland is a one-day holiday highlighted with a festive family dinner at noon featuring roast chicken, mashed potatoes and turnips and climaxed with a flaming steamed fruit pudding.[7]

But the merriest days on the Scottish calendar are Hogmanay and Robbie Burns' Night. Hogmanay is the day before New Year's and probably the only day in the year when everyone takes a holiday. This is the time for gifts and merry-making, for nibbling nuts and eating juicy imported oranges. It is also the time for the finest bakery from the kitchen – black bun, fragrant cherry and currant cakes, crispy delicate shortbreads – all to be accompanied with port wine, ginger wine or Scotch whisky. Later in the evening after midnight, all present enjoy a buffet meal of cold ham, roasted fowl and other meats, SCONES, BANNOCKS and sweet butter to be followed yet again by the array of cakes and buns till all are happily sated. Robbie Burns' Night is the celebration marking the birth of the great Scottish poet. It is celebrated on January 25 and is only slightly less important than Hogmanay. For public banquets both occasions may be marked with the almost-mystical preparation of the HAGGIS, served with great ceremony to the accompaniment of the pipes and many a nip of Scotch whisky.

FORTY-FOUR

Spanish

It is common to refer to anything we don't understand as being "mystical." And more than any other country, Spain has long been tagged with this cloudy term. The contrasts of the country, and the contradictory characteristics of the people, and the endless juxtaposition of the old and the new jar the sensibilities and make slick summaries all but impossible.

Spain's 33 million people are spread over nine regions, divided into fifty provinces and speak various dialects of four main languages. But one province subjugates them all.[1] Since 1469, Castile has dominated Spain linguistically, geographically and historically. For in that year, Isabella of Castile married Ferdinand of Aragon, launching not only Castile's influence over the rest of Spain, but also subtly but undeniably the dominance of women over men. It is interesting that their rule is referred to by Spaniards as the rule of the "Catholic Kings" in a phrase neatly depicting their strength and equality and the symbolism of "Spain's fervor for religious purity" that was to launch Christopher Columbus to the New World and herald Spain's global career, and at the same time catapult all of Spain into the degradation of the Inquisition.

The rule of the Catholic kings ended almost 800 years of Arab and Moorish occupation and united all the kingdoms of Spain. Probably because the Christians of that period identified all Moslems as Moors (inhabitants of what is today Morocco), the 800-year period is always called the Moorish period. Actually the first invasions were by Sunnites from Yemen and Shiites from Persia, and the combined Arab, Berber and Moorish occupation was not all bad. The rule was seldom a unified one, and there was as much fighting among themselves as there was with the Spanish princes. There were also long periods of amiable coexistence. Christians practised their religion and it was intellectual Arabs and Spaniards together who perfected new ideas in medicine, mathematics and astronomy and made Spain one of the most populous and wealthy countries in all of Europe at the time.[1,2]

The 800 years left not only an intellectual and economic imprint but a gastronomic one as well. Much earlier in Spain's history (about 1100 C.E.[2]) the Phoenicians had planted grape vines and olive trees. The olive oil supplanted the use of pork fat from Roman times, and the grapes added to the development of many wines. The Arabs, Berbers and Moors did some planting too. They added gardens of fragrant peach, apricot, lemon and almond trees as well as the thick-skinned bitter orange for which Seville was to become famous. Exotic seasonings of cinnamon, nutmeg, cumin and saffron found their way into Spanish dishes, and the planting of sugar cane and rice added new staples as well. Today Spanish PAELLA seems so indigenous to Spain that its roots in many exotic PILAUS of the Near East are all but forgotten.

Isabella and Ferdinand had launched Spain into an era of exploration, colonization and conquest. Spain swelled to encompass a vast overseas empire that included Cuba, Puerto Rico, colonies in South America, Guam and the Philippines. The world may remember that it was the Spanish *conquistadores* who brought corn, potatoes and tomatoes as well as chocolate and vanilla from the New World. But the world also remembers that these were the results of plunder and destruction abroad, while a degradation of another sort was taking place in Spain itself. The Inquisition, also launched by Isabella and Ferdinand, began slowly with the tormenting of *Conversos* and *Moriscos* in Spain for the sake of "religious purity and unity." It ended with torture, death and expulsion not only for Jews converted to Christianity (*Conversos*) and Muslims converted to Catholicism (*Moriscos*), both of whom thought to be secretly practising their own religions, but finally for every person of a faith other than Catholicism.

To this day, Spaniards speak well of the great reign of the Catholic kings that brought unity and an overseas empire. They speak as if it happened but recently, and they dismiss critics of the conquests and the Inquisition as all part of a "Black Legend." But the results of that Black Legend still ominously haunt Spain. For with the expulsion and deaths of the *Conversos* and *Moriscos* went some of the greatest minds of the country. There followed a gradual but undeniable slump in the country's intellectual, economical, cultural and political affairs and achievements. In later years Spain was left bereft by the declarations of independence by its colonies, the Treaty of Paris in 1898 which gave Puerto Rico, Guam and the Philippines to the United States. Internal strife – the continuing and fundamental conflict of the Liberalists and the Absolutists – and bitter sporadic civil wars gradually led to Spain's isolation from the rest of the world.[1,2]

Perhaps it is this isolation that furthers the image of the province of Castile as the symbol of Spain itself. Linguistically, Castilian Spanish is considered the purest, geographically Castile is located in the centre of Spain, aloof and impenetrable, historically and socially the Castilians consider themselves descendants of royalty whose manners and sophistication are unexcelled. Yet to describe all Spaniards in the image of Castilians would be a mistake. For though the provinces have been unified for more than 500 years, the areas are fiercely individualistic and regard themselves as Basques, Aragonists, Catalonians, Andalusians and so on. They treasure their linguistic differences as much as they savour their culinary specialties, and they cling to many old ways even as they enjoy materialistic changes.

Everywhere in Spain roads are shared by motorcycles, bicycles, Seats (the Spanish answer to the Italian Fiat), and mule-drawn Gypsy carts. Small scattered villages still store their daily water supply in earthenware jugs brought from the rivers while electricity lights their homes and television antennas bristle on their roofs. And in Madrid black-clad women jostle girls in mini-skirts, outdoor cafés serve unhurried coffees and snackers enjoy TAPAS (appetizers) in age-old bars with sawdust floors. But while relative prosperity seems to be merging the working class into the middle class, it is the Castilian legacy of rigid class structure that is making this inevitable movement a slow one. The old is never quite removed from the new: the mule carts stubbornly demand their share of the road, and water is still the most important and unsolved problem in all of Spain. While television draws the men perhaps more than philosophical conversations, they traditionally prefer to talk and think rather than to do.

Other things have not changed. Did the vital force of women's influence begin with the Castilian Queen Isabella? Surely she must stand as the single most important figure of Spain, for it is not only her Castile that has subjugated all of Spain, but for more than 500 years her impact has been felt, and is responsible for the quiet but driving force typical of Spanish women. Regardless of class or position, the Spanish male prides himself on his appearance, his authority and his own great self-esteem. It is with a patience born of centuries of intuitive understanding that the Spanish woman has resigned herself to the combination of Don Juan and Don Quixote that is her husband. While he fantasizes and philosophizes she quietly manages the finances and the household.

But time and influences from the outside world are making their inroads felt all over Spain, from the fertile lush lands of the Basque country to the mountains and hard plains of the Castile and Estremadura and even to the lazy, sunny coastal areas of Costa del Sol and San Sebastian. Gently the old forces, customs and patterns are making a place for the new as Spain herself emerges from the shackles of feudalism and the

Black Legend, from fantasies and philosophies into realities and the pursuit of material pleasures. Likely the mysticism will always be there, but the clouds are parting.

Home Life and Facilities

The kitchens of Spain mirror old traditions side by side with the newest conveniences. The mortar and pestle is being replaced by the electric blender and a place is being found for imported electrical refrigerators even if that place is in the living room.[4] Yet breads freshly baked in community hearth ovens and earthenware *ollas* (pots or casseroles) have not been cast aside. And as more and more women are entering business, professional fields and even part-time work, and as cooks and maids are becoming scarcer too convenience foods and electrical appliances that make cooking easier and quicker are quickly finding a place.

FOODS COMMONLY USED

The most common misconception about Spanish food is that it is spicy hot. In fact, Spanish foods are noted for their fresh natural flavours and a minimum of seasonings and many an authentic Spanish dish prepared elsewhere fails simply because of the lack of quality and freshness in the basic ingredients.

The staples of the Spanish kitchen include olive oil, tomatoes, garlic and onions. Fresh bread is always on the table not only for each meal but also for each course except dessert. Partly because they are the freshest, and partly because of regional pride and preferences, the Spanish cook adds local specialties from land or sea to the staples to produce distinctive regional dishes. COCIDA and GAZPACHO are national dishes of Spain, but have as many variations as there are kitchens, and each variation is stoutly defended as being the best. Fruits and subtle light seasonings, combinations of fruits and nuts with meats and fish and dishes based on rice are all influences from the Muslim times. But the oldest additions to Spain's table – wine and olive oil – have never lost their importance.

Milk and Milk Products

Milk as a beverage is almost non-existent in Spain except perhaps occasionally in some rural areas. Adults and children alike take coffee or chocolate (made with milk) for breakfast only. But milk is consumed in the form of cheeses and the favourite dessert, a caramel flan. Cheeses may be made from cow's, goat's or sheep's milk or combinations thereof. Spain's cheeses are not of exceptional quality but they are often eaten as TAPAS (appetizers) and with fruits for dessert. Condensed and evaporated milk is used as well as fresh whole milk for the preparation of the baked custard called FLAN which is so popular it is often a part of the dessert course even with pastries or fruits.

Fruits and Vegetables

The Arabs, Berbers and Moors brought with them not only a taste for fruits but the actual plants themselves. There is seldom a day in Spain when fruit has not been enjoyed either by itself as a snack, wine-soaked in SANGRÍA, nestled in a casserole with meat or fish, or served as a refreshing dessert perhaps with cheese. Oranges, lemons, peaches, apricots, many types of berries, grapes, melons, dried fruits (dates, raisins, figs), candied fruits and even candied vegetables are all part of the daily fare.

Vegetables are seldom eaten raw; salads tend to be simple greens with tomatoes dressed with olive oil, salt and perhaps vinegar. Pickled or cooked vegetables dressed with oil and vinegar and served chilled are often a part of the TAPAS or ENTREMESES, but more usually vegetables are served as a separate course, simple but well-cooked. A wide range of fresh vegetables are available almost year-round: potatoes, carrots, peas, fresh beans, cabbage, cauliflower, artichokes, zucchini, cucumbers, greens, eggplants and of course tomatoes, peppers, onions and garlic. As well as being served in salads and as appetizers, many vegetables are a part of soups and stews.

Meats and Alternates

Still another reason for the difficulty in duplicating Spanish dishes is the wide variety of game used: rabbit, hare, partridge, boar, etc., as well as the use of suckling lamb and pig only little more than three weeks old. Domestically produced meats are tough and lack flavour which is probably why the most popular method of cooking meat dishes is by stewing or braising. The national dish, COCIDA, varying as it does in its ingredients from area to area, nonetheless makes practical use of meats and vegetables to produce three courses: a clear soup, a platter of mixed cooked vegetables and finally a variety of boiled meats.

Fish and seafood abound in many varieties unknown in this country. Mussels, prawns, shrimps, clams and oysters vie in popularity with lobsters and crayfish, crabs, barnacles and sea spiders. Fish is a cornerstone of Spanish cuisine and is widely used because of its fresh availability and because it is inexpensive. Dried and salted cod (BACALAO) is also used, but the fresh fish include bream, hake, mullet, flounder, tuna, fresh cod, sea bass, sole and trout. Fish may be poached, fried or baked and is often prepared as a soup-stew. Common also in Spanish cookery is the combination of fish or seafood with meats or fowl in one dish such as hake with ham and eggs, lobster with chicken, or the famed PAELLA VALENCIANA which, though made in many versions, classically combines chicken and seafood with rice.[5]

Legumes, especially in the form of GARBANZOS (chick peas) and lentils are widely used as an ingredient of the COCIDA and often as a simple but hearty soup. Eggs are consumed most frequently as ingredients in other dishes such as omelets, soufflés and FLAN. Almonds are nibbled as a candied sweet, pounded and made into a beverage called HORCHATA, used in sauces, pastries and in fish and meat dishes.

Breads and Cereals
Except for the province of Galicia where a light bread is made from cornmeal and the Canary Islands where corn is a staple, all of Spain enjoys fresh, crusty, white wheat bread. Bread is the staple that is always on the table. Hot or cold cereals are not eaten in Spain.

Fats
Olive oil is unquestionably the staple fat in all of Spain except in Basque country (Las Vascongadas) where pork fat is mostly used. Butter is used in some desserts and pastries, and with breads.

Sweets and Snacks
Candied dried fruits, candied cooked fruits and even candied vegetables such as pumpkin and squashes as well as candied nuts, especially almonds, are favourite nibbles. Taking late afternoon tea or coffee with a variety of sweet pastries is customary in some areas. Almost everywhere, convents are famed for their sweet pastries and candies especially prepared for the frequent fiestas. The main meal of the day (*comida*) taken leisurely in the afternoon or the restaurant meal taken with friends is seldom complete without a sweet FLAN or pastries. Occasionally though, fresh fruit may complete the meal. Sweet flaky pastries and honey-drenched cakes reminiscent of the Muslim occupation are great favourites.

Seasonings
The lightest hand in seasonings is to be found in southern Spain; the garlic and onions become more pronounced as one moves northward. Saffron is almost indispensable in most rice dishes, cumin, nutmeg and cinnamon are found lightly flavouring desserts and sometimes meat and fish dishes. But the favourite seasonings universally used are garlic, onions and tomatoes.

Beverages
Coffee with hot milk and hot chocolate made with milk are the usual breakfast beverages. Red wines and varieties of sherries from Jerez include *finos* and *olorosos*. The *finos* include *manzanilla* and *amontillado*: pale in colour but with a rich dry flavour. The *olorosos* include "brown"

and "cream" sherries and their deep rich colour matches their flavour. Local wines are made everywhere in Spain and wines commonly accompany the *comida* to the enjoyment of young and old alike. SANGRÍA is the most known mixed wine drink consisting of sliced fruits marinated in brandy then combined with equal amounts of mineral or soda water and red wine. Another refreshing drink popular everywhere is HORCHATA. It is milky in appearance, only slightly sweet and its flavour is delicately almond. HORCHATA may be made from pounded melon seeds, chufa seeds (similar to almonds) or almonds themselves.

A specialty served in Las Vascongadas (Basque country) is a mixture of equal amounts of red wine, white wine and lemonade served chilled but without ice cubes and especially enjoyed with the Basque buffet called MERIENDA.

Regional Specialties

Central Plateau

Don Quixote's La Mancha is noted not only for windmills but also for wheat and olives. This southeasterly area of the Central Plateau can also boast some game: hare, rabbits and quail. MANCHEGO, a cheese made from goat's milk, is produced in the area.

The rest of the Central Plateau includes New and Old Castile and the general lack of game make very young lamb and piglets the specialties. Placed on an earthenware platter directly in an oven they are slowly roasted to an unbelievable tenderness. Together with ham, pork sausages, bacon and other pork products, veal is also commonly used. There are many versions of the Castilian COCIDA but most frequently it is made with varieties of sausages, cabbage, potatoes and vermicelli.

OLLA PODRIDA (literally "rotten pot") is a simple bean and pork stew, said to be the original COCIDA. But both the COCIDA and the PODRIDA are said to have their origins in an ancient Jewish dish called *adafina* which was a slow-cooked mixture of beef, vegetables and hard eggs. Set in a slow oven late Friday afternoon, it provided a hot meal for the Sabbath without breaking the Sabbath commandment against work. During the times of the Inquisition, the *Conversos* and even the *Moriscos* demonstrated their pious Christianity by substituting pork for the eggs. (No Muslim or Jew would eat pork.) In time, the simple dish gained many variations and came to be the staple of Spain.[4]

Other specialties of the area include SANGRÍA, a light wine punch with sliced brandied fruit; FLAN, a baked milk and egg custard usually with a caramel sauce; and SOPA DE AJO, "garlic soup" made basically of oil-browned garlic and bread crumbs and served with a whole egg.

Like the rest of the area, Madrid itself prefers light simple food, but the city boasts restaurants that can serve any of the finest regional

Spanish dishes. *Madrilenos* themselves are famed for their endless eating and lack of sleep. They rise early, nibble frequently and eat three or four meals a day, the last being anytime after 10:00 P.M.

Estremadura
The area west of the Central Plateau is dry, mountainous and sparsely populated. Even the name means "extremely hard." Because it is one of the poorest regions in Spain, pork and potatoes form the staples and the TORTILLA, a potato and onion omelet, is a specialty.

Galicia and Asturia
Located north of Portugal, in the northwest area of Spain, the province of Asturia is noted for its coal mining and the fine salmon that are caught from its rivers.

Galicia is the only place in Spain where the people play bagpipes and the provincial export is men. The area is so poor that the men leave their women to look after the few cornfields while they seek work elsewhere. The staple foods are pork, potatoes, greens (especially *grelos*, turnip greens) and a moist bread made from cornmeal. Apple cider is used as a beverage and frequently in cooking.

POTE GALLEGO, a specialty of Galicia, is a thick soup-stew made with any meat or vegetables available. CALDERETA ASTURIANA, a specialty of Asturia, is a type of bouillabaisse made from fish and seafood from the Bay of Biscay.

Most famous of all is the FABADA ASTURIANA, a stew of CHORIZO, ham and beef, cabbages, potatoes and white beans; and the EMPANADAS, meat or seafood pies, usually served cold, and shaped in small triangles or cut in wedges from a large pie.

Las Vascongadas
Near France in the north-central part of Spain lie the Basque provinces where it is claimed that the simplest and finest cooking in all of Spain can be found. Unlike the men in most of the rest of the areas of Spain, the Basques excel energetically in everything they do. The greenest fertile lands, the highest per capita income, the most industry, the most banks and the most beautiful women in all of Spain are said to be in Las Vascongadas. With all of that it is difficult to believe that it is here too that gastronomy is a masculine art and that somehow the men find time to belong to the many serious societies dedicated solely to good food and drink.

While the midday meal may be taken at home and most weekends spent with the wife and family, the Basque male will be found most evenings dining with his gastronomic society – if not actually cooking.

Their many courses include egg dishes, fish, fowl, meat, cheese, NATILLAS (soft custard tinged with cinnamon and lemon), fruits, pastries, coffee and brandy. Basque cooks are noted for the delicacy and unexcelled natural flavours of all of their dishes but especially cod. TXAKOLI is a dry white wine with a fresh apple-like flavour, the specialty of Las Vascongadas. Unfortunately, it does not travel well so is enjoyed only there.

Navarre
Hemingway made famous Pamplona, the capital city of Navarre, and tourists as well as Spaniards flock there in July for the festival of San Fermín, the running of the bulls. The day of excitement is ended with a late special meal of rabbit pie and tangy cheese.

Aragon
Bordering on France, Aragon shares France's love of sauces and dedication to fine foods and wines. CHILINDRÓN is a basic sauce similar to the SOFRITO used in many Spanish-speaking countries. It is a well-cooked blend of onions, garlic, tomatoes and meat – in Aragon the meat is SERRANO ham. This sauce is used with meats, game, fish or seafood. One of the secrets of many dark, rich Aragonese sauces is the last-minute melting in of chocolate to blend all the other flavours, especially in a meat or game sauce.

But the great favourite of the area and popular in much of Spain is the MIGAS, piping hot crisply fried croutons of stale bread. These are lightly salted and often fried and tossed with crispy bits of ham to make a light delicious appetizer, but the MIGAS also find their way into stews, soups and sauces.

Catalonia
Bordering the Mediterranean in the northeastern corner of Spain, the province of Catalonia is famed for its cosmopolitan and hard-working people who are said to be more like Europeans than any of the other Spaniards except perhaps the Basques. Here, it is said, "everything edible is eaten." Perhaps it is the distinctive ruddy ROMESCU sauce with its tangy sharp and sometimes hot flavour together with the ALI-OLI (garlic and oil sauce) that helps to make any fish, seafood or game palatable.

In any case the sauces are almost as famous as the fine fruits grown in the area: peaches, apricots, cherries, pears, sweet berries and especially the numerous melons. HABAS (broad beans) are widely used in soups and stews, and, while a ZARZUELA in most of Spain means an operetta, here in Catalonia it usually refers to a melodic blending of fish and seafood as a stew. The hearty Catalan appetites often consume brimming soup plates of ESCUDELLA, a hearty thick soup, made with a melange of pork products (ESCUDELLA COCIDA) or a variety of meats (ESCUDELLA I CARN D'OLLA), then go on to finish a meal of several more courses. Another specialty is POTAJE DE GARBANZOS Y ESPINACAS, a thick nourishing soup of spinach and chick peas. The Catalan version of the FLAN dessert is called CREMA CATALANA and is served on a wide flat plate, a layer of creamy custard resting under a crispy topping of burnt sugar.

Valencia

The fertile and even swampy lands of Valencia make it Spain's principal rice-growing area. So it is not surprising that rice is the staple food, the base for many meat and seafood dishes, is used in soups, and in flour form is used to prepare many cakes and pastries. Valencian women are renowned for their pastry skills.

Sweet Valencian oranges are enjoyed for their juice which is a common refreshment and oranges, like rice, seem to appear in many dishes: salads, desserts and in combinations with fish, seafood and meats.

But the most famous dish of all is the classic PAELLA VALENCIANA, a succulent melange of chicken, seafood and rice lightly flavoured with saffron and a small garnish of red pimientos and green peas. But that is only one version. There are as many PAELLAS in Spain as there are COCIDAS, and who can say which is the best? Here too as in Catalonia the garlic and oil sauce called ALI-OLI is used as a dip or sauce for meats, game, fish or seafood.

Andalucia

Sometimes it is difficult to believe that the Strait of Gibraltar actually separates Andalucia from Morocco, so alike are these areas in lifestyle, climate and appearance. Moorish architecture predominates, and the romantic Andalucians favour many originally Muslim dishes.

One of these is GAZPACHO, the quintessence of the Andalucian kitchen. At once light and refreshing yet satisfying, this now-classic soup of Spain actually has many variations. Occasionally grapes and even rabbit meat are added to the fresh vegetable base.[3] Originally the name GAZPACHO referred to a cold soup based on water-soaked bread; today it commonly refers to a cold soup made with fresh tomatoes and cucumbers added to the water-soaked bread and usually flavoured with at least a little garlic. Cold soups based on vegetables, garlic or almonds are favourites in this area where the temperature may reach 130 degrees F, and life of necessity moves slowly.

Purists argue that although GAZPACHO is made throughout Spain, it cannot compare with the Andalucian version. Madrid GAZPACHO is said to be too thick, Estremadura's is said to be too thin.[1]

A little further inland, cool wintery weather makes cities like Granada appreciative of hot, thick soups. Although garlic, olive oil and tomatoes are unquestionably the staples in this province, fish, seafood and fresh fruits are much enjoyed. POTE BLANCO is a thick, satisfying soup of cod, cream and potatoes. One of the most popular basic sauces is SALMOREJO made with garlic, eggs, bread crumbs, oil and wine vinegar. In Granada, the term *escabeche* means anything that is pickled.

Meal Patterns and Eating Customs

Spain's history has indelibly affected the life of her people. The Civil War of 1936-1939 was followed by a long period of isolation from the rest of the world. This was broken in 1951[2] by the signing of an aid and defence pact with the United States, the impact of which sent pulses of change throughout Spain and is still affecting the daily life of the people. The resulting trade and industrial explosion not only brought about the slow emergence of a middle class, but also the adoption of many Western patterns in clothing, foods, sports, television and the increasing emergence of women in the business and professional world. Increasingly young women went out unchaperoned. The availability of cars (the modest Seat) made travel easier with the result that Spaniards are getting to know each other as regional differences break down and communications increase.

No longer are regional food specialties only available in the respective provinces. No longer are Spaniards sipping only on wine and sherry; now tourists sip the sherry while natives enjoy international cocktails. Domestic help is becoming scarcer but luckily a range of electrical appliances is helping to fill the gap.

Men and women are enjoying greater freedom, but some things have not changed. There is an overall general lack of home life: the centre of the Spaniard's social life is not in the home. Guests or friends are invited to dine in restaurants, meet at a specific coffeehouse for *tertúlia* (meeting and talking leisurely over coffee and pastries), or spend an evening *chateo* (a touring of bars and enjoying drinks and snacks). There is no end to superb restaurants, and many of the coffeehouses are regular hangouts for specific groups, i.e. students, professors, doctors. But the age-old bars with their endless varieties of drinks and TAPAS are best for brief enjoyment. Usually the refreshment is taken standing up, debris is thrown on the sawdust floors and then the patrons move on.

While the Spaniard's hospitality is usually offered outside the home, an effusion of courtesy and compliments are offered everywhere even without provocation. It is never enough to say thanks: in compliments and courtesies superlatives are the rule. Prized even more than smiles, money or the polite gesture, verbal compliments are a cultivated art. Perhaps the pinnacle of the fine art of compliments is to be found in the *piropos*: those delightfully risqué remarks addressed by men to any passing female. Far from being insulted, a woman would be greatly upset if her walk elicited no *piropos*.

While the rural dweller's day and meal patterns are geared to his work and the seasons, the day of the *Madrileño* never ceases to astonish the tourist. The people of Madrid are early risers, beginning their day with a modest coffee or hot chocolate and a bread or pastry (commonly CHURROS, cinnamon-dusted spiral doughnuts.) An ample dinner followed by a siesta is taken in the early afternoon then work resumes about four and concludes in the early evening. The evening meal is usually taken no earlier than ten and often later. It is an incredible sight to see *Madrileños*, men, women and even small children, thronging the streets close to midnight, simply out for a walk. No one seems to know when they sleep. But what they lack in sleep they make up in appetite: meals, snacks and drinks are consumed in unbelievable quantities around the clock.

Special Occasions

Roman Catholicism is the state religion of Spain. In 1967 Spain passed a decree guaranteeing religious freedom; this affected about 30,000 Protestants and 7,000 Jews. Previous to this, dating from 1492, laws still in effect forbad public worship or advertising of religious services by other than Roman Catholics.[1,2]

It is not enough to say that fiestas abound in Spain, they are in fact an almost daily occurrence. Perhaps in no other country of the world (with the possible exception of Italy) are there so many holidays and festivities to honour personal and local saints and special rituals relating to the seasons, work, weddings and funerals. In fact it has been said that there is scarcely a day on the Spanish calendar that is not marked by a fiesta for some region, village or family.

These are a few of the main festivity days:

New Year's Day
Epiphany
March: Fallas de San José. Rice-planting festival in Valencia. Costumes, parades, every conceivable rice dish and varieties of fine pastries.
March 19: Feast of St. Joseph (San José) in rest of Spain.
Holy Week Celebrations
Good Friday
Holy Saturday
Easter Monday
Pentecost Monday
May 1
Ascension Day
Corpus Christi
June 24: Feast of St. John
June 29: Feast of St. Peter and St. Paul
July 1: San Fermín. The running of the bulls in Pamplona, Navarre.
July 18: National Feast Day.
July 25: Feast of St. James, patron of Spain.
Aug. 15: Assumption Day.
Sept. 24: Feast of Our Lady of Mercy, patron saint of Barcelona.
Oct. 12: Feast of Hispanidad.

Nov. 1: All Saints' Day. Pumpkin is the symbolic All Saints' Day food in both French and Spanish Basque areas.

Dec. 8: Immaculate Conception.

Dec. 19: Pregón de Navidad. The official opening of the Christmas festivities which last till January 6. Kings' Day or the Day of the Three Wise Men, the day of gift-giving to children.

Dec. 25 or 26: St. Stephen's Day or Christmas. Celebrated as a family occasion. Christmas Eve is celebrated with decorations of the manger, Spanish carols, midnight church services and a late family dinner with roasted pork, lamb or baked fish ending with special sweets prepared weeks ahead of time.

FORTY-FIVE

Swedish

Maintaining neutrality in two world wars, and historically the benevolent ruler of parts of the Baltic, Germany and Finland, Sweden stands today as the wealthiest, most cosmopolitan country of Northern Europe. Sweden's population of approximately 8 million makes her the fourth largest nation in Europe.[1,2] Despite the fact that only 9 per cent of her land is arable, Sweden is almost self-sufficient in agricultural and dairy products, meats and fish due to the efficient application of the most modern techniques of fertilization, mechanization, animal and poultry production and fishing procedures. In the late 1800s Sweden gradually emerged as one of the important industrial nations of the world, maintaining to this day a great respect in business circles and a high reputation for fine products from industrial steel to glassware and modern furniture.

The southern portions of Sweden enjoy moderate climate due to the prevailing westerly winds and the warming Gulf Stream. But the northern areas bordering on Finland and Norway and stretching into the Arctic Circle brave bitter temperatures and long dark winters, though they delight in two months of continuous daylight. The many lakes and long rivers contribute to a great potential of hydroelectric energy of which only a portion is presently used.

But making the most of her natural resources and industrial potential is only a part of Sweden's success story. The other part must be the Swedish people themselves. Known for their lilting musical language, which has borrowed words both from French and German roots,[2] the Swedes are also noted for their serene dispositions. Perhaps a part of their serenity stems from their confidence and pride in their country; perhaps a part stems from their ordered, relaxed daily way of life. Swedes have the enviable ability to enjoy each day. And rituals are an important part of that enjoyment. Everything from coffee-drinking to *skoal*, from table manners to holiday festivities, follow prescribed and predictable procedures. And although most Swedes are Lutheran, their relaxed attitudes extend also into their religious life. Holidays and festivities are more celebrated out of tradition and sheer enjoyment than out of any deep religious convictions.[3,4] In fact, the three most joyous festivals are pagan in origin, yet still observed even by Swedes living in Canada: May Day Eve (Valborgsmässoafton), Midsummer Night, on June 24, and, most beloved, St. Lucia Day on December 13.[5]

Home Life and Facilities
Swedes enjoy most modern kitchen facilities and appliances, use electricity widely, and should they lack anything, it is sure to be imported. Beautiful tableware is prevalent in all homes and there is scarcely a meal where flowers do not grace the table.

Enjoying a variety of produce in season and imported fruits and vegetables in the winter months, Swedes are said to be second only to the United States in their consumption of frozen foods.[1] Convenience products, delicatessens, canned and frozen foods all combine to make the Swedish kitchen as up-to-date as any in the world.

FOODS COMMONLY USED

The Swedish cuisine, like its people, is a cosmopolitan one. Indigenous Scandinavian cooking makes the most of fine dairy products, rye, wheat and barley grains, domestic meats, game and herring. All are prepared with the combination of centuries-old skills, concern for appearance and natural flavours, and the gentle intermingling of French and German dishes that have filtered down into daily use from the royal courts of old.

Swedes prefer the robust natural flavours induced and preserved by salting and smoking, stewing and simmering. Seldom are any Swedish foods deep-fried. And the pride of the Swedish cuisine – baked delicacies – take their flavour from fresh eggs, butter and cream gently enhanced with cardamom, ginger and grated citrus peel.

Great eaters of meat, potatoes and fish, the Swedes prefer to take their milk in the form of cheeses, and their grains in the form of pastries, light rye breads and crackers.

Milk and Milk Products
Children may take milk with their meals; adults prefer beer or coffee.

The main form of milk consumption is in a wide variety of mostly mild cheeses which are eaten for breakfast, as appetizers, as part of the *smörgasbord* (sliced cheeses and sliced meats), or for dessert with fruits.

Fruits and Vegetables

A wide variety of fruits and vegetables are used fresh in season, grown locally or imported; also canned, dried and frozen fruits and vegetables. The most popular of the fruits are apples and lingonberries, while the humble potato still outshines imported artichokes and white asparagus in most homes as the daily standby.[1] Fruit preserves and pickled and brined vegetables are much enjoyed the year round.

Meats and Alternates

Pork and pork products are most important, but other meats are used: veal, beef, lamb, offal products, chickens and geese. Game fowl and wild animals are quite plentiful. The Laplander's domesticated reindeer meat is sold frozen, fresh or smoked. Herring is the staple fish and is served fresh, salted, smoked, pickled, fried or with a variety of sauces such as onion, mustard, cream, etc.

Other fish used include RÄKOR (shrimp), SVÄRDFISK, smelt, sword-fish, perch, flounder, halibut, sole, haddock and LAX (salmon). Not only herring, but also these other fish are frequently served with sauces of which the most popular are white sauce, mustard sauce and horse radish sauce. Fish may be prepared by poaching, steaming, grinding and forming into balls; fish may be pickled, smoked, or smoked then baked, or made into soufflés. Only occasionally is fish served breaded and fried.

Eggs are consumed in baked goods, as omelets or soufflés, pickled or chopped into salads. The most-used legumes are the dried yellow peas made into the traditional Thursday soup: ARTER MED FLASK. Small white dried beans are used for Swedish baked beans, a traditional dish which is part of almost any *smörgasbord*. Nuts, especially almonds, are used in desserts and in sweet bakery and pastries.

Breads and Cereals

Rye breads and rye thin crispbreads are favoured. These may vary from very dark, heavy and sour breads to light breads that are slightly sweet in flavour such as the Swedish LIMPA bread. Cooked cereals, gruels and por-ridges are not used by the Swedes. The frequent serving of coffee is always accompanied with a selection of yeast coffeecakes, light plain sponge cakes and crisp plain cookies – after meals, between meals and as a form of hospitality.

Fats

Butter or pork fat (lard) is used in cooking and baking. Fats are also con-sumed in the many cheeses, in cream which is used generously and in whipped cream which is enjoyed with desserts. Only occasionally is sour cream used.

Sweets and Snacks
The Swedish sweet tooth is well-satisfied by all the delicately sweet baked goods that accompany the many daily cups of coffee. A supply of these in any Swedish home is considered as much a staple as bread for the table.

Seasonings
Brining, marinating and smoking are the favoured methods of flavouring and preserving meats and fish, while dill and onions are the favourite seasonings. Sometimes the addition of creamy sauces mellows the flavours of salt and smoke. Vegetables are cooked in soups or stews or otherwise well-cooked then sauced with mustard and/or horse radish the predominating flavours. Vegetables are also used in salads with a marinade of vinegar, onions and spices. Fresh eggs, sweet butter and cream lend their gentle rich taste to most bakery.

The centuries-old river trade with Kiev brought the first spices to Sweden: saffron, cardamom, cinnamon and cloves, cumin and coriander, anise and even pepper.[6] There is variety on the Swedish spice shelf, but the hand that measures spices has a light touch: natural flavours from good ingredients is the overall preference.

Beverages
Coffee is not only a staple in Sweden, it is a ritualized institution. No meal is complete without it, and it must be hot, strong and black. Similarly an evening appetizer or the famed *smörgasbord* is scarcely complete without the ritual of *skoal*: you hold an icy glass of AKVAVIT up high, eyeing your companion, say "*skoal*!" and down the drink in one gulp with a final nod to your companion as you display the emptied glass. Some Swedes like to follow the AKVAVIT with beer, most others blithely continue with more *skoal* punctuated with salty morsels from the appetizer trays.

Meal Patterns and Eating Customs
Once again, the predominant word for this discussion on meal patterns is ritual. Incredible as it may seem for such a sophisticated people, the Swedes delight not only in drinking according to prescribed ritual (as mentioned above) but they eat certain foods in a specifically prescribed way, and they prepare festive foods exactly in the traditional way following century-old patterns.

The ritual of the *smörgasbord* is but one example. Accompanied by suitable *skoals*, salty herring dishes with tiny potatoes are always the first foods eaten from the huge array of selections. Each subsequent "course" follows a special order (never varied) and is eaten from a separate clean plate: other fish dishes and cold marinated salads, cold meats and varieties of pickles, a selection of hot dishes containing meats, eggs, fish, and, finally, on still another plate, a dessert of sliced cheeses and fruits.

It is even more interesting that this type of ordered procedure also applies to individual dishes. The familiar Smaland OSTKAKA (previously made at home in a copper mold, but now purchasable everywhere in Sweden) is a rich but delicate molded cheesecake savoured as a special dessert. Even at a party, the custom is for each person to taste a spoonful of the various OSTKAKAS on display, but to take their taste from the centre of the mold so that the cake may be fruit-filled the next day and served as a new dessert.

The potato dumplings of northern Sweden demand their own special ritual, too. A wedge is cut into the dumpling and the centre filling of ground seasoned pork is removed to be immediately replaced with a golden lump of butter. As the butter melts in its warm potato cavern, the diner cuts off small pieces of filling and dumpling and after dunking each into the melted butter, pops them in his mouth.[1]

Aside from carefully preserved traditions in drinking and eating, the Swedes also have a cherished way of thanking their hostess for a meal. The guest to the left of the hostess expresses thanks first, followed in order by every person around the table.[4]

There are eating rituals for certain days of the week as well. Traditionally, on Thursday night, it is said that everyone in Sweden, from the king on down, enjoys a supper of yellow pea soup with pork, followed by tiny pancakes with lingonberry preserves. And on every Tuesday during Lent, the dessert can be counted on to be buns filled with almond cream enjoyed with a glass of milk.[4]

The Swedish day begins with coffee, which is essential for breakfast. One or two open-face sandwiches with coffee will likely take the hard-working Swedes happily off to their jobs, but the women and children will often have yeast coffeecakes or bread and butter with their morning coffee. Children often take milk.

Lunch is most likely to be a small basic version of the *smörgasbord* called simply *sos*, meaning herring, cheese and bread with butter. Or it may be the full splendour of the *smörgasbord* itself.

The evening meal, most often at home together with the family, is the hot meal of the day, often featuring a satisfying soup or a hearty meat or fish casserole always accompanied by potatoes.[3] It finishes with a dessert and strong black coffee.

Throughout the day, coffee and pastry shops, sandwich shops and fruit stands are all arrayed to tempt the unwary. For sure the Swede will have at least one coffee and pastry bread in the day. And at the close of a pleasant evening with guests, there is sure to be an offering once again of coffee and pastries or a savoury hot casserole with beer as a NATTMATT to assure that the guests will not suffer hunger pangs on the way home!

Special Occasions

Although tolerant of all religious beliefs, most Swedes are Lutheran. Church affiliation is begun almost at birth, but the members are not actively involved and even religious holidays carry more traditional ritual flavour than deep religious fervour.

Perhaps it is to allay the cold and the months of darkness, or an inextricable part of their penchant for ritual and order. Whatever the reason, the Swedish calendar is dotted with important reasons for special celebrations, each demanding special foods.

It is of particular interest to note that while Christmas and Easter are undoubtedly the most important festivals, several others are retained and joyously celebrated even though their roots lie in the pagan past. For even though Sweden can be classified as a modern sophisticated community, as recently as 100 years ago, almost 90 per cent of her people were rural–deeply bound up in the land, the changing seasons, and the path of the sun in the sky. With traditions such a deeply ingrained part of Swedish life, it will likely be a very long time before any of these fade, if indeed their warmth and symbolism are discarded at all.

Christmas

The Swedes accepted Christianity in 1537, and joined the celebration of Christ's birthday with the ancient festival of "greeting the returning sun."[3] Christmas actually begins on December 13 with the celebration of St. Lucia's Day. The early church assimilated the pagan tradition of Lussi Queen of Light with the Italian Saint Lucia. In the home, the oldest daughter rises early in the morning and, dressed in a special white gown, a wreath of burning candles in her hair, she delivers to her parents a tray of fragrant saffron buns (LUSSIKATOR) and fresh hot coffee. In the cities, a Lucia Queen is chosen and a huge party is given at which everyone enjoys the saffron buns and coffee.[5]

The very next day, the hectic baking and preparations for Christmas begin in earnest. In the Swedish countryside it was always customary to slaughter a pig for Christmas with every portion being utilized: fresh meat cuts, hams and bacon, with the blood, feet, head and offal all used in soups, sausages, puddings and pâtés. In the past these dishes were served specifically in the Christmas season, but today they are readily available in specialty stores.[4] In pagan times, pigs, symbol of fertility, were sacrificed during the mid-winter bacchanal, and the Christmas ham of today is a symbol of that tradition. In fact the noon meal before Christmas Eve follows the ritual of DOPPA I GRYTAN: dunking chunks of bread into the broth from the simmering ham and sausages. This too has its origins in the ancient belief that eating of certain parts of the animal recaptured the animal's vigour for the diner. Modern-day Swedes are likely unaware of the symbolism; they just happily enjoy the delicious flavours.

The highlight of the Christmas Eve dinner is the LUTFISK. There is a ritual to the preparation of this dish too. About three weeks before, the dried salted cod is set to soak in a daily change of fresh water. An immersion in lye and ashes for a period, then it is ready to be scrubbed and again immersed for at least seven days in a daily changing bath of fresh water.

Finally it is considered ready for gentle poaching then a glaze of velvety white sauce completes the festive fish. Boiled potatoes accompany the LUTFISK and then everyone is ready for the suspense of the dessert. Although it appears to be a simple creamy rice pudding, the dessert has one whole almond hidden in it. The lucky finder of the almond may win a special prize, and, if a girl, she will be wed in the next year. In some homes, no one may sample their rice pudding until they have recited a poem.

To complete the gaiety of Christmas Eve, the tree is decorated, gifts distributed and everyone enjoys delicious samplings of the many Christmas cakes and cookies all washed down with JULGLÖGG (hot spiced wine punch).[1,3,7]

At each place on the Christmas breakfast table a delectable JULHOG awaits demolishing: this is an edible stack consisting of rye bread, a sweet yeast ring, a currant saffron bun, a crisp flat cookie and finally a red apple on top. Add hot coffee and that is a Swedish Christmas breakfast.

The Christmas ham becomes the centre of what is really a magnificent feast: the Christmas *smörgasbord*. For even today, many Swedish women pride themselves in preparing all of the festive foods in traditional Christmas splendour. The centrepiece of fruits and nuts is a reminder of sacrifices made to the gods at this time to bless and provide plenty for the table.[7] Once again AKVAVIT is served with many *skoals*, although some prefer GLÖGG. Meanwhile the children eat, laugh and play happily with their gifts, comparing those from *Jultomte*, the Swedish elf-like version of Santa Claus. And the woven straw *julbocken* (Christmas ram woven of straw) will swing from the chandelier as a reminder that long ago a Swedish Christmas was celebrated with straw strewn all over the floor.

Annandagen
This is the name given to the days between Christmas and New Year's, days of parties, drinking, eating and, above all, gatherings of family and friends.

Epiphany
Epiphany, January 6, the solemn commemoration of the Three Wise Men, celebrated quietly in the home or in the church.

St. Canute's Day
This falls on January 13 and is also called affectionately, if a little sadly, Knut's Day. This is the day when all the festive decorations of the holiday

season are carefully put away. Even the Swedes know that there is a time to return to the realities of everyday living.

Shrove Tuesday

This is the day before Ash Wednesday, and throughout Sweden buns filled with almond paste and whipped cream or almond paste and hot milk are served for lunch. Each Tuesday through Lent the dessert will be these same buns.

March 25

Waffle Day was originally called *Var Fru*, meaning "Our Lady," to commemorate the Virgin Mary's Annunciation Day. Later the name became *Vaffer* and finally *Vaffel*. And for each of the three meals of that day waffles are served.[3]

Easter

Many old country superstitions have full sway at Easter time. After the house is cleaned the broom is locked up so that the Easter Witch cannot spirit it away. During Lent birch twigs are picked and placed in the house; if they sprout green leaves by Easter it is said to symbolize growth in nature. There are many more such legends, and most are not taken seriously but followed out of fun or for tradition's sake.

Good Friday is a quiet, solemn day; simple humble foods are eaten such as herring and boiled potatoes and a sweet soup of cardamom-flavoured ale is often the dessert. Easter Eve is celebrated with a *smörgasbord*, but this time the highlight of the table is the mass of hard eggs which the children share in delightful competition, to see who can eat the most. For eggs with all their symbolism of life, growth and vitality are an important Easter symbol.

Valborgsmässoafton

Also known as Walpurgis Night, the eve of May Day is celebrated with outdoor gatherings, singing and the lighting of a huge bonfire.[5]

Christ's Ascension Day

Celebrated forty days after Easter, it usually coincides with the fishermen's first good catch of the season, so the menu features fresh-caught fish with horse radish sauce.

Pingst or Whitsuntide

A happy flower-filled holiday, just ten days after Christ's Ascension Day. Most often celebrated with happy announcements of First Communion, engagements, etc. The menu invariably features fresh fish.

Midsummer Eve

The festival to celebrate the longest day of the year, June 23, features dancing and the crowning of the Midsummer Queen in most Canadian and American Swedish communities. In Sweden, however, this is the special night when spells can be cast and dreams dreamed. With a mystical sun dazzling for almost twenty-four hours and resting for a brief two hours of dusk anything can happen. So this is the night that young Swedish girls gather nine different flowers to tuck under their pillows to conjure special dreams of their lovers.

August

The last of the bright soft summer nights coincides happily with the crayfish season and outdoor parties abound. Lit by coloured lanterns or flickering candles, the diners gather around a table set with a huge platter of crayfish, bibs for everyone, beer and AKVAVIT. For more reasons than one, it may be difficult to tell whether it is night or day by the time the party ends.

Martinmas or St. Martin's Day

Martin Luther's Name Day, November 11, also happens to coincide with traditions much older than Christianity in Sweden. The slaughtering of animals, with all the attendant rendering of fat, smoking and sausage-making, began, in olden times, towards the end of October in order to prepare for the feast at the end of December. November 11 was the time for the geese slaughter, and to this day, Martinmas is celebrated with roast goose stuffed with apples and prunes, preceded by a rich soup made from the goose blood.[1,4] The spectacular dessert specialty of the day, SPETTKAKA, is a wondrously intricate cake baked by dribbling an egg and sugar batter on a rotating spit.

FORTY-SIX

Swiss

If the Swiss have a gentle but perceptible air of superiority, it is well-deserved. For over 675 years, Switzerland has maintained her status as an independent nation – no small feat for a nation in the heart of Europe.

Switzerland is made up of twenty-two separate cantons, each almost a country in miniature having its own history, food specialties, local government and even a distinctly local dialect. The 5.5 million Swiss profess membership in eighteen faiths (but predominantly Protestant), three main ethnic groups – Italian, German and French – and speak four languages – German, French, Italian and Romansh. Although German predominates, most Swiss can speak several languages, and the Latin-based Romansh is spoken mostly in the Grisons area.

This diversity in ethnic background and languages as well as the number of distinct areas is a unique situation, for no other country as small as Switzerland can claim such a patchwork and a peaceful one at that. In fact, it is probably because each Swiss is a member of a minority group that they are so tolerant of other nationalities, languages and life-styles. However, their national tolerance stops short at any indication of autocracy or bureaucracy; a true Swiss will sell his soul to no one.[1,2]

So loyal is each Swiss to his home town, that marriage outside of his canton is considered a "mixed marriage."[1] Emotional and traditional ties are strong: the family comes first, then the home town, the canton and finally Switzerland itself. Swiss society, like Swiss loyalty, is traditional and well-ordered, and perhaps this too is a factor in individual security and self-confidence.

The Swiss characteristically rise early and work hard and often late hours. They are scrupulously honest, and quality and value-for-money are basic concepts. They expect this same seriousness in work and basic honesty from everyone else and will not tolerate either shoddy work or inferior products. More than half the population is engaged in agriculture in small rural areas, the rest are involved in a diversity of specialized industries such as watchmaking and precision machines and tools. Yet Switzerland suffers from a chronic labour shortage and each year approximately half a million labourers are imported from other countries, even as far off as Greece and Turkey.

It is also no accident that some of the finest chef and hotel administration schools are located in Switzerland. Not only do the Swiss have a penchant for education and culture, but they are also famed for their hospitality and politeness. Customers are always considered as personal guests and their comfort and happiness are of prime importance. Guests enjoy warm, clean surroundings, bountiful food servings and a surfeit of "good days" and "thank yous" as well as the idyllic scenery of picturesque towns, green valleys and snow-tipped mountains. Yet although their chef schools teach "haute cuisine" and their hospitality is all-inclusive, the Swiss are quietly reserved in their friendships and home life and prefer the simplest of menus.[1]

Swiss life as Swiss food is very much influenced by neighbours: France, Germany, Austria and Italy. Specialty dishes from each of these neighbours have long been intertwined with local regional specialties to produce a simple but substantial cuisine centring itself on soups, breads and nourishing cheese, egg and vegetable dishes. Recent trends in foods have attempted more exotic fare adapted from Chinese and Malaysian cooking but retaining mildness in flavour. One of the most successful "food movements" was that started by Dr. Bircher-Benner in Zurich. He invented the MUESLI, a combination of toasted oats, shredded dried apples and nuts. His movement stresses the inclusion of fresh salads and whole grain cereals, but it is the MUESLI that has attained almost a worldwide reputation as a "Swiss breakfast."[1]

Switzerland is many things: mountains and lakes, specialized schools and industries, a peaceful mix of people and languages, a huge wheel of Swiss cheese or a chunk of smooth Swiss chocolate. But probably most of all, Switzerland is people. People that have learned more than any other nation in the world the consummate art of blending tolerance, honesty and politeness with innate simplicity, ending up with a subtle sophistication entirely Swiss. It is a phenomenon as incredible as their mix of foods adopted from other countries. Somehow, in Swiss hands, these foods become purely Swiss.

Home Life and Facilities
The Swiss reputation for hard work, orderliness and simplicity is evi-

denced in the home. Swiss homemakers are "scrubbers": every corner is scrupulously clean and ordered. Swiss kitchens vie with any in the Western world for efficiency, appliances and convenience, but gadgets are used only if they are truly time-saving. Shoddy materials and poor quality are as little tolerated in the kitchen as they are in industry.

Although the true origin of Swiss FONDUES is lost in antiquity, the fondue remains a favoured meal and a form of entertainment. Most Swiss homes have the necessary accoutrements: the *caquelon*, a shallow but sturdy earthenware casserole for heating the cheese fondue, a supply of long-handled forks for dipping and a practical stand and heat source usually for alcohol heating. For FONDUE FRITURE (dunking foods in hot oil), the Swiss home will be equipped with a deep heavy metal pot, wider at the base than at the top to prevent tipping and possible spattering while frying. For the newly-introduced chocolate fondue (introduced in New York by Beverley Allen for the Swiss Chalet Restaurant[1]), a small candle-heated earthenware pot is used.

Finally, for the delightful Swiss supper of RACLETTE, an efficient gadget that not only keeps plates warm but also holds a big wedge of cheese firmly in place for melting is also a part of culinary equipment. Mountain cheeses such as GOMSER, RACLETTE, BELALP, or BAGNES are best for melting.

The Swiss standard of living is very high and this is reflected in the many specialty shops for bakery and pastries, meats and fancy delicatessen. Preparation of foods, packaging and displays reach such a high standard that they can seldom be duplicated elsewhere. Huge varieties of imported goods of every type await the shopper and convenience foods abound. Even raw meats in butcher shops are displayed with artistry, garnished with sprigs of greens and trimmed and shaped so that the homemaker need only cook them. The long tradition of daily shopping to ensure the freshest produce and baked goods is slowly declining as more and more women join the work force. Even the sale of deep freezers is increasing.[1]

FOODS COMMONLY USED

Quality of ingredients and simplicity in preparation and serving of foods are typical of Swiss menus. There is a stress on the importance of soups and many dishes made from cheese. Much bread is consumed and is a part of all meals. Meats and fish are often expensive so are purchased and cooked with care, often extended with vegetables or cereal foods.

The recent food reform movement stressing fresh vegetable salads and the use of whole grained breads and cereals has made a definite impression; there is an increase not only in the fresh

vegetables eaten and whole grain bread preference, but also more concern for the cooking of vegetables.[1]

Staple foods include bread, potatoes and cereals with a good consumption of milk and cheese. Favourite methods of food preparation are soups, stews and simple casserole dishes.

Milk and Milk Products

There is no shortage of quality dairy products in the Swiss diet. Fresh milk is almost a staple food in the form of coffee and milk (CAFÉ AU LAIT or MILCHKAFFEE) which is served so frequently that it is considered more of a food than a mere beverage. Milk and cheese are almost daily a part of soups or quick dishes that make up light meals, while the FONDUES and RACLETTES of Switzerland are well-known.

There is scarcely a canton in Switzerland without its own special version of a cheese soup: thick, thin, or baked with bread as a pudding or casserole. Cheese is also an integral ingredient in soufflés, sauces, dumplings, fritters, croquettes and garnishes as well as pies and tarts. One of the oldest traditional dishes of all is FÄNZ, made like a thick white sauce with flour, milk, and butter and then eaten with bread and CAFÉ AU LAIT.[1,3]

Fruits and Vegetables

Orchards abound in Switzerland, but when fresh fruits are scarce, much use is made of canned or dried fruits. Fruits are served fresh in season, stewed or made into puddings or tarts. Apples and cherries are special favourites and these are made into fritters (FNUTLI, Basel apple fritters, or CHRIESITÜTSCHLI, fresh cherry bunches dipped in batter and delicately fried), puddings or fruit soups. A bowl of stewed fruit accompanied with CAFÉ AU LAIT is a popular finish to a meal. More recently fruits and yoghurt combinations have been gaining in popularity.

Green beans, spinach, Swiss chard, turnips, leeks, asparagus, cabbage, squash and many other vegetables are available in profusion but none can reach the popularity or versatility of the potato. Potato soups, dumplings, baked puddings, pancakes, fritters, cheese and potato casseroles – the number and variety of potato dishes is staggering. But one potato dish is supreme: KARTOFFELRÖSTI. It is so popular it is known everywhere as simply RÖSTI. Mealy parboiled potatoes are coarsely shredded, then are packed into a large hot skillet sputtering with butter. When the bottom is crisply browned the whole cake is inverted (easy if inverted on a platter held over the pan, then slid carefully back) to brown the second side. Served in wedges, the RÖSTI accompanies almost any meat, fish or even cheese dish and often stands alone as a light supper.

Meats and Alternates

Meat, fish and game are expensive in Switzerland and are purchased, cooked and eaten with care and respect. The amount consumed depends very much on the family income, but traditional frugality will usually result in every part of the meat being carefully utilized. Fats will be rendered, bones and trimmings will make soups, and meat will be generously accompanied with vegetables or cereals such as rice, cornmeal or pasta to extend the meaty flavour. In many areas, meat is for Sundays only, while the poor may taste it only once in a year. Only recently have *rotisseurs* (restaurants specializing in expensive broiled or roasted meats) become popular. Part of the reason may be that Swiss cattle are raised mainly as milk cows and work animals with the result that their flesh is too often tough and stringy and best suited to soup-making and the long simmering of stews or the well-seasoned mixtures that make sausages. Swiss sausages are so varied and so popular that they probably represent the favoured form of meat, and there is a type of sausage for every taste and use from mild to spicy, whether for snacking, picnicking, leisurely dining or light suppers. Meats used include veal and beef, pork, venison and kid. Chickens, affectionately called *guggeli* or *mistkratzerli* (manure-scratchers) in German-speaking Switzerland, form the base of many a soup or stew.

Fish is not a staple, but is considered a delicacy. It is cooked with simplicity: usually simply baked or poached and served with butter or lemon. Trout, salmon, perch and pike as well as eels and scampi are available, but mostly only in the cities.

Eggs and legumes are seldom eaten as individual dishes; mostly they are consumed as ingredients. Eggs are a part of most cheese and milk baked casseroles as well as soufflés, omelets and pancakes. Dried peas and beans are used in lesser quantities as part of soups.

Breads and Cereals
It is almost an impossibility to think of a Swiss table set for a meal without bread. Breads and rolls are often the main part of breakfast, they accompany soups, they crumble or cube into casseroles and puddings with cheese or fruits or even vegetables, they are squeezed with water or milk to form stuffings, dumplings, fritters, and chunks of bread are dunked into cheese fondues and even mop up creamy sauces and gravies.

Cereals have been a Swiss food staple from earliest times. Gruels, porridges and soups made from grains and flour are seldom used anymore except for the one traditional dish that has survived: FÄNZ. Now popular mostly with the shepherds, it is a thick white sauce made with milk, flour and butter and served with bread and MILCHKAFFEE and is considered a satisfying meal.

Noodles and many pasta forms are served in the Italian way and also in typically Swiss style: cooked noodles tossed with butter-browned onions and sprinkled with cheese. Pasta is also a frequent ingredient in soups and a popular means of stretching meat dishes. In the area of Ticino (close to Italy), cooked cornmeal or polenta is frequently served as a bread, side dish or as part of a baked dish with cheese. Rice is gaining in popularity and favoured as an emergency staple because of its versatility and excellent keeping qualities.

Not to be overlooked is the increasing use of whole grains in breads, rolls and especially in the popular breakfast dish of toasted oats, shredded dried fruit and nuts served with milk or yoghurt called MUESLI.

Fats
Considerable fats are consumed in the form of cream and of course in the many varieties of cheese. Butter is favoured for baking and cooking because of its flavour and abundant good quality, but the efficient homemaker makes good use of all fats whether beef drippings, chicken fat, lard or bacon fat. Oils are not widely used for cooking but are a salad dressing ingredient.

Sweets and Snacks
Confiseries, those exquisite pastry shops, are located frequently enough in the cities to tempt the unwary. There does exist a definite Swiss sweet tooth, but it is more often assuaged by bread and butter with jam, or a "sweet supper" (pancakes or dumplings with sweet sauce) than with or- nate rich pastries. Chocolate, however, to the Swiss mind is more food than treat and will often be a part of a child's lunch or a hiker's pack for "quick energy."

Seasonings
Depending on the area and the predominating influence, the spice shelf in the Swiss kitchen may look more familiar to a German, French or Italian cook. Dill, caraway, garlic, tarragon, white wine or tomatoes, garlic, basil, oregano or even a melange of all may be used in the Swiss kitchen.

Overall, Swiss foods are well-cooked and not strongly flavoured. Much use is made of MAGGI, a seasoning sauce similar in taste and colour to soy sauce, and AROMAT or FONDOR – popular trade names for monosodium glutamate, all of which are used frequently and sometimes overdone. But the array of bottles, jars and tubes of condiments, spices and herbs makes cooking in any language possible and probable in Switzerland.

Beverages
The most popular beverage is strong coffee mixed with hot milk called CAFÉ AU LAIT or MILCHKAFFEE. It may be served at any meal, to all ages, and fresh CAFÉ AU LAIT will always be prepared for guests. Hot chocolate is also a popular drink, mostly for breakfast. Teas of all types including herbal brews are also popular, especially after the evening meal. Switzerland's famed CHEESE FONDUE may be accompanied with a single

small glass of KIRSCH and followed by hot tea, never with cold drinks of any type as is so often the custom elsewhere. Those areas influenced by the French or Italian drink wines, while beers are favoured in the German-speaking areas. An overall sense of moderation in drinking alcoholic beverages predominates.

Meal Patterns and Eating Customs

Hotel administration schools and internationally famous chefs' schools may teach sophisticated cuisine while Swiss restaurants may cater to every taste sensation, but in the Swiss home, light and simple meals are the rule.

MUESLI and MILCHKAFFEE are a popular Swiss way to begin the day, but CAFÉ COMPLET or CHOCOLAT COMPLET are still traditional. With either CAFÉ AU LAIT or hot chocolate as the mainstay, this simple breakfast revolves around an assortment of breads and rolls served with fresh butter and an assortment of preserves.

The main meal of the day is at noon. Beginning with a hearty soup, dinner may go on to a main dish based on potatoes, cheese, fish or meat accompanied by a small salad and ending with fruit and cheese. The adults will usually have wine or water and the children will sip only water with the dinner.

A late afternoon snack about four called *zvieri* will consist of sausages or ham with pickles and bread together with a quenching drink of hard cider or perhaps beer. Children will snack on bread and butter, women sometimes on MILCHKAFFEE or one of many teas with simple cakes or buns.

The evening meal may be one of the lightest and simplest of the day, consisting of bread, cheese and CAFÉ AU LAIT, or a simple casserole of potatoes and a side salad and bread.

If these typical meal patterns sound too simplistic, then the reader is underestimating the quality of fresh foods and the consummate skill of preparation so typical of the Swiss cuisine. Probably no meal can be simpler than the RACLETTE. Here a wedge of fine mountain cheese is melted before a special heater or an open fire. Just at the right moment, the melted cheese is scraped onto a waiting hot platter and served at once accompanied with a crunchy sweet pickled gherkin and a few tartly sharp pickled onions. The final touch in both flavour and texture is a boiled mealy potato. Few dishes are simpler both in preparation and service and yet the contrasting flavours and textures are worthy of the most complex gastronomic masterpiece.

More widely known is the Swiss CHEESE FONDUE. There are many versions and variations but basically a shredded mixture of Swiss Emmenthaler and Gruyère cheeses are melted in simmering wine then lightly flavoured with a sniff of garlic (often just rubbed in the *caquelon*) and a splash of KIRSCH. Diners spear chunks of crusty bread and dip into the melted cheese mixture, giving a stir and a swirl at the same time. At the end of the meal, a tasty crust will have formed at the bottom of the pot and this should be lifted and served to all. A small glass of KIRSCH is served in the middle of the eating, while hot tea is usually served to complete the fondue dinner. Sometimes servings of sausages and pickles with bread may be added to the meal.[4]

Special Occasions

More than eighteen religious groups claim members in the 5.5-million Swiss population. By a slight majority, Protestants predominate.

The many festivities that dot the Swiss calendar focus on the change of seasons, the movement of the cattle, planting and harvesting and of course religious celebrations. All have in common an abundance of good food and a colourful flurry of regional costumes. Both Catholics and Protestants celebrate Christmas with a variety of special cakes and cookies but no special menu; the best that is available is served with pride. In the German-speaking areas, Christmas Eve is celebrated with gifts and a candle-lit tree. Customs and ceremonies in each home may be traced to either French, German or Italian influences, together with individual family preferences.

As in the Netherlands, the Swiss have no Santa Claus, but they do set aside December 6 as the special evening when St. Nicholas brings fruits and candies and small gifts to all deserving children, and for the naughty ones only a switch! This holiday has no religious connotation and is celebrated by almost everyone.

As in many other countries, Easter is celebrated with the fresh exuberance of approaching spring: chocolate bunnies, coloured eggs, special cakes and cookies – as well as the sober rejoicing accompanying church services. The many popular meatless dishes make Lent less of a hardship and one of the traditionally favourite dishes is BASLER MEHLSUPPE. This is a typical "brown roux soup" prepared by browning flour in butter, then adding water to form a stock. Often little more than a bit of seasoning is added, and in the case of the BASLER MEHLSUPPE the flavour is of bay leaf and cloves.[1]

FORTY-SEVEN

Turkish

The area of land occupied by present-day Turkey has an ancient history of conquerors and conquered, extending from the early Hittite peoples, through the 700-year Ottoman Empire to today's nation. For hundreds of years the area of Asia Minor has geographically, culturally and even linguistically bridged the gap between Asia and Europe.[1]

As early as 1900 B.C.E., the Hittites inhabiting the plains of Anatolia raised cattle and sheep and cultivated crops of wheat and barley. They were also adept at making pottery and metal objects and it is believed that they were among the first people to work in iron. About 1000 B.C.E. the Hittites succumbed to Assyrians and later to groups of Arameans and Phoenicians (present-day Lebanese) and then to Thracian tribes from Greece. These peoples encouraged great prosperity and this drew the attention of the neighbouring Persians who dominated the area for about 200 years, up to the early fourth-century B.C.E.[2,3]

Each of the early conquerors left some lasting influence, but none as much as the Greeks. Even the Persian conquest could not subdue the effects of Greek culture, the prosperity, or the vitality of Greek enclaves in the cities. To this day, ancient Greek ruins exist around the landscape, Greek words for fish and vegetables exist in the Turkish language, and many daily foods can be easily traced to Greek origin. So entrenched was Hellenism in fact, that even the Roman rule in the first century C.E. – which brought Christianity, roads, buildings and general unification – could not replace the general widespread acceptance of Greek culture.[3] The Christianity brought by the Romans lasted in the area in calm coexistence with Hellenism, paganism and the small Jewish communities for about 800 years.

It was the Romans who changed the name of Byzantium to Constantinople, made it the centre of the Eastern Roman Empire, and introduced Latin. But the coexistence of religions, languages and cultures was paralleled also by the interplay of Greek, Roman and Oriental influences in arts and architecture. Asia Minor not only bridged the Asian-European land-gap, it mirrored the cultural imprints of its conquerors.

Around the 900s C.E., there was a brief conquest in the area by the Armenians. But they in turn were quickly subdued by the powerful surge of Arab-Islamic conquests which reduced the Byzantine Empire to a small area around Constantinople. This remained mainly a market area for Oriental and Occidental trade of foods, cloths, pottery and spices.

The next conquerors – the semi-nomadic Seljuk Turks – ousted the last influences of the Roman-Byzantium-Christian rule. These were the peoples from Persia, the chiefs of the Turkomans, powerfully influenced by Islamic-Persian culture, who were to gain the longest and strongest hold on the coveted Asia Minor. Only the periodic raids of the Crusaders in the next 200 years delayed the firm establishment of Turk rule, but it was inevitable.

By the early 1200s C.E. the Seljuks were overpowered by the Turkomans whose leader, Osman, gave his name to the Ottoman Empire. During this period, there was some influence from the Genoese but more importantly from the Mongol raids. The Mongols, being mainly meat eaters, left the field crops in ruin and encouraged only stockbreeding.[3] Not only agriculture declined; the general prosperity of the area disintegrated as the Turkomans became attracted to conquests around the Mediterranean, leaving the Anatolian area exploited and neglected.

For the next 500 years, as the Ottoman Empire sprawled over the Balkans, Persia, parts of North Africa, Arabia, Yemen, Greece, Bulgaria, areas of southern Russia and Italy, the area of Asia Minor absorbed still other influences. Providing the subject peoples were "People of the Scriptures," the Muslims were tolerant rulers, yet wherever they lived they built their walled homes and walled cities often side-by-side or even surrounded by Christian or Jewish suburbs.[3] While Greek words had long been used for foods, gradually Italian words entered the language for shipping, commerce and banking and later French words were added to express ideas. The Ottoman Empire was ruled from its centre in Istanbul (Constantinople) by an educated group of bureaucrats so loyal to the Sultan that they commonly referred to the rest of the populace as *raya* (the herd).[1]

But Istanbul was not only the seat of Ottoman rule, it was also the stronghold of the Turkish culinary tradition. Historical documents dating as early as the 1400s C.E. record details of the special buildings constructed beside the Topkapi Palace by the Great Sultan Mehmet. These were specifically for food preparation and housing for the food artisans such as confectioners, tinsmiths (required to reline copper cooking vessels), vegetable chefs and yoghurt-makers.[4] Even the most cursory review of the dishes reflects clearly the cultural imprints of earlier times. Pilafs and yoghurt from Persian sources; rich sweet pastries such as BAKLAVA of obvious Greek origin, as well as the widespread use of the egg-lemon sauce so characteristic of Greek cooking; thick bean and lentil soups and flat Arabic breads from Egypt and areas of North America; layered vegetable casseroles and *çorbasi* so reminiscent of the Romanian classic *guvech* and *çorbas*; and an unquestionable echo of Maltese cookery in the Turkish version of meat BÖREK in a tray[4] so similar to the Maltese "cheesecake" with its layers of flaky puff pastry and meat or cheese filling. Even the popular confection called LOKUM or LUKUM (Turkish Delight) is well-known and beloved in all Arabic countries.

The lengthy periods of Ottoman excursions around the Mediterranean and their subjugation of other lands gradually declined in the 1800s, coinciding with two other gradually emerging influences: the strengthening of the neighbouring nations both nationalistically and militaristically, and the internal struggles occurring within Asia Minor. The latter included deteriorating finances, political power struggles and Muslim versus Christian domination.[2,3]

At this crucial point in Turkey's history a new ferment had begun. A group of Turkish patriots, counterpart of similar nationalistic movements in other lands, used their European education to bring about needed reforms in the ancient land. With the final dismemberment of the Ottoman Empire at the end of World War I and the proclamation of the Turkish Republic in 1923 with its new capital at Ankara, the stage was set for the new Turkey. It was largely the efforts of Mustafa Kemal that gained the Turks world recognition of their right to their own country and the need for the sweeping reforms which he instigated. Primarily he sought modernization by disentangling Islam for government (which brought changes in daily life-styles to everyone including women), and encouraged the return to Turkey of Muslim refugees from Greece, Bulgaria and even Chinese Turkestan.

In today's Turkey, more than 90 per cent of the people speak Turkish, are Muslims, and about 80 per cent of the populace are engaged in agriculture. The Ottoman Turks had a three-fold origin: Turkish, Arabic and Persian with a culture strongly influenced by the early Greeks. The origins and cultural influences remain, but a distinct Turkish society is emerging. The opposition to the newer ways come mainly from the Kurds, a strong Muslim minority who retain their predominantly oral tradition in dialects of Kermanji, Zaza, and Gurani and have a reputation for extreme and sometimes unorthodox devoutness.[1] Some of the Kurds are farmers, others are city-dwellers while a small group retain their ancient nomadic life-styles, roaming with their herds and ignoring national boundaries for their winter migrations. Still smaller minority groups include some Christians and Jews.

Home Life and Facilities

Largely due to the influence of Islam, the "true Turk" is devoted to Sunni Islam, speaks Turkish and makes family life the centre of his existence. But there is something more. An important value in Turkish life is *dürüstlük*, that sense of trust and reliability conveyed by personal contact. *Dürüst* can motivate business deals, family relationships, and can prove more important than wealth, education or ability.[1] Small rural communities are more influenced by these traditional values than are the Turkish communities in urban areas, yet changes are slowly occurring even in isolated regions. Urban Turks have modified their life-styles because of European influence, and the migrating Turkish workers returning to their small villages from European centres have also carried with them the seeds of change.

Yet despite outside influence, Turks do retain a strong preference for home styles and home life that is distinctly and traditionally Turkish. Middle-class Turks still delight in decorating their homes with fine carpets, copperware and ceramics and disdain the European penchant for paintings and sculpture;[1] rural homes still devote their first floor to animals and remove their shoes when entering the second floor of their homes which is designed for the family.[5] Larger homes still have separate facilities for men and for women; women are still rarely seen in public alone, and Turkish men still feel somewhat ill at ease with feminine company in public.[3]

While many homes have adapted western cookstoves and even some gadgetry, the work of willing hands still dominates in meal preparation. Foods and water are still kept cool in earthenware jugs and jars called *testi*. Homes have collections of brightly decorated wooden spoons used for cooking and eating.[3]

FOODS COMMONLY USED

The area of Asia Minor has an ancient history of fine agricultural produce including wheat, barley, fruits and vegetables.[3] To this day, the general basic diet includes unleavened breads made from wheat or rye flours, locally grown fruits and vegetables in season and a variety of cheeses and sour milk products. Barley is used mainly for brewing varieties of beer. Beef, mutton and lamb are enjoyed but are often too expensive to be a regular part of the fare. Muslims do not eat pork and many eschew shellfish and snails. Fish both fresh and dried and served in many ways are an important protein source especially in the coastal regions where they are plentiful. Even in difficult times, most Turks eat well from their small household gardens and the sheep and goats that are typical of homes in rural areas. Diluted yoghurt and buttermilk are widely consumed as beverages; beer is enjoyed and RAKI, make from fermented raisins and flavoured with anise, is considered to be the national beverage.

While the general adult population enjoys a well-balanced diet, malnutrition is still widespread among infants and small children mainly due to the practice of feeding them starchy water and cereal gruels upon weaning with no other additional foods.[1]

Milk and Milk Products
YOUGHT (yoghurt), believed by some to be a Turkish invention, is widely used as a finishing touch to soups, vegetable dishes and as a sauce. It is also used as a dressing mixed with chopped fresh or cooked vegetables and provides a cooling refreshment when taken as it is or diluted with ice water and lightly salted. Buttermilk may be used in the same way as YOUGHT.

Many varieties of local cheeses, both fresh and aged, are also widely used in many dishes. They are eaten in cubes as appetizers or may be a main part of a meal accompanied with bread and olives. Fresh milk is an important ingredient in the many types of sweetened desserts based on milk-cooked rice. (See also "Meal Patterns and Eating Customs.")

Fruits and Vegetables
Turkish peaches and figs are outstanding for quality and flavour, but because of the climatic variations, there are fresh fruits available in any season and these are enjoyed especially at the end of a meal.

Favourite Turkish vegetables are AUBERGINES (eggplant) and okra. These are prepared in many ways and always served well-cooked, as are tomatoes, onions, cucumbers, large-disc artichokes, zucchini, many varieties of squash, cabbage, cauliflower, beans of all kinds and canned or fresh peas. AUBERGINES are such a favourite that household fires are common when the vegetable's season is at its height. The cooking oil used to fry the slices of AUBERGINE readily catches fire and burns the wooden homes.[3]

Leaves of many kinds, but especially vine leaves (from grapes) are used to prepare rolled DOLMAS, but any available vegetable may be served cooked and filled. Small squash, tomatoes, COURGETTES, AUBERGINES, ASMA KABAGI (marrow) and tomatoes and cucumbers may all be prepared as DOLMAS. At all times vegetables are plentiful and are used generously.

Thick conserves prepared from sweetened fruits and even flowers are often a part of meals. Purple and green, fresh or dried figs, many varieties of large grapes (ÇAVUS), tiny perfumed strawberries and many colourful types of sweet melons grow throughout the area. Some regions are noted for their exceptional produce: peaches and apricots from Bursa; hard round pears from Ankara; Jaffa oranges from Fethiye and Hatay, and of course the dried figs exported all over the world from Izmir (Smyrna).

Meats and Alternates

Meats do not form a large or important part of the Turkish meals. Beef, mutton and lamb are the favourites. Pork is not used as it is against the Muslim dietary laws. Veal and poultry as well as occasional game are enjoyed when available. Most meats are prepared either by slow simmering in vegetable sauces, in soups, or marinated then cooked on skewers. A traditional Turkish specialty is the DÖNER KEBAB: marinated serving pieces of lamb threaded on a tall vertical spit that rotates slowly in front of a specially constructed DÖNER broiler; the huge oval of rotating broiled succulent lamb is sliced vertically to serve.[4] When chickens or turkeys are used, they are well-cooked and often stuffed with a PILAF of rice, pine nuts, and currants. Offal such as brains, kidneys, liver, lungs and tripe are used to add flavour to soups and vegetable dishes and stuffings.

Sea bass, mullet, swordfish, bluefish, dory and plaice are the most widely used fish. Fish is often prepared with a base of vegetables called a PILAKI, a well-chopped mixture of carrots, garlic and onions cooked in olive oil and flavoured with parsley, dill and tomato sauce. Fish may also be baked in parchment; dipped in oil then flour then deep-fried in more oil; poached with vegetables to form both a broth and a main dish; or steamed by baking in a covered casserole in the oven. KILICH SHEESH is a popular dish of cubed marinated swordfish broiled on skewers. Tuna, mullet and swordfish may also be smoked and served in pieces or thinly sliced. Lobsters, prawns, sea scorpions (*iskorpit*) and mussels are also used by some who are not so strict about Muslim dietary rules. Red roe, the luxury botargo (grey mullet roe) as well as the very expensive sturgeon caviar are used as appetizers; red roe is used to prepare TARAMA (a salty appetizer paste of Greek origin).

Eggs are not plentiful but are enjoyed when available. A favourite preparation is to cook a pan of chopped vegetables lightly then make "holes" and drop the eggs in to cook together with the vegetables.[4] Eggs are also blended with fresh lemon juice to form the tart egg-lemon sauce (of Greek origin) used to flavour so many dishes and soups.

Peas, beans and lentils are used to prepare thick and hearty soups and they are also served cooked and chilled then dressed lightly with seasonings, olive oil and lemon juice and enjoyed as a salad dish. Lightly toasted salted nuts, especially Turkey's famed hazelnuts, are a special snack treat.

Breads and Cereals

The importance of cereal grains in the Turkish diet can be readily seen by a glance at a typical full-course meal. Not only is the typical PIDA (Arabian flatbread) in evidence throughout the meal to serve as plate, cutlery and food, there will likely be at least one course featuring a BULGHUR (cracked wheat) or rice PILAF, and yet another offering hot baked and filled pastries made from wheat flour.

Wheat and rye flours are widely used for breads and the finer flours to create the many pastries of stretched doughs, noodle pastries (MANTI), and delicate sweets made from YUFKAS (paper-thin dough brushed with butter). Rice is the main ingredient in daily PILAFS of many varieties and may be cooked with consommés, vegetables, or the popular combination of nuts, currants and spices. Many favoured desserts are based on thick mixtures of rice that have been well-cooked in milk then sweetened. BULGHUR may replace rice in stuffings and PILAF dishes.

Fats

Olive oil is used not only as a cooking fat, but also dribbled over many cooked dishes to add a pleasing glossy finish and flavour. Olive oil is not only the basic fat, but it is used with a generous hand in almost every dish and bakery item. Second to olive oil is butter which is also used generously in the preparation of the many delicate layered pastries and sweets. Paprika-tinted butter melted to a glowing sauce is often used a garnish. KAYMAK, a rich thick clotted cream used as a topping for puddings and pastries, is yet another source of fat in the Turkish dietary. It should also be noted that even the milk and yoghurt used is preferred with a high fat content. Skim milk products have no place here.

Sweets and Snacks

While it is an easy matter to select random dishes and specialties in the Turkish cuisine and assign their likely origins, so popular are sweets that it is clear that the Turks have happily adopted the desserts and confections of almost every people with whom they have come in contact. The myriad varieties of shaped pastries either baked or fried then drenched in rich sweet syrup include SEKERPARE, TATLISI (of many types), KADAIFES and triangles of BAKLAVA. These would be as familiar to the Turk as to the Greek or Iranian. So would the meltingly tender cookies called KURABIYE and the sweet cake squares called HELVA. A popular dessert made of stewed pumpkin in rich syrup then served cold with walnuts would delight Turks and most peoples of North Africa. A final course of ripe fresh fruits and small dishes of salted toasted nuts is a familiar meal ending to most peoples living near the Mediterranean.

But sometimes the pang of between-meal hunger cannot be satisfied by sweets no matter how tempting. *Muhallebici* (milk shops) stand ready to serve light meals of soups, boiled chicken dishes, many types of milk and YOUGHT refreshments or servings of milk-rice puddings.[3] *Kebapçi* are restaurants specializing in small meals or snacks of various types of KEBABS. For those who have overindulged, *iskembeci* are the shops dedicated to serving a strong vinegar-garlic soup made from tripe and believed to soothe many ailments. Finally there are the Turkish coffee-houses, where everything from conversations to full-course meals is available – but mainly for males.

Seasonings
The delicate flavours of fine olive oil, fresh butter, sweet young vegetables and the tart overtones of YOUGHT and egg-lemon sauce predominate in the Turkish cuisine. Flavours are subtle and delicate with only the gentlest touches of mint, garlic and onions, dill and in some dishes the aromatically sweet cinnamon, allspice and coriander.

Beverages
AYRAN, diluted YOUGHT lightly salted, the staple drink of the Anatolian peasants,[3] is enjoyed by almost everyone. Local beer made from barley, wine made from grapes and RAKI distilled from fermented raisins are used everywhere. Some of the more devout Muslims follow the prohibition against wine, but freely use beer and RAKI. Thrace province produces some popular wines: BÜZBAG (red), KAVILKEDERE (red or white) and DOLUCA (dry white).[6] Whisky, gin, rum and brandy are also taken by many Muslims with the conviction that these couldn't be prohibited as they were not known in the Prophet's time.

In many areas of the Middle East coffee is referred to as "Turkish coffee" even though it originated in Arab lands and was brought to Asia Minor by devout Muslims who made it their staple beverage.[7] So important is coffee to the Turks that traditional marriage vows include a promise from the groom to provide his wife with coffee.[8] Basically, the Turks prepare their coffee from pulverized beans boiled with varying amounts of sugar and sometimes spices in a funnel-shaped pot and serve it still foaming in tiny cups from which it is slowly sipped, leaving the grounds at the bottom. Any excuse is reason enough for serving coffee in one of many ways: SADE is bitter; AZ SEKERLI is sweetish; ORTA is medium; while ÇOK SEKERLI is very sweet.

Regional Specialties
It is from the leisurely prepared meals in the Sultan's palaces in Istanbul that the cuisine of Turkey developed. Yet over the countryside favourite dishes and traditions still prevail. The province of Bursa, noted for its fine orchards and some of the best butter and cheeses, also prides itself on a simple and classic meal style including a first course of fresh vegetables dressed with olive oil, then a meat stew accompanied with some type of

seasonal DOLMA (whatever greens are in season) and ending with YOUGHT, a bowl of fresh fruit and a quiet session with the *narghile* (water pipe).[6] KAVURMA or HASLAMA are two typical types of country stews containing some meat, mostly vegetables and varying amounts of fats. Predominantly, meat is rare but vegetables and YOUGHT are in abundance. Olives are a daily familiar staple everywhere except near the Black Sea coast where walnuts are used. Circassian chicken is a dish prepared with a garnish of crushed, well-peppered walnuts. In the same area the HAMSI (small anchovy) is also widely used. In the southeast, hot KEBABS and spicy raw meatballs (ÇIG KÖFTE) are the favourites and pulses are used daily especially mashed seasoned chick peas.[3]

European customs and manners prevail in the Turkish cities, but traditional customs such as eating with bread, spoons and fingers from cloth-covered carpets prevail as does the custom of entering restaurant kitchens to inspect and taste foods before eating one's meal.

Meal Patterns and Eating Customs

Urban Turks may enjoy a simple European-type breakfast of breads, fruit and coffee; rural Turks will wake up to clear tea, breads and goat's cheese, olives and jam; Anatolian peasants will start their day with hot satisfying soup.[3] Typically throughout the day hunger will be sated with snacks from the many vendors and small shops and restaurants, which also provide small meals of MEZE (appetizers) and RAKI or simply hot soup.

Turks enjoy extending hospitality to respected guests, most especially those with education or *dürüst*. The traditional six-course meal is not a daily occurrence but will be reserved for special guests or special occasions. One or more of the courses may comprise a usual evening meal. MEZE and RAKI of themselves can be so elaborate and varied that they can constitute a meal known as RAKI SOFRASI. But for the traditional meal, they comprise but the first course: tidbits of meats, fish of all types, vegetables hot and cold, stuffed and dressed with oil in endless varieties, cheeses, breads, olives and salted nuts. LEKERDA, BALIK YUMURTASI, TARAMA, PASTIRMA (sun-dried beef spiced with paprika, cumin and garlic), MIDIA DOLMASI (stuffed mussels) and many others, add to the tasty varieties of appetizers.

The second course, HAMUR ISI, consists of varieties of stuffed pastries all served hot, some with sauces. Fillings may be of cheeses, rice, meats or vegetables. The meat course would be served next, usually a form of KEBAB, to be followed by a refreshing cold vegetable dish with olive oil.

The last two courses of a traditional dinner could be considered as the desserts, with a milky rice pudding or one or more forms of the rich syrup-soaked pastries coming first, to be followed by an array of fresh seasonal fruits and Turkish coffee.

While changes are occurring, traditionally women are more in the background socially, and in some homes and areas they may even dine separately from the men. But overall, the innate sense of generous hospitality is prevalent and the respected guest (education, authority and fine manners having priority over mere wealth[3]) can be assured of the finest that the family may have to offer.

Traditionally food was eaten from trays called *tepsi* which were placed either on carpets or on small low tables for each diner or several diners. Luxurious cushions and exquisite carpeting made dining, either sitting or squatting, a comfortable matter. Foods would traditionally always be prepared and served in such a way that diners needed only to use wooden spoons for eating, but more recently the European forks and knives have been used more widely.[3,9]

Special Occasions

It has already been noted that the great majority of Turks profess the faith of Islam: "There is no God but God, and Muhammad is His Prophet." Yet while the call of the *muezzin* is heard throughout the land, few Turks observe the daily set of five prayers or adhere to the ban on alcohol. Most do retain the ambition of the pilgrimage to Mecca and many observe Friday prayers although Mustafa Kemal decreed Sunday the day of rest. Further, few Turks will eat pork, seafood or snails, and those Muslims who follow the precepts of the Prophet's son-in-law Ali and call themselves *Alevi*, include also the dietary prohibition against eating hare.[1,3]

One of the most important religious festive occasions is the *Sünnet Düğünü* (circumcision) performed when a boy is about seven years of age (based on the Mosaic law of circumcision which is performed on the male infant at the age of eight days) to mark his initiation from infancy to adolescent. But the occasion is not just one of joyous family celebration for very often it contains also a heartwarming deed: wealthy families traditionally sponsor the circumcision of a poor boy as well.

Popular at *Sünnet Düğünü* is not only food, music and dancing but also the traditional *Karagöz*, a type of shadow-show featuring the adventures of witty characters and sometimes critical or even crude but humorous dialogues.

Turkish weddings or *düğün* are almost as festive as the circumcision but differ from the country to the city. City weddings are brief refined ceremonies followed by musical receptions where MEZE and sweetened soft drinks are served. Country weddings delight in ancient traditions which include the lively bargaining for the "bride-price," the *baslik* and the inclusion of as many guests and musicians as can be afforded all happily participating in processions, dancing, eating and drinking often throughout the night while the marriage is consummated.

The peak of religious observance for the Turks is the holy month of Ramazan when all fast (total refrain from food, drink, smoking) during the daylight hours. In many areas, drums waken the people one hour before sunrise so that a meal may be taken. And later at sundown, a cannon may sound to signify the end of the day's fast; traditionally the time break occurs when the light is such that a black thread cannot be distinguished from a white. A two-day period called *Seker Bayram* marks the end of the holy month with floodlit monuments and mosques, festivities for children, parades and exhibitions and family gatherings featuring lengthy traditional dinners.[10] Perhaps it is because of the sincere devotion to Ramazan that many consider the Turks to be "night people." Certainly every province and village has its favoured coffeehouses (for men only) where men and boys commonly spend the entire night during Ramazan, eating, drinking and being entertained by the great oral tradition of Turkey, the wandering folk poets, singers and balladeers accompanied by the *saz*, the three-string, lute-like instrument.[12]

Other special occasions include the Festival of Mevlana Konya, in memory of the founder of the whirling dervishes; *Kurban Bayrami*, especially celebrated in rural areas as the lamb sacrifice; and October 29 when the anniversary of the Turkish Republic is celebrated with parades and special events.

FORTY-EIGHT

Ukrainian

Known both as the "Mother of Russia" and the "Breadbasket of Europe," the Ukraine is presently the third largest republic in the Union of Soviet Socialist Republics.[1,2] Her earliest history is in effect the early history of Russia itself. Under Prince Yaroslav, about the year 1036, Kiev became an imperial capital of the Rus principality and the centre of culture, education and the institution of the first Russian law: *Russkaya Pravda.*[3]

But Yaroslav's attempts to consolidate the Russian Empire disintegrated after his death not only because of feuding between the Rus principalities, but also because of intermittent invasions by neighbouring Poles, Lithuanians and Teutonic knights. Subsequent divisions of the Ukraine lands found them alternately under control of Russia, Poland and later Austria. Each conquest left both the marks of suppression of Ukrainian nationalism as well as some cultural and gastronomic influences of the conquering nations. For example Galicia, once a state of the Ukraine, at first challenged the supremacy of Kiev and in later history ended up as a part of Poland, then Austria and finally today finds itself divided between Poland, Russia and Austria.

Despite the suppressions and reversals caused by the relentless path of history, the Ukrainian peoples have retained a distinct cultural, literary and language pattern that distinguishes them from other Slav nations, and one which they proudly maintain wherever they live.

Basically throughout history, the Ukraine was always a tempting acquisition for any nation because of her vast fertile steppes that produced not only an abundant variety of grain crops but also fruit- and nut-laden orchards and fine pastures for beef and dairy cattle. It was historically, as now, the great natural gifts of fertile land interlaced with many river systems and combined with a mild and moist climate that made the Ukraine – together with her population of sturdy, hard-working people – an asset to any conqueror.

Although the Ukrainians are Eastern Slavs together with the Great Russians and Byelorussians,[7] their language as well as many aspects of their culture and cuisine differs. Russians may insist that Ukrainian is nothing but a Russian dialect, but the Ukrainians feel that the historical events of 1918 have divided themselves from the Russians in outlook as well. The argument is explained by the Ukrainian's pointing to the fact that their language differs in appearance, sound and letters.[8] Further, the Ukrainians feel they differ in appearance and personality, tallness of stature, setting them apart from other Europeans, profound individualism being their noted characteristic.[8] Because of the influence of historical conquests, the Ukrainian cuisine contains many elements of Russian and Polish cookery but the BORSCH is claimed to be of Ukrainian origin[9,10] and the myriad breads baked by the Ukrainians are said to be unexcelled (though copied) elsewhere.[2,10]

Home Life and Facilities

The rural areas of the Ukraine have changed little from hundreds of years ago. Typically, families lived in small cottages surrounded by gardens and fences. Older cottages may have had only one or two rooms, more recently only an increase of rooms may be noted as modernization.[13]

The centre of the main room would be the stove built against one wall of clay or stone. The traditional stove would include ovens, cooking top, and an opening in the forepart called the *prychipok*, usually also made of clay or bricks. To one side of the stove would be a firebox, and to the other side a hanging cupboard with shelves for dishes and implements.[12] Kerosene or oil lamps would be used for light; in the North Ukraine, lit-wood splinters placed in a holder provided lighting. In wooded areas wood would be the fuel; straw and sweet rush were and are used as fuel in the southern parts; dried manure would provide fuel in the Eastern Ukraine.[12] More recently, electricity is spreading through the countryside, but as in olden times, running water and proper sewage facilities remain problems in the rural areas.[13]

Age-old methods of food preservation also prevail in country areas. Food storage is not a problem in the cities as frequent shopping is the rule. Winter food storage is crucial and much care is taken to assure adequate winter provisions. Hollowed tree stumps, wooden chests, and large bins or granaries are used for grain storage. Vegetables such as beets and potatoes are commonly stored by burying them in the ground.[12] In some areas funnel-shaped pits plastered with clay and straw are used to store grains and even sauerkraut. Fish and some vegetables could be preserved by drying in the wind and sun or over a fire; meats could be brined, smoked or dried.[12]

FOODS COMMONLY USED

Ukrainian cooking is primarily Slavic; it resembles Russian cooking in the eastern Ukraine and takes elements both from Polish and Czech cooking in the areas of the West.[7] Tea drinking, emphasis on substantial soups and KASHA as well as the ZAKUSKA preceding dinner are all threads of Russian influence; some flour mixtures such as noodles, honeycakes and certain breads may all be of Polish origin; while the judicious use of bread crumbs as well as dumplings could be traced to Czech origin. But the hearty soup of beets and/or cabbage the Russians call BORSCH and the Poles called BARSHCH is considered to have originated in the Ukraine.[9,10] Ukrainian baking of sweets and breads based on their fine quality of wheat and rye flours is unexcelled both in variety and quality. Ukrainians also use more garlic in their foods; pork is the favoured meat when available; but the general basic diet depends upon grains and vegetables, dairy products and occasionally fish.[9,10,12]

Milk and Milk Products
Dairy products form a daily part of the dietary. SMETANA (sour cream) is used as a topping for fresh chopped vegetables, in soups, with noodle and dumpling dishes and with cooked or fresh fruits. SMETANKA is the fresh sweet cream used in bakery, served with grains or fruit desserts. Fresh milk is used but sour milk, buttermilk, and HUSLYANKA (clabbered milk) are preferred as beverages and in cookery.

Pot cheese or dry curd cottage cheese is used widely as the base for many dishes and the filling in baked goods, noodle or dumpling dishes. Also available in the Ukraine are a number of varieties of hard and soft, fresh and aged local cheeses made from sheep or cow's milk.

Fruits and Vegetables
The vegetables staples are beets, cabbage and potatoes. In the western Ukraine corn is also an important staple where it may be classed both as a grain that is dried and ground and used as hominy or cornmeal and cooked into breads, gruels and cereals; or it may be eaten off the cob as a vegetable. Other vegetables used in much lesser quantities include carrots, turnips, onions, tomatoes, cucumbers, greens (spinach, sorrel), pumpkin, eggplant and many varieties of wild mushrooms. Garlic is important and used generously.

Vegetables are eaten coarsely chopped and raw in salads; well-cooked in soups. Many stuffed vegetable dishes utilize the leaves of cabbage, spinach, grape leaves or beet greens. Pickled, and brined vegetables such as dill pickles, beet relishes, fermented apples, sauerkraut and dilled green tomatoes, etc., are enjoyed.

A variety of cultivated fruits and wild berries are enjoyed in season or preserved as relishes or jams. Fruits may be eaten fresh in season but are more often preferred stewed with sugar in compotes; cooked and puréed then thickened with starch as in KYSIL; and cooked and sweetened to use as filling for VARENYKY (noodle dumplings). Fruits may also be simply stewed, sweetened and thickened, then served with SMETANKA or they may be prepared as sharply tart or else sweet-and-sour fruit soups.

Meats and Alternates

Favoured meats are pork and pork products; very occasionally veal or lamb may be used. Mostly, meats are considered expensive and are eaten on special occasions;[12] all edible parts are well-utilized.[10] Salt pork is considered the staple of the peasant's diet. Also used when possible are chicken, turkey, wild duck, geese, rabbits, pigeons, venison. Many types of sausages are widely used because they are economical and tasty. These include mildly flavoured veal and pork sausages; KYSHKA, a homemade or commercially prepared sausage containing mostly fat and flour; SARDELKY, a spicy sausage; and hunter's sausage, thin, hard, well-cured and durable.

A good supply of fresh-water (there are many rivers in the Ukraine) and sea fish include herring, perch, pike, sturgeon and carp. Fish is usually prepared by poaching, jellying, frying, pickling or baking. Eggs are produced abundantly and used unstintingly in baking. Eggs are occasionally served boiled or fried for a breakfast. Legumes are not used extensively, except dried peas may be used in soup. Nuts are used in bakery for a garnish and as a filling.

Breads and Cereals

The sheaf of wheat is a fitting symbol for the Ukrainian Republic. Grain is not only the basic ingredient for the KASHA and the breads that are a part of almost every meal, but grain is an important and holy symbol on many sacred occasions from the Christmas KUTYA (a mixture of cooked wheat grains, honey, poppyseeds and nuts) to the grains of rye that are often strewn in the coffins of the deceased.[12] Specially baked breads highlight each special occasion as well. (See "Special Occasions.") In fact, there is no aspect of Ukrainian life or after-life that is not celebrated with the holiness of grain.[2,7,10,12] If a daily meal has neither breads nor KASHA (which would be most unusual) it would have, for sure, noodles (LOKSHYNA) in some form, or the many types of PYROHY or VARENYKY, little noodle pockets of fruit, meat or vegetable filling served with cream, fruits or SMETANA, or floated in soups.

Fats
Lard, rendered salt pork and bacon ends add characteristic flavour to most Ukrainian cookery. Butter is used when available. There is a preference for whole milk rather than skim. Much fat is also consumed in the creams and cheeses. Vegetable oils, especially sunflower seed oil, and also oils from flax and hemp[12] are used especially by the Orthodox on fast days and Lent when meat or meat products are not traditionally used.

Sweets and Snacks
While Ukrainians from rural areas serve desserts only on special occasions, others consider a meal completed only when cakes or desserts have been served. Desserts with honey are a special favourite. Tea is often enjoyed Russian-style, with a small accompanying saucer of sweet fruit jams to spoon up with each sip. Because of the use of honey as a frequent sweetener, bee-keeping is important in the Ukraine. Toasted and salted sunflower and melon seeds are enjoyed as a snack.

Seasonings
Tart flavours, fermented sour flavours and the combination of sweet-and-sour are great favourites. Juice from pickles and relishes, the juice squeezed from sauerkraut, and a specially made fermented liquid called KVAS (from fermented rye bread or fermented beet juice) – any of these may be used to add that special touch to soups and other dishes.[8] And tart or soured pickled vegetables are frequent meal additions. In general cookery, foods are rich with well-cooked natural flavours enhanced occasionally with dill seeds or caraway seeds, dill, butter or SMETANA. Onions and mushrooms also add their touch to many dishes, but garlic is probably the most-used of all. Honey is the favourite sweetener.

Beverages
Tea is the most important beverage of all for Ukrainians. Milk and sugar may be added according to taste. KVAS, as well as being used for its flavour, is also a popular country beverage.[12] Coffee is enjoyed but considered to be a luxury. Ukrainian wine or vodka may be a part of the evening meal. Tea, water or bottled mineral waters are most usually taken with breakfast or lunch.

Meal Patterns and Eating Customs
The Ukrainian emphasis on grains permeates each meal and most customs and special occasions. The traditional four meals of the day – breakfast, dinner (before noon), *pidvechirok*, the afternoon snack,

and the evening supper – all feature bread. It is also said that in the Ukraine a meal would be incomplete without a soup course.[10] In fact, very often the nourishing thick soups together with KASHA (buckwheat or barley groats oven-baked so each grain is fluffy and separate) and bread are satisfying enough to be the entire meal. Typical country meals include large helpings of soup, KASHA and bread together with noodle or dumpling dishes that may sometimes include meat, fish or vegetables. Pickles and SMETANA complete the meal. Depending on the time and the financial position, the evening meals in the cities may include more courses or more elaborate dishes: herrings, cheeses, PASHTET (baked pâté served hot or cold), sliced meats, sausages, varieties of breads and dessert.[2]

Meals are traditionally served family style with the foods placed on platters and diners helping themselves. Hearty eating is encouraged and taking more than one helping is considered to be flattering to the hostess. Tables are often set with hand-embroidered cloths traditional to the various regions of the Ukraine.

Special Occasions

The principal religions of the Ukraine are represented by the Ukrainian (Greek) Catholic Church and the Ukrainian Greek Orthodox Church with others in various Christian denominations, as well as a small population of Jews. Most of the latter were listed variously as Poles, Ukrainians, Austrians or Russians in the immigration waves following the turn of the century and both world wars.

Although Christianity predominates in the religious feelings of the Ukrainians, many of the festivals are intertwined with agricultural celebrations and carry overtones of ancient Slavic festivals as well as local superstitions and mysticism.

The majority of the Galician Ukrainians belong to the Ukrainian (Greek) Catholic Church, distinctive from the Roman Catholic Church in many features but especially in allowing married men to be ordained as priests.[8] The majority of Ukrainians from Bukovina (southwestern Ukraine, now a part of Romania) belong to the Ukrainian (Greek) Orthodox Church. Since most Ukrainians not only attempted to live near their own peoples and preserve their language and customs, as well as retain their religious affiliation, the community and the church became an integral part of the social life.[8]

These are described here as traditionally celebrated in the Ukraine. It must be considered that religious observances are not encouraged in the Soviet Union; however, agricultural and seasonal festivities are celebrated by all. In America, most Ukrainians celebrate two Christmases: one on December 25 with a Christmas tree (*yalynka*) and gift giving, and the other more solemn occasion of January 6 when the traditions of Christmas together with the symbols of family unity, respect for the dead, and the importance of agriculture all intertwine in a memorable Christmas Eve celebration.

In the Ukraine, traditional folk customs and rites are connected with the "Folk Calendar," with each season bringing its special days which are interlaced with family, agriculture and religion, not excluding spells, sorcery and protection against evil spirits or the "evil eye."[12]

Winter festivals are mostly centred around Christmas and New Year's but begin with a special holiday for young men and unmarried girls on December 13. For this day special breads are baked, some concealing charms or coins which will tell the lucky finder that she will wed within the year. The breads are called BALABUSHKY. Games, the casting of spells and telling of fortunes are commonplace on this day, one of the favourites being the pouring of hot wax on cold water to predict the future. This special day ends with a huge honeyed cake called KALYTA which is tied and hung from the ceiling rafters and becomes the centre of games and teasing until finally eaten.

December 19 is called St. Nicholas' Day, St. Nicholas being considered the guardian saint of orphans, animals and the poor. His day is one of merry-making and gifts for the children.

January 6 is the start of the Christmas season which ends on January 19 with Epiphany. It is considered the most important family celebration and its preparations begin many weeks before. In the early morning of *Sviat Vechir*, the mother lights a new fire from twelve pieces of wood that have been carefully selected and dried for twelve days. The ritual evening meal will start with blessings and a speech from the father and the entire family will be present around the table with a special place even being set to remember the dead. Symbols of the sacredness of agriculture in the life of the family will be found in the farm implements that are placed under the dinner table, the sheaf of wheat placed in the holy corner under the icons, garlic placed on four corners of the table and finally hay or straw strewn over the entire floor and some under the tablecloth. In the centre of the table will be placed a special round loaf of bread (KNYSH[12] or KALACH[2]) with a lighted candle in the centre.

The ceremonial meal will begin with the KUTYA, a dish of cooked grain mixed with poppyseeds, honey and nuts. A handful of this may be mixed with the food for the animals in the stable because it is believed that on this night even the animals have the power of speech.[10,11,12] Another handful of KUTYA is thrown out of doors – "let the frost eat KUTYA" – and a last handful is flung up at the ceiling "so that the bees may swarm."[12] Finally, all at the table take some to eat and this ritual food is followed by eleven meatless dishes to complete the meal. The total of twelve dishes is said to be symbolic of the twelve apostles. Vegetables, fishes and grains are the basic ingredients of the twelve dishes which may include KASHA; boiled dumplings filled with fruit, grains or vegetables;

cabbage, peas, beans or potatoes dressed with oil and garlic; boiled corn (KOKOT); PYROHY, with poppyseeds; and fruit dishes. Children play an important part in this ritual meal for it is they who eagerly watch the sky to sight the first star – a signal that the ritual meal may begin.

The day of Christmas is celebrated usually with caroling, dancing and a roast suckling pig. The festivities continue till January 9.

New Year's Eve, January 13, is called *Malanka* or *Shchedryi-Vechir* ("Generous Eve") and is gaily celebrated with parties. Each area of the Ukraine prepares its specialty dishes, which may include PYROHY filled with meat or cottage cheese, buckwheat pancakes and sausages, and bagels or BUBLYKY. In addition, a plate of KUTYA completes the festive meal.[12] The following day the festivities continue with costumes and entertainment, dancing and fortune-telling.

January 19 and 20 ends the Christmas season more solemnly with church services commemorating Christ's baptism by St. John the Baptist in the Jordan River. This is called Epiphany or Jordan's Day and the evening meal is similar to that of Christmas Eve, ending this time with the KUTYA being "driven away."[10,12]

The many spring festivals are centred around Easter and Whitsuntide or the "Green Festival." *Miasnytsi* is the carnival period that precedes Lent; the favourite food, VARENYKY (boiled dumplings made with fine noodle pastry and filled with fruits, or cheese fillings), and HRECHANYKY are served.

This period is marked by intensive house-cleaning, washing, repairing and painting. Refuse is collected and burned. And all of this work is accompanied by prescribed rituals and incantations ending with the carrying of a plow around the village and the sacrificial burning of a black rooster. Although the cleaning takes place about the home, there seems to be an accompanying cleansing of the soul said to culminate in the burning of the rooster – perhaps symbolic of the end of evil deeds and sins.[12]

Since palm branches are not available, willow branches are substituted for blessing on Willow Sunday, the Sunday before Easter.

Maundy Thursday, the Thursday before Easter Sunday, is celebrated with a solemn *strasti* or "passion" service in the church with all the congregants hurrying home afterwards, each carrying a specially lit candle. This candle is considered to have special significance the whole year through; it is relit and placed near the icons during a severe thunderstorm and is lit and placed in the hand of a dying person. In the eastern Ukraine strong beliefs persist that the dead return on that night to hold a Divine Mass in the church.[12]

Easter Sunday's joyous service is ended with the congregants singing *"Khrystos Voskres"* ("Christ Is Risen") and hurrying home with baskets of foods and decorated eggs (PYSANKY and KRASHANKY) blessed by the priest. These are eaten as part of the festive meal: a fine array of sausages, smoked meats, roast suckling pig, cheeses, breads, relishes and the specialty Easter cakes, PASKA or BABKA.

Summer time is similarly laced with festivities that intertwine the mystical and the religious and pay special homage to the good earth which produces the bounties of the Ukraine. Young love, weddings and births, even funeral ceremonies are symbolic of the agricultural life of the people. Coffins may be strewn with rye so that the dead will not go hungry; poppyseeds may be sprinkled on the coffin so that the dead may rest peacefully. Sometimes food is left at the graveside, usually a dish of KOLYVO, a mixture of grains and honey. Traditionally upon returning from the funeral, no one must look back, and all must purify themselves by washing and touching the stove before eating the funeral meal which itself begins with the traditional KOLYVO.

A freshly baked loaf of bread topped with a small mound of salt is traditionally called KHLIB I SIL and is the age-old welcome for special guests and for newlyweds. Perhaps it comes as no surprise that a Ukrainian wedding cake is also replete with tradition. Seven bridesmaids grind flour taken from seven different sources and bake it into an ornamented loaf of bread called KOROVAI which will be tasted by each wedding guest at the wedding feast. The KOROVAI is considered to be the wedding cake.

Few Ukrainians in North America keep all the Old World traditions, but certain customs and rituals are held dear by some families. Many celebrate two Christmases and most celebrate Easter with all its joyous symbols.

FORTY-NINE

Vietnamese

The name Vietnam has historically caused confusion, and for good reason. The mixed ethnic population has seldom known long periods of freedom, social security, or peace. There is South Vietnam and North Vietnam – the latter known also as Viet Minh, presently a Communist country. Originally the area was known as French Indochina. In fact, just before 1800, the area presently known as South Vietnam used to be called Cochin China and South Annam while North Vietnam territory used to be known as Tonkin and North Annam.[1,2]

The huge S-shape of North and South Vietnam, curving from the Gulf of Tonkin and bulging outward to the South China Sea, is the home of a population made up of 90 per cent Annamite stock. These are the peoples who are believed to have migrated as a Paleomongoloid people from the area that is now Southeast China. The area they first settled is believed to be the flat wooded swamp of lower Tonkin, long ago called Yue state,[2] in the Vietnamese language, Viet state; and so the people came to be called Vietnamese. The first capital of the Vietnamese Kingdom of Nam Viet or South Yue was Hanoi. By 42 C.E. Nam Viet had become a Chinese province and in the almost one-thousand-year occupation by China both the people and the country reflected the powerful "elder brother" influence in every aspect of daily life.[2]

Chinese influence in the countryside remains to this day. Chinese-style villages, autonomous leadership, ancestor worship, and the patrilineal kinship system, coupled with a high degree of nationalism and individual reserve, characterize most of the South Vietnam villages. Dikes and canals constructed against annual floods, layout of irrigation patterns for the fields, the introduction of fertilizing the fields with human feces as well as the use of the iron plough share and the bucket-wheel all greatly increased rice production. In fact some areas were able to glean two annual crops with the use of these methods.[2] Chinese also introduced and helped to develop crafts and craft guilds, which promoted the rapid development and pride in creativity. To the basic animism, the Chinese introduced Taoism, Mahayana Buddhism, and the morals and philosophy of Confucianism. As in China, government officials were a hierarchy of Confucian intellectuals. Temples, pagodas and gracefully curved roof lines (warding away evil spirits) became a part of the skyline just as the Chinese vocabulary permeated the Austro-Asiatic language of the Vietnamese.[2]

Even today Chinese influence is clearly distinguishable at the table as well. Most Vietnamese eat their foods with chopsticks. Only in scattered mountainous regions, where the Chinese influence did not penetrate, do the people eat with their fingers as is customary in most of Southeast Asia.[3] Chinese cooking implements: charcoal braziers, ladles and stirring spoons, many bowls and woks, knives and choppers are as familiar and lovingly used as in any Chinese kitchen. The Vietnamese prefer their rice served plain and white – the Northerners showing a preference for long grain rice (TAMTHOM), the Southerners short grain rice (NANHCHON)[4] – rather than mixed with other foods.[3] Yet while the Vietnamese enjoy many fried foods and stir-fried dishes they have a further distinct preference for lean meats (lean chicken and pork) fatless soups, and a dislike for foods that taste greasy.[3] In fact, because of this, most dishes are steamed or boiled or very quickly stir-fried and all foods that may have any suspicion of grease are skimmed, trimmed, or otherwise handled to remove the grease.

By the late 900s C.E. the Vietnamese drove out the Chinese and extended their sense of strength by pressuring their southern neighbours in the Kingdom of Cham (predominantly under Indian influence) whose population of Malayo-Polynesian origin engaged in rice culture soon came under their domination. By the 1600s the Viets had annexed the entire "rice-bowl" of the Mekong Delta region. It is probable that the Viets might have even gone further in their "annexing" had it not been for the incredible influence of both the Catholic French missionaries and the development of the French East India Company in the 1600s, which helped to engage France's interest in this area.[2,5]

It was the French who moved into the Mekong Delta and established the colony of Cochin China and the protectorate of Cambodia in 1865. Gradual French influence was seen in the extension of industrialization and in the spread of Roman Catholicism.[2] Gradually too Vietnamese of means began sending their children to study in Europe. French culture, language, cuisine, and religion found a place in Vietnamese life-style. The growth of these overseas-educated led to a small middle class and a gradually burgeoning intelligentsia who were soon joined by Chinese moving into the cities and towns as traders, craftsmen, clerks, and merchants. Saigon's twin city of Cholon was founded by the Chinese.[2] It was not long before the growing minority ethnic groups of approximately six million Khmers, 2.5 million Laotians, three million mountain tribesmen and one million Chinese all came to view the thirty-three million Vietnamese with the same attitudes of hostility and fear as the Vietnamese traditionally had towards the Chinese.[2]

Although the French united much of the area for administrative purposes, a slow-simmering nationalism brewed. Ignoring the French extension of ports, canals, highways, and railroads, the Annamese pressed for independence of their Vietnam or "Indochinese Union," as it was called by 1900.[5] France's collapse to Germany in 1940, gave further impetus to the nationalistic tide but was quelled when the Allies divided Indochina arbitrarily into a northern zone to be held by the Chinese and a southern zone to be held by the British-Indian troops pending the arrival once again of the French. The embattled Vietnamese, torn by strife, starvation, and corruption from within, and tugged by opposing outside forces, became the pawn in a chess game called the "Cold War." In the belief that it could contain the Communists (under Ho Chi Minh in North Vietnam), the Americans poured men and arms into South Vietnam.

The upheavals of a violent history have left their mark on the land and the people. Ethnic antagonisms and the deep contrasts between the rich and the poor, the various religions and between the lowlanders and the mountain people will take kinder turns of history to heal.

Home Life and Facilities

The home life of the Vietnamese closely resembles that of traditional China even with the distinguishing characteristics of the village, town, and city. Close family life, respect for elders, and the dignified politeness of children are all apparent. Some elements of traditional animism, Taoism and Buddhism show in family celebrations and festivities and even in everyday affairs. Few Vietnamese homes fail to give at least cursory homage to several personal gods, especially the God of the Kitchen. Despite the modernization of the cities, the presence of French and later the Americans, despite even education abroad, old traditions hold dear. A child is considered one year old when he is born and counts birthdays not on the day of birth but on each New Year's; scholars still lead in the traditional hierarchy of society followed by agriculturalists, salaried workers, and finally merchants; belief in herbal teas and the medicinal qualities of certain foods persist.[6]

Similarly, Vietnamese kitchens and tables reflect much of China's influence. Facilities and utensils vary according to means: many small electrical appliances find a useful place in city kitchens while the age-old methods of food storage and meal preparation hold sway in traditional village kitchens. Women enjoy preparing their foods for meals in a separate kitchen that is often also a separate building from the main living quarters. This is not only practical from the standpoint of fire hazards, but also provides the women a special place for women talk.[3] Three-stoned stands set in clay or stone hearths hold charcoal embers and efficiently heat steamers, iron kettles, or woks. Sharp knives and cleavers make quick work of slicing, slivering, chopping, mincing, while quick and artful fingers carefully arrange platters of foods to be placed attractively on the meal table. While among the wealthy the cuisine of the household may be very continental and varied, with dishes from local and Western cultures, amongst all Vietnamese the dishes of Chinese origin (but given a special Vietnamese fillip) appear for all special occasions.[4]

Tradition persists not only in the home and the kitchen, but even in the diets of expectant mothers. Vietnamese women are fearful of eating too much food lest their baby becomes too heavy, and many fear that certain foods may be harmful to the fetus.[4] Rice, soy sauce, some vegetables and NUOC MAM (the fish-sauce condiment) are taken as required, but many believe that fish and meats may generate poisons in the child and refuse to eat them as part of the daily diet during pregnancy.[4] These are typical of food beliefs in the countryside and are not commonly found among women in Saigon.[4]

FOODS COMMONLY USED

The tropical-monsoon climate of most of Vietnam, the land and the fresh-water and inshore fishing contribute to bring the Vietnamese staples to the table: rice, NUOC MAM, fish, fruits and vegetables, pork and poultry. Rice is the most important food, present at all main meals but close in use and importance is the condiment added to most dishes at all times: NUOC MAM. This is made from salt and fish well fermented. The first liquid produced is the best quality NUOC MAM; the result of pressing the remaining fish and salt (stronger flavour and more pungent smell) is of lower quality.[3,4] Inland fishing is less costly than deep-sea, but every type of fish and seafood is enjoyed in the Vietnamese dietary. Both wild and cultivated fruits are abundant, and consumption of vegetables has increased since the North Vietnam refugees brought market garden culture to the southern "rice bowl." Both meat and fats come from hogs although some chicken and beef is also eaten. Almost as widely used as NUOC MAM is the spicy hot condiment NUOC CHAM – each cook preparing it in her own special way with chili peppers, garlic and onions, vinegar, and a sprinkle of citrus juice to heighten the tang.[3]

The Northerners prefer long grain rice, the Southerners round grain rice. Both areas also enjoy "hot-pot cookery" where a bubbling pot of broth centred at the table receives tidbits of foods held by chopsticks for quick-cooking. At meals, the diner assembles his own tidbits of meat, fish, fruits, and vegetables then wraps them in packets of edible rice paper, various green leaves, noodle dough, all to be sauce-dipped before devouring. Although these many similarities have been noted, Northerners and Southerners insist not only upon their rice preferences, but the Southerners enjoy more spiciness, the use of more fresh fruits and raw vegetables, simpler dishes and a lot of coconut. They will tell you this is because of their more tropical climate. However, while the Northerners consider the Southern food something less than subtle, the Southerners may counter that they think the Northerners' food flat![3]

Milk and Milk Products
The Vietnamese share the general Oriental distaste of milk and cheese. Some canned evaporated milk is used, but the quantity is small.[1] Soybean curd in the form of creamy-white sponge-like squares is used in many dishes and is sometimes called "Oriental Cheese." There is a growing tendency for milk and cream to appear at the tables of the well-to-do (milk for children and cream in coffee for adults) but not among the poorer country dwellers.[4]

Fruits and Vegetables
Consumption of fruits and vegetables varies according to location and income. Wild fruits are abundant and used either while green or when ripened. These include mangoes and bananas as well as coconuts and a range of common tropical fruits. Pineapples are enjoyed in season and by those who can afford this cultivated fruit.[4] Both fruits and vegetables may be mixed in different dishes containing meats or fish. Often fruits may be used and seasoned in the same way as vegetables: for example, green slices of papaya are eaten with a mixture of salt and chili peppers and a sprinkle of vinegar.[4]

All leafy green vegetables, onions, scallions, garlic, as well as many varieties of mushrooms, radishes, cabbages, are all enjoyed. Perhaps the only category of vegetables not a part of the Vietnamese diet are the roots and tubers such as yams and cassava.[4]

Fruits may be used in their green state in cooked dishes to impart a sour tang and enliven other flavours, or enjoyed for their own flavour addition. Other fruits may be served fresh as dessert. Most vegetables are served either raw, steamed, boiled, or stir-fried.

Meats and Alternates

In Vietnam cattle and buffalo are considered animals of burden rather than food sources. Hogs are the principal source of meat and fat for cooking. Chickens and ducks are seen everywhere but not scientifically produced, therefore the meat from them is generally lean and tough, and the production of eggs is not high.[4] Some beef is used in various dishes, especially in the larger towns and cities where tastes are more cosmopolitan and income higher; again the beef is lean and requires moist cooking or marinating to tenderize before grilling.

Fish is the most important protein in the Vietnamese diet. Since inland fishing is less costly, the majority of fish eaten is taken from inland water sources. Deep-sea fisheries are increasing. Fish may be steamed with vegetables and seasoning, poached, made into minced fish cakes, or barbecued over coals.

Both meats and fish are used in small quantities, cooked with great care to gain maximum flavour from minimal amounts, and served attractively. Many soups are prepared by the basic Chinese method of browning a few meat strips in a small amount of fat with some seasoning, then adding water to form the basic soup broth. Both meat- and fish-based soups may be prepared in the same way. The practice of thinly slicing or shredding meats or fish or seafood, or cooking them together with quantities of minced, sliced, or slivered vegetables also extends their flavour.

Oriental medicine ascribes great value to eggs, especially incubated eggs, and the Vietnamese are very fond of these although the high price and scarcity makes them only a small portion of the dietary. Eggs may also be pickled, boiled in tea (to colour), and served in slices or wedges as a garnish to other dishes or appetizers. Tiny pancakes, made basically with eggs, and the shredded egg pancake used as a soup garnish, are used according to income.

Soybeans are used in the Chinese way and in as many forms (see Chinese or Korean). Sprouted greens of many types of beans, as well as seasoned mashed beans, used in condiments and for fillings, and the popular soybean curd, served in many ways in soups and with vegetables (usually stir-fried) add to the protein consumption.

Breads and Cereals

Rice is the principal staple Vietnamese food and one of the most important crops. For the poor, rice with only a sprinkling of low grade NUOC MAM is considered a meal and an occasional addition of fish and few vegetables may be the whole dietary. For other Vietnamese, rice still comes first but the addition of fish, meats and poultry, as well as a variety of vegetables and fruits round out the diet more completely. Without rice – simply boiled white and fluffy – it is scarcely a meal.

Rice flour is used in the making of many dumplings and pastry dishes that are cooked usually by steaming. One such soft dumpling dish is called BANH CUON, made by rubbing a ball of soft dough over cheesecloth stretched tightly over a pot of boiling water. The steam cooks the circle of dough which is then lifted off, filled with a minced mixture of meat, fish, or vegetables, then rolled and dipped in NUOC CHAM before popping in the mouth. "Papers" of almost cellophane consistency are made usually commercially out of rice flour and are called "rice papers." Cut into small squares these are used at the table to wrap variously prepared tidbits, then a preliminary sauce-dunking makes them the special dish called CHA GIO.[3]

Some western-type breads and rolls are available in Saigon in restaurants catering to European or Western tastes but these are not a regular part of the Vietnamese dietary.

Noodle dishes, as in other East Asian countries, often form the basis of a quick lunch. Noodles may be prepared from rice, wheat, or buckwheat flours. As with almost every other type of dish, what makes it distinctly Vietnamese is the addition of NUOC MAM.

Fats
The only animal fat used is pork fat. All foods are served well-skimmed of any fats as Vietnamese do not like greasy foods. Coconut oil and groundnut (peanut) oil are also used.

Sweets and Snacks
Sweet chunks of juicy fruits in season and specially prepared sweet small cakes and steamed dumplings for festivities are the main sources of sweet foods for the Vietnamese. More recently, consumption of sweetened bottled beverages and imported candies has increased. Sugar is used in cookery much like another seasoning to heighten and distinguish flavours.

Seasonings
The Chinese seasonings of garlic, scallions and onions, fresh ginger root and soy sauce are all part of Vietnamese cookery. But what makes the cuisine most distinctive is the addition of two special condiment sauces used both in cookery and at the table: NUOC MAM and NUOC CHAM. These two sauces represent the essence of what separates Vietnamese cookery from most other eastern cookery. NUOC MAM is the liquid that is produced from layered salted fish which has been allowed to ferment in barrels. Almost equally important is NUOC CHAM and every cook has her own special recipe for the addition of fiery spices and pungent flavours to the basic NUOC MAM. Garlic and onions, chili peppers, black pepper, cayenne, sugar, citrus juices, coconut juice and vinegar may all be a part of the final hot combination. Both of these sauces are used as ingredients in many other dishes – almost the way Westerners use salt and pepper – or as added sauces or condiments for dipping savoury mouthfuls.

The delicate flavours of coconut and lemon grass also permeate many Vietnamese dishes. Peanuts, too, add a special flavour to many sauces.[3]

Beverages

Some upper-class city children drink milk as a beverage but this is not common. Flavoured and sweetened bottled beverages, sweetened or natural fruit juices, tea, coffee, and beer all take their place as meal-time accompaniments or as refreshments. Where French influence is evident, wines may be used. Vietnamese-grown tea is exported as is the high quality Vietnamese beer.

Meal Patterns and Eating Customs

The Vietnamese are the only peoples in the Pacific and Southeastern Asia region whose eating customs are dominated by Chinese influence. This is most evident in the use of chopsticks both for eating and as an aid in lifting, beating and stirring while cooking.[3] Table service also borrows heavily from traditional Chinese customs: white tablecloth, individual rice bowls and beverage glasses or tea bowls with most foods being served buffet style for the diners to help themselves.

The Vietnamese recognize three types of meals. Whenever rice is served with or without anything else it is considered to be a "filling meal"; a meal of refreshing beverages or sometimes only soup is considered to be a "cooling meal"; while a meal consisting of sweetmeats and locally-prepared delicacies is called a "greed meal." People in most other lands frequently enjoy the same types of meals but seldom label them. These three types of meals represent nutrition, refreshment, and pleasure.[4] Festive meals, or large meals in well-to-do homes, may well contain the elements of all three types but for most Vietnamese, one type at a time suffices. Street vendors are seen everywhere in stalls and along roadsides or carrying their wares upon their heads. Snacks and nibbles and drinks and even soups are always available to satisfy the faintest hunger pang. These may vary from slices of fresh fruit with dipping sauces, to bowls of hot soups, steamed dumplings, or local fish or specialties.

There is a difference not only in the foods eaten but also in the meal patterns among the well-to-do, the middle class, and the poor. Well-to-do families enjoy a wide variety of local dishes, western dishes as well as Chinese delicacies – the latter usually served daily on all festive occasions. Breakfast may feature eggs, breads, preserves, and coffee with cream and sugar. Lunch and dinner will likely be similar, with rice at both meals, and a variety of meat or fish, eggs, vegetables and fruits or fruit preserves or compotes for dessert. THIT-KHO (pork) is the favoured meat and may be served as sausages, minced raw or cooked, diced and fried and served with vegetables, noodles, or in steamed doughs. NUOC MAM and coconut juice will add flavour to almost all dishes, while soy sauce will flavour Chinese-type foods. Sugar and vinegar are also widely used. Tea, wine, or beer may appear at meals, and often the choice of all three is given. Some well-to-do homes may also include butter and quality oils at the table and in their cooking. Fruits in season may be offered as a refreshment to guests or for dessert.[3,4]

Middle-class homes prepare a varied menu combining local foods, Chinese, and even western-type foods. A typical breakfast may include a minced pork broth with HU-TIEN (rice noodles) – a Chinese soup that becomes definitively Vietnamese with the addition of NUOC MAM. Dinner and supper are usually similar, featuring rice and several dishes of vegetables plus meat, fish, poultry, or eggs. Vegetables are used more frequently and in more variety than fruits.[4]

The poorer class consumes mostly rice, but varies this by preparing both steamed rice or NEP, sticky rice.[4] Some vegetables or fish may be steamed on top of the rice or the fish may be sliced and eaten raw. More NUOC MAM is consumed by the poorer classes than the middle or upper classes, but it is of the lowest quality and pungently strong in flavour and odour. Cooking is done mostly with lard, occasionally with vegetable oils.

Special Occasions

Animism, Taoism, Buddhism, Confucianism, and more recently Christianity, have each in their turn influenced Vietnamese daily life. Even those professing Christianity vary their observances and may favour personal deities and household shrines and often on special occasions there may be a symbolic return to ancient traditions.

As in China, Korea and Japan, Vietnamese occasions may be divided into family, seasonal, as well as religious. Throughout, Chinese festivals, traditions, and foods predominate. Even the celebration of the traditional lunar New Year, called ONG TAO DAY, celebrated on the last day of the last month according to the lunar calendar, follows Chinese custom with parades, flags and sweetmeats. Typically Vietnamese is the paper image of ONG TAO attached to a paper bird, which is covered with a detailed report of a family's year-long activities. Beside the bird is an array of rich and sticky treats. It is hoped that while the fire is set to this special offering, the god will dine as he reads the report, then be forced to keep his mouth shut (at least in regard to any bad deeds) by the sticky candy.[6]

FIFTY

Welsh

The Welsh name for Wales is *Cymru*, "land of comradeship," and a place where traditions are deep-rooted and well-preserved, not only in the castles, customs, and philosophy of the people, but also in their love of music and poetry. The "musical" Welsh language seems natural for a people who love to sing and who are world famous for their voices.[1] In fact, of all people in the British Isles, it is the Welsh who are considered to be the "most truly British of all."[1] They proudly trace their ancestry to the original Celts who fled foreign invaders by hiding in the mountains and valleys of what is today called Wales. Here they carefully preserved their love of community and their kinship ties — to this day families proudly trace relationships "even to the 9th degree"[2] – and the early principles of Welsh society which always stressed unity rather than class distinction.

The earliest Welsh poetry is thought to be dated from the 500s C.E., and has served as a model of inspiration not only for other literary forms but also for language and even "masculine heroic ideals."[3] Queen Elizabeth, in 1563 C.E., insisted upon having the Bible and Common Book of Prayer translated into Welsh (in the hope of gaining Welsh sympathies), and that had the effect of preserving not only the Welsh language but Welsh nationalism as well. The early Calvinist churches deeply affected Welsh life by fostering a strong individualistic sense, which much later resulted in the development of radical and even socialist thought.[2]

Further effects of religious influence on Welsh life were to come later with the Methodist Movement, its exaggerated emphasis on "saving souls," its consideration of music and dance as "sinful occupations," even going so far as to insist that the Sabbath (Sunday) be a day of sanctity with no sound of music.

The good effect of these conflicting religious movements, the Calvinist and the Methodist, was twofold: it promoted a literate nation; and made the people strongly concerned with theology, politics, and literature. To this day, the stimulation of religious thinking, and the proud preservation of language, especially in the Sunday schools, has continued to unify the people and make *Cymru* much more than just a name. Despite the sweep of industrialization in the 1800s, despite repeated attempts by the English to integrate them, and despite many periods of dismal poverty, the Welsh have retained their solidarity and think of the whole of Wales as "home."[1] And their intense love of language, music, and poetry is reflected in their annual *Eisteddfod* festival in August: the Welsh national holiday honouring music and poetry.[4]

Although they are known in England as "Welshmen," the people distinguish themselves as North Walian and South Walian. Black is the prevailing colour of South Wales, for more than 50 per cent of the population is concentrated in the Glamorgan county famed for coal mining. As if to remove the blackness from their lives, every collier wears a bright white scarf when off work and every housewife has a fetish about whitewashed doorsteps![4] Intertwined with their religious feelings is more than a thread of respect for the supernatural, and with great wit, the South Walian loves to tell jokes on himself, and hair-raising ghost stories as well. North Wales is more industrialized and some claim that the greatest social reformers, statesmen, and orators were all born in the hills of North Wales.[4] But that is a matter for Walians to debate.

It is from their ancient Celtic inheritance that a linguistic link connects the Welsh with the Irish, Scots, Cornish, and even the Bretons of Brittany, France. In fact, there are many interesting culinary links between Wales and Brittany based on their mutual love of onions and leeks, pork, seafood, spices, and the presence of cheese, red wine, ale, and cider in so many of their traditional dishes. Many different forms of pancakes are common to all Celtic countries, differing only in the names: Scotland has thick DROP SCONES, Brittany enjoys delicate lacy cakes called CRÊPES DENTELLES, while the Welsh call them CREMPOG. Similarly, a raisin or fruit-flecked cake served well-buttered is called BARM BRACK in Ireland, SELKIRK BANNOCK in Scotland, and MORLAIX BRIOCHE in Brittany, while the Welsh call the same beloved cake, BARA BRITH. Here are some other similar dishes:

Brittany	*Wales*
FLAN DE POIREAUX	TARTEN GENNIN: leek tart
POMME DE TERRE À LA	
BOULANGÈRE	TEISEN NIONOD: onion cake

SAUCE VINAIGRETTE	SURYN CYFFAITH POETH: A potent and spicy garlic sauce served with veal.
CRÉPINE or CRÉPINETTES	FAGGOTS: called MOCK DUCK or SAVOURY DUCKS in English; meatballs of pig liver, seasoned and wrapped in lacy pig's flead or caul fat and baked.[5]

Home Life and Facilities

The most important room of the traditional Welsh stone and slate houses has always been the kitchen. Here the family gathers for meals around a table; a deal-top (similar to pine wood) table scrubbed to a glowing white and covered with a cloth for dinner and on Sundays.[7] If there were more children than could be seated at once, they quietly took their turns. Guests, whether relatives or strangers, were always seated on the hearth bench called *mainc y simnai*, where it would be warm, and bowls of soup were traditionally offered together with entertaining songs and stories. Family and visitor alike were warmed inside and out in the hospitality of the kitchen.

Traditional Welsh kitchens boast utensils of earthenware and wood. Earthenware mixing bowls and pudding bowls and many sizes of wooden spoons for beating, measuring, and mixing are a part of every kitchen. As in most Celtic countries, the griddle or bakestone is the utensil most used for preparing the popular quick breads and pancakes. Some bakestones have a removable handle, others are set on legs ready to be placed over an open hearth fire. Many homes still take pride in their home-baked breads and ancient stone ovens that result in crispy-crusted bread are still widely used.[5]

The area of the kitchen called the scullery includes the sink for washing and the shelves where dishes, pots, and pans are stored. Storage shelves may be openly displayed or covered with curtains. Perishable foods are stored in stone crocks, or in earthen cellars under the house. The week's bread may be suspended in a cage called a bread crate, hung from the ceiling and worked on pulleys. The bread is thus kept safe from animals or vermin. Sides of bacon and pieces of ham, carefully meted out for the week's meals, may also be kept in suspended cages hung from the ceiling.

Modern homes, especially those in the cities, boast electrical refrigerators and gas-heated ovens and cook tops. However, coal is still widely used in the country areas, both for heating and cooking. The thrifty no-nonsense approach that the Welsh use in every aspect of their lives, applies also to the kitchen: there is little use for frivolous gadgets or for unnecessary electrical conveniences.

FOODS COMMONLY USED

The staples of the Welsh table reflect the products of the land: pork and succulent lamb and mutton, oats and wheat for breads and cakes, local cheeses and buttermilk, homemade cider, ale and wine, locally-caught fish and seafoods, and seasonal vegetables and fruits and herbs. In poorest times, bread forms the staple food accompanied by milk or soups based on "drippings" (left-over rendered fats).[3] Meats, except on special occasions, are used thriftily, their flavour spread as far as possible in soups and stews and quick supper dishes based on breads, pancakes, or potatoes. Large cuts of meat are Sunday dinner specialties, together with two or three cooked vegetables and a slow-baked rice pudding to complete the meal. The Welsh enjoy sprightly seasoned cakes fragrant with lemon, caraway, cinnamon, and nutmeg. Wild mountain herbs such as mint, marjoram, thyme, rosemary, and wild garlic are used liberally in roasted meats, fish dishes, and casseroles as well as soups and stews.

Milk and Milk Products

Milk is considered by most Welsh to be a food and not a beverage, therefore water is commonly served with meals for children while milk is an ingredient in custards and puddings, and usually served with tea.[7] Breakfast coffee or cocoa is usually prepared liberally with milk, but the consumption of milk in the many daily cups of tea should not be underestimated. Soured milk and buttermilk are enjoyed, especially accompanied by pancakes of many kinds, potato dishes, or one of the many light supper dishes.

Wales produces and enjoys many fine local cheeses, fresh as well as aged. The most famous is Caerphilly cheese originating from Caerphilly in Glamorgan County. It is a moist mild cheese good both for eating and cooking.

Chunks of local cheese, fresh bread, and a few pickles together with a mug of ale constitute the famed PLOUGHMAN'S LUNCH, a popular meal in any pub. The well-known WELSH RAREBIT consists of cheese melted and poured over toast points then browned in a grill. Grated cheese often garnishes homemade soups and tops baked casseroles. But the most creative cheese dish of all is GLAMORGAN SAUSAGES or SELSIG MORGANNWG: a mixture of lightly-seasoned soft breadcrumbs and grated cheddar cheese bound with egg yolk, shaped like sausages, then dipped into beaten egg white and dried bread crumbs and fried to a golden crispiness. Served with creamed potatoes and peas, it is a hearty meal.[8]

Fruits and Vegetables

Fruits and vegetables are enjoyed fresh only in season. Salads of fresh vegetables are not a common part of the Welsh menu, nor are fresh fruit desserts, with the possible exception of berries. Pears, apples, and plums, as well as many types of berries: blackberries, elderberries, gooseberries, strawberries and blaeberries (similar to blueberries). Berries are served fresh, but are enjoyed still more in preserves, pastries, and desserts, where they are well-cooked and sugared.

Onions and leeks head the list of Welsh vegetables, followed very closely by potatoes – used in everything from soups and stews and the Sunday roast (TATWS RHOST) to many light supper dishes of layered potatoes, onions and bacon, even a moist potato "pastry" from which TEISEN DATWS is made: thick potato cakes cooked on the bakestone and served with butter and glasses of buttermilk. Pumpkin is a traditional Welsh favourite, pre-cooked then crumbed and fried and is also popularly cooked with mutton or spiced and baked in a pie.[5] Could it have been the early Welsh settlers who introduced pumpkin pie for Thanksgiving? Swedes (turnips), carrots, peas, and the vegetables in the cabbage family (cabbages, cauliflower, brussels sprouts), are all served well-cooked, mostly as a part of soups or stews.

Special mention should be made of CHIPS. There is scarcely a Welsh kitchen without a sturdy pot and a wire basket used especially for deep-frying potato strips called CHIPS. There is scarcely a meal served in a pub that is not accompanied by CHIPS: steak and chips, fish and chips, prawns and chips. Almost as ubiquitous are peas: considered almost as a garnish canned peas or well-cooked fresh peas nestle on plates of meat pies, casserole dishes, and quick supper dishes. A special Welsh favourite is LAVERBREAD or BARA LAWR. Called SLOKE in Scotland and Ireland, this is the fine silken seaweed, well-washed and cured (dried) and served well boiled. It can be eaten as is, or mixed with fine oatmeal and fried into cakes for breakfast; used as an appetizer; or made into a soup.[5,9] It is said to be an acquired taste that can become "a passion."[5]

Meats and Alternates

Pork, lamb, mutton, beef, and chicken as well as the occasional rabbit or rook, supply meat for the Welsh table. Great use is made of every part of the animal for soups, sausages, stews, and ground meat mixtures, and probably most popular of all is the sweet smoky flavour of ham and bacon. In fact, bacon is a staple of the Welsh kitchen and it not only forms the base of many quick supper dishes, it is often used as a garnish for dishes such as CARDIGANSHIRE SAVOURIES or TOCYN Y CARDI (flour and oat cakes fried in bacon fat and garnished with sliced tomatoes and rashers of bacon); as a flavouring for soups such as LEEK AND POTATO SOUP or SWP CENNIN A THATWS and the delicious BRITHYLL A CHIG

MOCH or trout laid and topped with bacon then oven-baked (known as TRUITES AU LARD in Brittany).[5]

Large roasts of meat are saved for Sunday dinner, when the roasted meat is accompanied by two or three well-cooked or roasted vegetables and the Sunday special rice pudding PWDIN REIS DYDDSUL[9] for dessert.

Pig's liver is used in many ways. The most well-known is probably in baked FAGGOTS or MOCK DUCK, called FFAGOD SIR BENFRO. Usually made around pig killing time, they are shaped into balls from a mixture of pig's liver, breadcrumbs and oatmeal, minced onions, and liberally flavoured with mace, sage, thyme, and salt and pepper. The minced balls are covered with the lacy fat-veined membrane called "pig's flead" or "caul fat" then baked in a pan till well done. They are good eaten hot or cold and are a popular dish for those carrying their lunch to work as well as those eating at home.[5]

Although special occasions may warrant a boiled ham served with parsley sauce (CIG MOCH WEDI EI FERWI A SAWS PERSLI), or Welsh salt duck with onion sauce (HWYADEN HALLT CYMREIG) or even a sage-stuffed roasted goose, - most Welsh meals contain small quantities of meats and these are carefully used to provide the most flavourful and satisfying meals.

Not to be overlooked are the fine salmon and trout in many varieties caught in local waters. Coastal areas, such as Swansea, are especially noted for their fine fresh seafood and Welsh enjoy a variety of clams, cockles, prawns, shrimp, mussels, and scallops. Herrings are used for sousing (pickling) and served in casseroles with potatoes for supper. Oyster soup, cockle cakes and cockle pie, potted herrings: baked with seasonings then pounded to a paste and served cold with oatcakes or toast, and trout baked with bacon are popular dishes. EOG RHOST (roast salmon) is a fine example of the Welsh sense of seasoning: nutmeg, cloves, and bay leaves spread with butter are rubbed and placed in the salmon cavity and it is roasted covered in paper or foil then served with the pan juices blended with more butter, thin orange and lemon slices, and a splash of vinegar. Another example of the Welsh touch with herbs and spices is to be seen in GRANVILLE SAUCE: the frequent accompaniment with fish made with sherry, pounded anchovies, pepper, nutmeg, and mace all smoothed into a creamy base of cream, flour, and butter.[5]

Beans are not a frequent part of the Welsh menu, but dried peas are. These are cooked in a cloth bag so that they swell and form a firm mold which is then served as a side dish with dinner (similar to the English PEASE PORRIDGE).[7]

Eggs may form part of a hearty breakfast menu, but more frequently are served as part of light supper: fried eggs, omelets, or pancakes.

Breads and Cereals
Bread is an important part of every meal: homemade bread with

homemade soup is considered a hearty meal. Bread forms the staple of the diet for rich or poor. Fine breads are made from white wheat flour or whole meal (whole wheat or whole grain), while many types of flat thin "cakes" are made from oats. The Welsh prefer the fine oatmeal rather than the rolled or flaked oakmeal popular in Canada and the United States. Fine oatmeal is also used to thicken soups, sauces, and stews and to coat foods for frying. Corn starch, called cornflour, is used to thicken puddings and desserts and sometimes in baked goods.

Every Welsh cookbook has a large section devoted to breads, quick breads, biscuits, scones, and cakes of many kinds. Few, however, are rich or very sweet: the simple natural flavours are most enjoyed and spices such as cinnamon, nutmeg, and ginger are widely used, while raisins, currants and caraway seeds dot and flavour many breads and cakes. Fancy baking is traditionally done on Saturdays so that there will always be something especially nice to serve at tea on Sunday afternoons.[7] Pancakes, crumpets and pikelets (variations of thin and quick breads) all prepared on the iron bakestone, are a tea-time favourite and are served with generous quantities of butter and sometimes preserves. PASTIES: savoury or fruit-filled pies and tarts are not only snacks but may also form the main part of a meal. Large pastie rounds may be oven baked or browned on a bakestone and carefully turned to brown the other side.[9] A traditional Welsh PASTIE is called TEISEN BLAT or HARVEST CAKE. This is a fruit-filled pastry but is unusual in that it is baked on a thick plate, then cut and served warm with buttermilk to drink.[5]

Fats
Lard and drippings as well as bacon fat are used to brown meats and vegetables before stewing or preparing as a soup[8] and in baking as well. Butter is used generously as a spread and for flavouring other foods from oatmeal porridge to vegetables and fish. Oil is used very little.

Sweets and Snacks
The Welsh sweet tooth is satisfied daily in the sugar taken in frequent cups of tea and in the sweet cakes and sweet breads that accompany most cups of tea. CYFLAITH or TREACLE TOFFEE is a special New Year's treat, but candies are not consumed in great amounts.

Seasonings
Welsh prefer to begin their cookery with fresh seasonal foods, adding spices and herbs in judicious but never in overpowering quantity. Ginger, nutmeg, mace, cinnamon, and cloves are the favoured spices, while sage, thyme, marjoram, parsley, mint, and wild garlic are the most used herbs. The smokiness of bacon and ham cannot be ignored as a flavour that delights the Welsh tongue, nor can the special touch of ale, cider, and red wine be ignored for they add much to treasured traditional

Welsh dishes. Currants, raisins, caraway seeds, and lemon add delicious taste and aromas to many cakes and special breads.

Beverages

Tea with milk and sugar is a meal-time and snack beverage, afternoon tea being a popular ritual in many Welsh homes. Coffee is taken rarely, mostly at breakfast if at all. Soured milk and buttermilk are preferred over plain milk as a beverage. At meals water is served and men usually drink ale.[7] Local ales, ciders, and wines are often prepared in homes. In fact, many unusual wine recipes are treasured traditions: wines prepared from elderberries, potatoes, rhubarb, oak leaves, pumpkin, beetroot, daisies, parsley, parsnip — the list seems endless.[9] Also – Ginger Beer (Diod Sinsir).

Meal Patterns and Eating Customs

The simplest and oldest traditional Welsh breakfast is a basin of FLUM-MERY: prepared from flour and milk like a soft porridge[3] or the more widely favoured bacon and eggs served with bread fried in the bacon fat till crisp. Plentiful cups of tea with milk and sugar complete the classic breakfast. Sometimes a porridge of fine oatmeal is prepared in winter and served with hot cocoa, or with coffee with milk.[7] Whatever the breakfast choice, the Welsh are seldom off to work without at least tea and bread and butter.

In some areas, businesses close between 1:00 and 2:00 P.M., when everyone goes home for the main hot meal of the day, consisting usually of fish or meat with two vegetables and a dessert of steamed or suet pudding, canned fruit with cream, trifle, or a custard. Tea with milk and sugar is taken by children and women, while most men prefer beer or ale with their meals.[7]

In the late afternoon a light quick meal, again with tea, is taken. This may be a plate of cold meats and pickles served with buttered bread, or anything cooked quickly: sausages and beans, fish and chips, warmed leftovers or sandwiches. So inconsequential is the evening meal, that many restaurants serve only the main hot meal at noon and close in the evening.[7]

Mid-morning snacks of tea with breads, pikelets, or little cakes are taken by almost everyone. This is similar to a snack time in the evening about 9:00 P.M.; when tea and something "small" is taken again. To the Welsh, tea is so satisfying that the kettle is always on, there is always a comforting cup of tea with milk and sugar available.

The Welsh prefer their foods served on individual plates. Food service is similar to the English style, with dessert eaten with a spoon and a fork.

Special Occasions

The great traditional Welsh family pride and communal interest, makes almost any occasion a special one. Helping hands are always available, whether it is for the hard work of harvesting, sadness of funerals, or the joy of weddings. TEISEN BLAT, fruit-filled PASTIES baked on old heavy China plates and traditionally served up in large quantities together with fresh cool buttermilk make all work seem lighter. When a neighbourhood wedding is in the offing, neighbours and relatives help with the preparations – pig-killing, fowl-plucking – and delicious smells from the many spiced breads and cakes fill the air. Light fingers of sponge cake, often tied in bundles with black ribbons, would be baked for funerals together with several caraway seed cakes, BARA CARAWE, all to be eaten with sips of wine or sherry for the mourners.[5]

The national holiday of Wales, the *Eisteddfod,* is a merry week-long celebration of what the Welsh hold dearest – music and poetry. To sustain the singers and orators, ale, cider, and wine accompany the many savoury PASTIES, especially KATT PIE, made from ground spiced mutton and currants, and the TREACLE TOFFEE.

Many other special foods help to mark special days on the Welsh calendar. When everyone gathers together to help shear the sheep, CACEN GNEIFO (also called SHEARING CAKE) is made in quantity. This dark cake is made with brown sugar and flavoured with nutmeg and caraway seeds. On All Hallow's Eve, October 31, it is traditional for costumed young men to go house to house collecting small gifts, and children chant old rhymes and are given fresh fruits. Eating oatcakes (BARA CEIRCH) near a blazing bonfire is the traditional way to celebrate May Day Eve, St. John's Eve and All Hallow's Eve. The purpose of the bonfire is to drive away all evil spirits. Various area specialties are prepared to help celebrate these occasions. Sometimes a meat and vegetable stew is shared after the huge bonfire, or a special sweet dish called WHIPOD, made of dried fruits, rice and white bread, would be enjoyed by all. Whatever the specialty, it would be followed by beer and dancing.[5]

The Feast of Epiphany or Twelfth Night is a more festive occasion than Christmas, which is usually observed quietly as a religious day. The Twelfth Night festivities are highlighted by the serving of a roast dinner, such as stuffed goose, two or three vegetables, and steamed pudding for dessert. The special TWELFTH NIGHT CAKE is a rich mellow fruitcake topped with almond paste and thick white frosting – and hidden somewhere in its fruity sweetness is a bean or pea, which is supposed to bring good luck to the finder.[5] An ancient Christmas tradition still followed in some homes is *Plygain,* a Christmas morning service held between 3:00 and 6:00 A.M., usually preceded by decorating the house, making TREACLE TOFFEE, or playing card games in between refreshments of various buttered cakes, PIKELETS, and tea. The *Plygain* ends about 8:00 A.M. with carol singing and feasting. The special foods enjoyed at this time include WELSH RAREBIT and ale, assorted cold meats and breads, BREWIS and other local specialties or family favourites.

New Year's is celebrated in some areas by young boys calling on houses carrying skewered apples or oranges gaily decorated with mistletoe and holly – said to be symbolic of fruitfulness in the coming year. Coins and gifts of little cookies called CALENNIG are presented to the boys after they offer verses. TREACLE TOFFEE (CYFLAITH) is the traditional New Year's sweet and everyone is greeted with: "Blwyddyn Newydd Dda!" (Happy New Year!).

Heralding spring, the fifth Sunday of Lent is called Pea Sunday (*Sul-y-pys*) and roasted peas or a soup made of dried peas form the traditional fare. Roasted lamb, chickens, and coloured eggs help celebrate Easter. Courtship is another special time in Welsh life that carries its own special traditions and superstitions. Most famous of all are the Welsh love spoons. It is customary for a young man to carve a wooden spoon with suitable symbols and designs to be presented to the girl he wishes to court. Some girls collected more than one, keeping them as treasured heirlooms, while others were lucky to have just one. Today these spoons are considered museum pieces for there are few carvers left.[9] Pricking a clean-picked blade bone of mutton nine times (a magical Welsh number) was used by girls to divine their future husbands – especially on the night of All Hallow's Eve. Similarly, stored onions would be named after suitable bachelors: the first one to sprout would become the loved one, while those that refused to sprout were designated as future bachelors! Various love potions presumed to increase the ardour of a loved one were also used. One of these was a mysterious mixture of herbs and wines placed into a drinking horn together with small crumbs of dough preserved from nine bakings. It was believed that this drink offered to a loved one would ignite the fires of passion.[5]

FIFTY-ONE

West Indian

"All mixed up and born in the islands . . ."[1] This phrase refers to one definition of the term "Creole." But it could so easily refer to the complex diversity that is the West Indies of today.

The West Indies are also known by two other names: the Greater and Lesser Antilles and the Caribbean Islands. Historically they have shared the same periods of conquest, piracy, oppression, slavery, and revolution. They also share incredibly beautiful landscapes of mountains, plains, and beaches and a remarkably stable climate warmed by the tropical sun and tempered by the easterly trade winds. It is these trade winds that are believed to have brought the many seeds, spores, and coconuts to the islands' fertile soils.[2] And it is these same trade winds that brought the European explorers.

Christopher Columbus landed on these islands in 1492. The 2,600-mile arc of islands enclosing the Caribbean Sea and arching outward to the Atlantic Ocean must have seemed like paradise itself to the European explorers. The beauty of the landscape and the pleasantness of the climate was marred only by the group of warring native peoples whom the Spanish called the Caribs, from the Spanish word meaning "cannibal." However the other native peoples, the Arawaks and the Ciboney, were peaceful and hospitable. They introduced the Europeans to their fruits: avocado, papaya, guava, pineapple, as well as their staple food crops of corn and cassava root. They taught the Europeans how to smoke tobacco and how to sleep in a hammock.[3] They even taught them a delicious way of cooking fish and fowl by coating with wet mud and burying them in hot embers (later to be known as clay-baking) and a method of cooking meat with a smoky flavour by laying thin strips of meat over green boughs placed atop burning embers.[1] The early settlers called this latter method of cookery, to *boucan*, while the Arawaks themselves called it *barbacoa*. From this, much later, came the term "buccaneer," identifying the men who sustained themselves by preparing their meats in this way.[1]

In spite of the sad fact that almost all strains of the original inhabitants of the West Indies today are almost extinct, their important culinary contribution to the culture of the islands cannot be forgotten because it is ever-present. Aside from the fruits and vegetables – and the distinctions between those that are edible and those that are poisonous – the smoking of tobacco and the use of hammocks as well as clay-baking and barbecueing, the Indians (as the Europeans called them) left two other important contributions. They taught the settlers how to make CASSAVA BREAD and PEPPER-POT. Presently, the few living Indians rely on these as their staples.[1]

Because the raw juice of the bitter cassava root is poisonous (containing prussic acid), the root is prepared for use by first grating then squeezing to extract the juice. The last moisture is removed by spreading the grated mixture to dry in the sun. From this, a coarse meal is prepared which, when mixed with water and "baked" on a metal griddle produces a satisfying crusty bread enjoyed to this very day. PEPPER-POT is also a sustaining food, especially important to the poorer people. A huge pot is kept simmering over coals; perhaps the simplest method of food preservation long before the development of refrigeration and easier than salting, drying, or smoking. Any available foods including meats, fish or fowl and a variety of vegetables plus water could be added to the constantly simmering PEPPER-POT. But most important was the seasoning of peppers and CASSAREEP: the boiled juice from the cassava root lending a peculiar bittersweet flavour.[1] Always the contents of the pot would be eaten in little amounts so as to leave a continuing source of food. In fact "a good pepper-pot is so highly valued that it may be willed from one generation to another."[2]

The Spanish were the first explorers and settlers in the area of the West Indies and they took over the islands of the Arawaks – Cuba, Hispaniola, Puerto Rico and Jamaica – ostensibly looking for gold.[3] The Papal Donation of 1493 allocated to Spain all territories (land and sea) west of a boundary set in the mid-Atlantic Ocean.[4] This did not last long. By the 1500s piracy was common, and France and England disputed the Papal rights coinciding with the decline in the Spanish marine powers.[4] The Netherlands allied themselves with the French and English naval powers against the Spanish, and even set up the Dutch West India Company in 1621. The Dutch were seeking not gold but salt. Portugal's union with Spain in 1580 had deprived the Dutch of the use of Portuguese sources of the salt vital for their fisheries and so an alternative source had to be found: the Dutch discovered the Araya saltpans of Venezuela and later those in Curaçao.[4] In the 1600s, the French settled in Martinique,

Guadeloupe, and Grenada.[3] The British acquired Jamaica around 1658 by defeating the bucanneers who had made it their headquarters; living on wild pigs and selling hides and smoked meats (BOUCAN) to passing ships and adding piracy for greater profits.[3]

Another group of people came to the West Indies in the 1600s. These were Sephardic Jews seeking to escape the Inquisitions of both Spain and Portugal and bringing with them some of the techniques of sugar processing and the capital necessary to establish the industry.[6] Many came from Brazil in the early 1600s; they had used their expertise and wealth to increase sugar production in Brazil, then under Dutch control, but when the Jews were pressed to become "new Christians" they moved northward to Barbados, Jamaica, and Nevis.[6] Ancient tombstones found on the islands testify to the early Jewish settlers.

Those who had settled on the lands – British, Spanish, Dutch, and French – all sought profitable crops that could be exported and so began the trade of cacao, cotton, coffee, tobacco, and sugar. It did not take long for the settlers to realize that their most profitable crop was sugar. It could be easily shipped (requiring no special care to prevent spoilage), it was a great luxury to the European market accustomed mainly to honey as a sweetener, and, most important, several crops a year could be harvested from the same piece of land.[3]

The first sugar plantation workers were Europeans hired as indentured labourers. This meant that they agreed to work for a given time period and then were given small areas of land of their own. But when sugar replaced tobacco as the important crop, the small land holders were literally wiped out. As using indentured workers became unfeasible, the growing shortage of labour and the huge sugar profits started a new trade – slavery. From 1698 onwards, more than forty English slave-trading companies were established on the west coast of Africa.[3]

It is important to note that the slaves were brought to the trading companies from many different areas of Africa.[2,4] Some masters favoured Africans from certain areas because of their purported characteristics. For example, the Mandingoes were said to be the most gentle, but other Africans included the Yorubas from West Nigeria, the Ashanti and Fanti from the Gold Coast, and the Ibos and Dahomians.[2] Although they shared the fact that they were Africans, they were forced to subdue their native cultures and, bonded by their common plight of slavery, they developed their own customs and language under the West Indian conditions.[4]

The slaves learned foreign languages rapidly and made their own adaptations of mixtures of languages. Many, forbidden to converse while working, learned to gossip while singing and thus were born the enchanting words and rhythms of calypso.[5]

They built their own homes from mud-plastered timber or woven leaves and grass. On tiny plots of land near their homes they carefully cultivated yams, sweet potatoes, and other vegetables and prepared dishes based on these and flavoured with bits of salt meat or salt fish supplied to them by their masters.[3] Often they were fed foods that were rejected by their masters, but often a taste from "home" could be evoked by preparing dishes from the plants of okra, callaloo, taro, and akee, that they had brought with them from Africa.[1] To make these simple foods more palatable, they made clever use of natural herbs and pungent spices, much as they had done in their homeland.

The slave and sugar trade was also called "the triangular trade."[3] The West Indies shipped mostly sugar but also cotton and tobacco to the British Isles. From the British Isles went ships carrying iron tools, kitchen utensils, and cutlery as well as wool and cotton cloths to be used for barter in return for the human cargo of slaves at the ports in West Africa. Ships laden with their unhappy cargo made for their markets both in the West Indies and also South America (particularly in Brazil where the Africans were to play a key role in the developing Brazilian cuisine.) The completion of the triangular voyage for one ship from the West Indies to the British Isles and then to Africa and finally back to the West Indies took twelve months.[3]

Wars and disputes continued among the marine powers, all vying for territories and hoped-for riches. Blockades often prevented the shipment of salt cod from the New England States in exchange for rum and molasses from the West Indies, so other foods had to be found to feed the slaves. Young akee trees were brought from West Africa, breadfruit trees from Tahiti (it was breadfruit trees that the much-maligned Captain Bligh on the *Bounty* was attempting to save with rations of the crew's water[1]), and mangoes from Asia.[3] For almost two hundred years, despite the human suffering involved, the slave and sugar trade was ruthlessly pursued so that the words, West Indies, sugar, and slaves became synonymous.[2]

However, changes came. Two seemingly unrelated occurrences were destined to change both "sugar" and "slavery" and thus, inevitably, the West Indies. In 1756, the arrival of the first missionaries from Germany (Moravian Protestants) was met by strong opposition from the plantation owners. With good reason: they feared the education of their slaves might lead to intermarriage and the consequences of being taught the precept that "all men are equal."[3]

At about the same time a German scientist, Marggraf, discovered sugar in beet juice and by the end of the 1700s many European countries unable to grow sugar cane were busily producing their own sugar from beets which could be easily grown.[1]

The combination of competition in sugar manufacturing and revolution among the slaves led, in 1772 in England, to the pronouncement that "a slave becomes free the moment he sets foot on English soil."[3] Other nations followed suit with the Portuguese, said to have been the first in the slave trade,[3] being the last in 1836 to put a legal end to it.[3] But the end of slavery was not an end to misery. Both the English and the Dutch seemed unprepared for the handling of the freed slaves and seemed to view the Black people's slavery as being synonymous with inferiority.[2] Spanish slaves, upon being freed, were treated generally as people who had suffered; while the French treated the freed slaves slightly less well than the Spanish but better than either the English or the Dutch.[2]

Although the general economy of the West Indies had slowed, the huge plantations still had nonetheless to be worked and labour had to be found. Many freed slaves became small independent farmers with fruits and vegetables as their produce. The answer was found in bringing in Chinese and East Indians as indentured servants, and they in turn brought with them their culture and customs and food preferences. The Chinese planted vegetables and the East Indians planted rice crops. Both groups came to be respected members of the community, many ending up as merchants and business people.[1,4]

Many East Indians settled in Trinidad and Tobago, introducing their flat bread called ROTI, and a taste for blended spices called "curry."[1] As the foods and tastes spread, the Dutch called it *kerry*, while the French gave it the name *colombo*; all agreeing that the perspiration caused by eating the spicy hot curries, caused them to feel cooler.[1]

The 1800s and early 1900s in the West Indies saw the development of racial stereotypes that persist in many areas to the present time: Africans showing disdain for the East Indians and Chinese arriving to undertake what they still consider to be slave labour. The close family life of these groups and their distinctive customs helped to intensify their separateness.[4] But more and more, children went to schools, women minded their homes and the men went to work: neither the African nor the European pattern of society was distinct, instead a loose family structure developed, often not even bound by formal marriage contracts.[4]

The 1930s witnessed a sudden blossoming in West Indian identity. Increase in population led to expansion of social services, growth of cultural groups, trade unions and political parties, and the surge for self-government.[4,6] Overpopulation in some islands led to emigration, causing, unfortunately, a loss of the most skilled. And during the Second World War when the United States used the West Indies as military bases, the inhabitants opened their eyes to higher living standards and labour-saving devices, all of which reinforced the need for development and change.[4]

Currently, the sovereign units in the West Indies include the following independent countries: Cuba; Hispaniola, which includes Haiti and the Dominican Republic; Jamaica, Trinidad and Tobago (as one area). The British West Indies include: Antigua; Bahamas; Barbados; Cayman Islands; St. Vincent; Virgin Islands; Grenada; Monserrat; St. Kitts; Nevis; and Anguilla; St. Lucia; the Turks; and Carcos. Netherlands Antilles include: Aruba; Curaçao; Bonaire; Saba; St. Eustatius; and part of St. Martin. Those under United States influence include: Puerto Rico and the Virgin Islands and other small areas.[7] Guadeloupe, Marie Galante, and Martinique remain strongly under French influence.

Although other islands can be clearly seen on the horizon from almost any one of the West Indian Islands, it is a curious phenomenon that the ties have in the past always been closer to the European country of influence rather than to a nearby island. A peculiar state of insularism and self-imposed isolationism still strongly persists.[2,6,7] Thus the culture, political ties, and even the food preferences and the language can be readily predicted by understanding the past ties of the island.

The diversity of the islands is further pointed out by the many religions, including those of the Muslim faith, Christians, Sephardic Jews and many varieties of primitive cults.[4] Many adapted form and rituals from Christianity to their own African-born religions and customs and so found solace for their woes.[2]

The population is diverse with black Africans dominating, followed by Afro-Europeans who are called "brown" or "coloured" while both these groups together may be called "creole."[4] The smaller minorities of Amerinds, Asians, and Europeans are "white": only in Puerto Rico is the majority of the population white (80 per cent) and the minority "non-white" (20 per cent).[4] Status is determined by material possessions and by colour and language.[4,7] The closer the language is to "white," the higher the status.[7]

Four hundred years of human influx, blending a diversity of colours, languages, customs, religions, and cultures and suffering a common history of oppression, slavery, and revolution has created a unique and interesting area. Diversified though their people and their pasts may be, there is a new pride in local culture and a movement towards unifying the complex elements of the West Indies. This is reflected in the establishment in 1957 of the West Indian Federation.[6] These include the proof that all peoples are capable of assuming all positions and class levels in human society regardless of colour, race or religion, and the sense that while a nation be small nonetheless its independence is important to its image and future.[4] It is further an example of each of the peoples adding their foods and food customs to those already established. Together with the influences of the early Amerinds, then the Europeans and the Africans, Chinese, and the East Indians, still another group is adding its influence: the tourists.[1] And it is the combination of the desire of tourists to taste "the real Caribbean flavours" and the pride of the West Indians themselves, regardless of traditional imperial ties, that causes the flowering and promotes the greatest appreciation of the West Indian cuisine.

Home Life and Facilities
Although there is a rapidly growing movement in all the islands to improve

living conditions, "most West Indians can afford only the meanest accommodations"[6] and status is undeniably linked to colour, with black being synonymous with being poor.[6] Lower classes tend to be matriarchal, middle classes (mostly the "coloured") tend to be patriarchal and the upper classes "agnostic and scientific."[6] Poverty, poor health, lack of medical services, and lack of sanitation are almost constant neighbours to examples of luxuriant living. But the fertile soil and the benevolent climate help to alleviate some hardships.

Most homes are wooden structures with galvanized metal roofs. Cooking and toilet facilities are usually separate from the main dwelling. Small coal pots and boards nailed between trees may serve as cooking and working areas. Most kitchens have the necessary tools for making cassava bread: a grater, and sifter, cloth and metal griddle for cooking. And most homes, too, depending on the area and the circumstances, will have a large heavy pot for the PEPPER-POT.[1,4] A treasured implement is the BATON LELE: an African swizzle stick used deftly as a whisk for beating and whipping.[1] The growing middle class is enjoying increasingly better accommodations and facilities, and in many areas modern supermarkets have an array of convenience foods as well as quality local produce.

In Puerto Rico, for example, the traditional kitchen stove will be shaped like a built-in box, made of cement, tiles, or brick with grates on top for cooking and using charcoal as the fuel. This is called the FOGÓN. Upper class homes will have a FOGÓN with a decorated ceramic tile and a hood above to collect smoke and odours and direct them through a chimney to the outdoors. Traditional kitchen utensils include a RALLO: a grater used especially for coconut; PILÓN Y MACETA: mortar and pestle to grind spices; CALDERO: a large heavy pot to cook rice; and HABICHUELAS GUISADAS: an aluminum covered kettle used to cook legumes. The latter two implements are indispensable for Puerto Rico's staples: rice and beans.[8] Although the implements may be similar from island to island, each area in the West Indies has its own name for each.

FOODS COMMONLY USED

Again, there may be different names used in different areas, but the staple foods of the West Indies bear a striking similarity from island to island.[1] The naturally grown fruits and vegetables, together with those brought and introduced by the waves of immigrants, blend together to form the culinary pattern. CASSAVA BREAD and PEPPER-POT, introduced by the earliest inhabitants, continue to form the staples of the poorer classes, especially in the south and southeastern areas of the West Indies. SALT BEEF, SALT PORK, and SALT FISH are widely used[9] and help to add needed protein to a dietary largely dependent on root and starchy vegetables such as cassava, taro, plantains, many varieties of squashes, yams, sweet potatoes, corn, and okra and a variety of greens.[1] Meats are added by those who can afford them, but fish does not play a large or important part in the cuisine.[1] Another important staple combination is beans and rice: the Jamaicans may call beans peas and cook a dish with coconut milk and red beans; to the Cubans black beans and rice are a specialty; and the Haitians cook a combination of local black mushrooms, rice, and lima beans; while the Puerto Ricans sauté their rice in hot fat and serve it with beans or peas such as cow peas, chick peas, or pigeon peas. However, for the Puerto Ricans, red or kidney beans are the favourites. Most popular beverages include cold fruit drinks of many types, while coffee with hot milk or hot chocolate are favoured for breakfasts. Tea is popular in the areas of English influence. Rum is the alcoholic beverage of the Islands. Desserts based on fruits, but especially coconut and bananas in many different forms, are popular everywhere.[9,1]

Milk and Milk Products
Milk as a beverage is not widely used in the West Indies, but canned evaporated milk or canned condensed milk is used in cooking and mostly for desserts, confections, and as hot milk in coffee or hot chocolate. Imported Dutch cheeses are used in the Islands of Dutch influence, French cheeses are preferred in the Islands of French influence, but there is little dairy product produced locally.

Fruits and Vegetables
All West Indians enjoy an abundant variety of native fruits, many unknown in other areas because of their short season, perishability and difficulty in transporting and storing. The more familiar fruits include: pineapples, coconut, guavas, bananas, mangoes, papayas, oranges, grapefruit, and limes. Others include: tamarind, soursop, otaheite, gooseberry, pomegranates, tangelo, ugli, star apple, passion fruit, cherimoya, hog plum, cocoplum, granadilla, sugar apple, and genip. Unusual as many of these are, they are catalogued as to nutrient composition by the Caribbean Food and Nutrition Institute in their pamphlet.[10] It should be noted that many of these fruits are not only used ripe but are also prepared while in their green state and often cooked as a vegetable. Papaya and mango are both used in their green state, cherished for their tart flavour, but also for the enzymes they contain that are known to tenderize meats.[1] Many fruits are eaten fresh while others may be used as preserves, made into many types of refreshing drinks, or prepared as fruit sherbets, or ice creams. Starchy fruits, roots, and tubers commonly form the main part of many meals and these include: breadfruit, plantains, taro (also called COCO or DASHEEN), yams, sweet potatoes, Irish potatoes,

cassava, yambean and yautia.[10] Squashes include those commonly known in temperate climates, such as pumpkin, but also others, such as calabaza, christophene, or chayote. Greens are also used: taro leaves, turnip and beet tops, mustard greens, endive, radish leaves. Akee is another vegetable-fruit frequently forming part of a main dish, while okra, an African favourite, is also used widely.

Most of the starchy roots and tubers and green fruits can be used in a variety of ways: boiling, mashing, frying, or made into specialty dishes. Corn is frequently prepared into a thick pudding similar to the Romanian MAMALIGA or the Italian POLENTA, only here it is called FUNCHI or FUNGEE. Curaçao is famed for its FUNCHI served with FISH CHOWDER. Other areas commonly serve okra plus FUNCHI and it is called COO-COO. Okra cooked with mashed plantains is called FOO-FOO.[1] FUNCHI, COO-COO and FOO-FOO are West Indian dishes originating in Africa.[1] Plantains too, enjoy great popularity as thinly fried crisp plantain chips, as MOFONGO, the Puerto Rican appetizer made by mixing ripe fried plantains with garlic and pork cracklings and spreading the mixture on bread.[1] Garlic, onions, scallions, leeks, avocados, LEREN (a root vegetable with a corn flavour), red peppers and green peppers, eggplant, tomatoes and cucumbers round out the list of widely used vegetables. Vegetables are seldom served raw or as salads; they are cooked as vegetable main dishes with highly seasoned sauces or have their flavour enhanced by the use of small amounts of salt meat or salt fish. Soups and stews also make use of well-cooked vegetables.[9,8]

Meats and Alternates
Although vegetables are cooked and eaten in common ways (though sometimes with different names throughout the West Indies[1]), the preparation and eating of meats differs by technique, climate, and influences of the European powers. It was the Spanish-speaking Islands that early in history imported cattle, horses, pigs, and sheep from Spain, and to this day, these same islands use more beef dishes than the others.[1] PICADILLO, ROPA VIEJA, and SANCOCHO are the classic dishes of the Spanish-speaking islands, but so too are LECHON ASADA: spit-roasted young pigs; CHICHARRONES: pork cracklings served as snacks; and PASTELES: meat mixtures wrapped in plantain leaves then steamed.[1]

Guadeloupe and Martinique favour the flavours of sheep and lamb, probably a preference inherited from Algeria via France. Surely their MECHOUI; spit-roasted sheep, points to indisputable Algerian influence.[1] Another French-influenced specialty is PÂTÉ EN POT: finely chopped sheep and lamb parts cooked to form a thick, rich soup generously seasoned with garlic and hot peppers and a whiff of cloves, thyme, bay leaf, and celery. Rich as this dish may be, it is usually served as the first course of a dinner, probably preceding a main course of roast mutton or lamb.

Barbados is often called "little England" and many English customs persist unchanged from the mother country. However, some acknowledgement to West Indian food culture may be noted in the use of rum as a meat marinade, and the festive CONKIES, similar to PASTELES, banana-leaf-wrapped meat mixture steamed before eating. Roast pork, roast lamb, and roast fowl are sure to grace the Sunday or festive dinner table.

The Dutch-owned islands favour two specialties, STOBÁ: a stew made from goat or lamb, well-seasoned with garlic, peppers, and spices, and the showy KESHY YENA: a scooped-out whole Edam cheese refilled with a mixture of chopped cheese, mixed beef, olives, onions, and tomatoes, all oven baked.

The PEPPER-POT of the more southern islands may be a blend of any available meats.

Although meats may be scarce on the menu of the poorer peoples, they are prepared as regional specialties and the favourite meats used include: beef, pork, chicken, duck, goat or kid, rabbit. The offals and variety meats of all types are carefully utilized in minced dishes, sausages and in soups and stews. Many areas consider kid and rabbit as special delicacies, while curried goat is a particular favourite in Jamaica.

While a glance at the map would indicate that fish and seafood must have an important place on the West Indian menu, the facts are otherwise. Lacking a history or tradition of seafaring or fishing, most West Indians are better suited to farming. Thus it is not surprising that the fishing industry is only carried out on a small and local scale. The lack of proper transportation, storage, and packing facilities aggravates the situation. Probably more fish and seafood is consumed by tourists than by local populace.[1]

Dating back to sugar and slave trade days, salt cod or baccalao is widely used and very popular. Mixtures of flour batter or batters made with any of the starchy vegetables plus flaked salt cod are prepared by frying in small patties. These are called STAMP and GO in Jamaica; MARINADES in Haiti; CODFISH CAKES in Barbados; ACRATS DE MORUE in Guadeloupe and Martinique; BACALAITOS in Puerto Rico and ACCRA in Trinidad.[9] Another favourite is conch (pronounced conk) and called by the Carib name: LAMBI or LAMBIE; by the Spanish name: CONCHA; or by the French name: CONQUE. By whatever name, the large white fleshy mollusc is first pounded then marinated to tenderize before cooking in soups or stews or serving cooked but chilled in salads.[9] The third most popular fish dish could be ESCABECHE: prepared by pouring a tangy dressing of oil, vinegar or lime juice and spices over pieces of grilled or fried fish. This may be eaten hot or cold and keeps well.[1] Fish chowders usually differ from the customary flavour because they are often prepared with coconut milk.[1]

Other available fish and seafood include: snapper, grouper, kingfish,

Caribbean dolphin (not related to the mammal type), Spanish mackerel, sea eggs, green turtles, Caribbean lobster and shrimp. Also popular are sea crabs and land crabs. These are usually prepared by steaming or boiling then removing the flesh and preparing it as a stuffing with crumbs and seasonings, served in the crab backs.[1]

Probably the most important protein source, and the most widely used, is legumes: lima beans, black beans, green beans, cow peas, chick peas, pigeon peas, all usually prepared from the dried legumes, and most frequently served together with rice – in many homes more of a staple than bread. Many soups are also based on legumes.

Eggs are not abundant because of low local production, but are used when available, baked or scrambled, or most frequently as omelets or TORTILLAS mixed with vegetables.[8]

Breads and Cereals

Rice as served with beans, breads made from cassava and wheat flours, cornmeal, served as FUNCHI or FUNGEE, provide the main sources of cereal staples. Many varieties of other breads such as banana bread, corn bread, coconut bread are used. White, brown and rye breads are also prepared but not as widely used by the populace as by the tourists. Cassava bread, rice with beans and peas and cornmeal pudding (FUNCHI) remain the West Indian bread and cereal staples.

Fats

Fried foods of all kinds are very popular, particularly those made from starchy vegetables into patties, fritters, and cakes. Lard is used most frequently for deep-frying but many seed and vegetable oils as well as margarine are also available. Butter is used at the table and for special baked goods, while GHEE (clarified butter) is a favoured fat used by the Muslims (East Indians). Jamaicans use coconut oil for sautéeing; French-speaking islands (e.g. Haiti) prefer butter and olive oil.[1]

Sweets and Snacks

Sweetened fruit drinks, icy fruit desserts, such as sherbets and ice creams, and many mousses, soufflés, custards, and flans use sugar and fruit as their base. Sweet confections made from sugar and coconut are traditional. Fresh fruits in combination are served frequently. Citron, cocoplum, guava, bitter orange, and other fruits are especially used in sweet preserves and jams. Pound cakes, simple light sponge, cakes, and caramel baked custards, called FLANS, are especially popular in the Spanish-speaking islands.[8] Puddings and desserts are also made from pumpkin, sweet potatoes, and rice. Brown sugar is commonly used.[11]

Snack foods are most likely to be nibbles in a great variety of crisply fried savoury treats: plantain chips, fried corn sticks (SURULLITOS), and the variety of East Indian fried vegetable specialties often sold by street vendors, especially in Trinidad: PALOURI, BARAS, KACHOURI, and BAIGANI (all vegetable fritters dipped in batter and fried crisply.)[1]

Seasonings

Although the Africans brought with them a taste preference for spicy hot sauces to add to their mild COO-COO and FOO-FOO and FUNCHI, the Amerinds also enjoy the use of spices. The East Indians added the taste for blended seasonings called curries, and while these became a favourite, most West Indians prefer to buy blended curry powder rather than crush and grind their own blends as the East Indians do so skilfully.[1] In the Spanish-speaking countries the basic sauce that finds its way to many dishes and adds its own distinct flavour and aroma is the SOFRITO: a highly-seasoned thick sauce based on tomatoes, garlic, onions, and peppers. Two other important ingredients in the SOFRITO, adding to its distinctiveness, are cilantro (also called Chinese parsley or coriander) and annatto seeds. In fact, cooking of the annatto seeds in lard to make a reddish-orange paste serves as a base for many dishes.[1,9] Annatto seeds are called *achiote* on the Spanish Islands. Annatto seeds or *achiote* were used by the Amerinds, the Caribs, the Ciboney, and the Arawaks to anoint and colour their naked bodies as a protection against insects and the sun.[1] Puerto Ricans also consider these seeds useful as a flavouring ingredient. ACEITE DE ACHIOTE is a preparation of annatto seeds cooked with olive oil until the colour is deep orange, then strained, cooled and bottled.[12]

The French-influenced islands of Martinique and Guadeloupe favour the seasonings of wines, herbs, and especially ONION PAYS, also called CIVE: an herb with an onion and garlic flavour.[13]

The southern islands, especially Trinidad, are strongly influenced by their large East Indian population. Thus, as in the East Indian cuisine, many fried vegetables served in appetizer form (PAKORIS), many Indian breads under the general name ROTI, and CURRIES are all popular. The distinction between "dry and wet" MASALAHS is also observed. (MASALAH is the correct East Indian term for any mixture of seasonings. See East Indian chapter.) GHEE, or clarified butter, is frequently used and adds flavour as well.

While there are definite seasoning preferences in the different areas, many seasonings are common to all. A PEPPER-POT without CASSAREEP could hardly be considered authentic. And a bottle of COUI SAUCE is as common on a West Indian table as salt and pepper is for Americans. COUI SAUCE is as often used in place of salt and pepper for it is a potent mixture of hot peppers and cassava juice. CASSAREEP and COUI are two more traditions from the Amerinds. Everywhere too, tomatoes and hot peppers are a favourite combination for many dishes. There is little doubt that the rich colour and flavour of these pungent seasonings help to make the simplest foods tasty: even meats and fish are commonly marinated with herb seasonings before cooking.[1] Ginger, cloves, allspice, and nutmeg are often included in soups, stews, meats and fish preparations. A most interesting custom is the common use of cinnamon. In fact, in many areas, cinnamon is synonymous with "spice".[1] Grenada is famed for its use of nutmeg and mace.

Beverages
While milk is not a popular or widely used beverage, the abundance of fresh and unusual fruits of the West Indies are made into a great variety of cooling fresh drinks and punches. Those that are alcoholic usually contain the local varieties (many types) of rum.[1] Puerto Rican drinks are familiar in all Spanish countries – HORCHATA: a cooling drink of milky appearance made from pressed almonds, melon seeds or sesame seeds then sweetened and diluted to taste[8]; CAFE CON LECHE: equal parts of hot milk and hot coffee, sweetened to taste, is a popular breakfast beverage, while hot chocolate is also an old favourite. In Puerto Rico, hot chocolate enriched with butter and egg yolks was a traditional hot beverage for weddings.[8] Two drinks that may be familiar only to the Spanish-speaking islands are: MABÍ, a fermented beverage prepared from a water extract of mabí bark, sweetened with brown sugar; and GARAPIÑA: a heady drink made from the peelings of pineapple allowed to ferment with water then strained, sweetened and served well chilled.[8]

The most famous beverage of all the islands is of course rum, prepared from sugar cane. What is not so well-known is the fact that rum comes in many varieties and each locality takes pride in its specialty.[1] Rum may be light, medium, or heavy. The light or clear rum is delicate in flavour and often used in cocktails, the heavy rum in strong punches, or by the experienced rum-toter. In the middle range are rums of every hue and flavour from deepest mahogany to a gentle yellowish tone. Rum is the only spirit distilled from sugar cane; most other spirits are made from grains and a few from grapes.

Meal Patterns and Eating Customs
Caribbean history produced a profound sense of isolationism in the islands that has only recently begun to withdraw its hold on the people. So it is not surprising to find that the sense of allegiance and influence of the European "owners" was felt at every level of culture and in the daily life, including at the table. If you would imagine that a Sunday Jamaican planter's table would bear some resemblance to an Englishman's Sunday table, you would be right. On both would appear an abundance of cooked vegetables together with a large roast ready for carving. But to the French mind, carving a huge roast at the table is not a part of the etiquette, and so the custom of presenting platters of sliced, ready-to-eat meats at the table will be seen in Martinique and Guadeloupe.

By simply adding the local produce, seasonings, the fresh fruit beverages, many concocted from rum, it is not difficult to conjure up

West Indian tables or eating customs. Add the colour of the tropics: clear, bright colours for tablecloths and flowers for centrepieces, the steel drums of Trinidad or the gentle calypsos of Jamaica, and you have a typical West Indian picture.

Special Occasions

People in the West Indies, like those the world over, enjoy a festive occasion. Arts and music festivals and local Independence Day festivities as well as special days to mark family and religious festivities all are characterized with feasting, drinking, and merry-making, with everyone decked out in their best clothes. Religious tolerance is characteristic of the West Indies. Many primitive cults, animism and others coexist with those professing the Muslim faith, Judaism and various forms of Christianity. Roman Catholic festive days predominate in the Spanish-speaking Islands, while the celebration of many Muslim festivities prevails in Trinidad and Tobago where approximately 36.5 per cent of the population are of Indian-Pakistan descent.[14]

Trinidad and Tobago mark Christmas with a fury of house cleaning and decorating – with balloons, tinsel, flowers and coloured electric lights – as well as by the sending of greeting cards and singing of carols. Children bursting bamboo and carbide-in-tins with loud noises and much laughter starts before Christmas and is punctuated by the friendly house-to-house visiting. While adults drink run, beer, and whisky, children enjoy sorrel, ginger beer, and sweet fruit drinks and great amounts of nuts, cakes, and fruits. The Christmas dinner is a buffet featuring chicken and turkey, ham, and goat meat.[14] New Year's in Trinidad and Tobago is a quieter festival celebrated especially the night before, which is called "Old Year's Night." An interesting tradition is to stay awake for midnight "to feel the New Year's breeze blowing in . . . ."[14] Many also attend midnight church services. During New Year's Day beach picnics are common and so are spectator sports.

The most famous festival of Trinidad and Tobago is the Carnival. Here, the cultural elements of French, African, and East Indian can be seen in the gaiest form. Held on the Monday and Tuesday preceding Ash Wednesday, Carnival is a raucous and colourful blend of brilliant costumes, steel bands, calypso singers, kalinda stickfighting, and competitions for the best of each.[14] To feed the masses of paraders, dancers, musicians and on-lookers, East Indians set up stands and booths and sell coconut confections, fruit beverages but most of all a tempting array of crisply-fried batter-dipped vegetable snacks. Other stands scoop steaming ladles of spicy stews and vegetable curries into ROTI to be gobbled up by the hungry revellers and fortify them for more singing and dancing.[1]

Easter weekend in Trinidad and Tobago also involves ancient pagan rituals and modern rites: on Good Friday it is traditional to pour the white of an egg into a glass of lukewarm water and analyze the shape formed to foretell a fortune; children make a Judas by stuffing old clothes with grass or dry leaves then beat it up. The stuffed image may also be called "Bobolee."[14] Easter Sunday may be spent as a beach day, or a time to attend a goat race or a boat race.

The Indian-Pakistanis of Trinidad and Tobago celebrate their own festivities with great colour and gaiety. These include Dewali, or the Feast of Lights, when hundreds of small *deeyahs* are prepared and lit during prayer sessions. Special baths are taken before the ceremonies, singing and dancing are interspersed with eating. Kartik Nahan is the ceremonial river-bathing for the devout, followed by eating of special foods and sweetmeats. Phhagwah or Holi Festival is characterized by the splashing of red paint (actually just a red liquid) on anyone that can be "caught." Food and drink are taken at various homes, while rhythmic pelvic dances and suggestive songs fill the merry time.[14] The whole month of Ramazan is spent with fasting from dawn to dusk with prayers, alms for the poor and visiting of friends and relatives. SAWINE is a special mix of noodles, milk, sugar, raisins, and spices. Curried chicken and goat meat eaten with PARATHAS (like pancakes) are the special foods of RAMAZAN.[14]

Many of the people of African descent in Haiti believe in ritual dancing, animal sacrifices, possession by *loas* (spirits), magical potions and charms, and Zombies or Jumbies who are characterized by their dazed expressions and servile mien. Many of the rituals are accompanied by specially-prepared offerings of food or drink.[2] Because of these traditional beliefs, a proper funeral may be of more importance to a Haitian than any material goal. Believing that a soul incorrectly mourned (and thus not freed) may remain in the area and turn evil, great care is taken to provide a good "wake." This means much loud weeping and wailing followed by the best foods and drinks available as well as songs and games so that the spirit may enjoy its last hours on earth. Traditional burials are held just before dawn with a devious route to the cemetery "to confuse the spirit about the way back to its house."[2]

Puerto Ricans celebrate their festive occasions with a Spanish touch. CENA DE NOCHEBUENA is the Christmas Eve supper served at midnight or after the family returns from mass services. It is an occasion for family gatherings and a special menu: eggnog or rich fruit punch followed by CRULLERS, HAYACAS, and TOSTONES. Then the family and relatives sit down to a festive dinner of chicken with rice or a whole ham baked in wine or stewed rice (with SOFRITO) and pigeon peas. PONQUE, nuts and raisins, coffee and more drinks will finish the great meal. Christmas Day and New Year's Day are spent quietly and are usually highlighted by a family meal of a stuffed roast turkey, a large chicken pie or a roast suckling pig. Side dishes of eggplant, plantain, or stewed beans give the meal the Puerto Rican touch for the tradition of the turkey is taken from the United States. Cakes, nuts, puddings, and flans end the meal on a sweet note and coffee marks the finish.[8] A special dish for most holidays and "essential" for feeding Christmas carolers, who go from house to house, are PASTELES: a mixture of chopped meats, raisins, almonds, and spices steamed in plantain leaves with a filling of mashed plantain or cornmeal. Fragrantly sweet and filling, PASTELES fortify the singers and traditionally must be kept hot for any hour of the evening that the singers may appear.[1] Perhaps most popular of all is the LECHÓN ASADO, or roast pig, special for Christmas but popular also for picnics or any outdoor family gathering: the blood is saved for sausage (MORCILLA) and variety meats used for a special stew, GANDINGA.[8] The pig is roasted on a pole and turned and basted with ACHIOTE, while charcoal burning over a stone bed keeps a constant heat.

Puerto Ricans also enjoy TRULLA, or Three Kings' Day, noted for singing groups that go from house to house and are greeted with the serving of SANGRÍA and appetizers, such as TOSTONES, CHICHARRONES, MORCELLA, sweets, and coffee.[8] Fish and egg dishes are most frequently eaten by the Puerto Ricans during Lent, when most devout do not eat meat. COCAS, sardine pies, fish stews and omelets as well as the more familiar vegetable dishes and rice and beans are served.

FIFTY-TWO

Yugoslavian: Croatian, Serb, Slovene, Macedonian

"Yugoslavia has six republics, five peoples, four languages, three religions, two alphabets – and one great desire for peace."[1,2]

There is scarcely a piece of writing on Yugoslavia that does not quote this country saying. For good reason. After more than 1,500 years of separate kingdoms, external dominations and influences, wars and suffering, these Southern Slavs, despite their many differences, agreed in 1929 to call the union of their lands Yugoslavia. But it was not until after the Second World War, on November 29, 1945, that the Federal Socialist Republic of Yugoslavia was proclaimed with Marshal Tito as the leader.

This picturesque, mostly mountainous land borders on seven European countries: Italy, Austria, Hungary, Romania, Albania, Greece, and Bulgaria, so it is not surprising that some of their customs and even some of their foods have crossed over into Yugoslavia. In fact, the earliest peoples in this area were first ruled by the Romans who divided the Southern Slavs into eastern and western regions. The Slovenes and the Croats in the west adopted Roman Catholicism and western ways, while the Serbs and Macedonians in the east adopted Eastern Orthodox and Moslem religions as well as traditions. In later years Turkish, Venetian, and Austro-Hungarian dominations took their turn in attempting to rule and subjugate the peoples but managed to leave only a few customs and some delicious foods.

Although all the Yugoslavian peoples are historically considered as Southern Slavs, very early in their histories they separated to become Serbians, Croatians, Slovenians, Bosnians, Montenegrins, and Macedonians – each group differing politically, religiously, culturally and even temperamentally.[2,3] A combination of favourable land and climate gives good production of grain crops, vineyards, orchards, and pasturelands for cattle and sheep. And although there have been hard times, generally food has not been a problem. Perhaps this is one of the reasons for the Yugoslavians' great enjoyment of life itself, easy living, strolling and talking, and enjoying the moment. Envious outsiders have called this the "shepherd's complex," but this easy approach to life may also be one of the reasons that in Yugoslavia, even the Communist regime differs from any other country: changes are gradual, never forceful.[1]

Strong regional differences persist, some general observations can be made. Although country festivals are still enjoyed, religious influence is diminishing, but Western clothing, business methods, skyscrapers and even cola drinks are becoming more prevalent. Yet despite the recent changes, Yugoslavia's gentle romantic soul predominates and it is still a country where "a poet can become a millionaire."[3]

Yugoslavia's six republics include (in order of size): Serbia, Croatia, Bosnia-Herzegovina, Macedonia, Slavenia, Montenegro. The five nations or peoples who formed this union are the Serbs, Croats, Slovenes, Macedonians, and Montenegrins but they speak the three languages of Serbo-Croatian, Slovenian, and Macedonian. But many people also speak Italian, Hungarian, Bulgarian, Greek, and currently English is popular and being taught in many schools. Both the Latin and Cyrillic alphabets are used, and in some areas it is even necessary to publish textbooks in three or four languages. Serbian Orthodox, Roman Catholic, and Muslim are the three principal religions, with a small minority of Jews and Protestants.[3,4,5]

Home Life and Facilities

As in most other countries, urban and rural life in Yugoslavia differ. As in most newly industrialized countries, the flow of people to the cities makes apartments scarce, and most often they are small in size. Kitchens are simply a designated space with the appliances, with even the cupboards having to be added by the tenants according to their means. Refrigerators and stoves are small by American standards as well as expensive and many households simply do without. Seldom can a family afford to devote one room to only one purpose so it is not unusual for the kitchen to be set up with a cot for sleeping, while table and chairs may be a permanent part of the living-room. Where space permits, some apartments may have the typical Yugoslavian ceramic-tiled stove, called a *peć* (commonly found in country peasant homes), used for heating as well as cooking. The *peć* may use oil or coal for fuel.

Food storage is no problem in the rural areas where sheds, cold pantries or even earthen pits may be used. In the urban areas there is no problem in winter: foods are simply kept in a cool place. In summer it is seldom a problem because the people prefer to purchase their foods fresh and marketing will be done on a daily basis.

Samo posluga, literally meaning "self-service," is the name given to the supermarkets. Foods are also purchased in outdoor markets. All foods are moderately priced, being fixed by government order. Some prepared and convenience foods as well as frozen foods are making their appearance and gaining in popularity because of the many women who work and have little time for food preparation at home – and few facilities as well.

Country people moving to the cities often adjust well to their new work, but retain a yearning for their own beehives, fruit trees and fresh produce. It is not unusual to hear of a family finding a place for their own chickens, to supply fresh eggs, and a goat for milk.

Country living is simple and casual, and the food is substantial. The ceramic-tiled *peć* is the centre of country homes, a vegetable garden, beehive, fruit trees and a few animals always nearby. There are few roadside cafés for tourists and all have one thing in common: a huge charcoal stove with a spit as the feature of the open-air kitchen. Grilled foods and hearty soup-stews are the usual fare.[6,7]

FOODS COMMONLY USED

Just as the people within Yugoslavia differ, so do their foods. Most Yugoslavian specialties are either grilled or slowly cooked in big pots or casseroles. Italian, Hungarian, Romanian, Bulgarian, Greek, and Albanian dishes all find a place in Yugoslavian cuisine but the strongest overall influence is that of Turkey. Stuffed vegetable dishes, grilled meats, enjoyment of dairy foods especially, soured milk and yoghurt, and many forms of curd cheese (fresh, salted, fermented), and a taste for syrupy and honey-drenched sweets, served with strong Turkish coffee, prevails. So does a taste and capacity for wine and strong brandies – the latter often a morning eye-opener. Strong flavours predominate: garlic and onions and spicy hot pickles. Strong alcoholic drinks and seasonings notwithstanding, Yugoslavs also have a keen sense of taste and appreciation for water. (Future chlorination and fluoridation of water supplies will likely meet with strong resistance.[4])

Country foods are usually simple and may be based mainly on curds, coarse breads, made of corn or coarsely-ground wheat, fresh fruits and raw vegetables, soups based on beans or potatoes, and homemade pastries and pastas. But always cheese, breads, and hot pickles will be on the table, and always there will be homemade wine to wash it all down.[5]

Milk and Milk Products
Dairy products find a frequent place on the menu and soured milk and

curds often form the staple protein foods of those with lower incomes. Buttermilk and yoghurt are eaten with meals and as snacks. Many types of local cheeses are used but most popular are fresh, salted or fermented curd cheese, made from cow's, goat's or sheep's milk. Cheeses are used as appetizers, condiments and often in bakery. Sweet, rich cream and sour cream are frequently a finishing touch to stews and oven-baked casseroles of vegetables and meat. In fact, it is difficult to think of a Yugoslav day without some form of cheese: as appetizers, spreads for bread, in dumplings and fritters, or in cheese-filled vegetables and bakery.[5,8]

Fruits and Vegetables

With the Yugoslav's great love and appreciation of nature, it is not unusual to see their corn fields interlaced with pumpkin vines, fruit orchards buzzing with beehives, and vineyards large or small almost everywhere.

Vineyards, fruit trees, and olive groves abound, but most of all, Yugoslavia is famous for fine plums. These are dried, preserved as jams, fillings and SLATKO (cooked fruit in very heavy syrup) and fermented into plum brandy called SLIVOVITZ and KLEKOVAČA, a plum brandy flavoured with juniper berries.

Apples, pears, peaches, apricots, sweet cherries, and sour cherries, figs, melons, berries (cultivated and wild) and several varieties of nuts are all enjoyed fresh when possible. Mostly, fruits are stewed with sugar for dessert or made into preserves or brandies. Pumpkin is used as a fruit for stewing, filling for bakery, and cooked in a heavy syrup as a special treat. There are many uses also for quinces: preserves, jellies, compotes, liqueurs and even a type of quince "cheese," prepared by drying a thick quince paste and topping it with nuts.[5]

Fruit juices are very popular and form a large industry, Yugoslavia being one of the first European countries to produce on a large scale quality juices and concentrates from a great variety of crushed fruits.

Vegetables are almost as varied and abundant as fruits. They are eaten raw (especially onions, scallions, cucumbers, radishes) or in the form of spicy hot pickles or else as well-cooked ingredients of a stew or soup. Favourite vegetables vary from potatoes and cabbage (also sauerkraut) in the north, to eggplant, tomatoes and zucchini, red and yellow peppers, green beans, and always onions and garlic. In many wooded areas, wild mushrooms are collected and form the basis of many special dishes, if not the whole meal.

Meats and Alternates

Depending on the area, pork and lamb are the favoured meats, but beef, veal, and occasionally poultry are also used. Legumes are used especially in the mountain areas for soups and slowly-cooked casserole meals. Fish is used only when fresh, mostly in coastal areas. Stews and grilled meats are most popular, and a restaurant specialty almost everywhere, especially in sidewalk cafés and garden restaurants, is grilled meats served with spicy hot peppers, chopped raw onions and bread.

From the Adriatic Sea the fishermen bring swordfish, tunny, sardines, anchovies, langouste, scampi, crayfish, octopus, squid, and mussels. Salmon and trout may be caught in the lakes and rivers. Carp and pike, sturgeon and sterlet, beluga and perch are also to be found in rivers and lakes. BRODET and ALASKA ČORBA are two types of classic fish soups that may be made with several types of fish or seafood and vegetables. Fish roe may be soaked in milk and served with chopped onions and a sauce of lemon juice, paprika, and olive oil poured over. Caviar is enjoyed with chopped onions and a squeeze of fresh lemon juice. Fresh caught fish may be baked in the oven over a bed of chopped fresh vegetables or else grilled over charcoal and seasoned with olive oil and lemon juice.[2,5]

Eggs are frequently combined with pot or cream cheese and used in bakery. They are also used as a topping with cream for the famed meat and vegetable stews, and sometimes eaten by themselves.

Breads and Cereals
Bread is a staple food and to be found on every table for every meal. Wheat, corn, rye, oats, and barley are all grown in various areas and breads are made from all of the grains. Corn and wheat are mostly used. Grains are not used as porridge, but may be a part of soups and stews or fillings for vegetables or pastries.

Fats
Fats are consumed in the form of sweet and sour cream as well as many varieties of cheeses. Cooking fats include olive oil, seed and vegetable oils, butter, pork or sheep's fat.

Sweets and Snacks
Sweets are always a special treat, but exactly which sweets depends on where one is indulging. Ice cream and sherbets, syrup- and honey-soaked crisp nut pastries, thick, sweet fruit preserves all are enjoyed in Yugoslavia and in the desserts as in all other foods, the influence varies from Austro-Hungarian to Italian, Greek, and Turkish. Even street vendors in the cities tempt walkers with trays of tiny sweet pastries, and a frequent urban afternoon snack is pastries and coffee.

Seasonings
Yugoslavian foods are all richly flavoured and seasoned without timidity. Onions and garlic are used in abundance: there is even a famous casserole dish, LONAC, made with whole *heads* of garlic. Sweet and sour soups of Romanian influence, sour fermented juices like RASOL made from sauerkraut, pickles made with brine or sugar-vinegar solutions and hot

spices, and salads (often made from cold cooked vegetables), dressed with lemon juice and olive oil testify to Slavic tastes, though of varied origin. Paprika, caraway, and poppy seeds are of Hungarian influence, and grace main dishes, while sugar and honey, fruits, and cheeses, all with their own distinct flavours, form the basis for the many cakes and pastries.

Beverages
Sweet, strong Turkish coffee served in tiny cups is taken at breakfast, afternoon snack times, and after dinner. Wine is plentiful and inexpensive and accompanies lunch (the main meal) and dinner. The locally made beer, PIVO, is quite popular but not considered as good as the wines, which are drunk in quantity.[1,8] SLIVOVITZ or SLIVOVKA, the clear, potent brandy made from plums, is the national drink and not only begins and ends many meals, but also begins and ends many days.

Regional Specialties
Yugoslavia is one country about which making generalizations is difficult and often unfair because of the distinctive characteristics, traditions, and historical backgrounds peculiar to regions that were separate kingdoms for so long. These differences are not only tolerated, they are consciously preserved, even treasured.

Serbia
Serbians form the largest racial group in Yugoslavia, almost 42 per cent of the population.[4] Most are members of the Serbian Orthodox (Greek) Church, although minorities of Muslims and Protestants do exist. Centuries of almost unceasing warfare and oppression by the Ottoman Empire finally ended in 1867 with the withdrawal of the last Turkish garrisons.[5] The Republic of Serbia borders on Hungary, Romania, and Bulgaria and contains a sizable minority of Hungarians in the north and Albanians in the southwest.

Although Yugoslavians in general have a reputation for being easy going, the Serbians are especially sociable, talkative, and fun-loving. Warm-hearted hospitality is evidenced particularly in two traditions originated in Serbia and popular in nearly all of Yugoslavia. These are the customs of drinking plum brandy (called variously: RAKIJA, SLIVOVKA, SLIVOVITZ, or KLEKOVAČA) with Turkish coffee as the first "meal" of the day, and the special way of preparing the coffee – often called SERBIAN COFFEE – and the greeting of guests with SLATKO.[5]

The preparation of SLATKO is the pride of every homemaker and a measure of her prowess. The finest fruits are selected to be simmered in a thick, sweet syrup. These may include any whole perfect fruits (or attractive slices) e.g. figs, green walnuts, cherries, apricots, and many exotic preserves are made only from flower petals such as from violets, roses, and acacia – chosen both for colour and fragrance. The SLATKO is served in tiny dishes arranged on a large tray with teaspoons and glasses of fresh cold water. Guests relish the perfection of the SLATKO and enjoy its rich sweetness contrasted with sips of icy cold water. This tradition is usually followed by serving tiny cups of coffee, and is a ritual enjoyed throughout Yugoslavia.

SERBIAN COFFEE is prepared in a lidless long-handled pot called a DŽEZVA. Finely pulverized coffee, water, and sugar are measured into the DŽEZVA and brought quickly to a boil. Some water is then poured off into a demitasse cup and the mixture allowed to foam up again over high heat for only half a minute, then the amount previously poured off is added again and the coffee is ready to serve. (See also TURKISH COFFEE as prepared in Bosnia.)

Serbian cookery is generally considered to be the richest in regional specialties: cheeses and cheese dishes, fine fish specialties and highly-seasoned meats cooked in lard.[3] Not only the SLATKO and SERBIAN COFFEE, but also the custom of stirring a spoonful of rich preserves – especially plum jam – into a cold glass of water as a refreshment, is widely copied in other regions of Yugoslavia. Similarly, the rich flavours of many Serbian dishes have also found wide popularity in Romania and Bulgaria. Particular favourites are the KISELA ČORBA: a slow-simmering soup (said to be Serbia's national soup) of lamb, chicken, and chopped vegetables, thickened with rice, and finished with a mixture of egg yolks, cream, and vinegar added just before serving; and GIBANICA, a Serbian pastry made with butter-drenched layers of phyllo pastry sheets filled with a smooth mixture of cream cheese and eggs, baked till crispy golden and served in diamond cuts with fresh fruits or sweet fruit preserves.

Many Balkan and Hungarian dishes are a part of the Serbian cuisine, pork the favourite meat, lard the favoured cooking fat, and a generous hand with paprika, garlic and onions, dill and caraway much in evidence.

Serbia is also fish and cheese country. The river fishermen are called *alasi*, and they bring in quantities of fresh sturgeon, carp, pike, sterlet, sheatfish, all of which may be simply baked with lemon and butter or as KEČIGA U "PROCEPU": the cleaned fish is wrapped in willow bark, packed with river mud, then cooked slowly over charcoal embers. When the mud and bark begin to crack, the fish is considered done.[5] The ALASKA ČORBA is a medley of simmered fish and vegetables with seasonings, strained then served with big pieces of cooked fish with the broth poured over. The broth itself is finished with the eggyolk-vinegar-cream mixture.

Soft white cheeses are served as *meze* (appetizers) with thin slices of smoked beef or pork called PRŠUTA. Cream and cottage cheeses are used in bakery, in yeast buns, pastries, dumplings, fritters. In this area, the Turkish filo or phyllo or strudel pastry is called PITA and is used in endless combinations just as it is used and enjoyed elsewhere. Most cheeses in Serbia are made from sheep's milk and are named for the area in which they are produced: JAVORSKI, LIPSKI, ZLATIBORSKI. More recently, many successful imitations of other European cheeses have been made: LIPTAUR, a cream cheese flavoured with onion, caraway, and paprika; IMPERIAL, a soft cream cheese further enriched with added butter; and GERVAIS, a soft delicately-flavoured cream cheese. A typical hard cheese with a pungent odour and flavour made everywhere in Yugoslavia is KAČKAVALJ. When this cheese is young it is eaten as *meze*, as it hardens with age it may be used grated or cut in pieces, batter-dipped and deep-fried.

A special Serbian dairy product, also much enjoyed in neighbouring countries, is KAJMAK. Boiled milk is cooled in special shallow wooden bowls called KARLICE. The cooled cream is skimmed off and layered in wooden tubs called ČABRICA. The freshly made KAJMAK is eaten as a spread on breads, especially the heavy farmer's bread made with fat, flour, and yeast, called POGAČA, or the SRPSKA PROJA (Serbian cornbread) made from cornmeal, fat, eggs, and milk. This latter bread may be made daily and split when half-baked, then returned to the oven to toast. Served warm with fresh KAJMAK and sauerkraut dishes or SARMA (stuffed vine or cabbage leaves) it makes a memorable country meal. When the KAJMAK is allowed to ferment with the addition of salt, a stronger flavour develops. This aged KAJMAK is often used in combination with fresh curd and cream cheeses in many baked dishes and pastries, but most especially for the GIBANICA. Yoghurts and soured cow's milk or sheep's milk are, together with the cheeses, a daily part of the diet in Serbia. These are prepared in every home and eaten not just as part of a meal but often as a snack.

Serbian food specialties are among the most widely copied elsewhere in Yugoslavia, and among the Serbs themselves their special dishes are so loved they are even considered "fit to cure the sick."[5]

Some Serbian specialties are:

CÉVAPČIĆI: of Turkish influence: grilled meat balls

ČORBA: classic soup throughout the Balkans: a rich broth made with meat or fish plus vegetables. Just before serving, the soup is strained. The clear broth is blended with a mixture of egg yolks, cream, and vinegar and served with choice pieces of the meat or fish.

DJUVEČ: Serbian version of the Romanian GUIVETCH: a layered casserole of a variety of meats and vegetables – sometimes with added rice – cooked slowly with water and oil. The dish may have a topping of eggs and cream poured over and baked just before serving.

GURABIJE: rich honey cake cookies.

MUSAKA: relic of the Turkish occupation: a baked casserole of layered eggplant and meats richly flavoured with garlic, onions, and tomatoes, sometimes cheese.

PIHTIJE: a natural aspic prepared from simmered calves' feet. The meat and vegetables from the broth are chopped and jelled.

PITA: the thin, translucent sheets of pastry used to prepare many strudels, pies, and appetizer dishes. The PITA is brushed with melted butter and filled with any mixture of flavoured meats, fruits, pumpkin, nuts, and layered, rolled, or folded, then baked.

PLJESKAVICE: grilled meat patties, often in oval or finger shapes.

PODVARAK: cooked meats served with a specially-prepared sauerkraut, made by simmering the kraut with onions then smothering the mixture with meat drippings and baking slowly in the oven till the mixture has caramelized throughout.

RAŽNJIĆI: grilled cubes of meat on skewers. Like all grilled meat dishes, this is served with chopped raw onions and tiny hot peppers.

SARMA: meat-and-rice-stuffed grape (vine) or cabbage leaves. Many variations of this dish exist. For example, the leaves may be pickled as sauerkraut then wrapped around meat and rice and ovenbaked with smoked spareribs with a *roux* (flour and fat) added near the end of cooking to thicken the juices. Tomato juice, cream, or broth may be used as the liquid to cook the SARMA.

SRPSKI AJVAR: "Serbian caviar," but actually a dish popular in so many countries it is difficult to name the origin. Cooked eggplant is cooled and mashed with pepper and garlic and served as a salad appetizer.

ŽITO: ground cooked wheat is mixed with sugar and chopped walnuts and patted into a round mound on a platter, the top is dusted with fine sugar and more walnuts. This dish was prepared by the ancient Slav tribes as an offering to their gods and is a tradition still held in any Slav country or household. In Serbia, it is prepared for Slava, the special day of the patron saint of each family, and though it dates from pagan times, it is still very much a part of Orthodox Serbian custom.

Croatia

The Croats are among the most artistic and literary members of the great family of Slavs. Artists, writers, philosophers, and efficient businessmen, they too have suffered through varying allegiances, dominations, and divisions of their land. At one time in their history, Dalmatia and Istria, along the Adriatic Sea, and also the central areas of Bosnia-Herzegovina were all part of Croatian territory. With the establishment of Yugoslavia they became separate areas and republics befitting their divergent histories.[3,9,10] Zagreb is the capital of Croatia, but the Dalmatian city of Dubrovnik, with its ancient walled area housing a mixture of Catholics, Muslims, and Orthodox Christians and Croats, Dalmatians, Macedonians, and Montenegrins – even a few Gypsies – speaks most eloquently of the historical past: Dubrovnik seems to be a microcosm of Yugoslav history.[10,11]

The Golden Age of Dubrovnik lasted about 300 years, from the 1400s to the 1700s. Despite continual political problems, it was a time of economic and intellectual flowering.[11] Despite religious pressures and dominance from the Turkish Empire, the Hungarian and later the Austro-Hungarian Empires, the Croats treasured their principles and traditions and avidly kept them alive. In smaller villages, even illiterate peasants could recite poetry.[9] It was these same traditions that served and continue to serve as inspiration to the Croats to preserve their identity. They always retained a reputation as being militarists and brave fighters but this prowess was never used to conquer, only to defend what was theirs.[9,10]

The majority of Croats are Roman Catholic, a few are Muslims. All are devoutly religious. Together with an innate love of arts and literature, and with a devotion to family and religion, the Croat is also known for two other traits that are often misunderstood. Family and home are so important, and jealously guarded, that the Croat is sometimes accused of "Croatian envy," a trait that can lead to feuds and vengeance. And their strong self-determination that has made them often successful businessmen, also serves to prevent unity in Croatian organizations: it is an individualism that often prohibits submission. It was Tito in 1945 who suppressed both religious zeal and political independence in the cause of Communism creating the first semblance of unity for the various religious and ethnic groups that form Yugoslavia.[9] Nonetheless, the cult of the family remains an integral part of Croatian life. There are currently ripples of change, but for the most part the families are patriarchal and relatives, even godparents, retain the lifelong concern of all family members. "Brothers-by-friendship," called *pobratimi*, and "sisters-by-friendship," called *posestrime*, are unique relationships and entered into by mutual agreement. The vow is taken seriously and the relationship is equally important as any other inter-familial bond.[9]

Although many areas of Yugoslavia retain oriental (Turkish) cultural characteristics, the 25 per cent of the population that are Croats are basically Western in outlook and culture both due to their early acceptance of Roman Catholicism and influence from the Latins and Germans. Earliest immigrants were sailors and fishermen, later ones were mainly labourers and peasants, but all took care to retain their language, their arts and even their *tamburitza* orchestra. (*Tamburitza* is a string instrument plucked with a pick.)[12]

Croatian cookery is simple, rich with eggs and cream, and for the most part resembles central European cuisine: that of the Austro-Hungarian Empire intertwined with Balkan favourites. The stuffed vegetable dishes vie with the grilled meats and layered casseroles, dumpling dishes and noodle specialties. In fact, noodles are such a favourite they are often eaten as a dessert sprinkled with walnuts and cinnamon sugar, or as a light main dish with pot cheese.[3] It is also not uncommon to taste GULYAS and PAPRIKAS, cherry, apple or poppy seed ŠTRUDLA, or the bread dumplings so typical of Czechoslovakian cookery.

The coastal area of Dalmatia differs. Although here too Balkan and Austro-Hungarian dishes may be found, the emphasis is on fresh fish from the Adriatic Sea prepared simply, often only with the addition of olive oil, or as a fish stew called BRODET. Recipes for the latter are local and family specialties are as varied as the 365 fish said to be in the Adriatic. Cornbreads and GNOCCHI, made from cornmeal and served with cheese and butter, seem to be "imports" from northern Italy, while a local predilection for swiss chard and spinach seem to be more typically Dalmatian.[5]

Favourite desserts in Dalmatia, as in Croatia, are usually fresh, stewed, or preserved fruits. Ice cream is one of the favourite Dalmatian desserts often served together with the abundance of fresh local fruits. Croatians have a more pronounced sweet tooth, which can only be satisfied by the famed Austro-Hungarian pastries and then only if they are accompanied with whipped cream.

Some food specialties of the area include:

DALMATIAN CHEESES: as everywhere in Yugoslavia fine local cheeses abound: PRIMORSKI, GRANIČKI, KRCKI, PAŠKI. They are sold as soft unripened cheeses, or allowed to age and used mainly for grating.

KNEDLA OD ZEMICKE: a soft mixture of eggs, milk-soaked bread and flour are kneaded together then shaped into a log and wrapped in a napkin for steaming. When done, the dumpling is sliced and served with butter and sour cream.

KNEDLE OD POVRĆA: cooked cubed vegetables and toasted croutons of bread are mixed with beaten eggs, milk, and flour then shaped into round dumplings and poached in water. Served with butter or butter-fried breadcrumbs and sour cream they, like other dumpling dishes, may form a meal with only the addition of a hot soup.

LIČKI KUPUS: from the Lika district of Croatia, a casserole of layered cabbage and smoked pork (ribs or chops), served with boiled potatoes.

MARASCAS: sour cherries

PAŠTA I FAŽOL: the spelling may vary slightly, but this dish of cooked pasta and beans, flavoured with garlic and onions, and sometimes a bit of smoked meat or cheese, is originally Italian.

POHOVAN PILE: Croatian specialty of breaded fried chicken.

SLAVONSKI CÉVAP: Croatian barbecue dish similar to many others in that it is made with cubed meats, peppers, onions, and tomatoes skewered and grilled. But the Croatian touch appears when the entire skewer is first wrapped in caul fat before grilling.

ZDENKA: a fine processed cheese served and sold everywhere in Yugoslavia, but especially popular in Croatia where it is served as a dessert cheese just before the fruit.

Slovenia

Located in a triangle area in northernmost Yugoslavia, Slovenia is bordered by Italy, Austria, and Hungary. The Southern Slav tribes, called Slovenes, settled in the area about 300 C.E., their strategically located land a veritable highway for the Germans and Huns. The Romans and finally Slovenia joined with the Hapsburgs in a struggle against the Ottoman Empire and ended up with a one-thousand-year domination by the Austro-Hungarian Empire.[3,13] It was a combination of their geographic location and their very early affiliation with the Holy Roman Empire and later the Austro-Hungarian Empire as well as its Roman Catholicism that gave the Slovenes a combination of Western culture, folklore, education, and even cuisine that is almost indistinguishable from that of its neighbours.

Slovenes retain the sociable easy going characteristics of most Yugoslavs, but because of their early affiliations, they are probably the most intellectual and sophisticated of all the Yugoslavs.[3] Slovenes are adept at languages, most being fluent in German and Italian, the intellectuals versed in French as well. Most children learn English in school. In spite of this inherent linguistic ability, many historians, and the Slovenes themselves, credit their very survival to the fact that above all, and indeed through all, they clung to their own ancient language, which is considered to be one of the oldest.[3]

Slovenian *bifes* (snack bars) and *slaščičarna* (tea shops) betray the national weakness for delectable cakes, tortes, strudels, and pastries, in seemingly endless procession. Sweet bakery is not only a national snack, it is a national preoccupation. When one considers that the selection includes the finest of Italian, Austrian, Hungarian, and Turkish sweets, it is difficult to imagine a more superior combination. With the frequent difficulty of which pastry to select, it could indeed become a preoccupation.

Turkish coffee, pastries, and grilled meats, Balkan sweets and hearty meat and vegetable casseroles, German varieties of excellent sausages, Italian sauces and pastas and risottos, the filling sweet dumplings and sweet noodle creations of the Austro-Hungarian Empire – with Slovenian cooks adept at all of these, it needs little further explanation that a slim waistline must be one of the most pressing national problems. CVIČEK, the omnipresent Slovenian rosé wine, is served everywhere with everything, although an excellent variety of red and white wines is also available, as is SLIVOVITZ.

Close in importance to the sweets are the Slovenian soups. Not only is a meal considered incomplete without soup, soup often is the entire meal, with only the minor accompaniment of bread and wine and perhaps a sweet noodle dish.[5]

The heavily-wooded areas of Slovenia yield game in abundance: quail, partridge, pheasants, hare, boar, venison. The Adriatic Sea supplies the ingredients for the numerous fish dishes, while the orchards produce not only peaches and apricots and sweet and sour cherries, but they are famed for their apples. Almonds, walnuts, and berries in generous amounts add their flavour to desserts. Mutton and pork are the favoured meats (aside from game) and many excellent cheeses are locally produced.

Some Slovenian specialties include:

CVIČEK: Slovenian rosé wine used in such quantity and frequency that it is poured from casks rather than bottles.

DUNAJSKI ZREZEK: the pounded veal cutlet or scallop after it has been egg-dipped and crumbed then fried to a crisp perfection, otherwise known as WIENERSCHNITZEL.

IDRIJSKI ZLIKROFI: small filled noodle pockets, poached and served with sauce. In Italy they would be called RAVIOLI.

KRANJSKE KLOBASE: German-style sausages in many varieties.

MLADIC SA PECURKAMA: whole baked river char stuffed with a bread and mushroom dressing. (Whether or not to use mushrooms in Slovenian cookery is not a problem. The problem is deciding which of the one hundred varieties to use.)

PALACINKE: those thin pancakes that the French call CRÊPES. Slovenians enjoy them mostly Hungarian-style with apricot preserves and chopped walnuts, or with any other number of sweet combinations.

POHANA PIŠKE: it doesn't matter what you call it, it is still breaded fried chicken. If the bird is not exactly tender, the dish may be finished by baking for a short time in the oven in the Austrian dish of BACKHENDL.

POTICA: from the Slovenian word *povitica*, which means literally "something rolled in." Usually it is taken to mean a many-layered coffee-cake with generous nut filling.

REZANCI: freshly-cooked noodles tossed with fresh curd cheese or poppy seeds or chopped walnuts. Whatever proves to be the choice, melted butter and sugar will also be generously added. This dish may be a snack or, with soup, may make a light meal.

RIČET: stewed barley flavoured with a small amount of smoked meat.

ŠTRUKLJI OD SIRA: one of the infinite varieties of dumpling: noodle dough is spread with a mixture of cottage cheese, egg yolks, sour cream and whipped egg white. It is then rolled and placed in a crumb-sprinkled napkin and poached. The cooked dumpling is removed from the napkin, then sliced and served with buttered crumbs.

VIPAVSKA ČORBA: a thick soup of pork, potatoes, sauerkraut, and beans, well-flavoured with onion and garlic and served with sour cream.

Bosnia – Herzegovina

This inland republic is bounded by other Yugoslavian republics and maintains a slow pace of living, the religion of Islam, and the serious outlook on life imprinted by the Turkish domination. The almost cloistered existence of the women, the haggling at the market place, and the narrow winding streets and walled courtyards exist today almost as they did several hundred years ago.

Some Balkan dishes find their way into the dietary, but the overall influence in the cuisine, as in the general way of life, is Turkish. Because of the Muslim restriction against pork, it is not used in this area. But the Mediterranean climate helps produce a variety of crops: grains, fruits, and vegetables, all generously used in a healthful cuisine rich in vegetables, soured milk, simple cheeses, fresh fruits, and some meat and fish. Turkish coffee begins and ends the day, accompanied with RAKIJA (clear potent spirits) and/or sweet Turkish pastries.

Some Bosnian-Herzegovian specialties include:

BAKLAVA: a Turkish pastry made with butter-drenched layers of thin phyllo pastry. The centre layers are sprinkled with chopped nuts, spices, and sugar. After baking, a hot spiced syrup is poured over and absorbed. The dripping sweet diamond cuts are eaten usually accompanied with Turkish coffee.

BOSANKE ĆUFTE: (ćufte is an Arabic word meaning minced or finely chopped.) Bosnian meatballs oven-baked and topped with an egg-yoghurt custard.

BOSANSKI LONAC: a casserole of cubed mixed meats layered with cubed vegetables (root), potatoes, onions and often whole heads of garlic all baked with wine or diluted vinegar.

BOSNIAN CHEESES: TRAVNIČKI is a soft cheese, both salty and sour. Others are SJENIČKI and LIVANJSKI.

HALVA: popular Middle East (Turkish) confection with semolina.

KADAIF: Turkish sweet of honey-soaked thin shreds of wheat.

MUSAKA: of both Greek and Turkish origin. A layered casserole of eggplant and meat with tomatoes, onions, and seasonings. Sometimes topped with cheese or an egg-yoghurt custard.

PITA: the general Yugoslavian name for most confections made with phyllo pastry. The Bosnian (and Macedonian) version is usually made in a round baking dish and cut in wedges like a big round cake. Similar to BAKLAVA.

RATLUK: also called LOKUM or TURKISH DELIGHT. Blandly flavoured (rose water or orange water) jelled confection cut in squares and dusted with icing sugar.

ŠIŠ-ĆEVAP: *šiš* (pronounced "shish") is the Turkish word for skewer. So this is a dish of skewered meat cubes, green peppers and tomatoes.

SOGAN-DOLMA: "*dolma*," means "stuffed" in Turkish, this is stuffed onions filled with ground mutton, rice, KAJMAK, and tomato paste.

SUVA-PITA: just like BAKLAVA. (Perhaps having many names for the same thing means you can order it more often without sounding greedy.)

TURKISH COFFEE: made the Bosnian way uses two DŽEZVAS (lidless, long-handled coffee pots), one to boil fresh water and the other to hold the coffee. Pouring from one to the other after the initial boiling increases the frothiness. Sugar may be added to the pot or crunched in the mouth while sipping the coffee.

URMAŠICE: a rich pastry of egg yolks, butter, yoghurt, and blended with flour. Small pieces are pulled off and shaped like fat dates. After baking, the rich cookies shaped like dates are soaked in honey-spice syrup.

Montenegro

A small republic on the Adriatic coast situated south of Dalmatia and north of Albania, Montenegro, as the name suggests, is a rocky and mountainous country with little arable land. Sheep graze on sparse pastures and here and there vineyards, orchards, and corn fields manage to produce the main food of the region: sheep and lamb, cheeses and yoghurt from the sheep's milk, fruits, wine, and corn for breads and pudding dishes. Beehives yield a fine honey that forms one of the main sweeteners used as it is and in a variety of spiced honey cakes and cookies such as MEDENJACI. The KAJMAK so enjoyed throughout Yugoslavia is also a favourite here and is eaten on coarse cornbread, layered between cornmeal puddings and as a filling in baked dishes.

The Montenegrans are tall gentle people, preferring their simple uncomplicated mountain life to the hustle and bustle of the urban world. From Muslim influence, they prefer lamb and mutton and eat no pork. There are also Venetian-inspired fish soups added to the basic cuisine of corn dishes and mutton.

Macedonian

Muslim and Greek Orthodox are the main religions and both Turkey and

Greece the main influences in this area where life is still for the most part poor and primitive. The Macedonians are a mixed group counting among their numbers Albanians, Greeks, Bulgarians and Serbians.

The variety of spices, especially tiny hot peppers, fresh herbs, garlic, onions, and leeks, so much a part of both Turkish and Greek cookery, are very evident in the Macedonian cuisine. In fact so spicy is their food that it is purported to be the reason why they eat such large quantities of bread with their meals.[5]

Many types of local fish and locally made cheeses, lamb dishes, stuffed vegetables, and a lush variety of fruits and vegetables add to their diet. Macedonia is considered to be the "Yugoslavian California," with a moderate climate conducive to a variety of produce. Okra, spinach, eggplant, zucchini, olives, tomatoes, and peppers all flourish. Rice as well as a pasta resembling rice, called TARANA (note similarity to the Hungarian TARHONYA) is used in soups and layered meat and vegetable dishes.

The Macedonians enjoy Turkish coffee and the sweet rich pastries so much a part of the Turkish and Greek cuisine, only some of the names differ. PITA is considered the Macedonian specialty and can be made with sweet or savoury fillings rolled or layered with KATMER, the phyllo pastry that is stretched, buttered and layered for all the PITA dishes.

Yoghurt is a snack food and an ingredient in many other dishes. FETA, MANDUR (a whey cheese in pear shape), and KEFALOTIR are the most popular cheeses. The latter is smooth and strong and favoured for *meze* (appetizers) with RAKIJA, olives, and salted nuts.

Olive oil is used instead of animal fats, and the egg-lemon sauce so popular in Greece is used here in soups, over fish or vegetables or casseroles.

Meal Patterns and Eating Customs

RAKIJA, SLJIVOVICA, SLIVOVITZ, or SLIVOVKA, whatever it is called, is the national drink, a clear, potent plum brandy: its potency rendering the uninitiated literally breathless. Yet it is the morning drink accompanied by TURSKA KAFA: a tiny strong sweet cup of Turkish coffee that sets most Yugoslavs on their daily routine. Some take a simple breakfast of coffee or weak tea and breads and jams or honey.

Almost everywhere in Yugoslavia the main meal of the day is at noon, followed by a rest period. The meal begins with soup, may include a fish dish or a meat and vegetable casserole, and probably ends with fresh or stewed fruits. Wine accompanies most meals. In some areas a course of cheese precedes the fruit dessert. The evening meal is usually a light one made up of dinner leftovers or soup and a sweet noodle dish or simply a vegetable casserole. Wine is a part of both dinner and the evening meal and bread is indispensable. Further, the meal would likely be considered incomplete without a small salad of cooked dressed beans or vegetables or at the very least a dish of tiny hot peppers.

In the early evening streets everywhere are most congested with strollers and people standing and talking. It is the time of the *korzo* (promenade). And no *korzo* is complete without a snack in a *kafana* (coffeeshop) where always SLIVOVICA, TURSKA KAFA, beer, or a SPRICER (wine and soda water) awaits. But who can drink without a little nibble? This is where all the many tidbits grilled on skewers over charcoal fires are so enjoyed with tiny salads of spiced cooked vegetables, chopped raw onions and hot little peppers. Snacks in the afternoons may be the same, or they may lean to the sweet side. In summer time the popularity of sherbets and ice creams is evident. Always coffee and sweet pastries tempt the passerby.

The enjoyment of guests and the generous hospitality of the Yugoslavs is of utmost importance. Slovenians like to offer guests small dishes of sweetened cooked fruit: apple sauce, mixed fruit compotes. Montenegrans will be likely to offer a fresh, cool glass of milk, while the Bosnian-Herzegovinians will present a tray of Turkish coffee and RATLUK. In Serbia and Macedonia Turkish coffee will be accompanied by RAKIJA. Almost everywhere, the offering to welcome guests may well be the ornate tray with SLATKO, with tiny spoons and glasses of fresh cold water. Eating and drinking together is the age-old symbol of friendship; to refuse would be a great insult.

Special Occasions

Serbian Orthodox, Roman Catholic and Muslim are the main religions in Yugoslavia. Also there are minorities of Protestants and Jews.

Throughout the year many local festivals, some church festivities, others related to fairs and agricultural celebrations, all offer good excuse for singing and dancing, eating and drinking.

A two-day New Year's holiday has been proclaimed by the Yugoslav government for January 1 and 2. It is widely celebrated with decorated trees, feasting, and partying, and the presentation of gifts to friends and family. Nova Godina is especially enjoyed by those with no religious affiliation. Christmas or Božić, however, is still the most important festival on the calendar. The Roman Catholics celebrate it on December 25, while the Serbian Orthodox members celebrate on January 7.

For the Orthodox Christians the day before Christmas Eve is considered a fast day and no meat is eaten. But the atmosphere in the house is special: a yule log burns while a special twenty-four-hour candle is lit and clean straw is scattered over well-scrubbed floors in memory of the manger scene. With the traditional Serbian Orthodox chant of "The Father, the Son, and the Holy Ghost, Amen," four whole walnuts are tossed, one into each corner of the room. The traditional evening meal will feature a soup, fish, and vegetables with bread and cheese and fruit – but no meat or meat fats. January 6, Epiphany Day, is considered to be the celebration of the visit of the three Wise Men and the Baptism of Christ. This holy day, believed to be a holiday long before December 25, was celebrated as Christmas, and is devoted to visiting with family and close friends. Especially important is the traditional Christmas cake cut in the shape of the Eastern Orthodox Cross with four "arms" and a centre wedge removed and set with a cup of wine to be symbolically tasted by all adults.

When the Slavs adopted Christianity in the 800s, each family took the name of a saint (on whose day the family was baptized) as their own patron saint. Coming soon after Božić in January, the Family Saint's Day or Krsna Slava is celebrated. A platter of ŽITO or KOLJIVO is prepared. This is a mixture of boiled crushed wheat mixed with sugar and nuts and decorated with more nuts and often raisins as well as candles. This ancient dish was prepared by early Slavs as an offering to their gods; with the acceptance of Christianity the Slavs present this offering to their own saint after first being blessed in the church.

Source References

CHAPTER ONE: AFRICAN

1. *Funk and Wagnalls Standard Reference Encyclopedia*. New York: Standard Reference Works Publishing Co., 1967.
2. "Army Rule Frequent in Africa." London Ontario: *London Free Press*, May 8, 1974.
3. "258 Civilians Killed by African Guerrillas." Toronto: *The Globe and Mail*, January 7, 1974.
4. Mendes, Helen. *The African Heritage Cookbook*. New York: The Macmillan Co., 1971.
5. De Andrade, Margarette. *Brazilian Cookery: Traditional and Modern*. Rutland, Vermont: Charles E. Tuttle Co., 1965.
6. Oka, Odinchezo. *Black Academy Cookbook*. Buffalo, N.Y.: Black Academy Press Inc. 1972.
7. *Immigration '73: Quarterly Statistics*. Ottawa: Department of Manpower and Immigration, 1974.
8. May, Jacques. *Ecology of Malnutrition in Middle Africa*. New York: Hafner Publishing Co., 1965.
9. Sandler, Bea. *The African Cookbook*. New York: World Publishing, 1972.
10. Gelfand, Michael. *Diet and Tradition in an African Culture*. Edinburgh: E. & S. Livingstone, 1971.
11. Van der Post, Laurens, et. al. *African Cooking*. New York: Time-Life Books, 1970.
12. May, Jacques. *Ecology of Malnutrition in Eastern and Western Africa*. New York: Hafner Publishing Co., 1970.
13. King, Maurice. *Nutrition for Developing Countries*. Nairobi: Oxford University Press, 1972.

14. May, Jacques. *Ecology of Malnutrition in the French-speaking Countries of West Africa and Madagascar.* New York: Hafner Publishing Co., 1968.
15. Wasserman, Ursula. "Afrique Gastronomique." *Gourmet*, November, 1962.
16. *Webster's New World Dictionary.* New York: The World Publishing Co., 1966.

CHAPTER TWO: ALBANIAN

1. Gottman, J. *A Geography of Europe.* New York: Holt, Rinehart and Winston. Vol. I, 3rd edition, 1960.
2. May, Jacques. *The Ecology of Malnutrition in East-Central Europe.* New York: Hafner Publishing Co., 1963.
3. Nelson, Kay Shaw. *The Eastern European Cookbook.* Chicago: Henry Regnery, 1973.
4. Seranne, Anne; and Gaden, Eileen. *The Best of Near East Cookery.* Garden City, N.Y.: Doubleday & Co., 1964.
5. Rowland, Jean. *Good Food from the Near East.* New York: Barrows and Co., 1957.

CHAPTER THREE: AMERICAN

1. Shenton, James P. *American Cooking: The Melting Pot.* New York: Time-Life Books, 1971.
2. Tannahill, Reay. *Food in History.* New York: Stein and Day, 1973.
3. Thomas, Gertrude I. *Foods of our Forefathers.* Philadelphia: F. A. Davis Co., 1941.
4. Krause, Marie V.; and Hunscher, Martha A. *Food, Nutrition and Diet Therapy.* Philadelphia: W. B. Saunders Co., 1972.
5. Hewitt, Jean. *New York Times Heritage Cookbook.* New York: G. P. Putnam's Sons, 1972.
6. Castle, Coralie, et al. *Peasant Cooking of Many Lands.* San Francisco: 101 Productions, 1972.
7. Walter, Eugene, et al. *American Cooking: Southern Style.* New York: Time-Life Books, 1971.
8. Seranne, Anne, ed. *The General Federation of Women's Clubs Cookbook: America Cooks.* New York: G. P. Putnam's Sons, 1967.

CHAPTER FOUR: ARMENIAN

1. *Encyclopedia Canadiana.* Toronto: Grolier of Canada, 1970.
2. Rowland, Joan. *Good Food from the Near East.* New York: M. Barrows and Co., 1957.
3. *Funk and Wagnalls Standard Reference Encyclopedia.* New York: Standard Reference Works Publishing Co., 1967.
4. Papashvily, Helen; and Papashvily, George. *Russian Cooking.* New York: Time-Life Books, 1969.
5. Polvay, Marina. "Cuisines of Russia." *Gourmet*, February 1974.
6. Leaf, Alexander. "Observations of a Peripatetic Gerontologist." *Nutrition Today*, September/October 1973.
7. Norman, Barbara. *The Russian Cookbook.* Toronto: Bantam Books, 1970.

8. Shenton, James P. *American Cooking: The Melting Pot*. New York: Time-Life Books, 1971.
9. Uvezian, Sonia. *The Cuisine of Armenia*. New York: Harper and Row, 1974.

CHAPTER FIVE: AUSTRALIAN
1. *Funk and Wagnalls Standard Reference Encyclopedia*. New York: Standard Reference Works Publishing Co., 1967.
2. Commonwealth Bureau of Census and Statisticis. *Australia at a Glance*. 1973.
3. Osborne, Charles, ed. *Australia, New Zealand and the South Pacific: A Handbook*. New York: Praeger Publishers, 1970.
4. Rabling, Harold; and Hamilton, Patrick. *Under the Southern Cross: The Story of Australia*. London: Macmillan and Co., 1961.
5. Marshall, Anne. *Australian and New Zealand Complete Book of Cookery*. Sydney: Paul Hamlyn, 1971.
6. Steinberg, Raphael, et al. *Pacific and Southeast Asian Cooking*. New York: Time-Life Books, 1970.
7. "Australians Told to Eat Less Steak, More Curries." London, Ontario: *London Free Press*, August 24, 1974.
8. Chambers, Elaine. *Australian Dried Fruit Cookbook*. Rigby Ltd., 1972.
9. Hembrow, Sally. *Outdoor Cookbook*. Rigby Ltd., 1972.
10. Howat, Val; and Mierisch, Gwen. *Presbyterian Women's Missionary Union Cookery Book*. Melbourne: Lothian Publishing Co., 1973.
11. Nation, Rhoda. *Mary Bought a Little Lamb and This Is How She Cooked It*. Wellington: A. H. and A. W. Reed, 1973.

CHAPTER SIX: AUSTRIAN
1. Wechsberg, Joseph, et al. *The Cooking of Vienna's Empire*. New York: Time-Life Books, 1968.
2. Langseth-Christensen, Lillian. *Gourmet's Old Vienna Cookbook: A Viennese Memoir*. New York: Gourmet Distributing Corp. 1959.
3. Rhode, Irma. *The Viennese Cookbook*. New York: Grosset & Dunlap, 1951.
4. Morton, Marcia Coleman. *The Art of Viennese Cooking*. Garden City, N.Y.: Doubleday and Co., 1963.
5. May, Jacques. *The Ecology of Malnutrition in Central and South-Eastern Europe*. New York: Hafner Publishing Co., 1966.
6. *Funk and Wagnalls Standard Reference Encyclopedia*. New York: Standard Reference Works Publishing Co., 1967.
7. *Encyclopedia Canadiana*. Toronto: Grolier of Canada, 1970.
8. Waldo, Myra. *Myra Waldo's Travel and Motoring Guide to Europe, 1974*. London: Collier Macmillan, 1974.

CHAPTER SEVEN: BALTIC PEOPLES
1. Florinsky, M. T., ed. *McGraw-Hill Encyclopedia of Russia and the Soviet Union*. New York: McGraw-Hill Books, 1961.

2. Papashvily, Helen; and Papashvily, George. *Russian Cooking*. New York: Time-Life Books, 1969.
3. *Funk and Wagnalls Standard Reference Encyclopedia*. New York: Standard Reference Works Publishing Co., 1967.
4. Ibid.
5. Gerutis, Albertis, ed. *Lithuania 700 Years*. New York: Manyland Books, 1969.
6. *Estonia, A Story of a Nation*. New York: Estonian House, 1974.
7. Aavik, Johannes, et al. *Aspects of Estonian Culture*. London: Boreas Publishing Co., 1961.
8. *Encyclopedia Canadiana*. Toronto: Grolier of Canada, 1970.
9. Suziedelis, Simas, ed. *Encyclopedia Lituanica*. Boston: J. Kapocius, 1972.
10. Norman, Barbara. *The Russian Cookbook*. Toronto: Bantam Books, 1970.
11. Gibbon, John Murray. *Canadian Mosaic: The Making of a Nation*. Toronto: McClelland and Stewart Ltd., 1938.
12. Ratsep, A. *Matkates Mooda Kodumaad*. Tallin, 1964.
13. Orav, Liia. *Eesta Rahva Vanu Kombeid*. 1965.
14. Sild, E. *Keedu-ja Majapidamis Raamat*. I Osa, Iosa.
15. Saviauk, V. *Tuhandeist Sudameist*. Tallin, 1956.
   NOTE: Thanks and sincere appreciation to Kaljo and Asta Loone and their daughter Hilja, of London, Ontario, for translating the above Estonian sources and providing much background material.
16. *The World Book Encyclopedia*. Chicago: Field Enterprises, Educational Corp., 1970.
17. Blodnieks, Adolfs. *The Undefeated Nation*. New York: Robert Speller and Sons, 1960.
18. Bilmanis, Alfred. "Latvia as an Independent State." Washington D.C.: Latvian Legation, 1947.

CHAPTER EIGHT: BELGIAN

1. Langer, William. *An Encyclopedia of World History*. Boston: Houghton Mifflin Co., 1952.
2. Beal, Doone. "The Appeal of Antwerp." *Gourmet*, February, 1973.
3. *Encyclopedia Canadiana*. Toronto: Grolier of Canada, 1970.
4. Hazelton, Nika. *The Belgian Cookbook*. New York: Atheneum, 1970.
5. Donovan, Maria Kozslik. "Gourmet Holidays: The Belgium Coast." *Gourmet*, April 1971.

CHAPTER NINE: BULGARIAN

1. Seranne, Anne; and Gaden, Eileen. *The Best of Near East Cookery*. Garden City, N.Y.: Doubleday & Co., 1964.
2. Nelson, Kay Shaw. *The Eastern European Cookbook*. Chicago: Henry Regnery Co., 1973.
3. May, Jacques. *Ecology of Malnutrition in Central and South-Eastern Europe*. New York: Hafner Publishing Co., 1966.
4. *Funk and Wagnalls Standard Reference Encyclopedia*. New York: Standard Reference Works Publishing Co., 1967.
5. *Encyclopedia Canadiana*. Toronto: Grolier of Canada, 1970.

6. Rowland, Jean. *Good Food from the Near East*. New York: M. Barrows and Co., 1957.
7. Castle, Coralie, et al. *Peasant Cooking of Many Lands*. San Francisco: 101 Productions, 1972.
8. Field, Michael; and Field, Frances. *A Quintet of Cuisines*. New York: Time-Life Books, 1970.
9. Perl, Lila. *Yugoslavia, Romania, Bulgaria: New Era in the Balkans*. Toronto: Thomas Nelson and Sons, 1970.

CHAPTER TEN: BYELORUSSIAN
1. *Funk and Wagnalls Standard Reference Encyclopedia*. New York: Standard Reference Works Publishing Co., 1967.
2. *Encyclopedia Canadiana*. Toronto: Grolier of Canada, 1970.
3. Norman, Barbara. *The Russian Cookbook*. Toronto: Bantam Books, 1970.
4. Stankevich, M. *Greatlitvanian (Byelorussian) Cookbook*. Ottawa: National Museums of Canada, 1972.

CHAPTER ELEVEN: CANADIAN
1. *Encyclopedia Canadiana*. Toronto: Grolier of Canada, 1970.
2. Eccles, W. J. *The Canadian Frontier 1534-1760*. New York: Holt, Rinehart and Winston, 1969.
3. Guillet, Edwin C. *Pioneer Days in Upper Canada*. Toronto: University of Toronto Press, 1964.
4. Tannahill, Reay. *Food in History*. New York: Stein and Day, 1973.
5. Clark, S. D. *The Developing Canadian Community*. Toronto: University of Toronto Press, 1962.
6. Magrath, C. A. *Canada's Growth and Some Problems Facing It*. Ottawa: The Mortimer Press, 1910.
7. MacGibbon, Duncan. *The Canadian Grain Trade*. Toronto: Macmillan Company of Canada, 1932.
8. Nightingale, Marie. *Out of Old Nova Scotia Kitchens*. New York: Charles Scribner's Sons, 1971.
9. Careless, J. M. S. *Canada: A Story of Challenge*. Toronto: Macmillan Company of Canada, 1972.
10. Barbeau, Marius. *Quebec: Where Ancient France Lingers*. Toronto: Macmillan Company of Canada, 1936.
11. Beaulieu, Mirelle. *The Cooking of Provincial Quebec*. Toronto: Gage Publishing Co., 1975.
12. Ladies' Auxiliary of the Lunenburg Hospital Society. *The Dutch Oven*. Lunenburg, Nova Scotia: Progress Enterprise Co. Ltd., 1953.
13. Canadian Citizenship Branch, Department of Secretary of State. *The Canadian Family Tree*. Ottawa: Queen's Printer, 1967.
14. Murray, Jean, ed. *The Newfoundland Journal of Aaron Thomas 1794*. Toronto: Longman Canada, 1968.
15. Guillet, Edwin C. *The Great Migration: The Atlantic Crossing by Sailing Ship since 1770*. Toronto: University of Toronto Press, 1963.
16. Reaman, G. Elmore. *The Trail of the Black Walnut*. Toronto: McClelland and Stewart, 1957.

17. Abrahamson, Una. *God Bless Our Home*. Toronto: Burns & McEachern Ltd., 1966.

18. Traill, Catharine Parr. *The Canadian Settler's Guide*. Toronto: McClelland and Stewart Ltd., 1969.

19. Waterston, Elizabeth. *Canadian Portraits, Pioneers in Agriculture*. Toronto: Clarke, Irwin and Co., 1957.

20. Benson, George. *Historical Record of the Edwardsburg and Canada Starch Companies*. 1958.

21. Peterson, Martin S.; and Tressler, Donald K. *Food Technology the World Over*. Westport, Conn.: Avi Publishing Co., 1963.

22. Lowenberg, Miriam, et al. *Food and Man*. New York: John Wiley and Sons, 1968.

23. Pyke, Magnus. *Synthetic Food*. London: John Murray Ltd., 1970.

24. Canada Department of Agriculture. *Canada's Agriculture, The First 100 Years*. Ottawa: Queen's Printer, 1967.

25. Lindal, Valdimar Jacobson. *The Saskatchewan Icelanders: A Strand of the Canadian Fabric*. Winnipeg: Columbia Press, 1955.

26. Rush, Gary B. *The Supermarket Storybook*. Vancouver: 1972.

27. Lawson, Jessie I.; and Sweet, Jean Maccallum. *This is New Brunswick*. Toronto: The Ryerson Press, 1951.

28. Hatheway, C. L. *The History of New Brunswick from Its First Settlement*. Fredericton: James P. A. Philips, 1846.

29. Wright, E. C. *The Loyalists of New Brunswick*. Available from the author, P. O. Box 7110, Wolfville, Nova Scotia.

30. Gesner, Abraham. *New Brunswick with Notes for Emigrants*. London: Simmonds & Ward, 1849.

31. *Olsen's Loyalist Day Scrapbook*. In Saint John Regional Library Scrapbook Collection, Saint John, New Brunswick.

32. Flowers, A. D. *Loyalists of Bay Chaleur*. Saint John, New Brunswick.

33. Deering, Rosemary. *Life of the Loyalists*. Toronto: Fitzhenry & Whiteside, 1975.

34. *The Newfoundland Journal*.

35. Mowat, Farley; and de Visser, John. *This Rock Within the Sea: A Heritage Lost*. Boston/Toronto: Atlantic Little, Brown Books, 1968.

36. Moyles, R. G. *Complaints is Many and Various But the Odd Divil Likes It: 19th Century Views of Newfoundland*. Toronto: Peter Martin Associates, 1975.

37. Smallwood, J. R. "Life Today in Newfoundland." *The Book of Newfoundland*. St. John's: Newfoundland Book Publishers Ltd., 1967.

38. Anderson, Olga H. "Boiled Dinner Still Preferred." *Canadian Hospital*, February 1962.

39. ____. "Posies and Doughboys." *Newfoundland Home Economics Association Newsletter*, May 1969.

40. Halpert, Herbert; and Story, G. M. *Christmas Mumming in Newfoundland*. Toronto: University of Toronto Press, 1969.

41. *Out of Old Nova Scotia Kitchens*.

42. Walworth, Arthur. *Cape Breton, Isle of Romance*. Toronto: Longmans Green and Co., 1948.

43. *The Dutch Oven*.

44. From information suppied by J. Estelle Reddin, associate professor, department of home economics, University of Prince Edward Island, Charlottetown, P.E.I.

45. Doiron, Nancy. "Fish and Seafood in P.E.I. Foodways." Student paper. Charlottetown: University of Prince Edward Island, 1975.

46. McAlduff, Angela. "Small Fruits and P.E.I. Foodways." Student Paper. Charlottetown: University of Prince Edward Island, 1975.

47. Doyle, Leona. "Festive Foods on P.E.I." Student paper. Charlottetown: University of Prince Edward Island, 1975.

48. Leechman, Douglas. *Native Tribes of Canada*. Toronto: Gage Publishing.

49. Assiniwi, Bernard. *Indian Recipes*. Toronto: Copp Clark Publishing, 1972.

50. Ritzenthaler, Robert; and Ritzenthaler, Pat. *The Woodland Indians of the Eastern Great Lakes*, Garden City, N.Y.: Natural History Press, 1970.

51. Quimby, George Irving. *Indian Culture and European Trade Goods*. Madison: University of Wisconsin Press, 1966.

52. Henrikson, Georg. *Hunters in the Barrens*. St. John's Newfoundland: Institute of Social and Economic Research, Memorial University of Newfoundland, 1973.

53. *Fort George, Quebec: Traditional Indian Recipes*. Cobalt, Ont.: Highway Book Shop, 1971.

54. Champlain, Samuel de. *Champlain: Voyages to New France* (1615-1618). Translated by Michael Macklem. Ottawa: Oberon Press, 1970.

55. Heidenreich, Conrad. *Huronia*. Toronto: McClelland and Stewart Ltd., 1971.

56. Reaman, George Elmore. *The Trail of the Iroquois Indians*. Toronto: Peter Martin Associates, 1967.

57. Parkham, Francis. *The Jesuits in North America in the Seventeenth Century*. Toronto: George N. Morang and Co. Ltd., 1900.

58. Quimby, George Irving. *Indian Life in Upper Great Lakes*. Chicago: University of Chicago Press, 1960.

59. Paget, Amelia M. *The People of the Plains*. Toronto: William Briggs, 1909.

60. Barbeau, Marius. *Indian Days on the Western Prairies*. Ottawa: National Museum of Canada, 1968.

61. Powers, William K. *Indians of the Northern Plains*. New York: G. P. Putnam's Sons, 1969.

62. Vanstone, James. *Athapaskan Adaptations: Hunters and Fishermen of the Subarctic Forests*. Chicago: Aldine Pub. Co., 1974.

63. Surtees, Ursula. *"LAK-LA HAI-EE": Interior Salish Food Preparation*. Lamont, -Surtees, Canada, 1974.

64. Wherry, Joseph H. *The Totem Pole Indians*. New York: Wilfred Funk, 1964.

65. McFeat, Tom, ed. *Indians of the North Pacific Coast*. Toronto: McClelland and Stewart Carleton Library, 1966.

66. Norris, John. *Strangers Entertained*. Vancouver: Evergreen Press, 1971.

67. Drucker, Philip. *Cultures of the North Pacific Coast*. New York: Chandler Publishing Co., 1965.

68. Stephanson, Vilhjalmer. "Food and Food Habits in Alaska and Northern Canada." *Human Nutrition Historic and Scientific*, edited by Iago Galston. New York: International Universities Press, 1960.

69. Schaeffer, Otto. "When the Eskimo Comes to Town." *Nutrition Today*, Nov./Dec. 1971.
70. Ellis, Eleanor. *Northern Cookbook*. Ottawa: The Queen's Printer, 1967.
71. Thompson, Charles Thomas. *Patterns of Housekeeping in Two Eskimo Settlements*. Ottawa: The Queen's Printer, 1969.
72. Houston, James. *The White Dawn*. New York: Harcourt Brace Jovanovich, 1971.
73. Benoit, Mme. Jehane. *The Canadian Cookbook*. Toronto: Pagurian Press, 1970.
74. Robotti, Frances D.; and Robotti, Peter J. *French Cooking in the New World*. Garden City, N.Y.: Doubleday and Co., 1967.
75. L'Association canadienne des Éducateurs de Langue Française. *Facets of French Canada*. Montreal: Editions Fide, 1967.
76. Gagne, Mme. Charles. *Quand les bateaux reviennent: Recettes typiques de la Gaspésie et des Îles-de-la Madeleine*. Ottawa: Leméac Inc., 1973.
77. Johnston, Charles M., ed. *The Valley of the Six Nations*. Toronto: University of Toronto Press, 1964.

CHAPTER TWELVE: CHINESE

1. Stokes, J.; and Stokes, G. *The People's Republic of China*. London: Ernest Benn Ltd., 1975.
2. Kolb, Albert. *East Asia: China, Japan, Korea, Vietnam: A Geography of a Cultural Region*. London: Methuen and Co., 1971.
3. Witzel, Anne. "Chinese Immigrants and China: An Introduction to the Multi-Medium Package on China." Research Department, Toronto Board of Education, 1969.
4. Munro, Ross H. "China Molds Minds of Minorities." Toronto: *The Globe and Mail*, June 2, 1976.
5. Spunt, Georges. *The Step-by-Step Chinese Cookbook*. Toronto: Fitzhenry and Whiteside, 1973.
6. Hu, Chang-Tu, et al. *China: Its People, Its Society, Its Culture*. New Haven: Hraf Press, 1960.
7. Hsu-Balzer, Eileen. *China Day by Day*. New Haven: University Press, 1974.
8. Winfield, G. F. *China: The Land and the People*. New York: Wm. Sloane Assoc., 1948.
9. Hahn, Emily, et al. *The Cooking of China*. New York: Time-Life Books, 1968.
10. May, Jacques. *The Ecology of Malnutrition in the Far and Near East*. New York: Hafner Publishing Co., 1961.
11. Wittfogel, Karl A. *Food and Society in China and India: Human Nutrition, Historic and Scientific*. New York: International Universities Press, 1960.
12. Miller, Gloria Bley. *The Thousand Recipe Chinese Cookbook*. New York: Grosset & Dunlap, 1970.
13. Ma, Nancy Chi. *Mrs. Ma's Chinese Cookbook*. Rutland, Vermont, and Tokyo, Japan: Charles E. Tuttle Publishers, 1970.
14. Wang, Lydia. *Chinese Cookbook*. Tokyo: Kamakura-Shobo Publishing Co., 1971.
15. Waley, Arthur. *Translations from the Chinese*. New York: Alfred A. Knopf & Co., 1941.

16. Yeung, David L., Cheung, Lillian W. Y., Sabry, Jean H. "The Hot-Cold Food Concept in Chinese Culture and its Application in a Canadian-Chinese Community." *Journal Canadian Dietetic Assn.*, Vol. 34, No. 4, Winter 1973.
17. Bodde, Dirk. *Annual Customs and Festivals in Peking*. Hong Kong: Hong Kong University Press, 1965.
18. Dore, Henry. *Researches into Chinese Superstitions*. Taipei: Ch'eng-Wen Publishing Co., 1966.
19. Ramondt, Joanne, "1,000 Londoners Celebrate Advent of Chinese 'Year of the Tiger'." London, Ontario: *London Free Press*, January 24, 1974.
20. Rosenberg, Monda. "Chinese Feasts Will Launch Year of Dragon." Toronto: *Toronto Star*, January 28, 1976.
21. Froud, Nina. *Far Eastern Cooking for Pleasure*. London: Hamlyn, 1971.
22. Castle, Coralie, et al. *Peasant Cooking of Many Lands*. San Francisco: 101 Productions, 1972.

CHAPTER THIRTEEN: CZECHOSLOVAKIAN

1. Castle, Coralie, et al. *Peasant Cooking in Many Lands*. San Francisco: 101 Productions, 1972.
2. Kane, Robert S. *Eastern Europe A to Z*. Garden City, N.J.: Doubleday & Co., 1968.
3. *Funk and Wagnalls Standard Reference Encyclopedia*. New York: Standard Reference Works Publishing Co., 1967.
4. Nelson, Kay Shaw. *The Eastern European Cookbook*. Chicago: Henry Regnery Co., 1973.
5. Wechsberg, Joseph. *The Cooking of Vienna's Empire*. New York: Time-Life Books, 1968.
6. May, Jacques. *The Ecology of Malnutrition in Central and South-Eastern Europe*. New York: Hafner Publishing Co., 1966.
7. Canadian Citizenship Branch, Department of the Secretary of State. *The Canadian Family Tree*. Ottawa: Queen's Printer, 1967.
8. Brizova, Joza, et al. *The Czechoslovak Cookbook*. New York: Crown Publishers, 1965.
9. Wechsberg, Joseph. "Traditional Czech Cookery." *Gourmet*, April, 1973.

CHAPTER FOURTEEN: DANISH

1. *Funk and Wagnalls Standard Reference Encyclopedia*. New York: Standard Reference Works Publishing Co., 1967.
2. Brown, Dale. *The Cooking of Scandinavia*. New York: Time-Life Books, 1968.
3. Hardisty, Jytte. *Scandinavian Cooking for Pleasure*. London: Paul Hamlyn, 1970.
4. *Encyclopedia Canadiana*. Toronto: Grolier of Canada, 1970.
5. Barry, Naomi. "Gourmet Holidays: Copenhagen." *Gourmet*, May 1970.
6. Castle, Coralie, et al. *Peasant Cooking of Many Lands*. San Francisco: 101 Productions, 1972.
7. Hazelton, Nika. *The Art of Danish Cooking*. New York: Doubleday & Co., 1964.

8. Fielding, Temple. *Fielding's Travel Guide to Europe.* 1973 ed. New York: Fielding Publications Inc., 1972.
9. Waldo, Myra. *Myra Waldo's Travel and Motoring Guide to Europe, 1974.* London: Collier Macmillan Publishers, 1974.

CHAPTER FIFTEEN: DUTCH

1. *Funk and Wagnalls Standard Reference Encyclopedia.* New York: Standard Reference Works Publishing Co., 1967.
2. *Encyclopedia Canadiana.* Toronto: Grolier of Canada, 1970.
3. Thomas, Gertrude I. *Foods of Our Forefathers.* Philadelphia: F. A. Davis & Co., 1941.
4. Brown, Dale. "A Dutch Celebration." *Gourmet,* December 1971.
5. Stirum, Countess Van Limburg. *The Art of Dutch Cooking or How the Dutch Treat.* New York: Doubleday & Co., 1961.
6. Field, Michael; and Field, Frances. *A Quintet of Cuisines.* New York: Time-Life Books, 1970.
7. Halverhout, Helen A. M. *The Netherlands Cookbook.* Amsterdam: De Driehoek, 1957.
8. Waldo, Myra. *Myra Waldo's Travel and Motoring Guide to Europe, 1974.* London: Collier Macmillan, 1974.
9. Mario, Thomas. "Hot Dutch Treat." *Playboy.*
10. Bennett, Margaret. "Tiptoe through the Spargel." *Gourmet,* June 1972.

CHAPTER SIXTEEN: EAST INDIAN

1. *Funk and Wagnalls Standard Reference Encyclopedia.* New York: Standard Reference Works Publishing Co., 1967.
2. Thomas, P. *Festivals and Holidays of India.* Bombay: Taraporevala Sons & Co. Private Ltd., 1971.
3. May, Jacques. *The Ecology of Malnutrition in the Far and Near East.* New York: Hafner Publishing Co., 1961.
4. Rau, Santha Rama, et al. *The Cooking of India.* New York: Time-Life Books, 1969.
5. Jaffrey, Madhur. *An Invitation to Indian Cooking.* New York: Alfred A. Knopf Inc., 1973.
6. Collins, Ruth Philpott. *A World of Curries.* New York: Funk and Wagnalls, 1967.
7. Singh, Dharam Jit. "Saffron, Sandalwood and Spice." *Gourmet,* September 1958.
8. Kaufman and Lakshmanan. *The Art of India's Cookery.* New York: Doubleday & Co., 1964.
9. Trotta, Geri. "Intriguing India." *Gourmet,* May 1974.
10. Grosvenor, Donna K.; and Grosvenor, Gilbert H. "Ceylon." *National Geographic,* April 1966.
11. Beyersbergen, Joanna. "Indian Nutritionist Claims Poverty Not 'Taboos' Cause of Poor Diet." London, Ontario: *The London Free Press,* June 15, 1974.
12. Zaener, R. C., ed. *The Concise Encyclopedia of Living Faiths.* New York: Hawthorn Books, 1959.

13. Lowenberg, Miriam, et al. *Food and Man*. New York: John Wiley and Sons, 1968.
14. Sekiguchi, Shindai. *Zen: A Manual for Westerners*. Japan Publications Inc., 1968.
15. ____. "Zen Diets Condemned." *Journal of the American Dietetic Association*, January 1972.
16. Sakr, Amid. "Dietary Regulations and Food Habits of Muslims." *Journal of the American Dietetic Association*, February 1971.
17. Norris, John. *Strangers Entertained: A History of the Ethnic Groups of British Columbia*. Vancouver: Evergreen Press, 1971.
18. Stroup, Herbert. *Four Religions of Asia*. New York: Harper and Row, 1968.
19. Lahnoy, Richard. *The Speaking Tree: A Study of Indian Culture and Society*. London: Oxford University Press, 1971.

CHAPTER SEVENTEEN: EGYPTIAN
1. Nickles, Harry G., et al. *Middle Eastern Cookery*. New York: Time-Life Books, 1969.
2. *Funk and Wagnalls Standard Reference Encyclopedia*. New York: Standard Reference Works Publishing Co., 1967.
3. Zane, Eva. *Middle Eastern Cookery*. San Francisco: 101 Productions, 1974.
4. Jacob, Heinrich Eduard. *Coffee: The Epic of a Commodity*. New York: Viking Press, 1935.
5. Rowland, Jean. *Good Food from the Near East*. New York: M. Barrows and Co., 1957.
6. May, Jacques. *The Ecology of Malnutrition in the Far and Near East*. New York: Hafner Publishing Co., 1961.
7. Seranne, Anne; and Gaden, Eileen. *The Best of Near East Cookery*. Garden City, N.Y.: Doubleday & Co., 1964.
8. Baldachin, Yolande. "Savoury Secrets from the Middle East." Toronto: *The Globe and Mail*, April 25, 1974.

CHAPTER EIGHTEEN: ENGLISH
1. *Lands and Peoples: Europe*. New York: Grolier Inc., Vol. 4, 1972.
2. Dunan, Marcel, et al. *Larousse Encyclopedia of Modern History: From 1500 to the Present Day*. New York: Paul Hamlyn, 1973.
3. Trager, James. *The Foodbook*. New York: Avon, 1972.
4. Hart, Roger. *English Life in Chaucer's Day*. London: Wayland Publishers, 1973.
5. Hutchins, Sheila. *English Recipes and Others . . .* London: Methuen and Co., 1967.
6. Evans, Hilary; and Evans, Mary. *The Victorians: At Home and at Work*. New York: Arco Publishing Co., 1973.
7. Bailey, Adrian, et al. *The Cooking of the British Isles*. New York: Time-Life Books, 1969.
8. Langer, William, ed. *An Encyclopedia of World History*. Boston: Houghton Mifflin Co., 1962.
9. Morris, Jan. "Rolls-Royceness." *The New York Times Magazine*, February 2, 1975.

10. *Know Your Foreigner: The British*. Toronto: Southam Business Publications.
11. English Tourist Board Information. *Traditional English and Regional Food*. London: British Government Office.
12. Ogrizek, Dore, ed. *Great Britain: England, Scotland and Wales*. New York: McGraw-Hill Book Co., 1949.
13. "Cumbria." *Lakeland Cookery*. Clapham, England: Dalesman Publishing Co., Ltd., 1973.
14. Spicer, Dorothy. *From an English Oven*. New York: Women's Press, 1948.
15. Pullar, Philippa. *Consuming Passions*. London: Hamish Hamilton, 1970.
16. Priestley, J. B. *The English*. New York: Viking Press, 1973.

CHAPTER NINETEEN: FILIPINO

1. De Roos, Robert. "The Philippines: Freedom's Pacific Frontier." *National Geographic*, September 1966.
2. *Funk and Wagnalls Standard Reference Encyclopedia*. New York: Standard Reference Works Publishing Co., 1967.
3. Steinberg, Raphael, et al. *Pacific and South-East Asian Cooking*. New York: Time-Life Books, 1970.
4. Froud, Nina. *Far Eastern Cooking for Pleasure*. London: Hamlyn, 1971.
5. "Filipino Family Sometimes Has to Live with No Income." London, Ontario: *London Free Press*, November 13, 1974.
6. Nelson, Raymond. *The Philippines*. New York: Walker and Co., 1968.
7. Day, Beth. "Philippine Fare." *Gourmet*, June 1974.
8. Wernstedt, Frederick L. *The Philippine Island World: A Physical, Cultural and Regional Geography*. Berkeley: University of California Press, 1967.
9. Castle, Coralie, et al. *Peasant Cooking of Many Lands*. San Francisco: 101 Productions, 1972.

CHAPTER TWENTY: FINNISH

1. Heinonen, Rev. Arvi I. *Finnish Friends in Canada*. United Church of Canada, 1930.
2. Ojakangas, Beatrice. *The Finnish Cookbook*. New York: Crown Publishers, 1974.
3. Simpson, Colin. *The Viking Circle*. London: Hodder & Stoughton, 1967.
4. *Funk and Wagnalls Standard Reference Encyclopedia*. New York: Standard Reference Works Publishing Co., 1967.
5. Castle, Coralie, et al. *Peasant Cooking of Many Lands*. San Francisco: 101 Productions, 1972.
6. Brown, Dale. *The Cooking of Scandinavia*. New York: Time-Life Books, 1968.
7. Waldo, Myra. *Myra Waldo's Travel and Motoring Guide to Europe, 1974*. London: Collier Macmillan, 1974.
8. Graves, William. "Finland, Plucky Neighbour of Soviet Russia." *National Geographic*, May 1968.
9. *Encyclopedia Canadiana*. Toronto: Grolier of Canada, 1970.
10. Fielding, Temple. *Fielding's Travel Guide to Europe*. New York: Fielding Publications, 1972.

CHAPTER TWENTY-ONE: FRENCH

1. *Funk and Wagnalls Standard Reference Encyclopedia*. New York: Standard Reference Works Publishing Co., 1967.
2. Sangster, Dorothy. "In Search of France's Nouvelle Cuisine." Toronto: *The Globe and Mail*, January 31, 1976.
3. *La Cuisine Française*. New York: The Cultural Services of the French Embassy, 1964.
4. De Gramont, Sanche. *The French: Portrait of a People*. New York: G. P. Putnam's Sons, 1969.
5. Root, Waverley, et al. *The Cooking of Italy*. New York: Time-Life Books, 1968.
6. Montagne, Prosper; and Gottschalk. Dr. *Larousse Gastronomique: The Encyclopedia of Food, Wine and Cooking*. London: Paul Hamlyn, 1961.
7. Waugh, Alec, et al. *Wines and Spirits*. New York: Time-Life Books, 1968.
8. Feibleman, Peter S., et al. *American Cooking: Creole and Acadian*. New York: Time-Life Books, 1971.
9. Curnonsky, Prince Élu Des Gastronomes. *Cuisine et Vins du France*. Paris: Larousse, 1953.
10. Child, Julia, Bertholle, Louisette, and Beck, Simone. *Mastering the Art of French Cooking*. New York: Alfred A. Knopf, 1968.
11. Barry, Naomi. "The Basque Country." *Gourmet*, July 1970.
12. Fisher, M. K. F., et al. *The Cooking of Provincial France*. New York: Time-Life Books, 1968.
13. Waldo, Myra. *Myra Waldo's Travel and Motoring Guide to Europe, 1974*. London: Collier Macmillan Publishers, 1974.
14. *McCall's Introduction to French Cooking*. New York: McCall Publishing Co., 1971.
15. Claiborne, Craig; and Franey, Pierre. *Classic French Cooking*. New York: Time-Life Books, 1970.

CHAPTER TWENTY-TWO: GERMAN

1. Fodor, Eugene, ed. *Fodor's Germany West and East, 1976*. New York: David McKay Co., 1976.
2. Morey, George. *West Germany*. London: Macdonald Educational, 1974.
3. Hazelton, Nika Standen, et al. *The Cooking of Germany*. New York: Time-Life Books, 1969.
4. Kahler, Eric. *The Germans*. Princeton, N.J.: Princeton University Press, 1974.
5. Reaman, George Elmore. *The Trail of the Black Walnut*. Toronto: McClelland & Stewart, 1957.
6. Langseth-Christensen, Lillian. "The Cuisines of Germany." *Gourmet*, June 1973.
7. Adam, Karl Hans. *The Wine and Food Society's Guide to German Cookery*. Cleveland: World Publishing Co., 1967.
8. Castle, Coralie, et al. *Peasant Cooking of Many Lands*. San Francisco: 101 Productions, 1972.
9. Morgan, Dr. Roger. *Germany 1870-1970*. London: BPC Publications, 1970.

10. Jacob, Heinrich Eduard. *Coffee: The Epic of a Commodity*. New York: Viking Press, 1935.
11. Sheraton, Mimi. *The German Cookbook: A Complete Guide to Mastering Authentic German Cooking*. New York: Random House, 1965.
12. May, Jacques. *The Ecology of Malnutrition in East-Central Europe*. New York: Hafner Publishing Co., 1963.
13. Nelson, Kay Shaw. *The Eastern European Cookbook*. Chicago: Henry Regnery Co., 1973.
14. Schuler, Elizabeth. *German Cookery: Mein Kochbuch*. New York: Crown Publishers, 1968.
15. Langseth-Christensen, Lillian. "Christmastime in Germany." *Gourmet*, December 1972.
16. Bielefeld, Dr. August Oetker. *Dr. Oetker German Home Baking*. Hannover, Germany: Ceres-Verlag Rudolf-August Oetker KG Bielefeld, 1970.

CHAPTER TWENTY-THREE: GREEK

1. Zotos, Stephanos. *The Greeks: Dilemma between Past and Present*. New York: Funk & Wagnalls, 1969.
2. Paradissus, Chrissa. *The Best Book of Greek Cookery*. Athens-Thessalonika: Estathiadis Bros., 1972.
3. Gage, Nicholas. *Portrait of Greece*. New York: American Heritage Press (McGraw-Hill), 1971.
4. Stubbs, Joyce. *The Home Book of Greek Cookery*. London: Faber & Faber, 1970.
5. Zane, Eva. *Greek Cooking for the Gods*. San Francisco: 101 Productions, 1970.
6. Nickles, Harry G., et al. *Middle Eastern Cooking*. New York: Time-Life Books, 1969.
7. *Lands and Peoples: Europe*. New York: Grolier Inc., 1972.
8. May, Jacques. *The Ecology of Malnutrition in East-Central Europe*. New York: Hafner Publishing Co., 1963.
9. *Encyclopedia Canadiana*. Toronto: Grolier of Canada, 1970.
10. Vlassis, George. *The Greeks in Canada*. Ottawa: 1942.
11. Rowland, Jean. *Good Food from the Near East*. New York: M. Barrows and Co., 1957.
12. Lianides, Leon. "Easter in Greece." *Gourmet*, April 1974.
13. *Selected Recipes of Greek Cooking*. Ottawa: Royal Greek Embassy, Press and Information Office, 1972.
14. Mahaffy, J. P. *What Have the Greeks Done for Modern Civilization?* New York: The Knickerbocker Press, 1909.
15. Seranne, Anne; and Gaden, Eileen. *The Best of Near East Cookery*. Garden City, N.Y.: Doubleday & Co., 1964.
16. *Report on the Greek Intercultural Seminar Held at St. Barnabas Anglican Church, Toronto, 1974*. Courtesy of Estelle Read, Ministry of Culture and Recreation, Citizenship Bureau, Toronto, Ontario.
17. Antoniou, C. *Greek Family Life*. Address presented at Greek Intercultural Seminar, Toronto, 1974. Courtesy Estelle Read, Ministry of Culture and Recreation, Citizenship Bureau, Toronto, Ontario.

18. Vickery, Kenton Frank. *Food in Early Greece*. Chicago: University of Illinois, 1936.

CHAPTER TWENTY-FOUR: HUNGARIAN

1. Lang, George. "The Pastries of Budapest." *Gourmet*, August 1971.
2. Lang, George. *The Cuisine of Hungary*. New York: Atheneum, 1971.
3. Isaacson, Rabbi Ben; and Wigoder, Deborah. *The International Jewish Encyclopedia*. Prentice-Hall, 1973.
4. Ausebel, Nathan. *Pictorial History of the Jewish People*. New York: Crown Publishers, 1962.
5. Bennett, Pogany and Clark. *The Art of Hungarian Cookery*. Garden City, N.Y.: Doubleday & Co., 1954.
6. Wechsberg, Joseph, et al. *The Cooking of Vienna's Empire*. New York: Time-Life Books, 1968.
7. *Hungarian Review*. Budapest, No. 10, 1974.
8. Timar, L. J. *A Short History of the Hungarian People in Canada*. Toronto: Across Canada Press, 1957.
9. *Funk and Wagnalls Standard Reference Encyclopedia*. New York: Standard Reference Works Publishing Co., 1967.
10. Kosa, John. *Land of Choice: The Hungarians in Canada*. Toronto: University of Toronto Press, 1957.
11. *Encyclopedia Canadiana*. Toronto: Grolier of Canada, 1970.
12. May, Jacques. *Ecology of Malnutrition in Central and South-Eastern Europe*. New York: Hafner Publishing Co., 1966.
13. Donovan, Maria Kozslik. "A Hungarian Rhapsody." *Gourmet*, August 1971.
14. Gundel, Károly. *Hungarian Cookery Book*. Budapest: Athenaeum Printing House, 1956.
15. Tannahill, Reay. *Food in History*. New York: Stein and Day, 1974.

CHAPTER TWENTY-FIVE: ICELANDIC

1. Simpson, Colin. *The Viking Circle*. London: Hodder and Stoughton Ltd., 1967.
2. Lindal, Valdimar Jacobson. *The Saskatchewan Icelanders: A Strand of the Canadian Fabric*. Winnipeg: Columbia Press, 1955.
3. Gjerset, Knut. *History of Iceland*. New York: The Macmillan Co., 1924.
4. Wylie, Betty Jane. "Paradise Revisited." *Gourmet*, March 1961.
5. Lindal, Amalia. *Ripples from Iceland*. New York: W. W. Norton and Co., 1962.
6. *Icelandic Food Specialities*. New York: Icelandic National Tourist Office.
7. Leaf, Horace. *Iceland, Yesterday and Today*. London: George Allen and Unwin Ltd., 1949.

CHAPTER TWENTY-SIX: IRANIAN

1. *Funk and Wagnalls Standard Reference Encyclopedia*. New York: Standard Reference Works Publishing Co., 1967.
2. "Iran Nation that Cannot Feed Itself: Government Has Program to Eliminate Poverty." London, Ontario: *London Free Press*, October 31, 1974.

3. *Funk and Wagnalls.*

4. Zane, Eva. *Middle Eastern Cookery.* San Francisco: 101 Productions, 1974.

5. *Funk and Wagnalls.*

6. Nickles, Harry G., et al. *Middle Eastern Cookery.* New York: Time-Life Books, 1969.

7. May, Jacques. *The Ecology of Malnutrition in the Far and Near East.* New York: Hafner Publishing Co., 1961.

8. Seranne, Anne; and Gaden, Eileen. *The Best of Near East Cooking.* Garden City, N.Y.: Doubleday & Co., 1964.

9. Mazda, Maideh. *In a Persian Kitchen.* Rutland, Vermont: Charles E. Tuttle, 1968.

10. Langseth-Christensen, Lillian. "Gourmet Holidays: Isfahan." *Gourmet,* March 1971.

11. Rowland, Jean. *Good Food from the Near East.* New York: M. Barrows and Co., 1957.

12. Iny, Daisy. *The Best of Baghdad Cooking.* Toronto: Clarke, Irwin and Co., 1976.

CHAPTER TWENTY-SEVEN: IRISH

1. *Facts about Ireland.* Dublin: The Department of Foreign Affairs, 1972.

2. Guillet, Edwin C. *The Great Migration: The Atlantic Crossing by Sailing Ship since 1770.* Toronto: University of Toronto Press, 1963.

3. Tucker, Gilbert. "The Famine Immigration to Canada." *American Historical Review,* April 1931.

4. *Encyclopedia Canadiana.* Toronto: Grolier of Canada, 1970.

5. Craig, Elizabeth. *The Art of Irish Cooking.* London: Ward Lock and Co., 1969.

6. Fitzgibbon, Theodora. *A Taste of Ireland.* Boston: Houghton Mifflin Co., 1969.

7. Bates, Margaret. *The Belfast Cookery Book.* Oxford: Pergamon Press, 1967.

8. Laverty, Maura. *Feasting Galore: Recipes and Food Lore from Ireland.* New York: Holt, Rinehart and Winston, 1961.

9. O'Hanlon, Thomas J. *The Irish.* Don Mills, Ont.: Fitzhenry and Whiteside, 1975.

10. Waldo, Myra. *Myra Waldo's Travel and Motoring Guide to Europe, 1974.* London: Collier Macmillan Publishers, 1974.

CHAPTER TWENTY-EIGHT: ISRAELI AND JEWISH

1. Hertz, Dr. J. H. *The Pentateuch and Haftorahs.* London: Soncino Press, 1972.

2. Ausubel, Nathan. *Pictorial History of the Jewish People: From Bible Times to Our Own Day throughout the World.* New York: Crown Publishers, 1962.

3. Raddock, Charles. *Portrait of a People: The Story of the Jews from Ancient to Modern Times.* New York: The Judaica Press, 1965.

4. Baron, W. Salo, et al. *Great Ages and Ideas of the Jewish People.* New York: The Modern Library (Random House), 1956.

5. Isaacson, Rabbi Ben; and Wigoder, Deborah. *The International Jewish Encyclopedia*. Jerusalem: Masada Press, 1973.
6. Gaster, Theodor. *Festivals of the Jewish Year: A Modern Interpretation and Guide*. New York: Wm. Sloane Ass., Publishers, 1953.
7. Epstein, Morris. *All about Jewish Holidays and Customs*. New York: Ktav Publishing House, 1959.
8. Eban, Abba. *My People: The Story of the Jews*. New York: Behrman House (Random House), 1968.
9. *Portrait of a People*.
10. Waugh, Alec, et al. *Wines and Spirits*. New York: Time-Life Books, 1968.
11. Cornfeld, Lillian. *Israeli Cookery*. Westport, Conn.: The Avi Publishing Co., 1962.
12. Nickles, Harry G., et al. *Middle Eastern Cooking*. New York: Time-Life Books, 1969.
13. Bar-David, Molly Lyons. *The Israeli Cookbook: What's Cooking In Israel's Melting Pot*. New York: Crown Publishers, 1973.
14. May, Jacques. *Ecology of Malnutrition in the Far and Near East*. New York: Hafner Publishing Co., 1961.
15. *Funk and Wagnalls Standard Reference Encyclopedia*. New York: Standard Reference Works Publishing Co., 1967.
16. Nahoum, Chef Aldo. *The Art of Israeli Cooking*. New York: Holt, Rinehart & Winston, 1960.
17. Perry, Ruth. "Cooking the Sephardic Way." *Women's League Outlook*. Spring 1974.
18. Seranne, Anne; and Gaden, Eileen. *The Best of Near East Cookery*. New York: Doubleday & Co., 1964.
19. Rowland, Jean. *Good Food from the Near East*. New York: M. Barrows and Co., 1967.

CHAPTER TWENTY-NINE: ITALIAN

1. Tucker, Ninetta. *Italy*. London: Thames and Hudson, 1970.
2. Cowell, F. R. *Everyday Life in Ancient Rome*. New York: G. P. Putnam's Sons, 1966.
3. Root, Waverley, et al. *The Cooking of Italy*. New York: Time-Life Books, 1968.
4. Fitzgibbon, Theodora. *A Taste of Rome: Traditional Food*. Boston: Houghton Mifflin Co., 1975.
5. Bodde, Dirk. *Annual Customs and Festivals in Peking*. Hong Kong University Press, 1965.
6. Barzini Luigi. *From Caesar to the Mafia: Sketches of Italian Life*. New York: The Library Press, 1971.
7. Fodor, Eugene, ed. *Fodor's Italy, 1976*. New York: David McKay Co., 1976.
8. Langseth-Christensen, Lillian. "To Genoa by Sea." *Gourmet*, June 1970.
9. Dilke, O. A. W. *The Ancient Romans: How They Lived and Worked*. Chester Springs, Pa.: Du Four, 1975.
10. Levine, Irving. *Main Street Italy*. Garden City, N.Y.: Doubleday and Co., 1963.
11. *Encyclopedia Canadiana*. Toronto: Grolier of Canada, 1970.

12. Candler, Teresa Gilardi. *The Northern Italian Cookbook.* New York: McGraw-Hill Book Co. 1977.
13. Mondadori, Arnoldo, ed. *Feast of Italy.* New York: Thomas Y. Crowell & Co., 1973.
14. Boni, Ada. *Italian Regional Cooking.* New York: E. P. Dutton and Co., 1969.
15. Andrieux, Maurice. *Daily Life in Venice in the Time of Casanova.* London: George Allen and Unwin Ltd., 1972.
16. Whelpton, Eric. *A Concise History of Italy.* New York: Roy Publishers Inc., 1964.
17. Lucas-Dubreton, Jean. *Daily Life in Florence: In the Time of the Medici.* London: George Allen & Unwin Ltd., 1960.
18. Jones, Evan. "Tastes of Tuscany." *Gourmet,* March 1971.
19. Muffoletto, Anna. *The Art of Sicilian Cooking.* Garden City, N.Y.: Doubleday & Co., 1971.
20. Castle, Coralie, et al. *Peasant Cooking in Many Lands.* San Francisco: 101 Productions, 1972.
21. Donovan, Maria Kozslik. "Epiphany in Italy." *Gourmet,* January 1973.

CHAPTER THIRTY: JAPANESE

1. *Funk and Wagnalls Standard Reference Encyclopedia.* New York: Standard Reference Works Publishing Co., 1967.
2. *Facts about Japan.* Public Information Bureau, Ministry of Foreign Affairs, Japan, Code no. 05103, April, 1972 (Geography of Japan).
3. *The Japan of Today.* Ministry of Foreign Affairs, Japan, 1972.
4. Skurka, Norma. "The Way of Tsutsumu: Design: An Art in Packaging." *The New York Times Magazine,* February 9, 1975.
5. *Facts about Japan.* Public Information Bureau, Ministry of Foreign Affairs, Japan, Code no. 05104, April, 1974 (Chronological Outline of Japanese History).
6. *Facts about Japan.* Public Information Bureau, Ministry of Foreign Affairs, Japan, Code no. 05502, March, 1973 (Religion).
7. Chie, Nakane. *Human Relations in Japan.* Ministry of Foreign Affairs, Japan, 1972.
8. Wenkam, Nao S; and Wolff, Robert J. "A Half Century of Changing Food Habits among Japanese in Hawaii." *Journal of the American Dietetic Association,* July 1970.
9. Steinberg, Raphael, et al. *The Cooking of Japan.* New York: Time-Life Books, 1969.
10. Oto, Tokihiko. *Folklore in Japanese Life and Customs.* Tokyo: Kokusai Bunka Shinkokai, 1963.
11. Trager, James. *The Foodbook.* New York: Avon Books, 1972.
12. Griffin, Stuart. *Japanese Food and Cooking.* Tokyo: Charles E. Tuttle and Co., 1968.
13. *Japanese and their Food.* Radio Japan News, June 1973.
14. "Briefly About Japanese Cooking," *Practical Japanese Cooking,* (sent from Japanese Trade Offices).
15. Castle, Coralie, et al. *Peasant Cooking of Many Lands.* San Francisco: 101 Productions, 1972.

16. *Facts about Japan*. Public Information Bureau, Ministry of Foreign Affairs, Japan, Code no. 05507, March, 1973 (Chanoyu).
17. *Funk and Wagnalls*.
18. Tanaka, Heichachi. "The Pleasures of Japanese Cooking." *Gourmet*, August 1963.
19. Shinojima, Tadashi. *Japanese Cookery*. Shufunotomo Cooking Text, Japan, 1968.

CHAPTER THIRTY-ONE: KOREAN

1. *Korea*. Seoul: International Publicity Corp., 1974.
2. *Facts about Korea 1974*. Seoul: Korean Overseas Information Service, 1974.
3. Kolb, Albert. *East Asia: China, Japan, Korea, Vietnam: Geography of a Cultural Region*. London: Methuen & Co., 1971.
4. Osgood, Cornelius. *The Koreans and Their Culture*. New York: The Ronald Press Co., 1951.
5. Castle, Coralie, et al. *Peasant Cooking of Many Lands*. San Francisco: 101 Productions, 1972.
6. Choong-Ok, Cho. *The Art of Korean Cookery*. Tokyo: Shibata Publishing Co., 1963.
7. Froud, Nina. *Far Eastern Cooking for Pleasure*. London: Hamlyn, 1971.

CHAPTER THIRTY-TWO: LATIN AMERICAN

1. Jacob, Heinrich Eduard. *Coffee: The Epic of a Commodity*. New York: Viking Press, 1935.
2. Montagne, Prosper; and Gottschalk, Dr. *Larousse Gastronomique*. London: Paul Hamlyn, 1961.
3. Adams, R. N. "Food Habits in Latin America: A Preliminary Historical Survey." *Human Nutrition, Historic and Scientific*. New York: International Universities Press, 1967.
4. Leonard, Jonathan N., et al. *Latin American Cooking*. New York: Time-Life Books, 1968.
5. *Funk and Wagnalls Standard Reference Encyclopedia*. New York: Standard Reference Works Publishing Co., 1967.
6. Carpenter, Allan; and Lyon, Jean C. *Enchantment of South America: Uruguay*. Chicago: Regensteiner Publishing Enterprises Inc., 1969.
7. Dobler, Lavinia. *The Land and People of Uruguay*. Philadelphia: J. B. Lipppincott Co., 1965.
8. Dirección National De Tourismo, Gráfica, Ham, S.A., *Argentina*.
9. *República Argentina*. Courtesy of the Embassy of Argentina, Ottawa, Canada.
10. *Funk and Wagnalls*.
11. De Andrade, Margarette. *Brazilian Cookery: Traditional and Modern*. Rutland, Vermont: Charles E. Tuttle Co., 1965.
12. Ortiz, Elisabeth Lambert. "Brazil." *Gourmet*, December 1973.
13. De Andrade, Margarette. "Brazilian Cookery." *Gourmet*, June 1963.
14. Castle, Coralie, et al. *Peasant Cooking of Many Lands*. San Francisco: 101 Productions, 1972.
15. *Funk and Wagnalls*.
16. *Chile*. Courtesy of the Embassy of Chile, Ottawa, Canada.

17. Guevara, Susan. "Memories of a Chilean Kitchen." *Gourmet*, September and October, 1960.
18. *Funk and Wagnalls.*
19. Consulate of Colombia. "Tasty Colombian Dishes." Reprinted from *Gourmet* (no date given). Colombian Information Service.
20. *Funk and Wagnalls.*
21. Autumn, Violetta. *A Russian Jew Cooks in Peru*. San Francisco: 101 Productions, 1973.

CHAPTER THIRTY-THREE: LEBANESE AND SYRIAN

1. Tannahill, Reay. *Food in History*. New York: Stein and Day, 1974.
2. Nickles, Harry, et al. *Middle Eastern Cooking*. New York: Time-Life Books, 1969.
3. *Funk and Wagnalls Standard Reference Encyclopedia*. New York: Standard Reference Works Publishing Co., 1967.
4. *Encyclopedia Canadiana*. Toronto: Grolier of Canada, 1970.
5. *Funk and Wagnalls.*
6. May, Jacques. *Ecology of Malnutrition in the Far and Near East*. New York: Hafner Publishing Co., 1961.
7. Allan, Donald Aspinwall. "Flavors of Lebanon." *Gourmet*, August 1974.
8. Corey, Helen. *The Art of Syrian Cookery*. Garden City, N.Y.: Doubleday & Co., 1962.
9. Rowland, Jean. *Good Food from the Near East*. New York: M. Barrows and Co., 1964.
10. Seranne, Anne; and Gaden, Eileen. *The Best of Near East Cookery*. Garden City, N.Y.: Doubleday & Co., 1964.
11. Zane, Eva. *Middle Eastern Cookery*. San Francisco: 101 Productions, 1974.
12. Casella, Dolores. "The Welcoming." *Gourmet*, March 1960.
13. Sakr, Ahmad H. "Dietary Regulations and Food Habits of Muslims." *Journal of the American Dietetic Association*, February 1971.
14. Zaehner, R. C., ed. *The Concise Encyclopedia of Living Faiths*. New York: Hawthorn Books, 1959.

CHAPTER THIRTY-FOUR: MALTESE

1. *Malta Handbook, 1974*. Issued by the Office of the Prime Minister, Kastija, Valletta, Malta.
2. Trotta, Geri. "Malta: A Journey through Time." *Gourmet*, December 1975.
3. Bradford, Ernle. "Democracy's Fortress: Unsinkable Malta." *National Geographic*, June 1969.
4. Interview granted by former Maltese citizen, Melrose Micallef Paquet.
5. Galizia Caruana, Anne; and Galizia Caruana, Helen. *Recipes from Malta*. Valetta, Malta: Progress Press Co.,
6. Carbonaro, Carmen. *Maltese Dishes*. Hamrun, Malta: Luxtrinting Press, 1967. (Translated and explained by Melrose Micallef Paquet).

CHAPTER THIRTY-FIVE: MEXICAN

1. Aaron, Jan; and Salom, Georgina Sachs. *The Art of Mexican Cooking*. New York: Doubleday and Co., 1967.

2. Booth, George C. *The Food and Drink of Mexico*. Toronto: Ward Ritchie Press, General Publishing Co., 1964.
3. DeLeon, Josefina Velasquez. *Mexican Cookbook*. Mexico City: Culinary Arts Institute, 1971.
4. Leonard, Jonathan N. *Latin American Cooking*. New York: Time-Life Books, 1968.
5. *Funk and Wagnalls Standard Reference Encyclopedia*. New York: Standard Reference Works Publishing Co., 1967.
6. Ortiz, Elisabeth Lambert. *The Complete Book of Mexican Cooking*. New York: Evans and Co., 1967.
7. Rojas, Pedro. *The Art and Architecture of Mexico*. New York: Paul Hamlyn, 1968.
8. Wason, Betty. *Cooks, Gluttons and Gourmets*. New York: Doubleday and Co., 1962.

CHAPTER THIRTY-SIX: MOROCCAN
1. Trotta, Geri. "Morrocco's Imperial Cities." *Gourmet*, February 1974.
2. *Funk and Wagnalls Standard Reference Encyclopedia*. New York: Standard Reference Works Publishing Co., 1967.
3. May, Jacques. *The Ecology of Malnutrition in Northern Africa*. New York: Hafner Publishing Co., 1967.
4. Szulc, Tad. *Portrait of Spain*. New York: American Heritage Press. Div. of McGraw-Hill Book Co., 1972.
5. *Funk and Wagnalls*.
6. Eban, Abba. *My People: The Story of the Jews*. New York: Behrman House, (Random House), 1968.
7. Ausubel, Nathan. *Pictorial History of the Jewish People*. New York: Crown Publishing Inc., 1962.
8. Englebert, Victor. "Trek by Mule among Morocco's Berbers." *National Geographic*, June 1968.
9. Wolfert, Paula. *Couscous and Other Good Food from Morocco*. New York: Harper and Row, 1973.
10. Zane, Eva. *Middle Eastern Cookery*. San Francisco: 101 Productions, 1974.
11. Feibleman, Peter. *The Cooking of Spain and Portugal*. New York: Time-Life Books, 1969.
12. Field, Michael; and Field, Frances. *A Quintet of Cuisines*. New York: Time-Life Books, 1970.
13. Castle, Coralie, et al. *Peasant Cooking of Many Lands*. San Francisco: 101 Productions, 1972.
14. Croft-Cooke, Rupert. "Tunisian Cookery." *Gourmet*, November 1970.

CHAPTER THIRTY-SEVEN: NEW ZEALANDERS
1. McCarry, Charles. "New Zealand's North Island: The Contented Land." *National Geographic*, August 1974.
2. *Facts about New Zealand*. Wellington: New Zealand Information Service, Tourist and Publicity Dept., 1974.
3. Benchley, Peter. "New Zealand's Bountiful South Island." *National Geographic*, January 1972.

4. *Funk and Wagnalls Standard Reference Encyclopedia*. New York: Standard Reference Works Publishing Co., 1967.
5. Hooper, Keith. "Booklet on Understanding Polynesians Prepared for White New Zealanders." London, Ontario: *London Free Press*, December 10, 1974.
6. Flower, Tui. *New Zealand Recipes*. Wellington: New Zealand Information Service, Tourist and Publicity Dept., 1973.
7. *Special New Zealand Recipes*. New Zealand Tourist Office, March 1956.
8. Nation, Rhoda. *Mary Bought a Little Lamb, and This Is How She Cooked It*. Wellington: A. H. and A. W. Reed, 1973.
9. *About New Zealand*. Washington, D.C.: New Zealand Embassy.
10. *New Zealand Background: Fish Recipes from New Zealand*. Wellington: No. 27, Government Publicity Division, 1965.
11. Rome, James; and Rome, Margaret. *New Zealand*. London: Ernest Benn Ltd., 1967.

CHAPTER THIRTY-EIGHT: NORWEGIAN

1. *Funk and Wagnalls Standard Reference Encyclopedia*. New York: Standard Reference Works Publishing Co., 1967.
2. Caraman, Philip. *Norway*. London: Longman's Green & Co., 1969.
3. Ovstedal, Barabara. *Norway*. London: B. T. Batsford Ltd., 1974.
4. Barry, Naomi. "Norwegian Journey." *Gourmet*, June 1959.
5. *Encyclopedia Canadiana*. Toronto: Grolier of Canada, 1970.
6. Langseth-Christensen, Lillian. "Bergen." *Gourmet*, July 1971.

CHAPTER THIRTY-NINE: POLISH

1. *Encyclopedia Canadiana*. Toronto: Grolier of Canada, 1970.
2. May, Jacques. *The Ecology of Malnutrition in East-Central Europe*. New York: Hafner Publishing Co., 1963.
3. Zeranska, Alina. *The Art of Polish Cooking*. New York: Doubleday & Co., 1968.
4. Field, Michael; and Field, Frances. *A Quintet of Cuisines*. New York: Time-Life Books, 1970.
5. *Funk and Wagnalls Standard Reference Encyclopedia*. New York: Standard Reference Works Publishing Co., 1967.
6. Castle, Coralie, et al. *Peasant Cooking of Many Lands*. San Francisco: 101 Productions, 1972.
7. Ochorowicz-Monatowa, Marja. *Polish Cookery: The Universal Cookbook*. New York: Crown Publishers, 1973.

CHAPTER FORTY: PORTUGUESE

1. Feibleman, Peter, et al. *The Cooking of Spain and Portugal*. New York: Time-Life Books, 1969.
2. Maas, Carl. "The Cookery of Northern Portugal." *Gourmet*, August 1973.
3. *Funk and Wagnalls Standard Reference Encyclopedia*. New York: Standard Reference Works Publishing Co., 1967.
4. Kempner, Mary Jean. *Invitation to Portugal*. New York: Atheneum, 1969.
5. Kolb. Albert. *East Asia: China, Japan, Korea, Vietnam: Geography of a Cultural Region*. London: Methuen and Co., 1971.

6. Spunt, Georges. *The Step-by-Step Chinese Cookbook*. Toronto: Fitzhenry and Whiteside, 1973.
7. Thomas, Veronica. "The Allure of the Algarve." *Gourmet*, May 1973.
8. Kelly, Marie Noëlle. *This Delicious Land Portugal*. London: Hutchinson & Co., 1956.
9. "Report on the Portuguese Seminar Held at St. Helen's Portuguese Community Centre, November 21, 1973," and "Adjustment Problems of the Portuguese Mother" by Fatima Pires.
10. Bridge, Ann; and Lowndes, Susan. *The Selective Traveller in Portugal*. London: Chatto & Windus, 1967.
11. Maas, Carl. "Beyond the Tagus." *Gourmet*, April 1974.
12. Waldo, Myra. *Myra Waldo's Travel and Motoring Guide to Europe, 1974*. London: Collier Macmillan, 1974.
13. Waugh, Alec. *Wines and Spirits*. New York: Time-Life Books, 1968.

CHAPTER FORTY-ONE: ROMANIAN

1. May, Jacques. *The Ecology of Malnutrition in Central and South-Eastern Europe*. New York: Hafner Publishing Co., 1966.
2. Mackintosh, May. *Rumania*. London: Robert Hale Ltd., 1963.
3. Matley, Ian M. *Romania: A Profile*. New York: Praeger Publishers, 1970.
4. *Funk and Wagnalls Standard Reference Encyclopedia*. New York: Standard Reference Works Publishing Co., 1967.
5. Seranne, Anne; and Gaden, Eileen. *The Best of Near East Cookery*. Garden City, N.Y.: Doubleday and Co., 1964.
6. Stan, Anisoara. *The Romanian Cookbook*. New York: The Citadel Press, 1969.
7. Levi, Avraham. *Bazak Guide to Romania*. Tel Aviv: Bazak Israel Guidebook Publishers, 1970.
8. Nelson, Kay Shaw. *The Eastern European Cookbook*. Chicago: Henry Regnery, 1973.
9. Perl, Lila. *Yugoslavia, Romania, Bulgaria: New Era in the Balkans*. Toronto: Thomas Nelson and Sons, 1970.

CHAPTER FORTY-TWO: RUSSIAN

1. Nicolaieff, Nina; and Phelan, Nancy. *The Art of Russian Cooking*. New York: Doubleday and Co., 1969.
2. Papashvily, Helen; and Papashvily, George. *Russian Cooking*. New York: Time-Life Books, 1969.
3. *Funk and Wagnalls Standard Reference Encyclopedia*. New York: Standard Reference Works Publishing Co., 1967.
4. *Funk and Wagnalls Standard Reference Encyclopedia Yearbook: Events of 1973*. New York: Funk and Wagnalls Inc., 1974.
5. Norman, Barbara. *The Russian Cookbook*. Toronto: Bantam Books, 1970.
6. Polvay, Marina. "Cuisines of Russia." *Gourmet*, February 1974.
7. *Rand McNally Premier World Atlas: New Census Edition*. Chicago: Rand McNally & Co., 1972.
8. Kropotkin, Alexandra. *The Best of Russian Cooking*. New York: Charles Scribner's Sons, 1964.

9. Petrova, Nina. *Russian Cookery*. Harmondsworth, England: Penguin Books, 1968.
10. Nelson, Kay Shaw. *The Eastern European Cookbook*. Chicago: Henry Regnery Co., 1973.
11. *Funk and Wagnalls Standard Reference Encyclopedia*. New York: Standard Reference Works Publishing Co., 1967.
12. Wren, Christopher, "Ho Ho Ho, Soviet Style." *New York Times*.
13. Stearns, Anna. *New Canadians of Slavic Origin: A Problem in Creative Orientation*. Winnipeg: Trident Press, 1960.
14. Castle, Coralie, et al. *Peasant Cooking of Many Lands*. San Francisco: 101 Productions, 1972.

CHAPTER FORTY-THREE: SCOTTISH

1. Cameron, Sheila MacNiven. *The Highlander's Cookbook: Recipes from Scotland*. New York: Ward Ritchie Press, 1966.
2. *Encyclopedia Canadiana*. Toronto: Grolier of Canada, 1970.
3. Barker, T. C.; McKenzie, J. C.; and Yudkin, J. *Our Changing Fare: 200 Years of British Food Habits*. London: Macgibbon and Kee, 1966.
4. *Funk and Wagnalls Standard Reference Encyclopedia*. New York: Standard Reference Works Publishing Co., 1967.
5. Costa, Margaret. "The Highlands of Scotland." *Gourmet*, August 1972.
6. Lindsay, Ann McColl. Proprietor of Ann McColl's Kitchen Shop, London, Ontario. (Interview).
7. Walker, Sara Macleod. *The Highland Fling Cookbook*. New York: Atheneum, 1971.
8. Bailey, Adrian, et al. *The Cooking of the British Isles*. New York: Time-Life Books, 1969.
9. Howells, J. Harvey. "Home to Arran: Scotland's Magic Isle." *National Geographic*. Vol. 128, no. 1. July 1965.

CHAPTER FORTY-FOUR: SPANISH

1. Szulc, Tad. *Portrait of Spain*. New York: American Heritage Press, Division of McGraw-Hill Book Co., 1972.
2. *Funk and Wagnalls Standard Reference Encyclopedia*. New York: Standard Reference Works Publishing Co., 1967.
3. Aguilar, Jeanette. *The Classic Cooking of Spain*. New York: Holt, Rinehart & Winston, 1966.
4. Feibleman, Peter, et al. *The Cooking of Spain and Portugal*. New York: Time-Life Books, 1969.
5. Hatheway, Maruja. *Authentic Spanish Cooking*. New York: Paperback Library, 1970.
6. Mitchell, Fanny Todd. "Buena Sopa." *Gourmet*, February 1973.
7. _____. "The Riches of Granada." *Gourmet*, February 1971.
8. McDonough, Jean. "All Ranks of Basques Work Gourmet Wonders." London, Ontario: *London Free Press*, March 21, 1974.
9. Wason, Betty. *Thirty-eight Delectable Dishes from Spain*.
10. Castle, Coralie, et al. *Peasant Cooking of Many Lands*. San Francisco: 101 Productions, 1972.

11. Fodor, Eugene; and Curtis, William; eds. *Fodor's Spain, 1969.* New York: David McKay Co., 1969.
12. Waldo, Myra. *Myra Waldo's Travel and Motoring Guide to Europe, 1974.* London: Collier Macmillan, 1974.

CHAPTER FORTY-FIVE: SWEDISH

1. Brown, Dale. *The Cooking of Scandinavia.* New York: Time-Life Books, 1968.
2. *Funk and Wagnalls Standard Reference Encyclopedia.* New York: Standard Reference Works Publishing Co., 1967.
3. Coombs, Anna Olsson. *The New Smorgasbord Cookbook.* New York: Hill & Wang, 1958.
4. Adlerbert, Elna. *Cooking the Scandinavian Way.* London: Paul Hamlyn, 1969.
5. Howard, Irene. *Vancouver's Svenskar: A History of the Swedish Community in Vancouver.* Vancouver Historical Society, 1970.
6. Langseth-Christensen, Lillian. "Swedish Yuletide Baking." *Gourmet,* December 1973.
7. Lindahl, Mac. " 'God Jul': A Swedish Christmas." *Gourmet,* December 1959.
8. Castle, Coralie, et al. *Peasant Cooking of Many Lands.* San Francisco: 101 Productions, 1972.
9. *Encyclopedia Canadiana.* Toronto: Grolier of Canada, 1970.
10. *Sweden.* Leslie Foods, 1963.

CHAPTER FORTY-SIX: SWISS

1. Hazelton, Nika Standen. *The Swiss Cookbook.* New York: Atheneum, 1967.
2. Kampfen, Werner. *Switzerland.* Zurich: Swiss National Tourist Office.
3. Field, Michael; and Field, Frances. *A Quintet of Cuisines.* New York: Time-Life Books, 1970.
4. Hofer, Heinz P. *La Fondue: A Collection of Authentic Fondue Recipes from Switzerland.* Switzerland Cheese Association, 1970.
5. ____. *Recipes from Switzerland.* Zurich: Swiss National Tourist Office, 1970.
6. Cowie, Donald. *Switzerland: The Land and the People.* Cranbury, N.J.: A. S. Barnes and Co., 1971.
7. Castle, Coralie, et al. *Peasant Cooking of Many Lands.* San Francisco: 101 Productions, 1972.

CHAPTER FORTY-SEVEN: TURKISH

1. Nyrop, Richard, et al. *Area Handbook of Turkey.* Washington, D.C.: U.S. Government Printing Office, 1973.
2. *Funk and Wagnalls Standard Reference Encyclopedia.* New York: Standard Reference Works Publishing Co., 1967.
3. Mango, Andrew. *Discovering Turkey.* New York: Hastings House Publishers, 1971.
4. Ertürk, Ilyas. *Turkish Kitchen Today.* Istanbul: Istanbul Matbasi, 1967.
5. Newman, Bernard. *Turkey and the Turks.* London: Herbert Jenkins, 1968.

6. Salter, Cedric. *Introducing Turkey*. London: Methuen and Co., 1961.
7. Jacob, Heinrich. *Coffee: The Epic of a Commodity*. New York: Viking Press, 1935.
8. Nickles, Harry G., et al. *Middle Eastern Cooking*. New York: Time-Life Books, 1969.
9. Seranne, Anne; and Gaden, Eileen. *The Best of Near East Cookery*. Garden City, N.Y.: Doubleday and Co., 1964.
10. Barish, Mort, et al. *Mort's Guide to Festivals, Feasts, Fairs and Fiestas*. International Edition. Princeton, N.J.: CMG Publishing Co., 1974.
11. Iny, Daisy. *The Best of Baghdad Cooking*. Toronto: Clarke, Irwin and Co., 1976.
12. Walker, Warren; and Uysal, Ahmet. *Tales Alive in Turkey*. Cambridge, Mass.: Harvard University Press, 1966.

CHAPTER FORTY-EIGHT: UKRAINIAN

1. *Funk and Wagnalls Standard Reference Encyclopedia*. New York: Standard Reference Works Publishing Co., 1967.
2. Papashvily, Helen; and Papashvily, George. *Russian Cooking*. New York: Time-Life Books, 1969.
3. *Funk and Wagnalls Standard Reference Encyclopedia*. New York: Standard Reference Works Publishing Co., 1967.
4. *Encyclopedia Canadiana*. Toronto: Grolier of Canada, 1970.
5. Statistics Canada. *1970 Immigration*. Ottawa: Canada Immigration Division, Department of Manpower and Immigration, Information Canada, 1971.
6. Canadian Citizenship Branch, Department of the Secretary of State. *Canadian Family Tree*. Ottawa: Queen's Printer, 1967.
7. *Webster's New World English Dictionary*. Toronto: Nelson, Foster and Scott, 1966.
8. Young, Charles H. *The Ukrainian Canadians: A Study in Assimilation*. Toronto: Thomas Nelson and Sons Ltd., 1931.
9. Norman, Barbara. *The Russian Cookbook*. Toronto: Bantam Books of Canada, 1970.
10. Stechishin, Savella. *Traditional Ukrainian Cookery*. Winnipeg: Trident Press, 1967.
11. Hawrish, Mary-Beth. "Age-Old Customs: Ukrainian Families Enjoy Christmas Twice." London, Ontario: *London Free Press*, January 7, 1974.
12. Kubijovyc, Volodymyr, ed. *Ukraine: A Concise Encyclopedia*. Toronto: University of Toronto Press. Vol. I, 1963.
13. Ibid. Vol. II, 1971.
14. Schopflin, George, ed. *The Soviet Union and Eastern Europe: A Handbook*. London: Anthony Blond, 1970.

CHAPTER FORTY-NINE: VIETNAMESE

1. *Funk and Wagnalls Standard Reference Encyclopedia*. New York: Standard Reference Works Publishing Co., 1967.
2. Kolb, Albert. *East Asia: China, Japan, Korea, Vietnam: Geography of a Cultural Region*. London: Methuen and Co., 1971.

3. Steinberg, Raphael, et al. *Pacific and South-East Asian Cooking*. New York: Time-Life Books, 1970.
4. May, Jacques. *The Ecology of Malnutrition in the Far and Near East*. New York: Hafner Publishing Co., 1961.
5. *Funk and Wagnalls Standard Reference Encyclopedia*.
6. Tao-Kim-Hai, André M. "Disciple of Ong Tao." *Gourmet*, June 1958.
7. Froud, Nina. *Far Eastern Cooking for Pleasure*. London: Paul Hamlyn, 1971.

CHAPTER FIFTY: WELSH

1. *Wales*. London: Alabaster, Passmore and Sons.
2. Jones, R. Brimley. *Anatomy of Wales*. Glamorgan, Wales: Gwerin Publications, Peterston-super-Ely, 1972.
3. Lloyd, D. M.; and Lloyd, E. M. *A Book of Wales*. London: Collins, 1954.
4. Ogizorek, Doré, ed. *Great Britain: England, Scotland and Wales*. New York: Whittlesey House, McGraw-Hill, 1949.
5. Fitzgibbon, Theodora. *A Taste of Wales*. London: Pan Books, 1973.
6. *Lands and Peoples: Europe*. Vol. 4. New York: Grolier Inc., 1972.
7. Interview with Mrs. James (Rhian) Haldane, President, London Welsh Society, London, Ontario. (1975).
8. Llewellyn, Sian. *The Welsh Kitchen: Recipes from Wales*. Swansea, Wales: Celtic Educational Services Ltd., 1972.
9. Welsh Gas Board. *Croeso Cymrig: A Welsh Welcome*. Cardiff: Tudor Graphic Ltd., 1963.

CHAPTER FIFTY-ONE: WEST INDIAN

1. Wolfe, Linda, et al. *The Cooking of the Caribbean Islands*. New York: Time-Life Books, 1960.
2. Harman, Carter, et al. *Life World Library: The West Indies*. New York: Time-Life Books, 1966.
3. Eneruwa, Linda. *The West Indies*. London: Longman's, 1962.
4. Waddell, D. A. G. *The West Indies and the Guianas*. Englewood Cliffs, N.J.: Prentice-Hall Inc., 1967.
5. Castle, Coralie, et al. *Peasant Cooking of Many Lands*. San Francisco: 101 Productions, 1972.
6. Lowenthal, David, ed. *The West Indies Federation*. New York: Columbia University Press, 1961.
7. Pearcy, G. Etzel. *The West Indian Scene*. Princeton, N.J.: Van Nostrand Co., 1965.
8. Cabanillas, Berta; and Ginorio, Carmen. *Puerto-Rican Dishes*. Puerto Rico: 1966.
9. Ortiz, Elisabeth Lambert. *The Complete Book of Caribbean Cooking*. New York: Evans and Co., 1973.
10. The Caribbean Food and Nutrition Institute. *Food Composition Tables for Use in the English-speaking Caribbean*. Kingston 7, Jamaica, 1974.
11. Horowitz, Michael M. ed. *Peoples and Cultures of the Caribbean: An Anthropological Reader*. Garden City, N.Y.: Natural History Press, 1971.
12. Ortiz, Elisabeth Lambert. "Puerto Rico." *Gourmet*, January 1973.

13. Ibid. "De Leyritz of Martinique." *Gourmet*, October 1972.
14. The Trinidad and Tobago Government Office. Toronto: Series of pamphlets, recipes, printed sheets, etc., prepared and presented courtesy of this office. (Particularly useful was M. P. Alladin's *Festivals of Trinidad and Tobago*, published by the Director of Culture, Ministry of Education and Culture, National Museum and Art Gallery, Trinidad and Tobago).

CHAPTER FIFTY-TWO: YUGOSLAVIAN

1. Goldring, Patrick. *Yugoslavia*. Chicago: Rand McNally, 1973.
2. Nelson, Kay Shaw. *The Eastern European Cookbook*. Chicago: Henry Regnery, 1973.
3. Fodor, Eugene, ed. *Fodor's Yugoslavia, 1970*. New York: David McKay Co., 1970.
4. May, Jacques. *The Ecology of Malnutrition in East-Central Europe*. New York: Hafner Publishing Co., 1963.
5. Markovic, Spasenija-Pata. *Yugoslav Cookbook*. New York: Lyle Stuart Inc., 1966.
6. Perl, Lila. *Yugoslavia, Romania, Bulgaria: New Era in the Balkans*. Toronto: Thomas Nelson and Sons, 1970.
7. Donovan, Maria Kozslik. "Yugoslavia II." *Gourmet*, June 1972.
8. Seranne, Anne; and Gaden, Eileen. *The Best of Near East Cookery*. Garden City, N.Y.: Doubleday and Co., 1964.
9. Esterovich and Spalatin. *Croatia: Land, People, Culture*. Toronto: University of Toronto Press. Vol. I. 1964.
10. Ibid. Volume II.
11. Wechsberg, Joseph. "Dubrovnik." *Gourmet*, June 1972.
12. *Encyclopedia Canadiana*. Toronto: Grolier of Canada, 1970.
13. Donovan, Maria Koszlik. "Yugoslavia I." *Gourmet*, January 1972.

Index

Note: When several page numbers follow an entry, the italicized number indicates the first page on which a definition is given.

Entries in boldface followed by the abbreviation "s.h." indicate section headings used throughout the book. For information on these topics the reader should consult individual chapters.

YOU EAT
WHAT YOU ARE